The Law of Charitable and Not-for-Profit Organizations

THIRD EDITION

The Law of Charitable and Not-for-Profit Organizations

THIRD EDITION

Donald J. Bourgeois, B.A., LL.B.

In Association with

Canadian Centre for Philanthropy ™
Le Centre canadien de philanthropie ᴹᶜ

The Law of Charitable and Not-for-Profit Organizations
© LexisNexis Canada Inc. 2002
April 2002

All rights reserved. No part of this publication may be reproduced, stored in any material form (including photocopying or storing it in any medium by electronic means and whether or not transiently or incidentally to some other use of this publication) without the written permission of the copyright holder except in accordance with the provisions of the Copyright Act. Applications for the copyright holder's written permission to reproduce any part of this publication should be addressed to the publisher.

Warning: The doing of an unauthorized act in relation to a copyrighted work may result in both a civil claim for damages and criminal prosecution.

Members of the LexisNexis Group worldwide

Canada	LexisNexis Canada Inc, 75 Clegg Road, MARKHAM, Ontario
Argentina	Abeledo Perrot, Jurisprudencia Argentina and Depalma, BUENOS AIRES
Australia	Butterworths, a Division of Reed International Books Australia Pty Ltd, CHATSWOOD, New South Wales
Austria	ARD Betriebsdienst and Verlag Orac, VIENNA
Chile	Publitecsa and Conosur Ltda, SANTIAGO DE CHILE
Czech Republic	Orac sro, PRAGUE
France	Éditions du Juris-Classeur SA, PARIS
Hong Kong	Butterworths Asia (Hong Kong), HONG KONG
Hungary	Hvg Orac, BUDAPEST
India	Butterworths India, NEW DELHI
Ireland	Butterworths (Ireland) Ltd, DUBLIN
Italy	Giuffré, MILAN
Malaysia	Malayan Law Journal Sdn Bhd, KUALA LUMPUR
New Zealand	Butterworths of New Zealand, WELLINGTON
Poland	Wydawnictwa Prawnicze PWN, WARSAW
Singapore	Butterworths Asia, SINGAPORE
South Africa	Butterworth Publishers (Pty) Ltd, DURBAN
Switzerland	Stämpfli Verlag AG, BERNE
United Kingdom	Butterworths Tolley, a Division of Reed Elsevier (UK), LONDON, WC2A
USA	LexisNexis, DAYTON, Ohio

National Library of Canada Cataloguing in Publication Data
Bourgeois, Donald J.

The law of charitable and not-for-profit organizations

3rd ed.
Includes index.
ISBN 0-433-43103-2

1. Nonprofit organizations – Law and legislation – Canada. 2. Charitable uses, trusts, and foundations – Canada. 3. Nonprofit organizations – Law and legislation – Ontario. 4. Charitable uses, trusts, and foundations – Ontario. I. Title.

KE1373.B69 2002   346.71'064   C2002-901076-4

Printed and bound in Canada
Reprint #1, 2004.

Preface

The first edition of this text was published in 1990. The period between the first and this third edition has seen substantial change and growth in the sector and its role in Canadian society. Just as other institutions and businesses in Canada have changed in response to information technology, globalization, economic difficulties, regulatory regimes, enhanced public scrutiny and public perception, so too have charities and not-for-profit organizations. Arguably, charitable and not-for-profit organizations had less capacity to make the changes required to survive and prosper than did most public or private sector organizations and, as a result, have had a more difficult transition.

This edition is, in many ways, a transitional work. Over the next several years, it is expected that there will be significant change to the legislative framework in which charitable and not-for-profit organizations operate. The Government of Canada and the Voluntary Sector are jointly working on changes to the *Canada Corporations Act* and the charity registration system under the *Income Tax Act* to improve accountability and — equally important — the capability and capacity of charitable and not-for-profit organizations.

These initiatives grew out of several reports in the mid- to late-1990s, including the Ontario Law Reform Commission's *Report on the Law of Charities* and the Panel on Accountability and Governance in the Voluntary Sector. Encouragingly, the Government of Canada has undertaken substantial work and consultation to modernize the legislative framework within its jurisdiction. Disappointingly — and without any cogent explanation — provincial governments, in particular the Government of Ontario, have been much less willing to do so. While the Government of Canada would appear to be taking a comprehensive approach (although at times one that is difficult to see), provincial governments would appear to have all but abandoned the sector to its own devices. Even small changes take too long and are not carried out in a coordinated manner or within a broader policy context.

There have been other factors leading to change in the sector. The advent of the internet has altered how people communicate. It has also made information available continuously, not just during business hours to the public but also to those in the charitable and not-for-profit sector. The ongoing downloading (and in some areas, abrogation) of government responsibilities to the "private sector" has created both opportunities and challenges. This downloading usually went hand-in-glove with substantial reductions in government support for the sector, at times with little or no notice. Organizations had to respond to survive in the short-term but at the cost of longer term stability and improvements. And, at a cost to society overall.

The discussion about what is or is not a "charity" was also prominent in the late 1990s. However, the courts expressed a reluctance to intervene in the debate without Parliament taking the first step. Court cases with respect to the obligations of charities to those injured by the actions of their employees or volunteers was also a significant topic, giving rise to greater focus on prevention. The *Christian Brothers* litigation in particular became and remains an outstanding area for legal debate.

The next five years will, no doubt, see continued developments in the sector. Some will be beyond the control of the sector. But it is important to note that the sector's leadership has responded through its own initiative. It is attempting, usually successfully, to take control of the challenges and to create capacity within the sector. The fact that there is now a "sector leadership" is perhaps one of the most profound changes that occurred in the 1990s, one that will allow the sector to stabilize, to respond and to grow in the future.

I would like to thank those who have provided comments on the third edition both in writing and in more casual conversation. Similarly, I would like to thank Gian-luca DiRocco, Peter Broder and Gordon Floyd for their comments and assistance. I also acknowledge and thank my spouse, Susan Campbell for her ongoing support and encouragement. Of course, I cannot forget Daphne, the snoring dog.

Don Bourgeois
March 2002

Table of Contents

Preface v

Table of Cases xvi

Chapter 1   **Introduction: Charitable and Not-for-profit Organizations** 1

A   Overview 1
B   Introduction 4
C   Defining Charitable and Not-for-profit Organizations 6
D   What is "Charitable" 9
      I   The English Law 9
           (1)   Defining "Charitable" 9
           (2)   Defining "Public Benefit" 14
           (3)   Relief of Poverty 17
           (4)   Advancement of Education 17
           (5)   Advancement of Religion 17
           (6)   Other Purposes Beneficial to the Community 18
      II   The Canadian Case Law 18
           (1)   General Comments 18
           (2)   Relief of Poverty 18
           (3)   Advancement of Education 19
           (4)   Advancement of Religion 21
           (5)   Other Purposes Beneficial to the Community 22
           (6)   Modernizing the Definition of "Charity" — Judicial Activism or Legislation? 27
      III   Politics and Business — Non-charitable Objects and Activities 30
           (1)   Political Objects 30
           (2)   Business Activities 32

Chapter 2   **Legal Structures for Charitable and Not-for-Profit Organizations** 37

A   Overview 37
B   Types of Legal Structures 38
      I   Trusts 38
      II   Unincorporated Associations 40
      III   Ontario Corporations and Co-operative Corporations without Share Capital 42
           (1)   Corporations without Share Capital 42
           (2)   Co-operative Corporations without Share Capital 45
      IV   Federal Corporations without Share Capital 46
C   Advantages and Disadvantages of the Legal Structures 48
      I   Introduction 48

	II	Liability of Members 49
	III	Legal Capacity 50
	IV	Relationship Among Members 51
	V	Advantages of Unincorporated Associations 52
	VI	Conclusion 53

Chapter 3   Incorporating a Charitable or Not-for-Profit Organization 55

A   Overview 55
B   Incorporation 57
     I   Ontario Corporations without Share Capital 57
         (1)   General Comments 57
         (2)   Application Process and Requirements 57
             (a)   Step 1 — Selecting and Searching a Corporate Name 57
                 (i)   General Comments 57
                 (ii)   Elements of a Corporate Name 58
                 (iii)   Prohibitions for a Corporate Name 59
                 (iv)   Restricted Words for a Corporate Name 60
                 (v)   Name for a Charitable Corporation 62
                 (vi)   NUANS Name Search and Report 63
             (b)   Step 2 — Application for Letters Patent 63
                 (i)   General Comments 63
                 (ii)   Head Office 65
                 (iii)   Directors 65
                 (iv)   Objects 66
                 (v)   Powers 66
                 (vi)   Special Provisions 67
                 (vii)   Special Corporations 69
             (c)   Step 3 — Establishing the Corporation 70
     II   Federal Corporations without Share Capital 70
         (1)   General Comments 70
         (2)   Types 71
         (3)   Application Process and Requirements 71
             (a)   Step 1 — Selecting and Searching a Corporate Name 72
                 (i)   Distinctive Name 72
                 (ii)   Prohibited Names 72
                 (iii)   Restrictions on Words in Corporate Names 73
                 (iv)   Change in Corporate Name 74
             (b)   Step 2 — Application for Letters Patent 74
     III   Co-operative Corporations 76
         (1)   General Comments 76
         (2)   Procedures for Incorporation 76
             (a)   Overview 76
             (b)   Name Selection and Approval 76

| | | (c) | Application for Articles of Incorporation............. 77 |
| | | (d) | Establishing the Co-operative Corporation .... 78 |

Chapter 4   **The Organization in Operation: Organizational By-Laws and Statutory Requirements**........................ 81

A	Overview... 81
B	General Comments on By-Laws... 82
C	Unincorporated Associations 85
D	Corporate By-Laws.. 86

    I   General Comments.. 86
    II   Ontario Corporations and Co-operative Corporations without Share Capital 86
        (1)   Corporations without Share Capital 86
        (2)   Co-operative Corporations without Share Capital 88
    III Federal Corporations without Share Capital........................... 89
    IV Organizational By-laws Under Other Provincial Incorporation Legislation.. 90
        (1)   Introduction.. 90
        (2)   Alberta... 91
        (3)   British Columbia 92
        (4)   Manitoba... 92
        (5)   New Brunswick.. 93
        (6)   Newfoundland 93
        (7)   Nova Scotia 93
        (8)   Prince Edward Island... 94
        (9)   Quebec.. 94
        (10)   Saskatchewan 94

E   Statutory Provisions... 95
    I   Auditors 95
        (1)   Ontario Corporations without Share Capital.............. 95
        (2)   Ontario Co-operative Corporations without Share Capital 97
        (3)   Federal Corporations without Share Capital 97
    II   Members 98
        (1)   Ontario Corporations without Share Capital.............. 98
        (2)   Ontario Co-operative Corporations without Share Capital 99
        (3)   Federal Corporations without Share Capital 99
    III Meetings 100
        (1)   Ontario Corporations without Share Capital............. 100
        (2)   Ontario Co-operative Corporations without Share Capital 100
        (3)   Federal Corporations without Share Capital 101
    IV Directors 101
        (1)   Ontario Corporations without Share Capital............. 101
        (2)   Ontario Co-operative Corporations without Share Capital 103

			(3)	Federal Corporations without Share Capital 103
	V	Officers 103
			(1)	Ontario Corporations without Share Capital.............. 103
			(2)	Ontario Co-operative Corporations without Share Capital 104
			(3)	Federal Corporations without Share Capital 104
F	Rules of Procedure or Rules of Order.. 104
	I	General Comments.. 104
	II	Content of the Rules of Procedure or Rules of Order 105
			(1)	Chair 105
			(2)	Procedure to Make a Decision 106
			(3)	Appeals from the Chair 107
			(4)	Quorum for Meetings 107
			(5)	Motions 108
			(6)	Debate and Its Role... 110
			(7)	Privileges 111
			(8)	Summary 112

Chapter 5 The Organization in Operation: Maintaining, Operating and Changing the Organization 113

A	Overview... 113
B	Maintaining the Organization.. 114
	I	Trusts and Unincorporated Associations.............................. 114
			(1)	Books and Records 114
			(2)	Filings 116
			(3)	Meetings... 117
	II	Corporations and Co-operative Corporations without Share Capital 117
			(1)	Ontario Corporations without Share Capital.............. 117
				(a) Books and Records.. 117
				(b) Filings 118
				(c) Members' Meetings 119
			(2)	Ontario Co-operative Corporations without Share Capital 121
				(a) Books and Records.. 121
				(b) Filings 122
				(c) Members' Meetings 122
			(3)	Federal Corporations without Share Capital 123
				(a) Books and Records.. 123
				(b) Filings 124
				(c) Members' Meetings 124
C	Financial Reporting 125
	I	Introduction... 125
	II	Accounting Records and Financial Statements..................... 126
			(1)	Financial Records.. 126
				(a) Introduction 126
				(b) Types of Accounts and Journals........................ 126

		(2)	Financial Statements 129
			(a) Introduction 129
			(b) Types of Financial Statements 130
			(c) Contributions — Restricted Fund Accounting Method and the Deferral Method 135
			(d) Reporting on Controlled and Related Entities .. 140
			(e) Other CICA Handbook Requirements 144
	III	Financial Records and the *Income Tax Act* 146
	IV	Auditing Charities 152
	V	Operating a Charity — Maintaining its Registration 155
		(1) Introduction 155
		(2) Official Donation Receipts 156
		(3) Charity Information Return 162
		(4) Not-for-Profit Information Return 173
		(5) Conclusion 175
D	Fundamental Changes 176
	I	Trusts 176
	II	Unincorporated Associations 176
	III	Corporations and Co-operative Corporations without Share Capital 177
		(1) General Comments 177
		(2) Ontario Corporations Without Share Capital 177
			(a) Supplementary Letters Patent 177
			(b) Dissolution 178
			(c) Amalgamation 180
		(3) Ontario Co-operative Corporations without Share Capital 181
			(a) Amendments to the Articles of Incorporation ... 181
			(b) Dissolution 182
			(c) Amalgamation 183
		(4) Federal Corporations without Share Capital 183
			(a) Supplementary Letters Patent 183
			(b) Dissolution 184
			(c) Amalgamation 186
	IV	Organizational Structural Change 186
		(1) General Comments 186
		(2) Structural Options for National Organizations 187
			(a) Overview 187
			(b) Association Model 190
			(c) Chapter Model 195
		(4) Parallel Foundations 197
		(5) Strategic Alliances 198
		(5) Foreign Activities 202
		(6) Carrying On Business and Political Activities 207

Chapter 6		**Officers, Directors and Trustees: The Standards of Care**	211
A	Introduction		211
B	Approaches to Governance		212
C	Standards of Care		221
	I	Introduction	221
	II	Defining the Standard of Care	223
		(1) Not-for-Profit Organizations	223
		(2) Charitable Organizations	226
	III	Duties and Obligations to the Organization	230
D	Trustees		234
	I	Introduction	234
	II	Duties to the Trust	234
		(1) Basic Duty of Care	234
		(2) Duty Not to Delegate	236
		(3) Conflict of Interest	236
E	Statutory Duties		238
	I	Introduction	238
	II	Common Statutory Duties	239
		(1) Employees and the Workplace	239
		(2) Taxes and Other Source Deductions	240
		(3) Environmental	241
		(4) Business Practices	241
F	Preventing Problems		241
	I	Effective Boards	241
	II	Due Diligence	245
	III	Checklist for Directors	247
G	Board Management of Risk		248
	I	Accountable Boards	248
	II	Policies and the Prevention and Minimization of Risk	249
		(1) What are Policies?	249
		(2) Policies Governing the Board	250
		(3) Policy Process	252
	III	Selected Policy Documents	253
		(1) Conflict of Interest	254
		(2) Code of Conduct	257
		(3) Personal Information and Privacy Policies	258
		(4) Financial Management Overview	265
		(5) Regulatory Compliance Management	267
		(6) Insurance and Indemnification	270
		(a) Directors and Officers	270
		(b) General Liability	273
		(7) Fiscal Management	276
		(8) Program Review	278
		(9) Investment Policy	280
		(a) Introduction	280
		(b) Investment of Charitable Property	281

		(c)	General Considerations... 283
		(d)	Ethical Investing... 284
		(e)	Commingling of Restricted Funds and Special Purpose Trusts 286

Chapter 7   Members and their Relationship with the Organization 289

A   Overview.. 289
B   Introduction 289
C   Common Law Provisions of the Contractual Relationship 291
       I   Property Rights.. 291
       II   Procedural Rights 294
D   Statutory Provisions of the Contractual Relationship 295
       I   Eligibility for Membership... 295
           (1)   Introduction... 295
           (2)   Types and Qualifications for Admission 295
       II   Specific Rights of Membership 298
           (1)   Right to Vote.. 298
           (2)   Right to Information.. 299
           (3)   Right to Attend Meetings.. 301
           (4)   Terminating and Suspending Membership................ 302
           (5)   Co-operative Corporations without Share Capital 303
               (a)   Membership Qualifications............................... 303
               (b)   Membership Rights 303
               (c)   Terminating Membership 304
                   (i)   Voluntary Leaving by the Member 304
                   (ii)   Administrative Termination by the Co-operative Corporation 304
                   (iii)   Expulsion of a Member by the Co-operative Corporation 304

Chapter 8   Taxation and Charitable and Not-for-Profit Organizations 307

A   Overview.. 307
B   Federal Income Tax Act... 309
       I   Exemptions.. 309
           (1)   Not-for-profit Organizations 309
           (2)   Charitable Organizations.. 314
       II   Registration as a Charitable Organization or Charitable Foundation 315
           (1)   Advantages and Disadvantages.................................. 315
           (2)   Application Process... 317
               (a)   Part 1 — Identification of Applicant................. 321
               (b)   Part 2 — List of Applicant's Directors or Trustees 322
               (c)   Part 3 — Organizational Structure 322
                   (i)   Internal Division... 322

			(ii)	Independent Organization 323
			(iii)	Unincorporated Associations 323
			(iv)	Designation 323
		(d)	Part 4 — Information about the Activities of the Applicant 325
			(i)	Description of Activities 325
			(ii)	Political Activities 328
			(iii)	Fundraising 329
		(e)	Part 5 — Financial Information 330
		(f)	Part 6 — Confidential Information 332
		(g)	Summary 333
C	Ontario Corporations Tax Act 334
	I Introduction 334
	II Exemption 334
D	Consumption Taxes 336
	I Goods and Services Tax/Harmonized Sales Tax 336
		(1)	Introduction 336
		(2)	Exemptions 337
		(3)	Registration 341
			(a)	Collecting and Paying the GST/HST 341
			(b)	Filings 341
	II Ontario Retail Sales Taxes 344
		(1)	Introduction 344
		(2)	Exemption 345
			(a)	Charitable Organizations 345
			(b)	Not-for-profit Organizations 347
E	Property Taxes 347
	I Assessment Act 347
		(1)	Other Taxes 350

Chapter 9   Supervision of Charitable Organizations 351

A   Overview 351
B   Role of Public Guardian and Trustee 352
    I   Introduction 352
    II Charities Accounting Act 353
    III Charitable Gifts Act 360
C   Doctrine of Cy-Pres 370
D   Judicial Supervision 372

Chapter 10   Fundraising 377

A   Introduction 377
B   Role of Directors 380
C   Ethical Standards 384
    I   Background 384
D   Developing the Strategy 389
    I   Introduction 389
    II Types of Fundraising Activities 389

	III	Professional Fundraisers 392
		(1) Deciding to Use and Selecting a Professional 392
		(2) Contracts with a Professional 395
	IV	Steps in a Campaign 397
E	Compliance with the Law 397
	I	Background 397
	II	Competition Act 398
	III	Personal Information Protection and Electronic Documents Act 402
	IV	Intellectual Property 402
	V	Charities Accounting Act and Charitable Gifts Act 406
	VI	Charitable Fund-Raising Act 407
	VII	Charities Endorsement Act 414
F	Defining "Gift" 414
G	Charitable Gaming 422
	I	Introduction 422
	II	*Criminal Code* and Charitable Gaming 425
	III	Types of Lottery Schemes 429
	IV	Terms and Conditions to Licences 431
		(1) Authority for Terms and Conditions 431
		(2) General Terms and Conditions 432
		(a) Introduction 432
		(b) Conduct of the Event 432
		(c) Bona fide Members 433
		(d) Lottery Trust Account, Proceeds and Expenses 435
		(e) Books and Records 438
		(f) Financial Reports and Financial Statements 439
		(g) Conflict of Interest 443
		(3) Specific Terms and Conditions 444
	V	Use of Proceeds 445
H	Special Events 447
	I	General Comments 447
	II	Risk Identification and Risk Management 449
		(1) Step 1 — Risk Identification 449
		(2) Step 2 — Risk Transference 449
		(a) Insurance 449
		(b) Waivers 451
		(3) Step 3 — Preparing for the Risks 452
	III	Planned Giving 454
		(1) Introduction 454
		(2) Kinds of Planned Giving 454
		(a) Bequests 454
		(b) Life Insurance 456
		(c) Capital Property 458
		(i) Real Property 458
		(ii) Securities 459

		(iii) Cultural Property... 460
	(d)	Remainder Trusts.. 461
	(e)	Annuities 464
	(f)	Interest-free Loan 466
I	Internet and Charitable and Not-for-Profit Websites............ 466

Appendix A:	Concordance of Legislation by Major Issues and Jurisdiction A — Incorporation Statutes 471
Appendix B:	List of Addresses 479
Appendix C:	Checklists 483
Appendix D:	Precedents 493

Index 593

Table of Cases

A

A.G. v. Marchant (1866), L.R. 3 Eq. 424 (Ch.) 16
Aberdeen Railway Co. v. Blaikie Bros., (1854), 2 Eq.
  Rep. 1281 (H.L) 230
Adamson v. Melbourne and Metropolitan Board of Works,
  [1929] A.C. 142 (P.C.) 14
Aikins v. Dominion Live Stock Assn. of Canada (1896),
  17 P.R. 303 (Ont. Div. Ct.) 49
Alberta Institute on Mental Retardation v. Canada, [1987]
  3 F.C. 286 (C.A.) 34, 208
Anderson v. Gislason, [1920] 3 W.W.R. 301, 53 D.L.R.
  491 (Man. C.A.) 293
Armstrong, Re (1969), 7 D.L.R. (3d) 36 (N.S. S.C.) 4, 22
Arrow 1st Cdn. Realty Inc. v. Winnipeg Real Estate Bd.
  (1991), 72 Man. R. (2d) 64 (Q.B.) 297
Ash v. Methodist Church (1900), 27 O.A.R. 602 (C.A.),
  affd. (1901), 31 S.C.R. 497 294
Ashbury Railway Carriage and Iron Co. v. Riche, (1875),
  L.R. 7 H.L. 653 (H.L.) 232
Asian Outreach Canada v. Hutchinson (1999), 28 E.T.R.
  (2d) 275 (Ont. S.C.J.) 229, 230, 357, 372
Atkinson, Re [1952] O.R. 685 (C.A.) 366
Auburn Retirement Village of Peterborough Inc. v.
  Peterborough (City) (1983), 22 M.P.L.R. 173 (Ont. Co. Ct.) 349
Auckland Harbour Bd. v. Commr. of Inland Revenue, [1959] N.Z.L.R.
  204 22
Augustinian Father (Ontario) Inc. v. Regional Assessment Commissioner
  Region No. 14 et al. (1985), 52 O.R. (2d) 536 (H.C.) 348

B

Baker v. Independent Order of Foresters (1897),
  28 O.R. 238 (H.C.), affd. (1911), 24 O.A.R. 585 (C.A.) 293
Baker, Re (1984), 47 O.R. (2d) 415, 17 E.T.R. 168 .... 353, 370
Ballard Estate v. Ballard Estate, (1991), 3 O.R. (3d)
  65 (C.A.) 363, 366, 367
Barrie v. Royal Colwood Golf Club, August 9, 2001,
  Doc. 01/2857, Edwards J. B.C.S.C. 302
Berry et al. v. Pulley et al. (2000), 48 O.R. (3d) 169 (C.A.) 291
Blackfoot Stock Assn. v. Thor, [1925] 3 W.W.R. 544 (Alta. C.A.) 50
Blainey v. Ont. Hockey Assn. (1986), 54 O.R. (2d)
  513 (C.A.), revg. (1985), 52 O.R. (2d) 225 297
Blais v. Touchet, [1963] S.C.R. 358 27

Bloorview Childrens Hospital Foundation v. Bloorview MacMillan
   Centre, [2001] O.J. 1700, May 2, 2001, Ontario Superior Court
   of Justice 201
Boldrini v. Hamilton Naturalists Club, [1995] O.J. No. 3321, Ontario
   Court of Justice (Gen. Div.), October 18, 1995 356
Bonar Law Memorial Trust v. Inland Revenue Commrs.
   (1933), 49 T.L.R. 220 17
Bowman v. Secular Society Ltd., [1917] A.C. 406 (H.L.) 17, 30
Brendzij v. Hajdij, [1927] 1 W.W.R. 301 (Man. C.A.) 293
Brewster v. Hendershot (1900), 27 O.A.R. 232 (C.A.) 292
Brooks, Re (1969), 68 W.W.R. 132 (Sask. Q.B.) 21
Brylinski v. Inkol (1924), 55 O.L.R. 369 (H.C.) 292
Burns, Re [1988] O.J. No. 2001, November 28, 1988,
   Ontario Surrogate Court 359

C

Campden Charities, Re (1881), 18 Ch. D. 310 16
Can. Aero Service Ltd. v. O'Malley, [1974] S.C.R. 592 .... 230, 232
Can. Morning News Co. v. Thompson et al., [1930]
   S.C.R. 338, [1930] 3 D.L.R. 833 50
Canada Trust Co. v. Ont. (Human Rights Comm.) (1990),
   74 O.R. (2d) 481, (sub nom. Leonard Foundation
   Trust, Re) 12 C.H.R.R. D/184, 69 D.L.R. (4th) 321,
   38 E.T.R. 1, 37 O.A.C. 191 (C.A.) 137, 297, 371, 422
Canada Trust Co. v. Ontario (Human Rights Commission)
   (1990), 20 A.C.W.S. (3d) 736 (Ont. C.A.); revg. (1987),
   61 O.R. (2d) 75, 42 D.L.R. (4th) 263 (H.C.) 11
Canada UNI Assn. v. M.N.R. (1992), 151 N.R. 4 (F.C.A.) 20, 32
Canada v. Corsano, [1999] 3 F.C. 173 .... 225, 226
Cannon v. Toronto Corn Exchange (1880), 5 O.A.R. 268 (C.A.) 302
Cdn. Foundation for Youth Action, Re (1977), 1 A.C.W.S. 282 359
Cencourse Project Inc. v. Regional Assessment Commissioner
   for Region 27 and Corporation of the City of Windsor (1991),
   5 O.R. (3d) 349 (Gen. Div.) 349
Centenary Hospital Assn. Re (1989), 69 O.R. (2d) 1 (H.C.)
   .... 37, 38, 165, 355, 359, 363, 364, 366, 373, 407
Centre Star Mining Co. v. Rossland Miners Union (1902),
   9 B.C.R. 190 (S.C.) 51
Chapman, Cocks v. Chapman, Re [1896] 2 Ch. 763 (C.A.) 235
Chartered Insurance Institute v. Corpn. of London, [1957]
   2 All E.R. 638 (D.C.) 17
Chase v. Starr, [1924] S.C.R. 495, [1924] 4 D.L.R. 55,
   44 C.C.C. 358 51
Chesterman v. Federal Taxation Commr., [1926] A.C. 128 (P.C.) 14
Chichester Diocesan Fund and Board of Finance Inc. v.
   Simpson, [1944] A.C. 341 14

Table of Cases xix

Christian Brothers of Ireland in Canada, Re (2000),
  47 O.R. (3d) 674 (C.A.) 281
Church of Christ Development Co. v. M.N.R., [1982]
  C.T.C. 2467, 82 D.T.C. 1461 (T.R.B.) 34
City Equitable Fire Insurance Co., Re [1925] 1 Ch. 407 (C.A.) 224, 227
Cocks v. Manners (1871), L.R. 12 Eq. 574 (H.L.) 18
Comeau v. Fundy Group Publications Ltd. (1981),
  24 C.P.C. 251 (N.S. T.D.) 50
Co-op College of Can. v. Sask. Human Rights Comm.,
  [1976] 2 W.W.R. 84 (Sask. C.A.) 20
Cooper v. McDonald (1909), 11 W.L.R. 173, 19 Man. R. 1 (C.A.) 50
Cotton Trust for Rural Beautification, Re (1980),
  9 E.T.R. 125 (P.E.I. S.C.) 23
Coulthurst's Will Trusts, Re [1951] 1 All E.R. 744 17
Cranston, Webb v. Oldfield, Re [1898] 1 I.R. 448 14
Cummings v. Ontario Minor Hockey Assn. (1979), 26 O.R.
  (2d) 7, 104 D.L.R. (3d) 434, 10 R.F.L. (2d) 121 (C.A.) 50

D

Daley Estate, Re (1987), 27 E.T.R. 291 (Sask. Q.B.) 371
D'Amore v. McDonald, [1973] 1 O.R. 845 (H.C.); affd.
  1 O.R. (2d) 370 (C.A.) 232
David Feldman Charitable Foundation, Re (1987),
  58 O.R. (2d) 626 (Surr. Ct.) 227, 359
Dom. Trust Co., Re (1917), 32 D.L.R. 63 (Ont. C.A.) 232
Dupriez v. Canada, [1998] 98 D.T.C. 1790 (T.C.C.) 416
Dutil v. Canada, (1991), 95 D.T.C. 281 (T.C.C.) 416, 418

E

Essery v. Court Pride of the Dominion (1882), 2 O.R. 596 (C.A.) 302
Everywoman's Health Centre Society (1988) v. M.N.R.,
  [1992] 2 F.C. 52 .... 30, 31

F

Faith Haven Bible Training Centre, Re (1988), 29 E.T.R. 198
  (Ont. Surr. Ct.) 228, 229, 237, 359
Fales v. Can. Permanent Trust Co., [1977] 2 S.C.R. 302 234
Finlay v. Black (1921), 60 D.L.R. 422, [1921] 2 W.W.R. 907
  (Y.T. S.C.) 49
First German Evangelical Lutheran Zion's Congregation
  v. Reiker, [1921] 1 W.W.R. 794 (Sask. T.D.) 293
Fitzpatrick; Fidelity Trust Co. et al. v. St. Joseph's
  Vocational School of Winnipeg et al.Re 371
Foran v. Kottmeier, [1973] 3 O.R. 1002, 39 D.L.R. (3d) 40 (C.A.) 51
Forgan, Re (1961), 29 D.L.R. (2d) 585 (Alta. S.C.) 19
French Protestant Hospital, Re [1951] 1 Ch. 567, [1951]
  1 All E.R. 938 (Ch. D.) 227, 380

Friedberg v. Canada, [1992] 1 C.T.C. 1, 92 D.T.C. 6031,
    135 N.R. 61 (F.C.A.) 416, 418
Fry v. Tapson (1884), 28 Ch. D. 268 236

G

Gilmour v. Coats, [1949] 1 All E.R. 848 (H.L.) 16, 18
Gold v. Maldaver (1912), 4 O.W.N. 106, 6 D.L.R. 333 (H.C.) 292
Grant v. Dom. Loose Leaf Co. (1924), 56 O.L.R. 43 (H.C.) 232
Guaranty Trust Co. of Can. v. M.N.R., [1967] S.C.R. 133 .... 18, 28
Gull Bay Development Corp. v. R., [1984] 2 F.C. 3 (T.D.) 25, 34
Gummerson v. Toronto Police Benefit Fund (1905), 11 O.L.R.
    194 (C.A.) 294

H

Harold G. Fox Education Fund v. Ont. (Public Trustee), Re
    (1989), 69 O.R. (2d) 742 (H.C.) 231, 237
Hart v. Felson (1924), 30 R.L.N.S. 109 (C.S.) 232
Haslam v. Haslam (1994), 3 E.T.R. (2d) 206 (Ont. Gen. Div.) 281
Heine v. Schaffer (1905), 2 W.L.R. 310 (Man. K.B.) 293
Henderson v. Toronto General Trusts Corp., [1928] 3 D.L.R.
    411 (Ont. C.A.) 50
Hennig v. Trautman, [1926] 1 W.W.R. 912, [1926] 2 D.L.R.
    280 (Alta. T.D.) 293
Hofer v. Hofer, [1970] S.C.R. 958 22
Hofer v. Waldner, [1921] 1 W.W.R. 177 (Alta. T.D.) 292
Hogle, Re [1939] O.R. 425 (H.C.) 22
Hopkinson, Lloyds Bank Ltd. v. Baker, Re [1949] 1 All E.R.
    346 (Ch. D.) 17
Hudson Bay Mining and Smelting Co. Ltd. v. R., [1986]
    1 C.T.C. 484, 86 D.T.C. 6244 (F.C.T.D.) 417
Huegli v. Pauli (1912), 26 O.L.R. 94, 4 D.L.R. 319 (H.C.) 293
Human Life International in Canada Inc. v. M.N.R., [1998]
    3 F.C. 202 (F.C.A.) 29
Hummeltenberg, Re [1923] All E.R. 49 (Ch. D.) 15
Hutterian Brethren Church of Wilson v. R., [1980] 1 F.C. 757
    (C.A.) 22, 34

I

I.R.C. v. Baddeley, [1955] A.C. 572 (H.L.) 9
Impenco Ltd. v. M.N.R., [1988] 1 C.T.C. 2339, 88 D.T.C.
    1242 (T.C.C.) 417
Income Tax Special Purposes Commrs. v. Pemsel, [1891] A.C. 531,
    [1891-4] All E.R. Rep. 28 (H.L.) 3, 13, 28
Incorporated Council of Law Reporting for England and
    Wales v. A.G., [1972] 1 Ch. 73, [1971] 3 All E.R.
    1029 (C.A.) 12, 13, 15

Incorporated Synod of the Diocese of Toronto and
  H.E.C. Hotels Ltd. et al., Re (1987), 61 O.R. (2d) 737 (C.A.) 355
International Bible Students Association of Canada et al. v.
  Halton Hills (Town) et al. (1986), 57 O.R. (2d) 42 (Div. Ct.) 348
Itter v. Howe (1896), 23 O.A.R. 256 (C.A.) 293

J

Jabs Construction Limited v. M.N.R., [1999] 99 D.T.C. 729
  (T.C.C.) 417
Jackson v. Phillips, (1867), 14 Allen 539 10
Jewish Nat. Fund v. Royal Trust Co., [1965] S.C.R. 780 22
Johnston, Re [1968] 1 O.R. 483 (H.C.J.) 22
Jones v. T. Eaton Co., [1973] S.C.R. 635 .... 18, 39
Jubilee Local No. 6 v. Carmen's Council Section "A", [1920]
  3 W.W.R. 781, 56 D.L.R. 318 (Man. T.D.) 292

K

Kaik v. Boraski, [1926] 3 D.L.R. 916 (Sask. K.B.) 292
Kay v. Nipissing Twin Lakes Rod & Gun Club (1993), 7 B.L.R.
  (2d) 225 (Ont. Gen. Div.) 180
Keech v. Sanford (1726), 25 E.R. 223 (L.C.) 236
Kemerer v. Standard Stock & Mining Exchange (1927),
  32 O.W.N. 295 (C.A.) 294, 302
Keystone Bingo Centre Inc. v. Manitoba Lottery Foundation,
  (1990), 76 D.L.R. (4th) 423 (Man. C.A.) 426, 436
Kinny, Re (1903), 6 O.L.R. 459 (In Chambers) 19
Kitchener-Waterloo and North Waterloo Humane Society
  and City of Kitchener, Re [1973] 1 O.R. 490 (C.A.) 349
Kowalchuk v. Ukrainian Labour Farmer Temple Assn., [1935]
  1 W.W.R. 529, [1935] 2 D.L.R. 691 (C.A.) 292
Kozlowski v. Workers' Benevolent Society of Can., [1933]
  2 W.W.R. 593, [1933] 4 D.L.R. 652 (C.A.) 292, 293

L

L.I.U.N.A., Local 57 Members' Training Trust Fund v. R.,
  [1992] 2 C.T.C. 2410, 92 D.T.C. 2365 (T.C.C.) 20, 312
Ladies of the Sacred Heart v. Armstrong's Point Assn. (1961),
  29 D.L.R. (2d) 373, 36 W.W.R. 364 (Man. C.A.) 50
Laidlaw Foundation, Re (1984), 44 O.R. (2d) 549 (Div. Ct.) .. 24, 327, 359
Lakeside Colony of Hutterian Brethren v. Hofer (1994),
  93 Man. R. (2d) 161 (Q.B.) 295
Lakeside Colony of Hutterian Brethren v. Hofer, [1992]
  S.C.R. 165, revg. (1991), 77 D.L.R. (4th) 202 (Man. C.A.) 294, 302
Lapointe v. Ont. (Public Trustee), (1993), 1 E.T.R. (2d) 203
  (Ont. Gen. Div.) 23, 371
LaRose v. Fleuty, [1971] 5 W.W.R. 515, 5 C.C.C. (2d) 528
  (Alta. S.C.) 426

Les Soeurs de La Visitation D'Ottawa v. Ottawa, (1951),
2 D.L.R. 343 350
Levy Estate, Re (1989), 68 O.R. (2d) 385 (C.A.) 24
Light-Haven Home Inc. v. Regional Assessment Commissioner,
Region No. 31 v. Bruce Mines (Town), unreported decision,
March 23, 1995, Doc. RE4807/94, Mandel J. Ontario Court
(Gen. Div.) 350
London (City) v. Byron Optimist Sports Complex Ltd.
(1983), 23 M.P.L.R. 10 349

M

Maillé v. Union des ouvriers boulangers (1897), 12 Que.
S.C. 524 302
Mason Estate, Re [1951] O.J. No. 40 (H.C.J.) 366
Matheson v. Kelly (1913), 15 D.L.R. 359, 5 W.W.R. 950
(Man. K.B.) 53
McDonald v. Linton, 53 N.B.R. 107, [1926] 3 D.L.R. 779 (C.A.) 50
McDonald, Re (1980), 105 D.L.R. (3d) 681 (B.C. S.C.) 19
McGovern et al. v. A.G. et al, [1982] Ch. 321, [1981]
3 All E.R. 493 (C.A.) 14, 32
McGovern et al. v. A.G. et al., [1981] 3 All E.R. 493, [1982]
Ch. 321 (Ch.) 17
McNab, Re [1995] O.J. No. 2581, Ontario Court of Justice
(Gen. Div.), August 4, 1995 352
Memory Gardens Ltd. v. Waterloo (Township), [1955]
O.W.N. 424 (H.C.) 348
Metallic Roofing Co. of Can. v. Amalgamated Sheet Metal Workers
Intn'l Assn., Local 30, (1905), 9 O.L.R. 171 (C.A.) 41, 51
Minister of Municipal Affairs of New Brunswick v. (Maria F.) Ganong
Old Folks Home (1981), 129 D.L.R. (3d) 655 (N.B. C.A.) 4, 19
Mizrachi Organization of Can. v. Ennismore (Township), Re
[1973] 1 O.R. 465 (H.C.) 348
Moorcroft v. Simpson (1921), 64 D.L.R. 231 (Ont. H.C.) 19
Morice v. Bishop of Durham, (1805), 10 Ves. 522,
32 E.R. 947, [1803-13] All E.R. Rep. 451 (L.C.) 3, 11

N

Nanaimo Community Bingo Assn. v. British Columbia
(Attorney General), (1998), 52 B.C.L.R. (3d) 284 (S.C.) 23, 436
Nat. Anti-Vivisection Society v. Inland Revenue Commrs.,
[1948] A.C. 31, [1947] 2 All E.R. 217 (H.L.) 14, 16, 371
National Ballet School v. Assessment Commissioner
No. 9 et al. (1979), 25 O.R. (2d) 50 (S.C.) 348
National Model Railroad Assn. v. Seventh Division,
Pacific Northwest Region M.N.R., [1989] 2 F.C. D-1,
31 E.T.R. 268 (C.A.) 23
Native Communications Society v. M.N.R., [1986] 3 F.C. 471 ... 24, 25, 26

Table of Cases xxiii

Northumberland & Durham v. Murray & Brighton
 Public School Trustees, [1939] O.W.N. 565 (H.C.J.) 22
Notre Dame de Grâce Neighbourhood Assn. v. M.N.R.,
 [1988] 3 F.C. D-39, 85 N.R. 73 (C.A.) 26, 30

O

Oblates of Mary Immaculate-St. Peter's Province v.
 Ontario (Public Trustee), [1994] O.J. No. 2757,
 Ontario Court of Justice (Gen. Div.), November 28, 1994 358
Olympia Floor & Wall (Que.) Ltd. v. M.N.R., [1970] Ex.
 C.R. 274, C.T.C. 99, 70 D.T.C. 6085 (Ex. Ct.) 417
Ont. Grand Commandery, Knights of St. John v.
 Goldkie (1921), 20 O.W.N. 86 (C.A.) 293
Ontario (Public Guardian and Trustee) v. AIDS Society for Children
 (Ontario), [2001] O.J. No. 2170, May 25, 2001 .... 373, 380, 396
Oppenheim v. Tobacco Securities Trust Co., [1951]
 1 All E.R. 31 (H.L.) 14, 17
Orchard v. Tunney, [1957] S.C.R. 436, 8 D.L.R. (2d) 273 41
Ottawa Lumbermen's Credit Bureau v. Swan, (1923),
 53 O.L.R. 135 (C.A.) 41, 50

P

Parker v. Lethbridge Real Estate Bd. Co-op Ltd. (1983),
 49 A.R. 279 (Q.B.), affd. (1986), 70 A.R. 61 (C.A.) 297
Payne v. Bradley, [1962] A.C. 343 (H.L.) 436
Pentecostal Benevolent Assn. of Ont. v. Scarborough (Borough)
 (1979), 26 O.R. (2d) 552 (H.C.) 349
Perin v. Carey (1860), 24 How. 465 10
Planned Parenthood of Toronto v. Toronto (City), Re (1979),
 27 O.R. (2d) 666 (C.A.) 349
Polakoff v. Winters Garment Co. (1928), 62 O.L.R. 40,
 [1928] 2 D.L.R. 55 (H.C.) 51
Polish Veterans Second Corps. v. Army, Navy &
 Airforce Veterans in Can. (1978), 20 O.R. (2d) 321 (C.A.) 292
Positive Action Against Pornography v. M.N.R., [1988]
 2 F.C. 340 (C.A.) 20, 30
Public Trustee and Toronto Humane Society et al., Re (1987),
 60 O.R. (2d) 236 (H.C.) 5, 33, 228, 237, 300

R

R. v. Assessors of the Town of Sunny Brae, [1952] 2 S.C.R. 76 28
R. v. Andriopoulos 425
R. v. Bata Industries Ltd., (1992), 9 O.R. (3d) 329; vard.
 (1993), 14 O.R. (3d) 354 (Gen. Div.) 241, 421
R. v. Burns, [1988] 88 D.T.C. 6101 (F.C.T.D.);
 affd. [1990] 90 D.T.C. 6335 (F.C.A.) 415
R. v. Brampton, [1932] 4 D.L.R. 209 (S.C.C.) 436

R. v. Furtney (1991), 66 C.C.C. (3d) 498, 8 C.R. (4th) 121 (S.C.C.) 426
R. v. Gladue (1986), 30 C.C.C. (3d) 308 (Alta. Prov. Ct.) 429
R. v. Hunt, unreported decision, January 20, 1998,
    Doc. GD98-426 (Ont. Gen. Div.) 427, 428
R. v. Kinsmen Club of Windsor, [1964] 1 C.C.C. 144
    (Ont. Mag. Ct.) 428
R. v. Kussner, [1936] Ex. C.R. 206 (Ex. Ct.) 232
R. v. MacKenzie (1982), 135 D.L.R. (3d) 174 429
R. v. McBurney, [1985] 2 C.T.C. 214, 85 D.T.C. 5433,
    62 N.R. 104, 20 E.T.R. 283 (F.C.A.) 415, 416
R. v. Miller, [1951] O.W.N. 230, 99 C.C.C. 79, 11 C.R. 324 (C.A.) 428
R. v. Rankine, [1938] 4 D.L.R. 201, 70 C.C.C. 354 (B.C.C.A.) 428
R. v. Salituro, [1991] 3 S.C.R. 654 29
R. v. Zandstra, [1974] C.T.C. 503, 74 D.T.C.
    6416 (F.C.T.D.) 415
Regal (Hastings) Ltd. v. Gulliver, [1942] 1 All E.R. 378 (H.L.) 230
Regional Assessment Commissioner et al. v. Zangari
    et al. (1985), 8 O.A.C. 294 (Div. Ct.) 348
Ritholz v. Optometric Society (Man.) (1957), 18 D.L.R. (2d)
    514 (Man. Q.B.) 297
Russell, Re; Wood v. R. (1977), 1 E.T.R. 285 (T.D.) 22
Ryegate (Tecumseh) Co-operative Homes Inc. v. Stallard,
    April 4, 2000, Doc. 898-1997, Ont. Div. Ct. 305

S

Scarborough Community Legal Services v. M.N.R., [1985]
    2 F.C. 555 (C.A.) 18, 33
Schoen, Re (1987), 19 C.P.C. (2d) 110 (Ont. Dist. Ct.) 355, 356, 357
Scottish Burial Reform and Cremation Society Ltd. v.
    Glasgow (City) Corp., [1967] 3 All E.R. 215 (H.L.) 15, 24
Seafarers Training Institute v. Williamsburg (Township) (1982),
    39 O.R. (2d) 370 (Dist. Ct.) 4, 20
Senez v. Montreal Real Estate Bd. (1980), 35 N.R. 545 (S.C.C.) 290
Shapiro, Re (1979), 6 E.T.R. 276 (Ont. S.C.) 20
Shaw (Public Trustee) v. Day, [1957] 1 All E.R. 745 14
Sons of Temperance of Ont., Re (1926), 8 C.B.R. 49 (Ont. S.C.) 292
Sosnowski v. Polish Fraternal Aid Society of St. John Cantius
    (1988), 55 Man. R. (2d) 222 (Q.B.) 302
Spencer, Re (1928), 34 O.W.N. 29 (S.C.) 19
St. Catharine's House, Re (1977), 2 A.R. 337 (C.A.) 4, 19
Stahl v. Ontario Society for the Prevention of
    Cruelty to Animals (1989), 70 O.R. (2d) 355 .... 355, 356
Stein v. Hauser (1913), 5 W.W.R. 971, 15 D.L.R. 223 (Sask. T.D.) 293
Stephen v. Stewart (1943), 59 B.C.R. 410, [1944] 1 D.L.R. 305,
    [1943] 3 W.W.R. 580 (C.A.) 51
Stern v. Larry Webb Hayes Training School, 381
    F. Supp. 1003, (U.S. Dist. Ct., D.C., 1974) 227

Stouffville Assessment Commr. v. Mennonite Home
 Assn. of York County, [1973] S.C.R. 189 .... 349, 350

T

Tamil Co-operative Homes Inc. v. Arulappah,
 May 10, 2000, Doc. C32908, Labrosse, Doherty,
 Austin JJ.A. Ont. C.A. 305
Temple v. Hallem (1989), 58 Man. R. (2d) 54,
 58 D.L.R. (4th) 541, [1989] 5 W.W.R. 660 (C.A.) 52
Tite v. M.N.R., [1986] 2 C.T.C. 2343, 86 D.T.C. 1788 (T.C.C.) 416
Toronto Humane Society v. Milne, [2001] O.J. 3890,
 October 2, 2001, Ontario Superior Court
 of Justice 119, 229, 293, 300
Toronto Humane Society, Re (1920), 18 O.W.N. 414 (H.C.J.) 22
Toronto Volgograd Committee v. M.N.R., [1988]
 3 F.C. 251 (C.A.) 25, 26, 31
Transamerica Life Insurance Company of Canada v.
 Canada Life Assurance Company (1996), 28 O.R.
 (3d) 423 (Gen. Div.) 194
Trow v. Toronto Humane Society, [2001] O.J. 3640,
 September 10, 2001, Ontario Superior Court
 of Justice 119, 293, 299, 375
Trustees of Greek Catholic Ruthenian Church of East Selkirk v. Portage
 LaPrairie Farmers Mutual Fire Insurance Co., 31 D.L.R. 33, [1917]
 1 W.W.R. 249 (Man. C.A.) 51
Trustees of Mary Clark Home v. Anderson, [1904] 2 K.B. 645 17

U

Underwriters' Survey Bureau Ltd. v. Massie & Renwick
 Ltd., [1940] S.C.R. 218, [1940] 1 D.L.R. 625 292

V

Vancouver Society of Immigrant and Visible
 Minority Women v. M.N.R., [1999] 1 S.C.R. 10 .... 4, 28, 29
Verge v. Somerville, [1924] A.C. 496 (J.C.P.C.) 14
Vick v. Toivonen (1913), 4 O.W.N. 1542, 12 D.L.R. 299 (T.D.) 292

W

Warkentin v. Sault Ste. Marie (Board of Education) (1985),
 49 C.P.C. 31 (Ont. Dist. Ct.) 51
Watkins v. Hamilton-Wentworth C.C.F. Council, [1947]
 O.W.N. 791 (Co. Ct.) 50
Wawrzyniak v. Jagiellicz (1988), 65 O.R. (2d) 384, 51 D.L.R.
 (4th) 639, 31 E.T.R. 45 (C.A.) 292
Weninger Estate v. Cdn. Diabetes Assn. (1993), 2 E.T.R. (2d) 24 (Ont.
 Gen. Div.) 371

Whelan v. Knights of Columbus (1913), 5 O.W.N. 432,
    14 D.L.R. 666 (H.C.) 293
Wirta v. Vick (1914), 6 O.W.N. 599 (Div. Ct.) 293
Wollmann v. Hofer (1989), 63 D.L.R. (4th) 473 (Man. Q.B.) 302
Wood v. R., [1977] 6 W.W.R. 273 (Alta. T.D.) 4, 20
Woolner v. The Attorney General of Canada, (1999),
    99 D.T.C. 5722 (F.C.A.) 415, 416
Wright, Re (1917), 12 O.W.N. 184 (H.C.J.) 23

CHAPTER 1

Introduction: Charitable and Not-for-profit Organizations

A OVERVIEW

The charitable and not-for-profit organizations witnessed substantial growth and change towards the end of the 20th century — and a number of developments strongly suggested that growth and change would continue. The growth seems to have continued a pattern over the previous decade where political and social dynamics and a stronger role for charitable and not-for-profit organizations in Canadian society required expansion of the sector.

Charitable organizations registered with the Canada Customs and Revenue Agency alone as of 2000 was more than 77,400. The Charities Directorate receives annually almost 4,000 applications for registration, of which close to 3,300 are registered.[1] The numbers of not-for-profit organizations is not known, but active ones probably exceed 175,000. Over just a few years, it is readily apparent how quickly the number of charities alone will increase — which will create its own dynamics for fundraising, volunteers, governance and other issues.

As an industry, charitable organizations are one of Canada's largest. The sector is involved in a wide array of activities and services, including public policy development, programme delivery and member services. Approximately 1.3 million Canadians are employed either full or part-time by charities alone. These charities have assets of over $100 billion and annual revenues of $90 billion. More than 7.5 million Canadians volunteer their time to charities and not-for-profit organizations — amounting to more than a billion hours each year. The volunteered time represents another 580,000 full-time jobs.[2]

Accountability received an enhanced focus. The sector itself recognized the importance of accountability and the public's perception that the sector was accountable. Accountability may mean different things in

---

[1] *Registered Charities Newsletter*, Newsletter No. 11, December 3, 2001, Canada Customs and Revenue Agency.
[2] These statistics are derived from *Working Together: A Government of Canada/Voluntary Sector Joint Initiative – Report of the Joint Tables*, August 1999, at pp. 16 to 19.

different contexts; nevertheless, organizations that provide public benefits and, in return, receive benefits from society, need to be accountable. They are accountable to their members but also to various regulators, donors, beneficiaries and, perhaps equally important, the public in general.

The sector moved on the issue of accountability in the late 1990s. The Ontario Law Reform Commission's *Report on the Law of Charities*[3] was a potential new beginning. It made significant recommendations on the reform of the law of charities and not-for-profit organizations — recommendations which the Government of Ontario seemed to have largely ignored. The Panel on Accountability in the Voluntary Sector was established in 1997 and broadly consulted the sector and the public. Its 1998 discussion paper, *Helping Canadians Help Canadians: Improving Governance and Accountability in the Voluntary Sector* and its final report, *Building on Strength: Improving Governance and Accountability in Canada's Voluntary Sector*[4] focussed attention on the importance of governance and accountability. The recommendations are discussed throughout this text.

A number of other institutions have also examined charitable and not-for-profit organizations and their role in Canadian society. The statistics compiled in *Caring Canadians, Involved Canadians: Highlights from the 1997 National Survey of Giving, Volunteering and Participating*[5] provided benchmarks and information about the sector that were necessary for public policy discussions and decisions. The Canadian Policy Research Networks carried out significant research and issued several background and discussion papers to better inform the overall discussion.[6]

These reports, and the work and discussion generated by them, had another important effect. They engaged the Government of Canada with the sector. Arguably, the late 1990s and early 21st century have led to a joint recognition between the federal government and the sector of the importance of working together to achieve mutual goals. Unfortunately, the provincial governments have largely declined to participate. Nevertheless, a "joint initiative" has arisen from the work of the federal government and the voluntary sector. Substantial work is being done at joint tables with representation from the sector's evolving leadership and relevant departments, including Industry Canada, the Canada Customs and

---

[3] (Toronto: Queen's Printer, 1996).
[4] Panel on Accountability in the Voluntary Sector (Ottawa, February 1999).
[5] Statistics Canada (Ottawa: Ministry of Industry, 1998, revised October 2000). A number of organizations were involved in preparing this survey, including the Canadian Centre for Philanthropy, Non-Profit Sector Research Initiative, Human Resources Development Canada, Canadian Heritage and Volunteer Canada.
[6] See, for example, K.M. Day and R.A. Devlin, *The Canadian Nonprofit Sector*, CPRN Working Paper No. 2 (Ottawa: Renouf Publishing Co. Ltd., 1997). Universities also became involved in the research and analysis. See, for example, P.J. Monahan with E.S. Roth, *Federal Regulation of Charities: A Critical Assessment of Recent Proposals for Legislative and Regulatory Reform* (North York: York University, 2000).

Revenue Agency, Ministry of Finance and so forth to find solutions to the issues and problems that exist in the sector.[7]

It is expected that over time — perhaps longer than desired — there will be reform in the law of charitable and not-for-profit organizations. The federal reforms may spur provincial governments into further action at that level. In the mean time, the legal system exists as is. And it is one that is confusing and often antiquated.

The legislative frameworks have not kept up with the growth in numbers or size of charitable and not-for-profit organizations. Essential concepts, such as what is "charitable", are based on the common law and not readily transparent or understandable to officers, directors and members of the organizations. This text attempts to assist those involved in the organizations and those providing legal and other advice to establish and maintain charitable and not-for-profit organizations within the legal framework.

Both charitable and not-for-profit (or "non-profit") organizations are operated on a "not-for-profit" basis. That is, neither may distribute profits to their members and must devote their resources to carrying out their objects. Both also provide some level of public benefit, although what is or is not a public benefit is much more restrictive for charitable organizations. A not-for-profit organization may, for example, be primarily a private, not-for-profit social club. This type of club would not normally be eligible to be a charitable organization.

Charitable objects are concerned with the relief of poverty, the advancement of education, the advancement of religion, or other purposes that are beneficial to the community. These four categories of charitable objects are based on the *Statute of Uses, 1601*[8] and the English common law.

The *Statute of Uses* was an early attempt to legislate charitable activities and to ensure that funds were not misapplied. The preamble listed a number of charitable objects. The list was used by the court in *Morice v. Bishop of Durham*[9] and its items became the generally accepted categories of charitable objects. A series of other cases, including *Income Tax Special Purposes Commrs. v. Pemsel*,[10] entrenched the four categories.

The Canadian courts have adopted much of the English law in carrying out their supervisory role over charities. These categories have also been accepted for use in various legislative and regulatory schemes. These categories, as interpreted by the courts, are used by the Canada Customs and Revenue Agency in deciding whether or not an organiza-

---

[7] *Working Together: A Government of Canada/Voluntary Sector Joint Initiative* (Ottawa, August 1999) set the initial stage for this joint activity.

[8] (Imp.), 1601, 43 Eliz. I, c. 4. See Hubert Picarda, *The Law and Practice Relating to Charities* (London: Butterworths, 1977) for a fuller discussion of the *Statute of Uses*.

[9] (1805), 10 Ves. 522, 32 E.R. 947, [1803-13] All E.R. Rep. 451 (L.C.).

[10] [1891] A.C. 531, [1891-4] All E.R. Rep. 28 (H.L.).

tion is a charitable organization.[11] The categories are also used in the *Charities Accounting Act*,[12] which provides the Public Guardian and Trustee with a supervisory jurisdiction over charities in Ontario.

The courts will look to the spirit and intent of the *Statute of Uses* in deciding whether or not an activity or object is charitable in nature. What is covered under "poverty", for example, has expanded to reflect changing social conditions.[13] The "advancement of education" is not restricted to teaching. It includes research if the research is of educational value to the person conducting the research or if it advances knowledge, which in turn may be taught.[14] More recently, the Supreme Court of Canada provided further insight into what "advancement of education" means in a modern, multi-cultural society.[15] The courts take a broad interpretation of the advancement of religion.[16] The fourth category, "other purposes beneficial to the community", is the category that is most subject to the changes that occur in society.

In all four categories, the objects or purposes must provide a general benefit to the public to be charitable. This benefit may be limited in its application to a portion of the community. If so, that portion must be significant. What is or is not significant will depend upon the context, including what the objects or purposes are and what the common understanding of the public is. The case law, especially the English case law, is extensive. Decisions are made on the basis of analogy to previous cases on the evidence that is before the court. The definition, however, is not static. Because it relies, in part, on the common understanding, it develops and evolves with society and its needs and conditions.

B INTRODUCTION

The law governing charitable and not-for-profit organizations is very confusing and generally underdeveloped. It is far from clear on a number of major issues, including the liability of directors, officers and members. The statutory provisions at the federal and provincial level are antiquated. Unlike the business corporations statutes, they have not been modernized for decades. Since the 1960s, attempts have been made to do so at both levels of government, but without very much success.

---

[11] See Information Circular No. 80-10R, "Registered Charities: Operating a Registered Charity" (Revenue Canada (Taxation), Dec. 17, 1985).
[12] R.S.O. 1990, c. C.10.
[13] *Minister of Municipal Affairs of New Brunswick v. (Maria F.) Ganong Old Folks Home* (1981), 129 D.L.R. (3d) 655 (N.B. C.A.) and *Re St. Catharine's House* (1977), 2 A.R. 337 (C.A.).
[14] *Wood v. R.*, [1977] 6 W.W.R. 273 (Alta. T.D.); *Seafarers Training Institute v. Williamsburg (Township)* (1982), 39 O.R. (2d) 370 (Dist. Ct.).
[15] *Vancouver Society of Immigrant and Visible Minority Women v. M.N.R.*, [1999] 1 S.C.R. 10.
[16] *Re Armstrong* (1969), 7 D.L.R. (3d) 36 (N.S. S.C.).

Instead of comprehensive legislated changes, problems have been addressed through policies and practices that have developed over the years within the existing legislative framework. At times, there have been inconsistencies in the legislation, leading to problems that have needed fixing. In the case of incorporation, the issuance of the letters patent is discretionary. Applicants for incorporation under the federal and provincial statutes do not have a right to become incorporated. An application may be refused if the applicants have not complied with the policy requirements. In Ontario, for example, all applications for incorporation by letters patent of a "charitable corporation" must receive prior approval of the Public Guardian and Trustee and include a number of clauses that restrict the objects and activities of the corporation. Unless the application includes those clauses, the letters patent will not be issued.

The confusion in the law and the failure to amend the statutory provisions to address and to take into account changes in society has made it more difficult for directors, officers and members to understand their legal obligations and roles. Individuals who participate in charitable and not-for-profit organizations are, for the most part, sincere in their attempts to make improvements to society, communities and institutions. They are not as often prepared for the potential legal, financial and practical consequences of their involvement. They may be "at sea" and unsure of what steps to take to address problems or issues. They may not have sufficient financial resources to pay for the expertise needed in an organization on an ongoing basis.

The confusion and underdevelopment of the law also make it difficult for lawyers to provide legal advice to clients. There are few texts on the subject. The cases often comment on the lack of legal developments in this area and the need to make analogies to other forms of law, including trust and business law.[17] The policies and practices may not be readily available or explicable. The law is not "transparent".

This text attempts to assist lawyers to better understand the complexities (legal and practical) of the law of charitable and not-for-profit organizations and to provide legal services to their clients in this area of law. It attempts to make the law, policies and practices more transparent. It distinguishes between "charitable" and "not-for-profit" organizations and reviews the options for legal structures (trust, unincorporated organization, corporation or co-operative corporation without share capital), and their advantages and disadvantages. It discusses the procedure for establishing and maintaining the legal structures, and provides precedents for each. The text also examines the major legal issues for officers, directors, trustees and members of charitable and not-for-profit organizations. Finally, it reviews the law of taxation as it applies to charitable and not-for-profit organizations and the procedures for ap-

---

[17] See, for example, *Re Public Trustee and Toronto Humane Society et al.* (1987), 60 O.R. (2d) 236 (H.C.).

plying for registration as a charitable organization with the Canada Customs and Revenue Agency.

The practice of law in this area is complicated by more than the lack of transparency in the law itself. Very often, the individuals organizing an association are unclear on what their objectives are, how they want to achieve those objectives and how to structure their organization. In some groups, there may be significant differences of opinion and principles that need to be resolved or at least recognized. It is not at all unusual for groups to be divided on what appear to be, to an outsider, relatively unimportant issues. In providing legal advice and services, a lawyer should take care to ensure that he or she understands the context of the charitable or not-for-profit organization and its members.

C DEFINING CHARITABLE AND NOT-FOR-PROFIT ORGANIZATIONS

There are no clear definitions of charitable or not-for-profit organizations that are used by all. Rather, the definitions used by various regulators, standards-setting bodies, and the courts and in legislation have evolved and continue to evolve. The federal *Income Tax Act*,[18] for example, defines a charitable organization, in part, in subs. 149(1) as "an organization whether or not incorporated, all the resources of which are devoted to charitable activities carried on by the organization itself ...". That subsection defines "non-profit organization" as a "club, society or association that, in the opinion of the Minister, was not a charity ... and that was organized and operated exclusively for social welfare, civic improvements, pleasure or recreation or for any other purpose except profit ...". A 1977 federal government proposal for a new *Canada Non-Profit Corporations Act* (which has not been enacted) would have defined charitable corporation more broadly to include any activities that were primarily for the benefit of the public.[19]

Section 118 of the Ontario *Corporations Act*[20] was amended in 1994 to broaden the possible objects of the corporation. Until the amendment, corporations were limited to objects that were charitable, educational, agricultural, scientific, artistic, social, patriotic and so forth. The 1994 amendment permits incorporation if the corporation "has objects that are within the jurisdiction of the Province of Ontario". The amendment would appear to permit corporations to have objects that are commercial in nature. However, the corporation is not a "business corporation". The corporate name cannot suggest that it is a business corporation and any profits from any commercial activities must accrue to the corporation for

---

[18] R.S.C. 1985, c. 1 (5th Supp.).
[19] "Detailed Background Paper for the Canada Non-Profit Corporation Bill" (Ottawa: Department of Consumer and Corporate Affairs, 1977).
[20] R.S.O. 1990, c. C.38, s. 118 [am. S.O. 1994, c. 27, s. 78(5)].

its objects. The profits from the commercial activities may not be distributed to other persons. The restrictions on charitable corporations from carrying on business activities are not affected by the 1994 amendment.

Section 154 of the *Canada Corporations Act*[21] retains the list approach for permitted objects. A corporation may be incorporated under Part II of the *Canada Corporations Act* for objects that are "of a national, patriotic, religious, philanthropic, charitable, scientific, artistic, social, professional or sporting character, or the like objects". In addition, the purposes to be carried out must fall within the legislative authority of the Parliament of Canada.

The Public Legal Education Society of Nova Scotia uses a less precise definition. It defines a not-for-profit organization as "any group of people acting together to achieve some purpose other than personal monetary gain".[22] It also notes that the term not-for-profit organization "can relate to many different groups with many different objectives".[23] The Nova Scotia *Societies Act* provides for the incorporation of a wide range of not-for-profit organizations that "promote any benevolent, philanthropic, patriotic, religious, charitable, artistic, literary, educational, social, professional, recreational, or sporting, or any other useful object, but not for the purpose of carrying on any trade, industry or business."[24]

Charitable and not-for-profit organizations are not, however, only those legal entities that are not "businesses". Legally, they have existed for centuries and have provided goods and services for their members and for the community that would otherwise not be as readily available. The legal restriction on distribution of profits does not necessarily mean that charitable or not-for-profit organizations do not or are not to operate in a business-like fashion. Efficiency and effectiveness in the provision of goods and services is as important to officers and directors of charitable and not-for-profit organizations as it is for business organizations. How well either charitable and not-for-profit organizations or business organizations operate will usually depend more on their governance than on their legal status.

Charitable and not-for-profit organizations have a number of characteristics in common. First, both are "not-for-profit" in nature. Neither a charity nor a not-for-profit organization are intended to make a profit or to distribute profits to their members. This characteristic clearly distinguishes them from other forms of associations or organizations which are intended to make profits, including business corporations, partnerships, limited partnerships and sole proprietorships.

Both types of organizations must usually be organized for some "public benefit", although this term is difficult to define with precision. Gen-

---

[21] R.S.C. 1970, c. C.32, s. 154.
[22] Thelma Costello, ed., *Non Profit Organizations: A Nova Scotia Guide* (Halifax: Public Legal Educational Society of Nova Scotia, 1983), at 2.
[23] *Ibid.*
[24] R.S.N.S. 1989, c. 435, s. 3(1).

erally, public benefit includes activities or objects that are intended to provide some benefits to the public or a specified or identifiable group of the public. What will be considered to be a public benefit is even more restrictive for charitable organizations. For example, a not-for-profit social club for members may be incorporated as a not-for-profit corporation but its social club objects are not charitable.

Charitable and not-for-profit organizations must devote their assets to furthering their objects and not to other purposes. As a result, the activities of these organizations are more restricted than those of, for example, a business corporation. If the charitable or not-for-profit organization operates any business activity, that activity must usually be incidental to the objects of the organization and the income and profits from the activity must be used to further the objects of the organization. Charitable organizations, in particular, are restricted in the types and size of business activities in which they may be involved. In Ontario, for example, the *Charitable Gifts Act*[25] regulates the ownership and sale by charities of business entities.

There are critical differences between charitable and not-for-profit organizations. Each is a distinct type of legal entity with different legal obligations and rights. Both types of organizations may be intended to be "not-for-profit" in the sense that they are not to distribute "profits" to their members. Organizations that have charitable objects, however, are more narrow in the types of public benefits that they will provide. In return, charitable organizations receive substantial privileges to carry out their objects.

A major privilege is the opportunity for registration with the Canada Customs and Revenue Agency as a charitable organization for purposes of the *Income Tax Act*.[26] Under the Act, the organization does not have to pay federal income tax on its income and it can issue charitable income tax receipts for donations received from others. Charitable organizations, in particular those that are registered with the Canada Customs and Revenue Agency, may receive additional privileges and exemptions from other forms of taxation, including provincial corporate taxes, goods and services taxes, retail sales taxes and municipal assessments.[27] Not-for-profit organizations may also receive some exemptions or privileges, but they are more restricted.[28]

---

[25] R.S.O. 1990, c. C.8.
[26] R.S.C. 1985 c. I (5th Supp.), s. 149.1.
[27] Part IX (Goods and Services Tax), *Excise Tax Act*, R.S.C. 1985, c. E-15 [am. S.C. 1990, c. 45]. See also *Corporations Tax Act*, R.S.O. 1990, c. C.40, s. 57; *Retail Sales Tax Act*, R.S.O. 1990, c. R.31, s. 9(2); R.R.O. 1990, Reg. 1012, s. 12; O. Reg. 1013/90, ss. 14 and 22; *Assessment Act*, R.S.O. 1990, c. A.31, s. 3.
[28] See Revenue Canada's Interpretation Bulletin, "Non-Profit Organizations," IT-496, February 18, 1983, for a discussion of the exemption from income tax for some not-for-profit organizations.

D WHAT IS "CHARITABLE"

I THE ENGLISH LAW

(1) Defining "Charitable"

The definition of "charitable" or "charity" is central to the distinction between charitable and not-for-profit organizations. The case law concerning charities is considerable, especially in England. In England, the Charity Commissioners were established by the *Charitable Trusts Act, 1853*.[29] The Commissioners were continued and modernized by the *Charities Act, 1960*[30] and more recently by the *Charities Act, 1993*.[31] The Charity Commissioners apply case law and legislation to perform a supervisory role over charitable organizations. This supervisory role arises out of the need to protect the public interest in charitable monies. There are no similar comprehensive legislative provisions governing Canadian charities. Only Ontario has legislation that is intended to administratively regulate certain aspects of charitable organizations — the *Charitable Gifts Act*,[32] the *Charitable Institutions Act*,[33] and the *Charities Accounting Act*.[34]

The *Charities Accounting Act* provides some guidance. It defines "charitable purpose" as being:

- relief of poverty;
- advancement of education;
- advancement of religion; or
- any other purpose beneficial to the community not falling under the other three purposes.

However, the statute does not provide a comprehensive definition of charity that is clear and apparent for most cases. The fourth purpose, in particular, is very wide in scope, open to interpretation and difficult to use with any precision.

Popular definitions of charity focus on the "poor" in society. The legal definitions of charity are somewhat broader, although no precise definition has been developed. A series of English cases attempted to define in rough terms what is charitable but "no comprehensive definition of legal charity has been given either by the legislature or in judicial utterance", according to Viscount Simonds in *I.R.C. v. Baddeley*.[35]

---

[29] (U.K.), 1853, 16 & 17 Vict., c. 137.
[30] (U.K.), 1960, 8 & 9 Eliz. 2, c. 58.
[31] (U.K.), 1993, c. 10.
[32] R.S.O. 1990, c. C.8.
[33] R.S.O. 1990, c. C.9.
[34] R.S.O. 1990, c. C.10.
[35] [1955] A.C. 572, at 583 (H.L.).

The generally accepted definition is that of Lord Camden found in *Jones v. Williams*.[36] Lord Camden defines charity as "a gift to the general public use which extends to the poor as well as to the rich". A later case, *Perin v. Carey*[37] did not advance the definition much further when Wayne J. commented that "charity, in a legal sense, is rather a matter of description than of definition".

American case law is no more conclusive. Gray J. in *Jackson v. Phillips*[38] said:

> A charity, in the legal sense, may be more fully defined as a gift to be applied consistently within existing laws, for the benefit of an indefinite number of persons either by bringing their minds or hearts under the influence of education or religion, by relieving their bodies from disease, suffering or constraint, by assisting them to establish themselves in life or by erecting or maintaining public buildings or works, or otherwise lessening the burdens of government.

The definitions used in the cases from the 19th century are "not broad enough" for some commentators.[39] The law recognizes a much wider definition of charity and the types of objects a charity may have. Objects that are recognized as being charitable in the twentieth century, for example, include the activities of humane societies and cultural organizations.

The issue of defining or classifying charitable objects and charitable purposes arose out of the *Statute of Uses, 1601*[40] (also known as the *Charitable Uses Act* and the *Statute of Elizabeth I*). The *Statute of Uses* was not enacted to define charity or charitable objects or purposes, but rather to reform the abuses in the law of uses, an early form of trusts. Prior to the sixteenth century, there was little need to regulate charities. Most of the charitable purposes in England were undertaken by the church or by local manors and guilds. Individuals would donate or bequeath property to the church, which would use the property for what would be recognized as charitable purposes. The ecclesiastical courts were responsible for the supervision of the administration of the property donated or bequeathed.

Changes to the institutional structure of medieval England resulted in a greater opportunity and need for other institutions to become involved

---

[36] (1767), Amb. 651; 8(1) Digest (Repl.) 322, as quoted in Herbert Picarda, *The Law and Practice Relating to Charities* (London: Butterworths, 1977), at 7; and, in *Halsbury's Laws of England*, 4th ed., Vol. 5(2) Charities (London: Butterworths, 1974), para. 505.

[37] (1860), 24 How. 465, at 494, as quoted in Picarda, *supra*, note 36, at 8.

[38] (1867), 14 Allen 539, at 555, as quoted in Picarda, *supra*, note 36, at 8. See also *Corpus Juris Secundum*, Vol. 14 (Brooklyn, N.Y.: The American Law Book, 1939), cited as 14 C.J.S. Charities 5.

[39] Picarda, *supra*, note 36, at 8.

[40] (Imp.), 1601, 43 Eliz. 1, c. 4. See Picarda, *supra*, note 36, for a fuller discussion of the *Statute of Uses*.

in social welfare. Gradually, by the early sixteenth century, the ecclesiastical courts lost jurisdiction over the supervision of the trusts to the Court of Chancery. Supervision was, however, lax and it became apparent that funds were being misapplied. This development, combined with the enactment of the Elizabethan "poor laws" and greater governmental interest in the relief of poverty, led to the *Statute of Uses*. The statute established an administrative framework to supervise the administration and allocation of property that was subject to a use or trust.

A list of charitable objects was included in the preamble to the *Statute of Uses*. The list was extensive and included:

> The relief of aged, impotent and poor people; the maintenance of sick and maimed soldiers and mariners, schools of learning, free schools and scholars in universities; the repair of bridges, ports, havens, causeways, churches, sea-banks and highways; the education and preferment of orphans; the relief, stock or maintenance of houses of correction; the marriages of poor maids, the supportation, aid and help of young tradesmen, handicraftsmen and persons decayed; the relief or redemption of prisoners or captives; and the aid or ease of any poor inhabitants concerning payment of fifteens, setting out of soldiers and other taxes.

Some scholars have noted the similarity between the list in the preamble of the statute and that in the *Vision of Piers Plowman*, a poem from circa 1377.[41] This similarity is consistent with the view that the definition of charity should reflect the values and needs of a society at any given time. These values and needs change. For example, today it is not generally acceptable to establish a scholarship fund for Caucasian, male, protestant students, yet it was in the early part of the twentieth century. This type of scholarship is now prohibited by the *Ontario Human Rights Code*.[42]

The *Statute of Uses* is not law in Canada; however, the list in the preamble has been used to assist in deciding what is or is not a charity, a charitable object or a charitable purpose. The first major attempt to use the preamble was in the English case of *Morice v. Bishop of Durham*.[43] The case arose from a will in which a testatrix bequeathed the residuary of her estate for "such objects of benevolence and liberalities as the Bishop of Durham in his own discretion shall most approve of". The bequest was challenged by the next of kin on the grounds that the bequest was not for charitable purposes because the objects were not certain.

Counsel for the Bishop argued that the prevailing view was that a trust need only result in a public benefit for it to be considered a charity. Sir

---

[41] Picarda, *supra*, note 36, at 9.
[42] R.S.O. 1990, c. H.19. See *Canada Trust Co. v. Ontario (Human Rights Commission)* (1990), 20 A.C.W.S. (3d) 736 (Ont. C.A.); revg (1987), 61 O.R. (2d) 75, 42 D.L.R. (4th) 263 (H.C.).
[43] [1803-13] All E.R. 451, at 453, 10 Ves. 522, 32 E.R. 947 (L.C.).

Samuel Romilly, for the next of kin, argued that the objects were not charitable because a public benefit would not necessarily be derived from the bequest. The court ruled, at trial, that charity in law must involve more than just a public benefit. On appeal, Romilly expanded on his argument that the definition must be restricted. He attempted to reconcile the case law into four categories:

> There are four objects, within one of which all charities, to be administered in this court, must fall. 1st, relief of indigent; in various ways: money: provisions: education: medical assistance: etc. 2dly, the advancement of learning: 3dly, the advancement of religion; and 4thly, which is the most difficult, the advancement of objects of general public utility.[44]

Lord Chancellor Eldon held that the trust in the *Bishop of Durham* case was not charitable in nature and that the legal definition of charity was restricted to those articulated in the *Statute of Uses* and other purposes that were analogous to those purposes. This overall approach to determining if an object is charitable remains the judicial and administrative approach today.

Although the *Statute of Uses* was replaced by the *Mortmain and Charitable Uses Act*[45] and by subsequent legislation reforming charitable law in England, it continues to be used as a guide. Russell L.J. commented in *Incorporated Council of Law Reporting for England and Wales v. A.G.*[46] that:

> The Statute of Elizabeth I was a statute to reform abuses; in such circumstances and in that age the courts of this country were not inclined to be restricted in their implementation of Parliament's desire for reform to particular examples given by the Statute: and they deliberately kept open their ability to intervene when they thought necessary in cases not specifically mentioned, by applying as the test whether any particular case of abuse of funds or property was within the "mischief" or the "equity" of the Statute.

> For myself, I believe that this rather vague and undefined approach is the correct one, with analogy, its handmaid, and that when considering Lord Macnaghten's fourth category in *Pemsel's* case ... the courts, in consistently saying that not all such are necessarily charitable in law, are in substance accepting that if a purpose is shown to be so beneficial or of such utility it is prima facie charitable in law, but have left open a line of retreat based on the equity of the Statute in case they are faced with a purpose (e.g. a political purpose) which could not have been within the contemplation of the Statute even if the then legislators had been endowed with the gift of foresight into the circumstances of later centuries.

---

[44] *Ibid.*, (All E.R.), at 455.
[45] (U.K.), 1888, 51 & 52 Vict., c. 42.
[46] [1972] 1 Ch. 73, at 88, [1971] 3 All E.R. 1029 (C.A.).

Lord Russell in the *Incorporated Council of Law* case referred to *Pemsel's Case* or the *Income Tax Special Purposes Commrs. v. Pemsel*.[47] *Pemsel's Case* is considered to be the major judicial approval of the classification of charitable purposes and charitable objects. In *Pemsel's Case*, Lord Macnaghten adopted Romilly's classification system. The case arose from a decision of the Inland Revenue Commissioners to restrict the types of charities that would not be subject to taxation on their income. Chancellor of the Exchequer Gladstone was concerned with the loss of tax revenue that resulted from the exemption. He also noted that the exemption amounted to a subsidy from the government to the wealthier charities. The less wealthy charities, which raised money through subscriptions, received little benefit from the tax exemption. Although no legislative action was taken at that time, the Inland Revenue Commissioners altered their administrative practice so that only those organizations that were involved in the relief of poverty were exempted. In 1886, the Commissioners refused to grant an exemption to the Protestant Episcopal Church, also known as the Moravian Church. The refusal led to *Pemsel's Case*.

The Moravian Church had received, in 1813, lands which were to be held in trust. The income from the lands was to be applied to the establishment and maintenance of missionaries. The Commissioners took the position that the legal definition of charity, for income tax purposes, did not include the purposes of the Moravian Church. Pemsel, the treasurer, took the position that charity should be given a broader interpretation, such as in trust law. Lord Macnaghten, writing for the majority of the House of Lords, ruled in favour of the Moravian Church. He commented:

> With the policy of taxing charities I have nothing to do. It may be right, or it may be wrong; but speaking for myself, I am not sorry to be compelled to give my voice for the respondent. To my mind it is rather startling to find the established practice of so many years suddenly set aside by an administrative department of their own motion, and after something like an assurance given to Parliament that no change would be made without the interposition of the Legislature.[48]

He outlined the four "principal divisions" of charitable purposes:

> "Charity" in its legal sense comprises four principal divisions: trusts for the relief of poverty; trusts for the advancement of education; trusts for the advancement of religion; and trusts for other purposes beneficial to the community, not falling under any of the preceding heads.[49]

---

[47] [1891] A.C. 531 (H.L.).
[48] *Ibid.*, at 591.
[49] *Ibid.*, at 583.

Lord Macnaghten emphasized in his judgment that there is a legal definition of "charity". By its nature, that legal definition may exclude some objects that non-lawyers might consider to be charitable in nature.[50] Unless the context requires otherwise, statutory references to "charity" are to be construed within the legal sense of charity that has been judicially developed.[51]

There are distinctions between the objects or purposes of the charitable organization, the means by which it is to carry out those objects or purposes and the consequences of carrying them out. A charitable organization may carry out its objects or purposes using powers that are not charitable.[52] For example, it may have the power to sell goods and services provided that it does so to carry out its charitable objects.

(2) Defining "Public Benefit"

The essential element in all four divisions of charitable objects or purposes is whether or not there is a public benefit. There must be a public benefit for the object or purpose to be charitable in its "legal sense". Whether or not an object or purpose has a public benefit is a question of fact based upon the evidence before the court.[53]

The public benefit, to be viewed as charitable, must benefit the whole community or a significant part of an appreciably important class within the community.[54] What is a sufficient or significant part of the community is not always clear. However, in *Oppenheim v. Tobacco Securities Trust Co.* the Court noted that the words "section of community" are a convenient indicator that: "the possible (I emphasize the word 'possible') beneficiaries must not be numerically negligible, and secondly, that the quality which distinguishes them from other members of the community ... must be a quality which does not depend on their relationship to a particular individual".

The assessment of this component of the test depends upon the charitable object or purpose that is being assessed. Certainly, the benefit cannot be a "private" one in which the numbers are so insignificant that the general public does not benefit from the object or purpose. For example, a community not-for-profit theatre may not be used by all members of a community; however, if it is available for general public use and

---

[50] *Shaw (Public Trustee) v. Day*, [1957] 1 All E.R. 745, at 752. See *Halsbury's Laws of England*, Vol. 5(2) Charities, for a thorough discussion of what is or is not charitable in law in England.

[51] *Pemsel's Case, supra*, note 47, at 580; *Chesterman v. Federal Taxation Commr.*, [1926] A.C. 128 (P.C.); *Adamson v. Melbourne and Metropolitan Board of Works*, [1929] A.C. 142 (P.C.).

[52] *Chichester Diocesan Fund and Board of Finance Inc. v. Simpson*, [1944] A.C. 341, at 371; *McGovern et al., v. A.G. et al.*, [1982] Ch. 321, [1981] 3 All E.R. 493 (Ch.).

[53] *Nat. Anti-Vivisection Society v. Inland Revenue Commrs.*, [1948] A.C. 31, [1947] 2 All E.R. 217, at 219 (H.L.).

[54] *Oppenheim v. Tobacco Securities Trust Co.*, [1951] 1 All E.R. 31 (H.L.); *Verge v. Somerville*, [1924] A.C. 496 (J.C.P.C.); *Re Cranston, Webb v. Oldfield*, [1898] 1 I.R. 448.

will be used by a substantial portion of the public, it would probably be viewed as providing a "public benefit". If the object or purpose has a general public utility and comes within the "spirit and intendment" of the preamble to the *Statute of Uses, 1601* it will usually be held to be charitable.[55]

The intention of any donor or of the persons establishing the charitable organization is not relevant in making the assessment. The court is concerned with its ability to control the administration of any charitable trust as a public benefit. Lord Russell, in *Re Hummeltenberg*,[56] concluded that the intention of the donor may be a factor in the assessment but it is not decisive. He commented that:

> So far as the views so expressed declare that the personal or private opinion of the judge is immaterial, I agree; but so far as they lay down or suggest that the donor of the gift or the creator of the trust is to determine whether the purpose is beneficial to the public, I respectfully disagree. If a testator by stating or indicating his view that a trust is beneficial to the public can establish that fact beyond question, trust might be established in perpetuity for the promoting of all kinds of fantastic (though not unlawful) objects of which the training of poodles to dance might be a mild example. In my opinion, the question whether a gift is or may be operative for the public benefit is a question to be answered by the court by forming an opinion upon the evidence before it.

The test of what is or is not a public benefit is not the opinion of the donor or creator of the charitable trust; nor is it the personal opinion of the judge reviewing the matter. Rather, it appears to be related to what most people in a society would view as being of a public benefit. Lord Simonds, in *National Anti-Vivisection Society v. I.R.C.*, reviewed several of the cases on public benefit. Quoting from earlier cases, he wrote:

> The question remained whether the object of the societies was charitable and after stating that the objects must be one by which the public, or a section of the public, benefits, the Lord Justice proceeds:
>
> ... but what is the test or standard by which a particular gift is to be tried with a view of ascertaining whether it is beneficial in this sense? I am of opinion that it does not depend upon the view entertained by any individual — either by the judge who is to decide the question or by the person who makes the gift.

---

[55] *National Anti-Vivisection v. Inland Revenue Commrs.*, [1947] 2 All E.R. 217, at 220 (H.L.). See also *Incorporated Council of Law Reporting for England and Wales v. A.G.*, [1972] 1 Ch. 73, [1971] 3 All E.R. 1029 (C.A.); *Scottish Burial Reform and Cremation Society Ltd. v. Glasgow (City) Corp.*, [1967] 3 All E.R. 215 (H.L.).

[56] [1923] All E.R. 49, at 51 (Ch. D.).

He answers the question by saying:

> There is probably no purpose that all men would agree is beneficial to the community: but there are surely many purposes which everyone would admit are generally so regarded, although individuals differ as to their expediency or utility. The test or stand is, I believe, to be found in this common understanding.[57]

The concept of public benefit would appear to be based on a common understanding within a society. What is or is not a public benefit, therefore, is not static but will develop as the common understanding evolves. It will depend upon the social conditions at the time of the assessment. What once was considered to be a public benefit may, in the 21st century, no longer be seen as such. As with the overall judicial approach to the term "charitable", the interpretation of "public benefit" evolves to accommodate changes in society and the needs of society.[58] Lord Simonds noted in *National Anti-Vivisection* that:

> A purpose regarded in one age as charitable may in another be regarded differently.... A bequest in the will of a testator dying in 1700 might be held valid upon the evidence then before the court, but, upon different evidence, held invalid if he died in 1900. So, too, I conceive that an anti-vivisection society might at different times be differently regarded. But this is not to say that a charitable trust, when it has once been established, can ever fail. If, by a change in social habits and needs, or, it may be, by a change in the law, the purpose of an established charity becomes superfluous or even illegal, or if, with increasing knowledge, it appears that a purpose once thought beneficial is truly detrimental to the community, it is the duty of the trustees of an established charity to apply to the court ... and ask that a *cy-pres* scheme be established.... A charity once established does not die, though its nature may be changed. But it is wholly consistent with this that in a later age the court should decline to regard as charitable a purpose, to which in an earlier age that quality would have been ascribed ... I cannot share the apprehension of Lord Greene, M.R., that great confusion will be caused if the court declines to be bound by the beliefs and knowledge of a past age in considering whether a particular purpose is today for the benefit of the community, but, if it is so, then I say that it is the lesser of two evils.[59]

In short, what is or is not a public benefit in law depends upon the conditions of society at any particular time and the common understanding within that society of what is or is not a public benefit.

---

[57] [1947] 2 All E.R. 217, at 237 (H.L.).
[58] See *Gilmour v. Coats*, [1949] 1 All E.R. 848, at 853 (H.L.); *Re Campden Charities* (1881), 18 Ch. D. 310; *A.G. v. Marchant* (1866), L.R. 3 Eq. 424 (Ch.).
[59] *Nat. Anti-Vivisection v. Inland Revenue Commrs.*, [1947] 2 All E.R. 217, at 238.

(3) Relief of Poverty

An object or purpose that is intended to relieve poverty will usually be charitable in nature. Poverty does not mean, however, that the individuals who will be eligible for assistance need to be destitute. Being "poor" is a relative term. It depends upon the overall economic and social conditions that exist in a society, the needs of individuals in that society and how society has changed.[60] The English case law is extensive on interpreting relief of poverty and applying it to different fact situations.[61]

(4) Advancement of Education

The advancement of education does not require an element of poverty, although assistance for the poor to become educated would, of course, be a charitable object or purpose. The advancement of education is a charitable object or purpose in and of itself. The intent appears to be to ensure that human knowledge continues to be improved and that the public finds out about these advances in knowledge.[62] The advancement of education, though, must have a public and not a private benefit. As a result, private research for private gain would not be a charitable purpose. The results of any research must be useful, be disseminated to the public, and benefit a sufficient portion of the public to be charitable.[63] The education of classes of persons within society may also be a charitable purpose.[64] Continuing education of professionals provides a private benefit and not a public benefit. As a result, it would not be a charitable purpose.[65] Similarly, education that is intended to advance a political point of view or party is not charitable.[66]

(5) Advancement of Religion

An object that is intended to advance a particular religion is charitable in nature, provided that the object is otherwise lawful.[67] The promotion of spiritual teachings generally or with respect to a particular religion fall

---

[60] *Trustees of Mary Clark Home v. Anderson*, [1904] 2 K.B. 645; *Re Coulthurst's Will Trusts*, [1951] 1 All E.R. 744, at 785.
[61] See *Halsbury's Laws of England*, Vol. 5(2), Charities, paras. 16–23, for a more detailed review of the cases.
[62] *Incorporated Council of Law Reporting for England and Wales v. A.G.*, [1971] 3 All E.R. 1029, at 1046 (C.A.).
[63] *McGovern et al. v. A.G. et al.*, [1981] 3 All E.R. 493, [1982] Ch. 321 (Ch.), quoting from *Re Besterman's Will Trusts*, an unreported case of January 21, 1980. See also *Halsbury's Laws of England*, Vol. 5(2), Charities, para. 24.
[64] *Oppenheim v. Tobacco Securities Trust Co. Ltd.*, [1951] 1 All E.R. 31, at 33 (H.L.).
[65] *Chartered Insurance Institute v. Corpn. of London*, [1957] 2 All E.R. 638 (D.C.).
[66] *Re Hopkinson, Lloyds Bank Ltd. v. Baker*, [1949] 1 All E.R. 346 (Ch. D.); *Bonar Law Memorial Trust v. Inland Revenue Commrs.* (1933), 49 T.L.R. 220.
[67] *Bowman v. Secular Society Ltd.*, [1917] A.C. 406 (H.L.); *Nat. Anti-Vivisection Society v. Inland Revenue Commrs.*, [1947] 2 All E.R. 217, at 220 (H.L).

within this category of charitable objects. As with all charitable objects, there must be a demonstrable public benefit to the religious object.[68] A purely contemplative order of nuns, for example, does not provide a sufficient degree of public benefit to be charitable.[69]

(6) Other Purposes Beneficial to the Community

The English case law with respect to the fourth category of charity — other purposes beneficial to the public — is very extensive.[70] As discussed above, there must be a general public benefit that falls within the spirit and intent of the preamble to the *Statute of Uses, 1601*. Private charities do not fall within this category. Gifts for a particular individual are also not charitable in nature.[71]

II THE CANADIAN CASE LAW

(1) General Comments

The four categories of charitable purposes developed in England formed the basic concept and definition of charity in Canada.[72] The courts and various departments and agencies of government categorize purported charitable and not-for-profit objects and organizations into one of the four divisions. Canadian commentators have noted that there is a wide acceptance that the first three divisions are of "public benefit". The fourth division, however, is vague and open-ended and has been used more out of convenience than always as a result of rigourous analysis. It probably includes any organization that would fall within the first three divisions because they are all, by definition, "beneficial to the community" or to the public. The problem is in determining what is not beneficial to the community or to the public in a charitable sense.[73]

(2) Relief of Poverty

The definition of what is or is not relief of poverty is fairly broad in Canada. There does not, for example, have to be a specific "public aspect" for a trust to qualify under this category of charity.[74] The type of suffer-

---

[68] *Cocks v. Manners* (1871), L.R. 12 Eq. 574, at 585 (H.L.).
[69] *Gilmour v. Coats*, [1949] 1 All E.R. 848 (H.L.).
[70] See *Halsbury's Laws of England*, Vol. 5(2), Charities, paras. 37–51.
[71] *Ibid.*, paras. 52–57.
[72] *Scarborough Community Legal Services v. M.N.R.*, [1985] 2 F.C. 555, at 577 (C.A.); *Guaranty Trust Co. of Can. v. M.N.R.*, [1967] S.C.R. 133.
[73] Professor Neil Brooks, "Charities: The Legal Framework," a background paper for the Secretary of State for Canada, 1983, at 21-22, 24.
[74] *Jones v. T. Eaton Co.*, [1973] S.C.R. 635; affg. [1971] 2 O.R. 316 (*sub nom. Re Bethel*) (C.A.).

ing or distress includes mental illness,[75] blindness[76] and the neglect of children.[77]

The relief of poverty category has expanded since the early twentieth century and is intended to reflect the changing needs of Canadian society. *Minister of Municipal Affairs of New Brunswick v. (Maria F.) Ganong Old Folks Home* is an example of how the category has changed with the times. It is also consistent with the approach taken in the English cases. Hughes C.J.N.B. commented that:

> Social conditions have vastly changed in this Province since 1934 when Mrs. Ganong's will took effect. Social security and other financial assistance provided by Government and otherwise have nearly extinguished the class of persons who formerly were regarded as "poor" or "needy"....
>
> Formerly the Courts held the view that if a gift for the benefit of aged persons was to be upheld there must be an element of poverty.... In recent years, however, the English Courts have departed from that view and I think it is now recognized that the words "aged, impotent, and poor" in the preamble to the Statute of Elizabeth I are to be read disjunctively so that aged persons need not also be poor to come within the preamble.[78]

Individuals should no longer be disqualified from receiving benefits under a charitable bequest because they also receive government assistance.[79] Courts must maintain currency with social conditions and realities, according to the Alberta Court of Appeal in *Re St. Catharine's House*.[80] The Court based its decision in part on "the liberal interpretations which the courts over the years [have] given to the word 'charity'". The Alberta Court of Appeal looked to the spirit and intent of the *Statute of Uses, 1601* and the subsequent case law to assist in reaching its decision.[81]

(3) Advancement of Education

The second category of charity, the advancement of education, has also received a broad interpretation in the Canadian courts. It includes the provision of financial assistance to students[82] and for publication of "an

---

[75] *Moorcroft v. Simpson* (1921), 64 D.L.R. 231 (Ont. H.C.).
[76] *Re McDonald* (1980), 105 D.L.R. (3d) 681 (B.C. S.C.).
[77] *Re Kinny* (1903), 6 O.L.R. 459 (In Chambers).
[78] (1981), 129 D.L.R. (3d) 655, at 663-64 (N.B. C.A.).
[79] *Re Forgan* (1961), 29 D.L.R. (2d) 585 (Alta. S.C.).
[80] (1977), 2 A.R. 337 (C.A.).
[81] *Ibid.*, at 348.
[82] *Re Spencer* (1928), 34 O.W.N. 29 (S.C.).

unknown Canadian author".[83] The advancement of education is not restricted to teaching, but includes research, provided that the research is of educational value to the person conducting the research or advances knowledge, which may in turn be taught.[84]

However, if the underlying purpose of the purported charity is not "exclusively charitable," but has economic or political objects, it may not fall within this category. For example, in *Co-op College of Can. v. Sask. Human Rights Comm.*,[85] the Saskatchewan Court of Appeal held that the college had educational purposes, but these were primarily to educate members of the co-operative and credit union movement. The educational purposes provided a private and not a public benefit. Similarly, if the educational purposes are inextricably connected to a political purpose, such as the promotion of social change with respect to pornography, the object will not be charitable.[86] A trust established by a trade union and an employer to retrain employees would not come within this category because it does not provide a sufficient degree of public benefit.[87]

The simple "presentation to the public of selected items of information and opinion on the subject of pornography ... cannot be regarded as educational in the sense understood by this branch of the law".[88] The activities contemplated by the objects or purposes must be more than just the provision of information about national unity. In order to qualify as an advancement of education, there must be some element of training or instruction in the dissemination of information.[89]

"Advancement of education" and what it means in a modern society was at issue in *Vancouver Society of Immigrant and Visible Minority Women v. M.N.R.*[90] The Supreme Court, in a 4 to 3 majority, dismissed the Society's appeal from the Minister and refused to register it as a charitable organization. The case is also important for the role of the court in keeping the common law definition relevant. However, all agreed with the following comments of Mr. Justice Iacobucci on what "advancement of education" means:

> In my view, there is much to be gained by adopting a more inclusive approach to education for the purposes of the law of charity. Indeed, compared to the English approach, the limited Canadian definition of educa-

---

[83] *Re Shapiro* (1979), 6 E.T.R. 276 (Ont. S.C.). But see the annotation of Professor John Smith, which argues that the trust does not satisfy the requirements because the money could be used to produce something that is not beneficial to the public.
[84] *Wood v. R.*, [1977] 6 W.W.R. 273 (Alta. T.D.); *Seafarers Training Institute v. Williamsburg* (1982), 39 O.R. (2d) 370 (T.D.).
[85] [1976] 2 W.W.R. 84 (Sask. C.A.).
[86] *Positive Action Against Pornography v. M.N.R.*, [1988] 2 F.C. 340 (C.A.).
[87] *L.I.U.N.A., Local 527, Members' Training Trust v. R.* (1992), 47 E.T.R. 29.
[88] *Positive Action Against Pornography v. M.N.R.*, [1988] 2 F.C. 340, at 349 (C.A.).
[89] *Canada UNI Assn. v. M.N.R.* (1992), 151 N.R. 4, [1993] 1 F.C. D-31 (C.A.).
[90] [1999] 1 S.C.R. 10.

tion as the "formal training of the mind" or the "improvement of a useful branch of human knowledge" seems unduly restrictive. There seems no logical or principled reason why the advancement of education should not be interpreted to include more informal training initiatives, aimed at teaching necessary life skills or providing information toward a practical end, so long as these are truly geared at the training of the mind and not just the promotion of a particular point of view. Notwithstanding the limitations posed by the existing jurisprudence, to adopt such an approach would amount to no more than the type of incremental change to the common of which the Court has approved in such decisions as *Watkins v. Olafson*, [1989] 2 S.C.R. 750, and *Salituro*.

To limit the notion of "training of the mind" to structured, systematic instruction or traditional academic subjects reflects an outmoded and under inclusive understanding of education which is of little use in modern Canadian society. As I said earlier, the purpose of offering certain benefits to charitable organizations is to promote activities which are seen as being of special benefit to the community, or advancing a common goal. In the case of education, the good advanced is knowledge or training. Thus, so long as information or training is provided in a structured manner and for a genuinely educational purpose - that is, to advance the knowledge or abilities of the recipients - and not solely to promote a particular point of view or political orientation, it may properly be viewed as falling within the advancement of education.[91]

The majority had some limitations to this interpretation. It was concerned that education not be broadened beyond recognition. There must be actual teaching or learning components. There must be some legitimate, targeted attempt at educating others whether through formal or informal instruction, training, plans of self-study or otherwise. An opportunity for people to educate themselves is not sufficient. Another concern is that while education may be directed toward a practical end, at some point it ceases to be an end and becomes an activity. That activity must be independently determined to be charitable.[92]

(4) Advancement of Religion

Although not all religious purposes are recognized as being charitable in Canada, the courts seem to take a very broad interpretation of what a valid religious purpose is. Religious purposes are charitable if they instruct or edify the public either directly or indirectly. In *Re Brooks*,[93] the

---

[91] *Ibid.*, at paras. 168 to 169. The dissenting opinion agreed with the definition of "advancement of education" set out in para. 169, at para. 77 of Mr. Justice Gonthier's opinion.
[92] *Ibid.*, at paras. 171 to 172.
[93] (1969), 68 W.W.R. 132 (Sask. Q.B.).

Saskatchewan Court of Queen's Bench held that a gift "to the work of the Lord" was charitable and not void for uncertainty. The Nova Scotia Supreme Court ruled in *Re Armstrong*[94] that a direction to a trustee to make payments to a church for ancillary projects was within the category where the projects were related to the activities of the church.

The courts have turned down some objects on the grounds that they were not for the advancement of religion. In *Jewish Nat. Fund v. Royal Trust Co.*,[95] the Supreme Court of Canada held that a bequest to the Jewish National Fund for the purpose of a tract or tracts "of the best lands available in Palestine, the United States of America or any British Dominion, and the establishment thereon of a Jewish colony or colonies" was not a trust for a religious purpose.

What is "religion" is a legal question, based on the evidence before the court. It is not necessarily dependent upon the religious beliefs of the individuals involved. Thus, a belief that farming is the only activity compatible with religious life does not make farming a religious or charitable activity.[96] A trust for the encouragement of the study of comparative religions also would not qualify as a charitable trust, although it could qualify under the second category, the advancement of education.[97] In order to qualify under the advancement of religion, the court must be able to answer the question "What religion does the organization advance and how does it advance it?"

(5) Other Purposes Beneficial to the Community

The fourth category of charity, for other purposes that are beneficial to the community, is the most broad and difficult to consider. Often charitable objects that fail to meet the criteria for the first three categories may be considered under this category. A bequest to a conservation group meets the requirements[98] as do humane societies.[99] Neither would have qualified under the first three categories of charitable objects and purposes.

A municipality in Canada is not a charity but an "artificial being" that is invisible, intangible and exists only in contemplation of law, according to *Northumberland & Durham v. Murray & Brighton Public School Trustees*.[100] A municipality is a political body and not a charitable organization

---

[94] (1969), 7 D.L.R. (3d) 36 (N.S. S.C.).
[95] [1965] S.C.R. 780, at 793.
[96] *Hutterian Brethren Church of Wilson v. R.*, [1980] 1 F.C. 757, at 759 (C.A.), quoting *Hofer v. Hofer*, [1970] S.C.R. 958, at 980. But see also Mr. Justice Ryan's discussion of this issue at 764-66 in *Hutterian Brethren*.
[97] *Re Russell, v. R.* (1977), 1 E.T.R. 285 (T.D.).
[98] *Re Hogle*, [1939] O.R. 425 (H.C.).
[99] *Re Toronto Humane Society* (1920), 18 O.W.N. 414 (H.C.J.); *Re Johnston*, [1968] 1 O.R. 483 (H.C.J.).
[100] [1939] O.W.N. 565 (H.C.J.); see also *Auckland Harbour Bd. v. Commr. of Inland Revenue*, [1959] N.Z.L.R. 204.

or a charity; a gift to a municipality for a local public purpose may be, however, a valid charitable bequest.[101] Although governments clearly provide services that are of a public benefit, their role in society is to govern. A government is not a charitable organization even if the services that it provides, if provided by a charitable organization, are a charitable activity. A sanitorium where the county treasurer held the endowment fund in trust for the benefit of the institution was charitable.[102] Similarly, a trust for the beautification of property within the view of public highways, controlled by a government department, could be a charitable trust.[103] In both cases, the "charitable trust" was only being held by the office holder; it did not make the office-holder a charitable organization.

In *Nanaimo Community Bingo Assn. v. British Columbia (Attorney General)*[104] the British Columbia court dealt with the distinction between charitable and government in context of the use of proceeds from lottery licences. The Attorney General argued that the use of proceeds by government for education and health care were charitable purposes. Mr. Justice Owen-Flood disagreed. He commented:

> I see no merit in this contention. While it may be true that the *Criminal Code* does not require that the same charitable or religious aim must exist between the licensee of the bingo event and the end to which the proceeds from that event are eventually put, it goes without saying that Government responsibility for health care and education is not a matter of charity but rather one of duty. It is a novel proposition of the respondent that government funds directed to health care and education constitutes an act of charity. In any event, just as it would have ill behooved Robin Hood to have robbed from charity to give to other charities, likewise, it ill serves Government, even with the best of motives, to in effect expropriate charitable and religious funds.[105]

Not all purposes that have a public benefit will be considered charitable. For example, an organization whose objects included encouraging awareness of railway history and preservation of railway structures and rolling stock could fall within this category. However, if the activities are too member-oriented and not oriented towards the public, it would not have the requisite public character to qualify.[106]

---

[101] *Re Wright* (1917), 12 O.W.N. 184 (H.C.J.).
[102] *Lapointe v. Ontario (Public Trustee)* (1993), 1 E.T.R. (2d) 203.
[103] *Re Cotton Trust for Rural Beautification* (1980), 9 E.T.R. 125 (P.E.I. S.C.). The government department, however, is obliged to use the funds only for the purposes set out in the trust document.
[104] (1998), 52 B.C.L.R. (3d) 284 (S.C.).
[105] *Ibid.*, at 21.
[106] *National Model Railroad Assn. v. Seventh Division, Pacific Northwest Region M.N.R.*, [1989] 2 F.C. D-1, 31 E.T.R. 268 (C.A.).

A gift may also be used for a charitable purpose outside Canada. In *Re Levy Estate*,[107] the Ontario Court of Appeal found that the executor of an estate may be limited in selecting objects in a foreign country that are charitable in Ontario, but that the charitable trust was still valid. The Court was not concerned with the practical arrangements in determining whether a charitable trust was created.

In *Re Laidlaw Foundation*, the Court recognized a broader view of what is or is not beneficial to the community. Mr. Justice Southey adopted the following statement defining community:

> The community must be a definite community or section of the community; it must be identifiable as such; it must be of appreciable importance; and it must not depend on any personal relationship to a particular individual or individuals.[108]

He continued that an Ontario court should not "pay lip service" to the preamble of the *Statute of Uses* because it is "highly artificial and of no real value in deciding whether an object is charitable". In this case, a donation to amateur sporting associations was an acceptable charitable donation under the *Charities Accounting Act* because amateur athletics promoted health, which has a public benefit.[109]

The Federal Court of Appeal has dealt with what is or is not included in this fourth category in a number of taxation cases. In *Native Communications Society v. M.N.R.* the Court summarized the case law (both English and Canadian):

> A review of decided cases suggests that at least the following proposition may be stated as necessary preliminaries to a determination whether a particular purpose can be regarded as a charitable one falling under the fourth head ...
>
> a) the purpose must be beneficial to the community in a way in which the law regards as charitable by coming within the "spirit and intendment" to the preamble to the *Statute of Elizabeth* if not within its letter.
>
> b) whether a purpose would or may operate for the public benefit is to be answered by the courts on the basis of the record before it and in exercise of its equitable jurisdiction in matters of charity.[110]

The Court quoted — with approval — Lord Wilberforce that "the law of charity is a moving subject".[111] The Court was also cognizant of a special

---

[107] (1989), 68 O.R. (2d) 385 (C.A.).
[108] (1984), 18 E.T.R. 77, at 113, 58 O.R. (2d) 549 (Div. Ct.).
[109] See also the annotation to this case in 18 E.T.R. 77, at 120–32.
[110] [1986] 3 F.C. 471, at 479–80 (C.A.). Case citations deleted.
[111] *Ibid.*, at 480. *Scottish Burial Reform and Cremation Society Ltd. v. Glasgow City Corpn.*, [1968] A.C. 138, at 154 (H.L.).

legal position in Canadian society occupied by Aboriginal peoples arising out of s. 35 of the *Constitution Act, 1982* and the large role that the state plays in their lives. It concluded that a newspaper that included political news, nonetheless, had objects within the fourth category. The newspaper was used for more than conveying news; it made the readers aware of cultural activities and attempted to foster language and culture. The Court commented that "it would be a mistake to dispose of this appeal on the basis of how this purpose or that may or may not have been seen by the courts in the decided cases as being charitable or not. This is especially so of the English decisions relied upon, none of which are concerned with activities directed toward aboriginal people".[112]

The special position of Aboriginal peoples was also addressed in *Gull Bay Development Corp. v. R.*[113] This case and *Native Communications Society* appear to stand for the proposition that because of the special relationship at law and in the Constitution between the federal government and Aboriginal peoples (in particular, status Indians), there may be a broader interpretation of what is or is not a public benefit in a First Nation community. However, both cases also noted that the activities must be carried out for charitable purposes. The achievement of the charitable purposes may have been inherently an indirect result of the organization's activities, however, there was still a requirement to do so. The organization could indirectly accomplish what could not be accomplished directly by the alternative structures, such as the Band Councils.[114] It is not clear to what extent these two cases reflect a substantive legal difference or would be available in other circumstances not involving Aboriginal persons. The cases used in *Gull Bay* would suggest that it does not represent a significant departure from the previous case law; it may, instead, build on the practical approach of the law of charities — what the results will be, not necessarily the method of achieving the results.

Mr. Justice Marceau in *Toronto Volgograd Committee v. M.N.R.* discusses the difference between "purposes" and "activities". He notes that the classification system used since the *Pemsel* case was with respect to "charitable trusts" and their purposes while the *Income Tax Act* is concerned with "activities". He comments that:

> When used with respect to *activities* and in the context of tax law, some adaptation will undoubtedly be required to make it capable of identifying those activities sufficiently beneficial to be entitled to the very special tax treatment conferred by the Act. For one thing, it seems to me obvious that the vagueness of the fourth heading is particularly troubling when applied

---

[112] *Ibid.*, at 482.
[113] [1984] 2 F.C. 3 (T.D.).
[114] See *Toronto Volgograd Committee v. M.N.R.*, [1988] F.C. 251, at 255 (C.A.). Mahoney J. refers only to the *Native Communications* case; however, his comment would appear to be consistent with the rationale set out in *Gull Bay Development Corp. v. R.*, *supra*, note 113, at 20-21.

to activities as it appears almost totally meaningless if not somehow reformulated with more precise language. But the point I really wish to make here is that, to be assigned validly and usefully to one of the four headings of the classification, activities must necessarily ... be considered with respect to their immediate result and effect, not their possible eventual consequence. In other words, the activity will draw its charitable quality from what it itself accomplishes not from what may eventually flow from it or be somehow indirectly achieved by it.

It is not clear how the courts will reconcile these different approaches and whether or not such will affect the special position of Aboriginal people. However, it is clear from the separate written reasons of the appellant judges that the activities undertaken by the purported charitable organization or proposed to be undertaken are relevant to the assessment, for income taxation purposes, of whether or not the organization is charitable.

An assessment of the activities would appear to provide a better basis on which to determine if the organization will be a charity. If reliance were placed only on the constituting documents, it would "enable an organization to conduct its affairs in a manner necessary to satisfy that test for the purposes of securing registration but allow it to pursue other activities authorized by its constituting documents although not charitable ones in the legal sense".[115] The Federal Court, in the *Native Communications*, *Gull Bay* and *Toronto Volgograd* cases appears to have taken a practical approach to determine charitability, at least for purposes of income taxation.

At least one case, *Notre Dame de Grâce Neighbourhood Assn. v. M.N.R.*, has considered expanding the principles set out in the *Native Communications* case to a non-Aboriginal situation. MacGuigan J. noted that the objects were ones which enlightened opinion would regard as qualifying under the advancement of education. He continued that:

> In light of this decision [*Native Communications*] there may well be an argument to be made that an organization similarly dedicated to the interests of the urban disadvantaged as the British Columbia society was to the interests of the native people should qualify as a charity. But, on the facts, this is not such a case.[116]

Its activities, and the ambivalence about its ultimate purposes, resulted in the Notre Dame de Grâce Neighbourhood Association not qualifying as a charitable organization, under either an "enlightened opinion" about the advancement of education or as a benefit to the public. Its purposes may

---

[115] *Ibid.*, at 268.
[116] 85 N.R. 73, at 77, [1988] 3 F.C. D-39 (C.A.).

have qualified; but its activities took it beyond either category into political activism.[117]

One must have regard to all circumstances to determine what types of activities, purposes or objects are within one of the four categories of charities. Analogies to objects that have or have not been accepted by the courts, the Canada Customs and Revenue Agency, the Ontario Public Guardian and Trustee or other regulatory bodies having jurisdiction over charitable matters are the best gauge of whether or not a contemplated object is charitable. Very often the decision is a result of drawing a fine distinction, a fact that the Supreme Court of Canada recognized in *Blais v. Touchet*[118] when it noted:

> Fine distinctions have been made from time to time and it is not always easy to see why in one case a court would decide that a case fell on the charitable side of the line and in another case on the non-charitable side.

These fine distinctions become even more difficult to draw if the charity is also involved in business activities or political activities.

(6) Modernizing the Definition of "Charity" — Judicial Activism or Legislation?

The Supreme Court, in *Vancouver Society of Immigrant and Visible Minority Women v. M.N.R.*[119] examined for modern times the concept of "advancement of education". The Society had applied for registration as a charity but was refused by the Minister of National Revenue, largely on the grounds that it had not constituted itself exclusively for charitable purposes.

This case became an important focal point for the reform of the law of charities as it wound its way to the Supreme Court of Canada. A number of intervenors were permitted by the Supreme Court who argued that the Court ought to take a role in revising the law of charities. Ultimately, however, the legal issue went before the Court, and the Society lost its appeals at the Federal Court of Appeal and Supreme Court of Canada levels. At the Supreme Court, the justices were split 4 to 3.

Mr. Justice Iacobucci wrote the majority opinion. He commented:

> Considering the law of charity in Canada continues to make reference to an English statute enacted almost 400 years ago, I find it not surprising that there have been numerous calls for its reform, both legislative and judicial. This appeal presents an opportunity to reconsider the matter. Not only is this Court invited to consider, for the first time in more than 25 years, the application of the law as it presently exists, but we also face the

---

[117] *Ibid.*, at 80.
[118] [1963] S.C.R. 358, at 360.
[119] [1999] 1 S.C.R. 10.

interesting questions of whether the time for modernization has come, and if so, what form that modernization might take. The answers to these questions will decide the ultimate issue before us: whether the appellant qualifies for registration as a charitable organization under the *Income Tax Act*.[120]

Mr. Justice Iacobucci continued that "the starting point for the determination of whether a purpose is charitable has, for more than a century, been Lord Macnaghten's classification, set out in *Pemsel* ... of the purposes of the common law had come to recognize as charitable."[121] He noted that the Supreme Court had implicitly adopted the *Pemsel* classification in *The King v. Assessors of the Town of Sunny Brae* and explicitly in *Guaranty Trust Co. of Canada v. Minister of National Revenue*.[122] He continued, with respect to the issue of "benefit to the public" that some confusion had been created where the Court commented in *Guaranty Trust* that the *Pemsel* scheme is subject to the consideration that the purpose must also be for the benefit of the community or of an appreciably important class of the community. This phrasing created confusion with the fourth head of charity.[123]

The issue of "public benefit" does appear to have a greater role in Canada than under *Pemsel*. Justice Iacobucci continued:

> The difference between the *Pemsel* classification and this additional notion of being "for the benefit of the community" is perhaps best understood in the following terms. The requirement of being "for the benefit of the community" is a necessary, but not a sufficient, condition for a finding of charity at common law. If it is not present, then the purpose cannot be charitable. However, even if it is present the court must still ask whether the purpose in question has what Professor Waters calls ... the "generic character" of charity. This character is discerned by perceiving an analogy with those purposes already found to be charitable at common law, and which are classified for convenience in *Pemsel*. The difference is also often one of focus: the four heads of charity concern what is being provided while the "for the benefit of the community" requirement more often centres on who is the recipient.[124]

He recognizes that this analysis is a difficult one. And that it has called for reform, including by Mr. Justice Strayer of the Federal Court of Appeal in *Human Life International in Canada Inc. v. M.N.R.* where Strayer J.A. comments that the definition of charity "remains ... an area crying

---

[120] *Ibid.*, at para. 127.
[121] *Ibid.*, at para. 144.
[122] *Ibid.*, at para. 147. Respectively, [1952] 2 S.C.R. 76 and [1967] S.C.R. 133.
[123] *Vancouver Society of Immigrant and Visible Minority Women v. M.N.R.*, *supra*, note 119, at para. 147.
[124] *Ibid.*, at para. 148.

out for clarification through Canadian legislation for the guidance of taxpayers, administrators and the courts".[125]

But what is the role of the courts in providing this clarification? It is a limited one, according to the majority. Essentially, the role of the court in modernizing the law is limited in a democracy to "those incremental changes which are necessary to keep the common law in step with the dynamic and evolving fabric of our society".[126]

The dissenting opinion of Mr. Justice Gonthier concluded that the Society was charitable. It disagreed with the majority opinion and found that the Society fell within the fourth head of charity and that its objects were not vague. However, importantly, it also commented on the modernization of the common law definition of charity. Mr. Justice Gonthier wrote:

> The Society and the intervenors invited this Court to modify the existing categorizations of charitable purposes set out in *Pemsel* in favour of a broader test. Given my view that the existing *Pemsel* classification scheme is sufficiently flexible to comprehend the Society's claim, and my view that the Society's purpose is charitable within that framework, we need not engage in such an exercise on the facts of this appeal. This is not to suggest that the courts are precluded from recognizing new charitable purposes, or indeed, from revising the *Pemsel* classification itself should an appropriate case come before us. The task of modernizing the definition of charity has always fallen to the courts. There is no indication that Parliament has expressed dissatisfaction with this state of affairs, and it is plain that had Parliament wanted to develop a statutory definition of charity, it would have done so. It has not. This leads me to conclude that Parliament continues to favour judicial development of the law of charity.[127]

To a large measure, the underlying issue in *Vancouver Society of Immigrant and Visible Minority Women* was not strictly a definition of charity at common law. Although this issue was important, it needs to be seen in context of the legislative regime that is in place, in which the common law plays a part. The provisions of the *Income Tax Act* also looked to the activities of the organization, not its purposes alone, in any assessment of eligibility for registration as a charitable organization. Nevertheless, from a modernization of the common law of charity, the judicial approach will clearly be a restrained one.

---

[125] *Ibid.*, at para. 149. *Human Life International in Canada Inc. v. M.N.R.*, [1998] 3 F.C. 202 (F.C.A.).

[126] *Vancouver Society of Immigrant and Visible Minority Women v. M.N.R.*, *supra*, note 119, at para. 150 quoting from *R. v. Salituro*, [1991] 3 S.C.R. 654 at 670.

[127] *Vancouver Society of Immigrant and Visible Minority Women v. M.N.R.*, *supra*, note 119, at para. 122.

III POLITICS AND BUSINESS — NON-CHARITABLE OBJECTS AND ACTIVITIES

Two areas have concerned the courts and regulators in interpreting the case law. Political objects and business activities have not usually been recognized as "charitable". Each is dealt with below.

(1) Political Objects

"Political" objects are not "charitable" objects notwithstanding that there may be a public benefit accruing from an organization entering into the political realm. Generally, an organization that is established with the purpose of altering the law will not be considered a "charitable" organization, regardless of the potential public benefits. In *Bowman v. Secular Society*,[128] the House of Lords noted that:

> The abolition of religious tests, the disestablishment of the Church, the secularization of education, the alteration of the law touching religion or marriage, or the observation of the Sabbath, are purely political objects. Equity has always refused to recognize such objects as charitable.... a trust for the attainment of political objects has always been held invalid, not because it is illegal, for every one is at liberty to advocate or promote by any lawful means a change in the law, but because the Court has no means of judging whether a proposed change in the law will or will not be for the public benefit, and therefore cannot say that a gift to secure the change is a charitable gift.

Similarly, a community legal services clinic is not a charitable organization if the essential part of its activities is devoted to influence the policy-making process.[129] An organization that was devoted to changing the law with respect to pornography was not undertaking charitable activities and was not, therefore, a charitable organization.[130] An activist neighbourhood association, even one devoted to the interests of the urban poor, would not qualify as a charitable organization.[131]

The courts do recognize, however, that a certain amount of political participation may be a legitimate, or at least not illegitimate, activity of a charitable organization. For example, a charitable organization that has only an "exceptional and sporadic activity" would probably not be deprived of its charitable registration for income taxation purposes "because one of its components or some incidental or subservient portion

---

[128] [1917] A.C. 406, at 442 (H.L.). Quoted with approval in *Everywoman's Health Centre Society (1988) v. M.N.R.*, [1992] 2 F.C. 52, at 70.
[129] *Scarborough Community Legal Services v. M.N.R.*, [1985] 2 F.C. 555 (C.A.).
[130] *Positive Action Against Pornography v. M.N.R.*, [1988] 2 F.C. 340 (C.A.).
[131] *Notre Dame de Grâce Neighbourhood Assn. v. M.N.R.*, [1988] 3 F.C. D-39, 85 N.R. 73 (C.A.).

thereof cannot, when considered in isolation, be seen as a charity".[132] An organization that is essentially a trust for the espousal of a political cause would not, however, benefit even if its objects were charitable in nature. A political cause, although laudable, is not a charitable cause.[133]

The courts, however, have not required that an organization provide services or undertake activities for which there is a public consensus in order to be considered "charitable". In the *Everywoman's Health Centre* decision, Decary J. commented that:

> With respect to the argument that there can be no charity at law absent public consensus, counsel for the respondent was unable to direct the Court to any supporting authority. Counsel was indeed at a loss to define what she meant by "public consensus", what would be the degree of consensus required and how the courts would measure that degree. To define "charity" through public consensus would be a most imprudent thing to do. Charity and public opinion do not always go hand in hand; some forms of charity will often precede public opinion, while others will often offend it. Courts are not well equipped to assess public consensus, which is a fragile and volatile concept. The determination of the charitable character of an activity should not become a battle between pollsters. Courts are asked to decide whether there is an advantage for the public, not whether the public agrees that there is such an advantage.[134]

Charitable organizations may, however, undertake limited political activities. The activities must be ancillary or incidental to the objects of the charitable organization and related to those objects. A charitable organization cannot lobby for a specific political party or donate to a political party. Its role appears to be limited and a charitable organization must be able to account for all expenditures.[135] The law is not very clear, however, on what constitutes ancillary or incidental political activities. It would appear that expenditures in excess of 10 per cent of a charitable organization's revenue would raise concerns with the Canada Customs and Revenue Agency. However, that figure is, at best, a rough guideline and not determinative of what is or is not "ancillary or incidental" to the charitable objects.

The Canada Customs and Revenue Agency, as part of its review of the law, has attempted to clarify the law in this area. Its predecessor, Revenue Canada, noted in its 1990 Discussion Paper[136] that the *Income Tax Act*

---

[132] *Scarborough Community Legal Services v. M.N.R.*, [1985] 2 F.C. 555, at 579–80 (C.A.).
[133] *Toronto Volgograd Committee v. M.N.R.*, [1988] 3 F.C. 251, at 275 (C.A.).
[134] [1992] 2 F.C. 52, at 68–69 (C.A.).
[135] Section 149.1, *Income Tax Act*, R.S.C. 1985, c. 1 (5th Supp.). For a discussion of this issue, see Information Circular No. 80-10R, December 17, 1985, "Registered Charities: Operating a Registered Charity" and Information Circular 87-1, "Registered Charities — Ancillary and Incidental Political Activities".
[136] Revenue Canada, "A Better Tax Administration", 1990 Discussion Paper, at 17–18.

was amended in 1986 to permit registered charities to engage in limited, non-partisan political activities to support their charitable mandate. It commented, by way of an example, that a charity established to care for abused children could "press for changes in the law to assist it in pursuing that aim".[137] It is important to note that for the Canada Customs and Revenue Agency, the "pressing for changes in the law" are, in effect, charitable activities. Furthermore, only limited resources could be used for that purpose. What might be acceptable charitable activity for one charity might be political and, thus, non-charitable activity for another.

The issue of what is a political activity versus a charitable activity became prominent during the 1992 constitutional referendum. To clarify its interpretation of the law, Revenue Canada issued a news release advising charitable organizations with respect to participation in the referendum debate. The news release stated that a registered charity would not compromise its status by affirming a position on the referendum. The organization could also make that position known publicly and be associated with a public information campaign. No funds that were raised for charitable purposes, however, could be used for such political purposes.[138]

(2) Business Activities

Another concern for the courts, the Canada Customs and Revenue Agency and other regulators is the level of business activities that are undertaken by charitable organizations. The underlying premise for charitable (and not-for-profit) organizations is that they are not intended to make profits but to provide "public benefits". In addition, the assets of organizations should not be at risk, as they would be normally in a business activity. Another policy consideration is that charitable organizations, which benefit from tax exemptions, should not be competing unfairly in the marketplace with commercial entities that are subject to taxation. Any business activities must be "related" to the objects of the charitable organization.

The courts have reviewed the issue of what types of business activities may be undertaken by a charitable organization. In *McGovern et al. v. A.G. et al*[139] the Court commented that:

> The distinction is thus one between (a) those non-charitable activities authorised by the trust instrument which are merely subsidiary or incidental to a charitable purpose, and (b) those non-charitable activities so

---

[137] *Ibid.*, at 17.
[138] "Charitable Organizations and the Referendum", Revenue Canada Taxation News Release, September 23, 1992. This position would appear to be consistent with the Court's decision in *Canada UNI Assn. v. M.N.R.* (1992), 151 N.R. 4 (F.C.A.). In that case, the purpose for the organization was to promote politically Canadian unity.
[139] [1982] Ch. 321, at 341, [1981] 3 All E.R. 493 (C.A.).

authorised which in themselves form part of the trust purpose. In the latter but not the former case, the reference to non-charitable activities will deprive the trust of its charitable status. The distinction is perhaps easier to state than to apply in practice.

The distinction has been very difficult to apply in Ontario. Anderson J. made a similar comment in *Re Public Trustee and Toronto Humane Society et al.* in which he stated that "the final statement is a classic understatement".[140] The *Charitable Gifts Act*[141] places statutory constraints on charitable organizations and their holding of shares or other interests of a business that have been gifted or vested to a charity. The term "business" and what it includes is not defined in that Act but has been considered in the cases. It would appear that a medical arts building owned by a public hospital may be an investment rather than a business undertaking.[142] An "exceptional and sporadic" activity probably would not be sufficient to deprive an organization of registration for income taxation purposes.[143] Assuming that the business activity is ancillary or incidental to the objects, and that it is not prohibited or restricted by the *Charitable Gifts Act*, any profits earned must be used exclusively for the charitable objects of that charitable corporation. In some cases, the profits may be used indirectly for charitable purposes. This issue is discussed further in chapters 9 and 10.

The Canada Customs and Revenue Agency has developed guidelines, based on the case law, to interpret what types of "related business" activities registered charities may undertake.[144] The business activity cannot become a substantial commercial endeavour. If the business activity is not a substantial commercial endeavour, it will be considered to be a "related business" activity where it meets the following four factors:

(1) The activity is related to the charity's objects or ancillary to them;

(2) There is no private profit motive, since any net revenues will be used for charitable activities;

(3) The business operation does not compete directly with other for-profit businesses;

(4) The business has been in operation for some time and is accepted by the community.

---

[140] (1987), 60 O.R. (2d) 236, at 254 (H.C.).
[141] R.S.O. 1990, c. C.8.
[142] *Re Centenary Hospital Assn.* (1989), 69 O.R. (2d) 1 (H.C.).
[143] *Scarborough Community Legal Services v. M.N.R.*, [1985] 2 F.C. 555 (C.A.). Although this case dealt with political objects and activities, its reasoning would appear to be equally applicable to business activities.
[144] "A Better Tax Administration", *supra*, note 136 at 13–14.

The Canada Customs and Revenue Agency also notes that in some circumstances a business activity may not meet all four factors, but will still be considered as "related". For example, a hospital may compete with privately operated parking lots in providing a parking lot for patients and visitors to use. The Canada Customs and Revenue Agency's approach was adopted from the majority decision in the Federal Court of Appeal in *Alberta Institute on Mental Retardation v. Canada*.[145]

The business activity must not have become an end in itself. For example, commercial farming by an organization that, on the evidence, was the main activity of the organization would result in the organization not being eligible for registration for income taxation purposes. A commercial farming operation for a profit does not become a charitable activity for the sole reason that it is being carried out by a charitable organization to raise funds for its charitable activities.[146] In this case, the court found that the Hutterian Brethren had a business purpose as well as a religious purpose. The motivation of the individuals may have been for religious purposes, but the corporate entity carried out those activities for business purposes.[147]

A charitable organization may, subject to the legislation and its constituting documents, invest funds that are surplus to its immediate needs to earn income to carry out the charitable activities. However, the investments should not become, in effect, an activity of the organization. If the investments take on the character of being inventory for the purpose of making profits from business, the organization may be considered to be carrying on a business activity. If so, the organization may lose its "charitable" character and become a commercial or business enterprise even if the "profits" are subsequently used for charitable purposes.[148]

The courts may also view, for purposes of the *Charities Accounting Act* and the *Charitable Gifts Act*, the ownership of a medical arts building as an investment and not a business. The courts recognize that the activities should not be viewed in isolation in making a determination of whether or not an activity is a business.[149] These sources of revenue will become increasingly important to charitable organizations as governments continue to restrict funding levels for community, social and health services and traditional fundraising efforts are less effective. Care must be taken

---

[145] [1987] 3 F.C. 286, at 298–99 (C.A.). But see the dissenting opinion of Pratte J. which would appear to have required a stronger relationship between the commercial activity and the charitable object for the business activity to be "a related business activity" for purposes of income taxation.

[146] *Hutterian Brethren Church of Wilson v. R.*, [1980] 1 F.C. 757, at 759 (C.A.). It is not easy, however, to reconcile this case with the *Alberta Institute on Mental Retardation v. Canada* case on this point.

[147] *Ibid.*, at 766, *per* Ryan J. This case is also not easily reconciled with the Trial Division's decision (Walsh J.) in *Gull Bay Development Corp.*, [1984] 2 F.C. 3, which considered but distinguished the *Hutterian Brethren* case.

[148] *Church of Christ Development Co. v. M.N.R.*, [1982] C.T.C. 2467, 82 D.T.C. 1461 (T.R.B.).

[149] *Re Centenary Hospital Assn.* (1989), 69 O.R. (2d) 1, at 19.

in drafting the objects of the organization and in implementing any business activities to ensure compliance with the law as it is interpreted and applied by the courts, the Canada Customs and Revenue Agency, the Public Guardian and Trustee and regulators.

CHAPTER 2

Legal Structures for Charitable and Not-for-Profit Organizations

A   OVERVIEW

There are four major legal structures that may be used to establish and operate an association, group, club or similar charitable or not-for-profit organization. These structures are:

- *Trusts*. A trust is usually established by a trust document or instrument. The trust document must include three essential components or "certainties" to be recognized by the courts as creating a trust — the certainties of intention, subject matter and object. The trust document typically will set out what the purposes or objects of the trust are, what property is to be held in trust, who the beneficiaries of the trust are or, if a charitable trust, what the criteria are that will be used to determine the beneficiaries or the purpose of the trust, and how the trust property is to be managed by the trustees for the benefit of the specified persons or for the specified purposes;
- *Unincorporated associations*. A memorandum of association or similar document sets out the purpose of the organization and how it is to be managed and operated. The memorandum of association is contractual in nature. It does not for most purposes and in most situations create a "legal person" but rather a legal relationship among the members;
- *Corporations without share capital*. Letters patent to incorporate a corporation without share capital may be issued under Part III of the Ontario *Corporations Act*[1] or Part II of the *Canada Corporations Act*.[2] A corporation is a separate legal entity or legal person independent of its members, officers and directors. As with any corpo-

---

[1] R.S.O. 1990, c. C.38 [as am. to S.O. 2001, c. 9, Sched. D, s. 5].
[2] R.S.C. 1970, c. C.32 [as am. to S.C. 1999, c. 3].

38   *The Law of Charitable and Not-for-Profit Organizations*

ration, it needs individuals to act on its behalf to carry out its objects.
- *Co-operatives without share capital.* A co-operative is a specialized form of corporation that carries on an enterprise on a co-operative basis. Co-operatives are established under the *Co-operative Corporations Act*[3] by articles of incorporation. A co-operative may be either one with share capital, similar to a business corporation, or without share capital and not-for-profit in nature. This text will deal with co-operatives without share capital.

The advantages and disadvantages of each type of legal structure should be assessed in light of the activities and risks of the organization. Are the risks of liability or refusal of funding from potential donors or granting bodies sufficiently high to warrant the costs of incorporation? Is a specific legal structure required to carry out the activities? Are the activities inherently risky or dangerous? How long do the members intend to maintain the legal entity? These questions are largely practical in nature and are concerned with the types of activities the members want to carry out. A legal structure is, ultimately, intended to meet the needs of its members and not third parties.

B TYPES OF LEGAL STRUCTURES

1 TRUSTS

Trusts are not common legal structures for most associations and clubs. Trusts may be used to establish a club, but trusts are more commonly used for charitable purposes, for tax purposes or to isolate funds being held by a person for the benefit of another from the assets of the person holding the funds. A typical use, where the potential risk level is normally low, is for the investment and administration of a scholarship or bursary.

A trust is created when one or more persons holds legal title to property, but another person or group of persons has the right to the enjoyment of or to benefit from that property.[4] A trust may arise from:

- the words or actions of a "settlor" which indicate an intention to create a trust, either express or implied;
- statutes which impose a trust; or

---

[3] R.S.O. 1990, c. C.35 [as am. to S.O. 2001, c. 8, ss. 6-17].
[4] See, for a fuller discussion of trust law in Canada, Professor D.W.M. Waters, *Law of Trusts in Canada*, 2nd ed. (Toronto: Carswell, Thomson Professional Publishing, 1984).

- the common law which imposes a resulting or a constructive trust, based on the equities of the situation.

There are three essential characteristics for all trusts, often called the "three certainties".[5] There must be certainty of intention to create a trust, either by words or actions. The subject matter, the property which is to be the subject of the trust, must be certain. Finally, the objects of the trust must be certain. The beneficiary of the trust must be readily apparent or ascertainable by name or class description.

The courts have modified the certainty of object to accommodate charitable activities. Instead of identifying the beneficiaries by name or class description, a charitable trust may include in its objects a purpose for the trust. The charitable purposes should be specific and enable the trustees to determine how the charitable activities are to be carried out. A charitable purpose cannot be vague or ambiguous. It must be certain and determinable in specific fact situations.[6]

The objects clause in a trust document must be carefully prepared. It should provide to the trustees a clear direction on who or what is included in the description of a class of beneficiaries. Trustees for charitable trusts may, however, be given discretion to make a determination about whether or not an individual is one of the intended beneficiaries.[7]

The courts have conferred other significant advantages on charitable trusts that are not applied to other types of trusts. The underlying policy rationale is that charitable trusts provide public benefits. For example, the rule against perpetuities does not apply (with some exceptions with respect to charitable gifts) provided that any gifts vest in the charity within the appropriate time period. The rule against inalienability also does not apply.[8] In order to assist charitable trusts to adapt, the courts will apply the doctrine of *cy-pres*. A charitable trust may apply to the court to change the terms of a trust and use the funds for other, court-approved charitable purposes as close as possible to the original purposes set out in the trust document.[9]

The trustees carry on the activities of the trust in their name as trustees of the trust. For example, the trustees could initiate a legal proceeding in their names as trustees of the trust. The powers and duties of the trustees are set out in the trust document. Trustees also have a number of powers that have been developed by the courts and that have been

---

[5] *Ibid.*, at 107–28.
[6] See, for a fuller discussion of this point, Part D, "What is 'Charitable'" in Chapter 1.
[7] *Jones v. T. Eaton Co.*, [1973] S.C.R. 635.
[8] See Professor D.W.M. Waters, *Law of Trusts in Canada*, 2nd ed. (Toronto: Carswell, Thomson Professional Publishing, 1984) for a fuller discussion of these legal issues. The rule against perpetuities and the rule against inalienability are too complex to discuss in any detail in this text.
[9] The doctrine of *cy-pres* is discussed in more detail in Chapter 9, "Supervision of Charitable Organizations".

set out in ss. 17 to 29 of the *Trustee Act*.[10] These powers are administrative and dispositive in nature. For example, s. 21 permits the trustee to purchase insurance to insure property, s. 22 to renew leases, s. 23 to pass the accounts in the Ontario Superior Court of Justice of his or her dealings with the trust property. Sections 26 to 28 provide for investments made by trustees or on their behalf. The revisions in the late 1990s and in 2001 provided a new approach to investment powers, which are discussed in more detail in Chapter 6. Instead of a permitted list of investments, trustees were authorized to make investments in accordance with the prudent investor approach.

The *Trustee Act* may be used to supplement the powers and duties of trustees; however, where possible, all of the trustees' major powers and duties should be clearly set out in the trust document. The trust document will usually be more familiar to trustees than the Act will be. The *Trustee Act* should not be relied upon to fill in the gaps in the trust document. It is often not sufficiently flexible to take into account the different types of purposes or methods of operation that many organizations want or need. The unique characteristics of an organization and how the trustees are to carry out the objects and purposes of the trust should be built into the trust document.

The relationship between the trustees and the charitable trust and its beneficiaries is a fiduciary one. The trustee has substantial obligations that arise out of this fiduciary relationship. Three basic duties have been imposed by the courts on trustees. First, a trustee must carry out his or her tasks honestly and with due care and attention. Second, the trustee must carry out the duties personally and not delegate to another person the responsibilities entrusted to him or her. There are exceptions to this duty — where the trust document permits delegation, for certain administrative matters and where otherwise authorized by law, such as the *Trustee Act*. Third, the trustee must place the interests of the beneficiaries or the purpose of the charitable trust first and not permit his or her own interests to conflict in any way with the duties to the beneficiaries or the purpose of the charitable trust.[11]

II UNINCORPORATED ASSOCIATIONS

An unincorporated association is a relatively common legal structure for a group of persons to use. It is, essentially, an agreement among a number of persons which articulates their common purpose, establishes an organization to achieve that common purpose and sets out how that organization is to be operated to achieve that purpose. The relationship

---

[10] R.S.O. 1990, c. T.23 [as am. to S.O. 2001, c. 9, Sched. B, s. 13].
[11] These duties are examined in more detail in Chapter 6, "Officers, Directors and Trustees: The Standards of Care".

among the persons is contractual in nature. The courts sometimes refer to these organizations as "voluntary associations".[12]

An organization is made up of "members" who agree, implicitly or explicitly, with the common purpose. Usually, the members are intended to receive some benefits from being members. This intent to benefit the members distinguishes an unincorporated association from a trust, which is usually, but not invariably, intended to benefit other persons or for specified purposes, in the case of some charitable trusts.

An association is not limited in the scope of its objects, provided that they are lawful objects. In contrast, a charitable trust must have only objects that are charitable in nature; and corporations without share capital cannot, for example, have any objects that suggest that the organization is a government entity. The association, therefore, is the most flexible organizational model because there are no restrictions on its objects, provided that they are not otherwise prohibited by law.

The organization may be set up formally or informally, depending upon the needs of the members. Associations may also evolve out of a relationship among a few individuals and, over time, take on the formal characteristics of an association. At the informal level, the relationship may be based on an "understanding" but later on a written constitution or by-laws are developed.

An association has some of the characteristics of a partnership but it is not one. A partnership is established with the intent of carrying on business and making a profit. An association may be used to discuss commercial matters, but its purpose is not to carry on business activities or to make a profit. In *Ottawa Lumbermen's Credit Bureau v. Swan*[13] the Court dealt with an organization that had an office and an employee and carried out credit negotiations for its members. The members contributed to a fund to pay the expenses of the organization, which included gathering information. The Court commented that:

> The members, therefore, act in common in gathering information, but it seems to be straining the words to call that carrying on business in common; and it seems to be straining them still more to call it carrying on business in common with a view of profit; for in what is done there is no idea at all of profit or advantage of any kind to the bureau — the only profit that there can possibly be is a profit (or an avoidance of loss) to the individual members in their individual businesses. Therefore I think that there is here no partnership in the proper sense of the term.

The courts have taken a similar approach in defining trade unions as voluntary associations.[14]

---

[12] *Orchard v. Tunney*, [1957] S.C.R. 436, 8 D.L.R. (2d) 273.
[13] (1923), 53 O.L.R. 135 (C.A.).
[14] *Metallic Roofing Co. of Can. v. Amalgamated Sheet Metal Workers Intn'l Assn., Local 30*, (1905), 9 O.L.R. 171 (C.A.).

III ONTARIO CORPORATIONS AND CO-OPERATIVE CORPORATIONS WITHOUT SHARE CAPITAL

(1) Corporations without Share Capital

The objects of a corporation without share capital incorporated under the Ontario *Corporations Act*[15] are very broad. Section 118 permits a corporation to be incorporated under Part III of the Act where it "has objects that are within the jurisdiction of the Province of Ontario". Corporations without share capital are incorporated for non-profit purposes and not for business purposes. Some may also be charitable in nature.

There are five basic types of non-profit corporations under the Act:

- general, such as neighbourhood associations, trade or business associations, community organizations and so forth,
- sporting and athletic organizations. If the organization is involved in the use of firearms, there are federal registration requirements for firearms and other requirements to ensure that the firearms are kept and used in a safe manner. Consultation with the appropriate law enforcement agency is recommended. If the organization is involved in organized sports, a number of associations are in place at the municipal, school board, provincial and national levels to ensure that there is appropriate safety and training in place for the sport or athletic activity. These associations of sporting organizations may also be representative of the sport to governments and international associations and membership in them may be necessary to participate competitively in the sport or athletic activity,
- social clubs, where the objects of the corporation are in whole or in part social in nature,
- service clubs, such as Knights of Columbus, Optimists, Rotary and so forth. If the corporation is to be affiliated with an established service club, permission from the parent is usually required. The use of the names of most of service clubs is protected as it is the intellectual property of those organizations. In addition, without the written permission to use the name, any proposed name would likely be seen as deceptively similar and not approved,
- charities, including religious organizations and other organizations whose objects are charitable.

Incorporation is usually a simple process, provided that the members have taken the time to review what they want. The process may take sev-

---

[15] R.S.O. 1990, c. C.38 [as am. S.O. 1994, c. 27, s. 78(5)].

eral weeks to several months from application to receipt of letters patent. The time period will depend in part on the application's completeness, whether or not there are any backlogs, whether or not the appropriate pre-clearances, approvals or reviews have been obtained, and whether or not changes to the application are necessary.

The costs of incorporation will include disbursements and fees of between $300 and $500, depending upon the need for government approval, and legal fees. The level of legal fees will depend upon the need for legal advice and services to meet the member's objectives and to obtain government approval. A relatively simple non-profit organization could be incorporated for about $1,000 to $1,500; however the actual costs in disbursements, fees and legal services will vary.

There are three major steps to the incorporation process: name search, submission of the application and receipt of the letters patent, and establishing the corporation. Each of these three steps is discussed in Chapter 3, "Incorporating a Charitable or Not-for-Profit Organization".

A number of corporations may have activities that are either regulated for public safety and protection or are related to various government programmes. If the corporation is intended to carry on activities that are regulated or intended to benefit from these programmes, it would be appropriate to consult with the relevant government ministry or agency. The Ministry of Consumer and Business Services previously circulated applications to relevant ministries within the Government of Ontario, but that practice ceased in 1993. In some cases, the government has also abandoned programme areas, such as social housing, where prior approvals were required from the relevant ministry or it had specific requirements in the letters patent and other documentation before the corporation would be eligible to benefit from the programme.

The Ministry of Community and Social Services provides funding for and regulates a number of services provided to members of the public. These services include nurseries, child care, child and family services, services for persons with disabilities and services for seniors. Where a corporation applies for a licence under the *Day Nurseries Act*,[16] the *Elderly Persons Centres Act*,[17] the *Charitable Institutions Act*[18] or similar legislation, or for funding under a ministry programme, the incorporators should consult with the Ministry.

The *Charitable Institutions Act* should be reviewed where the corporation will provide residential, sheltered or specialized or group care in buildings maintained and operated by the corporation. Several types of institutions are exempted from the Act where other more specific legislation applies. If the Act does apply, the approval of the Minister of Community and Social Services is required before the corporation operates the services. The Act and its regulation are detailed and provide

---

[16] R.S.O. 1990, c. D.2.
[17] R.S.O. 1990, c. E.4.
[18] R.S.O. 1990, c. C.9.

significant legal obligations on the corporation and its officers and directors. Both should be reviewed if the corporation intends to carry on activities under the Act.

The Ministry of Health regulates the provision of health services and facilities in Ontario. In some cases, the prior approval of the Minister of Health is required before the letters patent may be issued. Section 4(1) of the *Public Hospitals Act*[19] requires the Minister's approval prior to the issuance of the letters patent, as does s. 7 of the *Ambulance Act*.[20] Section 5 of the *Private Hospitals Act*[21] prohibits the incorporation of a corporation under the *Corporations Act* or the *Business Corporations Act*. It is prudent, where the corporation will be providing health services or facilities, to review a draft of the application for letters patent with the Ministry of Health.

The Ministry of Training, Colleges and Universities administers the *Post-Secondary Education Choice and Excellence Act, 2000*,[22] the *Private Vocational Schools Act*,[23] and the *Ministry of Training, Colleges and Universities Act*.[24] A letters patent corporation that is intended to provide educational or training services may fall within those statutes. The prior written approval of the Minister is required if the corporate name is to include the terms "university", "college" or "institute".[25] The Ministry's major concern is to ensure that members of the public are not misled with respect to any private college or institute.

The Ministry of Municipal Affairs administers the *Community Economic Development Act, 1993*.[26] That Act provides for the incorporation of two types of community economic development corporations: community investment share corporations (CISC) and community loan fund corporations (CLF). A CISC is intended to assist communities in developing and diversifying their local economies. Investors purchase shares in a community-based CISC and the funds are invested in shares of a new or expanding eligible business in the community. A CISC is, however, a for-profit business, usually incorporated under the Ontario *Business Corporations Act*[27] or the *Co-operative Corporations Act*[28] as a corporation or co-operative corporation with share capital.[29]

Community loan fund corporations are incorporated as non-profit corporations under the *Corporations Act* (or non-profit co-operative cor-

---

[19] R.S.O. 1990, c. P.40.
[20] R.S.O. 1990, c. A.19.
[21] R.S.O. 1990, c. P.24.
[22] S.O. 2000, c. 36, Sched.
[23] R.S.O. 1990, c. P.26.
[24] R.S.O. 1990, c. M.19 [as am. to S.O. 2001, c. 6 and c. 8].
[25] O. Reg. 181/90, subs. 3(1).
[26] S.O. 1993, c. 26.
[27] R.S.O. 1990, c. B.16.
[28] R.S.O. 1990, c. C.35.
[29] *Community Investment Shares Program Handbook* (Ontario: Ministry of Municipal Affairs, 1994).

porations under the *Co-operative Corporations Act*) to establish, finance and operate a community fund. The fund provides collateral loans to eligible borrowers. It may also provide business and other advice to these borrowers. The intent is to encourage the establishment and growth of small businesses in a community by providing loans to those businesses that lack the assets to secure a loan. The CLF provides the loan guarantee to an entrepreneur who uses the guarantee to obtain a loan from a financial institution that is in partnership with the CLF. The funds to provide the guarantee are raised from investors, pooled and then reinvested in safe investments. A wide variety of non-profit or government organizations may sponsor a CLF.[30]

An increasing number of Aboriginal organizations have incorporated corporations without share capital in order to be eligible for government funding or to assist in administering the programmes through Aboriginal controlled organizations. Incorporation may be a condition for grants and other support from various government programmes. Corporations without share capital have been established to provide not-for-profit housing, job and skills training, economic development (including infrastructure and corporations to operate local airports), social development and the delivery of programmes previously provided directly by the federal government.

The corporate form is a useful approach to establish a mechanism for Aboriginal organizations to control the administration of programmes. The objects of a corporation without share capital may not be political in nature. This form of legal entity should not be used to establish, for example, the "government" for a First Nation because governments are political in nature. It could be used, however, to establish one of the mechanisms through which a government may operate.

(2) Co-operative Corporations without Share Capital

A co-operative corporation is a specific type of corporation established by articles of incorporation under the *Co-operative Corporations Act*. Section 1 of that Act defines "co-operative" as a corporation "carrying on an enterprise on a co-operative basis". "Enterprise" is not a defined term but would appear to include both business or commercial activities and non-commercial activities. A co-operative may, however, be either a corporation with share capital or without share capital. A co-operative with share capital is more in the nature of a business corporation. This text will focus on co-operatives without share capital, which are similar in intent to corporations without share capital under the *Corporations Act*.

A co-operative is organized, operated and administered upon certain principles and methods. These principles and methods are set out in s. 1 of the Act. Each member has only one vote and no member may vote by proxy. The enterprise is to be operated as nearly as possible at cost after

---

[30] *Community Loan Fund Program Handbook* (Ontario: Ministry of Municipal Affairs, 1994).

providing for reasonable reserves. Any surplus funds, unless used to maintain or improve services of the organization for its members, are to be distributed to the members, unless the co-operative corporation is to be charitable in nature. Surplus funds may also be donated for community welfare or for the propagation of co-operative principles.

The co-operative legal structure has been used for the distribution of goods to members or to provide specialized services to members. For example, co-operatives have been established to provide farming supplies in rural areas, outdoors equipment to campers and hikers, and farm-fresh food to urban dwellers. Essentially, these types of co-operatives purchase in bulk and sell to members at a price that they would not be able to obtain on their own.

Co-operatives have also been popular methods for non-profit housing. In 1992, Ontario enacted amendments to the *Co-operative Corporations Act* to ensure that non-profit co-operative housing, which receives substantial benefits from the government, cannot be transformed into for-profit housing. The amendments set out mandatory provisions for their articles for all non-profit housing co-operatives, which are related to providing housing on a non-profit basis to the members. The Ontario Government, a few years later, abandoned its role in social housing, which substantially reduced if not eliminated the creation of not-for-profit housing co-operatives.

The amendments also permitted multi-stakeholder co-operatives. In a multi-stakeholder co-operative, control is shared among two or more distinct stakeholders, each of whom may have different interests. They work together on a co-operative basis and, at the same time, their respective interests are reflected in the operations of the co-operative. Each stakeholder, for example, will elect its own directors and must approve changes to the articles of incorporation or by-laws.

IV FEDERAL CORPORATIONS WITHOUT SHARE CAPITAL

Incorporation under Part II of the *Canada Corporations Act*[31] is appropriate where the organization will operate on a national level or in more than one province, or if the objects and activities fall within federal constitutional jurisdiction. If the objects and activities fall within provincial jurisdiction, the applicants should also consider incorporation under the Ontario statute and then obtain registration to operate as an extra-provincial corporation in other appropriate provinces.

Some incorporators of charitable corporations in Ontario prefer to incorporate under the federal legislation where possible. This approach avoids the need for prior approval or review by the Public Guardian and Trustee. It was thought by some that the process caused delays and unnecessary complications. However, the Public Guardian and Trustee has amended its procedures, including the development of pre-approved

---

[31] R.S.C. 1970, c. C.32.

object clauses for corporations without share capital, to reduce the time required for incorporation.

The federal Act provides for similar types of corporations as does the Ontario statute but is not as specific as is the Ontario legislation. A corporation without share capital may be a not-for-profit corporation that provides services to its members, such as a professional association. It may also be a not-for-profit corporation with charitable objects that does not intend to register as a charitable organization. Finally, the corporation may be a charitable corporation that does intend to register its charitable status.

Is a corporation that is charitable in nature required to notify the Public Guardian and Trustee of its existence under the *Charities Accounting Act*?[32] Although there may be an argument that it is not required to do so, it would appear that the Public Guardian and Trustee does claim jurisdiction over federally incorporated charitable corporations that carry on activities in Ontario.

Industry Canada is responsible for the administration of the *Canada Corporations Act*. Corporations without share capital are incorporated under Part II of that statute. The Department developed an information kit to assist applicants for incorporation under Part II.[33] The kit includes a sample application, model by-laws, a summary of the Department's policy on not-for-profit corporations, a checklist for use with the application and a fee schedule. A handbook is also being prepared to assist in the incorporation process.

The kit is intended to assist applicants in several ways. First, it sets out the requirements for incorporation under the Act. The policy summary also provides information on what is acceptable under the Act, including areas where the Act is not clear. Second, the use of the model by-laws will speed up the process for incorporation. The model by-laws include provisions on all the areas that must be in the by-laws under Part II of the Act. Adoption of the model by-laws avoids the need for departmental review of the by-laws. Where changes to the model by-laws are necessary, the list of requirements assists applicants to ensure compliance with the Act and the Department's policies. Third, the information kit provides information to applicants to understand the process of incorporation and the maintenance of a corporate entity.

Industry Canada consulted the sector in 2000 and 2001 on proposed changes to the incorporating legislation and processes. It is anticipated that legislation will be introduced that will permit "as of right" incorporation of corporations without share capital. The corporations would have objects clauses but would have broader powers, subject to appropriate limitations given the nature and purposes of these corporations. The legislation, it is expected, will also deal with matters that are absent in

---

[32] R.S.O. 1990, c. C.10.
[33] Industry Canada, "Information Kit on the Creation of Non-Profit Corporations", November 25, 1999.

the existing statutory scheme, confusing or obstacles to the use of federal corporations without share capital.

C ADVANTAGES AND DISADVANTAGES OF THE LEGAL STRUCTURES

I INTRODUCTION

The practical purposes for all four legal structures are to establish the organization and to provide for the rules of its operation. The choice of legal structure will depend upon the situation of each group. Each type of structure has its own legal and practical advantages and disadvantages. These advantages and disadvantages should be assessed in light of the particular circumstances of each group. This section discusses briefly the benefits and advantages of the different legal structures.

It is important to assess the particular circumstances of a group, its purpose and its expected activities and operations before deciding on which of the four legal structures is appropriate. The Initial Information Checklist may assist in making this assessment.

Some regulators require an organization to be incorporated. Additionally, the federal *Income Tax Act* seems to encourage corporate entities over unincorporated associations. Corporations without share capital may be exempt from taxation pursuant to subs. 149(1) of that Act, but income of an unincorporated association may be taxable in the hands of each member. A "club, society or association" may qualify under para. 149(1)(l) for an exemption from income taxation. The exemption may not, however, apply to any income from property owned by the club, society or association.[34]

The trust structure is not, in itself, expensive to establish or to operate. It is not usually a useful structure where the organization intends to own or lease real estate (such as a sports facility), enter into a number of contractual relationships, or if it will be exposed to a significant risk of liability arising from its operations and transactions. It is useful where the trustees are primarily to hold and invest funds or other similar property and to disburse the income from those funds or other similar property.

In comparison to other legal structures, the trust may increase the potential exposure of trustees. The obligations of a trustee are substantial. A trustee must:

- carry out his or her tasks with due care and attention and honesty;

---

[34] See, for a fuller discussion of this issue, the following two Interpretation Bulletins issued by the Canada Customs and Revenue Agency — "Non-profit Organizations," IT-496R, August 2, 2001 and "Non-profit Organizations — Taxation of Income from Property," IT-83R3, October 31, 1990.

- carry out the duties personally and not delegate to another the responsibilities entrusted to him or her; and
- place the interests of the beneficiary first and not permit his or her own interest to conflict in any way with the duties to the beneficiary.

Although these duties are similar in nature to the duties of a director of a corporation without share capital (especially a "charitable corporation"), the standard of care appears to be higher for trustees, in particular trustees of a charitable trust, than for directors and officers of a corporation or even of an unincorporated association. Trust law is also generally more complicated and may be difficult to understand for trustees who are not legally trained.

II LIABILITY OF MEMBERS

The basic legal difference between an unincorporated association and a corporation without share capital is not their purposes, but their legal characters. A corporation is a separate legal entity. An unincorporated association is not a separate legal entity and it usually has no legal status apart from that of its members. The members may, therefore, be held individually liable for the actions of the unincorporated association.

Members of an incorporated organization are in a different legal position. Under s. 122 of the Ontario *Corporations Act*:[35]

> A member shall not, as such, be held answerable or responsible for any act, default, obligation or liability of the corporation or for any engagement, claim, payment, loss, injury, transaction, matter or thing relating to or connected with the corporation.

Section 73 of the *Co-operative Corporations Act* has similar wording that limits liability of the members in their capacity as members of the co-operative.

By contrast, plaintiffs may properly look to the officers, directors or members of an unincorporated association for compensation for breach of contract, negligence or tortious actions in a number of situations. For example, the officers, directors and members of an unincorporated association may be liable where they assumed to act for the association, authorized or sanctioned a contract or otherwise led the plaintiff to believe that the contract would be honoured.[36]

---

[35] R.S.O. 1990, c. C.38. A comparable section is not found in the *Canada Corporations Act* but see para. 21(1)(d) of the *Interpretations Act*, R.S.C. 1985, c. I-21.
[36] *Finlay v. Black* (1921), 60 D.L.R. 422, [1921] 2 W.W.R. 907 (Y.T. S.C.); *Aikins v. Dominion Live Stock Assn. of Canada* (1896), 17 P.R. 303 (Ont. Div. Ct.).

It is probably prudent to advise clients that all of their personal assets are potentially exposed to meet contractual or tortious liabilities of an unincorporated association. The cases are, however, confusing and, at times, contradictory. The courts appear to have attempted to address the issues on an equitable basis, but this is far from certain. Additionally, the reported cases tend to come from certain specific fact situations involving fraternal societies (which provide insurance or similar benefits to members) or unions. The reported cases are also usually older cases, from the late nineteenth and early twentieth centuries. There are only a few modern cases that appear to deal with these issues.[37]

III LEGAL CAPACITY

An unincorporated association is not usually recognized in law. In common law, unincorporated associations cannot be sued or sue in their own names.[38] They cannot assert, for example, any position that is maintainable in law only by a legal entity. As a result, an unincorporated association is not legally recognized as a landlord or a tenant[39] and it cannot validly endorse a note to pass title.[40] A lease or an endorsement must be signed by all members of the association or, in some circumstances, the trustees. Any property rights that it has are to be held according to the rules of the association; but the property continues to be property of the members of the association.[41] It may maintain an action by a representative if the rules of court permit it to do so.[42] It also may not have legal status to appear before certain administrative law tribunals.[43] For example, an unincorporated association, other than an association of employ-

---

[37] For a good discussion of the liability issues for tort and fiduciary matters, see Robert Flannigan, "The Liability Structure of Nonprofit Associations: Tort and Fiduciary Liability Assignments", [1998] 77 Cdn. Bar Rev. 73.

[38] *Comeau v. Fundy Group Publications Ltd.* (1981), 24 C.P.C. 251 (N.S. T.D.). See also *Cummings v. Ontario Minor Hockey Assn.* (1979), 26 O.R. (2d) 7, 104 D.L.R. (3d) 434, 10 R.F.L. (2d) 121 (C.A.).

[39] *Can. Morning News Co. v. Thompson et al.*, [1930] S.C.R. 338, [1930] 3 D.L.R. 833; *Henderson v. Toronto General Trusts Corp.*, [1928] 3 D.L.R. 411 (Ont. C.A.); *Ottawa Lumbermen's Credit Bureau v. Swan* (1923), 53 O.L.R. 135, [1923] 4 D.L.R. 1157 (C.A.). But see *Watkins v. Hamilton-Wentworth C.C.F. Council*, [1947] O.W.N. 791 (Co. Ct.) where a lease was signed by two individuals on behalf of three political unincorporated associations. The associations, in that case, could be sued properly in action for possession.

[40] *Cooper v. McDonald* (1909), 11 W.L.R. 173, 19 Man. R. 1 (C.A.).

[41] *Wawrzyniak v. Jagiellicz* (1988), 65 O.R. (2d) 384, 51 D.L.R. (4th) 639 (C.A.), affg. (1988), 64 O.R. (2d) 81, 48 D.L.R. (4th) 688 (H.C.).

[42] *McDonald v. Linton*, 53 N.B.R. 107, [1926] 3 D.L.R. 779 (C.A.); *Blackfoot Stock Assn. v. Thor*, [1925] 3 W.W.R. 544 (Alta. C.A.).

[43] *Ladies of the Sacred Heart v. Armstrong's Point Assn.* (1961), 29 D.L.R. (2d) 373, 36 W.W.R. 364 (Man. C.A.). See *Statutory Powers Procedure Act*, R.S.O. 1990, c. S.22, subs. 1(2), which defines party for administrative tribunals.

ers or a union, is not a party in a proceeding before the Ontario Municipal Board.[44]

There are exceptions to the general rule. In the field of organized athletic activities, the law recognizes that an association may be named as a party to an action.[45] There may also be exceptions to the general rule where the organization is provided for under other statutory provisions. For example, if the organization includes a statutory trustee, the organization could probably be sued with respect to matters coming under that statutory trust. The basis for this approach appears to be that the statute creates an artificial person or quasi-corporation that may sue or be sued.[46]

An unincorporated association may still be more restricted in maintaining a legal action. For example, an illegal object or an object that is contrary to public policy may mean that an unincorporated association cannot maintain a civil action in Ontario.[47] If an illegal object can be severed, the civil action could be maintained.[48]

IV RELATIONSHIP AMONG MEMBERS

Generally, membership creates a contractual relationship between each member in an unincorporated association.[49] The terms of that contractual relationship will be found in the constitution adopted by the membership. Unless the contract provides otherwise, the terms of the contract as set out in the memorandum of association may not be altered unless all members agree to do so. However, rules or by-laws that are established by the directors, officers or a majority of the members probably could be amended in the same way as they were established if there are no amending provisions for rules and by-laws. If the rules or by-laws were not contractual in nature and were, for example, enacted by a majority of the directors to govern behaviour at meetings, the rules or by-laws could probably be amended by a majority of the directors.

As with any contractual relationship, a breach of the contract may give rise to damages and to a cause of action. A violation of the rules, how-

---

[44] See R. 1.03, *Rules of Procedure*, R.R.O. 1990, Reg. 889, under the *Ontario Municipal Board Act*, R.S.O. 1990, c. O.28.
[45] *Warkentin v. Sault Ste. Marie (Board of Education)* (1985), 49 C.P.C. 31 (Ont. Dist. Ct.).
[46] *Trustees of Greek Catholic Ruthenian Church of East Selkirk v. Portage LaPrairie Farmers Mutual Fire Insurance Co.*, 31 D.L.R. 33, [1917] 1 W.W.R. 249 (Man. C.A.). See also *Metallic Roofing Co. of Can. v. Amalgamated Sheet Metal Workers' Intn'l Assn., Local Union No. 30* (1903), 5 O.L.R. 424 (Div. Ct.), affd. (1905), 9 O.L.R. 171 (C.A.) and *Centre Star Mining Co. v. Rossland Miners Union* (1902), 9 B.C.R. 190 (S.C.).
[47] *Polakoff v. Winters Garment Co.* (1928), 62 O.L.R. 40, [1928] 2 D.L.R. 55 (H.C.).
[48] *Chase v. Starr*, [1924] S.C.R. 495, [1924] 4 D.L.R. 55, 44 C.C.C. 358.
[49] *Stephen v. Stewart* (1943), 59 B.C.R. 410, [1944] 1 D.L.R. 305, [1943] 3 W.W.R. 580 (C.A.); *Foran v. Kottmeier*, [1973] 3 O.R. 1002, 39 D.L.R. (3d) 40 (C.A.).

ever, will not necessarily give rise to a cause of action if there was no deliberate attempt to violate the rules.[50]

V ADVANTAGES OF UNINCORPORATED ASSOCIATIONS

There are a number of advantages to unincorporated associations. Unincorporated associations are usually easier to establish. For example, they do not usually require the approval of any government body as do corporations without share capital. The major exceptions are if the activities of the unincorporated association are regulated or if it is or is intended to be a charitable organization.

Unincorporated associations have few reporting requirements. They do not, for example, need to make any corporate filings as do corporations under the *Corporations Information Act*,[51] the *Co-operative Corporations Act*[52] and the *Canada Corporations Act*.[53]

Unlike trust or corporate law, the courts have not been extensively involved in reviewing unincorporated associations and their activities. There are few statutory provisions that are specifically intended to apply to unincorporated associations. As a result, while there is more flexibility in how unincorporated associations operate, there is also the potential for greater uncertainty. For example, there are no statutory requirements for the directors to provide to the membership the organization's financial statements. Under the *Corporations Act*,[54] directors of corporations without share capital are required to present to the membership the corporation's financial statements and the report of the auditor. The directors of a co-operative corporation must also present the co-operative's financial statements to the members. In trust law, trustees are required to account for the property being held in trust.

The absence of "fixed" rules provides greater flexibility to members to organize their relationship. An organization may be tailored very carefully to the needs and wants of its members. But it also means that the members, officers, directors and courts have few reference points to assist them when disputes arise or there is a need for an unanticipated change. For example, because the relationship is contractual in nature, absent a provision for amendments in the Memorandum of Association, all members must agree to a change in the relationship. To avoid the need for unanimity, the Memorandum of Association could set out the procedures and requirements for amendments, i.e., by resolution approved by a majority of the members voting at a meeting called for that purpose. It could also include the procedures and requirements for the

---

[50] *Temple v. Hallem* (1989), 58 Man. R. (2d) 54, 58 D.L.R. (4th) 541, [1989] 5 W.W.R. 660 (C.A.).
[51] R.S.O. 1990, c. C.39.
[52] R.S.O. 1990, c. C.35.
[53] R.S.C. 1970, c. C.32.
[54] R.S.O. 1990, c. C.38, s. 97.

dissolution of the organization, including what happens to any assets and liabilities. However, rules or by-laws that are established by the directors, officers or majority of the members probably could be amended through a similar procedure.

The lack of a statutory base for unincorporated associations means that any by-laws or rules must be based on the objects of the organization. The by-laws and rules may not be *ultra vires* the objects of the organization as set out in the Memorandum of Association or similar constating document.[55] The Ontario *Corporation Act* provides explicitly for the types of matters that may be in the by-laws[56] as does the *Co-operative Corporations Act*.[57]

Unincorporated associations are often less expensive to establish than corporations. For example, because no application is usually required, no application fees need to be paid. The lower costs to establish the organization may be an important factor in deciding whether or not to incorporate. In addition, because approval of the government is usually not necessary, they can be established faster than corporations.

The level of risk is also a factor in deciding whether or not to incorporate or operate as an unincorporated association. A major reason to incorporate an association or club is to minimize the risk of members' liability. As noted above, s. 122 of the *Corporations Act* and s. 73 of the *Co-operative Corporations Act* significantly minimize the risks of liability. However, not all activities give rise to a significant level of risk. The risk can also be minimized by other means, such as requiring waivers from participants in activities or purchasing liability insurance. Both of these methods to reduce the risk of liability, however, pose their own difficulties. The waivers, for example, must be informed and third-party liability insurance can be prohibitively expensive.

VI Conclusion

Each group should assess the level of risk given their particular circumstances before deciding whether or not to operate as an unincorporated association or to apply for incorporation. Although it is not possible to assess risk in the abstract, there are some activities that obviously give rise to concerns about the level of risk for potential liability. For example, activities that involve personal safety, such as physical activity or contact sports, or significant contractual obligations would raise legitimate concerns about risk of potential liability for both the officers and directors and the members of an unincorporated association. Similarly, if the organization owns real property, especially if the public is invited to attend, incorporation would be a worthwhile consideration. On the other hand, an organization that only meets socially or to discuss issues of the

---

[55] *Matheson v. Kelly* (1913), 15 D.L.R. 359, 5 W.W.R. 950 (Man. K.B.).
[56] R.S.O. 1990, c. C.38, ss. 129 and 130.
[57] R.S.O. 1990, c. C.35, ss. 21–24.

day arguably does not need to incorporate given the minimal risk involved.

CHAPTER 3

Incorporating a Charitable or Not-for-Profit Organization

A   OVERVIEW

The corporate form is a useful and common method for an organization to carry on charitable and not-for-profit activities. It provides limited liability for the members and is often the legal structure required by governments for an organization to be eligible for funding or to carry out certain activities. There are three major types of corporate forms available to charitable and not-for-profit organizations: corporations without share capital incorporated under the Ontario *Corporations Act*;[1] corporations without share capital incorporated under the *Canada Corporations Act*;[2] and co-operative corporations without share capital incorporated under the Ontario *Co-operative Corporations Act*.[3] There are other options for incorporation, such as private legislation; however, most not-for-profit or charitable corporations will be incorporated under one of these three statutes or the equivalents in the other provinces. The concordance in Appendix A identifies the relevant statutes and provisions for the other provinces. Appendix B provides a list of the government departments responsible for incorporating corporations and co-operative corporations without share capital.

Each statute serves a different purpose. The decision under which statute the organization will incorporate will depend upon the needs and desires of the members and on any legal requirements. For example, in order to be incorporated under the federal statute, the objects of the corporation should fall within federal jurisdiction or be national in scope. If the members want to operate a not-for-profit co-operative, to benefit from bulk sale purchases, for example, the provincial co-operative legislation is a more appropriate choice.

Within these three incorporating statutes, several different types of not-for-profit corporations or co-operative corporations may be incorporated. Historically, the major types have included a general not-for-profit

---
[1] R.S.O. 1990, c. C.38 [as am. to S.O. 2001, c. 9, Sched. D, s. 5].
[2] R.S.C. 1970, c. C.32 [as am. to S.C. 1999, c. 3].
[3] R.S.O. 1990, c. C.35 [as am. to S.O. 2001, c. 8, ss. 6-17].

corporation and charitable corporations. For Ontario corporations, not-for-profit corporations also included social clubs, service clubs and athletic or sporting clubs. In more recent years, not-for-profit and charitable corporations have been used to deliver government programmes and may need to comply with specific policy or legal requirements, some of which are reviewed in general terms in Chapter 2.

The application processes and requirements are generally the same for all three statutes, with minor variations or additional requirements depending upon the circumstances. Each statute requires that the proposed corporation have a name and not be just a "numbered company". The name must meet criteria set out in the relevant statute or its regulations. For example, the name must not be so similar to other corporate names as to mislead or deceive the public. There are also restrictions on what words can or cannot be included in the proposed corporate name or words that require the consent of a governing body. The name must be distinctive, descriptive and may include the legal status of the corporation. The process also requires the applicant to file a computerized name search report — the NUANS report — to ensure that the name is available.

The applications must include two original copies of the proposed letters patent or articles of incorporation, in the case of a cooperative corporation. The name of the corporation and its objects, first directors and their addresses and head office must be included in the application. Because the 1992 amendments provide that a co-operative corporation has the powers of a natural person, objects are not required for co-operatives. The special provisions may be used, however, to limit the co-operative's activities or objects, which could occur, for example, to comply with government requirements or programme criteria. Additional information may be required depending upon which statute is involved. For example, the federal legislation also requires the occupations of the applicants. Any consents should also be included with the application, such as the Public Guardian and Trustee's approval if the application is for letters patent for a charitable corporation under the Ontario *Corporations Act* — assuming that the pre-approved object clauses do not meet the needs of the organization. The federal statute also requires that the by-laws be included with the application for incorporation. Each application requires an application fee and may require a name reservation fee. These fees are subject to change but are less than those for the incorporation of a business corporation.

Once the corporation is incorporated, a copy is returned to the incorporators and must be kept with the corporate records. The other copy is maintained in the public records. The Ontario corporations and co-operative corporations are required to file an Initial Return or Notice which identifies the officers and directors, the head office and principal place of business, language of preference and activity classification. This notice is required under the Ontario *Corporations Information Act*.[4]

B INCORPORATION

I ONTARIO CORPORATIONS WITHOUT SHARE CAPITAL

(1) General Comments

The objects of a corporation without share capital incorporated under the Ontario *Corporations Act*[5] are very broad. Section 118 permits a corporation to be incorporated under Part III of the Act for the purpose of carrying on objects that are within the constitutional jurisdiction of Ontario. There are five types of not-for-profit corporations under the Act: general not-for-profit corporations, sporting and athletics organizations, social clubs, service clubs, and charitable corporations.

(2) Application Process and Requirements

Incorporation is usually a simple process, provided that the members have taken the time to review what they want. The process may take several weeks to several months from application to receipt of letters patent. The time period will depend in part on the application's completeness, whether or not there are any backlogs, whether or not the appropriate pre-clearances, approvals or reviews have been obtained, and whether or not changes to the application are necessary.

There are three major steps to the incorporation process: name search; submission of the application and receipt of the letters patent; and establishing the corporation. Each of these three steps is discussed below.

(a) Step 1 — Selecting and Searching a Corporate Name

(i) General Comments

The corporate name serves two functions. First, it reflects the desires of the membership and often indicates the types of activities that the corporation is involved in or the background of the members. Second, it distinguishes the corporation from other persons so that other parties know with whom they are dealing. Through the corporate name, other parties may find out more about the corporation and its directors and officers from various public records, including the application for letters patent, the corporate filings and personal property registration systems.

---

[4] R.S.O. 1990, c. C.39.
[5] R.S.O. 1990, c. C.38 [as am. S.O. 1994, c. 27, s. 78(5)].

There are a number of practical issues that members of an organization should consider before they choose a corporate name. First, the name should be memorable and easily recognized. A recognizable and memorable name is particularly important if the corporation will be dealing with the public, will be providing services to the community or intends to raise funds from the public. Second, the name should be short. Longer names tend to be more cumbersome and confusing than short names. Names that look or sound awkward may alienate the public. Names that are pejorative in nature or that appear to be discriminatory contrary to the *Ontario Human Rights Code* should be avoided. Third, the name should have a broad appeal among the members and within the community that the corporation intends to serve. The members and community should feel comfortable with the name and believe that it reflects the objects of the corporation.

A useful approach is to hold a brainstorming session to develop a list of several words or names. The Act and Regulation should be checked to ensure that none of the words or names are prohibited or restricted. Following this initial review, the list of names should be checked against several telephone directories, municipal directories, trade association directories and so forth to determine if anyone else is using the same or a similar name. The directories are generally accessible at public libraries. The name could also be checked against existing corporate names at the Ministry of Consumer and Business Services. These types of checks may eliminate names that are the same or similar to existing corporate and business names and avoid unnecessary expense and delay through additional NUANS name searches.

(ii)   Elements of a Corporate Name

There are three elements to a corporate name: it should be distinctive; it should be descriptive; and it should indicate the legal status of the corporation.[6] A name is distinctive if it is not too general, will not be confused with existing names in use and will not mislead or confuse the public. The name may be distinctive in and of itself or it may have acquired its distinctiveness over time. Coined words are usually distinctive, as are names that combine two or more generic words.

Names that include geographic references, numbers, initials or dictionary words are less distinctive than coined or combination words. A corporate name may not, usually, be primarily or only a geographic name. An exception exists if the name has been in continuous use for at least 20 years before the date of application or the name has, through use, acquired a meaning that renders it distinctive.[7]

---

[6] Ontario Ministry of Consumer and Commercial Relations and the Office of the Public Guardian and Trustee, *Not-For-Profit Incorporator's Handbook* (Toronto: Queen's Printer, 2000), at 12.
[7] R.R.O. 1990, Reg. 181, s. 5.

The descriptive element describes the nature of the main activity or undertaking of the corporation and should not be misleading about the activities or undertaking.[8] The legal element is optional. The use of the words "corporation" or "incorporated" or their abbreviations may be used but are not necessary.

(iii)   Prohibitions for a Corporate Name

Paragraph 13(1)(a) of the *Corporations Act* provides that a corporation shall not be given a name:

> that is the same as or similar to the name of a known corporation, association, partnership, individual or business if its use would be likely to deceive, except where the corporation, association, partnership, individual or person consents in writing that its, his or her name in whole or in part be granted ...

It is not uncommon for members of an unincorporated organization to decide to incorporate after a few years. The incorporation may take place for any of the reasons discussed earlier, including to minimize the exposure of the members and officers and directors to liability. If an unincorporated organization existed prior to the application for incorporation, a "consent and undertaking" from that organization should be included with the application. The consent and undertaking stipulates that the organization has consented to the incorporation and to the use of the name. The organization also undertakes to cease operations or to cease the use of the name within six months of incorporation.

If the corporation through inadvertence or otherwise is or has been given a name that is objectionable, subs. 13(2) of the Act provides the Lieutenant Governor with the authority to direct the issue of supplementary letters patent changing the name of the corporation to some other name. Prior to doing so, the Lieutenant Governor must provide written notice of his or her intention to do so.

A person who feels aggrieved by the giving of the name in the letters patent or by the change under subs. 13(2) of the Act may apply to the Ontario Superior Court of Justice for a review of the matter. The Court may make an order changing the name of the corporation to such name as it considers proper or may dismiss the application. The applicant must serve notice on the Minister and on such other persons as the Court directs at least seven days before the hearing. A corporation which fails to comply with an order of the Court is guilty of an offence and, on conviction, liable to a fine of not more than $200. Every director or officer of the corporation who authorizes, permits or acquiesces in any such failure is guilty of an offence and, on conviction, is liable to a like fine.[9]

---

[8]   *Ibid.*, s. 7.
[9]   Subs. 13(4).

Subsection 13(1) provides that the corporate name may not suggest or imply a connection with the Crown, a member of the Royal Family or the Government of Canada or of any province, or any department, branch, bureau, service, agency or activity of any such government without the written consent of the appropriate authority. If the objects of the corporation are of a political nature, the name may not suggest or imply a connection with a political party. Furthermore, the corporate name may not be objectionable on any public grounds.

The Companies Branch has established a process for dealing with objections to corporate names.[10] Once a formal objection is made, the Director exchanges correspondence with the objector and the corporation. A corporation that receives a letter from the director about a formal objection should respond thoroughly to the objection. A decision is made whether or not an inquiry should be held based on the objection letter and the response from the corporation. If there are no allegations of actual deception in the public and the names do not appear to be so similar as to be likely to deceive the public, a decision may be made without the need for an inquiry. A letter is sent to the objector that an inquiry will not be held.

Where the corporation's name is likely to deceive the public, an inquiry officer is appointed and a notice of inquiry is issued to the objector, the corporation complained of and any solicitors of record in the matter. The notice sets out the date, time and place for the inquiry, the purpose of the inquiry, and a statement of the consequences that may follow if the corporation is not represented at the inquiry. The objector is called upon to present its case to have the name changed. The objector may call witnesses and introduce documents. The witnesses may be cross-examined by the corporation's representative or lawyer, or by any other parties. The corporation or proponent is then called upon to present its case and may do so using witnesses and documents.

Based on the evidence and arguments presented at any hearing, the inquiry officer makes a decision using the authority delegated by the minister. If the inquiry officer concludes that the name is sufficiently similar, an order is issued requiring the corporation to choose a new name which is dissimilar to that complained about by the objector. If the corporation does not do so, the inquiry officer may change the corporation's name. The corporation may appeal any order to the Ontario Superior Court of Justice pursuant to subs. 13(3) of the Act in accordance with the Rules of Court.

(iv) *Restricted Words for a Corporate Name*

Several words are permitted but restricted in their use as part of the corporate name by subs. 3(1) of the Regulation. "Amalgamated", "*fusioné*" or

---

[10] Ontario Ministry of Consumer and Commercial Relations, "Companies Branch Directive", No. 8002, July 29, 1983.

any other related word or expression may not be used in a corporate name unless the corporation is an amalgamated corporation. Certain words may only be used with the consent of the appropriate body. For example, the words "college", "institute", "university" or their French language equivalents may only be used with the written permission of the Ministry of Training, Colleges and Universities. The Association of Professional Engineers of Ontario must consent to the use of the words "engineer", "engineering" and any variation or French language equivalent. The word "housing" and its French language equivalents may only be used if the corporation is owned by, sponsored by or connected with the Government of Canada, the Government of Ontario or a municipal government in Ontario. "Royal" may be used only with the consent of the Crown obtained through the Secretary of State for Canada. Numerals indicating the year of incorporation may only be used if the proposed corporation is a successor to a corporation with the same or similar name or it is the year of amalgamation of the corporation.

Subsection 3(4) provides that the word "veteran" or "*ancien combattant*" or any abbreviation or derivative may be used only if 95 per cent of the members of the corporation are war veterans, their spouses, same sex partners or children of war veterans, or if the name has been in continuous use for at least 20 years. "War veterans" is defined in subs. 3(5) as persons who served in the armed forces of any country while that country was in a state of war. This subsection was amended in 2000 to define "spouse" and "same sex partner". "Spouse" includes a spouse as defined in the *Family Law Act*[11] and two person of the opposite sex who live together in a conjugal relationship outside of marriage. "Same sex partner" are two people of the same sex who live togther in a conjugal relationship.[12]

The use of a name of another province or of Canada may be refused because it suggests that the corporation was incorporated in that jurisdiction and is, therefore, misleading. Paragraph 13(1)(b) of the Act requires that the applicant provide the consent in writing of the appropriate authority if the use of a word suggests or implies a connection with the Crown or any member of the Royal Family or the Government of Canada or the government of any province. This restriction extends to any department, branch, bureau, service, agency or activity of any such government.

At one time, the use of the word "association" or a similar word or expression that denotes that the corporation is a representative body was restricted. The word could be used only if the applicants could satisfy the director that two thirds of the persons represented by the corporation would be members of the organization. This restriction was deleted in 1993. However, the general rule that a name not be misleading to the public continues to apply. An objector could object to the name of a cor-

---

[11] R.S.O. 1990, c. F.2.
[12] O. Reg. 43/00, subs. 1(2).

poration that includes the word "association" or "federation" if, in fact, the corporation was not an association or federation of members.

A family name or the name of a particular individual who is living or who has lived within the previous 30 years may not be used without written permission of the individual or his or her heir, executor, administrator or guardian.[13] The prohibition does not apply if the proposed corporation is the successor or affiliate of a corporation that uses the family name and the first corporation consents in writing to the use of the name. The first corporation may also be required to consent to dissolve itself or change its name where the two corporations would have the same or similar name. The individual or family name may also be used if the consent cannot be obtained or the family name is of historic or patriotic significance and has a *bona fide* connection to the objects of the corporation.[14]

Names cannot exceed 120 characters in length, including punctuation marks and spaces.[15] Only letters from the Roman alphabet or Arabic numbers or combinations of the two may be used.[16] Only the punctuation marks and other marks as set out in subs. 8(2) of the Regulation may be used in a name.

Bilingual (English and French) names are permitted where the translation is exact. Minor changes may be made to ensure that the name is idiomatically correct. The translated name must not mislead the public into thinking that two separate corporations have been created. A translated name must be set out as a special provision with exact translations of the English and French names. Care must be taken in the use of acronyms.

Subsection 3(3) of the Regulation requires the name of a fraternal society incorporated under s. 176 of the Act to include the words "fraternal society" or its French language equivalent. Similarly, a pension fund or employees' mutual benefit society incorporated under s. 185 of the Act must use the words "pension fund society", "employees' mutual benefit society" or the French language equivalents. These two types of corporations are very specialized and, as such, are not dealt with in this text.

(v)   ***Name for a Charitable Corporation***

Where the corporation is to be a charitable corporation, the name should describe the charitable objects of the corporation.[17] The exception to this requirement is if the charitable corporation is a public or private foundation, in which case the name may include a reference to the name of

---

[13] O. Reg. 181/90, subs. 6(1).
[14] *Ibid.*, subs. 6(3).
[15] *Ibid.*, s. 9.
[16] *Ibid.*, subs. 8(3).
[17] *Not-for-Profit Incorporator's Handbook, supra*, note 6, at 33.

the individual or family. The term foundation may be used only if the objects of the charitable corporation are in the nature of a foundation.

(vi) NUANS Name Search and Report

The Ministry requires that the proposed name be cleared by a private search house. The search houses are operated by private sector companies that have obtained access to the NUANS computer database of corporate names, trade marks and business names. The NUANS database is owned and maintained by Industry Canada. The search house will produce, for a fee, an "Ontario biased" report that is submitted as part of the application to the Ministry of Consumer and Business Services. Some search houses will also advise on whether or not the name appears to be similar to another existing corporate name or registered trade name or trade mark.

The NUANS search report must be dated not more than 90 days before the application for letters patent is submitted.[18] Only the person who proposes the name may use the name identified in the computer search report unless a consent in writing has been obtained from the person who first proposed the name.[19] The NUANS search report is not necessary if the incorporation is required by a government authority as a condition to the awarding of financial assistance under a government program.[20]

(b) Step 2 — Application for Letters Patent

(i) General Comments

Charitable and not-for-profit organizations are often involved in activities that involve the delivery of government services or services that are regulated. An organization should review the requirements with the appropriate ministry or agencies prior to submitting an application for letters patent. Until January 1, 1993, the Ministry would circulate applications to relevant ministries for comment. This practice is no longer in place and the responsibility is on the applicants to obtain any pre-clearances, approvals or reviews that may be necessary or appropriate.

Subsection 1(1) of the Regulation does require that the application include any consent or consent and undertaking required by the Act or the Minister. The application should, therefore, include any consents required for the use of a corporate name or word in a corporate name. The applicants for incorporation are also required to ensure that the letters patent comply with any statutory provisions and any relevant policies and practices of the appropriate ministries or agencies. Any required

---

[18] O. Reg. 181/90, subs. 1(1).
[19] *Ibid.*, s. 2 [am. O. Reg. 625/93].
[20] *Ibid.*, subs. 1(3) [am. O. Reg. 625/93].

consents supplied by those ministries or agencies should be included in the application for letters patent.

In addition, the Public Guardian and Trustee's consent is required for the incorporation of a charitable corporation. Since November 1, 1989, the Ministry will accept an application for incorporation of a corporation that is or appears to be a "charitable corporation" only after it has received the approval of the Public Guardian and Trustee. The applicants must submit the application to the Public Guardian and Trustee and pay a $150 fee to obtain the pre-clearance of the letters patent. The Public Guardian and Trustee has, however, put in place a number of "pre-approved" objects clauses. If the pre-approved objects clauses and prescribed special provisions are used, there is no need to obtain the Public Guardian and Trustee's approval. The PGT fee is not, therefore, required and the time that would otherwise be used to obtain the approval is saved. Furthermore, Canada Customs and Revenue Agency has agreed to accept these pre-approved objects clauses for purposes of registration as a charity, resulting in additional time being saved. The downside is that there is no flexibility in the wording; the exact wording must be used for both the relevant objects clauses and the special provisions. However, the pre-approved objects clauses do cover most situations.[21]

The application should be completed in duplicate in the prescribed form.[22] Detailed instructions are included on the form. The form was simplified in 1993 and 1998 to take into account the amendments to the regulation and changes to the Companies Branch's administrative practices.[23] The form prescribed under the Regulations requires the name of the corporation, the address of its head office, the names and residence addresses of the first directors, the objects of the corporation, any special provisions and the names and residence addresses of the incorporators. The prescribed form also includes the following special provision:

> The corporation shall be carried on without the purpose of gain for its members, and any profits or other accretions to the corporation shall be used in promoting its objects.

Any additional special provisions, which may be required by a regulator or ministry, or to take into account the desires of the membership, would be included after this mandatory special provision. The application must be executed in duplicate. The second copy may not be, therefore, a photocopy of the original with signatures.

---

[21] *Charities Bulletin #2*, Public Guardian and Trustee, October 1999.
[22] *Ibid.*, s. 18.
[23] O. Reg. 625/93. The application form is available online at the Ministry's website <http://www.cbs.gov.on.ca>.

(ii) Head Office

Every corporation must have a head office, but it need not own or lease the premises. The intent is to provide a physical location that will be designated as the head office where records are kept and where persons may contact the corporation. Many smaller charitable and not-for-profit organizations use the home address of one of the applicants or the secretary or treasurer for this purpose.

A social club, which may maintain a club house or similar premises, should ensure before it files an application that the municipality will permit the land and premises to be used for that purpose. The organization should also consult with municipal authorities to ensure that premises comply with the Building Code,[24] the Fire Code[25] and the *Health Protection and Promotion Act*.[26] The application for letters patent as a social club no longer includes the club's address nor must it obtain prior written consent of the Minister to change premises. These requirements were revoked in 1994 and came into effect in 1995.[27] A genuine incorporated social club may be exempt from the definition of common gaming house if it is licensed by a provincial Attorney General or other authorized person and the club receives no consideration from the gambling. Prior to 1993, the application for letters patent had to include "bars and bolts" provisions to ensure access by police. This requirement probably arose out of the exemption under subs. 196(2) of the *Criminal Code*.[28] However, licences are no longer issued in Ontario.

(iii) Directors

Section 286 of the *Corporations Act* sets out the minimum standards for the first directors. A first director must be at least 18 years of age, a member of the organization or become a member within ten days of becoming a director, and not an undischarged bankrupt. The number of directors is fixed and must be at least three. The first directors remain as directors until they are replaced. The number of directors may be changed by a special resolution passed by the members voting at a meeting called for that purpose. The first directors shall have all the powers, duties and liabilities of elected directors. Any clause to authorize rotating election of directors must be set out in the special provisions of the letters patent in detail. It is not sufficient to leave this clause to the by-laws.

---

[24] *Building Code Act*, 1992, S.O. 1992, c. 23.
[25] *Fire Protection and Prevention Act, 1997*, S.O. 1997, c. 4.
[26] R.S.O. 1990, c. H.7. There are several Regulations under the Act. The most relevant for most club houses would be the Regulation dealing with the preparation and service of food and beverages, O. Reg. 562/90.
[27] *Corporations Act*, R.S.O. 1990, c. C.38, s. 278 [am. S.O. 1994, c. 27, s. 78].
[28] R.S.C. 1985, c. C-46.

(iv) Objects

The objects of the corporation are set out in the application for letters patent. They are intended to identify the purposes of the corporation in a concise fashion. The objects are not a list of proposed activities but a statement of the primary and secondary purposes. The objects may include a commercial purpose provided that the profits accrue to the corporation and are not distributed to members. If the intent is to make a profit for distribution, the organization should be incorporated under the *Business Corporations Act*[29] or similar statutes and not Part III of the *Corporations Act*.

A charitable corporation is more restricted in what types of business activities it may undertake. As discussed in Chapter 1, at common law and under the *Income Tax Act* charitable corporations may carry on business activities provided that these activities are incidental or ancillary to its charitable objects.

The difference between an object and an activity is important. An example may assist to understand the distinction. A corporation without share capital may have as one of its objects "to operate, equip and maintain a community theatre". In carrying out this object, the corporation could purchase lighting equipment for use in the theatre. When the equipment is not being used for a production in the theatre, the corporation could rent it out to others for use in another theatre. This activity is a business activity that is incidental and ancillary to its object and would usually be an acceptable activity for that corporation. Provided that the activity is only incidental and any revenues are used to carry out the objects of the corporation, for example, to purchase new equipment or to pay for the operation of the theatre, the activity would probably be valid.

The Ontario Racing Commission's written consent is required if the proposed objects include horse-racing.[30] The Commission has, under the *Racing Commission Act, 2000*,[31] a very broad regulatory jurisdiction over race-tracks and racing. Subsection 12(2) of the regulation prohibits the objects from including dog-racing. The objects may, however, include the breeding of race-dogs.

(v) Powers

Section 23 of the *Corporations Act* provides a number of ancillary powers. A corporation without share capital may, for example, enter into agreements with any public authority, purchase or lease personal or real prop-

---

[29] R.S.O. 1990, c. B.16. For-profit corporations may also be established under other parts of the *Corporations Act* and other statutes such as the *Co-operative Corporations Act*, R.S.O. 1990, c. C.35 and the *Loan and Trust Corporations Act*, R.S.O. 1990, c. L.25.
[30] O. Reg. 181/90, subs. 12(1).
[31] S.O. 2000, c. 20.

erty, pay all costs and expenses related to the incorporation, and do all such other things that are incidental or conducive to the attainment of the objects of the corporation as set out in s. 23 of the Act, the letters patent and any supplementary letters patent. There is no need to list the powers set out in s. 23 in the application for letters patent or for supplementary letters patent. Not all of the s. 23 powers, however, are applicable to Part III corporations without share capital. Subsection 133(1) provides that only paras. 23(1) (a) to (p), (s), (u) and (v) are applicable. Paragraphs 23(1) (q), (r) and (t) are concerned with shares of corporations with share capital incorporated under the Act.

(vi) Special Provisions

Subsection 23(2) provides that any of the ancillary or incidental powers may be withheld or limited by the letters patent or supplementary letters patent. Additionally, subs. 119(2) provides that any matter that could be the subject of a by-law could be included in the letters patent or supplementary letters patent. Clauses with respect to the terms and conditions of directors, the distribution of assets upon dissolution and the qualifications for membership are common special provisions included in letters patent. Restrictions on the powers of corporations without share capital may be required by the Ministry, other ministries or the Public Guardian and Trustee in several circumstances.

"Clubs" are generally considered by the Ministry to be "social" in nature, absent evidence to the contrary. A club that is purely athletic in nature and whose objects do not include any of the usual attributes of a social club, such as a club house, would not usually be considered to be a social club. At one time, the applications were referred to the Commissioner of the Ontario Provincial Police and to the local municipal police. This practice is no longer in effect. It is no longer necessary to have a minimum of 10 applicants; three are sufficient. The letters patent no longer set out the club house premises.

Restrictions on the powers of charitable corporations are also included as special provisions. These restrictions are intended to ensure that charitable corporations carry out activities that are only charitable in nature. The Public Guardian and Trustee, as part of its pre-clearance approval, requires that the following clauses be included as special provisions to ensure that the corporation carries out its charitable objects:

(1) The corporation shall be carried on without the purpose of gain for its members and any profits or other accretions to the corporation shall be used in promoting its objects.

(2) The corporation shall be subject to the *Charities Accounting Act* and the *Charitable Gifts Act*.

(3) The directors shall serve as such without remuneration and no directors shall directly or indirectly receive any profit from their position as such, provided that directors may be paid reasonable expenses incurred by them in the performance of their duties.

(4) The borrowing power of the corporation pursuant to any by-law passed and confirmed in accordance with s. 59 of the *Corporations Act* shall be limited to borrowing money for current operating expenses, provided that the borrowing power of the corporation shall not be so limited if it borrows on the security of real or personal property.

(5) If it is made to appear to the satisfaction of the Minister, upon report of the Public Guardian and Trustee, that the corporation has failed to comply with any of the provisions of the *Charities Accounting Act* or the *Charitable Gifts Act*, the Minister may authorize an inquiry for the purpose of determining whether or not there is sufficient cause for the Lieutenant Governor to make an order under subsection 317(1) of the *Corporations Act* to cancel the letters patent of the corporation and declare it to be dissolved.

(6) Upon dissolution of the corporation and after the payment of all debts and liabilities, its remaining property shall be distributed or disposed of to charities registered under the *Income Tax Act* (Canada), in Canada.

(7) To invest the funds of the corporation pursuant to the *Trustee Act*.

Or

(8) To invest the funds of the corporation in such manner as determined by the directors, and in making such investments the directors shall not be subject to the *Trustee Act*, but provided that such investments are reasonable, prudent and sagacious under the circumstances and do not constitute, either directly or indirectly, a conflict of interest.[32]

(9) For the above objects, and as incidental and ancillary thereto, to exercise any of the powers as prescribed by the *Corporations Act*, or

---

[32] These special provisions were drafted prior to the implementation of the prudent investor approach in amendments to the *Trustee Act*. It is not clear whether the optional (8) is required anymore as a result.

by any other statutes or laws from time to time applicable, except where such power is limited by these letters patent or the statute or common law relating to charities.

The Public Guardian and Trustee, in pre-clearing the application, does not certify the charitable corporation. The pre-clearance is intended to provide the opportunity to the Public Guardian and Trustee to determine if the objects of the corporation are charitable and therefore within the jurisdiction of the Public Guardian and Trustee under the *Charities Accounting Act*.[33] The legal authority for the Public Guardian and Trustee to pre-clear an application for letters patent appears to be based in the discretionary nature of the issuance of letters patent and the requirement that the application for letters patent include any consents required by the Minister.[34] The Public Guardian and Trustee charges a $150 fee for providing this pre-clearance.[35] The pre-clearance and payment of that fee can be avoided if the incorporators use the "pre-approved" object clauses and special provisions.

Unlike the Ontario *Business Corporations Act*,[36] the *Corporations Act* does not provide to applicants a legislative right to incorporation. The Minister exercises discretion in determining whether or not to incorporate a corporation by letters patent. The degree of discretion, however, has not been tested by judicial review.

The Public Guardian and Trustee has jurisdiction over charitable organizations at common law and pursuant to the *Charities Accounting Act*. It has broad discretionary power to refuse to approve the objects of a proposed charitable corporation where, for example, the objects are too vague, broad or not wholly and exclusively charitable. In other instances, the Public Guardian and Trustee has expressed an opinion that power clauses in an application went beyond the purposes of the charity; that the name did not reflect the purposes and objects set out in the application; that the organization was pursuing political purposes; that it would not be properly administered based on the previous failure of the incorporators to comply with the law with respect to charities; and that the financial statements of the predecessor indicated that too high a proportion of charitable funds were spent on noncharitable activities and administrative expenses.

(vii) ***Special Corporations***

There are a number of corporations that provide services that are regulated by other ministries, including the Ministry of Housing, the Ministry of Health, the Ministry of Community and Social Services, the Ministry

---

[33] R.S.O. 1990, c. C.10.
[34] O. Reg. 181/90, subs. 1(1).
[35] O. Reg. 1078/90 under the *Public Guardian and Trustee Act*, R.S.O. 1990, c. P.51.
[36] R.S.O. 1990, c. B.16.

of Education, the Ministry of Training, Colleges and Universities and the Ministry of Municipal Affairs. At one time, the Companies Branch would refer applications for letters patent to the various relevant ministries. As of January 1, 1993, this practice is no longer in effect. The applicants, however, remain responsible for ensuring that the letters patent and by-laws comply with the requirements of those ministries. It is advisable to review a draft application for letters patent and, if available, draft by-laws, with the relevant ministry prior to submitting it to the Companies Branch.

(c)   Step 3 — Establishing the Corporation

Once the letters patent have been issued by the Ministry, the first directors are required to take a number of steps to establish the operations of the corporation. The board of directors must meet and adopt the by-laws, make banking and financial arrangements, adopt the corporate seal, appoint the auditors and the officers of the corporation.

An Initial Return (Form 1) under the *Corporations Information Act*[37] must be filed within 60 days of the issuance of the letters patent. The Initial Return is placed on the corporation's public file to provide basic information to the public about the directors and officers of the corporation, including their names and residential addresses. The Initial Return also includes the location of the corporation's head office. A Notice of Change must be filed within 15 days of a change in the information contained in the initial return.

II FEDERAL CORPORATIONS WITHOUT SHARE CAPITAL

(1)   General Comments

Incorporation under Part II of the *Canada Corporations Act*[38] is appropriate where the organization will operate on a national level or in more than one province, or if the objects and activities fall within federal constitutional jurisdiction. If the objects and activities fall within provincial jurisdiction, the applicants should also consider incorporation under the Ontario statute and then obtain registration to operate as an extra-provincial corporation in other appropriate provinces.

Industry Canada is consulting the sector with respect to proposed legislative changes.[39] It appears that there will be draft legislation proposed that will substantially change the application process. For example, one option is that incorporation will be "as of right" as it is under

---

[37] R.S.O. 1990, c. C.39 [as am. S.O. 1995, c. 3].
[38] R.S.C. 1970, c. C.32.
[39] *Reform of the Canada Corporations Act: The Federal Nonprofit Framework Law*, Corporate Law Policy Directorate, Industry Canada, July 2000.

business corporation incorporating legislation, although object clauses will still be required.

(2) Types

The federal Act provides for similar types of corporations as does the Ontario statute but is not as specific as is the Ontario legislation. A corporation without share capital may be a not-for-profit corporation that provides services to its members, such as a professional association. It may also be a not-for-profit corporation with charitable objects that does not intend to register as a charitable organization. Finally, the corporation may be a charitable corporation that does intend to register its charitable status.

It is not certain whether a corporation that is charitable in nature is required to notify the Public Guardian and Trustee of its existence under the *Charities Accounting Act*.[40] Although there may be an argument that it does not on constitutional grounds, it would appear that the Public Guardian and Trustee does claim jurisdiction over federally incorporated charitable corporations that carry on activities in Ontario. Furthermore, under head 7 of s. 92 of the *Constitution Act, 1867*, charitable institutions are within provincial jurisdiction.

(3) Application Process and Requirements

Industry Canada is responsible for the administration of the *Canada Corporations Act*. Corporations without share capital are incorporated under Part II of that statute. The department developed an information kit to assist applicants for incorporation under Part II.[41] The kit includes a sample application; model by-laws; a summary of the department's policy on not-for-profit corporations; a checklist for use with the application; and a fee schedule.

The kit is intended to assist applicants in several ways. First, it sets out the requirements under the Act for incorporation. The policy summary also provides information on what is acceptable under the Act, including areas where the Act is not clear. Second, the use of the model by-laws will speed up the process for incorporation. The model by-laws include provisions on all the areas that must be in the by-laws under Part II of the Act. Adoption of the model by-laws avoids the need for departmental review of the by-laws. Where changes to the model by-laws are necessary, the list of requirements assists applicants to ensure compliance with the Act and the Department's policies. Third, the information kit provides information to applicants to understand the process of incorporation and the maintenance of a corporate entity.

---

[40] R.S.O. 1990, c. C.10.
[41] Industry Canada, "Information Kit on the Creation of Not-for-profit Corporations", November 25, 1999.

(a) Step 1 — Selecting and Searching a Corporate Name

The first step is choosing the corporate name for the corporation. As with the Ontario incorporation, the choice of a corporate name is important.

(i) Distinctive Name

The name must be distinctive. It distinguishes the organization and activities from others and their activities. In determining whether or not a name is distinctive, the Minister is to consider the whole name and not only its separate elements.

Section 19 of the Regulations provides that a name is not distinctive where it is too general; is only descriptive of the quality, function or other characteristic of the goods or services in which the corporation intends to deal; is primarily or only the name or surname used alone of an individual who is living or has died within 30 years preceding the date of request for that name; or is primarily or only a geographic name used alone. The name would be acceptable, however, if the applicant establishes that the name, through use, has acquired and continues to have a secondary meaning at the time of the request. A corporate name could include, as an element, the name of a family of an individual where the individual or his or her heir or legal representative consents in writing to the use of his or her name and the individual has or had a material interest in the corporation.[42]

(ii) Prohibited Names

The corporate name must not be the same or similar to the name of any other company, society, association or firm that is in existence, carrying on business in Canada or that is incorporated under the laws of Canada or any province. Furthermore, the name must not so resemble another name so as to be calculated to deceive. It may be the same or similar to another name if the existing company, society, association or firm is in the course of being dissolved or changing its name and has consented to the use of the name. The name may not otherwise be objectionable on public grounds.[43]

Section 16 prohibits the use of several elements in a corporate name. A corporate name is objectionable if it includes "Air Canada"; "Trans Canada Airlines" or "*Lignes aeriennes Trans Canada*"; "Canada Standard" or "CS"; "Co-operative", "co-op" or "pool" when it connotes a co-operative venture; "Parliament Hill" or "*Colline du Parlement*"; "Royal Canadian Mounted Police", "*Gendarmerie Royale du Canada*", "RCMP" or

---

[42] *Canada Corporations Regulations*, C.R.C. [1978], c. 424, s. 21.
[43] *Canada Corporations Act*, R.S.C. 1970, c. C.32, para. 9(1)(b) and subs. 28(1).

"GRC"; or "United Nations", *Nations Unies*", "UN" or "ONU".[44] A name is also objectionable if it connotes that the corporation carries on business under royal, vice-regal or governmental patronage, approval or authority unless the appropriate government department or agency approves the name in writing.[45]

The Regulation provides guidance on when a proposed name of a corporation shall be considered to be objectionable on the grounds that it is prohibited or deceptively misdescriptive.[46] Under s. 13, a corporate name would be considered to be confusing with a trade mark or a trade name if the use is likely to lead to the inference that the business carried on or intended to be carried on under the corporate name and the business connected with the trade mark or trade name are one business. It is not relevant whether or not the nature of the business of each is generally the same. The corporate name may be used if the other corporation has not carried on business during the previous two years and it has consented to the use of the name and undertakes in writing to dissolve itself or to change its name.[47]

(iii)   Restrictions on Words in Corporate Names

Section 17 of the Regulation includes other restrictions on the elements in a corporate name to avoid confusion or misleading the public. A name is prohibited if it connotes that the corporation is sponsored or controlled by or is affiliated with the Government of Canada, the government of a province, a foreign government or a subdivision or agency of any such government unless that government, subdivision or agency has consented in writing to the use of the name. Similar written consents are required from universities, associations of accountants, architects, engineers, lawyers, physicians, surgeons or any other professional association recognized by the laws of Canada or of a province. If the name connotes the carrying on of the business of a bank, loan company, insurance company, trust company, other financial intermediary or a stock exchange that is regulated by a law of Canada or a province, the written consent for the use of the name is required from the appropriate government department or agency.

Section 20 sets out the circumstances that are to be considered in determining whether or not a name is "confusing". These circumstances include the inherent distinctiveness of the whole or any element of a trade name or trade mark, the length of time a trade name or trade mark has been in use, the nature or the goods or services associated with the trade name or trade mark and the likelihood of competition, the nature of the trade with which a trade name or trade mark is associated,

---

[44] C.R.C., c. 424, s. 16.
[45] *Ibid.*, subs. 17(a).
[46] *Ibid.*, s. 11.
[47] *Ibid.*, s. 25. See also ss. 22 and 26.

the degree of resemblance in appearance or sound or the ideas suggested by them, and the territorial area in which the proposed corporate name or existing trade name is likely to be used.

A corporate name is also prohibited if it contains a work or phrase that is obscene or connotes a business that is scandalous, obscene or immoral.[48] A name may not be used if it misdescribes in any language the business, goods or services in association with which it is proposed to be used; the conditions under which goods or services will be produced or the persons to be employed in the production or supply of the goods or services; or the place of origin of those goods or services.[49]

The name may be in English or French. If the corporation has a name consisting of a separated or combined French and English form, it may use either the French or the English form of its name or both. The corporate seal must show the corporate name in both English and French forms or the corporation must have two seals, each of which is equally valid, for the English and French forms.[50] The corporate name may include alphabetic or numeric characters, initials, punctuation marks or a combination of these elements.[51]

(iv) *Change in Corporate Name*

Pursuant to subs. 28(2) of the *Act*, the Minister may change a corporation's name by supplementary letters patent if letters patent were issued to a corporation with a name that is not in compliance with the Act. Prior to issuing the supplementary letters patent, the Minister must provide notice of his or her intention to do so.

A corporation may also change its name. To do so, two-thirds of the votes cast at a special general meeting called for the purpose must sanction a by-law for the name change. The name change is to be confirmed by supplementary letters patent. If the Minister is satisfied that the change in name is not objectionable, he or she may direct that supplementary letters patent be issued. A notice of the issuance of the supplementary letters patent is to be published in the *Canada Gazette* pursuant to section 29 of the *Act*.

(b) *Step 2 — Application for Letters Patent*

An application must be made by at least three applicants, all of whom are at least 18 years of age. A corporation may not be one of the applicants. All applicants must be individuals. The contents of an application for incorporation by letters patent are set out in subs. 155(1) of the Act. The application must include:

---

[48] *Ibid.*, s. 18.
[49] *Ibid.*, s. 23.
[50] *Ibid.*, subss. 25(2) and (3).
[51] *Ibid.*, s. 24.

- the proposed name of the corporation;
- the purposes for which its incorporation is sought;
- the place within Canada where the head office will be situated;
- the names in full and the address and occupation of each of the applicants; and
- the names of the applicants, not less than three, who are to be the first directors of the corporation.

Subsection 155(2) requires that the by-laws shall accompany the application for incorporation. As noted above, the department provides model by-laws which may be used by the applicants. The model includes the matters that are required by subs. 155(2) to be covered in the by-laws and other matters that are required by policy. Any provision under subs. 155(2) could also be set out in the letters patent.

A completed application includes several documents. The department has established a format for the letters patent. The application includes an affidavit or statutory declaration of one of the applicants swearing to the truthfulness of the application. A Canada-biased NUANS report is to be filed with the application or, alternatively, the applicants may, for a fee of $15, request the department to search and to reserve a name. A bilingual name requires two scarches ($30).

If the applicants are satisfied with the model by-laws, a copy of the unsigned by-laws should be enclosed. If the applicant is not satisfied with the model by-laws, the proposed by-laws should be attached. The applicants should also include a completed checklist indicating the required provisions that have been included in the proposed by-laws.

A covering letter should set out the documents that are enclosed with the application. It should also specify the street address of the head office of the corporation. The filing fee of $200 for application for letters patent must be included. All cheques are payable to the Receiver General of Canada.

The corporation will have a number of incidental and ancillary powers which are set out in s. 16 of the Act. It is not necessary, therefore, to include those incidental and ancillary powers in the application for letters patent. The list is extensive and in most cases it is unlikely that any additional powers would be required. The letters patent could, however, restrict the corporation in the exercise of any incidental or ancillary powers.

III CO-OPERATIVE CORPORATIONS

(1) General Comments

Co-operative corporations are another form of legal entity that meet a particular purpose. Under the *Co-operative Corporations Act*,[52] a co-operative corporation may be incorporated with share capital or without share capital. This text is concerned only with co-operative corporations without share capital, which are similar in purpose to corporations without share capital under the *Corporations Act*. As with corporations without share capital, a number of government programmes may be implemented by co-operative corporations or the activities of the co-operative corporations may be regulated. The incorporators may want to consult with the relevant ministry or agency prior to initiating the incorporation process.

(2) Procedures for Incorporation

(a) *Overview*

A co-operative corporation is incorporated by Articles of Incorporation. The *Act* is administered by the Financial Services Commission of Ontario. The completed application includes two copies of a completed Form 2 (co-operatives without share capital), a NUANS report and payment to reserve the name and for the incorporation of the not-for-profit co-operative corporation, an affidavit of verification and Form 3 consents to act as first directors. The name is reserved, pursuant to section 13, for 90 days.

(b) *Name Selection and Approval*

The first step in the incorporation process is the choice of name and its approval by the Commission. As with the other forms of corporation, the Act and Regulations set out restrictions and prohibitions on the words in the corporate name. Section 7 of the Act requires that the word "co-operative" or its French equivalent be part of the name. No other person other than a co-operative corporation may use this word in their name.[53] The name must include the legal status, such as "Incorporated" or "Corporation" or corresponding abbreviation or French equivalent.[54] Section 8 provides the discretion to approve a name in another form or language.

---

[52] R.S.O. 1990, c. C.38 [am. S.O. 1992, c. 19; 1994, c. 17].
[53] Subsection 7(3). There are exceptions under subs. 7(4) for federally incorporated co-operative corporations or a corporation granted an extra-provincial licence and other similar exceptions.
[54] Subsection 7(5). "Limited" may only be used by co-operative corporations with share capital.

Section 9 provides general guidance on what words may be used in a name. As with s. 13 under the *Corporations Act*,[55] the name may not be the same as or similar to the name of a known corporation, association, partnership or individual. The name must not suggest or imply a connection with the Crown or Government of Canada, a municipality, or province without the written consent of the appropriate authority. The name must not suggest or imply a connection with a political party or leader, contain any word or phrase that indicates or implies it is incorporated for any purpose other than that set out in its objects or contain any word or phrase that is prohibited or restricted under any other Act unless the restrictions are complied with by the corporation. Finally, the name may not be objectionable on any public grounds, in the opinion of the Minister. Under subs. 9(2), the Minister may cause the name of the co-operative corporation to be changed after giving the co-operative an opportunity to be heard.

The Regulations provide some additional restrictions to the words used in the name. For example, the name should not be too general in character[56] or use the word "veteran" unless it has become established by a long and continuous prior use.[57] The name cannot include the word "condominium".[58] If the name uses initials or numerals, the Minister may require the addition of a distinctive element.[59] The restrictions set out under the Ontario *Corporations Act* would also apply, as a result of s. 9 of the Act, and the reader should refer to the discussion of name earlier in this chapter.

(c)   Application for Articles of Incorporation

Step two in the process of incorporation is the submission of the Articles of Incorporation. The information required in the Articles of Incorporation is prescribed by Regulation.[60] It must include the name of the co-operative; its head office location; the names, addresses and signatures of the incorporators; the number of directors; the names and addresses of the first directors; how the co-operative intends to finance itself (accepting loans from members or charging membership fees); the terms and conditions of the loans; and any special restrictions or provisions which apply to the co-operative. These restrictions or provisions may arise out of the type of co-operative or as a result of other government policies or programmes. For example, if the co-operative is to be a not-for-profit housing co-operative, certain special provisions are required to restrict the co-operative to those activities.

---

[55] R.S.O. 1990, c. C.38.
[56] O. Reg. 178/90, s. 5.
[57] *Ibid.*, s. 8.
[58] *Ibid.*, s. 9.
[59] *Ibid.*, s. 6.
[60] O. Reg. 178/90.

The fee schedule to the regulation sets out several of the restrictions that apply to co-operatives without share capital. In order to be eligible for the reduced fee, the following clauses must be included in the Articles of Incorporation:

- The co-operative shall carry on business without the purpose of gain for its members;
- The co-operative shall use any profit or other accretion for the purposes of promoting its objects;
- Upon dissolution and after the payment of all debts and liabilities, the co-operative's remaining property shall be distributed or disposed of to charitable organizations carrying on their activities solely within Canada; and
- The directors
  (a) shall serve without remuneration; and
  (b) shall not receive, directly or indirectly, any profit from their positions as directors but the articles may provide that the directors may be paid reasonable expenses incurred in the performance of their duties.

These required special provisions for co-operative corporations without share capital are intended to ensure that the co-operative operates on a not-for-profit basis, similar to corporations incorporated under the Ontario and federal statutes.

The application must include two other documents. A consent to act as a first director must be submitted for each first director who is not an incorporator (Form 3 under the Regulations). This form confirms that the individual has agreed to be first director. The application must also include an Affidavit of Verification. The Affidavit confirms who are the incorporators, their ages and that they will be members of the co-operative.

(d)   Establishing the Co-operative Corporation

Once the co-operative corporation is established, the co-operative must file an Initial Return under the *Corporations Information Act*.[61] The Initial Return includes information on the name, head office and business address of the co-operative and the names and addresses of the officers and directors. The Initial Return must be filed within 60 days of incorporation as a co-operative corporation.

A co-operative corporation without share capital may finance its operations through debt financing. The co-operative may, for example,

---

[61] R.S.O. 1990, c. C.39. See, also, the Commission's information pamphlet, Financial Services Commission of Ontario, *Filing Requirements and Record Keeping*.

borrow funds from its members. The membership loans may be a condition of membership in the co-operative. The maximum interest rate on the membership loans is limited to two per cent above the prime lending rate of the financial institution mentioned in the co-operative's by-laws. Membership loans must be repaid with any accrued interest when the member ceases to be a member.

The co-operative must file an offering statement with the Commission prior to soliciting the loans from the membership. Every prospective member must be given a copy of the filed offering statement and a copy of any filed material change statement before he or she makes the loan. The offering statement and material change statement are intended to ensure that full, plain and true disclosure is made about the co-operative, the risks associated with the loan and how the funds will be used, so that a potential member has the information that he or she needs to make an informed decision. The Commission provides a template for offering statements in Bulletin No. C-1/00, July 31, 2000.

Sections 34 to 37 of the Act set out the requirements for an offering statement. An offering statement is not required if the membership loans are a condition of membership and the value is less than $100 to each member and the total amount of membership loans held by a member is less than $1,000, or if the loans are offered to less than 25 persons.

A loan certificate must be issued to the member. The certificate must include the name of the co-operative and the fact that it is incorporated under the *Co-operative Corporations Act*, the name of the member to whom the certificate is issued, any restrictions on the transfer of the security, and whether the co-operative has a lien on the loan.

CHAPTER 4

The Organization in Operation: Organizational By-Laws and Statutory Requirements

A   OVERVIEW

By-laws are concerned with the management of the affairs of the corporation and set out the various rights and responsibilities of the members, directors and officers. They provide who may do what on behalf of the organization, the procedures for decision making, and a structure for the organization.

The content, detail and sophistication of an organization's by-laws should reflect the needs of the organization and the intentions of its members. The by-laws of an unincorporated association with limited objects and activities may be short and simple. The by-laws could also be included in the memorandum of association so that there is only one document that establishes the organization and governs the management of its affairs. It is important, however, to ensure that an appropriate amending provision is included in the by-laws. Because the relationship among the members of an unincorporated association is contractual in nature, absent an amending formula, all members (the parties to the contract) must agree on any amendment or dissolution.

The by-laws for a corporation under federal or provincial incorporating legislation must include certain provisions or address certain matters. As a result, the by-laws tend to be longer and more detailed than for unincorporated associations. The by-laws will also be more detailed and sophisticated if the membership is to be divided into groups with each group electing one director and directors at large or if the directors are to be elected on a rotating basis. As with unincorporated associations, the objective with by-laws is to ensure that the organization operates effectively, efficiently and in a manner that is consistent with the objects of the organization and the intentions of the members.

Certain issues should be addressed in the by-laws whether the organization is an unincorporated association or a corporation. The by-laws should include provisions on how decisions are to be made and by whom. The by-laws should, therefore, set out: how the directors are to be elected or appointed; for what term; what qualifications are necessary to be a director; and what will be the quorum for meeting. In addition, the by-laws should establish what officers are to be appointed or elected and what their functions will be. The classes of membership (if any), fees and dues, voting rights, general meetings, quorums and rights and responsibilities of members should be included in the by-laws. If there are any qualifications to be a member, these should be set out in the by-laws. By-laws will usually include provisions with respect to banking and financial arrangements, fiscal periods, the books and records to be maintained and the execution of documents, such as contracts. The by-laws should also include amending and repealing provisions, and a dissolution clause. Some of these matters may be set out in the memorandum of association for an unincorporated association or in the letters patent of a corporation.

Each province in Canada has enacted legislation to incorporate not-for-profit corporations. The statutory requirements and schemes vary from province to province. In some cases, such as Alberta and federal legislation, the by-laws must be included as part of the application for incorporation. Other provincial legislation, such as Ontario and Manitoba, set out only the matters that could or must be included in the by-laws. Although the details may differ, in general terms, the types of matters that should be addressed in by-laws are, not surprisingly, similar across Canada. Although the Ontario and federal legislative requirements are the focus of this chapter, some comments are also provided about the corporations without share capital in the other provinces. A concordance of the statutory provisions is included in Appendix A.

There are also several matters that are required by statutes to be considered in the organization and operation of a not-for-profit corporation. This chapter reviews the requirements under the Ontario and federal legislation for auditors, membership, general meetings, directors and officers in greater detail. The importance of rules of procedure or rules of order for meetings and their content is discussed at the end of the chapter.

B   GENERAL COMMENTS ON BY-LAWS

By-laws provide guidance to the members, board of directors, officers and staff members of charitable and not-for-profit organizations. They set out: who may do what on behalf of the corporation; the procedures for decision making; and provide further details on the organizational structure of unincorporated associations and corporations.

It is not necessary to have a lawyer draft the by-laws, especially for organizations that do not intend to incorporate and will have limited activities or time frames. Lawyers may, however, provide assistance to charitable and not-for-profit organizations, both corporate and unincorporated, in the design and drafting of the by-laws. If the organization is incorporated, if assets are likely to be owned by the organization, if the activities involve a degree of risk, or if the objects and activities may give rise to disputes among the members, officers and directors, it is advisable to retain a lawyer to draft the by-laws or to assist in their drafting. A lawyer may also deflect or resolve some of the disputes that arise during drafting by providing independent and disinterested legal or practical advice on the decision-making processes.

Whether the organization is an unincorporated association or a corporation, there are several issues that should be taken into account in drafting the by-laws. These issues include:

- if the organization is not applying for incorporation, do the members expect to do so later? If so, the closer the by-laws are to those required for corporations, the easier the transition will be;
- what size does the organization want to be, both geographically and in numbers? The larger the organization, the greater the impetus to provide for local chapters. Similarly, the larger the corporation in numbers, the greater the expense and effort in meeting the notice requirements and in achieving approval for the direction of the organization or changes to the legal structure of the organization;
- if the organization intends to operate in several geographic areas with independent or quasi-independent branches, will it do so using through associations or chapters,
- other requirements provided for in other legislation should be reviewed. The *Charities Accounting Act*[1] and the *Human Rights Code*[2] should receive particular attention. If the organization is to be active in certain areas, such as child care, the relevant legislation, regulations and government policies should be examined by the lawyers retained by the organization;
- zoning by-laws or other existing legal documents, such as a lease, may restrict the flexibility in drafting the by-laws. For example, attendance in a hall used as the head office of the corporation may be restricted by municipal by-laws or by the lease. If so, the organization's by-laws should provide flexibility in where the annual general meeting and other meetings of the members may take place;
- the organization may want to be active in a particular area or receive funding that requires approval of a ministry, department or municipality. If so, it may be prudent to review the proposed by-laws with that level of government to ensure that the provisions

---

[1] R.S.O. 1990, c. C.10.
[2] R.S.O. 1990, c. H.19.

will not preclude any funding. For example, a by-law that restricted membership to individuals with a particular background may not be contrary to the *Human Rights Code* but it could result in a government refusing to provide grants. Government policies will often restrict or prohibit grants to organizations that are not representative of the community or open to all individuals in the community;
- the organization may want to restrict the ability of its members or directors, current and future, to amend the by-laws by having certain provisions placed in the letters patent or supplementary letters patent rather than in the by-laws. Similarly, if an unincorporated association has both a Memorandum of Association and organizational by-laws, the Memorandum of Association may deal with those matters that require a greater level of approval before amendments may be made.

In any event, by-laws for both incorporated and unincorporated charitable and not-for-profit organizations should address the following matters:

- the objects of the organization and its activities, either directly or by reference to the letters patent, supplementary letters patents, memorandum of association or other constituting documents. The purpose of the by-laws are to provide the decision-making structure for the organization to carry out its objects. The by-laws should, therefore, complement and assist the organization to do so;
- the head office of the organization and an imprint of the corporate seal, if incorporated. Corporate seals were required at one time for many corporate acts. However, as legislation is modernized to recognize electronic commerce and other methods of transacting business, corporate seals are not always mandatory. Notwithstanding the changes, many corporations continue to obtain corporate seals to be safe;
- the board of directors, its size (if not in the incorporating documents), qualifications, election, removal, vacancies, committees (both standing and advisory) and indemnification;
- the appointment and removal of officers, agents and employees and their remuneration and responsibilities;
- membership qualifications, classes (if any), fees and dues, cards, transfer, suspension or termination of membership;
- meetings of the members and directors, including location, timing, notice and quorums and, for meetings of the directors, if the

meeting can be conducted through telephone conference call or other electronic methods;
- banking and financial arrangements, fiscal periods, books and records, and execution of documents. Financial institutions will normally provide a by-law for use by organizations that is consistent with the statutory requirements in that jurisdiction and the financial institution's policies and practices;
- amendments and repeal of the by-laws; and
- the winding up of the organization. The dissolution clauses will usually be in the letters patent, supplementary letters patent, memorandum of association or similar constituting documents. However, further details may also be contained in the by-laws.

The degree of detail and level of sophistication will depend largely on the objects of the organization, whether it is incorporated, its size and complexity, and any governmental requirements for a particular area of activities. As the by-laws provide a legal structure in which the members, officers, directors and staff will operate, it is important that the incorporating members take the time necessary in the preparation and review of the draft by-laws. The by-laws should ensure that the organization can carry out its objects in an effective and efficient way and that they meet the intentions of the members. They should also be sufficiently flexible for the organization to respond in a fair and appropriate way to changing circumstances, where the incorporating legislation permits.

C   UNINCORPORATED ASSOCIATIONS

The by-laws of an unincorporated organization are contractual in nature. The members agree among themselves to certain objects, procedures and structure. The level of complexity or sophistication in the by-laws reflects the purpose and structure desired by the members. An unincorporated association that is set up for a short period of time with a specific objective, such as lobbying for improvements to lighting on a neighbourhood street, does not require the same level of sophistication in the by-laws as would an association of professionals that intends to operate throughout Ontario and have different classes of membership. In the latter case, it is advisable and probably necessary to establish an organization with a clear structure and definitive lines of accountability. In the lobbying case, all that would probably be necessary in practice would be evidence, such as a petition or resolution signed by the majority of the residents, indicating that the organization is the political representative of the neighbourhood and that it has a mandate to speak on the issue on behalf of most, if not all, of the neighbourhood.

Whatever the purpose of the unincorporated association, it is important to ensure that its constituting documents include provisions on dissolution and for amendments. These provisions should be consistent with the intent of the members. For example, if the members after due deliberation conclude that any amendments to the by-laws should be restrictive, then this intention can be implemented. Because the relationship is contractual in nature in an unincorporated association, without an amendment provision, all members must agree to the change in terms of the contract. If there is a dispute, such agreement may be very difficult, if not impossible, to obtain. It is prudent, therefore, to include an amending power in the constituting documents, including any memorandum of association, by-laws or rules.

D CORPORATE BY-LAWS

I GENERAL COMMENTS

Corporate by-laws, on the other hand, have both a contractual basis and a legislative authority. The relationship among the members or incorporating directors is initially contractual in nature, with each person agreeing to perform certain services or functions for a common purpose. The incorporating legislation comes into play after incorporation, requiring that by-laws address specific matters and that they be approved by the membership.

This part of the chapter reviews the requirements for by-laws under incorporating legislation. It examines the requirements at the federal and provincial levels but provides greater detail for corporations incorporated under the Ontario *Corporations Act*,[3] the Ontario *Co-operative Corporations Act*[4] and the *Canada Corporations Act*.[5]

II ONTARIO CORPORATIONS AND CO-OPERATIVE CORPORATIONS WITHOUT SHARE CAPITAL

(1) Corporations without Share Capital

Section 129 of the Ontario *Corporations Act*[6] is concerned with the membership and their rights and obligations, the meetings of the corporation and of the board of directors, and the operations of the corporation. A by-law may be enacted, repealed or amended by the board of directors. It is effective until the next annual meeting of the members, at which time it ceases to have effect unless it is confirmed by the members. Only the board of directors may initiate by-laws and only the members may confirm, reject, amend or otherwise deal with a by-law submitted by the

---

[3] R.S.O. 1990, c. C.38.
[4] R.S.O. 1990, c. C.35.
[5] R.S.C. 1970, c. C.32.
[6] R.S.O. 1990, c. C.38.

board of directors. Any matter that may be the subject of a by-law may be included in the letters patent or supplementary letters patent.

The duality of functions between the board of directors and the members of the corporation in dealing with by-laws is important. It allows the board to manage the corporation and provides it with the flexibility to respond to new developments or operational problems, consistent with the legislation, the letters patent and any supplementary letters patent. It also retains in the members the ultimate control and direction of the corporation. The residual authority in the members is essential, especially if the rationale for incorporation is recalled — to limit liability of the members; to create an ongoing entity for the members to achieve their objectives; and to provide a legally recognized structure based on the agreement among the members. Incorporation facilitates the organization in attaining its objects. It is not intended to allow the board of directors to manage the corporation as the board would want, but rather as the law permits and the members have authorized.

If the by-law, its amendment or repeal is not confirmed by the members, no new by-law of the same or like substance has any effect until confirmed at a general meeting of the members. Confirmation of a by-law made pursuant to s. 129 requires a majority of the votes cast at the annual general meeting or a general meeting called to deal with the by-law. No act performed or right acquired under the by-law is prejudicially affected if the members reject, amend or otherwise deal with the by-law.[7] This provision provides a degree of certainty, especially for those persons who deal with the corporation as third parties or as members and who, in good faith, act on the basis that the by-law was valid.

Section 129 lists a number of items that may be the subject of by-laws. Any of these following items may also be dealt with in the letters patent or supplementary letters patent:

- the admission of persons and unincorporated associations as members and as *ex officio* members and the qualifications of and the conditions of membership;
- the fees and dues of members;
- the issue of membership cards and certificates;
- the suspension and termination of memberships by the corporation and by the member;
- the transfer of membership;
- the qualification of and the remuneration of the directors and the *ex officio* directors, if any;
- the time for and the manner of election of directors;

---

[7] *Ibid.*, subs. 129(3).

- the appointment, remuneration, functions, duties and removal of agents, officers and employees of the corporation and the security, if any, to be given by them to it;
- the time and place and the notice to be given for the holding of meetings of the members and of the board of directors, the quorum at meetings of members, the requirements as to proxies, and the procedure in all things at members' meetings and at meetings of the board of directors;
- the conduct in all other particulars of the affairs of the corporation.

By-laws made pursuant to s. 130 of the Act are concerned with the categories of members, either on a geographic basis or on the basis of common interest, and the election of delegates and directors. A by-law, or a repeal or amendment of a by-law, is not in effect until it is confirmed by at least two-thirds of the votes cast by the members. The reason for this more onerous level of confirmation by the members is that by-laws under s. 130 go to the heart of the ability of the members to control and direct the board of directors and staff in the implementation of the corporation's objects and in the conduct of its affairs.

An exception to the requirement of confirmation at a meeting called for a specific purpose exists during the corporation's first year of operation. Any by-law or resolution signed by all the directors is as valid and effective as if it were passed at a meeting of the board of directors.[8] A resolution signed by all members is also as valid and as effective as if passed at a meeting of the members. For an Ontario charitable or not-for-profit corporation, any by-law passed at any time during the corporation's existence may be confirmed in writing by all members in lieu of confirmation at a general meeting.[9] This provision of the Act provides a degree of flexibility to Ontario corporations in the confirmation of by-laws and may reduce expenses. It avoids, for example, the need for a meeting and the giving of notice. The signatures that purport to be the signatures of the directors or members are *prima facie* proof of the passing or confirmation of a by-law or resolution.[10]

(2) Co-operative Corporations without Share Capital

The *Co-operative Corporations Act*[11] takes a different approach with respect to organizational by-laws. Section 21 provides that the directors of the co-operative may pass by-laws that regulate the affairs of the co-operative. A by-law is not effective until it is passed by the directors and

---

[8] *Ibid.*, s. 298.
[9] *Ibid.*, subs. 298(2).
[10] *Ibid.*, subs. 298(4).
[11] R.S.O. 1990, c. C.35.

confirmed, with or without variation, by at least two-thirds of the votes cast at a general members' meeting called for that purpose.[12] This provision leaves greater immediate control in the hands of the members of the co-operative than exists for members of corporations without share capital under the *Corporations Act*.

The members of the co-operative may also require the passing of a by-law. Under s. 70 of the Act, 10 per cent of the members may requisition the directors to call a meeting of the directors for the purpose of passing a by-law or resolution. The requisition must set out the by-law or resolution. Once deposited at the head office, the directors must call a meeting for the purpose of passing the by-law or resolution. If the directors do not do so within 21 days, any of the requisitioners may call a general meeting of the members for the purpose of the passing of the by-laws or resolution. If the by-law or resolution is not passed at this meeting, no similar requisition may be made for at least two years.

In part, these provisions reflect the different purposes between corporations without share capital and co-operatives. Co-operatives may have a more direct impact upon the lives of individual members. For example, a co-operative corporation may provide housing for its members. The impact on the members of this type of co-operative will be more direct and immediate than on a member of a corporation without share capital incorporated under the *Corporations Act*.

The Act does not list the types of matters that may be included in a by-law, but they are similar to those for corporations. The authority under s. 21 is to pass by-laws that regulate the business and affairs of the co-operative. The only restriction on this authority is that the by-laws are subject to the Act and the articles.

There are two areas for which the Act does provide greater direction. A by-law on the remuneration of directors, under s. 23, shall fix the remuneration and the period for which it is to be paid. Section 24 sets out the types of by-laws that may be passed with respect to the election of directors. The directors may, for example, establish groups of members of the co-operative, either on a geographic basis or on the basis of common interest by passing by-laws. A special resolution of the members is required to do so. The election of directors may be based upon these groups.

III FEDERAL CORPORATIONS WITHOUT SHARE CAPITAL

Section 155 of the *Canada Corporations Act*[13] provides a similar legislative base for by-laws as do ss. 129 and 130 of the Ontario *Corporations Act*. However, under the federal Act, the approval of the Minister of Industry is required. The organizational by-laws are submitted with the application for letters patent and become effective upon approval by the Minis-

---

[12] *Ibid.*, s. 23.
[13] R.S.C. 1970, c. C.32.

ter. The Minister has discretion to refuse to approve the by-laws but, in practice, this discretion is exercised only for unusual provisions or if all the mandatory provisions are not included. Industry Canada provides a model by-law for use in drafting the by-laws for a federally-incorporated charitable or not-for-profit incorporation.

Subsection 155(2) provides that the by-laws should include the following matters:

- conditions of membership, including societies or companies becoming members of the corporation;
- mode of holding meetings, provision for quorum, rights of voting and of enacting by-laws;
- mode of repealing or amending by-laws with special provision that the repeal or amendment of by-laws not embodied in the letters patent shall not be enforced or acted upon until the approval of the Minister has been obtained;
- appointment and removal of directors, trustees, committees and officers, and their respective powers and remuneration;
- audit of accounts and appointment of auditors;
- whether or how members may withdraw from the corporation; and
- custody of the corporate seal and certifying of documents issued by the corporation.

The requirement for ministerial approval before an amendment to a by-law becomes effective may adversely affect the ability of the directors to manage the affairs of the corporation. It makes the organization less flexible and less able to change to new conditions. The department appears to recognize the situation. It includes in the model by-law a provision permitting the directors to prescribe rules and regulations. These rules and regulations must be consistent with the by-laws and must be confirmed at the next annual meeting of the members. If they are not confirmed, they are no longer in effect. This provision in the model by-law permits the directors to pass "by-laws" in all but name to elaborate on matters not detailed in the by-laws or to address other related issues that are concerned with the management and operation of the corporation.

IV ORGANIZATIONAL BY-LAWS UNDER OTHER PROVINCIAL INCORPORATION LEGISLATION

(1) Introduction

This section provides an overview of the by-law-making powers under the incorporating legislation in the other provinces. It is not intended to be comprehensive, but rather to set out who may make by-laws, whether or not they require approval of any governmental authority and the types of matters that should or must be included in the by-laws. The specific legislation should be consulted before the drafter prepares the by-laws. In addition, many of the provinces have prepared manuals, guidelines or model by-laws to be used in the preparation of by-laws.

The Alberta *Societies Act*,[14] the British Columbia *Society Act*,[15] the Nova Scotia *Societies Act*,[16] and the Prince Edward Island *Companies Act*[17] require that the proposed by-laws be included in the application for incorporation. The Saskatchewan *Not-for-profit Corporations Act*,[18] the Quebec *Companies Act*,[19] the Newfoundland *Corporations Act*,[20] the New Brunswick *Companies Act*[21] and the Manitoba *Corporations Act*[22] do not. In general, the different provincial legislation identify similar types of matters that may be or must be included in by-laws to those set out in s. 129 of the Ontario *Corporations Act*.[23]

(2) Alberta

Subsection 5(2) of the Alberta statute lists those matters that must be included in the by-law when submitting an application for incorporation. The information kit prepared for the applicants also includes a model by-law that may be used by applicants for incorporation.[24] The model is a very simplified version of a by-law but may be appropriate for some corporations with limited objects and activities and need only a simple decision-making process. The Registrar under the Act may strike out or modify any part of the by-law.[25] The by-law may not be rescinded, altered or added to except by special resolution of the members. The changes to the by-law are not in effect until they are registered by the Registrar under s. 11 of the Act. The Registrar may refuse to register the changes if he or she is of the opinion that the by-law is not in accordance with the application for incorporation or is contrary to law.

The by-laws may permit a person under 18 to be a member and to be appointed an officer of the corporation.[26] The by-laws may also provide for the arbitration of disputes arising out of the affairs of the society and

---

[14] R.S.A. 1980, c. S.18, subs. 5(1).
[15] R.S.B.C. 1996, c. 433, subs. 3(1).
[16] R.S.N.S. 1989, c. 435, s. 5.
[17] R.S.P.E.I. 1988, c. C.14, ss. 90(2).
[18] S.S. 1995, c. N.4.2.
[19] R.S.Q. 1977, c. C.38.
[20] R.S.N. 1986, c. 36.
[21] R.S.N.B. 1973, c. C.13.
[22] R.S.M. 1987, c. C225.
[23] R.S.O. 1990, c. C.38.
[24] "How to Form a Society", Alberta Municipal Affairs, March 1996.
[25] R.S.A. 1980, c. S.18, subs. 6(2).
[26] *Ibid.*, s. 16.

between members of the society.[27] Fines of up to $5 may be imposed under the by-laws for the contravention of a by-law of the society.[28]

(3) British Columbia

Section 6 of the British Columbia *Society Act*[29] sets out the requirements for by-laws and provides that they may be in the form prescribed under the legislation or in a modified form or another form altogether. Schedule B to the Act is more detailed than the model by-law for Alberta. Any restriction on minors becoming members or a provision to permit the transfer of membership should be set out in the by-laws.[30] If the by-laws do not provide otherwise, the society may only invest in the types of securities in which trustees are authorized by law to invest.[31]

The by-laws may be changed by special resolution of the members under s. 23 of the Act but are not effective until accepted by the Registrar. The members of the society may also establish rules at general meetings provided that the rules are not inconsistent with the by-laws. These rules may provide direction to the board of directors in the exercise of their powers.[32] The British Columbia guide, *Information for Incorporation of a British Columbia Society*[33] provides some assistance to incorporators and includes a copy of the sample by-law.

(4) Manitoba

The Manitoba *Corporations Act*[34] takes a similar approach to that of the Ontario legislation. The statute provides a list of matters that may be included in the by-laws or in the articles of incorporation. Unlike the Ontario legislation, there is no requirement for the members to confirm most by-laws or amendments to the by-laws. Unless the by-laws provide otherwise, the authority to pass and amend by-laws is exercised by the directors. The only exception is for by-laws under s. 277 with respect to the establishment of classes or groups of members. The by-laws should, therefore, clearly set out what matters may be dealt with by the directors alone and what matters require the approval of the members. The Manitoba guide includes a sample by-law.[35]

---

[27] *Ibid.*, s. 18.
[28] *Ibid.*, s. 19.
[29] R.S.B.C. 1996, c. 433.
[30] *Ibid.*, subs. 7(5) and s. 9, respectively.
[31] *Ibid.*, s. 32.
[32] Schedule B to the Act, s. 24.
[33] Ministry of Finance and Corporate Services, 1996.
[34] R.S.M. 1987, c. C225, ss. 275-276.
[35] "Filing Articles of Incorporation", February 1990.

(5) New Brunswick

The New Brunswick *Companies Act*[36] does not list in any section all of the matters that may be included in the by-laws. Section 96(1) of the Act authorizes the directors to make by-laws with respect to several matters, including the appointment, functions, duties and removal of agents, officers and servants; the holding of meetings; the imposition of fines; and "the conduct, in all other particulars, of the affairs of the company not otherwise provided for in this Act". In addition, throughout the statute, there are references to matters that may be dealt with by by-law. For example, under s. 39, the company's head office may be changed. The directors may apply for supplementary letters patent under s. 43 if authorized by by-law to do so. Sections 87 to 94 provide for by-laws governing the board of directors, their election and appointment. Amendments to the by-laws are only in effect until confirmed at the next general meeting of the members.[37]

(6) Newfoundland

Section 428 in the Newfoundland *Corporations Act*[38] sets out a list similar to that in Ontario's legislation of matters that may be the subject of a by-law. Section 429 permits by-laws with respect to the establishment of groups of members and their voting rights. A by-law under s. 429 requires the confirmation by at least two-thirds of the votes cast at a meeting called for that purpose. Sections 424 to 426 govern the number of members, admission to membership and voting by members in the absence of any provision in the articles of incorporation or the by-laws.

(7) Nova Scotia

The Nova Scotia legislation requires the by-laws to be submitted with the application for incorporation and to contain the provisions set out in Schedule B to the Act.[39] The Registrar may refuse to register the memorandum of association or by-laws unless they are in conformity with the Act.[40] Section 13 provides that the society may by special resolution make, amend or repeal the by-laws. The by-laws do not take effect until approved of by the Registrar. Under s. 14, a member may be fined for a breach of the by-laws. A sample by-law is included in the Nova Scotia guide.[41]

---

[36] R.S.N.B. 1973, c. C.13.
[37] *Ibid.*, s. 97.
[38] S.N. 1990, c. 36.
[39] R.S.N.S. 1989, c. 435, s. 5 and subs. 13(2).
[40] *Ibid.*, subs. 6(2).
[41] *Incorporating a Society Overview and Instructions*, Business and Consumer Services, Registrar of Joint Stock Companies.

(8) Prince Edward Island

By-laws must also be included with the application for letters patent under the Prince Edward Island *Companies Act*.[42] The matters to be included in the by-laws are similar to those required under other incorporation legislation. As with Ontario, a provision may be included in the letters patent rather than in the by-law. The PEI guide includes a sample by-laws.[43]

(9) Quebec

In section 91 of the Quebec *Companies Act*[44] the matters are similar to Ontario's legislation. Any matter that may be the subject of a by-law may be included in the letters patent.[45] The directors have the authority to make, amend or repeal by-laws under s. 91. The by-law may only be in effect until it is confirmed at a general meeting or at the annual general meeting.

(10) Saskatchewan

The Saskatchewan legislation, the *Not-for-profit Corporations Act*,[46] is one of the more recent statutes governing charitable and not-for-profit corporations. The statute does not explicitly set out what matters could or must be included in by-laws. Instead, there are references to by-law provisions in several sections of the Act. The articles of incorporation may include a matter that could be a by-law.[47] Unless otherwise provided, the directors under s. 90 and 91 of the Act may make, amend or repeal a by-law to regulate the activities and affairs of the corporation. The by-law is effective until it is confirmed at a general meeting or the annual general meeting. The Saskatchewan *The Not-for-profit Corporations Act, 1995 Incorporation Kit*[48] includes a model by-law.

A member may also propose a by-law or amendments to an existing by-law in accordance with section 127. This provision is not a common one in not-for-profit incorporating legislation. It would appear to assist in ensuring that the corporation remains, ultimately, an instrument of the members and that the directors remain accountable to the members.

---

[42] R.S.P.E.I. 1988, c. C.14, s. 90.
[43] Application for Incorporation of Not-for-profit (Part II) Companies.
[44] R.S.Q. 1977, c. C.38.
[45] *Ibid.*, s. 8.
[46] S.S. 1995, c. N.4.2.
[47] *Ibid.*, subs. 6(2).
[48] Corporations Branch, Saskatchewan Justice, October 1996.

E STATUTORY PROVISIONS

The Ontario *Corporations Act*,[49] the Ontario *Co-operative Corporations Act*[50] and the *Canada Corporations Act*[51] impose statutory provisions on corporations incorporated under the respective statutes. This part of the chapter reviews the more important provisions.

I AUDITORS

(1) Ontario Corporations without Share Capital

The *Corporations Act* requires that members appoint one or more auditors to hold office during the first annual meeting and, if the members fail to do so, the directors must make the appointment.[52] At each annual meeting, the members are to appoint an auditor until the next annual meeting. If an appointment is not made, the auditor shall continue in office until a successor is appointed. The directors have the authority to fill any "casual vacancy" that may be created between annual general meetings.[53]

The members may remove an auditor by a resolution passed by two-thirds of the votes cast at a general meeting where notice of the intention to pass such a resolution was given. The members must also approve of another auditor by a majority of the votes cast for the remainder of the term. The Minister may appoint an auditor on the application of a member for the year and fix the auditor's remuneration.[54]

The auditor appointed may not be a director, officer or employee of the charitable or not-for-profit corporation or of an affiliate corporation, or a partner, employer or employee of any director, officer or employee. These restrictions are an attempt to ensure that the auditor is independent and is seen to be independent of the board of directors and of any director, officer or employee. Independence is essential for an auditor to perform the auditor's primary duty — to make such examination as will enable the auditor to report to the members on whether the financial statements present fairly the financial position of the corporation and the results of the operations for the period under review in accordance with generally accepted accounting principles applied on a basis consistent with that of the preceding period.[55] These financial statements are also used by the Public Guardian and Trustee in carrying out its supervisory role, by financial institutions in making decisions about financial

---

[49] R.S.O. 1990, c. C.38.
[50] R.S.O. 1990, c. C.35.
[51] R.S.C. 1970, c. C.32.
[52] R.S.O. 1990, c. C.38, subs. 94(1).
[53] *Ibid.*, subs. 94(3) and, under the *Canada Corporations Act*, s. 130.
[54] *Ibid.*, subs. 94(6).
[55] *Ibid.*, subs. 96(2).

matters and by governments, corporations and charitable foundations to determine whether or not to provide grants or support to an organization and on what terms and conditions.

Financial statements and the role of the auditor are dealt with in greater detail in Chapter 5, "The Organization in Operation: Maintaining, Operating and Changing the Organization". However, it is important to note at this time that the role of the auditor is pivotal in ensuring accountability to the members and to the public in general. The expense of audited financial statements may be significant, especially for smaller charitable and not-for-profit organizations. The expense of an audit may also cause a charitable organization to exceed its allowable administrative expenses and, thereby, put at risk its registration as a charity with the Canada Customs and Revenue Agency.

Unfortunately, the Ontario *Corporations Act* does not permit the members to waive the audit requirements, unlike the Ontario *Co-operative Corporations Act*, the Ontario *Business Corporations Act*[56] and the *Canada Business Corporations Act*.[57] There is one, limited, exception to this requirement. A corporation with revenues of less than $10,000 may be exempted from the requirements if all of the members consent in writing for that year.

Under the *Public Accountancy Act*,[58] only a public accountant may conduct audits in Ontario. The *Canada Corporations Act* does not specifically address this issue, but as a matter of policy, a professional accountant is not required.[59] However, it is not clear that this policy would take precedence over the provincial statutory requirements that audits only be conducted by accountants under the *Public Accountancy Act*. A charitable organization may be caught in a difficult, if not impossible, situation — complying with the requirements for audited financial statements and, in doing so, expending its funds on administrative rather than charitable activities, and putting its registration at risk. The charitable organization would also be no better off if it had an accountant on its board of directors. That individual could not conduct the audit nor could any of his or her partners or employees. It appears that not all charitable and not-for-profit corporations are in strict compliance with the requirements of the Act as it applies to the preparation of audited financial statements.

Section 96 requires the auditor to make such examination as will enable the auditor to report to the members at the annual general meeting. The auditor's report must include the opinion of the auditor on whether or not the financial statements fairly represent the financial position of the corporation. The auditor is also obliged under subs. 96(4) to make such statements as the auditor considers necessary if: the financial state-

---

[56] R.S.O. 1990, c. B.16.
[57] R.S.C. 1985, c. C.44.
[58] R.S.O. 1990, c. P.37.
[59] See Corporations Directorate Not-for-profit Policy Summary in the "Information Kit for the Creation of Not-for-profit Corporations", November 25, 1999.

ments are not in agreement with the accounting records; are not in accordance with the requirements under the Act; the auditor has not received the information or explanations that the auditor has required; or, proper accounting records have not been kept. The auditor has a right of access to all such accounting records and may require from the officers and directors such information and explanations as the auditor considers necessary to enable him or her to report to the members. Under subs. 97(2), the auditor's report is to be read at the annual general meeting. The auditor has a right to attend this meeting or any other meeting of the members.[60]

(2) Ontario Co-operative Corporations without Share Capital

The requirement for audits is somewhat different for a co-operative incorporated under the Ontario *Co-operative Corporations Act*.[61] Under s. 124, the members are required to appoint an auditor at the first general meeting and each subsequent annual general meeting. Section 126 sets out similar criteria for disqualifying someone as are set out in the *Corporations Act*. The auditor, under s. 127, is required to conduct an audit and report on the financial statement at the annual meeting. The auditor's responsibilities and rights under s. 127 are similar to those under the Ontario *Corporations Act*. An audit is not required, however, if the co-operative has (a) fewer than 15 members and no more than $500,000 in capital, assets, gross revenue or sales, and all members agree or (b) between 16 and 51 members and no more than $500,000 in capital, assets, gross revenue or sales if the exemption is approved by a special resolution. Subsection 123(1.1) of the Act and s. 13.1 of the Regulations limit the exemption to smaller co-operatives and to co-operatives where no government grants have been provided.[62] This exemption provides a greater and more reasonable flexibility that was previously lacking for Ontario corporations.

(3) Federal Corporations without Share Capital

Section 130 of the *Canada Corporations Act* requires the members to appoint an auditor and also governs the auditor's removal and remuneration. If no auditor is appointed at an annual meeting, the auditor continues in office until a successor is appointed. Under subs. 130(3), Notice of Intention to nominate another person to be auditor is necessary. The directors may fill any casual vacancy[63] and the Minister may appoint an

---

[60] Subs. 96(6).
[61] R.S.O. 1990, c. C.35.
[62] O. Reg. 495/92. The Regulation prescribes $500,000 base for capital, assets or gross revenues or sales.
[63] Subs. 130(4).

auditor and fix the remuneration to be paid on application of a member.[64]

Section 131 disqualifies any director, officer and employee of the corporation or of an affiliated corporation from being an auditor. Any partner, employer or employee of any such officer or director is also disqualified. The department's policy for not-for-profit corporations does not require the auditor to be a professional accountant. Furthermore, the policy also permits a director, officer or employee of the corporation or an affiliated corporation associated with that director, officer or employee to be the auditor if 100 per cent of the members consent.[65] The policy provides greater flexibility to not-for-profit corporations than Ontario corporations and is consistent with subs. 131(2) of the federal legislation.

The auditor must make such examination as will enable him or her to report to the members on the financial statements of the corporation.[66] The auditor's report is to be laid before the members at the annual general meeting and is to set out the auditor's opinion. In order to carry out his or her duty, the auditor has the right of access to all business records of the corporation. The auditor's responsibilities and rights under s. 132 of the Act are similar to those for auditors under the Ontario *Corporations Act*.

II MEMBERS

(1) Ontario Corporations without Share Capital

An applicant for letters patent is automatically a member of the corporation upon incorporation.[67] Unless the letters patent, supplementary letters patent or the by-laws state otherwise, there is no limit to the number of members the corporation may have.[68] Persons may be admitted to membership by resolution of the board of directors or as provided for in the letters patent, supplementary letters patent or by-laws.[69]

Membership qualifications are common for charitable and not-for-profit organizations and may be linked to the objects of the organization. There may also be more than one category or class of membership, with each having different voting rights.[70] Membership is deemed to be non-transferable, to lapse and to cease on the member's death, resignation or

---

[64] Subs. 130(7).
[65] Corporations Directorate Not-for-profit Policy Summary in the "Information Kit on the Creation of Not-for-profit Corporations", November 25, 1999.
[66] Subss. 132(1) and (2).
[67] *Corporations Act*, R.S.O. 1990, c. C.38, s. 121.
[68] *Ibid.*, s. 123.
[69] *Ibid.*, s. 124.
[70] *Ibid.*, ss. 120 and 125.

otherwise in accordance with the by-laws, such as suspension or termination for failure to pay fees.[71]

(2) Ontario Co-operative Corporations without Share Capital

The Ontario *Co-operative Corporations Act*[72] may result in economic rights for members. For example, in co-operative housing, an occupant of the unit may also be a member of the co-operative. Similarly, in a housing co-operative, an occupant of a unit may also be a member of the co-operative. Because co-operatives are voluntary associations, no person may be required to remain a member. A member will also usually have a right to the return of their investment. A co-operative is required to redeem a member's loans at their par value plus any premium with six-months' notice.[73]

However, the co-operative may also expel the member by resolution passed by the majority of the board of directors. The member must have been given written notice of the proposed resolution together with the grounds for the expulsion and an opportunity to make submissions at the meeting called for that purpose.[74] The section sets out how the member's interest is to be redeemed. The co-operative may also terminate a membership if it has not been used for a period of two years or more.[75]

If the co-operative is a not-for-profit housing co-operative, under ss. 171.8 and 171.23 of the Act, there are two ways to terminate a membership. If the member does not have occupancy rights, he or she is terminated in accordance with s. 66 of the Act. A member with occupancy rights, though, has greater procedural protection under the Act in recognition of the fact that the unit may also be the member's residence. A writ of possession under s. 171.13 is also required before the terminated member may be evicted.

(3) Federal Corporations without Share Capital

The *Canada Corporations Act*[76] is less specific than the Ontario *Corporations Act* and provides less guidance to the organization. By-laws under subs. 155(2) must set out the conditions related to membership and provisions on voting rights, and whether or how members may withdraw from the corporation. The model by-law prepared by the department sets out a simple version for membership and resignation, suspension and termination. Although this model by-law may be used, it may be more appro-

---

[71] *Ibid.*, subs. 128(1).
[72] R.S.O. 1990, c. C.35.
[73] *Ibid.*, s. 64.
[74] *Ibid.*, s. 66.
[75] *Ibid.*, ss. 32 and 49.
[76] R.S.C. 1970, c. C.32.

priate to prepare a by-law that is consistent with the specific objects of the corporation, provided all mandatory provisions are included and the by-law is in accordance with the department's policies.

III MEETINGS

(1) Ontario Corporations without Share Capital

The first annual meeting of charitable or not-for-profit corporations must be held not later than 18 months after the incorporation and subsequently not more than 15 months after the last preceding annual meeting.[77] Directors may call a general meeting at any time, provided that notice of the general nature of the business is given to the members.[78] A minimum of 10 per cent of the members entitled to vote at the meeting may request that the directors call a meeting, the general nature of which shall be specified in the notice calling the meeting.[79]

Section 93 of the Ontario *Corporations Act* governs the handling of meetings, in the absence of any other provisions in the by-laws. A notice of meeting must be given not less than ten days in advance of the meeting to each member, usually by mail. A notice of meeting for a corporation whose objects are exclusively charitable may be given by publication of the notice at least once a week for two consecutive weeks prior to the meeting in a newspaper or newspapers circulated in the municipality or municipalities in which the majority of the members reside.[80]

Meetings are to be held at the head office of the corporation unless the by-law provides for meetings to be held elsewhere. Typically, a by-law will provide that meetings may be held at any place in Ontario. For a meeting to be held outside Ontario the letters patent or supplementary letters patent must include an enabling provision. Members may vote by proxy under s. 84 of the Ontario *Corporations Act*.

(2) Ontario Co-operative Corporations without Share Capital

The first annual general meeting must be called within 18 months of incorporation and subsequent annual general meetings no more than 15 months after the last general meeting.[81] Directors may call a meeting at any time with appropriate notice[82] and 10 per cent of the members may require a meeting to be called with respect to a by-law and 5 per cent for other purposes.[83] Notice of a meeting must be in writing and provide a

---

[77] *Corporations Act*, R.S.O. 1990, c. C.38, s. 293.
[78] *Ibid.*, s. 294.
[79] *Ibid.*, s. 295.
[80] *Ibid.*, subs. 133(2).
[81] *Co-operative Corporations Act*, R.S.O. 1990, c. C.35, s. 77.
[82] *Ibid.*, s. 78.
[83] *Ibid.*, ss. 70, 71 and 79.

minimum of ten days notice but no more than 50 days notice.[84] The meetings must be held at the head office unless the by-laws provide otherwise and in Ontario unless the articles of incorporation enable meetings to be held outside Ontario.[85]

Co-operative corporations are intended to be democratically-controlled and involve the members in the decision-making process. As a result, members may not vote by proxy with one exception. Under s. 76, a corporate member may authorize, under its corporate seal, an officer or director to vote on its behalf. Delegates for groups of members may vote under s. 24 on behalf of the group, but may not do so by proxy. The delegate voting is not itself proxy voting but rather a system of voting set up in accordance with the by-laws.

(3)   Federal Corporations without Share Capital

Section 102 of the Act requires that the first annual meeting be held within 18 months of incorporation. Subsequent annual meetings must be held each calendar year and no more than 15 months after the last one held.

The federal policy statement sets out requirement for notice of general meetings. The notice must be reasonable, in writing and provide sufficient information that the members know what business is to be transacted at the meeting.[86] The model by-law includes a 14-day written notice period for the calling of meetings. The model by-law also provides that five per cent of the members may requisition a meeting to be called by the directors. The meetings may be held anywhere in Canada. The policy also permits the members to resolve that meetings may be held outside Canada. Although the Act does not specifically address proxy voting, the by-laws may include provisions with respect to proxy voting by members.

IV DIRECTORS

(1)   Ontario Corporations without Share Capital

A charitable or not-for-profit organization is managed by a board of directors. The board of an Ontario corporation must be composed of at least three persons. A change in the number of directors requires a special resolution of the members.[87] The normal practice is to have the number of applicants for incorporation correspond to the number of directors that is desired for the corporation.

---

[84] *Ibid.*, s. 75.
[85] *Ibid.*, s. 74.
[86] Corporations Directorate Not-for-profit Policy Summary in the "Information Kit on the Creation of Not-for-profit Corporations", November 25, 1999.
[87] Ontario *Corporations Act*, s. 285, as am. S.O. 1998, c. 18, Sched. E, s. 75.

A quorum of the board is required for the conduct of the business of the corporation. Should there be a vacancy or vacancies on the board, the directors may exercise the powers of the board provided there is a quorum of the board. A majority constitutes a quorum unless otherwise provided for in the by-laws, but a quorum shall not be less than two-fifths of the board of directors.[88] A vacancy may be filled by a quorum of directors in office for the remainder of the term of the director who is being replaced. If no quorum exists, the remaining directors must call a general meeting to fill the vacancies. If no directors remain, any member may call a meeting to elect a board of directors.

Directors are elected by the members at a general meeting by ballot or as otherwise provided for in the by-laws. Section 286 provides that the minimum level of qualifications are that the director must be a member (or become one within ten days of election), 18 years of age, and not an undischarged bankrupt.

The by-laws may provide for *ex officio* members of the board.[89] Paragraph 129(1)(f) permits the by-laws to set out the qualifications of an *ex officio* director and this provision may allow for prior approval of an *ex officio* director before the election. The use of *ex officio* directors is important and a common practice, especially where the charitable or not-for-profit corporation carries out certain government-related activities, such as providing hospital care, animal control, or administering social welfare programmes. They are also used where the corporation receives funding from a municipal government. In these cases, a municipality may nominate a member of the municipal council for director, who is then elected to the board of directors by the members.

The board may find it useful to establish an executive committee where the number of directors is large. Section 70 of the Act permits the by-laws to allow for the establishment of an executive committee where there are more than six directors. The executive committee must have a minimum of three directors and may be delegated powers of the board. A quorum may not be less than a majority of the executive committee's members. The by-law requires the confirmation of at least two thirds of the votes cast at a general meeting called specifically to pass this by-law. Any other committees of the board may only be advisory in nature. The board may not delegate any of its powers to any advisory committee.

The by-laws may also indemnify the directors. Section 80 of the Act permits the indemnification of directors (and their heirs, executors, administrators and estate and effects) if the members consent. Section 93 of the federal statute also permits the corporation to indemnify directors. In the case of charitable corporations, any indemnification such as through the purchase of insurance to protect the directors and officers, must be done in accordance with the provisions of the *Charities Accounting Act* or by court order in Ontario.

---

[88] *Ibid.*, s. 288.
[89] *Ibid.*, subs. 124(2).

(2) Ontario Co-operative Corporations without Share Capital

Co-operative corporations have similar requirements for directors. Directors must be at least 18 years of age, not bankrupt and be a member of the co-operative. *Ex officio* directors are not permitted. A majority of the board of directors must live in Canada.[90] The directors are usually elected at the annual general meeting. Members may vote once for each candidate regardless of the number of positions to be filled. Directors may be elected for terms of up to five years and on a rotating basis.[91] There must be a minimum of three directors, but the articles of incorporation may specify a range of directors to be elected. Unless the articles of incorporation provide otherwise, a quorum of directors may fill any vacancy on the board.[92]

(3) Federal Corporations without Share Capital

The federal legislation does not provide as much detail about directors as the Ontario statute. Subsection 155(1) establishes a minimum of three directors, all of whom must be at least 18 years of age and have the power under law to contract. The number of directors may also be a range rather than a set number as required by the Ontario legislation. A director is not required, however, to be a member of the corporation, although the by-laws may require this. The policy directive provides that the power to manage the corporation rests with the board of directors. The policy directive also permits the election or appointment of *ex officio* directors, but they need not have a right to vote. There are no specific provisions for committees of the board. The model by-law does, however, include provisions for an executive committee with authority delegated by the board of directors and for the establishment of other committees of the board.

V OFFICERS

(1) Ontario Corporations without Share Capital

The officers are responsible for specific functions of the corporation. The directors are required by s. 289 of the Ontario *Corporations Act* to elect from among themselves a president, a secretary, and other such officers. The secretary and other officers need not be members of the corporation. If the letters patent, supplementary letters patent or by-laws provide, the officers may be elected or appointed at the general meeting of the members. The acts of an officer are valid, notwithstanding any defect

---

[90] Ontario *Co-operative Corporations Act*, s. 89.
[91] *Ibid.*, ss. 90 and 91.
[92] *Ibid.*, s. 92.

that may afterwards be discovered in his or her appointment or qualifications.

(2) Ontario Co-operative Corporations without Share Capital

The officers of a co-operative corporation may include the chair of the board, president, treasurer, secretary and general manager. Other officers may also be established in the by-laws or by directors' resolutions. If a chair is to be an officer of the co-operative corporation, the by-laws must set out the responsibilities and how he or she is to be elected or appointed. The president and chair must be members of the co-operative corporation but other officers need not be.[93]

(3) Federal Corporations without Share Capital

The Act itself provides little direction with respect to officers of a Canada corporation. Most of the guidance is set out in the departmental policy for not-for-profit corporations and in the model by-law.[94] There is no limit to the number of officers that a federally-incorporated corporation may have.[95] Their duties and responsibilities must, however, be set out in the by-laws. The officers need not be directors nor members of the corporation, unless otherwise required by letters patent or the by-laws.

F RULES OF PROCEDURE OR RULES OF ORDER

I GENERAL COMMENTS

The board may want to put in place a policy with respect to the running of a meeting. These provisions are more procedural in nature and are often called rules of procedure or rules of order. Typically, an organization will adopt rules of procedure. There are several different versions of these rules. However, it is questionable whether the adoption of such rules of procedure is the best approach. The adoption of "Robert's Rules" or similar rules of order is made by reference in a by-law but without any thought as to the appropriateness for the organization. Simpler rules of procedure that are developed in the context of the organization are preferable, where the time can be devoted to preparing them. And too often nobody knows what the Rules say because a copy was never actually obtained.

---

[93] *Ibid.*, ss. 105 to 108.
[94] "Information Kit on the Creation of Not-for-profit Corporations", November 25, 1999, Corporations Directorate, Industry Canada.
[95] Subsection 3(1) of the *Canada Corporations Act* defines "officer" as the "president, chairman of the board of directors, vice-president, secretary, assistant secretary, treasurer, assistant treasurer or any other person designated an officer by by-law or by a resolution of the directors".

II CONTENT OF THE RULES OF PROCEDURE OR RULES OF ORDER

Rules of procedure or rules of order — either as provided for in the by-laws or in separate rules of procedure or rules or order — will cover a number of matters, which are discussed below.

(1) Chair

The election or appointment of chair for the meeting and any substitute or temporary chair and the removal or vacating of the chair is an important step. The duties of a chair are significant and occur before, during and after any meeting. The chair needs to be aware of and knowledgeable about the organization's constating documents, by-laws and the rules of procedure. The chair will normally prepare or cause to be prepared notice of the meeting and an agenda for the meeting. The chair should also ensure that the accommodation for the meeting are appropriate for the anticipated attendance and that any appropriate amenities are available, such as refreshments.

During the meeting, the chair is to call the meeting to order, ensure that the meeting is properly constituted and that those in attendance have a right to be there. He or she will ensure that notes are taken, which will be used for the preparation of minutes.

The chair is also responsible for conduct during the meeting. Meetings are productive only if proper order is maintained. However, balanced against the need for order is the need for open and full discussion of issues and a recognition that, at times, tempers can flare and passions can arise. A chair needs to enforce decorum in a responsible, even-handed and reasonable way. He or she should insist on discipline and respect for opposing views and, if necessary, adjourn the meeting to bring order back. If somebody becomes excessive, the chair has a duty and a right to expel that person from the meeting.

The chair also has a duty to act fairly, in good faith and without malice. Although tempers may flare, the chair needs to remain calm and collected. The chair decides who will speak — when and for how long (subject, of course, to any express rules otherwise). The chair should keep the meeting moving along and on agenda, whenever possible. At times, an agenda item will take longer than anticipated and adjustments need to be made. The chair may canvas the meeting on this point or make an assessment and decision on his or her own.

The chair may or may not have a vote. Some organizations prohibit the chair of the meeting from voting, others provide a vote to the chair and a casting vote (second vote in case of a tie), or a vote only if there is a tie (which is different from a casting vote where the chair votes twice because the tie occurs without the chair's vote) or only has a vote as do others. Normally, for a motion to pass, the motion must receive a majority of the votes. The by-laws, constating documents or incorporating legislation may provide that certain matters require a two-thirds or other majority. In any event, if the vote is tied, usually the motion fails. The chair also declares when the meeting is ended. Usually, there will be a motion to end the meeting.

(2) Procedure to Make a Decision

The usual method of making and documenting a decision is by resolution which is recorded and voted upon. Resolutions are made by motion, which is seconded, discussed or debated, and voted upon. The chair should consider the wording of the motion to ensure that is appropriate (not disrespectful or substantially the same as one that has already been dealt with) or out of order because contrary to the law or the organization's constating documents. A motion could be made before discussion occurs or after an issue has been discussed. Often, the appropriate action to take only comes to light after a full and frank discussion has occurred. In any event, the chair has a role to ensure that the discussion occurs, to determine when sufficient discussion has occurred, to determine the sense of the meeting and to call for a vote and declare the results.

The chair usually cannot move or second a motion or amendment while acting as chair. It may be possible for the chair to temporarily vacate the position to do so. Some rules provide that the chair may move or second a motion when only one other person is present who is qualified to do so. The chair normally should not discuss the merits of a motion. However, human nature makes this restriction very difficult to enforce. It also depends upon the culture of the organization. A chair may, however, want to vacate the position if he or she will be taking a strong or controversial position on the subject. It is also not uncommon for chairs to participate more fully in a meeting if the meeting is a board meeting or committee meeting where the sense is that it would be appropriate. An annual general meeting or public meeting is different from the monthly finance committee meeting.

After the meeting, the chair is responsible for ensuring that the minutes are prepared. Often the secretary is designated to prepare the minutes by the by-laws or otherwise. However, the chair has a responsibility to ensure that the minutes are prepared and accurately reflect the meeting. There are several approaches to minutes — they can be very detailed, blow-by-blow report of the meeting or simply a record of who attended, who was absent and what decisions were made, or anything in between.

It is common practice for municipal councils to pass "confirming by-laws" as measure to attempt to cure procedural irregularities that may have occurred during the previous council session. In theory, there is nothing to prevent not-for-profit or charity boards from following the same practice, although the legal validity of such a measure might not survive scrutiny.

(3) Appeals from the Chair

Some rules of procedure provide for appeals from procedural rulings of the chair. Normally, these appeals are not necessary but an appeal process may be appropriate for some organizations. If there is an appeal process, there will be an obligation to follow it in a fair manner. The appeal could be to those in attendance at the meeting or to the board. If there is to be an appeal process, the process should clearly identify what could be appealed, when and under what circumstances. It should be done immediately at the meeting or as soon as possible to another body, such as the board. It requires a second, is not open to debate (other than brief statement of reasons for the appeal and a response by the chair) and should, then, be voted on. In rare circumstances, somebody could apply to the courts. If it is intended that this process be available, it should be noted in the rules. These provisions would be very unusual in procedural rules for the board's decision-making process.

(4) Quorum for Meetings

Quorum requirements are typically set out in the incorporating legislation and/or in the by-laws of the organization, but the rules may sometimes repeat the quorum requirements or refine them. Normally, quorum is not less than two-fifths of the positions on the board of directors, i.e., if the number of positions of directors is 10, quorum will be at least 4. If the number of positions is 11, quorum would be 5. Quorum could be higher than two-fifths, such as a majority or even more, but practical experience will provide some guidance. A higher percentage may encourage more directors to attend, otherwise they will feel guilty if quorum is not reached and no decisions can be made. On the other hand, an excessively high quorum will lead to frustration as quorum is not reached and those in attendance have wasted their time. If the constating documents do not state what quorum is, it is generally taken to be the majority of positions.

Recent changes to legislation and policies have permitted directors to attend through conference call or similar telecommunications methods. All boards ought to consider using this technique not only for quorum purposes but also to encourage a full participation in meetings with the most minimal cost to those involved. Whatever the method used, each person must be able to clearly hear each other, otherwise, the conditions of having a "meeting" will not be present.

A few issues arise from quorum. Are *ex officio* directors included or not? If the *ex officio* director does not have voting rights, is he or she still part of quorum? What about honorary directors? If these individuals have voting rights and rights to attend and participate at meetings, arguably they are part of quorum. This fact is sometimes overlooked in preparing by-laws which allow for *ex officio* directors. What happens, for example, if the mayor of a municipality is an *ex officio* director but never attends the meetings? If the by-laws are silent on the matter, decisions taken at the meeting may be subject to challenge if achieving quorum turned on the *ex officio* director's attendance.

Some organizations also are unclear about who is included in quorum. If there are 9 positions of director but only 7 are filled, and quorum is a majority, is quorum 5 or 4? Quorum in this case would be 5 as quorum is based on the number of positions, not the number of positions filled. A majority of 9 is 5. Again, lack of clarity could leave scope for decisions to be challenged.

Another issue that periodically arises is what happens if quorum disappears? This can occur especially where a meeting is lengthy. Unless the constating documents or by-laws provide otherwise, if quorum disappears, no further business may be transacted at the meeting. It is common, therefore, to provide that once quorum is reached, quorum will be maintained for the remainder of the meeting. On a related issue, quorum will be deemed to continue regardless until somebody raises the issue. If no quorum count is taken or demanded, quorum once reached is presumed to continue. Query, however, if there are only 5 members out of the 9 and the quorum-making director leaves. The chair may be obliged to raise the issue if he or she is aware quorum is no longer present.

If quorum is lost and the by-laws do not permit quorum to continue, what happens? Or, if quorum is never obtained, can the meeting continue? Yes and no. There is nothing necessarily wrong if those in attendance discuss the issues, provided that it is understood that no business may be transacted. It may be possible for those in attendance to take a position on the matter, which can be brought to the next board or committee meeting. That meeting's notice and agenda would include the item, any motions that were developed and so forth and the subsequent meeting could transact the business.

(5) Motions

Motions present a wealth of opportunities for weird and wonderful things to occur. The rules should provide for types of motions and when they may be made. Several types of motions are recognized in rules of procedure. These include:

- main motions, which are substantive in nature. These motions will direct or authorize somebody to do something, or adopt, ratify, approve, confirm or reject something that has been done. They can also be used to express the opinion of the meeting or of the organization. A main motion should be seconded before it is open to debate. If it fails to be seconded, it does not go to the next step. Main motions may be amended (which may be a friendly amendment that the mover accepts) or unfriendly. If unfriendly, the amending motion ought to be debated and voted upon first be-

fore the originating motion is voted upon or debate is continued on it,
- amendment motions, which are intended to amend motions and resolutions,
- subsidiary or procedural motions, which address the conduct of motions. A procedural motion takes precedence to an amendment motion or the original main motion. Procedural motions may deal with objections to the matter being considered, that the matter be put to a vote immediately, that discussion or debate be closed or postponed, or that the motion be referred to another committee or be referred back to the initial committee, or that the rules be suspended,
- motions to close, recess or to adjourn the meeting. An adjournment may be to a fixed date or a date to be scheduled, and
- motions for the election or appointment of directors, officers and similar positions.

Different rules of procedure or rules of order will use different classes of motions and may also categorize them in varying ways. In some rules, a motion to amend is a subsidiary motion, as are motions to table a motion, to close, limit or extend debate, to postpone to a definite or indefinite time, or to refer to a committee. Incidental rules are those that involve appeals to the chair, points of order, procedural inquiry or information, suspensions of the rules, withdrawal or modification of a motion and so forth.

Statutes sometimes also require that certain by-laws or changes to the constating documents may only be made by "special resolution" requiring a two-thirds majority. Certain matters may also be raised as motions but are more in the nature of a demand or privilege. For example, if somebody is questioning whether or not quorum is present, a quorum count may be requested. There may also be points privilege (personal or general), points of information or of procedure or of order that may arise. The more formal the rules of procedure, the more likely these types of motions or points will be covered.

Typically, rules of procedure will provide that only one motion may be on the floor and open to debate and vote at any given time. This procedure ensures that people have a better chance of knowing what is being debated and what the vote is for.

Motions should be informative and form the basis for debate or discussion and a vote. A motion will include the subject under discussion. It should be within the power and scope of the meeting and the organization's lawful authority. Motions should be affirmative, not offensive or argumentative. Historically, motions have had words included, such as "whereas" but these words are not required. Indeed, the fewer the words and simpler the language, usually the better. Motions that do not comply with the rules are to be ruled out of order.

Motions require a seconder. If no seconder is willing to do so, the motion dies. However, this rule has been a matter of convention and is not for the most part a legal requirement. Indeed, many of the rules of procedure or rules of order are based on conventions that have developed over the years — some of which may no longer be relevant in the 21st century or to the organization. Some rules of order permit the chair to second a motion if there is no other eligible person to do so. The secondment of a motion is really a test of whether or not there is any interest to debate the matter.

Motions may be divided, especially if there is more than one proposition in the motion which can stand or fall independently of the others. For example, a motion to support something in principle could be divided from a motion to support something in principle and to provide funding for it at that time. A motion to divide the main motion must be seconded. It cannot be amended and is debated solely on the issue of dividing the main motion. The debate and vote on any motion to divide a main motion is done before debate or a vote continues on the main motion. If there is more than one motion to divide, each is taken in turn until one is acceptable. Any remaining motions to divide are not followed up as the division has already been made.

A motion may also be withdrawn by the mover before it is seconded or the chair states it. After that point, the motion is in play and the meeting will decide its fate — to permit the withdrawal on consent of the meeting, to be deferred, to be voted on or otherwise considered. A motion to withdraw is like any other motion and requires a seconder. It is not open to amendment and is not debated.

Amending motions are useful to allow the meeting to consider alternatives to the motion that is currently before the meeting. There may be several amendments to substantive motions as the meeting considers different approaches or wording. But, each amendment must be dealt with in turn — including any subamendments to an amendment to a substantive motion. On contentious matters, the number of motions, amendments and subamendments (including those designed to kill or neuter the original substantive motion) can multiply and try the skills of the chair. The chair needs to keep things moving and to ensure that proper order and procedure are followed for fairness. However, at some point, proper order also means bringing matters to a conclusion.

(6) Debate and Its Role

The essence of meetings and motions is to promote discussion and debate of issues with a view to a decision or resolution. Openness is particularly key for not-for-profit and charitable organizations because of the nature of their mandates. With the advent and widespread public popularity of the *Charter of Rights and Freedoms*, Canadians have become more conscious of issues like "free speech" and "due process". An organization can rarely do itself harm by allowing full and frank discussion of the issues it faces, though admittedly this process can, at times, be taxing. But a far greater danger lies in stifling debate, which can hurt not only the organization itself but also reflect poorly on the voluntary sector as a whole. Canadians pride themselves on the democratic principles set out in the *Charter of Rights and Freedoms* and in other constitutional and legal documents. The terms "free speech" and "democracy" are sometimes used during meetings and board meetings of organizations. Canadians are inculcated with the concept and it has become bred to the bone.

Generally, discussion or debate should be open. However, the chair needs to ensure that no one person or group of persons so dominate a meeting as to hijack it. A debate by its nature means that more than one view point is put forth and considered. Some people become intimidated or are shy to speak their minds. Opportunities should be made to ensure that all persons can express their views in a fair and full manner. Once that view is expressed, it is common practice to limit any further discussion by the same person until after all others who want to speak have had the opportunity to do so. The chair could also limit any supplementary discussion by a previous speaker to responses to new information or points of view and not permit an ongoing repetition of the same information or opinion. Similarly, if the same view is being expressed repeatedly by a series of speakers, the chair may want to consider limiting any further comment to new perspectives or for new information. While speakers have a "right" to speak — it is a constrained one.

The concept of the "floor" is an important one in promoting an orderly debate or discussion of an issue. People should be recognized by the chair before they speak, especially in larger meetings. It may be less formal in smaller meetings — and, indeed, the culture of the organization may mitigate against formalities such as putting up one's hand to be recognized. Speakers deserve a fair opportunity to make their points in a concise and forthright fashion without fear of heckling, undue interruption or disruption. A speaker could be interrupted for example on a point of order or procedural matter. Once that matter is dealt with, the floor returns to that speaker, assuming of course that the point of order or procedural matter did not result in him or her no longer having the floor.

(7)   **Privileges**

There are several procedural motions that may arise in relation to a substantive motion. For example, somebody may object to the substantive motion on the grounds that the action contemplated is illegal, contrary to the organization's constating documents, repetitive, unwise, not needed or for other reasons. The individual may bring a motion to object to the consideration of the substantive motion. This motion must be brought at the time the agenda is being reviewed or when the substantive motion is brought and before another speaker starts on the motion. This type of motion does not require a seconder because it is more in the nature of a demand that any requirements for the motion to be dealt with be met.

There are also a variety of privileges that may be considered at a meeting. For example, an individual who feels that he or she has been insulted or subjected to abuse may raise a point of personal privilege. A point of general privilege may also be raised if, for example, the speaker cannot be heard, or the room is uncomfortable or too crowded. A point of information may be raised if the information is being provided in good faith and is not intended to divert the discussion or to be argumentative. Finally, points of procedure may be raised, provided they are raised in good faith and are not argumentative. A point of order may also be raised if the agenda is not being followed or there is a similar irregularity. All of these demands or privileges are to be considered immediately before ongoing debate of a motion continues.

(8) Summary

There are a number of very good rules of procedure or rules of order. An organization may adopt one of them or it may develop its own rules. The above discussion was intended to canvas the major issues that are covered in such rules and to identify some matters that have been and will be contentious in the future. Whatever "policy" for meetings is selected by the board, the overriding principle is that it should be fair and allow all members an opportunity to participate in the discussion of an issue and to do so without any fear or abuse. The role of the chair is crucial and, as a result, the chair must remain as neutral as possible. He or she needs to understand the sense of the meeting and, at times, be courageous to ensure that there is a proper balance of "free speech" with effective and efficient decision making.

CHAPTER 5

The Organization in Operation: Maintaining, Operating and Changing the Organization

A OVERVIEW

The purpose of any organization is to carry out its objects through permitted activities. In order to do so, the organization must:

- be maintained as a legal entity; and
- change to reflect the needs of its members, the community that it serves and new circumstances.

This chapter deals with both aspects of operating an organization — maintaining itself as a legal entity and adapting itself to changing circumstances.

The chapter is divided into three main parts. The first part is on the basic administrative matters that must be undertaken to maintain the organization. The second part discusses financial reporting, including accounting records and financial statements and their uses. The third part reviews the major types of amendments that may occur in order to reflect the changing circumstances and needs and several types of arrangements to carry out objects.

The maintenance of a trust, unincorporated association or a corporation without share capital is administrative in nature. It is, however, essential that the administrative work be conducted regularly, as required and with due diligence. The holding of members' meetings, the filing of any required forms under various statutes, and the keeping of records are necessary steps in the maintenance of an organization. An effective board of directors or board of trustees requires the financial statements, for example, to manage the affairs of the organization. The members have a right to information about their organization, information which is located in the books and records, financial statements, minutes and resolutions of the organization. Regulators require the information to ensure that the trusts and organizations are in compliance with the law and regulatory requirements, including the annual Charity Information Return which is filed with the Canada Customs and Revenue Agency

(CCRA). Third parties may need the information in the public records to determine with whom they are dealing.

Any organization will encounter changing circumstances. It may accommodate itself to these circumstances through administrative or fundamental changes, depending on the needs. The administrative changes may be relatively minor ones, such as amending the by-law to alter procedural rules at the annual meeting. Alternatively, the circumstances may require more substantial or fundamental changes. The organization may want to amend its objects or special provisions in order to undertake a new direction; or it may want to amalgamate with other organizations or dissolve itself. This chapter reviews the more usual forms of fundamental change and the procedures used to do so. Chapter 4, "The Organization in Operation: Organizational By-Laws and Statutory Requirements", discusses the procedures for organizational by-laws in more detail. It also reviews a number of structural options, ranging from agreements with foreign entities to affiliated foundations.

B MAINTAINING THE ORGANIZATION

This part of the chapter reviews the legal requirements for the keeping of books and records, for filings and for the holding of meetings for each legal form of organization — trusts, unincorporated associations, Ontario and federal corporations without share capital and co-operative corporations.

I TRUSTS AND UNINCORPORATED ASSOCIATIONS

The requirements for the regular maintenance of trusts and unincorporated associations will depend upon the terms of the trust and of the constituting documents for the unincorporated association. The types of books and records, procedures for managing the affairs of the trust or organization, and the holding of meetings may be set out in those documents.

The lack of statutory requirements for many trusts and unincorporated associations provides for flexibility in the types of books and records that will be maintained and in the holding of meetings. This flexibility, however, may create problems where the basic maintenance of the organization does not occur.

(1) Books and Records

The *Income Tax Act*[1] requires that certain books and records be maintained by registered charities, whether they are incorporated, trusts or unincorporated associations. Subsection 230(2) requires a registered

---

[1] R.S.C. 1985, c. I (5th Supp.).

charity to keep records and books of account at the designated address which contain:

(a) information in such form as will enable the Minister to determine whether there are any grounds for the revocation of its registration;
(b) a duplicate of each receipt containing prescribed information for a donation received by it; and
(c) other information in such form as will enable the Minister to verify the donations for which a deduction or tax credit is available under this Act.

Although subs. 230(2) is drafted in broad terms, it is readily apparent that normal accounting books and records must be kept. In addition, the Minister would probably require the constituting documents (including by-laws), minutes of meetings, resolutions and records of revenues and expenditures in order to determine if there are grounds to revoke the charity's registration. The requirements under the *Income Tax Act* are discussed in more detail below.

The legal requirement to keep normal accounting records may also apply to not-for-profit organizations. Paragraph 149(1)(l) provides an exemption to specified not-for-profit organizations from the payment of income tax. However, as of the 1993 tax year, if the not-for-profit organization has a specified income in a tax year of more than $10,000 or assets of more than $200,000, it must file a return for that tax year and each subsequent tax year. The type of income that triggers this provision is interest, rentals or royalties.[2] These types of income are, it would appear, commercial in nature rather than other types of income, such as membership fees or donations. In order to complete the Information Return, the usual types of books and records must be maintained. Similarly, in order to benefit from the goods and services or harmonized sales tax rebates, an eligible organization must maintain the required books and records.

Subsection 230(1) of the *Income Tax Act* provides that every person who is carrying on business and every person who is required by or pursuant to the Act to pay or collect taxes or other amounts "shall keep records and books of account". They must be kept in a form and contain the information necessary to enable the department to determine the taxes payable under the Act or the taxes or other amounts that should have been deducted, withheld or collected. Under subs. 230(7), the Minister may also require any person to keep books and records, including vouchers for verification purposes, where it is necessary in the Minister's opinion for the administration of the Act.

---

[2] *Ibid.*, subs. 149(12).

There are few other statutory requirements that provide guidance on what books and records must be kept maintained by trustees and unincorporated associations. The *Trustee Act*[3] does not, for example, explicitly state what books and records must be maintained. However, in order for the trustees to pass their accounts under s. 23 of the Act, books and records of account are necessary. The *Charities Accounting Act*[4] does require charitable organizations to provide the information requested by the Public Guardian and Trustee. The Public Guardian and Trustee may require, for example, the filing of the financial statements for the charitable organization, which could be prepared only if the usual books and records were maintained.

Trustees must account for the assets entrusted to their care. In order to do so, it is prudent for the trustees to ensure that proper books and records are kept and maintained with respect to all transactions. Minutes of meetings of the trustees should be kept and maintained to ensure that decisions have been documented. Decisions on the affairs of the trust should be evidenced through resolutions or similar documents. Similarly, unincorporated associations should ensure that books and records are kept and maintained, that minutes of meetings are kept and maintained and that decisions are documented.

The safest approach is to use the requirements for corporations without share capital as a model and follow those requirements with whatever modifications are appropriate. For example, it is probably not necessary to have audited financial statements for an organization that meets to discuss issues of the day and has a budget of only a few hundred dollars for refreshments. A balance sheet, statement of revenue and expenses, statement of change in financial position and the appropriate ledgers and receipts may be sufficient.

(2) Filings

Any charitable organization in Ontario may be required to file with the Public Guardian and Trustee, whether it is a trust, unincorporated association or corporation pursuant to the *Charities Accounting Act*. The Public Guardian and Trustee requires that the charitable organization provide a copy of the constituting documents and, in subsequent years, any amendments to it, a list of trustees, officers and directors and their addresses, a summary of assets and liabilities, and the financial statements. If the organization or trust is registered as a charity, an annual filing with the Canada Customs and Revenue Agency is required. As noted above, not-for-profit organizations that have an income of more than $10,000 from interest, rental or royalties or assets of more than $200,000 or have been required to file previously, must file an annual return with the Canada Customs and Revenue Agency.

---

[3] R.S.O. 1990, c. T.23.
[4] R.S.O. 1990, c. C.10.

(3) Meetings

The holding of meetings is an important mechanism to manage the affairs of an organization and to carry out its objects. The number of meetings that are necessary for a trust or unincorporated association will vary, depending upon its activities, objects and needs. However, at least one meeting of the members should be held each year. This meeting should be used to report to the members on the financial position of the organization, to review the previous year's activities, to discuss the future of the organization and to confirm or authorize any changes to the organization that are required or appropriate. If the organization's constituting documents provide for the election of directors, officers or trustees by the members, the annual meeting is usually the most appropriate time to do so.

II CORPORATIONS AND CO-OPERATIVE CORPORATIONS WITHOUT SHARE CAPITAL

(1) Ontario Corporations without Share Capital

The Ontario *Corporations Act*[5] provides for the maintenance of the corporation through the holding of annual meetings, the keeping of books and records, the preparation of and reporting on financial statements and reporting requirements. The *Corporations Information Act*[6] requires that the public record on the corporation be kept up to date.

(a) Books and Records

Section 302 of the Act requires the corporation to keep proper books of account and accounting records for the corporation's financial and other transactions. These books and records include a record of all monies received and disbursed, sales and purchases, the assets and liabilities of the corporation, and all other transactions affecting the financial position of the corporation.

The corporation must keep a copy of the letters patent and any supplementary letters issued to the corporation and copies of all by-laws and special resolutions of the corporation. A register of members, in alphabetical order, for the previous ten years and their addresses must be kept. A register of all directors, addresses, callings and dates on which each became and ceased to be a director must be kept.[7] Section 299 of the Act requires that a minute book of all proceedings of the members, directors and of any executive committee must be kept.

---

[5] R.S.O. 1990, c. C.38.
[6] R.S.O. 1990, c. C.39.
[7] R.S.O. 1990, c. C.38, s. 300.

It is an offence to make or assist in the making of any entry in the minutes, registers or books of accounts and accounting records that is untrue. Any director, officer or employee who knowingly does so, is guilty of an offence and liable to a fine of up to $1,000 and a term of imprisonment of three months.[8]

Records are to be kept at the head office of the corporation or at another location provided that the records are available for inspection during regular business hours at the head office by means of a computer terminal or other electronic technology.[9] A portion of the accounting records may be kept at a place where the corporation carries on business that relate to those operations, assets or liabilities. Sufficient records must be kept at head office to enable the directors to ascertain, on a quarterly basis, with reasonable accuracy the financial position of the corporation. The records, in any event, must be open for inspection during normal business hours of the corporation.[10]

Sections 306, 307 and 308 deal with the making of copies of lists of members and their uses. A member may obtain a copy for purposes in connection with the corporation. A person may also apply under s. 309 to have his or her name added or deleted from the minutes or registers if it has been omitted or entered without sufficient cause. A member may also apply to the court under s. 310 for the appointment of an inspector to investigate the affairs and management of the corporation. Section 310 does not appear to have been used very often, although it is an alternative to a complaint to the Public Guardian and Trustee and an application for an order directing the Public Guardian and Trustee to carry out an investigation.

(b) Filings

The *Corporations Information Act*[11] requires each corporation to file an Initial Return (Form 1) within 60 days of incorporation and, within 15 days, notice of every change to the information. A corporation without share capital must file a return annually with the Minister on the anniversary of its incorporation or amalgamation, whichever is later, or within 60 days of the anniversary pursuant to subs. 3.1(3). The return is physically delivered to the Minister of Finance who transmits the information to the Minister of Consumer and Business Services for purposes of recording the information under s. 8. The Minister may, under s. 6, require that the corporation make a special filing for the purposes of maintaining an electronic record database under s. 9.

Subsection 150(1) of the *Income Tax Act* requires all corporations, except registered charities, to file an annual return within six months of the

---

[8] *Ibid.*, s. 303.
[9] *Ibid.*, s. 304.
[10] *Ibid.*, s. 305.
[11] R.S.O. 1990, c. C.39, s. 2.

corporate year end. Registered charitable corporations must file the Charity Information Return. A registered charity and certain other not-for-profit corporations are exempt from filing under the *Corporations Tax Act*.[12]

(c)   Members' Meetings

An annual meeting must be held within 18 months of the incorporation and subsequent annual meetings must be held not more than 15 months after the last meeting.[13] Unless the by-laws provide otherwise, the annual meeting must be held at the corporation's head office. The by-laws may provide for the meeting to be held anywhere in the Province of Ontario and the letters patent or supplementary letters patent may provide for meetings anywhere outside of Ontario.[14]

The members have a right to adequate notice of the annual meeting.[15] In the absence of a provision in the by-laws, notice must be not less than ten days before the date of the meeting in writing by pre-paid mail to each member at the last address shown on the books of the corporation. The notice must state the date, time, location and purpose of the meeting. It would be useful to attach a copy of the draft agenda to the notice in order to provide full notice of the business that is to be conducted at the meeting. Subsection 133(2) permits charitable corporations to provide notice of the annual meeting in municipal newspapers where a majority of members reside, according to addresses in the corporation's books. The notice must be published at least once a week for two consecutive weeks.

Certain business must be conducted at the annual meeting. The minutes of the previous annual meeting should be read and adopted. The draft agenda should also be adopted and may form the basis for the conduct of the meeting. The directors must present the financial statements to the members and the auditor's report.[16] The board of directors is to be elected,[17] the past acts of the directors and officers could be confirmed, and an auditor is appointed for the next year.[18] Changes to the by-laws and any special resolutions may be passed or confirmed at the meeting.

---

[12]   R.S.O. 1990, c. C.40, s. 57.
[13]   R.S.O. 1990, c. C.38, s. 293.
[14]   *Ibid.*, s. 82.
[15]   The definition of adequate notice is reviewed in *Trow v. Toronto Humane Society*, [2001] O.J. 3640, September 10, 2001, Ontario Superior Court of Justice and *Toronto Humane Society v. Milne*, [2001] O.J. 3890, October 2, 2001, Ontario Superior Court of Justice, both of which are discussed in Chapter 7.
[16]   *Ibid.*, subss. 97(1) and (3).
[17]   *Ibid.*, subss. 287(1) and (2).
[18]   *Ibid.*, subs. 94(2). The members may authorize the directors to fix the remuneration to be paid to the auditors pursuant to subs. 94(7).

The meeting should also be used to discuss any other business that could be raised at an annual meeting. It is common, for example, for organizations to use the annual meeting to discuss future direction for the organization. The annual meeting is and should be used as the main opportunity for members to assess what has happened during the previous year and where the organization is going and should be going in the future.

The *Corporations Act* requires that the members appoint an auditor. The directors are obliged to make the appointment if the members fail to do so.[19] The directors are also authorized by subs. 94(3) to fill any casual vacancies in the position of auditor.

The auditor is an essential mechanism for membership control over the direction of the corporation. The members may, therefore, remove an auditor by a resolution passed by two thirds of the votes cast at a general meeting where notice of the intention to pass such a resolution was given. The members may also approve of another auditor being appointed by a majority of votes cast. On the application of a member, the Minister may appoint an auditor for the year and fix the auditor's remuneration.[20]

The auditor may not be a director, officer or employee of the corporation or of an affiliate corporation, or a partner, employer or employee of any director, officer or employee. These restrictions are an attempt to ensure that the auditor may carry out its functions independently and be seen to do so. The independence is essential not only to the members but also to any regulators, such as the Public Guardian and Trustee, who may need to use the audited financial statements.

The Ontario statute does not exempt corporations from auditing the financial statements, with one exception. Under s. 96.1, a corporation may be exempt from the requirements of appointment and duties of an auditor if it has annual income of less than $10,000 and all members consent in writing to the exemption for that year. The exemption is, obviously, very limited in its scope.

The audit requirement poses some practical difficulties for most corporations without share capital — they cannot afford to retain an auditor to conduct the audit in accordance with generally accepted accounting principles.[21] Under the existing *Public Accountancy Act*,[22] only a public accountant may perform an audit. Subsection 95(1) of the *Corporations Act* prohibits a public accountant who is a director of the corporation from conducting the audit. Unless the corporation can prevail upon a public accountant to conduct the audit for free or at a reduced rate, the corporation may not have the financial resources to comply with the audit requirements.

---

[19] *Ibid.*
[20] *Ibid.*, subs. 94(6).
[21] *Ibid.*, subss. 96(1) and (2).
[22] R.S.O. 1990, c. P.37, ss. 1 and 24.

Charitable corporations are in a particularly difficult position because they are restricted by their objects from expending significant amounts of money on administrative expenses. It is understood that the problem has been recognized by regulators.

(2) Ontario Co-operative Corporations without Share Capital

The basic maintenance elements that are required for Ontario corporations without share capital apply to co-operative corporations. There are some differences, however, to reflect the more "democratic" nature and role of co-operatives.

(a) Books and Records

Section 114 of the Act requires the co-operative to keep a number of records. These must be kept at the head office of the co-operative and be available during normal business hours to the directors[23] and to the members and creditors.[24] The accounting records, directors' resolutions and the minutes of proceedings at meetings of directors and any executive committee need not be available to members and creditors. The Minister may also approve the keeping of records at a place other than the head office.

The following records must be kept:

- a copy of the articles of incorporation of the co-operative;
- all by-laws and resolutions, including special resolutions;
- a register of members in alphabetical order or alphabetically indexed for the appropriate categories of membership. In the case of a co-operative without share capital, the register shall include all persons who are or have been members within ten years and the addresses of all members. All persons who are holders of debt obligations must be registered. The register must also include their addresses, the class or series of debt, and the principal amount of the debt obligations held by that person. Under s. 115, the co-operative is also required to keep a register of transfers for all registered securities, including debt obligations, and the date and other particulars of the transfer. A co-operative may appoint a register and transfer agent under s. 116 to keep this register at a place as is appointed by resolution of the directors;
- a register of directors, including their names and residence addresses while directors and the names of all persons who are or

---

[23] R.S.O. 1990, c. C.35, s. 118.
[24] *Ibid.*, s. 119.

have been directors and the dates on which they became or ceased to be a director;
- proper accounting records in which are set out all financial and other transactions of the co-operative. The Act requires that the accounting records include records of all sums of money received and disbursed and for what matters, all sales and purchases of the co-operative, the assets and liabilities of the co-operative, and all other transactions affecting the financial position of the co-operative; and
- the minutes of all proceedings at the meetings of members, directors and any executive committee.

(b)   Filings

Co-operative corporations without share capital have the same filing requirements as do Ontario corporations without share capital. A co-operative must also file financial statements. If a co-operative moves into another municipality, it must file a certified copy of the by-law authorizing the move.

(c)   Members' Meetings

A co-operative's first annual meeting of its members must be held within 18 months of its incorporation. Subsequent annual meetings must be within 15 months of the last meeting.[25] Meetings of the members are to take place where the head office is located, unless the by-laws provide for meetings to be held elsewhere in Ontario. A meeting may be held outside Ontario only if the Articles of Incorporation permit and must specify the places.[26]

Notice of a meeting must include the time and place of the meeting and must be sent to each person who is entitled to vote by pre-paid mail to the person's last address. The notice must be given at least ten days in advance but no more than 50 days before the date of the meeting.[27] A member may, though, waive notice of the meeting and attendance at the meeting constitutes a waiver unless the member is attending for the purpose of objecting to the transaction of any business at the meeting on the grounds that it was lawfully called.[28]

The members have a right to hear and examine the auditor's report (if required) on the co-operative's financial position and the results of its

---

[25] *Ibid.*, s. 77.
[26] *Ibid.*, s. 74.
[27] *Ibid.*, s. 75. Subsection 75(1) provides the default provisions where the articles of incorporation or the by-laws are silent on the matter.
[28] Ibid., ss. 75(2.1) and (2.2), as am. S.O. 2001, c. 8, s. 15.

operations and to obtain and review the financial statements.[29] They may also discuss any other issues that are on the agenda for the meeting. The appointment of the auditor for the subsequent year is made by the members at this time. The election of the board of directors is usually held at this time. Minutes of the meeting must be maintained with the corporate records.[30]

All questions proposed for the consideration of the members shall be determined by a majority of the votes cast.[31] A poll of votes may be required, but if it is not, an entry in the minutes of the meeting that the chair declared the motion to be carried is admissible in evidence as proof of the fact, absent other evidence to the contrary. Because of the democratic nature of co-operative corporations, a member has only one vote.[32]

The directors may call other meetings at any time to deal with matters affecting the co-operative.[33] Under ss. 70, 71 and 79, the members may requisition or petition the directors to do certain things. A requisition of 5 per cent of the members is sufficient to require the directors to call a meeting within 30 days. The requisition must indicate the reason for the meeting. Five per cent of the members may also ask the directors to circulate a members' resolution related to the co-operative's business for consideration at a members' meeting. A directors' meeting to pass a by-law or resolution may be requisitioned by 10 per cent of the members. If the directors fail to do what the requisition asks, the members who signed the requisition may cause a meeting to be called.

(3)   Federal Corporations without Share Capital

The *Canada Corporations Act*[34] has similar requirements to those under the Ontario statute. Industry Canada's model by-laws fill in a number of gaps.

(a)   Books and Records

The corporation must maintain books of record. The books shall, under s. 109 of the Act, include a copy of the letters patent, by-laws and any supplementary letters patent. The names of all members and former members shall be maintained in alphabetical order, with their addresses and callings. The names of all persons who are or have been directors, their addresses and occupations and dates at which each became or ceased to be a director are to be included in the books. A list of members

---

[29] *Ibid.*, ss. 127 and 128, as am. S.O. 2001, c. 8, s. 17.
[30] *Ibid.*, s. 114.
[31] *Ibid.*, para. 75(1)(b).
[32] *Ibid.*, subs. 76(1). A corporate member may appoint under corporate seal one of its directors to vote on its behalf. Other than this exception, no proxy voting is permitted under subs. 76(2).
[33] *Ibid.*, s. 78.
[34] R.S.C. 1970, c. C.32.

may be obtained by any person, subject to the Regulation, pursuant to s. 111.1 of the Act.

The corporation shall also keep minutes of all meetings of the members, directors and of any executive committee.[35] Section 117 requires that books of account and accounting records also be maintained. The records are to be kept at the head office or at such other place in Canada as the directors think fit. They must be available for inspection.

(b)   Filings

Subsection 133(1) of the Act requires a corporation to file an annual return on or before June 1. The annual return is to set out information, as at March 31, in a summary form. The information includes the corporate name, date of incorporation and how it was incorporated (letters patent), the complete postal address of the head office, the date and place of the last annual meeting, the names and complete postal addresses of the directors, and the name and complete postal address of the auditor. The summary must be signed and certified by a director and filed in duplicate. The second copy is returned to the corporation for its records. Federally incorporated corporations have the same filing requirements under the taxing statutes as do Ontario corporations.

(c)   Members' Meetings

Subsection 102(1) requires that a meeting be held within 18 months of incorporation and subsequently once every calendar year and not more than 15 months after the holding of the last meeting. The meeting shall be called in accordance with the by-laws. The model by-laws require notice by pre-paid mail at least 14 days prior to the meeting. A notice may also be published in a newspaper where the majority of members reside and where there are more than 500 members, if the by-laws permit. Where a meeting has not been called, a member may apply to the court under subs. 102(2) for an order calling for the holding of an annual meeting.

The annual meeting serves the same purpose as it does under the Ontario statute. The audit provisions are, however, slightly different. An auditor must still be appointed by the members.[36] If the members fail to appoint an auditor, the directors must do so. The members may remove an auditor, under subs. 130(5), at a meeting called for that purpose where two thirds of the votes cast sanction the removal. The auditor must present the audited financial statements at the annual meeting.[37]

Industry Canada's not-for-profit policy statement indicates that the auditor need not be a professional accountant, provided that he or she

---

[35] *Ibid.*, s. 112.
[36] *Ibid.*, s. 130.
[37] *Ibid.*, subs. 132(2).

otherwise is qualified under s. 131 of the Act. It is unclear whether or not the federal policy statement would take precedence over the *Public Accountancy Act* requirements that audits may be conducted only by public accountants.

C FINANCIAL REPORTING

I INTRODUCTION

Charitable and not-for-profit organizations are established for a particular purpose or set of purposes. In almost every case, the organizers intend that some level of "public benefit" be derived from the organization. An organization must be able to know if it is fulfilling its purposes. Equally important, it must satisfy others, including its members, government agencies and donors, that it is doing so. Being able to do so is dependent, in part, on the maintenance of proper accounting records and the preparation of financial statements.

The financial statements are the end result of the accounting records. They will assist the charitable or not-for-profit organization to demonstrate that it is meeting the requirements of the law, to develop plans for its operations, and to determine whether or not it is fulfilling its objects in an efficient manner. Financial reporting is a major mechanism for members of a charitable or not-for-profit organization to ensure that the organization is achieving its objects and that the trustees, directors or officers are accountable to the members.

Charitable organizations are under pressure to be more business-like in their approach to accountability and to the presentation of financial information. These organizations have legal and moral responsibilities to the community and to their donors and members. Donors are demanding greater accountability for the funds that are donated or granted to ensure that the funds are spent properly and in an appropriate fashion. A British study noted the importance of financial information:

> Quite apart from their duty to be accountable for the funds they hold and use, charity trustees [and organizations] will want to work in the light of day and to provide as much information as is practicable and useful to the public they serve and indeed to the public at large. Informative and easily understood accounts — and indeed annual reports — will ensure the purpose of averting suspicion and overcoming ignorance and should positively encourage support, not just for individual charities but charity at large.[38]

---

[38] Institute of Chartered Accountants of England and Wales, *Accounting by Charities*, as quoted in D. Kincaid and G. Colin, "The State of the Art in Financial Statements", *Legal and Tax Issues Affecting the Charitable Sector* (Toronto: The Canadian Centre for Philanthropy, 1984), at 7; C.I. Torres, "Generally Accepted Accounting Principles for Non-Profit Organizations: A University Perspective" (1989), 4 The Philanthropist 29.

The Canadian Institute for Chartered Accountants (CICA) has come to similar conclusions in developing standards for charitable and not-for-profit organizations in Canada.

II ACCOUNTING RECORDS AND FINANCIAL STATEMENTS

(1) Financial Records

(a) Introduction

The maintenance of proper accounting records and the preparation of financial statements is the basis for financial accountability. The financial statements are the end result of the accounting records. They will assist a charitable or not-for-profit organization to demonstrate that it is meeting the requirements of the law, to develop plans for its operations, and to determine whether or not it is achieving its objects in an efficient manner.

There are several basic records and statements that charitable and not-for-profit organizations should maintain and prepare, irrespective of their legal form or their size. The level of sophistication of the records and statements will vary and reflect the needs of the organization. An organization with revenues of $20,000 per year is unlikely to need, or be in the position to afford, a computerized record-keeping system. A large charity may, on the other hand, benefit from such a system.

The maintenance of proper accounting records is almost invariably a legal requirement. For example, the *Canada Corporations Act*[39] and the Ontario *Corporations Act*[40] both require corporations without share capital to keep accounting records. A failure to do so is a breach of those statutes and the directors may be held personally liable for any damages that occur as a result of the failure. Trustees of a trust are also required by common law to maintain accounting records. Similarly, the *Income Tax Act*[41] requires that books and records be maintained.

(b) Types of Accounts and Journals

There are five classifications of accounts:[42]

- Assets — the economic resources owned or controlled by the organization, including cash, accounts receivable, inventory, furniture, equipment and so forth. Current assets are cash and other assets that can be readily converted into cash, such as accounts re-

---

[39] Section 117, R.S.C. 1970, c. C.32.
[40] Section 302, R.S.O. 1990, c. C.38.
[41] R.S.C. 1985, c. I (5th Supp.).
[42] *CICA Handbook*, 1999, paras. 1000.25 to 1000.40.

ceivable. Long term assets are less readily converted into cash and include fixed assets.
- Liabilities — the debts of the organization, including accounts payable, mortgages and loans are liabilities. Current liabilities are liabilities that will be retired or paid off in the near future, for example, an invoice from a supplier. Long-term liabilities have a longer period before being paid off, such as a mortgage.
- Equity/Net Assets — the difference between assets and liabilities, which may be either a surplus (assets are greater than liabilities) or a deficit (liabilities are greater than assets). Unlike business entities, charitable organizations may not distribute equity to members. Most not-for-profit organizations will not distribute equity to its members, with the possible exception of a winding-up of the organization. Instead, any remaining equity or net assets would normally be distributed to another charity upon dissolution after payment of all debts and liabilities. Implicit in this category are gains and losses. A gain is an increase in the equity/net assets of the organization from transactions, including operations and contributions and a loss is a decrease. Typically, where revenues exceed expenses, there will be a gain; if expenses exceed revenues, there will be a loss.
- Revenue — the money received or to be received by the organization, including membership fees, donations, grants and sales. Revenue is recorded in one of two ways — on a cash basis as it is received by the organization or on an accrual basis, as it is earned by the organization. Increasingly, the accrual rather than the cash basis is being used to comply with the generally accepted accounting principles.
- Expenses — the costs incurred to operate the organization and to carry out its objects. As with revenues, expenses may be recorded on a cash basis as the expense is paid or on an accrual basis as it is incurred.

The generally accepted accounting principles require that general purpose financial statements for charitable and not-for-profit organizations be prepared using the accrual basis.[43] The rationale for doing so is that it recognizes the effect of the transactions and events in the period in which the transactions and events occur. General purpose financial statements should be based, therefore, on accounting records that use the accrual basis. General purpose financial statements are financial

---

[43] *Ibid.*, para. 1000.46.

statements that are intended to be used by external users and to meet their needs.

Special purpose financial statements could be prepared using either the cash or accrual basis. Additionally, if day-to-day accounting records are kept on a cash basis, they could be adjusted as at the reporting date to prepare the general purpose financial statements. It is sometimes easier for smaller organizations to keep the accounting records on a cash basis and to make the necessary adjustments in preparing the financial statements.

Some larger organizations will use a code system for each of the accounting classifications. Subcodes would be used to identify different types of expenses, such as administrative, office supplies, salaries and benefits. Care should be taken in the use of codes, especially with respect to what is considered "administrative" given restrictions on administrative expenses for charitable organizations. Coding is also usually necessary for computerized systems. In recent years, various software programs have been developed which are affordable even for smaller organizations. These programs can be used not only to record transactions but as a tool for directors and for senior management in preparing budgets, assessing in-year status and so forth. Whatever methods or systems are used, it is important to keep in mind that the purpose is to provide information that is useable in a manner that is cost effective.

Several books of account will be necessary and should be maintained by charitable and not-for-profit organizations. The following books are commonly used to record the transactions related to the five classifications of accounts:

- Cash Receipts/Disbursements Journal — to record all revenue received and all payouts made, usually by cheque. Some organizations will maintain separate journals where the number of transactions warrant.
- Payroll Journal — to record employee wages, payroll deductions (such as pensions, Canada Pension Plan premiums, employment insurance premiums and income tax), net pay and any other deductions. This journal is obviously not needed if the organization does not have employees.
- General Journal — all entries made to adjust necessary accounts, usually on a monthly basis, that are not recorded in other journals are made to the General Journal. An organization may also keep other types of journals, such as a Petty Cash Journal, to record specific types of transactions.
- General Ledger — to record the changes to revenue, expenses, assets and liabilities and equity accounts. The General Ledger will be related to the subsidiary ledgers for specific matters, such as

accounts payable, travel expenses or other subsidiary ledgers appropriate to the organization.

An organization may also maintain other types of books of account and journals, that are useful to it, its major funders and regulators, that are otherwise required by law. An organization may also maintain books of account for specific projects, programs or activities so that the revenues and expenses for a project, program or activity can be readily identified. Care should be taken when designing the books of account to ensure that the directors and senior management have the information that they need for accountability purposes and to manage the affairs of the organization, assess progress in meeting the organization's goals and objectives, and to plan. On the other hand, the amount of information or its presentation should not overwhelm and should be kept in context of the overall organization. Directors and senior management need to see and understand both the forest and the trees.

The financial records include the various supporting documents that are used to produce the account books. For example, an invoice or receipt should be available to support the expenditure of any funds. This type of document is also important for purposes of goods and services tax rebates that are available to registered charities and to some not-for-profit organizations. Each expenditure should be supported by a document to substantiate that the expenditure was made. In addition, receipts, deposit slips and similar documents should be available to substantiate the receipt of revenues.

(2) Financial Statements

(a) Introduction

Financial statements may be for general purposes or for specific purposes depending upon the intended user. In either case, up-to-date bookkeeping and accounting records are necessary to prepare financial statements in order to ensure that the information provided to the user of the financial statements is accurate and complete and fairly represents the financial position of the organization and its financial transactions. Financial statements are intended to provide information about (i) the economic resources, obligations and equity/net assets of an organization, (ii) the changes in the organization's economic resources, obligations and equity/net assets, and (iii) the economic performance of the organization.[44]

---

[44] *Ibid.*, para. 1000.15.

(b)   Types of Financial Statements

The names given to the different types of financial statements will vary. However, in general, the following types of financial statements should be prepared — regardless of the name used to describe them:[45]

- statement of financial position. The purpose of this statement is to identify the economic resources that are available to the organization. It should include the following information:

    - net assets invested in capital assets,
    - net assets that are subject to restrictions requiring that they be maintained as endowment funds,
    - other restricted net assets,
    - unrestricted net assets, and
    - total net assets.[46]

The nature of the restrictions should also be disclosed. An organization may impose restrictions on itself (internal restrictions) or the restrictions may be externally imposed. Internal restrictions are more readily removed by the organization, in most cases, than are external restrictions. An internal restriction could be, for example, a reserve fund that is established by the organization to cover 12 months of operating expenses during a period of change. Once the rationale for the reserve fund is over or a more urgent use develops, the board could remove the internal restriction and reallocate the funds.

Donors or funding agencies may also restrict the use of funds donated, say, for a building fund or for scholarships. The organization cannot, on its own, remove an external restriction and, as a result, those assets are not as flexible. They could not, for example, be used for other programs delivered by the organization or for general operating expenses.

The existence of external restrictions is not necessarily a negative. Most donors want to ensure that their gift is used appropriately and will have a positive impact in the areas that are of concern to them. The fact that the organization has in place the accounting systems to identify, monitor and comply with external restrictions — and audited financial statements to verify that it does — is itself a potential selling point for donors.

The issue of restricted assets is discussed below as part of "restricted fund accounting" and "deferred contributions". Any restrictions on an asset's use must be disclosed. The *CICA Handbook* provides two ap-

---

[45] *Ibid.*, para. 4400.05.
[46] *Ibid.*, paras. 4400.18 to 21.

proaches for charitable and not-for-profit organizations to use to disclose this information — restricted fund method or deferral method.[47]

- statement of operations. This statement presents information about the changes in the organization's resources and obligations over the period, such as a fiscal year. It includes information about the revenues and expenses of the organization's operations. It will also disclose the source of revenues, for example, from operations or from contributions such as donations. Expenses may be described by object, function or program. Expenses should be classified in a manner that provides the most meaningful information for the users — including for the organization's own use. The information should also be recorded and used in a manner that is efficient for other purposes.[48]

A registered charity will need to complete the annual Charity Information Return and will usually want to minimize the need to make changes to its accounting information to comply with the requirements of the Canada Customs and Revenue Agency. The information is important both for purposes of presenting information about the organization but also for budget and planning purposes.

Revenues and expenses should be reported as gross amounts.[49] The use of "net amounts" does not provide a clear picture of the transactions and financial position of the organization. For example, if the organization only reports on the net amount earned or lost from a fundraising event or from a program that incurs costs and receives revenues, it does not provide the user of the financial statements with an understanding of the exposure that the organization had, its true costs or similar information. It also does not assist in determining the efficiency and effectiveness of the project, program or activity — something that all boards of directors should know.

The disclosure could occur as a note to the financial statements. In this way, the net amount could be reported as part of the statement but a note would set out details about the revenues and expenses. While there may be circumstances in which the reporting of gross amounts would distort the true picture of the organization and its financial position, the decision not to report the gross amount should be taken with specific accounting advice.

---

[47] *Ibid.*, para. 4400.02.
[48] *Ibid.*, paras. 4400.30 and 31.
[49] *Ibid.*, paras. 4400.37 to 40.

If the organization uses the deferral method to account for restrictions on funds, the statement of operations should present the following information:

- for each financial statement item, a total that includes all funds reported, and
- total excess or deficiency of revenues and gains over expenses and losses for the period.[50]

If the organization uses the restricted fund method, the following information would be presented in the statement of operations:

- the total for each financial statement item recognized in the general fund,
- the total for each financial statement item recognized in the restricted funds, other than the endowment fund,
- the total for each financial statement item recognized in the endowment fund,
- excess or deficiency or revenues and gains over expenses and losses for each of the general fund, restricted funds other than the endowment fund.[51]

- statement of change in net assets. This statement is sometimes called the statement of changes in fund balances. It is often combined with the statement of operations. Whether separate or integrated into the statement of operations, the information that is typically presented includes:

  - net assets invested in capital assets,
  - net assets subject to restrictions requiring that they be maintained permanently as endowments,
  - other restricted net assets,
  - unrestricted net assets, and
  - total net assets.[52]

If the organization uses fund accounting, it should provide a description of the purpose of each fund.[53] This information apprises

---

[50] Ibid., para. 4400.33.
[51] Ibid., para. 4400.35.
[52] Ibid., para. 4400.41.
[53] Ibid., para. 4400.06.

the user about important information on any restrictions that apply to the fund and the types of expenses that are reported in the fund. If there are any interfund transfers, those should be presented in the statement of changes in net assets. The amount and purpose of the interfund transfer should also be disclosed. If any interfund loans are made or remain outstanding, these too should be disclosed, including the amounts, terms and conditions.[54] A fund could include, for example, a reserve fund which is not restricted by external sources but which the board has established out of prudence.

- statement of cash flows. This statement reports on the total changes in cash and cash equivalents from the organization's activities and is intended to provide information about the source and uses of cash by the organization. It is also called a statement of changes in financial position. The purpose of this statement is to provide information about the source of cash and its uses. It allows users to assess the organization's ability to generate cash, either from internal (from operations) or external sources. It can also be used to assess management's abilities to manage the organization in a fiscally prudent manner. Donors and granting agencies will also use the statement of cash flow to determine if the organization used the funds that it received from them for the purpose that it was given and intended to be used.

The statement of cash flows will distinguish at the least the following:

- cash from operations and
- the components of cash flow that came from financing and investing activities.[55]

The financial statements will normally include "Notes to the Financial Statements". These Notes provide information on issues necessary for the reader to understand fully the information contained in the financial statements.[56] The notes will typically include a statement of the organization's major accounting practices, the legal structure of the organization, whether it is a registered charity, and any contingencies, such as outstanding litigation. Several accounting practices should be disclosed, including

---

[54] *Ibid.*, paras. 4400.12 to 15.
[55] *Ibid.*, paras. 4400.44 to 46.
[56] *Ibid.*, para. 1500.04.

how the organization treats donated property, plants and equipment, materials and services; how pledges are accounted for; how fixed assets are accounted for; what restricted resources are included in the financial statements and an indication of the nature of the restriction; and the income tax status of the organization. The notes to the financial statement are an integral part of the financial statements.

The financial statements may include supporting schedules, such as a more detailed schedule of expenses for important projects. Often, a more detailed schedule is included for fundraising activities, which will assist in determining the efficiency and effectiveness of different types of fundraising activities. The schedules are intended to provide supplementary information that is not necessarily required to comply with generally accepted accounting principles but that is nonetheless informative for users of financial statements.

If the financial statements are audited, the "Auditor's Report", prepared by an independent auditor, will present an opinion on the accuracy of the financial statements. The auditor may express an unqualified opinion ("clean audit"), a qualified opinion or deny providing an opinion, depending on the auditor's professional assessment. In carrying out the assessment and issuing an opinion, the auditor must comply with the standards established by the Auditing Standards Board and the generally accepted auditing standards.

The auditor may make such enquiries as is necessary to enable him or her to report on whether the financial statements fairly present the financial position of the organization and the results of its operations for the period under review in accordance with generally accepted accounting principles applied on a basis consistent with that of the preceding period. In some cases, where changes have occurred, the auditor will note that changes were made and the financial statements will represent the financial information from the previous period on a consistent basis.

Financial statements and the presentation of financial information must meet a number of qualitative characteristics to comply with the requirements set out in the *CICA Handbook*. They must be understandable by the usual external users; relevant in that they have predictive value and feedback value and are timely; reliable in that they present the transactions and events faithfully, verifiably, neutrally and conservatively; and comparable so that like information can be compared. The *Handbook* does recognize that trade-offs among these qualitative characteristics may be necessary. But these trade-offs are themselves the subject of professional assessment and judgment.[57]

---

[57] See paras. 1000.17 to 1000.24 to review these issues in detail.

(c) Contributions — Restricted Fund Accounting Method and the Deferral Method

The *CICA Handbook* addresses in a separate section what is a contribution and different types of contributions that may be made to organizations. The *Handbook* requires that contributions be recognized either in accordance with the deferral method or the restricted fund method.[58]

A contribution is defined in the *Handbook* as:[59]

> ... a non-reciprocal transfer to a not-for-profit organization of cash or other assets or a non-reciprocal settlement or cancellation of its liabilities. Government funding provided to a not-for-profit organization is considered to be a contribution.

This definition is, not surprisingly, generally consistent with the approach taken in the *Income Tax Act* and by the Canada Customs and Revenue Agency for a donation to be eligible for the issuance of a receipt for income tax purposes. There are some nuances, however, that are not entirely consistent but which are probably not decisive. For example, the Canada Customs and Revenue Agency would distinguish between a gift and a sponsorship where the business is allowed to provide some materials about itself. It is receiving something in return for the sponsorship. The business could, in that circumstances, treat the "contribution" as a business expense. It is not as certain that it is, for accounting purposes, a "reciprocal contribution". In some cases, a charity may consider the sponsorship in that circumstance to be a non-reciprocal contribution from the perspective of the charity.

Three types of contributions are identified in the *Handbook*:[60]

- a restricted contribution, where there are external restrictions on the uses of the asset. For example, the donation of cash may be for a building fund and for no other purpose. There are some examples where the restriction may be to prohibit certain uses. Charitable gaming is one example where the terms and conditions of a lottery licence may limit the use of funds to certain approved uses;
- an endowment contribution, which is a specific type of restricted contribution. An endowment contribution is to be part of a permanent fund and the organization is to use the revenue from that fund. The specific assets in the endowment fund may change as

---

[58] *Ibid.*, para. 4410.10.
[59] *Ibid.*, s. 4410.02(b).
[60] *Ibid.*

investment climates and opportunities change, unless, of course, a particular donation provides otherwise;
- unrestricted contribution, which can be used for any purpose or activities within the objects of the organization.

The recognition of a restricted contribution may be deferred in the financial statements until the organization incurs the relevant expense. This deferral makes sense from a conceptual perspective. If the contribution has restrictions such that the organization cannot use the donation until it is ready to construct a building or purchase equipment, then it is not, in one sense, an "asset" of the organization until it incurs the expense. Once it incurs that expense, it can gain access to the restricted contribution. As a result, if this approach is taken, the restricted contributions could be accumulated as deferred contributions and not increase the net assets of the organization.[61] The financial statements would include a note or schedule on the accumulated deferred contributions.

Alternatively, the organization could report restricted contributions on the restricted fund accounting basis. Contributions would be recorded and increase the net assets of the restricted fund. Once the building is constructed or the equipment purchased, the payment for that transaction would be recorded against the restricted fund account.[62]

Endowment funds are a special form of restricted fund. These contributions are permanently maintained on a separate basis. The contributions themselves are not intended to be available to be used for the organization's operations. Instead, the income from the endowment fund is intended to be used to pay for the operations, or, in some cases, for specific programs. An endowment fund could, therefore, be an "unrestricted" one or a "restricted" one. In either case, the endowment fund is reported on as a separate fund and the assets are accumulated separately from the other resources of the organization.[63]

It is critical that the board of directors and senior management of the organization be aware of and comply with the various restrictions that may exist on funds. There may be legal obligations to do so, in addition to the general fiduciary duties of directors. A failure to do so may expose both the organizations, and, equally important, the directors and officers, to legal difficulties. The organization itself may be irreparably harmed if the directors allow a reputation to be established that the organization does not comply with restrictions. Aside from the potential breach of trust implications, such a reputation could seriously undermine the organization's credibility and its future ability to obtain support — financial or otherwise — in the future.

---

[61] *Ibid.*, para. 4410.28.
[62] *Ibid.*, para. 4410.57.
[63] *Ibid.*, para. 4410.05(e)(ii) and paras. 4410.29 to 30 for the deferral method and paras. 4410.60 to 61 for the restricted fund method.

The board also needs to be aware of the restrictions for planning purposes. How could a board of directors develop its strategic direction, and long and short term plans if it does not know what restrictions may exist on the funds? Could it prepare a budget or plan cash flow if it does not know that certain funds are restricted? Or, that certain events must occur for the restriction to be lifted? Obviously, it would be extremely difficult if not impossible for the board to do so and directors are probably not fulfilling their fiduciary duties if they are not aware of such restrictions or do not operate within them.

The board also needs to know and understand the potential impact that a restriction may have on its operations or strategic direction. There are some circumstances in which a board may decide not to accept a donation because the restrictions are impractical or, in a worse case situation, illegal or unethical. A board in Ontario in the 21st century would be very hard-pressed to accept a donation for a scholarship fund if it could use the revenue solely for scholarships for caucasian, Protestant males.[64] Some boards will put in place policies or make decisions on a case-by-case basis with respect to the source of contributions. For example, some health charities will not accept contributions or participate in sponsorships from businesses that create, in the charity's opinion, health risks.

There are special considerations around grants or other funding from governments. The government grant may be based upon the budget provided by the organization and the organization is required to report on its expenditures on an ongoing basis.[65] Often, the organization may not spend the grant unless it obtains matching funding or only if it makes a specific, agreed upon purchase. Any unused grant sometimes must be returned to the government agency. Government grants may also be received prior to the intention to spend the money or the start of the organization's fiscal year. In this case, the organization may decide to treat the grant as a restricted fund until the fiscal period in which the monies are to be spent.

Accounting, to some extent, is an exercise of determining when to "recognize" revenues and expenses. The generally accepted accounting principles provide guidance on making the proper determination. The need to do so is to ensure that the financial information provided to users accurately and fairly represents the financial position and the transactions of the organization. As noted above, an organization may recognize restricted contributions either on a restricted fund or deferral basis.

If the organization does not report on a restricted fund accounting basis, then restricted contributions would be recognized in the fiscal period in which the related expenses are incurred. If the restricted contribution was for expenses to be incurred in a future fiscal period, it would not be

---

[64] See *Canada Trust Co. v. Ont. (Human Rights Comm.)* (1990), 74 O.R. (2d) 481, (*sub nom. Leonard Foundation Trust, Re*) 12 C.H.R.R. D/184, 69 D.L.R. (4th) 321, 38 E.T.R. 1, 37 O.A.C. 191 (C.A.).

[65] *CICA Handbook*, paras. 4410.08 to 09.

recognized as revenue until that future fiscal period. It would be a deferred contribution. The funds would, therefore, be segregated from the organization's current fiscal period's statement of revenues and expenses. It would be recorded as a deferred contribution, which in turn may be accumulated over a number of fiscal periods. The deferred contribution would then be recognized or included in the fiscal period when the event that triggers the removal of the restriction occurs.

If the restricted contribution is for the purchase of capital assets, the capital asset may be amortized over more than one or two fiscal periods. If so, the contribution should be deferred and recognized on the same basis as the amortized expense. Amortization is used to reflect the cost of a capital asset over that asset's useful life.[66] The organization will benefit from the capital asset not only in the fiscal period in which it was purchased, but over a longer period of time, such as 5 or 10 years. Of course, if the capital asset is not amortized, it would be recognized when the capital purchase is made.[67]

The alternative to recognizing restricted contributions in the manner discussed above is for the organization to use restricted fund accounting.[68] The organization's financial statements would include an unrestricted fund for its operational expenses and one or more restricted funds. The restricted fund records the receipt and use of funds that are subject to restrictions. As noted above, an endowment fund is a special type of restricted fund because its purpose is to be a permanently restricted fund to generate income for use by the organization. With restricted fund accounting, a restricted contribution is recognized in the fiscal period in which the contribution is made, but in the restricted fund. The contribution is, therefore, revenue for the restricted fund and would increase the net assets of that restricted fund. Any expenditures that are made from that restricted fund would need to comply with the restrictions. For example, a contribution for the building fund would be recognized in the fiscal period in which it was made by the donor and increase the net assets. If the building is constructed that same period, the expenses would be recognized and reduce the net assets. If the building were constructed two years later, the expenses would be recognized in that latter fiscal period.

Pledges and bequests are common forms of contributions and fundraising campaigns are sometimes developed around them. Pledges and bequests are "contribution receivables" and should be recognized in the financial statements when:[69]

- the amount to be received can be reasonably estimated; and

---

[66] *Ibid.*, paras. 4410.33 to 37.
[67] The accounting for capital assets is the subject of a separate section in the *CICA Handbook*. Section 4430 deals with most capital assets and section 4440 with collections.
[68] *CICA Handbook*, paras. 4410.57 to 77.
[69] *Ibid.*, para. 4420.03.

- ultimate collection is reasonably assured.

To some extent, these two criteria involve both accounting and legal advice. If the organization is advised that it was left a bequest, it may not be in a position to recognize that bequest at that time. It may be necessary for the estate to go through probate. Others may object to the bequest or contest the amount. There may be insufficient funds in the estate to pay the bequest. Until the cash is in hand or there is sufficient evidence, including a legal opinion, that the amount will be collected, a conservative approach would be not to recognize the bequest in that fiscal period.

Similarly, a pledge should not be included in the fiscal year in which it is made unless there are reasonably strong assurances that the property will be transferred. Campaigns, especially capital campaigns, often involve pledges over a period of years. The law around pledges is not entirely clear, but it would be very difficult to enforce a pledge as there is usually no contract between the donor and the organization. For a contract to exist, there must be mutual consideration. If of a significant value, consideration could mean that the contribution is not "non-reciprocal".

In any event, downturns in the economy, personal problems and so forth will affect the ability and willingness of the individual or business to fulfill its pledge. The donor may also be disturbed by how its previous donations were used and decline to fulfill the pledge. There are many reasons why a donor will not fulfill a pledge and these reasons will normally increase over time. The longer the period of the pledge, the greater the risks that it will not be met. Unless the organization can be reasonably assured that the payment will be made, based on an assessment of the circumstances and relevant previous experiences, the pledge should not be recognized for purposes of the financial statements.

Government funding, on the other hand, is more readily fulfilled.[70] Although there are circumstances in which a government will not provide the grant that it committed to provide, those usually are based on the actions or failure to act by the organization. For example, if the organization did not incur the expenses for which the grant was intended or the organization did not obtain the required matching funds from other sources, the government grant may be withheld.

The contribution is not always "cash". Often, a donor will give materials or services to the organization. The organization should only recognize such donations in its financial statements if a fair market value can be determined for the donation.[71] Furthermore, if the donor is donating services, it is important to remember that a receipt for income tax purposes cannot be provided for the contribution of services — although, if

---

[70] *Ibid.*, para. 4410.08.
[71] *Ibid.*, paras. 4410.16 to 18.

the organization pays for the services, the service provider could in turn donate the equivalent amount to the charity and the charity could issue a receipt for income tax purposes.[72]

The date of determining the fair market value may be different between an accounting and tax perspective, although only in some situations. The fair market value of a gift of equipment, for example, is to be determined as of the date the charity receives it for purposes of the *Income Tax Act*. For accounting purposes, the date is the date on which fair value can be reasonably determined if fair value can be reasonably estimated.[73] In most cases, the difference is not relevant, but if the property were securities in a volatile period on the stock market, there could be a relevant difference for which specific legal and accounting advice is required.

(d)   Reporting on Controlled and Related Entities

Organizations will sometimes control or be related to other entities. The *CICA Handbook* addresses these situations in a separate section for accounting purposes.[74] Of course, if the organization is a registered charity, it will need to address the issue of "associated charity" for purposes of the *Income Tax Act*.

Control is defined as the "continuing power to determine ... strategic operating, investing and financing policies without the co-operation of others".[75] This definition is broad and is not limited to "legal control". Obviously, the levers of control will also be different from those normally encountered in a business context where a "parent" will "control" its "subsidiaries" through ownership of shares. However, if the reporting organization has the authority to appoint a majority of the directors of the board of the other organization, it will be presumed to exercise control.

The *Handbook* also discusses "economic interests" as opposed to ownership. An economic interest exists if one organization holds resources that must be used to produce revenue or provide services for the other or the reporting organization is responsible for the liabilities of the other organization.[76] This situation could occur, for example, in the endowment foundation scenario where a foundation is established to be used to raise an endowment fund. The revenue from the endowment fund is donated to the associated charity. It is increasingly common to use this approach for fundraising purposes, especially there is a risk to the endowment fund for purposes of liability or for other reasons.

---

[72] Para. 30, "Registered Charities: Operating a Registered Charity", Information Circular 80-10R, December 17, 1985.
[73] *CICA Handbook*, para. 4410.19.
[74] *Ibid.*, para. 4450.
[75] *Ibid.*, para. 4450.02.
[76] *Ibid.*

If the reporting organization controls another organization, it should report on the controlled organization by one of the following methods:[77]

- consolidating the controlled organization in the reporting organization's financial statements;
- providing disclosure as provided for in section 4450.22;
- providing disclosure as provided for in section 4450.26 where the organization is one of several organizations that are immaterial. In this situation, each of the individual organizations are insignificant or immaterial. A judgment call must be made whether or not the expense and effort of adapting financial information from these individual organizations that are insignificant or immaterial or incorporating into consolidated financial statements will result in materially relevant information for the users of the organization's financial statements. If the organization does not exercise any control over these other organizations, it is questionable that any additional expense or effort would be justified.

The following information should be disclosed, regardless of which approach is taken:[78]

- the policy followed in reporting the controlled organization;
- a description of the relationship with the controlled organization;
- a clear and concise description of the controlled organization's purpose, its intended community of service, its status under income tax legislation and its legal form; and
- the nature and extent of any economic interest that the reporting organization has in the controlled organization.

If the reporting organization has significant influence over another organization, it should disclose the following information in its financial statements:[79]

- a description of the relationship with the significantly influenced organization;
- a clear and concise description of the influenced organization's purpose, its intended community of service, its status under income tax legislation and its legal form; and

---

[77] *Ibid.*, para. 4450.14.
[78] *Ibid.*, para. 4450.15.
[79] *Ibid.*, para. 4450.40.

- the nature and extent of any economic interest that the reporting organization has in the significantly influenced organization.

In some cases, the organization may also have a significant influence over for-profit entities. Indeed, operating or being part of a business is a major method of raising funds for some organizations. If an organization has significant influence over a profit-oriented enterprise, it must disclose that investment in accordance with the long-term investments rules in the *Handbook*.[80] Similarly, if it has an economic interest in a not-for-profit organization that does not amount to control or significant influence, it must disclose the nature and extent of the interest.[81] In both cases, the intention is to provide the user with relevant information about the relationships that the organization has, the resources and obligations that may exist and the risks that may flow from such relationships.

Organizations will often have an interest in controlled profit oriented enterprises. An organization should report each controlled profit oriented enterprise in one of two ways:[82]

- by consolidating the controlled enterprise in its financial statements, or
- by accounting for its investment in the controlled enterprise using the equity method. In this situation, the organization would report for each controlled enterprise or group of similar controlled enterprises by disclosing the total assets, liabilities and shareholders' equity at the reporting date, and revenues (including gains), expenses (including losses), net income and cash flows from operating, financing and investing activities reported in this period. The recommendations with respect to presentation and disclosure of long term investments in Section 3050 and for consolidated financial statements in Section 1600 would apply.

The directors must keep in mind that any investments of this nature must comply with the requirements of the *Trustee Act*[83] with respect to investments and, in Ontario, with the restrictions on ownership of shares under the *Charitable Gifts Act*.[84] All charitable organizations need to comply with the common law and the requirements for income taxation with respect to business activities, if the investments are in the nature of business activities.

---

[80] *Ibid.*, paras. 4450.43 to 44.
[81] *Ibid.*, para. 4450.45.
[82] *Ibid.*, paras. 4450.30 to 35.
[83] R.S.O. 1990, c. T.23, as amended.
[84] R.S.O. 1990, c. C.10.

The organization may also be involved in joint ventures — either for profit purposes or as part of the delivery of the organization's objects. The organization should report on these joint ventures by accounting for its interest. The organization may use the proportionate consolidated method or the equity method.[85] In either case, the policy followed in reporting the interest and a description of the organization's relationship with the joint venture should be disclosed. The information to be disclosed is, not surprisingly, similar to that for profit oriented enterprises.[86]

These types of investments can be complicated and the resulting obligations to accurately report the organization's interest and the financial implications of that interest may be correspondingly complicated. The purpose here is not to set out in detail how the organization's accountants ought to do so; rather, to apprise the directors of the need to do so. Also, this type of information is important for directors and senior managers to assess the risks that exist for the organization and the potential need to minimize those risks. In some cases, those risks may include personal liability if, for example, the investment was outside the legal authority of the organization to make the investment. This issue is particularly (but not solely) important for charitable organizations, which have both statutory and common law restrictions with respect to "carrying on business".

Organizations in the charitable and not-for-profit sector are often involved in a number of related party transactions. A related party relationship will exist when one party has the ability to exercise control, joint control or significant influence over another party — which may be done directly or indirectly by the organization. A related party relationship could be created through one having an economic interest in the other or through common or joint management. If the organization has related party transactions with another organization, i.e., the transfer of economic resources or obligations, it is important for those transactions to be disclosed in the financial statements.[87]

There is a judgment call that must be made on whether or not the parties are related. Several factors may be used to make this determination. If they are, and a related party transaction occurs, the organization should describe the relationship and the transaction (whether or not consideration was exchanged), the recorded amount of the transaction classified by financial statement category, the measurement basis used for recognizing the transaction in the financial statements, the amounts due to or from the related parties and the terms and conditions, contractual obligations with related parties and any contingencies amount related parties.[88] This type of information is needed so that the user of

---

[85] *CICA Handbook*, para. 4450.36.
[86] *Ibid.*, paras. 4450.37 and 38.
[87] *Ibid.*, para. 4460.03.
[88] *Ibid.*, para. 4460.07.

the financial statements can determine, among other things, whether or not the transactions were for fair market value. It may also provide information about the relative levels of exposure to risks and any changes to risk levels from one year to another.

(e) Other CICA Handbook Requirements

The discussion thus far has focussed on the areas of financial accountability that are unique to charitable and not-for-profit organizations and the presentation of the information in financial statements. There are a number of other sections of the *CICA Handbook* that are not specific to the sector but that are applicable. Several provisions in the *Handbook* apply to all entities — regardless of their legal character or nature of the entity — because they are necessary to ensure that financial information is presented fairly, accurately and in a consistent manner. These provisions include, for example, the basic financial statement concepts discussed earlier in this chapter.

The *Handbook* itself identifies the following sections as being generally applicable:

- Financial Statement Concepts — Section 1000
- General Standards of Financial Statement Presentation — Section 1500
- Disclosure of Accounting Policies — Section 1505
- Accounting Changes — Section 1506
- Measurement Uncertainty — Section 1508
- Current Assets and Current Liabilities — Section 1510
- Contractual Obligations — Section 3280
- Contingencies — Section 3290
- Subsequent Events — Section 3820.

There are several sections that apply to organizations in the sector if they have relevant transactions. These sections include the following:

- Consolidated Financial Statements — Section 1600
- Foreign Currency Transactions — Section 1650
- Cash — Section 3000
- Temporary Investments — Section 3010
- Accounts and Notes Receivable — Section 3020
- Impaired Loans — Section 3025
- Inventories — Section 3030
- Prepaid Expenses — Section 3040
- Long-Term Investments — Section 3050
- Leases — Section 3065

- Deferred Charges — Section 3070
- Long-Term Debt — Section 3210
- Revenue — Section 3400
- Research and Development Costs — Section 3450
- Employee Future Benefits — Section 3461
- Discontinued Operations — Section 3475
- Extraordinary Items — Section 3480
- Non-Monetary Transactions — Section 3830
- Interest Capitalized — Disclosure Considerations — Section 3850
- Financial Instruments — Disclosure and Presentation — Section 3860
- Future-Oriented Financial Information — Section 4250.

A detailed review of these types of provisions is beyond the scope of this chapter and text. However, another text is this series will provide a more detailed analysis of financial accounting and the requirements of organizations in the sector.

Financial accountability is at the crux of accountability and governance in any organization — for-profit, not-for-profit or charitable. As the users of financial information and the community become more aware and demanding, the level, accuracy and fairness of the financial information will increase. New standards for information will inevitably develop. Furthermore, as organizations become more global in nature — or participate in joint ventures or other projects with similar organizations elsewhere — the depth and sophistication will also increase. Organizations may need to comply not only with Canadian GAAP but GAAP in other jurisdictions, such as the United States and Europe. There has been some movement towards international standards for GAAP in the for-profit sector and it can be expected that this movement will also occur in the charitable and not-for-profit sector.

Whatever the specific standards or requirements that may be in place, the end product will remain the same:

- to provide financial and related information that accurately and fairly presents the financial position and transactions of the organization; and
- to provide useful and timely financial and related information for planning and assessment purposes.

This information is fundamental to the proper stewardship of an organization and to demonstrate good governance and accountability.

III FINANCIAL RECORDS AND THE *INCOME TAX ACT*

A number of books and records must be maintained under the *Income Tax Act*[89] and for the time specified under that statute and the *Income Tax Act Regulations*. The requirements for retention for purposes of the *Income Tax Act* are set out in Information Circular IC78-10R3.[90] The requirements discussed in that Information Circular apply to charitable and not-for-profit organizations. Other statutes, regulations or contracts for grants may impose other requirements. The *Corporations Act*[91] also imposes minimum requirements for books and records as do statutory regimes for specific areas of activities, such as child care centres or nursing homes. In the fundraising area, the *Trustee Act*,[92] *Charities Accounting Act*[93] and *Charitable Gifts Act*[94] are relevant.

"Records" is broadly defined by subs. 248(1) of the *Income Tax Act* and includes "an account, an agreement, a book, a chart or table, a diagram, a form, an image, an invoice, a letter, a map, a memorandum, a plan, a return, a statement, a telegram, a voucher, and any other thing containing information whether in writing or in any other form". This definition clearly encompasses accounting books and records but arguably extends beyond those records that are traditionally viewed "accounting" to include operational records. The breadth of the definition makes some sense when considering what the *Act* is intended to do. Although the *Act* does not state specifically what books and records are to be maintained for all purposes, they must meet the following criteria:[95]

- permit the taxes payable or the taxes or other amounts to be collected, withheld or deducted by a person to be determined. Although a charitable or not-for-profit organization may be exempt from the payment of income tax, if it employs anybody, it would be required to collect, withhold or deduct taxes and other payroll deductions;
- substantiate the qualification of registered charities for registration under the *Act*. It is important to note with respect to this criterion that qualification for registration is based on the common law as it has developed in Canada and includes the activities of the

---

[89] R.S.C. 1985, c. I (5th Supp.).
[90] "Books and Records Retention/Destruction", The Canada Customs and Revenue Agency, October 5, 1998.
[91] Section 307, R.S.O. 1990, c. C.38.
[92] R.S.O. 1990, c. T.23, as am.
[93] R.S.O. 1990, c. C.10.
[94] R.S.O. 1990, c. C.8.
[95] "Books and Records Retention/Destruction", Information Circular 78-10R3, The Canada Customs and Revenue Agency, October 5, 1998, at para. 6.

organization. The charity must, therefore, be able to demonstrate that its activities are charitable;

- permit the verification of all charitable, athletic and political donations received for which a deduction or tax credit is available. This criterion is obviously important in the fundraising activities of the organization; and

- be supported by source documents that verify the information in the records and books of account. Verification through original receipts, invoices and so forth is important. Verification is also part of the overall accountability of an organization. These source documents would also be examined as part of an audit of the financial statements on a random basis or, in the case of a forensic audit, more thoroughly to trace the transactions. Source documents include sales or purchase invoices, cash register receipts, contracts, credit or debit card receipts, delivery slips, deposit slips, word orders, dockets, cheques, bank statements, tax returns and general correspondence.

The records and books of account must be kept at the place of business in Canada or another place designated by the Minister.[96] In the case of many charitable and not-for-profit organizations, the records and books of account are kept at the treasurer's residence, especially where the organization has no specific place of business. Access is direct physical access, therefore, in the case of electronic records, access must be to the medium on which the information is stored. That medium, whether tape, disc or other medium, must be in Canada.[97]

The Canada Customs and Revenue Agency recognizes traditional, paper format records and books of account and electronic format. A record or book of account is electronic if the information is entered directly into any device for electronic storage, processing and/or manipulation or electronic or optical media, which can be reproduced on paper. The electronic format must be readable and be related back to supporting source documents. Both the electronic records and the source documents, in turn, must be supported by a system that is capable of producing accessible and readable copy.

The intention in this Chapter is not to review in detail the record-keeping systems that may be used. The Agency sets out its general standards for the imaging or microfilming of records and books of account, including supporting source documents, in the Information Circular. If the information was kept electronically, the organization must maintain the electronic format even where there is a paper version of the information. The organization must report any loss, damage or destruction

---

[96] *Ibid.*, at para. 8.
[97] *Ibid.*

to the Director of the local tax services offices and recreate the electronic record within a reasonable period of time. If an electronic image of a source record is produced such that an intelligible reproduction of that record can be made, than the paper source document may be disposed of and the image kept as the permanent record.[98]

Charitable and not-for-profit organizations that are on the "cutting edge" of fundraising using the Internet and similar electronic methods of raising monies (and paying expenses) may want to consider the feasibility of using electronic imaging. If so, the systems and reproductions must meet the standards established by the Canadian General Standards Board in *Microfilm and Electronic Images as Documentary Evidence*.[99] Of course, the organizations must maintain books of account and records for all of its fundraising activities.

The Agency has established the following requirements for any imaging program for the books of account and source documents:[100]

- the program will be part of the usual and ordinary activity of the organization's business and the organization has confirmed this fact in writing;
- systems and procedures are established and documented. Presumably, the organization must also be able to demonstrate that those systems and procedures are followed;
- a logbook is kept showing the date of the imaging, signatures of the persons who authorized and who performed the imaging, a description of the records imaged and whether the source documents are destroyed or disposed of after imaging and the date on which a sourced document was destroyed or disposed;
- an index must be maintained by the imaging software so that any record may be immediately located. The software must also inscribe the imaging date and the person who did the imaging;
- the images must be of a commercial quality and be legible and readable when displayed on a computer screen or reproduced on paper;
- a system of inspection and quality control must be established to ensure that the logbook, index and inscription and quality are maintained; and
- equipment in good working order is available to the Agency to view or, if feasible, to reproduce a hard copy of the image. The

---

[98] *Ibid.*, at paras. 15 to 18.
[99] CAN/CGSB-72.11-93.
[100] "Books and Records Retention/Destruction", Information Circular, 78-10R3, The Canada Customs and Revenue Agency, October 5, 1998, at para. 18.

Agency will provide reasonable notice to make sure the equipment is available.

Many of these requirements will be beyond the expertise and resources of most charities and not-for-profit organizations. However, contracting out the functions may be difficult, especially if the contractor is outside of Canada. The organization must maintain the medium in Canada, at its place of business. If the activities are carried out by a business entity, can the organization argue that it is maintaining the books of account and records at its place of business? If the service provider is outside of Canada, can the organization comply with the *Income Tax Act* and its regulations?

Similar requirements are in place for electronic records in general. These requirements include the following:[101]

- documentation describing the physical, environmental and system controls that exist or existed to prevent unauthorized alteration or loss of records. The documentation would include flow charts and policy and procedures manuals or instructions which document the flow and treatment of transactions from initiation to closure and storage in the accounting system;
- an audit trail from the source documents (paper or electronic) to the financial accounts must be maintained. If an electronic data interchange or similar system is used and no paper source document is available, the electronic records with functional acknowledgements must be kept. The organization must ensure that the EDI or similar transaction records are trustworthy and readable.

Although it is not clear, a public key infrastructure (PKI) or similar system for use in the Internet may comply with this requirement. PKI is a sophisticated electronic system that allows for the independent certification of the sending and receipt of electronic information from one specific party to another specific party. PKI is also intended to provide a high level of security to avoid tampering:

- the records should be stored in a way that is appropriate for the media being used to record the information. If the media that can be overwritten or the information can be deleted or erased, a back-up copy is necessary. The media should be physically secure. For example, computer discs should not be stored near magnetic fields, in direct light or near excessive heat;

---

[101] *Ibid.*, at paras. 19 to 25.

- if the record keeping function is contracted out to a third party, the organization remains responsible for ensuring that the contractor complies with the requirements. The organization must also ensure that the requirements are met if the contractor makes any changes to the system it uses or if it becomes bankrupt. The integrity must also be maintained and the requirements complied with if the organization changes service suppliers or decides to maintain the records in-house;
- if the organization uses existing software to keep books and records, it must satisfy itself that the software and the resulting records and books of account will be compliant with the requirements. For example, if the back-up procedures are inadequate, the organization must augment them to ensure compliance. The organization would also need to maintain documentation on the data entry procedures, the reports produced and any features that alter standard reports or create new reports;
- if the records are converted from one format to another, the organization must ensure that the converted records are trustworthy and readable. Anybody who has converted records, even text, from one word processing format to another will recognize the problems that can be created. The information can become corrupted or unuseable. At times, files can no longer be opened, much less read. The organization must be able to demonstrate that there is no loss, destruction or alteration of information and data relevant to the determination of taxes payable, collected or withheld once the records are converted.

The use of electronic records will increase over time, especially in fundraising. It is already prevalent because the systems create efficiencies and add value. Information can be more readily compared and, where appropriate, manipulated to produce reports on how effective different types of campaigns are on target audiences. Nevertheless, the records are essential for other purposes and must be kept, maintained, retained and safeguarded in order to comply with the *Income Tax Act* and the *Income Tax Act Regulations*. A failure to do so is an offence under the *Act*.

If the organization does not maintain adequate records, the Minister may under subs. 230(3) of the *Act* specify that records and books of account will be kept by the organization. The Agency will usually request a written agreement that the books and records will be maintained. It will then follow up within a month to ensure compliance has occurred. If compliance does not occur, a formal requirement letter is issued. Failure to comply may lead to prosecution by the Agency. There is a minimum fine of $1,000 on conviction under the *Act*. No minimum is provided if the charges are brought under the *Employment Insurance Act*[102] or the *Canada Pension Plan Act*.[103] A person who destroys or otherwise disposes of records or books of account to evade the payment of tax may be charged under s. 239 of the *Income Tax Act*. A charge, although unlikely, may also be possible under the business records provisions of the *Criminal Code of Canada*.[104]

Part 5800 of the *Income Tax Act Regulations* set out the retention period for books of account and records for purposes of paragraph 230(4)(a) of the *Act*. The records must be maintained for at least six years from the end of the last tax year to which they relate. The tax year is the fiscal period for corporations and the calendar year for others. In the case of employment insurance and Canada Pension Plan records, the minimum period is six years from the end of the calendar year to which the books and records relate.

Certain books and records have more specific retention periods under Part 5800 of the *ITAR*. These are:

- for a corporation, two years from the date of dissolution of the corporation;
- for any non-incorporated business, six years from the end of the tax year in which the business ceased. This requirement would be relevant, for example, if a charitable organization as part of its fundraising operated a business that was ancillary to its charitable objects. It would also apply to not-for-profit organizations, such as artists cooperative stores;
- for duplicate donation receipts of a registered charity or registered Canadian amateur athletic association, two years from the end of the calendar year in which the donations were made, other than for donations of property that are to be held for a period of not less than ten years;
- other records of registered charities and registered Canadian amateur athletic associations must be held for two years from the date the registration is revoked. These records include minutes of meetings of the board or executive of the organization, minutes of meetings of the members, all documents and by-laws governing the organization;
- if any return required under section 150 of the *Act* is filed late, the six-year time period runs from the date the return is filed.

---

[102] S.C. 1996, c. 23.
[103] R.S.C. 1985, c. C.8.
[104] R.S.C. 1985, c. C.46. Several sections of the *Criminal Code*, such as ss. 397 to 402, are intended to prohibit the destruction or falsification of business records.

A charitable or not-for-profit organization may apply to the Minister for permission to destroy or dispose of records earlier than the retention period. The request must be made in writing by the authorized representative of the organization. It should clearly identify what books, records or other documents are to be destroyed and for what tax years, details of the special circumstances that justify the destruction earlier than normally permitted and any other relevant information.

IV Auditing Charities

The Canada Customs and Revenue Agency has an auditing program for charities in place. It has also published an information pamphlet explaining the program so that charities can be prepared for an audit.[105] Audits are not necessarily something to be feared. The Agency may have determined that an audit is appropriate on a random basis. Or, concerns may have been raised from the information contained in the annual Charity Information Return. Or, if the annual filing has not occurred, the Agency may have concerns about the organization. Whatever the reason for the audit, there are two approaches that may be taken by the organization:

- recognize that monitoring by the Agency is part of the privilege of having a registration and part of the overall accountability structure;
- ignore it, not cooperate and attempt to divert the Agency's attention.

The first approach will usually result in the audit being completed quickly and with a level of trust that helps overcome any issues that may be identified. Even the best run organizations will slip; government regulators usually recognize this fact. It is how the organization reacts that is as important — does the organization have a good explanation? Is it attempting to rectify the problem? Will the problem be ongoing? Did it try to hide the problem? Did the officers and directors carry out their fiduciary duties to the organization by dealing with the problem?

The second approach will seldom work and creates suspicions. It is more likely to raise additional concerns on the part of the Agency and could lead to further actions. A lot is on the line if the organization and its officers and directors decide to take this approach — including the registration of the organization and the potential exposure of the organization and its officers and directors to legal proceedings. Depending upon how obstructionist the officers and directors may be, charges are also possible.

---

[105] "Auditing Charities", Canada Customs and Revenue Agency, T4118 1252.

Cooperation does not mean, however, caving in to whatever the Agency says. If the organization has a reason for doing what it did (or did not do), normally it should put forth that reason. If the directors, on rational grounds, are of the view that the corrective action suggested by the Agency's staff is an over-reaction, those grounds should be set out and argued. The position of the Agency is that if an audit reveals a problem, it notifies the charity of the problem and provides the opportunity for the charity's side to be heard. The Agency will also provide advice on how to comply with the law.[106]

The information obtained during an audit is confidential. The issue of confidentiality is an important one to charitable organizations. Information can damage an organization — whether or not the information is complete or interim. Indeed, for some potential donors, the mere fact that the organization is being "audited" can raise concerns even if the audit was a result of random selection rather than for any specific cause or due to a complaint.

The Agency has the ability to carry out a very broad audit. It is not always just limited to the financial affairs of the charity. The auditing staff will also examine other materials and records to determine whether or not the organization is fulfilling its legal obligations under the *Income Tax Act* — in particular, to ensure that it is operating as a charity. This type of audit is a field audit and can involve one auditor or team of auditors; can be short in duration or continue for some time depending upon the nature of the audit and the complexities. The auditors will review the ledgers, journals, bank accounts, expense accounts, investments, agreements, contracts, annual reports, minutes of board and staff meetings and any other document that is relevant to the charity's activities and the nature and scope of the audit. The auditor has statutory rights to demand information, if cooperation is not forthcoming.

It may be to the charity's advantage to readily provide information to the auditor. For example, senior staff and a member of the board or the president could meet with the auditor to provide an overview of the operations of the charity prior to the field audit. Auditors will be involved in a number of files and, given the nature of their function, it is important to ensure that the auditor sees both the forest and the trees.

The auditor would normally review preliminary findings with the charity's representative. This review stage provides another opportunity for the charity to put forth its position on any issues that may be identified. The completed audit report is provided to Charities Division, which may follow up for more information. The Agency subsequently writes to the charity setting out the results of the audit. The letter may confirm that the results were satisfactory or it may identify concerns that have been raised. Where concerns are raised, the Agency is to identify them specifically, explain the legal requirements and provide suggestions on appropriate steps to take to correct the problems.

---

[106] *Ibid.*, at 2.

Most people recognize that any operation, especially one that is run by volunteers with limited time and resources, will encounter problems. This recognition is not a condoning of any errors but a reflection of reality. However, clearly, there are situations in which the problems are systematic or too serious for the Agency to consider only corrective action; it may be necessary to move to revoke the charity's registration. The Agency takes into account the following considerations in making that determination:[107]

- were the inappropriate actions intentional or inadvertent?
- how significant are these actions when compared to the charity's goals?
- is the charity willing and able to change its practices to comply with the law? Clearly, the level of cooperation that the charity provided during the audit would be a factor in assessing the charity's willingness and ability, and its credibility under this consideration.
- what is the impact of the charity's inappropriate actions on its donors and beneficiaries, and on the community as a whole? The situation may be different if the beneficiaries were injured as a result of the failure to comply than if nobody suffered.
- how much money is involved?
- is this a repeat offence?

The issue of revocation is beyond the scope of this text. It is important, however, to understand the audit process and the expectations on the charity in any fundraising activities. There are two sides to the charitable "ledger" — carrying out the charity's charitable objects and raising the funds necessary to do so. The Canada Customs and Revenue Agency must be satisfied that both sides of the charitable ledger are in compliance with the law.

The Canada Customs and Revenue Agency is considering an audit protocol or agreement between a registered charity and the CCRA. The protocol sets out the expectations of the CCRA and its staff, and the registered charity. The protocol identifies four typical outcomes from the audit:

- confirmation of compliance letter noting that the audit is complete and the charity is in full compliance,
- education letter where the audit uncovers minor areas of noncompliance; the letter is intended to educate on ways to correct. No response would normally be required from the charity,

---

[107] *Ibid.*, at 5.

- undertaking letters where the non-compliance is serious but not so serious as to lead to revocation. The charity would be required to provide a written undertaking detailing its intentions to correct the situation. If a later review indicates that the charity has not complied or did not fulfill its undertaking, an administrative fairness letter would be issued,
- administrative fairness letter, which is issued where there are serious issues of non-compliance that are sufficient to consider revocation or undertakings have not been fulfilled. The charity is presented with an opportunity to make submissions within 30 days. If the matter is not resolved to the CCRA's satisfaction, a notice of intent to revoke registration would be issued. That notice has its own process.

In return, the CCRA will agree not to select the charity for a random audit for a period of at least three years.

V Operating a Charity — Maintaining its Registration

(1) Introduction

There are a number of specific issues that arise in the operation of a charity from an *Income Tax Act* registration perspective. In some cases, the charity must ensure that it operates in accordance with certain provisions and standards. In other cases, there are changes that may occur of which the charity must advise the Agency or for which it must obtain its permission. Many of these issues are directly related to the fundraising activities of the charity.

A charity must be able to demonstrate the following in order to maintain its registration:[108]

- it devotes its resources (financial and human) to charitable purposes and activities;
- it does not pay or otherwise make available its income to any of its members other than for payment of reasonable salaries or to reimburse reasonable out-of-pocket expenses;
- it issues official donation receipts in accordance with the *Income Tax Act* and the *Income Tax Act Regulations*. This issue is discussed below in more detail as it is a significant fundraising issue;

---

[108] "Registered Charities and the Income Tax Act", Canada Customs and Revenue Agency, RC4108, at 4.

- it keeps proper books and records and provides these and other relevant information to the Agency as required by the *Act*. The books and records requirements have been reviewed above;
- it files the annual information return on time. The annual information return is reviewed below as it includes information about fundraising and fundraising activities;
- it meets its disbursement quota, and does not do so by exchanging gifts with other registered charities.

A charitable organization or public foundation may, in addition, carry on business activities, but only if they are related to the organization's or foundation's objects. The carrying on of business activities is a form of fundraising.

A public foundation and private foundation must not acquire control of other corporations, which is defined as owning 50 per cent or more of that other corporation's issued share capital. Either may do so if it had bought up to five per cent of the shares and was given additional shares that increases the holdings to more than 50 per cent. Furthermore, public and private foundations cannot acquire debts other than those related to current operating expenses, the purchase and sale of investments or the administration of charitable activities.

(2) Official Donation Receipts

The purpose behind the official donation receipt is to acknowledge receipt by the charity of a donation of property — usually cash but also in-kind gifts such as real property, equipment, securities and so forth. A donation of "services" is not a donation of property. The donor is able to use the receipt for purposes of a credit on his or her payment of income tax or as a deduction in the case of a business.

There are three elements to a donation, all of which must be present before an official receipt for income tax purposes may be issued by the charity:[109]

- the property must be transferred by a donor to the registered charity;
- the property must be given voluntarily by the donor. The donor cannot be obliged to make the donation of the property;
- no consideration is being provided in return for the donation. For example, the donor cannot expect anything in return, such as some form of benefit to the donor or to somebody designated by the donor as a result of the gift.

---

[109] *Ibid.*, at para. 29.

A number of donations do not qualify as gifts for purposes of the *Income Tax Act* and an official donation receipt may not be issued for such contributions.[110] There is no prohibition on the contribution being made (subject to any other limitation on the charity accepting the donation) but no receipt for income tax purposes may be issued by the charity. These gifts include:

- admission fees to an event or program;
- membership fees that convey a right to attend events, receive literature or services or to have entitlements, such as free access to buildings. A membership fee could be considered a gift if the only benefit received is the right to vote at a meeting. The donor could also receive reports on the charity's activities for free if such reports are otherwise available for free;
- the cost of a lottery ticket, in whole or in part;
- payment of tuition fees, except as permitted under the *Income Tax Act*;[111]
- contribution of services. However, if the charity pays for the services provided to it, the service provider could accept the payment and subsequently make a donation of all or part of that amount. In that situation, there is a transfer of property by the donor and a receipt for income tax purposes could be issued;
- payment by a business if it receives material promotional or advertising benefits in return. An acknowledgement of the payment will not usually be a material promotional or advertising benefit. If there is a material promotional or advertising benefit, it would likely qualify as a business expense for purposes of income taxation;
- a gift that is subject to a direction by the donor that the charity transfer the funds to a specified person or family. The charity, in that situation, is not the true recipient of the gift but is being used as cover to obtain a receipt for income tax purposes for a gift that was intended by the donor to go to the individual or family;
- a gift subject to a direction by the donor that the charity give the funds to a non-qualified donee. This gift is disqualified for similar reasons as a gift that is subject to a direction that it be made to an individual or family;

---

[110] *Ibid.*, at 6. See also "Registered Charities: Operating a Registered Charity", Canada Customs and Revenue Agency, December 17, 1985, Information Circular 80-10R.

[111] See "Tuition Fees and Charitable Donations Paid to Privately Supported Secular and Religious Schools" (Canada Customs and Revenue Agency, September 29, 1975), Information Circular 75-23.

- a pledge, except for that portion of the pledge that was donated. An undertaking to make a donation by the transfer of property may or may not be legally enforceable depending upon the terms of the pledge. In any event, until the amount pledged is received and accepted by the charity, there is no transfer of property and the charity cannot issue an official receipt for income tax purposes. This approach is also consistent with the *CICA Handbook* on the recognition of pledges as a contribution.

The "general rule" of what is a gift is also articulated in the Canada Customs and Revenue Agency Interpretation Bulletin 110R3.[112] It notes that there must be a transfer of property, that the transfer is voluntary and is made without expectation of return. The Interpretation Bulletin continues, however, with exceptions to the general rule that are "in recognition of certain widely accepted fund-raising practices".[113]

The Agency accepts that a gift is made in certain very specific circumstances with respect to a "dinner, ball, concert or show" or "like event" for the difference in price between the purchase price of a ticket for a "dinner, ball, concert or show" and the fair market value of the food, entertainment and so forth.[114]

A receipt could be issued for this difference, presumably on the basis that the donor received something in return (fair market value) but also made a donation. The Agency notes that this exception will not be extended beyond the four enumerated events or a "like event". A "like event" is defined as "an event which provides services and consumable goods, the equivalent of which are readily available in the marketplace and which by their very nature are necessarily purchased with the intention that they be used on a specific date in the near future by the ticket purchaser (and guests) and which, if not used, have no resale value". The Agency notes that an auction would not be considered a "like event" nor would be a dinner coupled with an auction, unless people are invited to bid and can bid without paying the admission fee for the dinner.

The charity, essentially, considers that the purchase price is comprised of two payments. One payment is for the fair market value of admission. The second payment is for the "gift" to the charity. The fair market value is calculated by making a comparison with the regular or usual charge for the same or similar function or event where a donation is not solicited. If the charity does not have a comparable function or event, it can calculate the fair market value based on the estimated price that would have been charged for a function or event if it were carried out as a profit-making venture.[115]

---

[112] "Gifts and Official Receipts", June 20, 1997.
[113] *Ibid.*, at para. 4.
[114] *Ibid.*, at para. 5.
[115] *Ibid.*, at paras. 6 and 7.

This exception does not apply, however, if the dinner, ball, concert or show also includes participation in a lottery or draw for prizes or awards if the prizes or awards have more than a nominal value. The Agency considers the difference between the purchase price and the fair market value of the food and entertainment in that situation to be the consideration to participate in the lottery or draw.[116]

The Interpretation Bulletin also identifies other circumstances that are exceptions to the "general rule". These are:

- if a taxpayer honours a personal guarantee made to a charity or honours a pledge, the amount paid by the taxpayer may be considered a gift even though it is being made to honour an obligation. To be eligible, the donor must have entered into the obligation voluntarily and without consideration.[117] This situation could arise if, for example, a member guarantees a loan made by an arm's length financial institution to the charity, the charity is unable to pay the loan when it is called or due, and the financial institution calls on the personal guarantee of the member;
- certain types of planned giving, such as annuities purchased from a charity and the donation of insurance policies, which are discussed in Chapter 10; and
- the payment of tuition fees to privately supported secular or religious schools.[118]

A fundamental premise of any gift, in order to be eligible for a receipt for income tax purposes, is that it is a transfer of title of the property by the donor to the charity and the gift is accepted by the charity. Once the charity accepts the donation, it becomes an asset of the charity and all of its assets by law must be used to carry out its objects. As a result, in most circumstances once a gift is made, it is made and cannot be returned.

There are a few circumstances in which a donation could be returned, where, for example, there is a legal requirement to do so. If the charity solicits funds from the public for a project and only for that project and the project is either over-subscribed or does not proceed, there may be a legal obligation to return the funds. The property could be returned based on the common-law if the project becomes impossible to fulfill. However, it is important to note that the charity may want to make a *cypres* application. The superior court has the common-law and equitable jurisdiction to apply the donation to another charitable object or activity. However, prevention of the problem is better and solicitations should

---

[116] *Ibid.*, at para. 8.
[117] *Ibid.*, at para. 9.
[118] *Ibid.*, at para. 10. See also Information Circular 75-23, "Tuition Fees and Charitable Donations".

indicate for what the property will be used if the project is oversubscribed or does not proceed.

There may also be other situations in which the charity accepted the donation illegally, i.e., where it cannot hold the property due to restrictions in its letters patent. Or, the property was initially obtained by the donor by theft and must be returned to the rightful owner. Obviously, these situations are unusual and will be unique to the specific facts of the case. Before any donation is returned, especially after a receipt has been issued for income tax purposes, the charity and its legal counsel should discuss the matter with the Charities Division of the Canada Customs and Revenue Agency.

The *Income Tax Act Regulations* set out a number of mandatory elements for a receipt to be considered an "official receipt for income tax purposes".[119] The following information must be included on the document:

- a statement that it is an official receipt for income tax purposes. This statement clearly distinguishes it from other forms of receipt that a charity or any entity may use in carrying out its day to day operations;
- the charity's Business Number (BN), which is also its Registration number, name and address in Canada as recorded with the Charities Division. Each registered charity has been issued a Business Number, either when it obtained registration or if it was registered before the change-over, during the transition period in the mid-1990s. Charities should use receipts with the Business Number. Older stock may continue to be used if the incorrect information is crossed out by stamp or by hand, however this rationale is rapidly disappearing over time;
- the serial number for the receipt. Each receipt must have a unique number that identifies it from other receipts. A registered charity may issue computer-generated receipts, provided that the receipts are readable, contain the mandatory information and the reliability of the computer data entries is protected. This issue is discussed earlier in this chapter;
- the place or locality where the receipt was issued;
- for a cash donation, the date on which or the year during which the donation was received by the charity, which may be a different date than the donor made the donation. If the donation was mailed, the charity may use the date that is postmarked on the envelope. As a result, a charity may issue a receipt for a donation

---

[119] Sections 3500 to 3501, *Income Tax Act Regulations*.

for Year 1 if the envelope is postmarked December 31, Year 1 but the envelope is not delivered until January 3, Year 2;
- for a gift in-kind, the receipt must include the date on which the charity received the donation, a brief description of the gift, and the name and address of the appraiser of the property if an appraisal was done. If the gift in-kind was less than $1,000, an appraisal would not normally be needed, provided somebody is in the position to set out the fair market value of the gift in-kind;
- the date on which the receipt was issued, if different from the date on which the gift was received by the charity;
- the name and address of the donor. For individuals, the charity should use the first and last name and initial of the donor;
- the amount of the cash donation or the fair market value of a gift in-kind at the time the gift was made; and
- the signature of the person who authorized the issuance of the receipt. The signature may be a facsimile signature if it is imprinted distinctly with the name, address and Business Number of the charity and it is serially numbered by a printing press or numbering machine.

The charity may issue a replacement receipt to a donor if the original receipt was lost or spoiled. If the charity is satisfied that the receipt has been lost, it may issue a second receipt, noting clearly that it cancels and replaces the original receipt (which should be identified by receipt number) on the second receipt. The charity's copy of the original receipt must be retained and marked "cancelled". The donor must return a spoiled receipt and the charity retains both copies and marks them "cancelled". If the official receipt contains incorrect or illegible information with respect to the day the donation was received, the year in which the donation was received, or the amount of the donation, it will be regarded as a spoiled receipt.

There are circumstances in which the receipt for income tax purposes may be included in the T4 slip issued by an employer to an employee. Where a system of payroll deduction has been established, either using an Employees' Charity Trust or through a written agency agreement between the employer and the charity, the *Income Tax Act Regulations* permit the T4 slip to be used to set out the donations. An Employees' Charity Trust is a registered charity that has been established for the purpose of receiving payroll deductions and to disburse those funds to registered charities in accordance with the directions of the relevant employee.

The registered charity, such as the United Way, could alternatively enter into a written agency agreement with the employer. The agreement would specify that the employer is acting as the registered charity's agent using the employer's payroll deduction system. The employer, as agent, agrees to deduct through the payroll deduction system the funds that each employee has agreed to donate and to remit those funds to the registered charity. The employer must also verify that the contributions for each employee that is reported on the T4 slip is reconciled to the amount that was remitted to the registered charity. The employer also agrees to provide the charity's auditors such verification as the auditors require.

(3)   **Charity Information Return**

Every registered charity must file an annual Charity Information Return no later than six months after the end of the charity's fiscal period. The Canada Customs and Revenue Agency does mail out each year a copy of the Charity Information Return to the last address on file for the charity, under the *Income Tax Act*, it is the responsibility of the registered charity to file the Return without notice or demand. Failure to file the Return could lead to revocation of registration. A charity would no longer be able to issue receipts for income tax purposes and it may be subject to a tax equivalent to the full value of its remaining assets.

The Charity Information Return has a number of parts. Form T3010 includes information of general interest and its Schedules A, B and C to deal with more technical matters. The charity is also required to file its financial statements as part of the overall Charity Information Return. The information required in Form T3010 and its schedules have been divided into information that is publicly available and that which is not. Any person may request and receive a copy of the completed Form T3010. The Agency does not release Schedules A to C of the Return pursuant to the confidentiality provisions in the *Income Tax Act*.

The charity decides whether or not its own financial statements will be released to the public. The decision to permit the release the financial statements is one that should be taken after consideration of the issues. Many charities already provide copies of their financial statements as part of an annual report to members. The public may have access to the information. The release of financial information does demonstrate an openness with the public and provides for a higher level of accountability. On the other hand, some charities may be reluctant to permit the release for any number of reasons. Overall, the trend has been towards greater accountability and charities are generally encouraged to permit the Agency to release the financial statements.

The purpose of this section is not to review the filing of the Charity Information Return in whole. Rather, there are a number of fundraising issues that are identified in the Return and the focus will be on those issues. These issues are highlighted for each part of the Return below.

Section A of the Return requests information about the registered charity. If the charity has previously filed a Return, some of the information will be included in a preprinted label, similar to the approach taken with individual tax returns. It is common for a registered charity to use either a shortened version of its legal name or another name that is better known for fundraising purposes. If it does, it must identify the other names in Question A2.

Section B asks for information about the directors or trustees of the organization, including names, positions, postal codes, occupations and months of service. No specific "fundraising" information is requested in this Section.

Section C covers the activities of the organization, including where it carried out its charitable activities. It is important to ensure that the answers accurately and fully identify how the registered charity is implementing its charitable purposes or objects through its activities. The potential audience for this information includes donors who may be considering making a donation to the organization.

Section D is concerned with financial information. The charity's financial statements are included in this Section and are in addition to the information about financial matters requested in Section D. The financial statements submitted by the charity, at minimum, should consist of a statement of receipts and disbursements and a statement of assets and liabilities. If the income is more than $250,000, the Agency recommends that the statements be audited. Charitable corporations incorporated under the Ontario *Corporations Act* are required to have their financial statements audited, regardless of the amount of receipts or expenditures.[120]

The financial information requested in Section D is similar to that contained in the charity's own financial information. However, the information requested in Section D is more focussed on the issues considered important by the Canada Customs and Revenue Agency. Depending upon the accounting policies used (for example, accrual versus cash basis), there can also be differences in the financial information and its presentation.

There are a number of fundraising issues inherent in the information requested in Section D. For example, if an asset is donated to a charity, it should be included in the statement of assets and liabilities at its fair market value on the date the charity received it, which is the amount that was used for purposes of any official receipt for income tax purposes, if a receipt was issued. Any restricted funds could be included in "other assets" and specified in line 57.

The statement of receipts and disbursements requires information about donations and gifts. "Gift", whether receipted or not, is broadly defined to include all cash donations, cheques, cash-surrender value of life insurance policies donated to the charity and the amount of premiums the donor paid directly to the insurance company on behalf of the charity, gifts received under a will, gifts that are subject to a trust or

---

[120] Section 96, unless the audit requirements may be waived pursuant to s. 96.1. Under the *Ontario Public Accountancy Act*, R.S.O. 1990, c. P.37, only a public accountant may audit financial statements.

written direction to hold for a period of not less than 10 years, amounts from foreign donors (converted at the exchange rate when the charity received the gift).

The questions clearly separate out "tax-receipted" gifts from other gifts. Any gift for which a receipt for income tax purposes was issued must be included in the total amount for "tax-receipted" gifts on line 100. Any gifts made the charity for which an official receipt for income tax purposes was not issued is recorded as a separate item on line 102. This line would include, therefore, a not-for-profit organization that does not require a receipt for income tax purposes as it does not pay income taxes, an anonymous gift or collections of funds where the individual donor cannot be identified, e.g., loose collections. If it received gifts from other charities, those gifts need to be identified on a separate line (101). It is important to recall that charities ought not to issue receipts for income tax purposes to other charities (charitable organizations, public foundations, private foundations). If a receipt was issued in error, the amount should be included on the line for "tax-receipted" gifts and identified.

If funds were received from another charity and recorded in "total other gifts" for which a receipt for income tax purposes was not issued, the form still requires that the amount received be recorded on a separate line (103). The requirement to identify and record the amounts received from other charities is presumably to ensure that any errors in the issuance of receipts are identified and corrective action taken, and to ensure that there is not a misuse of the privileges under the *Income Tax Act* whereby charities would flow monies to each in order to fulfill — on paper — the disbursement quota.

Government grants are recorded separately as a total (line 108) and for each level of government (lines 103 to 107). A number of other sources of revenue are included in lines 109 to 117. These include:

- membership fees where the member receives an entitlement to privileges or services in addition to a right to attend and vote at meetings or to receive a newsletter (line 109). If the member receives only these nominal "rights" a receipt presumably could be issued,[121]
- rental income from real property (land and buildings), including rents received from carrying out its charitable activities. For example, if the charity operates a nursing home, any rents paid by the residents would be included on line 110. That line would also include ancillary income earned from charitable property when it is not being used for charitable purposes, such as a parking lot for a church which earns extra income during the week. If the property is not being used at all to carry out its charitable purposes, the income

---

[121] See "Registered Charities: Operating a Registered Charity", at para. 30.

is also recorded on line 110, but an explanation should be included in the charity's own financial statements which are submitted with the Charity Information Return. In addition, in Ontario, the period of time for which a charity may own property that is not used for charitable purposes is limited by statute,[122]

- receipts from governments for the purchase of goods and services. For example, a charity may enter into an agreement to provide services for offenders released on probation or parole. This type of revenue would be recorded on line 111,
- fees and income earned from other sources where the charity provides goods or services on a regular basis (line 112). These sources could include fees for daycare services, tuition fees for schools, operations of an ancillary business activity and so forth. In the case of tuition fees, the amount recorded on this line would not include any amount that was considered to be a donation for which a receipt for income tax purposes had been issued in accordance with the Information Circular 75-23, *Tuition Fees and Charitable Donation Receipts Paid to Privately Supported Secular and Religious Schools*. The receipted amount would be recorded on line 100,
- payments from fundraising not otherwise reported. The amounts recorded on line 113 include the gross amounts raised from fundraising events, activities or campaigns that are conducted on an occasional basis. If the event was a dinner or "like event", and a receipt was issued for income tax purposes for the difference between the fair market value of the meal and the price of the ticket, that difference would be included on line 100 as a receipted donation,
- interest and dividends are recorded on line 114. All amounts should be recorded in gross amounts, regardless of whether or not any withholding taxes were imposed. Any amounts received in another currency should be converted into Canadian dollars at the exchange rate in effect when the charity received the funds,
- capital gains or losses are recorded on line 115. A capital gain or loss will be incurred when a charity sells capital property, such as real property, shares or similar property. If the property sells for more than the charity paid for the property, there is a capital gain; for less, a capital loss. What the charity paid for the capital property, though, is based upon the adjusted capital cost of the property,

---

[122] *Charities Accounting Act*, R.S.O. 1990, c. C.10, s. 8. See also the *Charitable Gifts Act*, R.S.O. 1990, c. C.8. The applicability of these limitations has been restricted in the case of public hospitals, if not other similar public institutions, in *Re Centenary Hospital Assn.* (1989), 69 O.R. (2d) 1, 33 E.T.R. 270, 59 D.L.R. (4th) 449 (H.C.), additional reasons at (1989), 69 O.R. (2d) 447.

which includes the purchase price, legal fees and surveys associated with the purchase, the cost of any capital improvements to the property and the costs of selling the property. If the charity takes back a mortgage, the gain will be spread out over the term of the mortgage and the charity, for purposes of the line 115 calculation, would include the amounts the charity received during the fiscal period. A capital gain or capital loss could be incurred with gifted property, which should be reflected in the financial information.
- other income in lines 116 and 117 are for any other gross income that have not already been recorded on lines 100 to 115. Rebates on GST or similar payments are not included in these lines.

Section D of the Charity Information Return also requests information about the charity's disbursements. In most cases, these disbursements will be related to the operations of the charity and to the delivery of its charitable programs and activities. Lines 120 to 124 identify five different types of expenditures. It is important to note, as does the Canada Customs and Revenue Agency,[123] that most charities will have recorded the information in their books and records in a method that is more functional for the charities. Nevertheless, the Agency does expect that information on the five categories to be reasonably accurate and, if the books and records were properly maintained, the information could be extrapolated.

The five categories are:

- expenditures on charitable work (line 120),
- gifts to qualified donees (line 121),
- management and general administration (line 122),
- fundraising (line 123),
- political advocacy (line 124).

Lines 125 to 127 are for other expenditures not already included in the five categories of disbursements. The Agency requests that any category of disbursements be identified separately if it amounts to more than 5 per cent of the overall disbursements. These disbursements could include premiums to maintain life insurance policies that have been donated, costs of rental property that the charity does not use in its charitable programs or for fundraising, and the costs of producing and selling goods and services not included in the charitable programs. Any amounts that had been accumulated with the Agency's permission in previous years and recorded on a previous Schedule B and now expended would be recorded on one of these lines.

---

[123] "Completing the 2000 Registered Charity Information Return", Form T4033.

The five categories are broad ones. Any single employee or asset might be used for more than one of the five purposes. For example, it is common for an employee to be employed in carrying out charitable activities but also for some management and general administration functions or even in fundraising. If so, an appropriate allocation of the salaries, benefits and other expenses ought to be made for each of the relevant categories. In some cases, it may be difficult to decide when to allocate the salary and benefits of, say, an executive director, to management and general administration as opposed to fundraising. Any allocation ought to be demonstrably reasonable and based on the financial information.

The fundraising expenditures are the most relevant for purposes of this text. Any expenditure or disbursement made with a view to raising funds should be included in the information recorded on line 123. These disbursements would typically include the salaries and benefits of employees, overhead costs, the costs of promotional materials, campaign supplies, electronic data processing (if any), office expenses and so forth. Promotional expenses would be included if the primary purpose was for fundraising as opposed to, for example, information. Other fees that would be included in line 123 are postage for a mail campaign, fees paid to outside consultants, costs of running a bingo event and so forth.

The issue of publications and similar materials can become complicated and a matter for judgment. Is the brochure intended to provide information to the public on the charity and its programs available to the public or about a social or medical issue? Or is it intended to raise funds? If the former, the costs would have been included on line 120, even if there is an incidental fundraising purpose. If the latter, it is fundraising and should be recorded as a cost on line 123. The intended audience may be determinative of the issue — a very information and educational brochure that is used mostly in a solicitation campaign for donations, would likely be considered a fundraising expense rather than a charitable activity.

It is important to categorize the expenses properly on the Information Return. In addition, the information becomes part of the test of whether or not a charity is, in fact, carrying on as a charity. The ultimate purpose and public policy behind "charities" is to ensure that charitable programs are delivered to the public. If the financial information discloses that the charity is spending an inordinate amount on fundraising or on administration, it may no longer be a charity at common law. In some cases, there may be a valid explanation, such as the organization is expanding and undergoing some initially high administration or fundraising costs. This explanation would be much less credible if offered a second or third year in a row.

Section E focusses on additional amounts that have been received from fundraising, business activities and so forth. If the charity reported more than $30,000 in receipts on line 118 (total of "amounts received from other sources"), it must complete Section E. Most of Section E is a checklist of questions for which there is a "Yes" or "No" answer for 18 specific types of activities and another for the charity to identify.

Notwithstanding the "yes/no" nature of the questions and answers, completion of Section E will provide a good profile of the charity's activities. The list of 18 is fairly representative of the types of activities that charities in Canada undertake. Combined with the information provided in Section D, the Agency is in a position to make ongoing, preliminary assessments of whether or not the organization is, in fact and in law, charitable. This information may also be cross-checked against the charity's other filings with the Agency, such as its GST/HST filings or application for rebate of GST/HST paid if the organization is not also registered for GST/HST purposes. Because this part of the Charity Information Return is a public document, others, including potential donors, have access to the information.

Question E2 is concerned with whether or not the charity charged fees for or otherwise received regular revenue from a number of activities. Question E3 asks for the gross and net revenue from these activities. The gross amount includes the revenues obtained from all of the activities for which the answer was "Yes". The net revenue is the amount less expenses for those activities. The charity may allocate overhead and other indirect costs of the activity on a reasonable basis. For example, a gift shop in a hospital would incur costs for heat, hydro and maintenance and a reasonable proportion could be allocated. The charity should have a valid basis for the allocation, one which it could justify in an audit.

Depending upon the objects and purposes of the organization, these activities could be charitable in nature, an ancillary business activity or a problem. For example, a charity that is established to relieve poverty could sell donated clothing, furniture and other used goods to the poor. This activity could be seen as part of its charitable purposes. Similarly, a medical clinic that provided dental care and charged the patient a fee for the services could also be a carrying out its charitable activities, especially if the fees were less than the true costs of the services.

In other cases, the activity could be an ancillary business activity. Many hospitals operate gift shops that sell flowers, books and so forth that are purchased by visitors for the use of patients in the hospital. Although the gift shop is a business activity, it is related to and ancillary to the charitable activities and purposes of the hospital, the caring of patients. A church that rents parking spaces during the week may also be operating an ancillary business.

An issue does arise if the amounts earned by the charity from these other sources is out of proportion to its other revenues or if the activity is too far removed from its charitable purposes. For example, a charity that is intended to provide programs for the relief of poverty would probably have difficulty justifying that ninety per cent of its revenue came from product endorsements. It would also have significant problems trying to justify a substantial level of revenue from the sale or lease of its membership or donor mailing lists.

The answers to Question E2 are, in some ways, an opportunity for the board of directors to ensure that the organization is carrying out its mandate. If the board finds that there are some problems with the sources of its "other revenues", it should consider corrective action. The problem may be an over reliance on one source of revenue, an ethical concern that may arise from the source or a legal concern about the impact on the organization's "charitableness".

Question E4 asks about the charity's fundraising methods using the "Yes" or "No" approach. In this case, fundraising does not include the activities dealt with in Questions E2 and E3, which are ones in which the charity regularly charged a fee or earned income. Question E4 covers 14 specific types of fundraising methods and requires the charity to identify any other methods used which were intended to raise funds. The list includes auctions, mail campaigns (including using e-mails), telephone solicitation, door-to-door canvassing, sales, collection boxes, advertisements, posters, flyers, and radio and TV commercials, telethons, anonymous donations and loose collections, bingos and casino nights, walk-a-thons and similar activities, draws and lotteries, fundraising dinners, galas and concerts, tournaments and sports events.

Interestingly, the break-down of the list seems to highlight some fundraising methods that are the subject of specific concern to the Agency or of information bulletins. For example, fundraising dinners and sports tournaments have been problematic in the past and are identified as separate methods of fundraising for reporting purposes. A number of these methods are difficult to audit and are sometimes open to accounting concerns. Again, the board of directors ought to review the list and determine for its own purposes whether or not there are any issues that it needs to address. For example, if a high proportion of its revenues comes from "loose collections", what measures are in place to ensure that all of the funds collected are forwarded?

Question E5 asks for the total amount raised from the fundraising methods for which the charity answered "Yes". The amount to be recorded is the gross amount, without any deductions for expenses. If the charity retained an outside fundraising professional, it must answer the questions in E6. An outside fundraiser is paid either on a commission basis or on a fee basis. The charity must identify which method was used to pay the outside fundraiser and the total amount paid to or retained by the fundraiser. There may be some concerns that arise from the method of payment and who controls the funds, especially if any receipts for income tax purposes are issued.

While commission-based fundraising is not illegal, it is generally considered to be disadvantageous to charities. There may be circumstances in which it is appropriate to use a commission-based fundraising method. If it is used, particular attention needs to be paid to the contract for services and who controls the funds and the information collected. Clear accountability and verifiability must be built into the contract to protect the charity.

The charity must also report on what its major fundraising method was. The Agency defines "main" to mean the method that earned the most revenue before expenses. It wants to know what the activity was and how often it took place. For example, bingo could take place on a regular basis (weekly) or on an occasional basis. The charity must also estimate the percentage of people who were unpaid volunteers working on behalf of the charity at the event. If a professional fundraiser was involved, the charity must report on the amount that the fundraiser received. Finally, it must record the net proceeds or loss from the activity.

Question E8 focusses on planned giving. Planned giving has become an important fundraising method, especially for larger or more established charities. The overall intention of planned giving is to maximize the amount of gifts to a charity while at the same time accommodating the financial and personal interests of the donor. The financial interests of the donor would include the donor's tax situation which may be an overarching purpose for planned giving — in addition, of course, to the desire to contribute towards the improvement of one's community.

In planned giving, the donor makes a deferred gift in order to obtain a receipt for income tax purposes but the charity will receive the property at a future date. The form asks about four traditional forms of planned giving — bequests, annuities, life insurance policies and residual interests or charitable remainder trusts. The Agency is interested to know if the charity has in place a planned giving program in which the charity provides advice to potential donors on how to participate.

Section F asks for information about remuneration and benefits paid by the charity. If the charity had employees who were fundraisers, as opposed to outside professional fundraisers who are independent contractors, it should include those employees in the information recorded in Section F.

Question F4 raises an odd issue for charities and fundraising. At common law and under the *Income Tax Act*, charities are to devote their assets to carrying out their charitable objects or purposes. A transfer of income or assets to another person is inconsistent with this fundamental legal principle. However, on occasion, as part of a fundraising campaign, the charity may provide token gifts of recognition to volunteers or to staff. If this type of gift is made, it should be reported as a "Yes" to the relevant question and an explanation should be provided in an attachment.

Section G requires further information about political activities. Normally, political activities and fundraising are not related and ought not to be related to each other. There may be occasions, though, in which a fundraising campaign has political overtones. A brochure may have several functions — informational and carrying out charitable activities, raising political awareness of an issue, and fundraising. Charities should take care to ensure that any brochures normally not fall into Section G as attempts to influence opinion, legislation or policy. If they do, the issue must fall within the charity's charitable objects (such as a Children's Aid

Society advocating improvements to child welfare legislation) and is incidental to its overall operations and activities. In addition, if a charity has a need to complete Section G, the Ontario *Lobbyist Registration Act, 1998*[124] and the federal *Lobbyist Registration Act*[125] may apply.

Section H requires a list of gifts that were made to qualified donees, including an associated charity. Associated charities are two or more charities where the Minister has designated them as associated.[126] The charities must have similar charitable objects, such as a hospital and a hospital foundation. If an amount is recorded in Section H as a gift to a qualified donee that is a charity, an equivalent amount should be recorded in the recipient charity's Charity Information Return in Section D for the fiscal year in which the gift is received. Similarly, if the charities decide to use the specified gift option, the amounts would be recorded in the Charity Information Returns for both the donating charity and the recipient charity.

Section I on expenditures on programs outside Canada. Normally, there would be no fundraising issues raised in Section I, which is concerned for the most part with the expenditure of funds by a registered charity on programs outside of Canada, either directly or through agents or by contract. Although it is conceivable that a charity may expend monies on programs outside Canada for fundraising purposes, it would be in very odd circumstances for which specific legal and accounting advice ought to be obtained prior to taking any steps to do so.

The Return is certified to be correct and complete in Section J. The individuals who sign must be satisfied that the information is accurate and complete and that they have made such enquiries as are necessary to be able to certify the Charity Information Return. They must also have authority to sign on behalf of the registered charity, either in the by-laws or by specific resolution of the board. In addition, if they identify concerns arising from the information, they may have a fiduciary duty to raise these concerns with staff and/or at the board level for clarification and resolution. The document is an essential part of the overall accountability scheme that is in place for registered charities and it should be considered as such. If there are lessons to be learned, there is a duty to do so.

The Charity Information Return includes three schedules which are not publicly available documents. Schedule A is a checklist, Schedule B is a statement of accumulated property and Schedule C is the form to calculate the disbursement quota.

---

[124] S.O. 1998, c. 27.
[125] R.S.C. 1985, (4th Supp.).
[126] See "Registered Charities: Application for Designation as Associated Charities", The Canada Customs and Revenue Agency, Form T3011 and Information Circular IC77-6, "Registered Charities Designation as Associated Charities" Canada Customs and Revenue Agency, April 18, 1977.

Schedule A is a list of 23 questions, some of which apply only to public or private foundations. The questions are mostly "yes" or "no" and are intended to identify if the charity did something wrong or is otherwise not in compliance with the *Income Tax Act* and its regulations. The "wrong" answer indicates that a problem exists and an explanation may be required. For example, Question 1 asks if the charity has made any changes to its governing documents that it has not previously reported to the Agency. If it has, it must answer "yes" and submit an official copy of the changes. Depending upon what changes were made, the organization's eligibility to be registered or its category as registration (organization, public foundation or private foundation) may be affected.

In some cases, the "wrong" answer may direct the charity to the proper way to do things. For example, Question 2 asks if the charity issued tax receipts only when it received gifts of property as opposed to contribution of services. As discussed above, a receipt for income tax purposes may not be issued for a contribution of services, although there are legitimate ways to pay for the services and then obtain a donation of an equivalent amount from the service provider. If the charity did issue a receipt for the contribution of the services rather than for the donation of an equivalent amount of money, the charity is referred to the guide which discusses this issue.

Several of the questions deal with the issue of receipts for income tax purposes — for what purposes were receipts used, when they were issued, and so forth. In other cases, the questions focus on particular areas of concern to the Agency where abuses could occur or where there is a higher risk of errors — for example, in fundraising dinners, tuition fees, business sponsorships and so forth. Two of the questions deals with specific types of donations (gift of cultural property and gift of ecological property) for which there are separate approval processes for any dispositions. Two other questions deal with charitable remainder trusts and non-qualifying securities, again, to ensure compliance with the specific requirements for those types of gifts.

There are also questions that deal with books and records. For example, if the charity had employees, did it issue T4 slips to those employees? Similarly, if it awarded scholarships, did it file a T4 summary and a T4A Supplementary for each payment? The charity is also asked about where it keeps its complete books and records in Canada and who prepared the Charity Information Return.

There are questions directed at public and private foundations which reflect some special compliance issues for them. For example, did the foundation acquire control of a corporation? Or has it incurred debts other than for current operating expenses for the purchase and sale of investments and for administering charitable programmes? In the case of a private foundation, did the foundation hold any shares, rights to hold shares or debts owing to it that were non-qualified investments?

Schedule B is a statement of property accumulated. A charity must have prior written approval from the Minister to accumulate property for purposes of the disbursement quota.

Schedule C involves the calculation of the disbursement quota for the charity. The disbursement quota is based upon the revenue for which a receipt for income tax purposes was issued in previous year and other prior years, if relevant. Registered charities must expend each year the disbursement quota or draw on previous years' disbursement excess.

(4) Not-for-Profit Information Return

Not-for-profit organizations that are not registered charities are also exempt from the payment of income tax, in most circumstances, under subs. 149(1) of the *Income Tax Act*. Because they are not registered charities, they have not historically been required to file an annual return with the Canada Customs and Revenue Agency. However, if the organization meets any of the following conditions, it must file a Not-for-Profit Information Return:

- the organization received or is entitled to receive dividends, interest, rentals, or royalties totalling more than $10,000 in the fiscal period,
- the total assets of the organization were more than $200,000 at the end of the immediately preceding fiscal period, or
- the organization filed a Not-for-Profit Information Return in the previous fiscal period. In effect, once the organization has filed its first return on the income or asset test basis, it must do so in future years.

An organization may also be required to file other returns, such as the T2 Corporation Income Tax Return or the T3 Trust Income Tax and Information Return, depending upon their operations and financial circumstances. A not-for-profit organization that is otherwise exempt under subs. 149(1) from paying income taxes may be required to pay income taxes on specific types of income — rental income, a deemed *inter vivos* trust or investment income are some examples.[127]

The form is similar in some ways to the Charity Information Return but requires substantially less information. Indeed, it is only two pages (plus attachments) as opposed to thirteen pages plus attachments for charities.

In Section A — Identification — the organization provides information about itself, name and address, Business Number and Trust (T3) Number, if any, type of organization, fiscal period and if the final return.

---

[127] See "Non-profit Organization — Taxation of Income From Property", Canada Customs and Revenue Agency, Interpretation Bulletin IT83R3 October 31, 1990.

There are ten different types of organizations — recreational or social, professional association, boards of trade or chambers of commerce, organizations operated for civic improvement, agricultural organizations, educational organizations, multicultural organizations, arts or cultural organizations, and other types.

In Section B — Amounts Received During the Fiscal Period — the form requires information in summary form about several types of revenue — membership dues, fees and assessments (line 100), grants and payments from federal, provincial or municipal governments (line 101), interest, taxable dividends, rentals and royalties received (line 102), proceeds of disposition of capital property (line 103), gross sales and revenues for organizational activities (line 104), gifts (line 105), and other receipts, which are to be specified (line 106).

On line 102, all receipts from interest, including on bank accounts, is to be included even if no information slip was provided. If the investment income was from non-arm's length transactions, it is also to be included. Dividends are to be reported whether from a corporation residing in Canada or residing outside of Canada. No deductions for expenses are to be deducted from the receipts from rental.

Royalties must be recorded regardless of the source — on intellectual property or from natural resources, from Canadian sources or foreign sources. Any foreign receipts are to be reported in Canadian funds using the exchange rate in effect when the funds were received. If capital property (real property, securities and works of art are typical examples) is disposed of by sale or otherwise, the proceeds must be reported. The proceeds may have been from the sale or from compensation for property that was damaged or destroyed. If the proceeds are not money, the fair market value of the proceeds should be reported.

Gross sales and revenues from organizational activities is recorded on line 104. This figure includes monies from programs, services and fundraising. No expenses are to be deducted from this figure. If the organization received gifts of any kind, including bequests or subject to a trust from any source (Canadian or foreign) it is to be reported on line 105. Any other receipts are reported on line 106 and must be specified.

In Section C — Statement of Assets and Liabilities at the End of the Fiscal Period — the organization must identify the method used to record its assets and liabilities — accrual or cash basis. The types of assets to be reported include cash and short-term investments (line 108), amounts receivable from members (line 109), amounts receivable from others (line 110), prepaid expenses (line 111), inventory (line 112), long-term investments (line 113), fixed assets (line 114) and other assets, which are to be specified (line 115). If the asset is depreciable, the book value (cost less accumulate depreciation) should be reported. Liabilities to be reported are amounts owing to members (line 117), amounts owing to others (line 118) and other liabilities, which are to be specified (line 119).

In Section D — Remuneration — the remuneration paid to employees and officers is to be reported on line 120. Remuneration includes salaries, commissions, bonuses and benefits for employees, directors' fees and other perquisites, such as housing loans. If the remuneration is paid to a member, as an employee or as a director, this information is to be reported on line 121. Other payments to members are reported on line 122. Section D also asks for the number of members and the number who received remuneration. This information is intended, no doubt, to make the assessment of whether or not the organization is, in law based on the facts, a non-profit organization under the *Income Tax Act*. If, in fact, the organization is distributing its assets or profits to its members, it may not be exempt from the payment of taxes under subsection 149(1).

In Section E — Organization's Activities — the organization must describe its activities both in Canada and any activities that are outside Canada.

In Section F — Location of Books and Records — the organization must provide the location where its books and records are maintained, and give the name of the contact person.

In Section G — Certification — one current officer of the organization must certify that the information given in the Non-profit Information Return is complete and correct.

(5) Conclusion

Charitable and not-for-profit organizations benefit from a number of privileges that others in society do not have. These privileges are provided as part of an overall package — in return for the privileges, society expects charities and not-for-profit organizations to carry out their objects. Charities receive a greater level of privilege, including the ability to issue receipts for income tax purposes, because of the greater social benefit that accrues.

Privileges, though, come with a price. That price is a requirement that the charities and not-for-profit organizations be accountable to their members, donors, regulators, the courts and the public. Accountability starts with, but does not end with, financial accountability. Organizations are also accountable for the quality and relevance of their programs. However, without financial accountability, the other levels of accountability are not likely to be achieved. Given that an organization must raise funds first, before it can spend them, financial accountability in fundraising is necessarily an important function of the board of directors of any organization — from both a legal and an ethical perspective.

D FUNDAMENTAL CHANGES

I Trusts

A trust document may be amended by the trustees if the document includes a provision permitting the trustees to do so. The provision would be read narrowly to ensure that the intention of the settlors of the trust were complied with by the trustees. Where the document does not include an ability of the trustee to make amendments to the terms of the trust, the trustees of a charitable trust may make an application for *cy-pres* to the Ontario Superior Court of Justice under the *Trustee Act*[128] and R. 14.05 of the *Rules of Civil Procedure* to change the terms of the trust.

An application for *cy-pres* may be granted where the original purposes of the trust can no longer be met and an order to change the terms is appropriate. The court will apply the trust funds for other purposes that are as near as possible to the original purposes. The doctrine applies to all charitable trusts, whether held by trustees or by charitable organizations and is discussed in more detail in Chapter 9, "Supervision of Charitable Organizations".

A variation in the trust may also be possible under the *Variation of Trusts Act*.[129] The trustee may also apply for the opinion, advice or direction of the court under s. 60 of the *Trustee Act* with respect to the management or administration of the trust property.

II UNINCORPORATED ASSOCIATIONS

An unincorporated association and the relationship among its members are contractual in nature. Absent an amending clause in the memorandum of association, any changes must be agreed to by all of the members. If the association has also established by-laws or rules, those by-laws or rules can normally be amended using the same procedure for their establishment. For example, if the memorandum of association authorizes the directors to establish rules governing the affairs of the association, the directors could amend those rules.

III CORPORATIONS AND CO-OPERATIVE CORPORATIONS WITHOUT SHARE CAPITAL

(1) General Comments

The most common changes to a corporation without share capital are amendments to the by-laws, application for supplementary letters patent, application for amalgamation and application to dissolve the corporation. The procedures for amending the by-laws have been dealt with in Chapter 4, "The Organization in Operation: Organizational By-Laws and Statutory Requirements". This section will deal with amendments by supplementary letters patent, dissolution and amalgamation.

The Public Guardian and Trustee's approval is required for any changes to the objects of a charitable corporation. If the revised objects for a not-for-profit corporation are charitable in nature, it may be neces-

---

[128] R.S.O. 1990, c. T.23. See D.W.M. Waters, *Law of Trusts in Canada*, 2nd ed. (Toronto: Carswell, Thomson Professional Publishing, 1984), at 611–32.

[129] R.S.O. 1990, c. V.1. See also Waters, *supra*, note 128, at 1055-86.

sary to advise the Public Guardian and Trustee pursuant to the *Charities Accounting Act*. If the charitable corporation is registered as a charitable organization under the *Income Tax Act*, the Canada Customs and Revenue Agency's approval will be required. A change to the objects may also require an application for *cy-pres*.

(2) Ontario Corporations without Share Capital

(a) Supplementary Letters Patent

A corporation without share capital may apply under subs. 131(1) of the Ontario *Corporations Act* for supplementary letters patent for the following purposes:

- extending, limiting or otherwise varying its objects;
- changing its name;
- varying any provision in its letters patent or prior supplementary letters patent;
- providing for any matter or thing in respect of which provision may be made in letters patent under the Act;
- converting it into a company;
- converting it into a corporation with or without share capital.

An application is made to the Lieutenant Governor and the issuance of the supplementary letters patent is discretionary. An application must be authorized by a special resolution,[130] with the exception of conversion. Any application for conversion, however, must be authorized by a resolution of the board of directors and confirmed by the members. Under subs. 131(3), the confirmation must be confirmed in writing by 100 per cent of the members or, at least 95 per cent of the members where a 21-day notice of the application was sent to the members and none dissented in writing to the corporation. The application must be made within six months of the confirmation of the resolution by the members. The application must include information required in subs. 131(4) of the Act with respect to any shares where the corporation is being converted into a company. The Act was also amended in 1994 to permit a corporation without share capital to apply to the Minister of Finance to be continued as a co-operative corporation.[131]

An application for supplementary letters patent must be made in the prescribed form (Form 3).[132] The application requires information about the corporation (name, Ontario corporation number, date of incorporation), the date that the members confirmed the resolution authorizing

---

[130] R.S.O. 1990, c. C.38, subs. 131(2).
[131] Section 313.1 [as am. S.O. 1994, c. 17, s. 31].
[132] O. Reg. 181/90, subs. 19(1).

the application and what the supplementary letters patent are to provide. The application must be in duplicate.

If the application is to change the name of the corporation, the application must include a statement that the corporation is not insolvent within the meaning of subs. 19(4) of the Regulations.[133] A corporation is insolvent where its liabilities exceed the realizable value of its assets or if it is unable to pay its debts as they become due.

(b) Dissolution

A corporation without share capital may be dissolved by the Minister or the Lieutenant Governor, be wound up under the Act or, it may apply to surrender its charter. The Lieutenant Governor may terminate a corporation in several situations:

- where the corporation does not go into actual operation within two years after incorporation or for any two consecutive years does not use its corporate powers;[134]
- where the Minister is satisfied that a social club is operating an illegal common gaming house, has prevented inspection by police or fire officers, or has fitted the premises for gaming.[135] Prior to 1993, the regulations under the Act required that social clubs include "bars and bolts" provisions in the letters patent. Although newly incorporated social clubs do not require these provisions, they continue to apply to those corporations that have them in their letters patent and provide an additional ground for dissolution by the Minister;
- where a corporation has fewer than three members and, after notice has been provided, refuses or neglects to bring the number to three;[136]
- where sufficient cause is shown.[137] The Minister may authorize any officer of the Ministry to conduct an inquiry to determine if there is sufficient cause; and
- where a corporation has failed to make a filing required under the *Corporations Information Act*[138] and the corporation has been pro-

---

[133] *Ibid.*, subs. 19(2).
[134] R.S.O. 1990, c. C.38, subs. 315(1).
[135] *Ibid.*, s. 316.
[136] *Ibid.*, subs. 311(3).
[137] *Ibid.*, s. 317.
[138] R.S.O. 1990, c. C.39.

vided 90-days' notice to do so by registered mail or in *The Ontario Gazette*.[139]

A corporation may also be dissolved voluntarily by application to surrender the letters patent. The Lieutenant Governor may accept a surrender under s. 319 of the Act where he or she is satisfied that:

- the surrender has been authorized by a majority of the votes cast at a meeting called for that purpose or by such other vote as the letters patent or supplementary letters patent provide or by the consent in writing of all of the members entitled to vote at such a meeting;
- the corporation has no debts, obligations or liabilities, or its debts, obligations or liabilities have been provided for or protected, or the creditors or other persons having interests in its debts, obligations or liabilities have consented. Where a creditor or its location is unknown, the corporation may pay to the Public Guardian and Trustee an amount equal to the debt to be held in trust for the creditor by the Public Guardian and Trustee pursuant to subs. 319(4) of the Act. The Public Guardian and Trustee may also hold in trust any member's property under subs. 319(3) of the Act;
- there are no proceedings pending in any court against it;
- any remaining property has been distributed in accordance with its letters patent or supplementary letters patent or to its members rateably if there is no provision in the letters patent or supplementary letters patent. If the corporation is a charitable corporation, the remaining property must be distributed to another charitable organization; and
- notice of its intention to surrender its charter has been published in *The Ontario Gazette* and once in a newspaper published at or near the place in which the head office is located.

The application must be made in the prescribed form (Form 9) and shall include the letters patent and supplementary letters patent. If the letters patent or supplementary letters patent are lost or cannot be located, an affidavit of an officer or director to that effect must be filed with an undertaking to return them if they are located.[140] If any property is being held in trust by the Public Guardian and Trustee for a member or for a creditor, the application should include a statement setting out that information.[141]

---

[139] R.S.O. 1990, c. 38, subs. 317(9).
[140] O. Reg. 181/90, s. 23.
[141] *Ibid.*, subs. 23(3).

If the Lieutenant Governor accepts the surrender, he or she declares the corporation to be dissolved on a date to be set in the order. If the corporation is a charitable corporation, the Public Guardian and Trustee must consent to the dissolution.

A corporation may also be wound up under s. 230 of the Act or by order of the court. Part VI of the Act provides for the procedures for a corporation to do so voluntarily or by order of the court, for the appointment of inspectors and of a liquidator, and for the distribution of the property. Although the winding up provisions do not appear to be used very often, they are useful where the members of a not-for-profit corporation cannot agree on how to disburse the remaining property or where a deadlock has ensued.[142]

In cases where the corporation has been dissolved by the surrender of the charter or by the Lieutenant Governor, the Act does provide for the continuation of certain powers, for the revival of the corporation in certain circumstances and under specified conditions, and for legal proceedings to be initiated or continued.

If a corporation is to be revived under subs. 317(10) of the Act, the application must be made in the prescribed form (Form 10). The Act was amended in 1994 to remove the previous five-year limitation for revival.[143]

(c)   Amalgamation

Amalgamation is a process by which two or more corporations are reconstituted into one legal entity. Under the law, the amalgamating corporations "continue as one" corporate entity. Under subs. 113(1) of the Act, the corporations must have the same or similar objects to be amalgamated.

Although amalgamation is not a common change for corporations without share capital, it does occur and may be useful in certain circumstances. First, it provides a legal sanction to the combination of the operations of two or more corporations. Second, it permits the amalgamated corporation to retain the assets of the amalgamating corporations. Third, it can allow for a more efficient and effective operational structure for organizations that are associated with each other. Once the amalgamation is approved, the amalgamated corporation possesses all the property, rights, privileges and franchises and is subject to all liabilities, contracts, disabilities and debts of each of the amalgamating corporations. As a result, if one of the corporations has a particularly beneficial asset that cannot be assigned to another corporation, an amalgamated corporation would retain that asset.

Subsection 113(2) of the Act requires the amalgamating corporations to enter into an Amalgamation Agreement. That agreement sets out the

---

[142] *Kay v. Nipissing Twin Lakes Rod & Gun Club* (1993), 7 B.L.R. (2d) 225 (Ont. Gen. Div.).
[143] Subsection 317(10) [am. S.O. 1995, c. 27, subs. 78(11)].

terms and conditions of amalgamation, the mode of amalgamation, the name of the amalgamated corporation, the names, callings and residences of the first directors and how and when subsequent directors are to be elected. The Agreement must also include any other details that are necessary to perfect the amalgamation and to provide for the subsequent management and working of the amalgamated corporation.

The Agreement must be submitted to the members at a general meeting called for the purpose of considering the Agreement. It must be approved of by two thirds of the votes cast by members at that meeting. The secretaries of each amalgamating corporation certify that the Agreement was adopted by the members of the amalgamating corporations. Once the Agreement is adopted by the members of all the amalgamating corporations, the amalgamating corporations jointly apply to the Lieutenant Governor for letters patent confirming the Agreement and amalgamating the corporations.

(3) Ontario Co-operative Corporations without Share Capital

(a) Amendments to the Articles of Incorporation

A co-operative corporation may amend its articles of incorporation under ss. 151 to 155 of the *Co-operative Corporations Act*.[144] The amendments may be used to change its name, vary its objects, increase or decrease a membership fee or the minimum amount of member loans, delete or vary any provision in the articles or provide for any other matter or thing that could be in the articles or in the by-laws under the Act. The members must approve of the changes by resolution passed at a meeting called for that purpose.

The articles may also be amended under subs. 151(1) to convert the co-operative without share capital into a co-operative with share capital or vice versa, into a business corporation or into a corporation without share capital. Any amendment that is intended to convert the co-operative must also be confirmed in writing by at least 60 per cent of the members.[145] A not-for-profit housing co-operative cannot, however, convert itself into a co-operative with share capital, business corporation or corporation without share capital. Under subs. 151(5), it also cannot amend its articles to do anything that would result in it no longer being a not-for-profit housing co-operative.

The application for amendment to the articles must be made in Form 7 within six months of the members' resolution. The application is made in duplicate and includes an affidavit setting out the name of the co-operative, certified copy of the resolution and the date of confirmation of the resolution. If the name is being changed, evidence that the co-

---

[144] R.S.O. 1990, c. C.35.
[145] But see s. 152 which permits the Minister to convert the co-operative into a business corporation with only the special resolution being adopted.

operative is not insolvent must also be submitted. Under s. 155, the co-operative may also apply to have the articles restated.

(b) Dissolution

The members of a co-operative may voluntarily dissolve the co-operative under s. 163 of the Act. A majority of the members have to vote for a resolution to dissolve the co-operative at a meeting called for that purpose. The co-operative may also be dissolved if all the members consent to it in writing. If the co-operative has been incorporated for less than two years and has not undertaken any business or accepted members' fees or loans, a majority of the incorporators may authorize the dissolution.

Section 164 sets out the type of information that must be provided in the application for dissolution. This information is similar to that required to dissolve a corporation without share capital. The information is intended to ensure that the debts and liabilities of the co-operative are provided for and that the remaining assets will be distributed in accordance with its Articles of Incorporation. A not-for-profit housing co-operative may not distribute any of the property to its members on dissolution, other than to repay members' loans and pay any patronage returns. It must distribute the remaining property, in accordance with its articles, to one or more other not-for-profit housing co-operatives or charitable organizations.

Sections 190 to 220 and 222 to 236 of the Ontario *Business Corporations Act*[146] apply to co-operative corporations. Those sections provide for the winding up of a corporation.

(c) Amalgamation

Two or more co-operative corporations may be amalgamated under s. 156 of the Act. That section requires that the amalgamating co-operatives enter into an Amalgamation Agreement which is approved of by the members of each co-operative by special resolution. The documentation, process and legal results of amalgamation under the Act are similar to those for corporations without share capital. Under subss. 156(7) and (8), not-for-profit housing co-operatives may amalgamate only with other not-for-profit housing co-operatives.

(4) Federal Corporations without Share Capital

(a) Supplementary Letters Patent

Subsection 20(1) of the *Canada Corporations Act*[147] permits a corporation to apply for supplementary letters patent to extend the objects of the

---

[146] R.S.O. 1990, c. B.16.

corporation to such further or other objects for which a corporation may be incorporated under Part III of the Act or to reduce, limit, amend or vary the objects or powers of the corporation or any provisions of the letters patent or supplementary letters patent. The members must authorize the application by a by-law sanctioned by two thirds of the votes cast at a special meeting called for that purpose. The application must be made within six months of the sanctioning by the members.[148] A similar application to change the corporate name may be made under s. 29 of the Act.

The corporation must satisfy the Minister that the by-law has been passed, which is usually done by affidavit or statutory declaration.[149] Once the Minister is satisfied, the Minister has discretion to issue the supplementary letters patent. Notice of the changes are to be published in *The Canada Gazette*.[150]

The application for supplementary letters patent includes the following documents:[151]

- an application document prescribed by Industry Canada;
- an affidavit or statutory declaration of an officer stating that the required by-law was passed on the specified date by the directors and members;
- two certified copies of the by-law, which must be less than six months old except in the case of a name change;
- the $50 filing fee, except where the purpose of the change is to add an English or French version to the name;
- if a name change, a Canada-biased NUANS name search report not more than 90 days old or a $15 filing fee for each name search; and
- a covering letter.

(b)   Dissolution

A corporation's charter is forfeited under subs. 31(1) of the Act if it does not go into actual *bona fide* operation within three years of incorporation or for three consecutive years does not use its corporate powers. The Attorney General may apply to the court for an order winding up a corporation under s. 5.6 of the Act where it:

- carries on business that is not within the scope of the objects set forth in the letters patent or supplementary letters patent;

---

[147] R.S.C. 1970, c. C.32.
[148] *Ibid.*, subs. 20(3).
[149] *Ibid.*, subs. 20(4).
[150] *Ibid.*, subs. 20(5).
[151] "Information Kit on the Creation of Non-profit Corporations", Industry Canada, November 25, 1999.

- exercises or professes to exercise any powers that are not truly ancillary or reasonably incidental to the objects set forth in the letters patent or supplementary letters patent; or
- exercises or professes to exercise any powers expressly excluded by its letters patent or supplementary letters patent.

The costs of the winding up are to be paid by the corporation or by any directors who personally participated or acquiesced in the corporation acting outside its letters patent or supplementary letters patent.

The corporation may also be dissolved if it fails to file its annual returns for two consecutive years, as required by s. 133 of the Act. The Minister may, under subs. 133(9), provide one-year's notice to a corporation that where it has not filed for two consecutive years an order for dissolution will be issued unless the annual returns are filed.

The Attorney General may also apply under s. 150 of the Act for an order to wind up the corporation. The application may be made under the federal *Winding-Up Act*[152] where the corporation has not held an annual meeting for two or more consecutive years, fails to comply with s. 128 of the Act or defaults for more than six months to file an annual return under s. 133 of the Act. Any costs for the application are to be paid by the corporation or the directors who were responsible for the corporation's failures or defaults.

The corporation may also apply to surrender its charter under s. 32 of the Act. It may do so where it has satisfied the Minister that:

- it has no assets and that, if it had any assets immediately prior to the application, the assets have been divided rateably among its members after the payment of any debts, liabilities or other obligations or where they have been provided for and protected and where the corporation is a charitable corporation, the remaining assets have been properly disbursed; and
- the corporation has given notice of the application in *The Canada Gazette* and in a newspaper published at or near the location of its head office.

The Minister may direct that the charter be cancelled and on the date fixed the corporation is dissolved.[153]

The application for dissolution should include the following documents:[154]

- an application as prescribed by Industry Canada;

---

[152] R.S.C. 1985, c. W.11.
[153] R.S.C. 1970, c. C.32, subs. 32(3).
[154] "Information Kit on the Creation of Non-profit Corporations", Industry Canada, November 25, 1999.

- a certified copy of the by-law or resolution authorizing the surrender of the charter, including the date that it was passed by the members;
- a certificate or statement of an officer of the corporation attesting that the by-law or resolution was passed by the members;
- an affidavit or statutory declaration of an officer certifying that the facts in the application are true;
- a statement by an officer certifying that the corporation has no assets and no debts, liabilities or other obligations. If any assets were remaining after the payment of any debts, liabilities or other obligations, the statement should indicate that those assets were divided rateably among the members or distributed among other corporations in Canada having the same or similar objects. If the corporation was a charitable corporation, the remaining assets are to be distributed among charitable organizations;
- the original letters patent and supplementary letters patent or, if lost, an affidavit or statutory declaration stating that they have been lost; and
- a copy of the newspaper and *The Canada Gazette* publication, including the date of publication.

Members remain jointly and severally liable to any debtors for one year after dissolution.[155]

(c) Amalgamation

There are no provisions in the Act for the amalgamation of two or more corporations without share capital.

IV ORGANIZATIONAL STRUCTURAL CHANGE

(1) General Comments

The directors should periodically undertake a holistic review of the organization's structure. A comprehensive review may also be triggered by the organization embarking on a new and significant activity or venture, when there are organizational or financial problems or issues, and when strategic alliances are proposed. The intention is to ensure that the assets of the organization, especially for charitable organizations, are being used in the most effective and efficient manner and that risks are managed in an appropriate manner. Appropriate structures can influence and even dictate the success of meeting these organizational objectives.

---

[155] R.S.C. 1970, c. C.32, s. 33.

An organizational structural review may be limited to the organization itself and how to achieve these objectives through better by-laws, amendments to the letters patent and similar changes that are discussed above. It could involve a broader approach that relates to the organization to others of like mind or interests in their community, across Canada or throughout the world. The review could, therefore, be fundamental in the sense that it results in a significant change for the organization.

The board will want to consider a number of factors for any organizational structure:

- what options exist that would improve the efficiency of the use of the assets
- what options exist that would make the organization and its programs more effective in fulfilling the organization's mandate
- how best to protect the assets held by the organization, including its intangible assets such as good will and its reputation
- how best to minimize risks, manage the risks and minimize liability
- what opportunities exist for expansion
- what opportunities exist to coordinate efforts and to cooperate with other organizations.

There may also be a dichotomy or balancing of "control" and who will have control over the assets and operations with "liabilities" and how to minimize existing or potential liabilities.

(2) Structural Options for National Organizations

(a) Overview

Fundamental to establishing a multiple national structure is the concept that a not-for-profit organization does not permit equity ownership and therefore cannot be controlled through the usual means of share ownership.[156] With a profit making share capital corporation, effective control can be maintained over a multiple corporate structure by the parent corporation owning a majority of the shares in subsidiary corporations. Variations on this relationship can involve a parent/subsidiary corporate model or a holding/operating company model. However, with a not-for-profit corporation, there are no shares that can be bought or sold and

---

[156] This portion of the chapter is based on a paper by T.S. Carter, "National and International Charitable Structures: Achieving Protection and Control" in *Fit to be Tithed 2*, (Toronto: Law Society of Upper Canada, 1998). The materials were edited and reproduced with permission of the author.

therefore no ability to control the corporation through the means of equity ownership.

Instead of having shareholders or owners, a not-for-profit corporation has only members, whether the corporation is incorporated at the federal level in accordance with the *Canada Corporations Act*[157] or at the provincial level in accordance with applicable provincial legislation, such as the Ontario *Corporations Act*.[158] However, corporate members are not the owners of the not-for-profit corporation or its assets. Instead, a not-for-profit corporation has no legal owner, equitable or otherwise, except itself. It is its own self contained legal person that cannot be bought or sold. As there is no ability to "own" a not-for-profit corporation in the normal meaning, it is essential that there be effective mechanisms implemented to control member organizations by establishing either integrated corporate structures or expedient contractual relationships.

The characteristic that is common to all national organizations is that their operations extend beyond the boundaries of only one province. It can do so through one of two options:

- Chapter Model

   The chapter model involves one legal entity acting as a single organization across Canada, normally involving multiple divisions at either the provincial level, the regional level, or at the local level. Those divisions are often referred to as chapters or branches. However, none of the chapters or branches are themselves separate legal entities. Instead the chapters or branches are a part of a single monolith legal entity. In some cases, such as registered Canadian amateur athletic associations, this approach may be required for income tax purposes.[159]

- Association Model

   The association model involves multiple legal entities, as opposed to only one corporation, that are organized at various levels, such as incorporated provincial associations or incorporated local organizations. The association model will have a governing body, normally established as a federal corporation, to act as the umbrella body over its member organizations, whether those members are corporations or unincorporated associations. An example would be local churches of a large national denomination. A member organization will nor-

---

[157] R.S.C. 1970, c. C.32.
[158] R.S.O. 1990, c. C.38.
[159] See A.B. Drache, *Canadian Taxation of Charities and Donations*, (Toronto: Carswell, 1996) at 10 to 12 for a discussion of this issue.

mally have either a name or charitable purpose that is similar to that of the governing national association.

Although it is not difficult to draw a distinction in practice between the chapter model involving a single corporation and the association model involving multiple corporate entities, distinguishing between the two in practice is not always as easy. In fact, some national organizations currently operate without knowing whether they are a single corporation operating through local chapters or an association made up of separately incorporated members. A national organization that does not know whether it is organized as an association model or a chapter model will often perpetuate the confusion by encouraging local organizations to apply to become a chapter while at the same time creating a functional dichotomy by permitting or encouraging member organizations to be separately incorporated.

Even when it is clear that member organizations need to be separately incorporated as part of an association model, it may not be evident how those member organizations are to relate to the larger national structure. This is often the case with religious denominations that have seminaries, bible colleges, camps, or other related ministries that are expected to operate functionally "in sync" with the national denomination but without any corporate or contractual documentation in place to set out that relationship.

Significant problems can arise. For example, the board of directors of a member organization may strongly disagree with the direction being determined by the national board. The national board may be surprised to find that it has no legal means to stop the board of directors of the member organization from adopting a policy or course of action that was totally contrary to what was acceptable at the national level. When this happens, it will normally be too late to do anything about the lack of control over the renegade organization. The time to do something to avoid the loss of control is before the disputes arise with a member organization by developing and implementing an effective structural plan.

The most significant benefit of the chapter model is that by requiring only one corporation, it is much easier to maintain a higher degree of control over chapters or branches without the necessity of contract or licence agreements that are otherwise required with the association model. In addition, by utilizing only one corporation to carry on operations on a national basis, there is generally more symmetry and coherency over day-to-day operations and control of personnel.

A chapter model also does not run the risk of losing its assets, goodwill, donor base, or trade-marks to a "renegade" member organization, since legally everything is owned by the single national corporation. A chapter or branch would have no legal right to take any assets on its own if it was to leave the national organization.

The most fundamental problem inherent in the chapter model is that by having only one corporation, the liabilities that occur in the operations of one chapter will expose all of the assets of the national organization to claims arising out of activities of that one chapter even though other chapters may have had nothing to do with the incident in question. Similarly, even if the incident involves a national program involving all chapters, there is no ability to protect specific assets of the national organization, since all assets are owned by the national organization.

Even if the national organization was to set up individual charitable trusts to fund specific programs, the assets contained in those charitable trusts could still be subject to claims by those who were able to establish a causal connection between the trust fund and the incident that allegedly led to the injury or abuse that they had suffered.[160] Given the increased exposure to liability faced by charities arising out of claims associated with sexual abuse, every national organization that is currently organized on a chapter model should carefully review whether or not it can afford, from a risk management context, to remain as a single legal entity. For national charitable organizations that have programs involving low exposure to liability there will understandably be less reason to change from a chapter model structure.

(b)   Association Model

There are a number of advantages in utilizing the association model over that of the chapter model. The primary benefit is that of reduced liability exposure for the organization by containing the liability attributable to each member organization within a separate corporate entity so that the claims made against a member organization do not effect the assets of other member organizations or that of the governing body. In the event that one member organization owns real estate that is subject to toxic contamination, the cost associated with the clean-up of the contamination will generally be limited to the incorporated member organization as opposed to affecting the assets of other member organizations or of the governing body of the national association.

If a member charitable organization was to become involved in activities that resulted in its deregistration as a registered charity with the Canada Customs and Revenue Agency, only the charitable status of that member organization would be at risk instead of the charitable status of other member organizations or the national association itself. For national charitable organizations that carry on operations in Ontario, the creation of a separate charitable corporation in Ontario to oversee On-

---

[160] The Ontario Court of Appeal decision in *Re Christian Brothers of Ireland in Canada*, (2000), 47 O.R. (3d) 674, leave to appeal to Supreme Court of Canada denied, may have extended the potential liability by eliminating even the need for a causal connection. However, the full impact of this decision is difficult to discern and, arguably, it may be limited to situations in which the corporation is being wound-up due to insolvency. Further case law will be necessary to determine how far the Court of Appeal's decision goes.

tario activities would mean that the jurisdiction of the Public Guardian and Trustee in Ontario would generally be limited to only the assets of the Ontario charitable organization instead of affecting those of the national association or member organizations in other provinces.

Another benefit of establishing a separate corporation in Ontario is that the operations of the national organization that are carried on outside the province of Ontario through separate corporations in other provinces would not be subject to the provisions of the *Charities Accounting Act*.[161] Subsection 6(8), for example, permits an individual to apply for an *ex parte* order to require a public inquiry by the Office of the Public Guardian and Trustees in the event of complaints concerning the solicitation of funds and the manner in which those funds are utilized. Similarly, a national organization may be able to avoid the investment power provisions in the *Trustee Act*.[162]

There are several disadvantages with the association model. The most obvious problem is that a governing body can easily lose control over its separately incorporated member organizations if appropriate steps are not implemented to ensure that the member organizations are subject to appropriate contractual and/or licensing control mechanisms. Often a member organization will need to utilize the name or trade-marks of the national association. However, if the name and/or logos of the national association have not been protected by obtaining trade-mark registration, or the usage of the trade-marks by member organizations is not properly documented through trade-mark licence agreements, then the ability of the national organization to protect and enforce its trade-mark rights may be seriously prejudiced due to unintentional infringement of trade-marks by member organizations as well as others.

If the member organizations have names that are similar to that of their national associations, there is frequently confusion that occurs in gifts given to the wrong charitable organization, particularly where testamentary gifts fail to properly describe whether the national association or the member organization is the intended beneficiary. This confusion could result in the estate having to apply for a *cy-pres* court application to determine which charitable organization is legally entitled to the testamentary gift.

Effective utilization of the association model requires the creation of multiple corporations and the implementation of numerous and sometimes complex control provisions. The complexity in the relationship could result in serious confusion unless the control mechanisms are carefully crafted and consistently applied. Failure to take appropriate steps in this regard could result in a state of confusion that might be even more problematic than the liability risks associated with the chapter model.

---

[161] R.S.O. 1990, c. C.10.
[162] R.S.O. 1990, c. T.23.

Since each member organization within a national association will be a separate legal entity, it is essential that the matter of control over those member organizations be carefully addressed and that it be done in the early planning stages in the creation of a national association or during restructuring. Once member organizations have been created and are operational, it is generally very difficult for the national association to "rewrite the rules" and require that member organizations relinquish some measure of control back to the governing body. The national governing association will have little ability to exercise control over member organizations unless those organizations have agreed to operate under the control of the governing association by either amending the internal corporate documents of the member organization or entering into appropriate contractual or licence arrangements.

A frequently used method of indirectly controlling member organizations is through *ex officio* directors. The by-laws of the member organization would provide for *ex officio* directors who are either directors of the national governing board or alternatively hold officer positions in the national governing board created for the specific purpose of allowing those individuals to become qualified to sit as national representatives on the board of the member organization. Although the utilization of *ex officio* directors is an effective means of maintaining control, it should not be relied upon as the only means of doing so. It does not encompass contractual relationships that can articulate the expectations between a governing association and its member organizations or licensing considerations involving intellectual property. Furthermore, *ex officio* directors will owe a duty to act in the best interests of the corporation to which they are directors, which may create conflicts with their duties to the national organization.

A second approach is the "franchise" model. A parallel can be drawn between the relationship of a franchisor and its franchisees and the relationship between a national governing association and its member organizations. Just as a national governing association cannot control member organizations by owning the "shares" or other equity interest of a member organization, a franchisor, in a business context, is not the owner of shares in the franchisee corporation. As such, the franchisor must establish an alternative means of control over the franchisee. This is done through the contractual relationship of a franchise agreement.

The governing body of the national association can establish an effective contractual relationship between the governing association and its member organizations involving key factors, such as what are the requirements of membership in the association and the consequences of losing that membership. It can authorize the licensing of trade-marks and copyrights of the national organization. *Ex officio* directors and a franchise approach can be used to complement each other or be used independently, depending upon the circumstances.

The basic components involve:

- an effective association agreement,
- the inclusion of appropriate control provisions within the incorporating documents of member organizations, and
- the implementation of a licensing arrangement to deal with intellectual property.

The ability to enforce the various agreements and arrangements is central to this approach. Unless they can be enforced effectively and in a timely manner, they will not yield the necessary control over critical matters.

A national organization that is currently structured as a single legal entity based on the chapter model may at some point in the future decide to convert its operating structure to that of the association model.

The process of restructuring is decentralization because it involves a decentralization of a single national organization in favour of multiple separately incorporated members.

The process of decentralization is complicated by numerous legal factors. These include the following:

- if the member organization is to receive a transfer of assets from the national governing association, then those assets need to be set out in a bill of sale or other form of transfer agreement. In the case of a charitable organization, a transfer to a member organization presupposes that the member organization is already registered as a charitable organization, either because it previously obtained charitable status as an "associate" of the parent charity, or has applied and received separate charitable status when the member organization initially became incorporated
- if the property being transferred consists of real property, then a title search will need to be completed to determine if there are any restrictive trusts attached to the deed for the property being purchased that need to be complied with as part of the transfer. Restrictions in this regard could include a requirement that the church property only be used in accordance with a particular statement of faith or religious practice. If there are restrictive trusts, then the transferee organization, such as a local church, would need at the very least to agree in writing to comply with the terms of the restricted trust set out in the title documentation for the property
- when donor restricted trust funds are being transferred, such as when an estate endowment fund states that is to be used for a particular local purpose, the investment powers that apply to those funds will need to be identified and complied with by the transferee member organization. In addition, the transfer of do-

nor restricted special purpose trust funds will generally require court authorization for a change of trustees or in accordance, in Ontario, with the *Charities Accounting Act*
- if the transfer of assets involves real property that may be subject to toxic contamination, as may occur from a leaking underground oil tank, the transfer of real property should not take place until an environmental audit has been conducted and the directors of the transferee member organization have acknowledged in writing that they understand their potential exposure to personal liability arising out of the transfer of the property in the event that the property is subsequently found to contain contaminated materials
- if the transfer of real property to a member organization is to be subject to a reversionary interest in favour of the national governing association, then the deed to the member organization would need to include an appropriate provision to establish a reversionary interest
- if there are liabilities that the transferee member organization is to assume as part payment for the assets being received, such as the assumption of an outstanding mortgage or unsecured debts, such as bonds or promissary notes, then there should be a clear description of what those liabilities are together with the consent of the creditors or secured party, if necessary.

A fundamental reason for the association model is to limit liability within a single corporate entity. While the concept of limited liability protection is still the general rule for corporate entities, whether the corporation is in the form of a share capital or a corporation without share capital, there are a few instances where the governing body of a national association might be found to be liable for the actions of a member organization.

The law is not very clear on when the court will "pierce the corporate veil". In *Transamerica Life Insurance Company of Canada v. Canada Life Assurance Company*,[163] the court held that it is difficult to define precisely when the corporate veil can be lifted but that the lack of a precise test does not mean that a court is free to act as it pleases on some loosely defined "just and equitable" standard. In that case, the court went on to state that the separate legal personality of a corporate entity will only be discarded when it is completely dominated, controlled and used for fraudulent or improper conduct. "Complete control" involves more than ownership. It must be shown that there is complete domination and that the subsidiary company does not, in fact, function independently of the other corporation.

---

[163] (1996), 28 O.R. (3d) 423 (Gen. Div.).

Although the context of this case was a business corporation one, it does provide some guidance for an association model approach. The board of directors of both the national governing association and the member organization should avoid circumstances that might lead to allegations of complete domination and control by the governing association over the operations of the member organization. Some of the factors suggesting "central control" are:

- common bank accounts or investments shared between the national governing association and the member organization
- explicit or implicit representation that the national governing association is responsible for the operations of the member organization
- both organizations occupying the same location for either operational or administrative activities
- using the same officers or employees unless there is documentary evidence establishing that one organization is invoicing the other organization for the services provided by the employees of the other organization
- having either the national governing association or member organization use the land, buildings or property of the other organization
- having the executive director of the member organization act on the direction and in the interest of the national governing association
- failing to observe the legal formal requirements of the member organization in its operations and direction
- having the same individuals serving on the board of directors or key committees of both the national governing association and member organization
- indicating directly or indirectly on letterhead, signs, brochures or other documentation that the member organization is an operating division of the national governing association
- having the governing body pay the salary and other expenses or losses of the member organization
- having the national governing association and member organization use the same lawyers or accountants on a regular basis
- failing to have loans from the national governing association to the member organization properly documented and formalized through proper corporate formalities and authorization by board resolutions.

This list of factors is not intended to suggest that there cannot be some similarity in operations or some overlapping in control between a national governing association and a member organization. However, it is essential that the board members and key executive officers of both the national governing association and the member organizations understand that both organizations must operate as separate and distinct charitable corporations and, as such, must respect the autonomy and internal integrity of each organization.

(c)   Chapter Model

When a chapter or branch is established, it operates as a division of the national organization instead of having created a new legal entity. However, often the members of the local chapter or branch do not understand that their establishment is simply an extension of the national organization and that the branch or chapter does not have a separate existence outside of the national organization.

To clarify the relationship and to provide certainty concerning the establishment, operations and expectations of a chapter or branch, it is important that the national organization ensure that an appropriate agreement, usually referred to as a chapter or charter agreement, is in place when the chapter or branch is established. Some of the key considerations that should be part of a chapter agreement would include the following:

- recognition that the chapter or branch is an operating division of the national organization as opposed to being a separate legal entity on its own. As such, the continued existence of the chapter or branch will be at the discretion of the board of the national organization and dependent upon the branch or chapter complying with the chapter agreement,
- recognition that the organizational structure for the chapter or branch is to be reflected in the general operating by-law of the national organization,
- an explanation of the expectations of a branch or chapter, including those related to copyright and trade-mark usage, the minimization of risk and adherence to the policies and procedures put in place by the board of directors at the national level,
- an explanation of the circumstances under which the corporate name, trade-marks and logos of the national organization can be utilized by the chapter or branch,
- statement that all donations and income received by the chapter or branch is the property of the national organization and under its control, and is therefore to be accounted for in the consolidated financial statements for the national organization. The re-

quired financial accountability will necessitate that regular reports by chapters or branches be given to the national organization, preferably on a monthly basis, or as frequently as is necessary in the circumstances. There may be issues with respect to the use of any charitable gaming proceeds and the books and records for a lottery scheme conducted and managed by the branch or chapter. Typically, those must remain within the province that issued the licence,

- an explanation of the circumstances under which the grant of a charter will be terminated and the consequences that will flow from such termination. Some of those consequences would include the chapter or branch turning over all of "its" property to the national organization, ceasing to carry on operations and agreeing not to use the corporate name, logos and other trademarks of the national organization. In addition, the chapter or branch would be required to return all donor lists and agree not to contact any donors in the future,
- in the event that a chapter or branch obtains its own charitable registration number with the Canada Customs and Revenue Agency, it would be required to apply for "associate" status to allow for a transfer of funds between the chapter or branch and the national organization in excess of the normal 50% maximum of receipted donations for the previous year. The local chapter or branch should be required to submit its application for charitable registration to the national organization for approval before it is made to the Canada Customs and Revenue Agency,
- identify whether the chapter or the national office is to obtain general liability insurance for the operations of the chapter. Normally this should be done by the national office, since the national organization is the insured legal entity. It is important to ensure that the name of the national organization as well as all related chapters or branches are shown on the general liability insurance policy. Further, if directors' and officers' liability insurance is obtained, then the names of the members of the controlling board for each local chapter or branch should be shown on the policy in addition to the name of the directors of the national organization.

(4) Parallel Foundations

Parallel foundations are public foundations that are established by a charitable organization.[164] The charitable organization is intended to carry out the charitable activities and the parallel foundation raises funds to assist that charitable organization in doing so. The foundation may also carry out charitable activities on its own, which may or may not be broader than those of the charitable organization. The parallel foundation is registered as a charity pursuant to paragraph 149.1(1)(a) of the *Income Tax Act*.

Under that Act, the foundation must be either a corporation or a trust, and must be created and reside in Canada to comply with the statute. The majority of its directors or trustees must, therefore, be residents of Canada. More than 50 per cent of the directors, trustees, officers or officials must deal with each other arm's length and not more than 50 per cent of the contributed capital can come from one person or group of persons not dealing at arm's length. If not, the foundation will be a private foundation.

There are a number of reasons to establish a parallel foundation:

- establishment of an endowment fund - Because it is a foundation, it can create an endowment fund for the benefit of the charitable organization more readily and easily than the organization can. The foundation can produce a regular source of revenue for the organization or for special projects that require longer term development. There are disbursement quotas for public foundations, but compliance with those quotas can still be accomplished while meeting this objective.
- segregating funds. The board may want to do so for several reasons, including minimizing the risks to those funds being claimed to pay for any liabilities (although issues around the *Bankruptcy and Insolvency Act* need to be addressed if there is a transfer from the organization to the foundation and the organization was or becomes insolvent), distinguishing to donors between fundraising for operational purposes and for capital purposes, protection of surplus funds from future decisions by boards of directors or to reduce surplus funds so that the organization becomes eligible for other funding or granting programs.

Parallel foundations are not for all organizations. They are more appropriate if the organization has received or anticipates receiving larger

---

[164] See R. J. Burke-Robertson, "Establishing a Parallel Foundation: Why (or Why Not) and How", in *Fit to be Tithed: Risks and Rewards for Charities and Churches*, (Toronto: Law Society of Upper Canada, Continuing Legal Education 1994).

donations or bequests that are surplus to the current requirements. Similarly, if the organization has or is setting up a planned giving program, the foundation could be the target for those funds. However, the parallel foundation approach is probably not worthwhile for smaller organizations given the expenses involved in establishing and operating the foundation.

The board, if it decides to do so, should consider a number of issues. For example, will it be a trust or corporation? Will the beneficiaries be limited to the "parent" organization or broader? There is an argument that the beneficiary should not be limited to the parent organization but also permit the foundation to carry out charitable activities or to provide funding to other complementary charitable organizations.

How should the organization be controlled? Given that at least 50 per cent of the trustees or directors must be at arm's length from each other, there is a legal issue of who from the "parent" organization is on the board of the foundation. Also, if the relationship and control is too strong, it may be possible to pierce the corporate veil should the "parent" organization run into difficulty. The factors discussed above with respect to national structures are equally applicable to parallel foundations. In addition, the foundation may want to avoid allegations or actual conflicts of interest by having an independent committee make recommendations on grants.

(5) Strategic Alliances

Strategic alliances are common place in the commercial sector. The purpose of a strategic alliance is to permit two or more organizations, usually with a common or complementary interest or common or complementary assets, to work together to achieve a specific result. A deciding factor to enter into a strategic alliance is whether or not the organizations will be able to achieve the common or complementary purpose more efficiently and effectively than they could apart from each other.

There are a variety of strategic alliances, some of which are more formal than others. In assessing the value of a strategic alliance, the boards of directors may want to consider the range of options that are available. Each of them will have their own legal and practical issues that will need to be resolved. In some cases, the toughest issues will be related to the emotional ties people have to a particular asset or program or to the "independence" of an organization, an independence that was maintained through the hard work and diligence of its members. A clash of "corporate cultures" may also be another constraint on the success of a more integrative strategic alliance.

The range of strategic alliances include:

- advisory committees to assist in the delivery of programs by one or the other organization in a strategic alliance,

- committee that would develop joint recommendations for programs, including budget, annual plans and so forth,
- contractual relationship between two or more organizations for the delivery of services by one organization to the others, such as administrative services,
- "joint venture" in which the organizations have a share or interest in the asset, such as a building that is used by several organizations,
- "joint venture" in which each organization will contribute to and participate in a project, which is discussed further below,
- separate legal entity, such as another corporation without share capital or business corporation, that operates certain programs for several organizations, such as an office building,
- establishment of another corporation without share capital to operate programs on behalf of two or more organizations. Each of the organizations would enter into an agency or contractual arrangement by which the new corporation would deliver the charitable services, but it would do so in a more collaborative manner than would otherwise be possible,
- merger or amalgamation of two or more organizations.

There are several issues for a board to consider before it embarks on any of these paths. First, does the board have the political support to do so? In other words, does it have any mandate from its members and other stakeholders? This mandate will not usually be there explicitly but the board needs to be sufficiently comfortable that it will obtain approval before proceeding too far down that road. There may also be obstacles at the staff level towards any form of strategic alliance. If the organizations have been historically in competition with each other, have different styles, or have little in common, there may be significant cultural issues to address, especially where the strategic alliance is further along the spectrum towards merger.

Second, there are many legal issues that may arise, especially for charitable organizations but also for not-for-profit organizations. A particularly difficult scenario may arise where one organization is a registered charity and the other is not. Whatever approach to a strategic alliance is taken — and there is merit in taking small steps to test the waters — lawyers and accountants should be involved. There is a need for a full canvas of the legal and accounting issues and for a solid documentation of the agreements that are reached, with supporting and background materials. The legal issues will be broad and can be far-reaching even with relatively small transactions. There may be a need for expertise in employment law, labour relations, tax law, trust law, corporate law and the law of real property. And both or all parties will need their own independent legal counsel. Without independent legal counsel, the directors would be hard-pressed to demonstrate that they exercised due diligence in the transaction on behalf of their organizations.

There will be a long list of areas the will need to be examined, in particular for those alliances that are closer to a merger than an advisory committee.[165] These areas run the gamut of the topics reviewed in this text, including:

- review of the constating documents and incorporating statute or statutes to determine if there is the legal authority to do what is contemplated. A merger may be more difficult to achieve if one corporation is provincially incorporated and the other under the *Canada Corporations Act*,
- review of financial position of the organizations and the financial ability of each to meet its obligations. This review would also include an analysis of any restricted funds or special purpose trusts, investment polices, insurance, outstanding litigation or contingencies for litigation,
- listing of assets, such as real property, personal property and intellectual property, with any encumbrances on the property,
- status of the organizations as corporations or otherwise to ensure, for example, that the corporation remains in existence and is in compliance with its incorporation legislation,
- review of compliance with any regulatory requirements, including those related to the environment, human rights, taxation (income, property, goods and services, retail), registration as a charity, employment-related statutes and any specific regulatory requirements for areas of activity of the charitable organizations,
- analysis of the legal rights of employees — whether in a unionized or non-unionized workplace. There may be complications where one workforce is unionized and the other is not or if there are different unions representing the employees. The analysis should include a review of various human resources policies, benefit plans (to ensure no outstanding liabilities that have not been accounted for or are not funded), outstanding grievances or similar proceedings, and status of payments for wages, salaries and vacation and remittances to governments for taxes and employment-related premiums and taxes,

---

[165] See L.J.A. Greig and M.E. Hoffstein, "Issues in Mergers and Fusions of Charitable Organizations", in *Fit to Be Tithed 2* (Toronto: Law Society of Upper Canada, 1998) and R.J. Burke-Robertson, "Strategic Alliances in the Voluntary Sector in Canada", in *Fundamental New Developments in the Law of Charities in Canada*, (Toronto: Canadian Bar Association — Ontario, 2000).

- status of material contracts and with whom the contracts are. There may be opportunities for greater efficiency in administrative services, but those cost savings may be reduced substantially if there are long term leases that "unbreakable" and result in significant operating expenses,
- regulatory approvals that are required — or regulatory agencies who would want to be informed early in the process. There may also be funding ministries, agencies or foundations that need to be consulted or advised in order to comply with the funding agreements. A major regulatory agency for charitable organizations will be the Canada Customs and Revenue Agency and, in Ontario, the Public Guardian and Trustee.

The courts will not, however, necessarily rely on the regulators. In *Bloorview Childrens Hospital Foundation v. Bloorview MacMillan Centre*,[166] Croll, J. commented:

> I do not agree with the submission of the Bloorview Foundation that all interests are adequately represented by the Centre and the Public Guardian and Trustee. While the MacMillan Foundation and the Centre may take a similar or overlapping position on many of the issues, they are different entities with different functions and corporate objects. The MacMillan Foundation has knowledge and an understanding of charitable fundraising and fund receiving that it can contribute to these proceedings. It brings a unique perspective, different from that of the Centre and from that of the Public Guardian and Trustee, who represents the children who are cared for, directly or indirectly, by the Centre. By virtue of its own charitable mandate and experience, I am satisfied that the MacMillan Foundation can bring useful and fresh submissions to the proceedings.

The legal status of the organizations will have a bearing on many of these issues. For trusts to merge, for example, requires a court order and may not be possible in law to obtain. An application for *cy-pres* to change the objects of a trust is not necessarily approved by the court unless it can be shown that the charitable objects can no longer be fulfilled. For most trusts, it may be more fruitful to explore one of the less formal approaches to a strategic alliance. However, it may be possible for the trustees to obtain private legislation to accomplish the objectives. Similarly, with unincorporated associations, there may be difficulties in finding a sufficient legal authority to do what is desired unless the memoranda of association permits amendments and, preferably, amalgamations or strategic alliances.

---

[166] [2001] O.J. 1700, May 2, 2001, Croll J., Ontario Superior Court of Justice, at para. 25.

(5) Foreign Activities

Organizations may want to carry on activities outside of Canada. Provided that their constating documents are sufficiently broad to permit it, organizations could do so. The organization may, however, need to obtain legal status in that jurisdiction in order to operate legally in that jurisdiction. Many jurisdictions have some form of registration or licensing scheme to authorize an extra-territorial entity to operate in the jurisdiction.

There may be restrictions on the organization that make it difficult to operate outside Canada. For example, the letters patent may limit its operations to Canada; or it may be limited in using its assets outside of Canada. If the organization obtained a substantial portion of its assets using charitable gaming revenues, it may be prohibited from using those assets outside of the province as the funds are to be used for the benefit of the residents of the province.

Charitable organizations face other legal issues with respect to operations outside of Canada. There is no all-encompassing prohibition against charitable organizations carrying on their activities in other countries. But the organizations must meet certain requirements in order to do so legally for purposes of the *Income Tax Act* and to maintain their registrations as charities under that Act. A charitable organization must use its assets to carry out its own charitable activities.

It is not always easy to determine how a charitable organization is carrying out its own activities in another country. In order to comply with the Act, the organization would normally do so:

- by using its own employees to carry out the work,
- by entering into a principal/agent agreement in which the agent agrees to be retained by the charitable organization and to act as its agent in carrying out the work and the specific duties assigned to it. Agency agreements are potentially high risk, especially given concerns with respect to terrorist activities. The use of an agency agreement may place the charitable organization in a very difficult situation under the *Anti-Terrorist Act*.[167] As the principal, it will be held liable for the actions of its agent, a principle of agency law. Charitable organizations should ensure that a thorough due diligence has been carried out on any proposed agent and that very strict monitoring is maintained over the agent,
- by entering into contractual arrangements for others to carry out the work,

---

[167] S.C. 2001, c. 41.

- by entering into other arrangements that will ensure that the charitable organization is accountable for how the resources are used with appropriate controls.

This last method is a relatively new approach and can be tied into joint venture agreements with government agencies, such as the Canadian International Development Agency. Any organization using this approach would also expect to be more closely monitored than organizations that use their own employees to carry out the work.[168] The Registered Charity Information Return requires additional information from the charitable organization each year about its activities and how those activities were carried out in foreign jurisdictions.

Fundamentally, the organization must be able to demonstrate that it is in control of its own resources and that it is directing how they are used. This fundamental principle is applicable to arrangements to operate outside Canada and to any strategic alliance within Canada. A charitable organization must be able to demonstrate to the Canada Customs and Revenue Agency[169] that it meets the following requirements:

- the charity must maintain direction, control and supervision over the application of its funds by the agent,
- the charity's funds must remain apart from those of its agent so that the charity's role in any particular project or endeavour is separately identifiable as its own charitable activity,
- the financial statements submitted in support of the charity's annual information returns must include a detailed breakdown of expenditures made in respect of the charitable activities performed on behalf of the charity by its agent(s),
- adequate books and records must be kept by the charity by its agent(s) to substantiate compliance with these conditions.

Generally, regardless of the legal approach taken by the various charitable organizations, the Canadian charity needs to show that

- it has obtained reasonable assurances before entering into agreements with individuals or other organizations that they are able to deliver the services required by the charity. This assurance can be obtained by virtue of reputation, years of experience, expertise or by a due-diligence investigation,

---

[168] "A Better Tax Administration in Support of Charities: A Discussion Paper", (Ottawa: Minister of National Revenue, 1990). See also D. Amy, "Foreign Activities by Canadian Charities", in *Fundamental New Developments in the Law of Charities in Canada* (Toronto: Canadian Bar Association — Ontario, 2000).

[169] "Registered Charities: Operating a Registered Charity, Information Circular" Information Circular No. 80-10R, (CCRA, December 17, 1985).

- all expenditures will further the Canadian charity's formal purpose and constitute charitable activities that the Canadian charity carries on itself,
- an adequate agreement is in place,
- the charity provides periodic, specific instructions to individuals or organizations as and when appropriate,
- the charity regularly monitors the progress of the project or program and can provide satisfactory evidence to the Canada Customs and Revenue Agency,
- where appropriate, the charity makes periodic payments on the basis of the monitoring rather than lump sum payments and maintains the right to discontinue payments at any time if it is not satisfied.

An agreement must include the following elements:[170]

- the names and addresses of all parties,
- the duration of the agreement or the deadline by which the project must be completed,
- a description of the specific activities for which funds or other resources have been transferred in sufficient detail to clearly outline the limits of the authority given to the recipient to act for the Canadian charity or on its behalf,
- provision for written progress reports from the recipient of the charity's funds or other resources, or provision for the charity's right to inspect the project on reasonably short notice or both,
- provision that the Canadian charity will make payments by instalments based on confirmation of reasonable progress and that the resources provided to date have been applied to the specific activities outlined in the agreement,
- provision for withdrawing or withholding funds or other resources at the Canadian charity's discretion,
- provision for maintaining adequate records at the charity's address in Canada,
- in the case of agency agreements, provision for the Canadian charity's funds and property to be segregated from those of the agent and for the agent to keep separate books and records,
- the signatures of all parties and the date.

---

[170] "Registered Charities: Operating Outside Canada, RC4106", October 16, 2000.

If the charitable organization participates in joint ventures with other organizations (Canadian or foreign) that advances its own charitable objects, a similar approach is necessary. It must be able to demonstrate that it exercises ongoing control in a joint venture through:

- presence of members of the Canadian charity on the governing body of the joint venture,
- presence in the field of members of the Canadian charity,
- joint control by the Canadian charity of foreign assets and property,
- input by the Canadian charity into the venture's initiation and follow-through, including the charity's ability to direct or modify the venture and to establish deadlines or other performance benchmarks,
- signature of the Canadian charity on loans, contracts, and other agreements arising from the venture,
- review and approval of the venture's budget by the Canadian charity, availability of an independent audit of the venture and the option to discontinue funding,
- authorship of procedures manuals, training guides, standards of conduct and so forth by the Canadian charity,
- on-site identification of the venture as being the work, at least in part, of the Canadian charity.

The requirements for a charitable organization to operate outside Canada are significant. There is a substantial investment at the start of any such initiative and, on an ongoing basis, in legal and accounting expertise. However, that investment does allow a Canadian charitable organization to have influence beyond its size and own resources through appropriate organizational relationships with others.

Recent legislation, however, has reinforced the need to know what is going on in the foreign country. Parliament amended several statutes in late 2001 to enact measures to combat terrorism. The *Anti-terrorism Act*[171] includes a number of amendments and new legislation, some of which is directly applicable to registered charities, and others that are of general application. The measures were enacted in order to bring Canadian law into compliance with United Nations and other international arrangements.

"Terrorist activity" is broadly defined in the legislation. Every person who directly or indirectly, wilfully and without lawful justification or excuse, provides or collects property intending that it be used or knowing that it will be used, in whole or in part, in order to carry out a terrorist

---

[171] S.C. 2001, c. 41.

activity is guilty of an indictable offence under section 83.02 of the *Criminal Code of Canada*. Additional related offences are created under ss. 83.03 (providing or making available property or services for terrorist purposes), and 83.04 (using or possessing property for terrorist purposes).

Under s. 83.05, the Governor in Council may establish a list of entities recommended by the Solicitor General of Canada. The list may include entities that the Governor in Council is satisfied that there are reasonable grounds to believe that the entity has knowingly carried out, attempted to carry out or participate in, or facilitate, a terrorist activity; or is knowingly acting on behalf of, at the direction of or in association with an entity on the list. An entity on the list may apply to be removed from the list but it will not likely have access to the information that formed the basis for the Solicitor General's determination. Rather, the entity may apply to a judge (the Chief Justice of the Federal Court or a judge of the Trial Division designated by the Chief Justice) to examine any security or criminal intelligence reports considered in listing the applicant and other materials provided by the Solicitor General.

The applicant is to receive a statement summarizing the information available to the judge so as to enable the applicant to be reasonably informed of the reasons for the decision. The applicant is to be provided a reasonable opportunity to be heard. The judge then makes a determination on the information available to the judge whether or not to order that the applicant no longer be a listed entity. Clearly, the ability of the applicant to be delisted is limited.

The legislation authorizes the freezing, seizure and forfeiture of property that is used for terrorist purposes. It provides for very broad investigative powers, some of which require organizations and individuals to testify, including where it may be against their own interests. It creates criminal offences for participating with, facilitating, instructing or harbouring a terrorist, and facilitating a terrorist activity.

While it is unlikely that most registered charities in Canada that operate overseas will participate in terrorist activities deliberately, the wording of the legislation is broad and it is possible that *bona fide* charities may inadvertently fall within the scope of the legislation. It is critical that organizations that operate outside Canada — and those that operate in Canada where there is any uncertainty at all with respect to use of property by others — have in place measures that will protect themselves. Organizations need to conduct due diligence reviews of their operations with legal counsel to assess any risks. The directors need to ensure that there is review and monitoring in place of how and from whom funds and other property is obtained. They must ensure that the organization is not being used as an illegal conduit to a terrorist organization — in particular where there are any international relationships such as third-party agents or contracting parties.

(6) Carrying On Business and Political Activities

Charitable and not-for-profit organizations are restricted in how they carry on business activities. A fundamental position is that neither are intended to be "in business", that is to make and distribute profits. Charitable organizations are more severely restricted than are not-for-profit organizations in this regard.

Any business activity would need to fall within the objects of the organization, charitable or not-for-profit. For example, a not-for-profit organization that is intended to advance the interests of artists could operate a retail store. However, it is far from clear how it could operate a gas station or other extraneous retail outlet. There may also be problems if the only artists permitted to use the retail store are members, especially if they receive "profits" from the operation. If any surpluses or profits are distributed to members, the organization would appear to have crossed over the line from being not-for-profit to becoming a for-profit or business entity.

The Canada Customs and Revenue Agency takes the position that an organization will not be "not-for-profit" but "for-profit" if its principal activity is the carrying on of a business or trade.[172] It looks to the following factors in making its assessment of whether or not the activities of the not-for-profit organization are on the other side of the line:

- its activities are a trade or business in the ordinary meaning, that is, it is operated in a normal commercial manner,
- its goods or services are not restricted to members and their guests,
- it is operated on a profit basis rather than a cost recovery basis,
- it is operated in competition with taxable entities carrying on the same trade or business.

A charitable organization should also be able to illustrate how any business activity is carrying out its charitable activities. Historically, charitable organizations whose mandates are to relieve poverty have operated stores to sell low-cost clothing and other goods to the poor. But when does a charitable organization cross over the line if its primary market are not the poor but those with middle or high incomes who simply want cheaper goods?

Paragraph 149.1(3)(a) of the *Income Tax Act* only permits a charity to carry on "related business activities".[173] What is or is not a related business is not always an easy thing to determine. The former Revenue Can-

---

[172] "Non-profit Organizations", IT-496R, August 2, 2001.
[173] *The Alberta Institute on Mental Retardation v. Canada*, [1987] 3 F.C. 286 (F.C.A.) may have extended the circumstances for business activities to include fundraising purposes. However, this case may not prove to be as expansive as initially considered.

ada (now the Canada Customs and Revenue Agency) attempted to provide clarification in its 1990 Discussion Paper on charities. It commented that if the business activity does not become a "substantial commercial endeavour" the activity will be considered related if:

- the activity is related to the charity's objects or ancillary to them,
- there is no private profit motive since any net revenues will be used for charitable purposes,
- the business operation does not compete directly with other for-profit businesses,[174]
- the business has been in operation for some time and is accepted by the community.

In Ontario, the *Charitable Gifts Act*[175] and the *Charities Accounting Act*[176] place significant obstacles to a charitable organization operating businesses that do not have a clear relationship to the charitable objects of the organization. Section 2 of the *Charitable Gifts Act* prohibits most charities in Ontario from owning more than ten per cent interest in a business. If the charity does so, it must divest itself of the excess within seven years.

The *Charities Accounting Act* requires a charity to sell any real property that it does not use for charitable purposes and use the proceeds for its charitable purposes. As a result, with few exceptions such as hospitals that are governed by other statutory schemes in Ontario, most charitable organizations would not be able to hold real property for investment purposes, such as an apartment building or commercial building. It may be able to lease out some surplus space in its own building which is otherwise used for its charitable activities, but care must be taken even in that case.

Political activities pose another problem for charitable organizations. Lobbying and advocacy for political change is not a charitable activity. There are some recognized exceptions to this general statement; for example, a child welfare agency may lobby for changes to child welfare legislation to a reasonable extent.[177] Not-for-profit organizations are not

---

[174] The CCRA and this approach does not address a developing issue — what happens to this criterion where the business activity of the charitable organization creates a new industry or commercial activity and for-profit businesses subsequently enter the field. Arguably, this situation has occurred with respect to used clothing and household goods.

[175] R.S.O. 1990, c. C.8.

[176] R.S.O. 1990, c. C.10.

[177] See several of the Canada Customs and Revenue Agency publications for further discussion of this issue, including, "Registered Charities: Political Objects and Activities", Information Circular 78-3, "Registered Charities — Ancillary and Incidental Political Activities", Information Circular 87-1, and "Registered Charities: Education, Advocacy and Political Activities", RC4107 (Draft).

limited in this area and there are a number of organizations that lobby and carry out significant political activities as part of their mandates.

There are obvious restrictions, but, are there any options to permit, from a broader context, the organization to carry out either business or political activities? To a limited extent, there are some models that may do so and allow for a level of activities that could not occur within the charitable or not-for-profit organization. However, the board of directors ought to receive legal and accounting advice and to ensure that operationally there are clear distinctions made and maintained between the charitable or not-for-profit organization and the business or political entity. The issues discussed above about control and piercing the corporate veil are relevant factors to consider in structuring any such relationships.

The major options available for business activities[178] include the following:

- business corporation. A business corporation could be used to carry out any business activity. This option is available to both charitable and not-for-profit organizations, but the method implementing this option will vary as between the two, especially for charitable organizations in Ontario. A thorough review of the income tax implications would need to be made to ensure that any tax liability in the hands of the business corporation is minimized, either through an appropriate level of donations to the registered charity or through the size of the corporation.

    In the case of the charitable organization, it may be able to structure the ownership of the shares through intermediaries to avoid the restrictions in the *Charitable Gifts Act*. For example, a not-for-profit corporation could be incorporated to hold the shares of the business corporation and, in turn, forward the "profits" to the charitable organization. However, this type of scheme may be seen as a sham and that the statute purports to extend to direct and indirect ownership. But, it still may be possible to work from within the statutory scheme, i.e., hold the shares for up to seven years or have several charitable and not-for-profit organizations each hold less than ten per cent of the shares.

- business trust. A business trust is also a taxable entity under the *Income Tax Act* but it can be used to make distributions to charitable or not-for-profit organizations, which are not taxable entities. One difficulty with this option is that the trustees would be exposed to personal liability, which could be a significant deterrent.

---

[178] See R.J. Burke-Robertson, "Charities Carrying on Business Activities — The Legal Considerations", in *Fit to be Tithed 2*.

There are also timing limits to the use of a business trust. Every 21 years, there will be a deemed realization of the assets, which may trigger capital gains.

Both of these options may also give rise to other complications with respect to goods and services taxation, potential liability for the charitable or not-for-profit organization or its directors (especially if not all the procedures are followed and maintained), ongoing maintenance and record-keeping. Depending upon the type of business that is established, there may also be employment law, environmental law, tax law, regulatory law, securities law and other statutory and common law concerns that need to be addressed. The board also needs to be concerned with the *Income Tax Act*'s provisions with respect to anti-avoidance measures.

Neither of these options should be considered without expert legal and accounting advice and only if the potential benefits exceed the costs and potential costs. In addition, the payment of that legal and accounting advice needs to be justified as a reasonable and necessary expense for purposes of the charitable organization.

CHAPTER 6

Officers, Directors and Trustees: The Standards of Care

A   INTRODUCTION

The directors are any organization's primary asset. This statement may seem to be inconsistent with other pronouncements on what is most important. For example, it is common for private sector, public sector and voluntary sector employers to state that their employees or volunteers are their greatest assets. Others argue that an organization's major asset is its reputation. All of these statements and others are likely accurate in general and for specific organizations.

Directors are, however, unique. An organization is a legal artifice. It exists in law and as a legal concept for practical purposes. An organization allows people to structure their internal relationships and external dealings with others in an efficient and effective manner. Nobody can touch, feel, see or hear an organization; it has no physical reality. It becomes real through the actions of people. And directors are responsible for making sure that the organization relates to people in accordance with the law, that it acts in a fiscally prudent manner and that it is effective in achieving its purposes.

The organization itself may exist as a separate legal entity. Corporations, for example, are established by law as "legal persons". A large number of organizations, however, have little or no "legal personalty". These organizations are unincorporated associations which are not legally "persons". In some cases, the common law or statutory law recognizes a limited legal personalty to these unincorporated associations, for specific purposes. In other cases, the organizations may be "trusts", in which the assets are held in trust by legal persons, such as individuals or corporations.

Regardless of the legal structure, it takes real people for an organization to act. The law — in the form of the courts, regulators and governments — and the public look to directors and officers as the primary method by which organizations act and for accountability purposes. The law and the public have developed expectations that directors and officers will ensure that the organization achieves its goals, complies with the law that applies to the organization and operates in a fiscally prudent and effective, efficient manner. The method for doing so is often called "governance".

B APPROACHES TO GOVERNANCE

The legal, governmental and public expectations of organizations are articulated and summarized in a number of ways — but they always focus on the organization and how it is governed by its directors. The terms "governance" and "stewardship" are used in *Building on Strength: Improving Governance and Accountability in Canada's Voluntary Sector*.[1] This seminal report was the work of a panel of distinguished Canadians with experience and knowledge of the voluntary sector. The panel was established by several national organizations to provide guidance on governance and accountability. The report is seminal because it became the basis for ongoing work in modernizing the voluntary sector, its regulatory framework and making it more effective.

"Governance" for the panel is a combination of both the overall processes and the structures that are used in directing and managing the organization's operations and activities. "Stewardship" is the responsibility of the board of directors of an organization and involves the active oversight by the board of the organization's governance. These two concepts are easily stated, but a great deal is packed into them — something that is readily apparent by the length and complexity of the panel's report and background materials.

The need for such a panel grew out of several dynamics that were at play in Canada (and throughout the world) in the late 20th century. Most of these dynamics were and remain beyond the control of the voluntary sector as a whole and certainly of individual organizations. The panel was struck in part to help the sector to respond to these dynamics and to provide guidance to organizations on how to do so. These dynamics include:

- changing role of government from a service deliverer and direct provider of services to a standard setter, although international events and events in Canada have caused some to reassess this changed role;
- the downloading of what had been government activities and functions onto the voluntary sector and the private sector. The federal, provincial, territorial and municipal levels of government may each take their own approach, but "alternative service delivery" and "private/public partnerships" are clearly the trend;

---

[1] Panel on Accountability and Governance in the Voluntary Sector, Final Report, (February 1999).

- changing social and economic realities facing communities and groups within communities — not the least of which are the impact of the "new economy", "globalization" and new international structures;
- an increasingly diverse population and cultural backgrounds in Canada;
- a movement from philanthropy by the private sector towards "sponsorships" and marketing;
- a trend towards "strategic donating" where the donation is part of a strategic approach of the donor rather than the charitable organization;
- a reduction in overall support by governments of organizations and a refocusing of what remains from core-funding to project funding. This dynamic together with the movement away from philanthropy by the private sector appears to have led many organizations towards activities that will receive funding but which may or may not be consistent with the organization's and its members' sense of priorities;
- increased competition in the "charity" marketplace — be it for grants from governments or foundations, contracts for the delivery of services, donations and sponsorships from businesses, donations by individuals, or the operation of for-profit "business activities". This competition has led to a highly sophisticated fundraising industry within the voluntary sector in which larger and more established and recognized institutions (such as hospitals, universities and major health organizations) have a substantial edge over others in the sector;
- greater demands for accountability by governments, funders and the general public. Accountability is defined not only in terms of proper use of funds but in the effectiveness and efficiency of the organization and in meeting the needs of the community;
- more knowledgeable volunteers who have specific "wants" from their volunteer experiences;
- greater reliance on directors and a resulting increased concern about potential liability.

There are two conceptual approaches to "governance" and "stewardship". The more traditional approach is that the directors "manage" the affairs of the organization. The board would make most substantive decisions based on materials provided for board meetings and the discussion or debate at the meeting. The second approach is based on an "oversight" role for the directors to ensure that the organization is effective and is accountable. The oversight role relies more on the development of operational and other "policies" by the board of directors, which then looks to the officers and staff to implement.[2] The two approaches are sometimes labelled the "administrative governance board" model and the "policy governance board" model.

In reality, most organizations have operated and will continue to operate using a mixture of these two approaches. If the organization has staff, by-laws would, for example, often permit the executive director to manage staff in accordance with board-established human resource policies. Often, the by-laws or board resolutions determine the authority of the executive director to spend money within a budget set by the board. For larger organizations, these policies have typically included human resources, financial operations, advocacy, programming and so forth. Staff would be required to report to the board or a committee of the board on compliance with and deviation from the policies and on issues that arise for which greater direction is required.

There are both practical and legal limits to the extent to which boards may "delegate" their responsibilities through the issuance of policies. Boards will always have an "oversight" role in any organization but boards of corporations must be able to demonstrate that they "manage the affairs" of the corporation. Subsection 283(1) of the Ontario *Corporations Act*, for example, provides that the directors are to manage the affairs of the corporation.[3]

The proper mixture of "management" and "oversight" through policies is organization and time specific. There are practical limits to the abilities of directors to manage the affairs of large organizations with many employees. It is physically impossible for these directors to make all of the decisions that are required to be made on a day-to-day basis. Arguably, these directors could be negligent if they attempted to do so because decisions would not be made by the person most competent to do so, the decisions would not be made in a timely manner and the directors would be wasting the skills and talents of its employees. The same argument, however, could not be made for a small organization that has no employees and has no significant day-to-day activities. Although that organization may want policies in place to guide the board's decision-making, the board would continue to make most if not all decisions.

There is a spectrum between the two models of administrative governance and policy governance. Where on that spectrum an organization lays will depend upon a number of factors:

---

[2] John Carver is the major proponent of this approach, which gained prominence with the publication of his *Boards that Make a Difference: A New Design for Leadership in Nonprofit and Public Organizations* (San Francisco: Jossey-Bass Publications, 1991). Although not necessarily new conceptually, the text became an important opportunity for boards and organizations to re-examine how they operate and what structures were more appropriate for their circumstances. "Carverizing" became a touchstone for some as a solution to many problems.

[3] R.S.O. 1990, c. C.38.

- the legal authority of the directors and officers and of the organization itself,
- statutory or common law obligations or restrictions,
- letters patent, by-laws, constitution or other constating documents,
- culture of organization, which is often at variance with the organizational documents and at times with the legal requirements,
- views and perspectives of key stakeholders, who sometimes are not sensitive to the legal niceties or are overly demanding of compliance with policies that are not relevant to the organization,
- skills, competence and training of staff (assuming the organization has staff),
- size and type of operations and activities carried out by the organizations and their complexity, and
- due diligence requirements of the directors and of the officers.

There is no clear legal articulation of what is meant by "manage the affairs" of an organization. It will differ depending upon the issue, the circumstances and the organization. There are also certain decisions that are so fundamental to the affairs of any organization, that only the board should be making those decisions. For example, the budget of any organization ought to be, at the very least, approved by the directors and the board or a committee of the board ought to be involved in the preparation of the budget for larger organizations. In other situations, the law may require that the board be involved other than through policy statements — either directly or indirectly where the ramifications are such that no prudent director would consent not to be involved.

The panel on governance and accountability recognized that there is no "one size fits all" approach to governance and stewardship. It recommended "a good practice guide for effective stewardship" for large and medium-sized organizations, which is also intended to be a checklist for smaller organizations. The panel concluded that there were eight tasks that were key to effective stewardship by boards:

1) *Mission and Strategic Planning*, which involves the definition of the fundamental goals and strategy of the organization. It considered this task the most important duty for the board because it established the basis for accountability — the basis on which to determine the appropriateness of the board's actions, performance of management and the success of the organization. The mission and strategic planning, though, must be consistent with the letters patent and by-laws of the organization (or as they are amended in accordance with the law), any external restrictions on the use of the organization's assets, fiscal prudence and responsibility and

any statutory, contractual or other legal obligations. Too often, organizations have developed very good mission statements and strategic plans — but ones that bear little if any relationship to what the organization can legally do.

For example, a church group incorporated for missionary purposes may not have the legal capacity to operate a summer camp, regardless of the usefulness of the summer camp.[4] If the letters patent establishing the corporation do not extend to this type of operation, the organization would be acting *ultra vires* or outside its legal capacity and the directors and officers could be personally liable for any damages to the corporation. These damages could include losses on the operations or from closing down the operation once it was determined that it could not operate the summer camp.

There are several components to the mission and strategic planning. The directors need to establish the mission, communicate it with the organization's members and stakeholders, and review it periodically to ensure that it is appropriate. A mission, if it is to be used to guide the organization's subsequent decision-making, will be an important statement and the board should consider the level and type of consultation it will undertake with the members, its employees, clientele, funders, and the public. There ought to be a significant degree of up-front buy-in or comfort if the mission statement is to be accepted and become effective. The board also needs to develop strategic plans to implement the key elements of the mission statement; mission statements, like organizations themselves, can only become a reality to people being served through actions.

The board also needs to consider what the risks are and how to manage those risks. Any action involves risk and the board has a duty to anticipate risks, to understand those risks, to address them and to manage them. The board does not have a duty to avoid all risks; the only way to do so would be to do nothing in life, which defeats the very purpose for the organization to exist.

The board needs to oversee and monitor the mission on a regular basis. It can do so by establishing measurable goals. The panel

---

[4] See *Volunteers & the Law A Guide for Volunteers, Organizations and Boards* (Vancouver: The People's Law School, 2000), at 54 for an example of this situation.

preferred "desired outcomes" or "impacts": over "inputs or activities" but it is not always clear how this could be accomplished.

2) *Transparency and Communication*, which help to ensure that the organization's activities are open and transparent and that there is communication between the organization and its members and stakeholders. This communication should be both ways. Openness and transparency, however, should not preclude appropriate confidentiality. For example, a board should not normally negotiate the purchase of a building in public, permitting the seller to know what the board's bottom line price is.

Transparency and communication includes a number of elements. The board should establish policies for communication and feedback with stakeholders, a code of ethical conduct, and a complaints and grievance procedure that is effective. The board must meet regularly for discussion of matters and the making of decisions. Proper minutes and other documents must be kept to maintain the collective memory. Indeed, for corporations, the board has an obligation to do so and all organizations must do so under the *Income Tax Act*.[5] The organization should also respond appropriately to requests for information, recognizing that different requesters will have a different level of access to such information and differing needs.

However, not all requests are reasonable or *bona fide*. Furthermore, information may be proprietary or confidential and organizations need to protect those types of information. The level of the information that is provided to those requesting ought to be appropriate and take into account any restrictions — legal or practical — that may exist on the information and the context in which the person is making the request.

3) *Organizational Structures* should reflect the needs of the organization and its culture. Some organizations are part of a larger federation of organizations and its structure will likely be different from a stand-alone organization. Size and activities will also dictate differing structures. For example, a large organization may want an executive committee with decision-making powers. Care must be taken to ensure compliance with any legislative require-

---

[5] R.S.C. 1985, c. 3 (5th Supp.).

ments or restrictions around committees. For example, if an executive committee is to be established, the Ontario *Corporations Act* has specific requirements that need to be in place. Furthermore, only an executive committee under that Act can make decisions; all other committees can at most be advisory.

The panel recommended that the structure reflect at least three elements: (i) that the board be capable of objective oversight, (ii) that there be an independent nominating committee to ensure appropriate succession of the board, and (iii) that an audit committee be established. The purpose of the audit committee would be to report on whether or not the organization is complying with the laws, rules, regulations and contracts that govern it and to review whether the management, information and control systems are organized and implemented to carry out these rules and regulations. The audit committee is also responsible for supervising external financial reporting. Whether there is one committee or more will be dependent on each organization.

This type of structure may not be appropriate for most organizations. The size of the organization and the scope of its operations may suggest a less sophisticated approach to organizational structure. Each organization needs to develop its own approach, and the more sophisticated approach may be more in keeping with a policy governance board model than one in which the board makes most of the decisions.

4) *Board's Understanding of Its Role* requires that the board members have a shared understanding of the role of the board and of the directors, officers and staff. An effective board is a major method to prevent problems from occurring and to address those when they do occur. The success or failure of an organization is dependent upon the board understanding its role and carrying out that role — however that role has developed in law or in practice. The effectiveness of a board of directors is discussed below.

5) *Fiscal Responsibility* is a cornerstone of accountability. The board must ensure that the organization is in a financially sound position and that it has the resources necessary to carry out its activities. If these two objectives are not possible, the board has two options from which to choose:

- locate and put in place the resources that are necessary, or

- alter the organization's programs to fit the resources that are available.

While any human activity — not-for-profit or for-profit — is not without risk, the board should not put the assets of the organization at unnecessary or unknown risk. Risk is part of life but the board needs to know and understand the likely risks and put in place the tools to minimize and manage those risks.

The directors have both statutory and common law duties towards the organization and often to third parties to ensure that the organization is operated in a financially prudent manner. These duties are sometimes referred to as some of the "fiduciary duties" of directors. The board, in fulfilling its duties, ought to put in place:

- a budget that is based on the mission and strategic plan of the organization and its priorities, consistent with its legal obligations and limitations, and on a realistic estimate of revenues and expenses.
- mechanisms to monitor and control expenditures. These mechanisms will normally include the accounting books and records that are required to be kept by law and by generally accepted accounting principles, financial statements (including audited statements where required) and reports on a regular basis. In the case of a registered charity, the *Income Tax Act* establishes certain requirements for record-keeping.
- tools to ensure that the assets of the organization are managed appropriately and consistently with the organization's legal obligations and that any liabilities do not become excessive or unmanageable.

Boards too often fail to devote the resources that are necessary to ensure that prudent financial practices occur. However, without the resources being available and properly managed, the organization cannot fulfil its objectives and the underlying purpose of the organization is not possible. Human nature being what it is, it is also to financial prudence that others look in making their decisions about an organization. Organizations that become insolvent or that have substantial losses due to defalcation or misuse of funds that could have been avoided are not trusted. The voluntary sector operates on the basis of "trust" — both trust in its legal sense and in its human sense.

6) *Oversight of Human Resources* is necessary because human resources are an important asset of the organization. Human resources includes staff and volunteers. The oversight of human resources requires the directors to ensure that the human resources have appropriate skills, training and backgrounds for the positions they occupy. Proper recruitment processes, job descriptions and performance appraisals are the responsibility of the directors — either directly or through management staff reporting to the directors. These processes ought to be fair and open.

The board must also ensure that the organization complies with the various statutory schemes that are in place, including employment legislation, workplace safety, labour legislation, collective agreements, and human rights codes. There should be codes of conduct, including conflicts of interest. Appropriate screening processes should be in place for both staff and volunteers, especially where they deal with children, the elderly or vulnerable in the community.

7) *Assessment and Control Systems* are based in large measure on the accounting books and records. However, the systems often include codes of ethical conduct, an effective monitoring and complaints procedure, a framework for internal regulations (such as a constitution or by-laws), compliance audits and an evaluation of the board as a whole.

8) *Planning for Succession and Diversity* is important for organizations. In addition, organizations should reflect the diversity of the community in which they operate.

These concepts are not new but restated for a changing Canada. Others have articulated similar tasks in slightly different ways.[6] In one case, the author identified the following ten "responsibilities" of directors:[7]

- determine the mission,
- select the executive,
- support and evaluate the executive,
- lead planning,

---

[6] See, for example, M.A. Paquet, R. Ralston and D. Cardinal, *A Handbook for Cultural Trusts* (Waterloo: University of Waterloo Press, 1987) and S. Kreiger, *Duties and Responsibilities of Directors of Non-Profit Corporations* (Toronto: Canadian Society of Association Executives, 1989).

[7] R.T. Ingram, *Ten Responsibilities of Non-Profit Boards* (Washington: National Center for Non-profit Boards, 1988).

- secure adequate resources,
- manage resources,
- set and monitor programmes,
- public relations,
- "court of appeal",
- self-assessment.

C STANDARDS OF CARE

I INTRODUCTION

Officers, directors and trustees of charitable and not-for-profit organizations have duties and obligations to the organizations themselves, to the members and to employees and the public. The potential for personal liability arises in the execution of such duties. Unfortunately, there is no simple definition of potential liabilities or of the standard of care for officers, directors and trustees. Instead, officers, directors and trustees are faced with a confusing amalgam of statutory and common law rights, duties, obligations and standards, some of which vary depending upon the activities and legal status of the organizations and the individual's background.

The confusion is exacerbated by uncertainty about which standard of care is to be applied. Moreover, different persons or authorities may have jurisdiction to apply differing standards or to have the rights, duties and obligations enforced. These persons and authorities include: members of the organization; members of the public; the department incorporating the corporation; the Canada Customs and Revenue Agency; provincial revenue departments; departments responsible for labour and environmental legislation; the Attorneys General; the Public Guardian and Trustee in Ontario and the courts.

The level of personal liability of an officer, director or trustee will also vary depending on whether or not he or she acted within the scope of the objects of the organization and the terms and conditions of his or her office. Statutory provisions may impose personal liability for, among other infringements, unpaid wages or taxes that have not been remitted. Directors may also be liable for prosecution for a breach by the corporation if the director authorized, permitted or acquiesced in the breach or knowingly allowed the breach to occur.[8] Under the Ontario *Corporations Act*, these breaches include the following examples:

---

[8] *Corporations Act*, R.S.O. 1990, c. C.38, s. 332; *Co-operative Corporations Act*, R.S.O. 1990, c. C.35, s. 176; and *Canada Corporations Act*, R.S.C. 1970, c. C.32, s. 149.

- failure to file with the Minister and to publish in *The Ontario Gazette* a notice of resolution requiring the voluntary winding up of a corporation;[9]
- failure to give notice to the members of any resolution that may properly be moved and is intended to be moved at a meeting and to circulate a statement of not more than 1,000 words with respect to the matter referred to in any proposed resolution or with respect to any business to be dealt with at the meeting;[10]
- failure to keep the records of proceedings, documents and registers, and books of account and accounting records at the head office of the corporation or at another authorized location so that the records may be open for inspection during normal business hours;[11] and
- failure to allow a person entitled to undertake an inspection to inspect the minutes, documents or registers that are to be open for inspection during normal business hours.[12]

This list is obviously not a thorough list of statutory offences. However, it is important to note that in the incorporating legislation, the offences primarily involve a failure to provide members with required information or access to books and records that they have a right to. These offences highlight the importance that the statute places on accountability of the officers and directors to the members of the organization. The corporation is the members' organization and not that of the officers and directors.

The officers and directors of a co-operative corporation are at risk of personal liability in some unique areas that reflect the nature of co-operative corporations. Under s. 17 of the *Co-operative Corporations Act*,[13] a co-operative corporation may not approve a type of financial assistance to directors, members and employees that is not normally available to all members. An officer or director who approves financial assistance is liable to the co-operative corporation and its creditors for any losses. Similarly, under s. 99 the directors who voted in favour of repayment of loans where repayment is prohibited under the Act are liable to the co-operative corporation for the amount involved.

There will, of course, be other statutory duties and obligations of officers, directors and trustees. Some of these are reviewed later in the chapter with respect to taxation, employees, business practices and the

---

[9] *Corporations Act*, R.S.O. 1990, c. C.38, s. 231.
[10] *Ibid.*, s. 296.
[11] *Ibid.*, s. 304.
[12] *Ibid.*, s. 305.
[13] R.S.O. 1990, c. C.35.

environment. A thorough list is not, however, possible. Some organizations may have statutory obligations under specific legislation under which they operate; others may operate facilities and are required to meet zoning by-laws and building codes or to fulfil contractual obligations. Legal advice that is sensitive to the character and circumstances of the specific organization should be obtained.

II Defining the Standard of Care

(1) Not-for-Profit Organizations

The standard of care that officers and directors must meet is difficult to define. In most jurisdictions, a common law standard of care is applied. The common law standard is one that has been and will continue to be reinterpreted by the courts to meet changing circumstances. It was originally developed for all corporations, including business corporations. That standard of care is subjective in nature. For business corporations, legislative changes have established an objective standard of care to ensure appropriate levels of governance are undertaken by directors of corporations.

Although the standard was subjective in nature, the courts were reluctant to enforce the standard too rigorously in circumstances where, for example, the director was not involved in managing the affairs of the corporation. However, in recent years, the courts have placed greater responsibility on officers and directors to fulfil their duties and obligations. Although there do not appear to be reported cases in Canada where the courts have imposed personal liability on directors of not-for-profit corporations, it is expected that courts will reflect the greater emphasis on corporate governance that has developed for business corporations in the 1980s and 1990s.

It is unclear in law what standard of care will apply to officers and directors of unincorporated associations. Unless the constituting documents provide otherwise, it is likely that the standard of care developed at common law and applied to officers and directors of corporations without share capital will probably apply to officers and directors of unincorporated associations. In any event, it is prudent for officers and directors of unincorporated associations to meet common law standards for officers and directors of corporations without share capital.

The common law standard has been modified by legislation in some provinces. In British Columbia, the *Society Act*[14] sets out a statutory standard of care. Neither the Ontario *Corporations Act* nor the *Canada Corporations Act* provide for a similar statutory standard of care, although the more recent business corporations legislation do. The Ontario *Business Corporations Act*[15] provides for an objective test that requires every officer

---

[14] R.S.B.C. 1979, c. 390.
[15] R.S.O. 1990, c. B.16, s. 134.

and director to act honestly and in good faith with a view to the best interests of the corporation. In doing so, he or she must exercise the care, diligence and skill that a reasonably prudent person would exercise in comparable circumstances.

The test set out in the business corporations legislation is one of the "reasonably prudent person", an objective test. This test has also been enacted for co-operative corporations without share capital, the only type of charitable or not-for-profit organization that has this objective test. Section 108 of the *Co-operative Corporations Act*[16] provides that:

> Every director and officer of a co-operative shall exercise the powers and discharge the duties of his or her office honestly, in good faith and in the best interests of the co-operative, and in connection therewith shall exercise the degree of care, diligence and skill that a reasonably prudent person would exercise in comparable circumstances.

The standard of care that applies to Ontario and federal incorporated corporations without share capital, however, is a common law standard that is subjective in nature, not objective. In *Re City Equitable Fire Insurance Co.*,[17] the Court concluded that the degree of skill required of a director is what "may reasonably be expected from a person of his knowledge and experience". This test means that the standard of care will differ as between two persons. A lawyer, for example, will be required to meet a higher standard of care than another director on the same board who has no legal training. Or, for example, a person with substantial business experience will have a higher standard of care than a person who has no business experience.

Individuals who are sought after to be directors on the basis of their skills and experience are, therefore, subject to a higher standard of care than others, which may in turn disincline them from serving on the boards of charitable or not-for-profit corporations. The common law standard of care seems to make it more difficult for these organizations to obtain the voluntary services of persons for the very reasons that they should be on the boards — the skills that will assist the organization in meeting its objects and carrying out its activities are the grounds on which they will be judged.

As noted above, legislation may establish a statutory standard of care. Periodically, some argue that directors of charitable or not-for-profit corporations ought to be held to a different standard because they do not benefit personally from the position. The Federal Court of Appeal dealt with directors of a "not-for-profit" corporation with respect to income tax liability and the standard of care expected in *Canada v. Cor-*

---

[16] R.S.O. 1990, c. C.35.
[17] [1925] 1 Ch. 407, at 428 (C.A.).

sano.[18] The statutory standard of care in the *Income Tax Act* is similar to that in many other statutes, i.e., reasonably prudent person.

The trial court had decided that the directors were not vicariously liable for unpaid taxes owed by the corporation. The corporation had failed to remit the federal income tax for employee wages, which it was obliged to do as an employer. The corporation was a not-for-profit corporation and one of the arguments made in defence was that a different standard of care should be used for directors of these corporations. On the facts, different directors had differing levels of knowledge about the failure. Justice Letourneau commented on this argument:

> The learned Tax Court Judge was of the view, at page 2041 of his decision, that the standard of care applicable to a not-for-profit corporation, such as the Louisbourg Harbourfront Park Limited Corporation (Corporation) was a standard less rigorous than one governing the directors of corporations run for profit. He relied upon the decision of this Court in Soper v. Canada ... that he understood to mean that there were "different standards of care applicable to inside and outside directors". I note in passing that this Court in Soper expressly stated that it did not establish a different standard of care for inside and outside directors. ...
>
> Relying upon the decision in Soper, the respondents argued that the standard of care found in subsection 227.1(3) of the Act is inherently flexible and, therefore, there are different standards to meet different situations. Accordingly, there would be one standard for inside directors, one for outside directors, one for directors of a not-for-profit corporation, one for volunteer directors and another for paid directors. To accept this approach begs the thorny question: which of all these different standards should a court apply if one is, at the same time, an outside director acting without remuneration in a not-for-profit corporation?
>
> It is true that in Soper, this Court wrote that "[t]he standard of care laid down in subsection 227.1(3) of the Act is inherently flexible". It is obvious, however, on the reading of the decision, that it is the application of the standard that is flexible because of the varying and different skills, factors and circumstances that are to be weighed in measuring whether a director in a given situation lived up to the standard of care established by the Act. For, subsection 227.1(3) statutorily imposes only one standard to all directors, that is to say whether the director exercised the degree of care, diligence and skill to prevent the failure that a reasonably prudent person would have exercised in comparable circumstances.
>
> I agree with counsel for the appellant that the rationale for subsection 227.1(3) is the ultimate accountability of the directors of a company for the

---

[18] [1999] 3 F.C. 173, 2 C.T.C. 395 (F.C.A.), leave to appeal dismissed by Supreme Court of Canada, S.C.C. Bulletin 2000, at 753.

deduction and remittance of employees' taxes and that such accountability cannot depend on whether the company is a profit or not-for-profit company, or I would add whether the directors are paid or not or whether they are nominal but active or merely passive directors. All directors of all companies are liable for their failure if they do not meet the single standard of care provided for in subsection 227.1(3) of the Act. The flexibility is in the application of the standard of care since the qualifications, skills and attributes of a director will vary from case to case. So will the circumstances leading to and surrounding the failure to hold and remit the sums due.[19]

The Federal Court was dealing with a statutory obligation on the part of directors. That obligation established a standard of care of prudence on the part of directors. How that standard of care would be applied has some flexibility, but it does not create separate standards for different classes of directors — and certainly not on the basis of being a director of a not-for-profit corporation. A director is a director is a director.

(2) Charitable Organizations

The directors of a charitable corporation must meet an even higher standard of care, that of or almost that of a trustee. The higher standard of care is imposed indirectly through the *Charities Accounting Act*[20] and through the operation of trust law as it applies to charitable organizations. The Public Guardian and Trustee takes the position that the corporation holds the charitable assets in trust for charitable purposes. The directors, in turn, have fiduciary duties to the corporation to ensure that it fulfils its obligations as a trustee. The directors would appear to have the standard of care of a trustee in managing the charitable trust and the property that is subject to the trust.

Importantly, this standard of care would not appear to be limited to officers and directors of corporations that were incorporated as "charitable corporations" or that are registered with the Canada Customs and Revenue Agency as charitable organizations. In the case of charitable corporations and registered charities, by law all of the assets must be used to carry out the charitable objects of the organization. However, subs. 1(2) of the *Charities Accounting Act* would appear to apply to "any corporation incorporated for a religious, educational, charitable or public purpose". The subsection deems the corporation to be a trustee and that any real or personal property acquired by it shall be deemed to be property within the meaning of the Act. Statutorily, the ambit of the Act would appear to apply not only to property that was received subject to a "charitable trust" but also to property that would not otherwise be considered to be "charitable" in nature or intent.

---

[19] *Canada v. Corsano*, [1999] 3 F.C. 173, at 188-189.
[20] R.S.O. 1990, c. C.10.

Some of the case law provides an argument against the Public Guardian and Trustee's apparent position that the corporation holds the assets in trust for the charitable purpose and that the officers and directors, by extension, have duties of or similar to those of a trustee. In *Re City Equitable Fire Insurance Co.*,[21] Romer J. commented that:

> It has sometimes been said that directors are trustees. If this means no more than that directors in the performance of their duties stand in a fiduciary relationship to the company, the statement is true enough. But if the statement is meant to be an indication by way of analogy of what those duties are, it appears to me to be wholly misleading. I can see but little resemblance between the duties of a director and the duties of a trustee of a will or of a marriage settlement.

This position would seem to be consistent with the American case law. In *Stern v. Larry Webb Hayes Training School*,[22] the Court decided that:

> The charitable corporation is a relatively new legal entity which does not fit neatly into the established common law doctrine of corporation and trust ... the modern trend is to apply corporate rather than trust principles in determining the liability of the directors of charitable corporations, because their functions are virtually indistinguishable from those of their "pure" corporate counterparts.

The position in Ontario is not clear. The courts have discussed the question of whether or not a charitable corporation and the directors and officers are in their nature trustees. In *Re David Feldman Charitable Foundation*,[23] the Court concluded that the letters patent created both the foundation and a charitable trust. Mr. Justice Kerr commented that the "directors are also trustees of the foundation". He continued, quoting from the British case *Re French Protestant Hospital*:[24]

> The property of the charity is, of course, vested in and held by the corporation. It is a perpetual person which exists, however, only according to the rules of law, and it is not an actual person capable of acting on its own motion in any way whatever. It seems to me that in a case of this kind the court is bound to look at the real situation which exists in fact. It is obvious that the corporation is completely controlled under the provisions of the charter by the governor, deputy governor and directors, and that those are the persons who in fact control the corporation and decide what shall be done. It is plain that those persons are as much in a fiduciary position as trustees in regard to any acts which are done respecting the corporation

---

[21] [1925] 1 Ch. 407, at 426 (C.A.).
[22] 381 F. Supp. 1003, at 1013 (U.S. Dist. Ct., D.C., 1974).
[23] (1987), 58 O.R. (2d) 626 (Surr. Ct.).
[24] *Ibid.*, at 631. *Re French Protestant Hospital*, [1951] 1 Ch. 567, [1951] 1 All E.R. 938 (Ch. D.).

and its property. It is quite plain that it would be entirely illegal if they were simply to put the property, or the proceeds of the property of the corporation into their pockets and make use of it for their own individual purposes or for their purposes as a whole, and not for the purposes of the charitable trust for which the property is held. Therefore it seems to me plain that they are, to all intents and purposes, bound by the rules which affect trustees.

Mr. Justice Kerr concluded that the directors were in a conflict of interest and thus committed a breach of trust by authorizing a loan to a director even where the transaction was not unlawful. The breach of trust occurred even where there was no loss to the charitable trust and the Public Guardian and Trustee could require the repayment of the loan under the *Charities Accounting Act*.[25]

If the directors had applied under s. 61 of the *Trustee Act*,[26] the court would have had jurisdiction to authorize reasonable and fair allowances to trustees for their care, pains and trouble and their time expended to carry out their duties as directors of a charitable corporation. The court may also excuse any breach of trust under s. 35 of the Act.[27] There was, therefore, an appropriate mechanism to authorize or obtain approval for what the directors did in that case.

In *Re Public Trustee and Toronto Humane Society et al.*,[28] Mr. Justice Anderson found that a director is a fiduciary and not, therefore, entitled to make a profit from his or her office or to allow himself or herself to be placed in a position where his or her interests and duties conflict. Anderson J. noted that:

> Whether one calls them trustees in the pure sense (and it would be a blessing if for a moment one could get away from the problems of terminology), the directors are undoubtedly under a fiduciary obligation to the Society and the Society is dealing with funds solicited or otherwise obtained from the public for charitable purposes. If such persons are to pay themselves, it seems to me only proper that it should be upon the terms upon which a trustee can obtain remuneration, either by express provision in the trust document or by the order of the court.[29]

The case turned on two important points:

---

[25] But see *Ontario (Public Guardian and Trustee) v. Unity Church of Truth* [1998] O.J. No. 1291, March 24, 1998, Ont. Ct. of Justice (Gen. Div.) where the court declined to order that the church pass its accounts as no useful purpose would be served. An accounting would not provide any further illumination to the materials already before the court.
[26] R.S.O. 1990, c. T.23.
[27] *Re Faith Haven Bible Training Centre* (1988), 29 E.T.R. 198 (Ont. Surr. Ct.).
[28] (1987), 60 O.R. (2d) 236 (H.C.).
[29] *Ibid.*, at 247.

1) The *Charities Accounting Act* provides that any corporation incorporated for a religious, educational, charitable or public purpose shall be deemed to be a trustee within the meaning of the Act and any real or personal property acquired by it shall be deemed to be property within the meaning of the Act. That Act does not necessarily create for all purposes a trust relationship between the directors and the charitable corporation or the charitable property; and
2) The substance of the issue before the Court was narrow, dealing with the remuneration of a director who derived personal benefit from the office. It was not necessary to characterize the director as a trustee, but rather as a fiduciary.

The *Toronto Humane Society* case complicated an already confused situation. It would appear that directors are in a fiduciary relationship with charitable corporations, rather than in an explicit trust relationship. The relationship is, however, similar in nature to that of a trustee. The rules that apply to trustees regarding how they carry out their duties would appear to apply to directors of a charitable corporation. A director or officer of a charitable corporation would probably be prudent to exercise the same level of care that he or she would as a trustee.

The difference between the duty of a director as a trustee or as fiduciary was also addressed in *Re Faith Haven Bible Training Centre*. The Court commented that:

> In law, Faith Haven held its net assets as a trustee for that purpose. Whether the directors — the only body through whom the corporate trustee could carry out the trust — should be designated as trustees as well or whether they should be classified as fiduciaries bound to see to the execution of the trust is surely a sterile consideration. In either capacity they have the same obligations as the corporation itself.[30]

Mr. Justice Cullity reiterated these statements in *Asian Outreach Canada v. Hutchinson*. In that case, he reviewed the case law and commented:

> The confusion has sometimes arisen is a consequence of the fact that the equitable jurisdiction of the Court includes both the enforcement of trusts and the supervision of charities whether the latter are established under wills or trust instruments inter vivos, or as corporations. As many of the general principles applied by the courts in supervising charitable trusts have also been applied to charitable corporations there was a tendency, particularly in 19th Century cases in England, to find the basis of the jurisdiction over charities in the law of trusts. This does not appear to be cor-

---

[30] (1988), 29 E.T.R. 198, at 207 (Ont. Surr. Ct.).

rect historically and it is clear that it does not represent the present state of the law in this jurisdiction.[31]

While Justice Cullity was discussing the supervisory jurisdiction of the superior court and the issue of beneficial ownership of property for general purposes of the corporation or for specific charitable purposes, it illustrates the background to the confusion.

III DUTIES AND OBLIGATIONS TO THE ORGANIZATION

Directors and officers of an organization, such as a corporation, have fiduciary obligations to the organization. These obligations or duties require officers and directors to act with a reasonable degree of prudence, to be diligent, to act in good faith, honestly and loyally, and to avoid conflicts of interest.

The courts have applied, for example, the common law duty of loyalty to corporate officers and directors. In *Can. Aero Service Ltd. v. O'Malley*[32] Chief Justice Laskin concluded that a director, as a fiduciary, had a duty to act loyally, honestly, in good faith and to avoid personal profit. Liability does not turn on whether or not the director acted in bad faith. Rather, no fiduciary may "have an interest that possibly conflicts with the interests of those whom he is bound to protect", according to *Aberdeen Railway Co. v. Blaikie Bros.*[33] In *Regal (Hastings) Ltd. v. Gulliver*,[34] the House of Lords decided that the test is whether or not the director has a personal conflict. If there is a personal conflict, the director could be liable to account for any profits he or she makes. The rationale is that the director has a fiduciary relationship to the corporation and out of that relationship the director made a profit.[35]

The Supreme Court of Canada took a similar approach in the *Can. Aero* case. The Court looked to the circumstances to determine whether or not a conflict existed. The types of factors that the court should consider include the:

> ...position or office held, the nature of the corporate opportunity, its ripeness, its specificness and the director's or managerial officer's relation to it, the amount of knowledge possessed, the circumstances in which it was obtained and whether it was special or, indeed, even private, the factor of time in the continuation of fiduciary duty where the alleged breach occurs after termination of the relationship with the company, and the circum-

---

[31] *Asian Outreach Canada v. Hutchinson*, [1999] 28 E.T.R. (2d) 275 (Ont. S.C.J.).
[32] [1974] S.C.R. 592.
[33] (1854), 2 Eq. Rep. 1281 (H.L.).
[34] [1942] 1 All E.R. 378 (H.L.).
[35] *Ibid.*, at 385.

stances under which the relationship was terminated, that is whether by retirement or resignation or discharge.[36]

In practical terms, a prudent director or officer of a not-for-profit organization, either incorporated or an unincorporated association, should probably avoid having an interest in any contract of the corporation. An exception exists if the director declares an interest in the contract at the board meeting where the contract is considered or arises and refrains from voting or participating in the discussion or attempting to influence the vote.[37]

If the corporation is a charitable corporation, the director should avoid any interest in any contract with the corporation because directors are held, at least nominally, to a higher standard of conduct that is akin to that of a "trustee". An exception to this general rule would be where, with the court's approval, the corporation is paying for professional services that are additional to the director's duties.[38] Unless both conditions have been met, it is not prudent for a director to charge or receive professional or other fees from the charitable corporation. In the case of lawyers, accountants and similar professionals, the restriction from charging for professional services probably applies not only to the individual lawyer or accountant who is the officer or director but to all the partners and employees of the firm.

The prudent course would be for a professional firm not to charge or receive commissions for any professional services that it provides to the charitable corporation. This restriction would apply to any services provided not only by the officer or director in his or her professional capacity but also to the services provided by partners and employees. Obviously, this situation may result in greater difficulty for charitable organizations to attract officers and directors who can provide assistance to the organization.

The *Charities Accounting Act* was amended to permit certain types of transactions by directors. Section 5.1 was added to the Act[39] and authorized the Attorney General to make regulations on the advice of the Public Guardian and Trustee that would otherwise require the approval of a superior court justice. A regulation was enacted in 2001 that permits, for example, the purchase of indemnification insurance.[40]

In some cases, fees are paid by a third party and not by the charitable organization. For example, a financial consultant or investment advisor

---

[36] [1974] S.C.R. 592, at 620.
[37] The incorporating statutes usually provide for this approach. See, for e.g., s. 71 of the Ontario *Corporations Act*, R.S.O. 1990, c. C.38; s. 98 of the Ontario *Co-operative Corporations Act*, R.S.O. 1990, c. C.35; and s. 98 of the *Canada Corporations Act*, R.S.C. 1970, c. C.32.
[38] *Re Harold G. Fox Education Fund v. Ont. (Public Trustee)* (1989), 69 O.R. (2d) 742 (H.C.).
[39] S.O. 1999, c. 12, Sched. B, s. 1(4).
[40] O. Reg. 4/01.

will often be paid a commission by a financial institution on the sale of an investment instrument. If the same or similar investment could have been obtained for less money where the commission was not paid, it is apparent that the advisor probably has a conflict of interest with his or her role as a director. The situation is less clear if the payment of the fee does not affect directly the value of the investment of the charitable organization. A prudent director would probably consider donating the commission to the charitable organization in either situation.

There are a number of acts on the part of a director or officer that will give rise to liability. A director who breaches his or her duty to be honest in the exercise of powers and discretion would be liable for any damages to the corporation that result from the breach. Examples of this type of breach include: misuse of corporate funds;[41] misappropriation of corporate property;[42] improper loans to directors;[43] or appropriation of a corporate opportunity.[44] A breach of the duty of honesty involves misfeasance or active error and not merely inactivity or nonfeasance.[45] However, given the standard of care for officers and directors, turning a "blind eye" or not exercising due diligence where the director is aware or ought to be aware of misfeasance on the part of another director or another person could give rise to liability to the corporation.

It would appear that officers and directors would not be liable if they were acting within their authority as officers and directors. An officer or director who acts outside his or her authority is in a different situation. In some cases, the acts may be confirmed by the corporation, if the acts themselves were within the objects and powers of the corporation. The director involved should not vote on the ratification or confirmation of any such acts, since there would be, in all likelihood, a conflict of interest between his or her duty as a director and his or her personal interests.

Certain acts that are outside the authority of the director may also be beyond the objects and powers of the corporation, as set out in its letters patent, constituting documents or the applicable legislation. In *Ashbury Railway Carriage and Iron Co. v. Riche*,[46] the House of Lords held that ratification was not legally possible if the contract was beyond the scope of the corporation's powers. Similarly, if an activity is within the capacity of the corporation but is otherwise prohibited by law, the director's act cannot be ratified.[47]

In Ontario, corporations under the *Corporations Act*, the *Co-operative Corporations Act* or the *Canada Corporations Act* are "persons". A co-operative corporation, since the amendments in 1992, has the powers of

---

[41] *Re Dom. Trust Co.* (1917), 32 D.L.R. 63 (Ont. C.A.).
[42] *Hart v. Felson* (1924), 30 R.L.N.S. 109 (C.S.).
[43] *R. v. Kussner*, [1936] Ex. C.R. 206 (Ex. Ct.).
[44] *Can. Aero Service Ltd. v. O'Malley*, [1974] S.C.R. 592.
[45] *D'Amore v. McDonald*, [1973] 1 O.R. 845 (H.C.); affd. 1 O.R. (2d) 370 (C.A.).
[46] (1875), L.R. 7 H.L. 653 (H.L.).
[47] *Grant v. Dom. Loose Leaf Co.* (1924), 56 O.L.R. 43 (H.C.).

a natural person, unless those powers are otherwise restricted in the articles of incorporation or by statute. Corporations without share capital under the Ontario *Corporations Act* and *Canada Corporations Act* do not have all of the powers of a natural person or of a business corporation. They are generally treated as persons within the context of their objects. The legislation provides for ancillary and incidental powers which cover most of the needs of a corporation. Unless the incorporating documents place a restriction on the powers or the capacities of the corporation (as with charitable corporations, for example), there are few occasions that would give rise to the director's acts being *ultra vires* the corporation. It could occur, for example, if a charitable corporation attempted to ratify the acts of a director that were intended to cause gain to the members of the corporation. Similarly, a charitable corporation could not ratify a donation to a political party. Such a donation would be outside the powers of a charitable corporation and, as a result, is *ultra vires*. A director who caused, agreed to or acquiesced in an *ultra vires* act on the part of the corporation would be exposed to personal liability on the grounds that he or she breached the director's duty to ensure that the corporation complied with the law.[48]

The officers and directors owe a duty of diligence to the corporation. They should attend meetings and be prepared for the business at hand. Attendance and preparation are particularly important because most of the decisions that affect charitable and not-for-profit organizations must be under-taken at meetings and the responsibility for making decisions rests with the directors, more so than in business corporations. In business corporations, much of the decision making is left to the management of the corporation and implemented by employees; boards of charitable and not-for-profit organizations are usually substantially more involved in the operations of the organization.

The duty of diligence involves participating in decision making. Directors should not rely on the opinions of others, but should ask questions and be certain in their own minds and on reasonable grounds that a decision is appropriate in the circumstances. The director should be involved as fully as possible, asking for clarification when uncertain about an issue or the impact of a proposed decision.

Officers and directors must also balance the objects of the organization against its ability to attain the objects. They must be cognizant of the financial integrity of the organization to ensure that it is preserved and able to carry out its activities in the future. Accountability of officers and directors means that the organization not only achieves its objects but that it does so in a manner that does not unduly place the organization at risk. Indeed, officers and directors who knowingly place a charitable

---

[48] E. Blake Bromley and G.B. MacRae, "The Duties and Public Liability of Directors of British Columbia Societies", in *Charities and Non-Profit Organizations* (Vancouver: The Continuing Legal Education Society of British Columbia, 1985).

organization at risk, financially or otherwise, may be breaching their duties to the beneficiaries of the trust.

D TRUSTEES

I INTRODUCTION

A trustee is obliged to discharge his or her duties in accordance with the terms of trust. The terms of trust are usually set out in the trust instrument. However, as noted above, s. 1 of the *Charities Accounting Act*,[49] deems corporations that are incorporated for a religious, educational, charitable or public purpose to be trustees. It would appear that the officers and directors of corporations to which the Act applies have duties comparable to those of a trustee. The following discussion would, therefore, be relevant to officers and directors of those corporations. The trustee has three duties to the trust and its beneficiaries — to carry out his or her tasks with due care and attention; not to delegate; and not to permit his or her own interests to conflict with his or her duty to the beneficiaries of the trust.

In carrying out their duties, the trustees have a number of powers under the trust instrument, at common law and by legislation, such as the *Trustee Act*.[50] The powers are administrative and dispositive in nature and are intended to permit the trustees to carry out their duties. For example, the trustees may appoint new trustees,[51] sell property,[52] renew leases[53] and insure property. The Act also provides for investment of the trust assets, which is discussed in more detail. The statute was amended in Ontario to put in place a prudent investor rule as opposed to the more traditional list of permitted investments.

II DUTIES TO THE TRUST

(1) Basic Duty of Care

A trustee has the duty to carry out his or her tasks with care and attention. A trustee must exercise the level of diligence and care that an ordinary prudent person of business would in conducting his or her own business. The trustee must exercise "vigilance, prudence and sagacity".[54] A trustee may be held liable if he or she carries out the tasks negligently

---

[49] R.S.O. 1990, c. C.10.
[50] R.S.O. 1990, c. T.23.
[51] *Ibid.*, ss. 3 and 4.
[52] *Ibid.*, ss. 17 and 62.
[53] *Ibid.*, s. 22.
[54] *Fales v. Can. Permanent Trust Co.*, [1977] 2 S.C.R. 302, at 318. See also Ontario Ministry of Consumer and Commercial Relations and the Office of the Public Guardian and Trustee, *Not-For-Profit Incorporator's Handbook* (Toronto: Queen's Printer, 1998), at 56.

by omission or commission. The duties must be exercised to carry out the objects of the trust.

The trustee must act in "good faith" at all times, which complements the basic duty of care. "Good faith" is not an easily defined term. He or she must have an honest belief that what he or she is doing or proposes to do is proper and appropriate.[55] If not, the trustee may be accountable for any losses. The trustee is not, however, an insurer and proof of loss on its own is not sufficient to bring about personal liability. There must be evidence of wrong doing or failure to exercise his or her duties properly for a trustee to be held liable.[56]

Interestingly, the standard of care that is applied to any given situation would appear to be an objective one and not the subjective one that seems to apply to officers and directors at common law. The level of skills of the individual trustee or how he or she handles personal business affairs are not relevant to a determination of whether the trustee met the requisite standard of care. Rather, the courts will ask the question "did the trustee act as an ordinary prudent person of business would have acted in the same circumstances?" If not, and a loss resulted from the failure to do so, the trustee will be personally liable for the loss.

The rationale for this test seems to be an assumption that individuals will take the greatest care with their own business affairs. Whether they do take such care in their own business affairs is not relevant. The courts do exercise an "excusing" power to avoid unfairness where the individual trustee is inexperienced or does not have the skills or experience of "an ordinary prudent person of business". In *Fales v. Can. Permanent Trust Co.*, the Supreme Court of Canada took into consideration the fact that one of the trustees was not experienced and relieved that individual trustee from liability for the breach of trust committed by a co-trustee.[57]

It is not clear how the intrusion of this subjective standard into the otherwise objective standard for trustees will affect the duties of trustees of charitable organizations. Furthermore, what is the affect of the objective standard on the subjective standard that would appear to exist for officers and directors at common law? On the face of it, a director of a corporation that has charitable objects to which the *Charities Accounting Act* applies may have to meet an objective standard rather than the subjective standard. This area of law is clearly one that requires clarification, presumably by statute.[58]

---

[55] Ontario Law Reform Commission, *Report on the Law of Trusts*, Vol. 1 (Toronto: Ontario Ministry of the Attorney General, 1984), at 24.
[56] *Re Chapman, Cocks v. Chapman*, [1896] 2 Ch. 763, at 775 (C.A.).
[57] [1977] 2 S.C.R. 302.
[58] The Ontario Law Reform Commission in its 1984 *Report on the Law of Trusts* concluded at 29 that the test of the prudent person of business should not be lowered for the inexperienced or nonprofessional trustee. If the individual did not have the experience or skills, the report argued, he or she should not assume the duties.

(2) Duty Not to Delegate

The trustee has a duty not to delegate, which arises from the creation of the trust itself. The trust already provides for a delegation of the power to the trustees to control and manage the property for a specified purpose. The trustee must carry out his or her duties personally and may not sub-delegate the power to control and manage the property.

A power could be delegated if the terms of the trust permit it to be delegated in accordance with the terms. Furthermore, the trustee may delegate at common law certain administrative functions where the nature of the task necessitates the delegation, or if it is common business practice to do so in the circumstances. Where a trustee seeks the advice of a professional, the trustee must act prudently and exercise care before relying upon that advice.

The *Trustee Act*[59] permits the trustee to delegate certain functions. For example, s. 20 provides that a trustee may appoint: a solicitor as an agent to receive and give a discharge for any money or valuable consideration or property receivable by the trustee under the trust; or a manager or a branch manager of a chartered bank; or a solicitor to be an agent to receive and give a discharge for any money payable to the trustee under or by virtue of a policy of assurance or otherwise. The trustee may also seek the advice of professionals or others to assist in making decisions. The trustee should be satisfied, though, that the advice is sound before relying upon it. The trustee has a duty to act prudently and to exercise care before relying upon the advice.[60] The delegation of power with respect to investment decisions is discussed below.

(3) Conflict of Interest

A trustee has a duty to avoid conflicts of interest. A trustee must avoid a conflict of interest between his or her own personal interests and those of the trust and its beneficiaries. A trustee may not, for example, profit from the trust, a rule which is strictly applied.[61] The issue is not whether the trustee acted with or without integrity or if the benefit would have accrued to the trust; rather, the issue is whether the trustee was in a position where his or her duty could be in conflict with the duty to the trust when the profit was made or the gain acquired. A prudent trustee would, without authority otherwise, avoid the receipt of commissions from third parties on investment instruments or at least donate those commissions to the trust.

Courts apply the rule strictly because they cannot readily determine what motivated the trustee. A motive can be indirectly determined when there is evidence of a profit that was received or that a gain occurred.

---

[59] R.S.O. 1990, c. T.23.
[60] *Fry v. Tapson* (1884), 28 Ch. D. 268.
[61] *Keech v. Sanford* (1726), 25 E.R. 223 (L.C.).

However, an exception to the rule exists if the trustee has explicit authority to make a profit or gain. The authority may be provided by the trust document, by the beneficiaries or by the court. Authorization by the trust document to make profit or gain is circumscribed by the Public Guardian and Trustee's apparent position that trustees not receive any remuneration from a charitable trust or charitable corporation.

In the case of a charitable corporation, this restriction is implemented by the inclusion of the mandatory special provisions in the letters patent. If the terms of the trust do not permit payments to a trustee, a court order is required for trustees of a charitable trust to be paid for services that he or she supplies to the charitable trust.[62] Section 35 of the *Trustee Act* provides some protection to trustees. If the breach of trust was technical in nature, the trustee acted honestly and reasonably and the court considers it to be fair to excuse the trustee for the breach, the court may relieve the trustee from any personal liability.[63]

The Public Guardian and Trustee has identified a number of duties, responsibilities and powers of trustees.[64] The following duties would apply both to trustees of a charitable trust and to the officers and directors of a charitable corporation:

- duties on appointment as a director or trustee — a new director or trustee should know the purposes of the charity, be familiar with the general requirements of charities law and the *Corporations Act*, if incorporated, and review the past administration of the charity. There is a duty to investigate any suspicious circumstances which suggest that the charity's property was not used properly and to take action to correct any problems;
- duty to be reasonable, prudent and judicious — the directors and trustees must handle the charitable property with the care, skill and diligence that a prudent person would use. This duty includes treating the property in the way a careful person would treat his or her own property and to protect the property from undue risk of loss. They must also protect the property from excessive administrative expenses;
- duty to carry out the charitable purposes — this duty is two-fold: first, to ensure that the property is used only for purposes of the charity and no other purposes; but secondly to use the property to carry out the charitable purposes. The assets are not to be left un-

---

[62] *Re Harold G. Fox Educational Fund v. Ont. (Public Trustee)* (1989), 69 O.R. (2d) 742 (H.C.). See also *Re Public Trustee and Toronto Humane Society et al.* (1987), 60 O.R. (2d) 236 (H.C.) and *Not-For-Profit Incorporator's Handbook*, at 56.
[63] See *Re Faith Haven Bible Training Centre* (1988), 29 E.T.R. 198 (Ont. Surr. Ct.) for a case in which s. 35 was considered.
[64] *Charities Bulletin #3*, Public Guardian and Trustee.

used. In addition, if some of the assets are for specific purposes, those assets may only be used for those purposes;
- duty to avoid conflict of interest situations — directors and trustees are obliged to avoid conflicts of interests. The interests of the charity must be placed before any personal interests. This duty also includes the avoidance of any appearance of a conflict of interest. Decisions on who benefits from the charitable trust, if discretion is in the directors or trustees, ought to be fair;
- duty to act gratuitously — other than as permitted by law or court order, a director or trustee may not be remunerated or compensated for acting as a director. There are some exceptions which have been established by statute or through the common law. For example, directors or trustees may be reimbursed for reasonable and legitimate expenses incurred on behalf of the charitable organization and the charity may, in accordance with the regulation, purchase indemnification insurance;[65]
- duty to account — because directors or trustees are responsible for the charitable property, they must be able to account for the uses of that property. This duty includes the maintenance of proper books and records, preparation of audited financial statements where required by law and to provide information when requested to do so by the Public Guardian and Trustee;
- duty to manage the charity's assets — the directors and trustees, not employees, have this duty. They may retain appropriate staff or consultants but, subject to the investment policy provisions, they must control the assets.

These duties are not exhaustive; however, they are a useful summary of what the Public Guardian and Trustee and the courts would consider in reviewing the activities of trustees of charitable trusts and officers and directors of charitable corporations and other corporations in Ontario to which the *Charities Accounting Act* applies.

E STATUTORY DUTIES

I INTRODUCTION

There are approximately 100 federal and Ontario statutes that impose some statutory duties on the officers and directors of charitable and not-

---

[65] See O. Reg. 4/01 under the *Charities Accounting Act*.

for-profit corporations.[66] It is not possible to review all of these statutes. The common statutory duties, however, arise in four general areas: employees and the workplace; taxation; environmental legislation; and business practices. An officer or director who breaches the statutory duties or causes the corporation to do so may be personally liable for any losses and may also be subject to prosecution.

II COMMON STATUTORY DUTIES

(1) Employees and the Workplace

The *Employment Standards Act, 2000*[67] sets out statutory duties that employers have towards employees. In addition, a collective agreement under the *Labour Relations Act, 1995*[68] and the *Employers and Employee Act*[69] may also apply to the organization as an employer. The *Occupational Health and Safety Act* (OHSA),[70] the *Workplace Insurance and Safety Act, 1997*,[71] the *Pension Benefits Act*,[72] the *Pay Equity Act*[73] are also applicable to charitable and not-for-profit organizations as employers. The OHSA also incorporates the federal Workplace Hazardous Materials Information System to provide protection to workers in the handling of hazardous materials.

Officers and directors are required to exercise due diligence, at the very least, to ensure that the corporation complies with any of its statutory obligations. In some cases, such as s. 32 of the OHSA, the statute may also require directors to take all reasonable care to ensure that the corporation complies with the Act. Officers and directors of any organization may also be subject to the penalty sections of those statutes where the officer or director caused or acquiesced in the breach of the organization's statutory duty to its employees.[74]

The officers and directors may also be held personally liable for certain wages and benefits owed to employees. The Ontario *Corporations Act*,[75] the Ontario *Co-operative Corporations Act*[76] and the *Canada Corpora-*

---

[66] See A.D. Wolfe, "Liability of Directors and Officers of Non-Share Corporations" in *Fit to Be Tithed: Risks and Rewards of Charities and Churches* (Toronto: Law Society of Upper Canada, Continuing Legal Education, 1994) and S.D. Saxe, *Ontario Employment Law Handbook: An Employer's Guide*, 5th ed., (Toronto: Butterworths Canada Ltd., 2000).
[67] S.O. 2000, c. 41.
[68] S.O. 1995, c. 1.
[69] R.S.O. 1990, c. E.12.
[70] R.S.O. 1990, c. O.1.
[71] S.O. 1997, c. 16, Sched. A.
[72] R.S.O. 1990, c. P.8.
[73] R.S.O. 1990, c. P.7.
[74] See, for example, s. 110 of the *Pension Benefits Act*; s. 26 of the *Pay Equity Act*; s. 79 of the *Employment Standards Act*; and s. 66 of the *Occupational Health and Safety Act* for different approaches to establishing a statutory basis for prosecution.
[75] R.S.O. 1990, c. C.38, s. 81.
[76] R.S.O. 1990, c. C.35, s. 103.

tions Act[77] set up statutory schemes for employees to sue directors for unpaid wages. The schemes are similar in all three statutes — the directors are liable jointly and severally for up to six months in wages, and vacation pay for 12 months in the case of the Ontario statutes. A director will be liable if the corporation has been sued for the debt and the debt has not been satisfied or the corporation is bankrupt or insolvent. The director must be sued personally while he or she is a director or if the person ceased to be a director, within six months in the case of an Ontario corporation without share capital, two years for a co-operative corporation and one year for a Canada corporation without share capital. The limitation period for lawsuits is six months after the debt became due. There does not appear to be a statutory or common law due diligence defence for directors.

(2) Taxes and Other Source Deductions

There are several statutes that create an obligation for employers to collect and remit taxes or similar assessments to the governments. The more prominent among these are the *Income Tax Act*,[78] the *Canada Pension Plan*,[79] the *Employment Insurance Act*[80] and, in Ontario, the *Employer Health Tax Act*.[81] The organization may also be liable for taxes that it collects and is obliged to remit on the sale of goods and services, such as the goods and services tax, imposed under the *Excise Tax Act*[82] and retail sales taxes under the *Retail Sales Tax Act*.[83] The directors may also be liable for any taxes that are owed by the corporation on income that it has earned where it is not exempt from the payment of taxes under the *Income Tax Act* or the Ontario *Corporations Tax Act*.[84]

All of these statutes establish an obligation on the directors to ensure that the appropriate taxes are collected and remitted to the government. The statutes will usually have both a penalty section under which an officer or director may be charged with an offence under the statute and a statutory requirement to pay any amounts owing by the corporation. Any director who cannot demonstrate due diligence may be convicted and/or be held personally liable for the amount owed.[85] As discussed above, the standard of care is not less for directors of charitable or not-for-profit organizations.

---

[77] R.S.C. 1970, c. C-32, s. 99.
[78] R.S.C. 1985, c. I (5th Supp.).
[79] R.S.C. 1985, c. C.8.
[80] S.C. 1996, c. 23.
[81] R.S.O. 1990, c. E.11.
[82] R.S.C. 1985, c. E-15.
[83] R.S.O. 1990, c. R.31.
[84] R.S.O. 1990, c. C.40.
[85] See, for example, s. 227.1 of the *Income Tax Act*, which applies to the *Canada Pension Act*; s. 323 of the *Excise Tax Act*; s. 43 of the *Retail Sales Tax Act*.

(3) Environmental

Officers and directors are being held increasingly responsible, both in statutes and by the courts, for ensuring that corporations comply with environmental protection legislation. Section 194 of the Ontario *Environmental Protection Act*[86] provides that:

> Every director or officer of a corporation that engages in an activity that may result in the discharge of a contaminant into the natural environment contrary to this Act or the regulations has a duty to take all reasonable care to prevent the corporation from causing or permitting such unlawful discharge.

The courts, in *R. v. Bata Industries Ltd.*,[87] have convicted a director for failure to comply with the statutory duty and with a similar statutory duty in the *Ontario Water Resources Act*.[88] Those directors that could demonstrate that they had exercised due diligence were not convicted. Although the corporation was a business corporation, the principles would appear to apply to corporations without share capital and co-operative corporations.

(4) Business Practices

The Canada *Competition Act*[89] and the Ontario *Business Practices Act*[90] prohibit a number of practices that are intended to or have the effect of misleading purchasers. The *Competition Act* also prohibits certain practices that are anti-competitive in nature. Officers and directors may be prosecuted under these statutes if they participated in the commission of an offence or caused or acquiesced in the commission of an offence. If the corporation is involved in the sale of goods or services, the directors should be aware of the need to be fair and honest in the corporation's dealings with others. The *Competition Act* is reviewed in more detail in Chapter 10 as it applies to fundraising activities.

F PREVENTING PROBLEMS

I Effective Boards

In general, the board is responsible for overseeing the day-to-day operations of the organization. The directors have a duty to manage the or-

---

[86] R.S.O. 1990, c. E.19.
[87] (1992), 9 O.R. (3d) 329; vard. (1993), 14 O.R. (3d) 354 (Gen. Div.).
[88] R.S.O. 1990, c. O.40.
[89] R.S.C. 1985, c. C-34.
[90] R.S.O. 1990, c. B.18.

ganization — but they also have a duty to operate it, i.e., to ensure that it has activities that carry out its objects. It may do so through the development and implementation of policies and programs that meet the objectives of the organization. The directors are also responsible for ensuring that the organization complies with its common law and statutory obligations — which include those related to the area in which it operates (such as child care), employment law, environmental law, taxation and other statutory requirements.

The board is, however, made up of individuals. This fact is sometimes overlooked and individuals have differing views and personalities. One of the critical, practical roles of the board is to ensure that the board and the directors that comprise this human institution work in an effective and efficient manner — at the same time, recognizing and taking into account the different backgrounds, cultural and personal experiences, interests and personalities of the individuals.

There are several important "policies" or statements that should be in place so that existing and new directors understand what their roles are and what limits exist. These statements should first set out whether or not the board is to operate on the basis of "policy governance" or "administrative governance". The policy governance model gained favour in the 1990s. The board is intended to carry out its legal obligations by setting policies and monitoring the implementation by staff. Staff, in this model, are authorized to make decisions within the stated policies. An administrative governance model leaves decision-making with the board, which retains responsibility for implementation of its decisions. Obviously, the policy governance model is feasible only where there is staff — and staff that has the skills and training necessary to carry out the functions. It is more appropriate for larger, very sophisticated organizations and where the directors cannot make and implement all the decisions.

Increasingly, boards are also establishing codes of conduct to ensure that directors understand their roles and that they behave in an appropriate manner. The codes may include a conflict of interest policy, or that policy may be separate. There may also be "job descriptions" for directors, which identify expectations of each director with respect to, for example, fundraising or public speaking. Just as with staff, it is a good idea to include criteria to assess board performance and how well a director carried out his or her duties.

The overall purpose of the board is to provide the direction to the organization to permit it to carry out its objects, to ensure that the organization meets its legal obligations (including maintenance of its status) and is financially responsible. The board must plan on how it intends to carry out the objects of the organization and to use the available resources to do so.

The board should allocate specific functions and tasks to specific positions, which are filled by individuals. Typically, the by-laws will do so for the president, vice-president, treasurer and secretary, and for larger organizations, for certain staff, such as the executive director. The individuals filling those positions are responsible to the board for their performance of the functions and tasks.

Boards often operate through committees, both standing and *ad hoc* committees. Care must be taken to ensure that any committees that are established comply with the governing law. For example, the Ontario *Corporations Act* permits the establishment of an executive committee with decision-making powers in certain circumstances but all other committees may be advisory only. The committees should each have terms of reference, even if it is functioning only in an advisory capacity.

The proper and respectful conduct of the board meetings is essential for the board to fulfill its obligations. If decisions are to be made by the board of directors — either to establish policies and monitor their implementation as a "policy governance board" or to make day-to-day decisions as an "administrative governance board" — there must be a controlled forum in which to make those decisions.

The affairs of the organization are transacted at meetings and those meetings should be run in an effective manner. There is no single rule on how to ensure that meetings are effective but a number of techniques may be highlighted:

- clarity of purpose of the organization — all in attendance should know and understand what the purpose of the organization is, its activities and the issues at hand. New directors should receive orientation so that they can contribute as soon as possible,
- clarity of purpose of the meeting — the purpose of the meeting, be it a regular monthly meeting or a special meeting, should be clear. A well drafted agenda will indicate the topics for discussion, for decision and for information, the priorities of the meeting and the allocated times. Background materials should be sufficient for the directors to understand the issues, to contribute to the meeting and to make any necessary decisions.
- clarity of the rules — rules or procedures are used to facilitate a meeting to allow it to be conducted smoothly and to avoid confusion and unfairness (actual or perceived). While strict enforcement of the rules should not stifle or kill debate, they should not be so loosely enforced that effective decision-making or debate is lost. The rules need to be clear, explicit and understood by all.
- unwritten rules — in most organizations, there are unwritten rules or norms that people take for granted. These have sometimes been developed to avoid conflict or to accommodate the specific needs of individuals. While these unwritten rules assist the board, newer directors may not be aware of them. A process should be in place to acquaint new directors with these unwritten rules — and other directors should be cognizant that it is very difficult for newer directors to know about an unwritten rule if it is not made

known to them. In any event, the board should take care to ensure that any such unwritten rules are not in conflict with the law and the organization's by-laws and written rules.
- enjoyable meetings — individuals should find the meetings overall to be enjoyable, worthwhile and effective. This objective is true for any meeting but it is particularly important where the individuals are giving up their time for the public good. They want and deserve a level of personal satisfaction and enjoyment from the meetings — always within the context of what their jobs are as directors. The sense of enjoyment may be enhanced by a better meeting place or modest amenities, such as refreshments.
- skills of the chair — effective meetings depend upon the skills of the chair. The chair needs to be in control of the meeting and have prepared for the meeting. A lack of preparation and ineffectiveness will have a negative impact on the meeting. The chair should be and be seen to be fair and even-handed in dealing with matters as they arise — including any personality conflicts that may occur. The chair needs to ensure that all directors have a fair opportunity to participate in the meeting and to avoid excessive or repetitive participation by a few. The skills necessary to chair a meeting are ones that are developed with experience and time and tolerance on the part of others.

Effective boards are possible.[91] They generally have mechanisms in place to assess the community need for the organization so that it remains relevant. At times, these mechanisms may reveal that the organization is no longer needed and that its resources could be better used elsewhere. However, more often the organization will identify a better way to operate in the community or to alter itself to meet the needs in a more effective manner. Sometimes, changes to the organization's by-laws, letters patent, or, more simply, to its policies will be needed. The board is responsible for undertaking such assessments on a periodic basis or as needed.

The board must also plan within the context of the organization's mission and strategic plans. These plans are used to state what activities the organization will carry out and what outcomes are expected, what tasks are to be done and by whom, and how these plans relate to the organization's objects and resources and the budgetary process. They are intended to ensure that the organization's priorities are being met, in accordance with its legal obligations. It is useful to identify options during

---

[91] See D. Abbey-Livingstone and B. Wiele, *Working with Volunteer Boards: How to Improve Their Effectiveness* (Toronto: Ontario Ministry of Citizenship and the Ontario Association of Volunteer Bureaux/Centres, 1994).

the planning process and the pros and cons for each option so that the directors can determine which activities best meet and affect the organization's objects and resources.

The implementation of the plans involves the carrying out of the tasks identified in the plans and the ongoing coordination of the tasks. The board must be sensitive in implementing the plans should circumstances change. An unanticipated shortfall in revenues, for example, will require that the board either locate new resources, reallocate resources or amend the plan. The board should also evaluate plans and how they were implemented — both for purposes of accountability and monitoring, and to learn from what worked and what did not work. The evaluations will also assist in determining how relevant and effective the organization is in the community which it serves.

Boards should also manage relationships. They need to communicate internally and externally to stakeholders. Conflicts need to be managed so that they become productive outcomes or are resolved. If conflict is not managed, the board will have difficulty in developing and implementing plans and in carrying out the objects of the organization. Relationships with others outside the organization are equally important — be they regulators, governments, funders, corporate partners, clientele or the general public. Management of volunteers and their proper motivation is also part of the role of the board.

II Due Diligence

The first opportunity for a director to exercise due diligence is before he or she becomes a member of the board, either by election or by appointment. A potential director or officer should develop a good understanding of the organization and the area in which it operates before agreeing to be appointed or elected. For example, the individual should determine and understand:

- the objects and activities of the organization. These objects should be set out in the letters patent or similar document incorporating the organization, in the trust deed if the organization is a trust or in the other constating documents, such as a memorandum of association, if an unincorporated association. The activities would usually be identified in an annual report, strategic plan, report to funders, financial statements, brochures or similar document,
- the statutes, regulations and policies under which the organization operates. The first step is to review the incorporating legislation, if the organization is a corporation. In addition, it is important to understand the legal framework that may exist for the organization, including taxation legislation, supervisory statutes and similar statutory regimes. These statutes will often set out or define

- obligations and thus areas for potential liability for the organization and for individual directors,
- the regulators who have jurisdiction over the organization. What are the formal and informal expectations of the regulators? Is the organization in compliance with the requirements? Has the organization completed its annual filings?
- financial position of the organization. This type of information is usually (or ought to be) available in the financial statements, reports to regulators (including the Canada Customs and Revenue Agency) and to funders. There may be restrictions on the use of funds, either by statute, contract or internal decisions. In addition, the potential director would want to determine if there is any outstanding or potential litigation involving the organization, its directors or its officers for breach of contract, statute or other legal obligation.

Once the individual is a director, he or she must exercise due diligence in carrying out his or her fiduciary duties. Due diligence is both a question of fact and of law. What is due diligence will depend on the circumstances, the type of organization and the activities undertaken. In general, directors or officers will meet their obligations if they act reasonably, prudently and sagaciously and within the law, including the objects of the organization and the scope of their position or office. They should participate fully in the decisions of the organization. Participation means attending meetings and being prepared for those meetings by reviewing and understanding the materials and issues. Directors should also express their views and participate in the discussion of issues and information. Minutes of meetings should accurately reflect the discussion and the decisions.

The Ontario Public Guardian and Trustee has summarized the general duties of the directors of charities as follows:

> Directors and trustees must handle the charity's property with the care, skill and diligence that a prudent person would use. They must treat the charity's property the way a careful person would treat their own property. They must always protect the charity's property from undue risk of loss and must ensure that no excessive administrative expenses are incurred.[92]

This summary is designed for directors and trustees of charities, but it is illustrative of the duties of directors of other organizations in the voluntary sector.

---

[92] *Charities Bulletin No. 3* — Duties, Responsibilities and Powers of Directors and Trustees of Charities (Toronto: Office of the Public Guardian and Trustee, July 1999).

III CHECKLIST FOR DIRECTORS

- always act with a view to the best interests of the organization;
- understand and comply fully (in spirit and letter) with the conflict of interest policy;
- be informed about your organization's mandate, its constating documents (letters patent, trust deed, memorandum of association, by-laws) and its incorporating statute if incorporated;
- discuss matters that are before the board fully and with frankness and candidness;
- actively avoid conflicts of interest and, where a conflict arises, disclose the conflict and do not participate in the decision;
- exercise due diligence, care and skill in carrying out responsibilities as officer or director;
- fulfill fiduciary duties of good faith, honesty and loyalty;
- get independent or outside advice where it is required to ensure that decisions are well-informed;
- ensure effective internal monitoring and reporting systems are in place, including for financial matters but also in areas where there is high risk or regulatory requirements;
- attend meetings and, if not available, be informed about the issues and decisions through minutes and agenda items and any required follow-up;
- keep abreast of the organization's activities and how those activities fit within its mandate and its strategic plan and annual plan;
- ensure that the resources are available or become available to implement decisions;
- monitor compliance with statutes and regulations, especially those that regulate directly the fields in which the organization operates, e.g. day care;
- never forget that the role of the director is to manage the affairs of the organization;
- obtain confirmation that source deductions (taxes, EI, CPP and other pension benefits) have been remitted and that any taxes collected on behalf of governments are remitted;
- prepare adequately for all board and committee meetings;
- question whether the matters being discussed are within the mandate of the organization and the decision is authorized by the by-laws;
- if there are any concerns or objections, state them clearly and ensure that they are recorded in the minutes, especially if there is a reason to believe there may be a contravention of the law or a risk of liability;

- test treatment of assets against the standards of what a reasonably prudent person would do in comparable circumstances if he or she were dealing with his or her own assets — which may be a higher standard than what individuals actually do with their own assets; and
- examine your own performance objectively and determine if you meet your expectations of what a good director does or ought to do.

Nobody is perfect; but that statement cannot excuse a director from making an honest and good faith effort to meet their legal and moral obligations. Evidence of good faith goes a long way to satisfy a court and regulators.

G BOARD MANAGEMENT OF RISK

I ACCOUNTABLE BOARDS

If the role of the board of directors is to manage the affairs of the corporation, including managing risks; and if boards make decisions at meetings, the logical place to start any discussion about boards and management of risk is at the board meetings. The first step towards management of risks is to ensure that the board meetings operate effectively and efficiently and within the law.

An effective board of directors or trustees is a major method to prevent problems from occurring and, as a result, to minimize the potential for personal liability. The success or failure of an organization is also dependent in large measure on the board being effective. The overall purpose of the board is to manage the affairs of the organization. In doing so, the board provides direction to the organization to permit it (through staff, volunteers and agents) to carry out its objects and to ensure that the organization meets its legal obligations, maintains its status and is financially responsible. The board is to plan how the organization will carry out its objects, to use the resources available to it, and to manage any risks.

The board should, in carrying out its responsibilities, allocate specific functions and tasks to specific individuals. Those individuals as president, vice-president, treasurer, secretary (or whatever other title is used) are accountable to the board for the performance of those functions or tasks.

Boards often operate through committees, both standing and *ad hoc*, for membership, budget, audit, fundraising, human resources, volunteers, special projects, strategic planning and so forth. The types and numbers of committees should reflect the needs of the organization and permit it to carry out its objects in an effective and efficient manner. Terms of reference should be prepared and adopted for each committee, including membership on the committee. It may be useful, for example, to have non-board members on the committee. However, it is important to recall that committees are generally advisory only. It is the responsibility of the board of directors to manage the affairs of the corporation. The committees ought to provide advice and/or carry out the directions of the board.

It is also important that the committees not become a parallel or duplicative accountability mechanism for staff, confusing the lines of accountability. If staff reports to the executive director and the executive director reports to the board or a committee of the board, that is the line of accountability. There is a danger if committees assume that staff report to them alone or in addition to the executive director. This may occur more often where the committees parallel staff functions or departments. The risk is probably greater with a "policy governance" board because of the natural inclination of people to want to get involved. Directors in this situation should curb their inclinations.

Much as people may dislike meetings, it is at meetings that matters are discussed, issues debated and decisions made. Modern telecommunications make it easier for directors to meet while physically in different places. Legislative amendments have permitted, for example, meetings to be held through conference calls and in some cases through the internet.

II Policies and the Prevention and Minimization of Risk

(1) What are Policies?

Boards make decisions, but do not always implement them in person. One way to ensure implementation is to put in place policies that must be followed by staff, volunteers and agents in carrying out their respective duties. A policy is a governing principle. It allows the board to delegate to others (staff, volunteers or agents) the authority to act on behalf of the organization, but does so in a way that maintains the board's control. Essentially, it establishes the framework on what is to be done. Policies are often philosophically based, providing a brief statement of the board's views or approach on the matter. It may set out beliefs, values and desires. A policy allows staff, volunteers, agents and others to know what the board wants and expects and why.

Usually, a policy will identify the direction but leaves the methods to those implementing the policy. However, this need not always be the case. As discussed earlier, there are different approaches to governance — the "policy governance" and "administrative governance". There is no right or wrong approach. In reality, most organizations will (or ought to) find a comfortable and appropriate place along the spectrum between the two approaches — which place may move as the organization matures, undergoes stress or change in senior staff, or is adapting to a new environment.

There is another factor that mediates against full acceptance of the "policy governance" approach. Volunteers want to do good, which is why they volunteered in the first place. Directors are no different in this regard than any other volunteer. It is very difficult to get personal satisfaction on an ongoing basis from having adopted a good policy on some matter. Those who developed the policy may obtain a higher level of personal satisfaction, but merely approving a policy after some discussion does not usually make one's heart flutter with happiness. People want — and will — attempt to participate in decision-making whenever they can. Not to recognize this factor ignores the human dynamic in organizations.

On the other hand, this factor also mediates against adopting the full "administrative governance" approach. Policies are intended, among other things, to bring a reasoned approach to a particular matter or issue. They also assist in bringing consistency and overall fairness to decisions. They encourage (or should encourage) full consideration of all relevant factors before a decision is made on the merits of any particular matter. Indirectly, a policy will also carve out areas of responsibility so that those who know and do the job best are the ones who have the responsibilities to do so. Directors will be discouraged from getting involved in decisions for which they bring little or no expertise, knowledge, understanding or value.

This factor leads one to another purpose of policies — accountability. If the policy identifies who is to do what, when and what results are expected, then the policy also provides a basis for evaluation of the "doer" and for accountability. The staff or volunteer should know what is expected of him or her and he or she can be assessed against that standard.

(2) Policies Governing the Board

The board is also subject to "policies". These policies are more process, planning and decision making in nature. Traditionally, they have not always been seen as policies and have been called by other names. For example, a basic policy that all organizations must have are by-laws, that set out who does what, when and how often. By-laws will cover such matters as financial affairs, record-keeping, timing of and conduct at meetings and so forth. Yet, too often, boards will forget about or even worse not be aware of the by-laws.

Policies are also set out in resolutions of the board. These resolutions may set up committees or identify methods by which the board will operate. The resolutions may prescribe certain approaches to issues or document how certain decisions are to be made or even what the decisions will be in similar situations. For example, a board that decides on who gets a scholarship or bursary may set out by resolution what the eligibility criteria will be for applicants to be considered. Several of the policies have already been discussed in previous chapters. For example, the strategic plan is an essential policy that will govern resource allocation, partnerships and so forth for the organization.

What types of policies ought to be in place or considered? Context, is obviously important to answering this question. If the organization does not have employees or volunteers, there is no point in having human resource policies. There are a number of possible policies for most organizations:

- Governance Policies

    - letters patent, memorandum of association, trust deed or similar constating document;
    - by-laws, organizational structure or chart, especially if the organization is larger and has employees. This chart should set out decision-making levels so that it is clear who (or what position) makes what types of decisions. A "job description" for each position would also assist in making clear who does what;
    - board structure, including executive committee and its role and responsibilities, standing and *ad hoc* committees and their terms of reference and lines of accountability. Often, this information will also be in the by-laws and may be required in some cases. For example, for corporations in Ontario, if there is an executive committee that will make decisions, it must also be referenced in the letters patent;
    - rules of procedure or rules of order at meetings;
    - conflict of interest policies, either as a separate document or as part of a code of conduct for directors;
    - communications policy, both internal and with outside stakeholders. This policy could include advocacy; and
    - access to information and privacy policy. This area of policy is becoming increasingly important as a result of legislative changes and an increased focus on privacy in a wired world. Clearly, organizations that have employees or who provide social services will have a greater need for a policy in this area than an organization that puts on the occasional play.

- Strategic Planning

    - mission statement that is based on the letters patent or other constating document;
    - statement of goals and objectives;
    - business plans; and

- budgets and resource allocations based on plans.

• Operational Policies

- financial management, such as cash management, internal procedures, banking arrangements, internal audit;
- compliance management to demonstrate compliance with significant regulatory requirements that face the organization;
- human resource management, which would include policies with respect to workplace and sexual harassment, hiring, promotions and retention, volunteer management, training, discipline and conflict of interest (including use of the assets of the organization, such as computers); and
- program management, which will include review of programs to ensure that they are meeting their objectives. The programs ought to include overall assessment criteria so that it is easier to determine if and when a program is successful or requires further adjustment, refinement, resources or elimination.

(3) Policy Process

The development of policies and their approval, implementation and evaluation are separate but integral components in the policy process. The following checklist is intended to assist in the process, but it is not "the final word". Policies need to flow from the strategic plans of the organization, its legal obligations and what it can do from a practical perspective. A legitimate use of a policy is to minimize risks. However, if the policy is so sophisticated and resource intensive that it is not followed, it may instead lead to increased risk because the organization did not follow its own policy on the matter and that failure directly or indirectly caused injuries to another person.

The size, nature and level of sophistication of an organization, its context and the expertise of its staff (if any) need to be taken into account in how any such policy process actually works. The overall "governance approach", i.e., policy governance or administrative governance will also be an important factor in how the board addresses the policy process. In any event, the following elements could be included in a policy process:

- identification of a need for a policy, which may include a corporate policy to review all policies on a periodic basis or to require senior management to do so and identify areas that require new policies or revisions to existing policies;

- terms of reference for the committee or person who is to prepare the draft policy, including membership, time allocated for the preparation, consultation and so forth. In many cases, it is probably desirable to include staff and senior staff representation on the committee or, at least, consult with them. A committee may also need to retain external expertise, such as a lawyer, accountant or management consultant;
- format to be used for policies, in particular where consistency is desired for clarity purposes;
- research into the policy issue, assessment of current situation and its risks, need for policy and the proposed content of the policy. The research should also examine what options are available with respect to the policy and how any policy proposal will inter-relate with other policies and the overall mandate of the organization;
- review of any legal requirements or standards that are applicable;
- drafting of policy for review and comment, including any background materials that will assist the board in making a decision on the proposed policy. The board may want to consult on the draft policy, in particular where internal and/or external input have not been provided;
- discussion of the draft policy and preparation of final version;
- development of an implementation plan, which may include communications with staff and volunteers and with external stakeholders, training, allocation of resources for implementation, scheduling of activities, allocation of responsibilities and determination of who is accountable for implementation;
- approval of the policy and implementation plan and any related requirements, e.g., resource allocation; and
- evaluation of the policy after a prescribed period to determine if it is effective and addresses issues.

The policy ought to identify clearly what the issue is, the goals for the policy, the fundamental values or beliefs being advanced by the policy and how they relate to the mandate of the organization. It should also identify who is responsible for the policy and its implementation — both initially and on an ongoing basis.

III SELECTED POLICY DOCUMENTS

There are a number of policy areas that have become or are becoming particularly important in the governance of charitable and not-for-profit organizations. These policies have developed either from legal requirements or from a consensus around the need for such policies. The remainder of this chapter will examine policies for conflict of interest of directors; the collection, use and disclosure of information; financial management and regulatory compliance management; and indemnification and insurance.

(1) Conflict of Interest

Conflicts of interest are inevitable. The very people that most organizations want to attract to their boards and to be active as officers or chairs of committees are the ones most likely to be active elsewhere in the community. They have interests that are varied — both in the sense of things that are of interest to them and in the sense of interests with which they are involved. The issue in any conflict of interest policy is to ensure that any legal requirements are being complied with and that the policy is reasonable.

There will be commonality of elements in any conflict of interest policy in the sector. However, charitable organizations will generally have more stringent policies because of the influence of the law of charity. The issue of whether or not the director is a trustee or akin to a trustee raises its head again with respect to conflicts of interest. In Ontario, there are particular issues that arise from the positions taken by the Public Guardian and Trustee, such as the purchase of insurance.

If the organization is a corporation without share capital (not-for-profit), the incorporating legislation usually addresses at least one form of conflict of interest. Section 98 of the *Canada Corporations Act* and s. 71 of the Ontario *Corporations Act* provide statutory processes for a director to disclose and deal with a situation in which a director has a direct or indirect interest in a contract with the corporation or that is proposed. The director has a duty to disclose his or her interest at a meeting of the board of directors. If the contract is proposed, it shall be declared at the meeting at which the question of entering the contract is first taken into consideration or at the next meeting if the director is not at that meeting. If the director becomes interested in a contract after it is made, the declaration is to be made at the first meeting of directors held after the director becomes so interested. However, nothing stops the director from making an earlier disclosure.

The director could also make a general disclosure that he or she is a shareholder or otherwise interested in any company or a member of a firm and thereby has an interest in any contract to be made with that company or firm. It may be appropriate, though, for the director to remind his or her colleagues of this fact should a contract or proposed contract arise. A declaration made several years ago may not be immediately remembered or the various interconnections of businesses may not be readily apparent from the general disclosure.

The director is not permitted to vote in respect of any contract or proposed contract in which he or she has a direct or indirect interest. If the director does vote, that vote is not to be counted. There are some exceptions under the federal legislation, such as contracts by or on behalf of the corporation to give to the directors security for advances or by way of indemnity, if there is no quorum of directors in office who are not so interested, and the director holds shares in the other business only to qualify to be a director or officer of that corporation.

If the director has complied with the statutory provisions on conflict of interest, he or she will not be held accountable to the corporation for the contract or proposed contract by reason only of holding the office or of the fiduciary relationship established for any profit realized by the contract. If the contract is confirmed at a meeting of the members called for that purpose, the director will also not be liable.

In the case of the Ontario statute, there is also an offence under subs. 71(6). If the contract was voidable only by reason of the director's interest, he or she is liable upon conviction to a fine of not more than $200. While this fine is not large, it does indicate the seriousness with which this type of conflict of interest is held.

The statutory provisions would not appear to apply as readily to charitable corporations, where the directors are seen to be trustees or akin to trustees. Any interest, direct or indirect, would appear to be prohibited. There are obvious difficulties with such an iron-clad position. For example, would it prohibit a director from renting a facility operated by the charitable corporation for a family event? For a business event? If the director has shares in mutual funds and the mutual fund holds shares in a business that contracts with the charitable corporation, is there a conflict of interest? At some point, the rubber band of conflict of interest becomes too stretched to make sense. While the director could always bring an application to the court to remedy any such "breach of trust", it seems ludicrous to do so where the contract is not material. Though if there is doubt as to the contract being material the director may want to obtain a legal opinion that it is not.

There are other complications that may arise, which indicate a need for further reform of the law in this area. If the corporation without share capital has a charitable object but is not exclusively charitable, what are the rules? Is it sufficient for the director to comply with the statutory provisions? Or does he or she need to comply with the "charitable" requirements? Does it matter if the contract is not concerned with the charitable assets? Or can the charitable assets really be so easily divorced from the analysis?

A conflict of interest policy should have the following elements in it:

- definition of what is a conflict of interest. This definition should incorporate the legal requirements in any incorporating statutes, such as personal interest in a contract. The issue of family relationships may also be relevant for some organizations. For example, a director may be the spouse, parent or child of another director or of an employee of the organization. Or, the family member has an interest in a contract with the organization, either as a supplier of goods or services or as somebody who receives goods or services from the organization. The issue of receipt of goods and services may be relevant in many organizations. For example, directors are usually members of the organization. Could directors receive the same discount on tickets for a production as do other members? Could they rent the organization's clubhouse for a personal event just as any other member?

- what information must be disclosed about a conflict of interest? This factor may be very sensitive. If a director is in a personal relationship with somebody, that information may be very sensitive. Or the conflict may arise out of a confidential business dealing. On the other hand, without full disclosure of information, it is not possible to assess whether or not a conflict of interest does exist and, if it does, how to address the conflict. Not all conflicts necessarily lead to resignation; there are many steps in between that could be considered, including removing oneself from the decision making process and having no participation in the discussion of the matter.
- to whom must the information be disclosed? It may not be necessary or appropriate to inform everybody about the conflict or the facts surrounding the conflict. Many organizations have a staged process, whereby a director discloses to the chair the conflict and the relevant factors. The chair or director may inform the board of the existence of the conflict and how it has been resolved. In other cases, the board may need to know more about the conflict, especially where the integrity of the board or its decision or decision making process is at stake. In addition, if the director has a personal interest in a contract, most incorporating statutes set out a procedure to address that type of conflict.
- range of remedies to address a conflict. As noted above, resignation is one remedy but recusing oneself is another. The remedies will be influenced by whether or not the organization is not-for-profit or charitable. The nature of the conflict will also affect the type of remedy that may be available. The remedies should also consider the materiality of the conflict. Some conflicts are trivial; others are fundamental.
- penalties for breach of the conflict of interest policy. Although this element is related to remedies, it assumes that there has been a failure (deliberate or otherwise) to comply with the policy. For example, what is to happen to a director who knows that he or she has a conflict, does not disclose and benefits personally as a result? The board may want to consider having the corporation take

legal action if the matter is sufficiently serious against that director in order to protect the corporation and their own integrity.
- disclosure of information to members. In some cases, it may be appropriate to disclose the conflict to members at the annual general meeting. This approach may also be mandated by incorporating statutes with respect to material contracts. An auditor may also need to know about any such material contracts as part of the audit of the financial statements.

Conflicts of interest may be real or they may be perceived. They may be actual or potential conflicts. Where a conflict has not occurred but the director is aware that there is potential for it to occur, the director may want to disclose or at the very least avoid any involvement with the issue. The board and director should also consider public and member perception of conflicts of interest. There may, in fact, be no conflict of interest because the director has arranged his or her affairs to avoid any. However, a reasonable person could still perceive a conflict to exist, based on the information that is available to him or her. He or she may not know or have access to relevant information about how the conflict was avoided. These types of conflicts will probably need to be dealt with on a case by case basis, but the board needs to be aware of perception in how it deals with conflicts.

There are also some built-in conflicts. For example, if *ex officio* directors are appointed, as discussed earlier, conflicts may develop that are inherent to why the person is a director. Similarly, people may be directors because of a broader interest in the community. They are directors because of involvement in related matters. If so, care must be taken to avoid conflicts.

(2) Code of Conduct

A code of conduct is another useful policy to regulate the behaviour of the directors. It allows directors to understand their roles and the limits to those roles. It also assists in ensuring that meetings and activities are carried out in a civil manner, with a view to making appropriate decisions in a timely manner.

A code may include the conflict of interest policy. Or it could be separate to emphasize the importance of both policy areas. In any event, a code of conduct could include the following matters:

- "job" descriptions for the director and for the officer positions;
- information about the organization, its programs, strategic plans and so forth;
- expectations that the board has of all directors, including those related to fundraising (which may include personal donations),

community relations, contributions of time, work on specific committees or projects (such as policy development);
- requirement that directors prepare for, attend and participate in meetings of the board and of the relevant committees. The code could establish a minimum standard for attendance which if not met could trigger a review of that director's ongoing appointment;
- lines of accountability and what the director may or may not do with respect to staff;
- information on the essential policies of the organization and agreement to comply with those policies, including workplace harassment and discrimination;
- criteria for assessing whether or not the director is doing a good job as a director. This topic could be expanded to include the board's evaluation of its collective performance; and
- behavioural guidelines, such as acting in the best interests of the organization, comply with the principles of fairness, act in a civil manner, when acting on behalf of the board in public to do so with integrity, duty to participate fully and frankly at meetings, maintain confidential the confidential business of the board and so forth.

Codes of conduct can be used to reinforce the objects of the organization as well as the duties that directors must meet.

(3) Personal Information and Privacy Policies

Organizations collect and use personal and other information as part of their activities. Different types of organizations will, obviously, collect varying amounts of information. The degree of sensitivity of the information may also vary from organization to organization or within an organization. A social services agency that delivers care to the elderly, for example, will have access to very personal and sensitive information, much more so than that of a community theatre group that usually only needs to know addresses and past theatre experience.

Similarly, an organization that has employees will collect personal information, some of which will be very sensitive. How sensitive that information is may be dependent upon events beyond the control of the organization. For example, the address of an employee in normal circumstances may not be very sensitive and can usually be located in the telephone directory. But it is easy to envision situations in which the employee will not want others to know where he or she lives.

An organization may also need to collect information about its volunteers. If the volunteer is working with children, youth, the elderly or vulnerable people, the type of information may be very personal. An organization that provides services to children, for example, may want to know whether the volunteer has any convictions or findings of guilt for criminal offences. That type of information is obviously sensitive but necessary to safeguard the child and the organization.

A word about "criminal records searches". The typical criminal records search is not as informative as most people think. Typically, the individual will either obtain the records search or authorize the organization to obtain it. This authorization is required because the records are subject to confidentiality provisions in federal and provincial legislation and contractually as between law enforcement agencies in Canada. The search will normally provide information about convictions in the previous three years. What will likely be missing from the search document obtained by the individual or the organization are any findings of guilt (absolute or conditional discharges where the conditions have been met), charges that were not proceeded with for substantive or procedural reasons, peace bonds and any convictions for which a pardon has been given. What certainly will not be included are any police intelligence information. Also, these records are only as good as the information that has been entered into the computer system. If, for whatever reason, the information about a conviction was not entered, it obviously will not be on the search document.

The search is not comprehensive in other ways. If the volunteer is to drive children or others to sports events or medical appointments, the volunteer's driving record would certainly be relevant information. Does the volunteer have a practice of driving too fast? Or not signal when making turns? Or drive without insurance? Or drive while the licence is suspended? The criminal records search will not likely provide any of this information unless it is tangential to a criminal conviction or resulted in criminal charges and conviction. Requesting a copy of the driver's licence will not tell the organization whether or not it is suspended or was cancelled for non-payment of fines. Yet, in many situations, this information will be of more practical assistance to an organization in protecting itself and those under its care than information about a 20-year-old conviction for shop-lifting as a teenager.

There has been, in recent years, substantial pressure on all institutions in Canada to protect personal information and to justify its collection, use and disclosure. Federal legislation, which will govern throughout Canada unless similar legislation is enacted in a province, is the most recent example of this pressure. Although it does not apply fully to charitable and not-for-profit organizations, it would be a mistake for these organizations to ignore the legislation and the public sensibilities behind it. In addition, the statute will apply whenever certain information is transferred across provincial borders. Provincial legislation may also go beyond the federal legislation, which will place even greater pressures on organizations to comply with the law and the spirit of the law.

The *Personal Information Protection and Electronic Documents Act* is intended:

... to establish, in an era in which technology increasingly facilitates the circulation and exchange of information, rules to govern the collection, use and disclosure of personal information in a manner that recognizes the right of privacy with respect to their personal information and the need of organizations to collect, use or disclose personal information for purposes that a reasonable person would consider appropriate in the circumstances.

The Act applies very broadly to organizations that collect, use or disclose personal information in the course of commercial activities, or if the personal information is about employees and that the organization uses the information in connection with the operation of a federal work, undertaking or business. Few charitable or not-for-profit organizations would fall within the second part of s. 4, dealing with federal work, undertaking or business. However, the legislation includes a provision that contemplates the Act applying to provincial transactions (where there is commercial activity), at a future date if substantially similar provincial legislation is not enacted before that date. Although this provision may be subject to challenge as an infringement on provincial jurisdiction, prudence dictates that organizations assume their treatment of personal information is highly likely to be subject to some form of regulation in the foreseeable future, and put appropriate measures in place. The Canadian Standards Association Privacy Principles incorporated in the federal legislation are the recognized benchmark in this area and are likely to be reflected in provincial legislation enacted. Accordingly, they are a good starting point for any organization developing a privacy policy.

"Organization" includes an association, partnership, person and trade union and would, therefore, include most, if not all charitable and not-for-profit organizations. There may be an issue with respect to "trustees" but it is likely that the statutory definition of "organization" is sufficiently broad to include that form.

The critical definition is "commercial activity". That phrase is defined in subs. 2(1) as:

> any particular transaction, act or conduct or any regular course of conduct that is of a commercial character, including the selling, bartering or leasing of donor, membership or other fundraising lists.

It is clear that charitable and not-for-profit organizations will fall within the ambit of the Act if they sell, barter or lease any of these lists. "Personal information" means information about "an identifiable individual". It does not include the name, title or business address or telephone number of an employee of an organization.

But the statute will apply to the personal information collected, used or disclosed by an organization for other commercial activity. One of the ambiguities in the Act is the applicability of the requirements to revenue-generating transactions carried on by not-for-profit or charitable organizations in fulfilment of their mandates. For example, would the Act apply to a community theatre that collects the home address, e-mail address, telephone number and opinions of patrons about a show? What if the community theatre wanted to use that information to add the patron to its mailing list for upcoming productions? Would it matter if the community theatre is "in competition" with a for-profit commercial theatre in the community? Or if the community theatre organization is going to add the patron to its list for fundraising purposes?

What about a charity that operates a store to sell used clothing? Is that a commercial activity? Could it collect and use information about its customers? Would the type of use matter? For example, if the store employee collected information to confirm the identity of a patron who is paying by cheque? Could that same information be used to add the patron to the mailing list for upcoming specials? Or to the fundraising list?

If the organization participates in any revenue-generating activity, it is likely that personal information collected in connection with this activity will fall within either the federal or provincial legislation (if enacted). Where provincial governments enact legislation it could even apply in circumstances where there is collection of personal information unrelated to commercial activity (at least one province has contemplated developing privacy legislation of general application rather than triggered by commercial or revenue-generating activity). Accordingly, organizations and their boards ought to be evaluating their collection and treatment of personal information with a view to putting protocols in place that will comply with present or future privacy legislation.

Section 5 of the Act requires that every organization shall comply with the obligations set out in Schedule 1. That schedule is based upon the CSA International's *Model Code for the Protection of Personal Information*. The obligation to do so in 2000 for federally-regulated organizations and for the international and inter-provincial trade in personal information, and in 2004 for organizations that operate solely within a province. If the relevant province enacts comparable legislation, then the organization is exempt from the federal legislation but must comply with the comparable provincial legislation. The exemption, though, will only apply to intra-provincial transactions. The federal Act will continue to apply to any international or inter-provincial trade in personal information.

The CSA International *Model Code* has ten principles, which are followed by a number of notes. The ten principles are set out below. After each principle, a possible "policy" is provided. None of these sample policies is intended to be the answer for any particular organization; rather they are there to illustrate how an organization could meet its legal requirements. Different organizations will have different needs.

- Accountability — An organization is responsible for personal information under its control and shall designate an individual or individuals who are accountable for the organization's compliance with the following principles.

ABC is responsible for personal information of its members, employees and donors under its control. The board of directors has appointed a chief privacy officer who is accountable to the board and reports directly to the chair of the board on ABC's compliance with this privacy policy.

- Identifying Purpose — The purposes for which personal information is collected shall be identified by the organization at or before the time the information is collected.

ABC will identify the purposes for which personal information is collected by us at or before the time the information is collected. An individual can choose not to provide all or some of the personal information to ABC that is requested. However, where the information is required to provide the services or is legally required to be collected (for example, to issue a receipt for income tax purposes), ABC will decline to provide the services. The individual will be informed so that he or she may decide whether or not he or she still wants the services and will provide the information required.

- Consent — The knowledge and consent of the individual are required for the collection, use or disclosure of personal information, except where appropriate.

The individual's knowledge and consent are required for the collection, use or disclosure of personal information. ABC will only collect or disclose personal information for purposes that are appropriate under the circumstances or to comply with any other legal requirements.

- Limiting Collection — The collection of personal information shall be limited to that which is necessary for the purposes identified by the organization. Information shall be collected by fair and lawful means.

ABC will only collect personal information that the board has determined is necessary for the purposes identified by ABC. Information will be collected only in accordance with the law. The board has reviewed and will review annually the specific purposes for which personal information is collected from its members, employees and users of its services.

- Limiting Use, Disclosure, and Retention — Personal information shall not be used or disclosed for purposes other than those for which it was collected, except with the consent of the individual or as required by law. Personal information shall be retained only as long as necessary for the fulfilment of these purposes.

ABC will not use, disclose or retain personal information for any other purpose than for which it was collected, except if the individual has consented or it is required by law. ABC will not sell, rent, barter, exchange or otherwise deal membership, donor or other fundraising lists. ABC will only disclose to third parties personal information where the individual has consented to such disclosure or ABC is required to do so by law.

- Accuracy — Personal information shall be as accurate, complete and up-to-date as is necessary for the purposes for which it is to be used.

ABC shall keep personal information as accurate, complete and up-to-date as it can. Information about members shall be confirmed annually as part of the member's annual renewal. Information about employees shall be confirmed each year as part of the employee's performance appraisal. Records shall be corrected or up-dated within 5 business days of notification of the error or update.

- Safeguards — Personal information shall be protected by security safeguards appropriate to the sensitivity of the information.

Personal information will be kept in a manner that is secure having regard to the sensitivity of the information and other legal requirements. Sensitive personal information shall be kept in a locked cabinet and, in electronic format, shall be accessible only by an authorized user. Access to sensitive information shall be tracked using sign-out sheets and, in electronic format, through password access in accordance with the privacy procedural manual.

- Openness — An organization shall make readily available to individuals specific information about its policies and practices relating to the management of personal information,

ABC shall provide to individuals a copy of its policy on privacy and make available a summary of its procedural manual.

- Individual Access — Upon request, an individual shall be informed of the existence, use and disclosure of his or her personal information and shall be given access to that information. An individual shall be able to challenge the accuracy and completeness of the information and have it amended as appropriate.

An individual may request in writing access to information being held by ABC. ABC will inform the individual of the existence, use and disclosure by ABC of any personal information. The individual will be provided access to that information, provided such access is not prohibited or restricted by law. If the information is not accurate or complete, the individual may provide the correct or complete information and the changes shall be made where the changes are substantiated.

- Challenging Compliance — An individual shall be able to address a challenge concerning compliance with the above principles to the designated individual or individuals accountable for the organization's compliance.

Challenges concerning compliance by ABC with its privacy policy may be made to the chief privacy officer, whose decisions shall be final. The chief privacy officer shall inform the chair of the board of the context of any such challenge and the resolution, but shall not disclose to the chair the name of the challenger unless it is necessary to do so in the circumstances.

The *Model Code* includes lengthy notes for each of these principles. Unfortunately, the Act includes a number of modifications to the *Model Code* and those notes, which makes it difficult at times to assess the impact in any particular fact situation. The federal Privacy Commission has prepared a more detailed analysis and guide to the *Model Code* and the statute to assist businesses and organizations identify and meet their legal obligations.

The Act also gives the Privacy Commissioner a role in the handling of complaints. The Commissioner may investigate a complaint under s. 12 of the Act and has substantial powers to carry out the investigation. For example, the Commissioner may summon and enforce the appearance of a person before the Commissioner and compel him or her to give oral or written evidence on oath and to produce any record or things that the Commissioner considers necessary to investigate the complaint. The Commissioner may also attempt to resolve complaints.

Complainants have a number of possible remedies. The Commissioner is obliged under s. 13 to prepare a report that sets out the Commissioner's findings and recommendations, any settlement that was reached and, if appropriate, a request that the organization give the Commissioner notice of any action taken or to be taken to implement the recommendations or reasons why not. Subsection 13(2) authorizes the Commissioner not to issue a report in certain specific circumstances where other remedies or procedures are available, the complaint is too dated, or the complaint is trivial, frivolous or vexatious or made in bad faith. Under s. 14, a complainant may, after receiving the Commissioner's report, apply to the court for a hearing into the matter. The court has broad powers to issue an order under s. 16, including to correct the practices in order to comply with the Act and to award damages.

Finally, the Commissioner may also carry out audits on organizations under ss. 18 and 19 of the Act.

The Act is a strong disincentive to organizations to sell, barter or lease their membership, donor or other fundraising lists — if that is the only "commercial activity" under which the organization would fall. If they intend to do so, they must comply with the *Model Code*, as it is amended by ss. 6 to 9 of the Act. The organization would need to obtain the consent of the individuals to disclose the information, which may be difficult to do after the fact. If the organization intends to sell, barter or lease its lists, it should obtain the express permission to do so in advance. And it should set up its systems in a manner that allows it to comply with this legislation.

There are some issues that need to be resolved. Could chapters of a national organization exchange their lists? It is not clear from the legislation that they could without complying with the Act. This situation may cause difficulties for some national or inter-provincial organizations that share their lists for mutual benefit.

Organizations may also fall under the Act if they carry on other forms of commercial activities. For example, if the organization carries on a business activity, it would need to comply with the Act if it uses the information in more than one province. This compliance may be an extra cost of business that the organization cannot justify.

There is another important but less easily understood impact of the Act. It has raised the bar for charitable and not-for-profit organizations. Increasingly, donors and prospective donors will come to expect organizations to comply with the federal or provincial requirements as a matter of course. Charitable and not-for-profit organizations should consider compliance in areas in order to meet the developing expectations of donors and prospective donors.

Equally important, employees of organizations will come to expect compliance with the *Model Code* whether or not strict compliance is required by law. All employers owe common law duties to their employees and former employees to maintain personal information confidential and to use only for *bona fide* purposes. But with the codification of "rights" into the *Model Code* and its use as a basis for legislative enactment, it can be expected that employees will demand a more rigorous protection of their rights. Volunteers are also likely to have similar expectations. And all of these expectations are growing at the same time as the need to "screen" employees and volunteers increases to avoid liability from inappropriate employees or volunteers.

(4) Financial Management Overview

The board should establish some level of financial overview of the affairs of the organization either as a board function or a committee function. The level will depend upon the size and sophistication of the organization. The level of review, for example, need not include detailed analysis of the procedures used by management unless there have been problems with those procedures. The board or a committee may assess the integrity of the internal controls and information systems of the organization but it would leave the day-to-day monitoring to management.

Typically, in larger organizations, a committee of the board will be responsible for the ongoing overview of the finances of the organization. An "audit committee" is often established for that purpose and is recommended by the Panel on Accountability and Governance in the Voluntary Sector. This committee would be responsible for the financial affairs of the organization, at the initial stage, and accountable to the board in that regard.

The board's policy on financial overview would be set out in the terms of reference for the audit committee. The terms of reference for an audit committee could include the following:

- review of the accounting principles and their application to ensure that they are appropriate. If any changes are proposed, review any changes that may have a material impact on current or future years. In doing so, it is important to consider the reasons for the change and the views of the organization's auditor on the changes;
- consider whether or not the accounting policies and procedures being used are similar to those used by others in the sector and, if not, why not;
- review significant accounting policies that may be controversial or that may have recently been addressed by the CICA or others. In some cases, funding agencies may suggest certain accounting policies or approaches to be consistent with their own requirements; in other situations, it may be that the Canada Customs and Revenue Agency has identified issues or a new matter has arisen;
- review the use of the deferral or restricted fund accounting method and, in particular, ensure that the method used is carried out properly and is consistent with providing the most useful information;
- review any significant litigation, claims or contingent liabilities with a view to ensure that they are properly disclosed and that appropriate provisions are being made where possible to cover them;
- review any differences of opinion between management of the organization and the external auditor and consider how to resolve such differences of opinion;
- review any material adjustments that have been made to the financial statements by the external auditor and understand why they were made;

- compare operating results on an ongoing basis to previous years and to budget and satisfy self as to why there are differences or deviations;
- review interim financial statements or financial forecasts on a quarterly or monthly basis;
- review with the external auditor his or her involvement and any issues that arise;
- review management's suggestion for external auditor and the terms of engagement, including audit fees;
- review circumstances in which a material mis-statement could occur in the financial statements and the planned audit steps to prevent any mis-statement;
- determine the role of the external auditor in other matters in the financial management process, i.e., preparation of the financial statements;
- determine if the auditor should be involved in any "compliance" audit activities, such as compliance with the board's policies or with internal controls mechanisms;
- meet with external auditor and make sure coordination is present with internal accounting or audit staff;
- review and follow-up on any auditor's recommendations and management's responses;
- review internal audit arrangements, such as the terms of reference for internal audit;
- assess whether or not the internal audit staff are competent, objective and qualified;
- review and approve the budgets for internal audit; and
- review the results of any internal audit reports and management's responses. If necessary, resolve any disputes.

(5) Regulatory Compliance Management

The board has a role to ensure that any regulatory requirements are complied with in the operations of the organization. It may do so as a board or through a committee that reports to the board, such as the audit committee or a compliance committee. What those regulatory requirements are and how they will be monitored will depend upon the activities of the organization and its status. For example, corporations are obliged in their incorporating statutes to maintain certain books and records. The responsibility for doing so will lay with either the treasurer or the secretary, depending upon the by-laws and the nature of the books and records. The secretary will normally also be responsible for any corporate information filings and the treasurer any financial filings, such as the charity information return by registered charities with the Canada Customs and Revenue Agency.

There will be other regulatory requirements that are applicable to all entities or in certain sectors of the economy. For example, all employers have legal requirements to collect and remit income taxes and certain other employment-related taxes and premiums for employment insurance and the Canada Pension Plan. A failure to do so can result in charges against the officers and directors, and in personal liability. A board of directors will want to put in place measures to avoid such liability. Similarly, there may be environmental laws that apply to the organization. These may apply generally or as a result of the activities of the organization.

If the organization is involved in activities that are specifically regulated, it will need to comply with any such regulation. Most health care providers are regulated. Many social service agencies are regulated. These regulations may arise either directly by statutes or indirectly through contractual obligations. For example, an organization may agree by contract to comply with certain standards in the delivery of services.

The variety of regulatory obligations is too great to provide a one-size fits-all policy. However, certain elements ought to be included in a regulatory compliance policy:

- identification of regulatory measures that apply to the organization. This identification could be done by class;
- requirements that arise out of generally applicable legislation, such as the *Competition Act* or consumer protection legislation;
- requirements of incorporating legislation and from constating documents;
- requirements as an employer, such as employment standards, occupational health and safety, human rights code, *Income Tax Act* and similar statutes;
- environmental laws that apply, including those that are applicable at the federal, provincial, municipal or conservation authority levels. If the organization owns property, there is a higher likelihood that environmental issues will arise but almost all organizations will use property and, in doing so, may cause damage to the environment;
- if a charity, requirements that are unique to charities, such as those under the *Income Tax Act* with respect to books and records, receipts for income tax purposes and, in Ontario, with respect to the *Charities Accounting Act* and *Charitable Gifts Act*;
- requirements that arise from specific sectoral regulations, such as in day care or nursing homes;

- requirements that may not be statutory but are industry standards. For example, although community theatres are not regulated, there are industry standards that apply for health and safety;
- requirements that may be set out by CSA International or other standards setting bodies. In some cases, these bodies may also provide accreditation; and
- requirements that are set out in contracts, including funding agreements.

There will be other sources of requirements and the listing of relevant and applicable requirements may be very daunting — especially if there has not been ongoing regular activities in that regard. The first step in the policy process may be simply to get a complete list of these requirements or at least a list of where the requirements are located:

- prioritizing of the requirements based upon relevance, potential damage should the requirements not be met and assessment of risk. Not all requirements are equally important. It is essential to determine which ones are more important to the organization than others;
- identification of who is responsible for ensuring compliance with the requirements. Clearly, staff and senior staff will have substantial responsibility for ensuring that there is compliance. However, certain officers may also be responsible, such as the treasurer for financial matters, the secretary for corporate records and filings and so forth. The key is to have the correct person in place who has the skills, status and resources required and who will be accountable for doing so;
- identification of what information is to be provided to the board or a committee of the board with respect to compliance. In some cases, the information may be periodic, e.g., quarterly reports, or where an incident occurs;
- identification of what information is to be provided to senior management with respect to compliance;
- identification of the format that the information will be provided. It may be that the board will want the executive director to prepare a certificate stating that all income taxes and employment-related premiums have been collected and remitted to the Canada Customs and Revenue Agency and the appropriate provincial ministry;
- identification of what internal control mechanisms and quality control mechanisms will be in place to ensure that the information is accurate and complete;

- identification of what will be subject to internal or external audit, including a compliance audit where appropriate;
- allocation of responsibilities for follow-up on any deficiencies; and
- allocation of resources in order to implement policy on regulatory compliance management.

Each organization will need to determine for itself and in its own context how to handle regulatory compliance management. However, there may be useful examples within the organization's sector or industry standards that are applicable. The policy needs to be reasonable and rationally based. The board also needs to keep in mind that the information provided must be relevant, timely and useful.

There are also some practical matters; the organization is intended to carry out activities. Regulatory compliance is important, but the resources devoted to compliance and compliance management need to bear a relationship to the risks involved, the chance of the risk occurring and the need to carry out the mandate. When in doubt, the board ought to consult or have management consult with the regulator or contracting party to ensure that the compliance management policy will meet everybody's needs.

The *Anti-Terrorism Act*[93] has enhanced the need for some organizations to ensure compliance with the law. This statute amends several other statutes and is discussed elsewhere in this text. Nevertheless, it is important that directors of organizations that carry on activities outside of Canada ensure that there is compliance not only by their own organization but by any person who acts on the organization's behalf, as agent or contractor. Similarly, the organization will need to be careful to ensure that its own operations do not give rise to concerns under the Act.

(6) Insurance and Indemnification

(a)   Directors and Officers

Insurance and indemnification are usually dealt with as methods of protecting officers and directors from liability. However, from another perspective, these practices can be seen as protecting the assets of the organization. Insurance and indemnification are flip sides of the same coin.

Indemnification in law is the saving of one person harmless or to secure against loss or damage.[94] Normally, when indemnification and directors and officers are discussed, the topic is indemnification of the directors and officers by the organization. To this end, incorporating leg-

---

[93] S.C. 2001, c. 41.
[94] *Black's Law Dictionary*, revised fourth ed. (St. Paul, Minn.: West Publishing Co., 1968), at 910.

islation provides that the corporation may indemnify the directors. Section 80 of the Ontario *Corporations Act* and s. 93 of the *Canada Corporations Act* provide for similar authority to indemnify directors out of the assets of the incorporation.

The form of the indemnification is essentially the same in those two statutes and in similar statutes in other provinces. The officers and directors may be indemnified for all costs, charges, and expenses that the director or officer sustains or incurs as a result of a law suit or other legal proceedings arising out of the execution of his or her duties of office. The wording of the typical section in a by-law for an Ontario-incorporated corporation reads:

> The corporation shall indemnify and save harmless the directors, their heirs, executors and administrators, and estates and effects, respectively from time to time and at all times from and against:
>
> all costs, charges and expenses whatsoever that he or she sustains or incurs in or about any action, suit or proceeding that is brought, commenced or prosecuted against him or her, for or in respect of any act, deed, matter or thing whatsoever made, done or permitted by him or her in the execution of the duties of his or her office; and
>
> all other costs, charges and expenses that he or she sustains or incurs in or about or arising from or in relation to the affairs except costs, charges or expenses thereof as are occasioned by his or her own wilful neglect or default.

The standard by-law under the *Canada Corporations Act* is slightly different and reflects the statutory provisions under that legislation. But in principle, the by-law provisions are comparable.

The purchase of insurance — often called errors and omissions insurance or officers and directors insurance — is one method to provide such an indemnification. The assets of the organization may not be adequate to provide any realistic level of indemnification to the directors. Also, the tying up of the assets for that purpose would prohibit the assets from being used for the carrying out of the objects of the organization. If the building had to be sold to honour an indemnity to the directors, that asset would no longer be available to provide services.

This factor gives rise to a question, especially with respect to charitable organizations — Are those provisions legal? Some question has arisen in Ontario, at least, as to the legality of the indemnity provision for charitable corporations. The argument is that as the directors are trustees or akin to trustees, the clause would improperly put at risk the trust assets for the benefit of the directors as directors. They, of course, cannot personally benefit and, so the argument goes, the charitable corporation ought not to indemnify them. This issue would not apply to not-for-profit corporations that are not charitable; however, if the argument is valid, it would apply to deeds of trust and the trustees who are appointed to manage the affairs of the trust and to incorporated associations that are charitable.

It is far from clear that the argument is correct. The statutes make explicit provision for the indemnities. Letters patent filed pursuant to Ontario legislation include provisions at odds with other Ontario legislation governing charitable corporations. These mandatory provisions, one would think, ought to have similarly excluded the indemnification authorization if that was the intention.

However, the Public Guardian and Trustee in Ontario has argued that the indemnification is a form of "remuneration" paid to the directors which the mandatory provisions prohibit. While this position might have some merit with respect to the purchase of insurance by the charitable organization (corporation, trust or unincorporated association), the strength of the argument is less obvious in an indemnification. There are, in addition, protections in the standard by-law that would avoid the assets being used to indemnify if the directors did not act in good faith.

In the Ontario context, this issue has been addressed in amendments to that province's *Charities Accounting Act*[95] which would appear to allow for the indemnification of directors. The regulations under that Act allow for the indemnification of directors and officers and the purchase of liability insurance by the charity.[96] The board must, however, consider a number of issues before it authorizes the indemnification and/or purchase of liability insurance. The board must consider:

- the degree of risk to which the executor, trustee, director or officer is or may be exposed,
- whether, in practice, the risk cannot be eliminated or significantly reduced by means other than the indemnity or insurance,
- whether the amount or cost of the insurance is reasonable in relation to the risk,
- whether the cost of the insurance is reasonable in relation to the revenue available to the executor or trustee,
- whether it advances the administration and management of the property to give the indemnity or purchase the insurance.

There are other conditions to the purchase of insurance or the payment of the indemnity. For example, subs. 2(6) prohibits the purchase of insurance if, at the time of the purchase, it unduly impairs the carrying out of the religious, educational, charitable or public purpose for which the executor or trustee holds the property. No indemnity shall be paid or insurance purchased if doing so would result in the amount of the

---

[95] Section 5.1 to the *Charities Accounting Act* was enacted by the *Courts Improvement Act*, S.O. 1996, c. 25, subs. 2(2).

[96] O. Reg. 04/01.

debts and liabilities exceeding the value of the property or, if the executor or trustee is a corporation, render the corporation insolvent. The indemnity must also be paid or the insurance purchased from the property to which the personal liability relates and not from any other charitable property.

The sense of these conditions precedent and restrictions are far from clear. It is even less clear what happens to the indemnity or the insurance policy if, at some time in the future, the Public Guardian and Trustee or a court determines that the board did not adequately determine if in practice the risk could otherwise be eliminated or significantly reduced before approving the indemnity or purchase of insurance. Getting even muddier is the issue of the timing. Would insurance purchased prior to the promulgation of the regulation be valid? Would new by-laws be required? What happens to incidents that arise from the period before the regulation came into affect?

In other Canadian jurisdictions, where there is no equivalent body to the Public Guardian and Trustee overseeing charities, directors and staff still need to be wary of the ambiguities in the law detailed above. It is quite conceivable that they could see insurance or indemnification measures that they had in place challenged in an application or action brought to enforce their organization's charitable purposes. If successful, such a challenge could leave directors and the organization exposed to considerably increased liability.

Given the lack of clarity in the law, boards are well-advised to obtain legal counsel and engage in thorough discussion of these issues with their insurer or broker before considering indemnification or insurance measures. There may be legal steps needed to bring the organization onside. Certainly, the conditions precedent need to be addressed before any new by-law is put in place to indemnify the directors.

The issue of indemnification and insurance should be seen as one that is intended to protect the assets of the organization, whether that organization is charitable or not-for-profit. Many of the individuals who can provide the skills and expertise needed by organizations are those with a real and reasonable interest in protecting their personal assets. Also, it is not so much the payment of damages that gives rise to the issue but rather the retention of a lawyer and others to defend oneself. Legal fees, the hiring of experts and so forth can be expensive, an expense that the organization will need to bear in any event to some degree.

(b)   General Liability

Insurance also extends beyond the officers and directors. Insurance is an important part of any "asset protection" policy of a board. Insurance protects the assets in two ways — (i) should an event cause damage to the asset; (ii) should the organization be held liable for damages to another person. The board should, therefore, consider the following matters with respect to insurance:

- maintain historical record of insurance coverage;
- type of insurance coverage, i.e., occurrence basis versus claims made. If the policy is an occurrence basis one, it is particularly important to keep records of the insurance policies to determine what the coverage was at the time of the occurrence and who the insurer was;
- list of insurers and list of insurance brokerages used;
- annual report on existing coverage and recommendations from insurance broker. The broker is a professional who is there to provide advice to the organization. The insurance coverage should be reviewed at least annually to make sure that it is still appropriate or if additional (or less) coverage is required;
- review and upgrade property insurance. This review should determine if the policy provides replacement cost if it is needed, and whether or not the property coverage is adequate. There may be a need to upgrade the endorsements. For example, if the organization has started to serve liquor at its events, it should probably have an endorsement for that purpose, which may be less expensive than obtaining separate coverage for each event. There may be exclusions to coverage that should be reviewed and eliminated or, to save costs, added where the risk is minimal;
- review general liability coverage;
- ensure it is adequate to cover future claims;
- need to provide written disclosure of all changes in material risks to the broker;
- liability insurance will provide coverage for negligent actions but does not generally provide coverage for intentional acts, criminal acts, fines and penalties, punitive and exemplary damages, wrongful acts of directors and officers (e.g., discriminatory practices or breach of fiduciary duty), pollution and contamination or liability for contractual breaches;
- specific areas of liability may also be considered during a review to ensure that coverage is part of the insurance policy. For example, does the policy cover sexual or workplace harassment? The review should examine the coverage from the perspective of the activities of the organization and its employees and volunteers and assess where the risks are and whether or not coverage is available and appropriate;
- who is covered is another issue for review. A board would want to consider whether the directors and committee members who are not directors, the general membership of the organization, volunteers, spouses (who often are coerced into volunteering) and so

forth are covered by the policy and under what circumstances. The geographic coverage may also be an issue, especially if the employees or volunteers travel outside of Ontario;
- coverage for non-owned automobiles may be appropriate, in particular if volunteers or employees use their own or rental vehicles;
- fiduciary liability coverage is available and may be appropriate for organizations at significant risk for decisions or actions taken with respect to fiduciary responsibilities (i.e., where the transaction has, or could be imputed to have, the character of a trust) should consider obtaining this type of insurance;
- professional liability coverage for specialized services, including counselling services. If there are any professionals who are employees or volunteers, consideration should be given to any insurance coverage that is available through their professional or regulatory associations; and
- are legal defence costs part of or in addition to the coverage limit?
- officers and directors insurance has other considerations, which parallel those of the general policy:

    - is the coverage justifiable? This issue would arise with or without the list of considerations mandated by the Attorney General in Ontario for charitable organizations. It is difficult to justify $2,000 for insurance out of a budget of $5,000 whether or not the organization is a charitable organization;
    - is the coverage adequate and appropriate to the risk?
    - several areas are usually excluded from coverage, such as criminal acts, fines and penalties, libel and slander, wrongful dismissal, personal injury including mental anguish and distress, pollution and contamination. Directors and officers ought to be reminded that insurance is not necessarily as comprehensive as they may think, and that it does not allow them to do things they otherwise ought not to do;
    - is coverage for the directors and officers or is it for corporate indemnification? The difference may matter to the directors and officers as to who is being insured and who has rights under the insurance policy;
    - are former officers and directors covered or only existing ones?
    - are there any limits to geographic area of coverage?
    - are legal defence costs part of or in addition to the coverage limit?

- should the same insurer be used as for the general liability insurance? There may be advantages to using a different insurer. Also, some officers and directors may have independent access to insurance through their existing employment (if participation on the board is seen as part of their employment duties) or their professional association. Similarly, officers and directors may be able to obtain an endorsement for coverage under their home-owner's policy.

If the organization owns property there will be a number of other insurance issues that will arise. The organization may want to consider purchasing additional coverage to protect against pollution and contamination, either from their property or migrating to their property.

(7) Fiscal Management

Fiscal management is the board's management of the financial affairs of the organization. It is primarily concerned with issues such as cash-flow and ensuring that the cash is there when the invoices are due. There are, however, obvious connections to other management matters, including investment policy, program management, review and so forth. Fiscal management is critical to the short- and long-term success of the organization. If the cash is not there, the operations cease — no matter what the long term prospects may have been.

The board ought to be concerned about several factors in fiscal management. These include:

- the regular payment of salaries or wages, benefits and any deductions which are to be remitted to governments or for pension benefits. As discussed earlier, the directors have a high standard of care with respect to these matters and directors may be held personally liable under the relevant statutes should salaries or wages and remittances remain unpaid. It may be worthwhile to treat the remittances for income tax and other employment-related taxes and premiums (employment insurance and Canada Pension Plan) and benefits as "trust" funds and deposit into a designated account for that purpose if there is any question of having the cash to make the remittances when due. The board may also want a regular statement from the executive director certifying on a monthly or quarterly basis that all taxes and remittances have been made and that all salaries, wages and benefits have been paid;
- is the organization operating a deficit and, if so, for how long? The source of the deficit needs to be determined. It could be as a result of previous deficits which were financed and the payments

on the loans are causing the annual deficit. Expenses may exceed the budget or revenues may be lower than what was budgeted. In some cases, it may simply be a cash-flow issue — a grant or contractual payment not having arrived. Or the board may have approved a deficit for good, or bad, reasons. Or investments may not be doing as well as expected, or poor investments were made resulting in poor returns.

Boards need to take into account cash-flow issues in preparing budgets and in managing the fiscal situation during the year. The audit committee or, if no audit committee, the board needs to monitor the cash-flow on a regular or as needed basis. Banking arrangements and lines of credit may be appropriate, especially if there are regular peaks and valleys in revenues or expenses. A strong working relationship that is open and honest with its financial institution will help an organization to manage these peaks and valleys through various loan arrangements.

If the source of the problem is that expenses are too high, the board needs to examine its options to reduce those expenses. It may mean cutting programs or putting off other expenditures until the cash is available. Or the board may need to identify new funding or revenue sources, taking care to ensure that they are within the law and within the mandate of the organization.

- there are different ways to fund deficits. The board needs to review its incorporating statute, constating documents (such as its letters patent, trust deed or memorandum of association) and by-laws to determine what the organization may or may not do. Charitable organizations in Ontario are limited in their authority to borrow monies. Section 59 of the *Corporations Act* permits the corporation to borrow money, but a mandatory provision in the letters patent for charitable corporations limits borrowing for current operating expenses. The borrowing power of the charitable corporation is not limited if it borrows on the security of real or personal property.

There are a number of financing options, all of which should be considered with legal and accounting advice. The organization could mortgage its real property, issue promissory notes that are not secured, issue bonds and debentures that are secured or unsecured, establish longer payment periods with its creditors or borrow against its accounts receivable. If the organization intends to issue securities, such as bonds or debentures, it needs to ensure that it has the legal authority to do so and that it has complied with any relevant securities legislation.

No security should be issued by the organization without adequate legal advice. Even if the organization is exempt from the securities legislation in the province, the holder of the security will have common law and other rights to full and proper disclosure. The level of disclosure and how it is made is one that requires both expert legal and accounting advice. A full and frank assessment of the risk of an investment in a security is a significant part of disclosure. Individuals who lose their investment in a security issued by the organization may not be content with a simple "sorry". They may want to go after the directors who approved of the prospectus or disclosure document to recoup their losses.

- the board should consider establishing a sinking fund to retire debt. The sinking fund approach allows for the orderly repayment of debt. The board could also consider allocating any operating surpluses to the repayment of debt or to bring the level of debt to a manageable level. Similarly, the organization may receive an unexpected donation, which could be used to repay debt. Of course, if the donation is for a specific purpose, the organization needs to honour the donor's intentions.
- the board should also be vigilant in ensuring that no improper uses of funds occurs. Deficits and large debt place stress on people. Individuals may be more apt to use improper fundraising techniques, to use special trust funds for other purposes, or to divert remittances for a few months in order to manage the cash flow.

(8) Program Review

Program review is an important part of the board's responsibilities. Program review is a periodic review of an organization's programs to determine if the program is achieving the desired outcomes. A program review may also assess whether or not it is doing so in the most effective and efficient manner. While a program may be achieving its stated outcomes, if it does so at a cost that is bankrupting the organization, it will be unsustainable and may be considered reckless by the directors.

Program review also helps to determine what "assets" the organization should have to carry out its activities. The review may identify assets that could be better used for other purposes or assets that are required to do the job better. If a charitable organization has real property, it needs to make sure that the property is being used for charitable purposes. In Ontario, a program review will assist the charitable organization to meet its obligations under the *Charities Accounting Act*. In most cases, a charitable organization is prohibited from owning real property as an investment, although it may divest itself of the investment within three years. If the property is not being used for the charitable purposes of that charitable organization, it will be considered to be an investment. The common law would also seem to support this position, in particular if the charitable organization had significant investments in real property to the point at which it was no longer really a charitable organization devoting all of its assets to charitable activities but an investment company. The proceeds from the sale of any such property are to be used for the charitable purposes of the organization.

The Panel on Accountability and Governance in the Voluntary Sector[97] identified program outcomes as an important method to demonstrate that an organization is doing good in a good way. It suggested that organizations look to assessing results and impacts of programs as an accountability tool and a planning tool. It adopted the definition of outcomes as being benefits or changes for participants during or after their involvement in a program. This definition is dramatically different from the traditional approach to measuring success, for example, program outputs which measured the number of people who participated in or used the services.

Of course, the traditional method has its value, in particular in determining costs on a per user basis. It also is more easily adapted by a wider range of organizations. Outcomes based assessment and how it is to be implemented is not always readily apparent. It may be easier to use in social services agencies (although there would be debates within that sector) than, say, for cultural agencies. How did a play change an audience? Is that measurable? Can the organization collect the information that it needs to measure the outcomes over a period of time? Can it do so while complying with privacy rights of its audience members?

These comments are not intended to be critical of outcomes-based assessment. Rather, to illustrate that any new method to measure success will have its difficulties in design and implementation. There are limitations to any measurement tool and a board must understand those limitations before it adopts one approach over another. Indeed, it may need to use more than one approach in order to obtain a true assessment of the program and its value to its members or to the broader community.

Whatever approach is used, boards will need to grapple with three tasks:

- identifying the goals for the program, whether outcomes based or the more traditionally based. The goals need to be realistic and achievable. There is little point in having "prolonged world peace and happiness" as a goal under either the outcomes based or traditional approach to measurement. That goal is unrealistic and certainly beyond the capacity of any single charitable or not-for-profit organization.

---

[97] *Building on Strength: Improving Governance and Accountability in Canada's Voluntary Sector*, Ottawa, 1999.

- identifying or developing how to measure progress. The goals are just that, goals; the issue is how far towards those goals an organization has come. The goals may, over time, also adjust either as they are achieved or it is recognized that the goal cannot be achieved or is not relevant to the organization. The measurement of progress will be dependent on the collection and analysis of data that is relevant to the organization and to its goals.
- disseminating the information to those within the organization and those outside who have an interest in the results. The information should also be used in the planning process, including making decisions of whether to continue with the program, maintain as is or adjust it, to change the goals or the resources allocated to the program.

In response to calls from the public and funders for greater accountability, Canadian charitable and not-for-profit organizations are in the process of seeking better and more consistent means to measure success. Organizations have an opportunity to advance this process through finding or creating appropriate tools to measure their own success in meaningful ways, and through cooperation with others in determining and promoting evaluation standards.

(9) Investment Policy

(a) Introduction

Organizations will have a number of reasons to invest, whether they are charitable or not-for-profit in nature. Although charitable organizations may be more restricted in their investments, boards of both need to take due consideration in designing and implementing an investment policy and in monitoring its implementation and investments.

The first step in any investment policy is to determine what is to be invested or what the investments are. This step is not necessarily as easy as it sounds. What is an "investment"? Is it the temporary use of an asset, such as cash, for investment prior to it being used for its final purpose? Or is it a capital asset, such as real property, that is used for purposes of the organization? Or is it the use of assets in an endowment fund which is intended to generate revenue for the organization's operational expenses?

All of these three examples could be considered investments for either a charitable or not-for-profit organization. The intention here is to focus on the temporary or interim use of assets, in particular cash or cash equivalents, and endowment funds.

(b) Investment of Charitable Property

Over the last several years, issues around investments have become particularly problematic, especially for charitable organizations and others holding charitable property. Because charitable property is "trust" property, the laws of trust applied to the property, both the common law and statutory law. Organizations may also hold charitable property in general or for special purposes. While it was long thought that charitable property held for special purposes was "special", recent case law has forced a reassessment of this view.[98]

It seems that many charitable organizations and their investment counsellors operated on the assumption that the organization could make its investments in a simple manner. For example, the board could authorize an investment company to decide on what investments were appropriate. Often, these investments included mutual funds, especially if the desire was to take advantage of a rising market for stocks or bonds. However, a series of cases in the 1990s proved that approach to be in error.[99]

The legal situation was not tenable. Boards of directors were obliged to make investment decisions but could not delegate that decision. But many boards did not have the expertise to do so or could not meet in time to take advantage of opportunities or to reduce risks of losses in existing investments. Although the boards could obtain expert advice, the decision on individual investments remained with them. But the boards could not invest in mutual funds, an increasingly important method of investing which had several advantages — spreading of risk, expertise in investment decisions, broad choice in the marketplace and so forth. An investment in a mutual fund was an improper delegation of the investment decision.

The potential exposure to directors was substantial even where the directors would appear to have acted in good faith, carried out due diligence in selecting an investment firm, provided reasonable and reasoned parameters of investments to the firm and monitored specific investment decisions. Because the directors had improperly delegated the investment decision, in Ontario at least, they had breached their duties as trustees or persons akin to being a trustee under the *Trustee Act*[100] and at common law.

Legislative amendments were introduced in Ontario to manage this situation. The amendments permitted the board to adopt a more mod-

---

[98] See *Re Christian Brothers of Ireland in Canada*, (2000), 47 O.R. (3d) 674 (C.A.). That case, arguably, has reversed centuries of charitable purpose trust law. See, for a full discussion of this issue, D. Stevens, "Exigibility of Special Purpose Charitable Trusts: The Christian Brothers Ontario Court of Appeal and British Columbia Supreme Court Decisions", in *Fundamental New Development in the Law of Charities in Canada*, Canadian Bar Association — Ontario, Continuing Legal Education, October 27, 2000.

[99] *Haslam v. Haslam* (1994), 3 E.T.R. (2d) 206 (Ont. Gen. Div.).

[100] Sections 26 and 27, R.S.O. 1990, c. T.23.

ern "portfolio model" of investing. This approach moves towards an overall process for assessing investments and away from the prudence of making a specific investment.

The amendments to the *Trustee Act* came into effect on July 1, 1999. The *Trustee Act* requires a board to establish an investment policy on the basis of the "prudent investor rule". The board must consider the following statutory criteria:

- general economic conditions;
- the possible effect of inflation or deflation;
- the expected tax consequences of investment decisions or strategies;
- the role that each investment or course of action plays within the overall trust portfolio;
- the expected total return from income and the appreciation of capital;
- the needs for liquidity, regularity of income and preservation or appreciation of capital; and
- an asset's special relationship or special value, if any, to the purposes of the trust or to one or more of the beneficiaries.

The board must also consider the need for diversification in the investment. In doing so, it would look to the requirements of the trust and the general economic and investment market conditions. Obviously, the board may want expert advice and is authorized to obtain it and to rely upon it if a prudent investor would rely on the advice under comparable circumstances. Although this provision is helpful, it may leave some more sophisticated board members in a difficult position where they may have a higher standard of care than other directors.

There are some remaining fish-hooks in the amendments. For example, the list of criteria may be difficult to implement in reality. The list places a high premium on the ability of directors to understand the criteria and to work with them. Even sophisticated directors may have difficulty in understanding and applying the criteria.

A few fish-hooks that had been identified with the 1998 amendments were addressed by amendments in 2001. One of the amendments authorized the investments in not only mutual funds but also pooled or segregated funds under variable insurance contracts. If the trustees invest in mutual funds, pooled or segregated funds, then the "delegation" provisions in the new ss. 27.1 and 27.2 do not apply.[101]

Sections 27.1 and 27.2 authorize trustees to delegate any of the trustee's functions relating to investment of trust property to an agent. The amendments limit the delegation to the condition that it must be "to the

---

[101] S.O. 2001, c. 9, Sched., subs.13(2) and (3).

same extent that a prudent investor, acting in accordance with ordinary investment practice" would authorize.[102] There must be an investment plan or strategy that is in writing which complies with s. 28 of the Act and is intended to ensure that the functions will be exercised in the best interests of the beneficiaries of the trust. There must also be a written agreement between the trustee and the agent which requires the agent to comply with the plan or strategy and to report to the trustee at regular stated intervals. A trustee must exercise prudence in selecting an agent, in establishing the terms of the agent's authority and in monitoring the agent's performance to ensure compliance with the terms. While these provisions permit appropriate delegation to experts, it is equally clear that the trustees — be they directors of charitable corporations or otherwise — are not relieved of substantial responsibility.

Subsection 27.1(5) sets out what the trustee must do, at minimum, to meet the prudence in monitoring the agent's performance. The trustee must review the reports, review the agreement on a regular basis and consider appropriate changes to the plan or strategy. Trustees must also consider giving directions to the agent and to the revocation of the appointment and if required to do so.

Section 27.2 sets out the duties of the agent. He or she is required to carry out the functions with the standard of care expected of a person carrying on the business of investing the money of others and to do so in accordance with the agreement and the plan or strategy. The agent may not sub-delegate to another person. Subsection 27.2(3) also provides for proceedings against the agent by either the trustee or the beneficiaries of the trust.

(c) General Considerations

The board of an Ontario charitable organization, in reviewing a draft investment policy needs to consider the criteria set out in the *Trustee Act*. Boards of charities in other jurisdictions will be governed by their province's trust legislation, which may afford them less guidance than the Ontario provisions. Manitoba,[103] New Brunswick,[104] Newfoundland and Labrador,[105] Nova Scotia,[106] Prince Edward Island[107] have also taken a "prudent person" approach for investments, with Newfoundland's and PEI's statutory provisions being very similar to Ontario's. Under the Alberta *Trustee Act*[108] British Columbia,[109] trustees are provided with a list

---

[102] *Ibid.*, subs. 13(5).
[103] Sections 68 and 69, R.S.M. 1987, c. T160.
[104] Section 2, R.S.N.B. 1973, T.15, as amended by S.N.B. 2000, c. 29, s. 1.
[105] Section 3, R.S.N. 1990, T.10, as amended by S.N. 2000, c. 28, s.1.
[106] Section 3, R.S.N.S. 1989, c. 479, as amended by S.N.S. 1994-95, c. 19, s. 1.
[107] Sections 2, 3, 3.1 to 3.5, R.S.P.E.I. 1988 T.8, as amended by S.P.E.I. 1997, c. 51, s. 1.
[108] Sections 5 and 7, R.S.A. 1980, c. T-10.
[109] Sections 15 and 18, R.S.B.C. 1996, c. 464.

of investments that are authorized for trust funds, generally conservative in nature including government bonds and debentures, stocks in approved corporations and so forth. Other types of investments may be made only pursuant to a court order.

But all boards — charitable and not-for-profit — should take into account overall strategic direction of the organization and the context in which that direction was developed and adopted by the board. It should take into account its overall financial situation. Does the organization have a debt load that is excessive? If so, the best use of any funds may be to reduce that debt load. However, the funds may be impressed with a special purpose trust, such as for endowment fund purposes or for the operations of a particular program. If so, the board may not be in a position to use those funds for debt reduction.

The board should look to its medium and longer term revenue position. What financial return will be needed from the investments to meet any cash flow shortfalls? Or is the investment intended to fund longer term program development? The board may want to include in its investment policy a discussion of how it intends to address any shortfalls through other mechanisms, such as greater fundraising activities or reduction in operating expenses. This type of information can be used both to guide investment decisions and to justify those decisions. The prudent investor rule focusses on the process used to make investment decisions and the investment policy ought to demonstrate clearly that the board was prudent, reasoned and reasonable in developing its investment policy, whether the organization is charitable or not-for-profit.

The board will probably want to identify its primary objectives from the investments so that they tee-up with the strategic plan of the organization. For example, if an important feature of the strategic plan is to build a new facility for the operations of the organization in five years, that factor may be critical to the types of investments that will be made under the investment policy. On the other hand, if the organization is investing surplus cash solely on a short-term basis to generate some additional interest or other revenue, it may want to restrict investments to those that can be cashed in on short notice without penalty. The objectives of the investment policy need to be clearly articulated so that the investments can be related to the objectives.

The investments made under the policy ought to be monitored by a committee of the board or by the board itself. If the investments are not meeting the objectives, the board may need to address the issue.

(d)   Ethical Investing

A board may also be faced with concerns about its investments. A number of organizations, because of their objects or the religious or ethical background to the organization, may prefer not to invest in certain types of investments. Or, it may articulate its desires in a more positive manner, i.e., to make investments in only certain types of investments that advance its objects or that are consistent with its objects. This investment approach is sometimes called "ethical investing". "Ethical procurement" is another aspect of the overall approach that is developing within the sector.

The law is not clear on the issue. Indeed, in the 1980s, the lack of clarity caused Ontario to enact the *South African Trust Investments Act*[110] which effectively relieved trustees, including directors of charitable organizations, from any liabilities for deciding not to make investments in South African investments or to dispose of any such investment.

Short of legislative enactment, there is no clear common law position on ethical investments. Manitoba has permitted trustees to consider non-financial criteria in making investments.[111] Arguably, the board could consider the objects in its letters patent or other constating documents to determine whether or not the investment was within or outside those objects. For example, a medical health charity could argue that investments in tobacco companies were *ultra vires* because it was using charitable assets for a purpose inconsistent with its objects, i.e., to advance the medical health of Canadians. Similarly, a religious charity could argue on the grounds of religious freedom that it ought not to take into account only financial criteria in making investment decisions.

There are significant legal issues with this approach. First, the board will also be judged on the same basis for other investments. If the board decided against investments in tobacco companies, why did it invest in liquor companies? Second, in Ontario, the charitable organization will still need to marry up its investment decisions against the criteria set out in the Ontario *Trustee Act*. The organization will need to be able to argue that any ethical investments fall within those explicit statutory criteria.

The board of directors may be able to bolster its argument (and this time it would be only an argument) on the basis of consultation with its members and regulators, evidence that the ethical investments were not materially detrimental to the organization, evidence that donors would decide against donating to the organization because of such investments, evidence that the investment would be inconsistent with its objects or evidence that it is contrary to its strategic plans. Similarly, there may be evidence that the investment in a "non-ethical" product will damage the organization's reputation. And reputation is a critical intangible asset of most charitable organizations, without which they could not survive or prosper.

A factual basis must be in place to justify an investment policy based on ethical considerations. Any investment policy that is based on non-financial criteria will need to be very well thought out and only carried out with legal advice. But the final test is how well the investment does. If

---

[110] R.S.O. 1990, c. S.16. The statute was repealed in 1997 by s. 12 of the *Government Process Simplification Act (Ministry of the Attorney General), 1997*, S.O. 1997, c. 23.
[111] Section 79.1 of the *Trustee Act*, R.S.M. 1987, c. T160, as amended by S.M. 1995, c. C.14, s. 3.

the investment has comparable returns to other investments that may be available to the charitable organization, there may be no losses on which to base an argument that there has been a breach of duty.

This argument would probably be stronger with respect to new investments as opposed to selling an existing investment. Any investor is faced with a vast number of options, even a charitable investor. It would likely be easier to demonstrate that a new investment meets the statutory and common law requirements. However, in selling an existing investment (especially if a loss would occur on the investment), it will be much more difficult to justify that sale than a decision not to purchase.

(e)   Commingling of Restricted Funds and Special Purpose Trusts

Charitable organizations may have a number of special purpose trusts that need to be managed or that are otherwise restricted. There is an argument that the "contributed property" (cash or other property) could only be invested on its own and not with other investments. This argument posed serious practical difficulties. Organizations would be required to invest separately the $5,000 fund for scholarships, the $500 donation for an endowment fund and so forth. The book keeping requirements alone could be depressing to any treasurer. Technically, the funds could not even be kept in the same bank account and each would need its own account, increasing banking and administrative costs for the charitable organization. In addition, the commingling of these types of funds permitted more prudent investments, which spread the risk and allowed for better returns.

In Ontario, a regulation under the *Charities Accounting Act* authorizes the combination of restricted or special purpose funds with other property received for another restricted or special purpose.[112] The regulation allows the organization to combine the property in one account or in an investment, but only if doing so advances the administration and management of each of the individual properties. All gains, losses, income and expenses must be allocated rateably on a fair and reasonable basis to the individual properties in accordance with generally accepted accounting principles.

The board must also ensure that the following records are maintained for each individual property, in addition to other record keeping requirements:

- the value of the individual property immediately before it becomes part of the combined property and the date on which it becomes part of the combined property;
- the value of any portion of the individual property that does not become part of the combined property;

---

[112] Section 3, O. Reg. 04/01.

- the source and the value of contributed property relating to an individual property and the date on which the contributed property is received;
- the value of the contributed property immediately before it becomes part of the combined property and the date on which it becomes part of the combined property;
- the amount of revenue received by the combined property that is allocated to the individual property and the date of each allocation;
- the amount of the expenses paid from the combined property that are allocated to the individual property and the date of each allocation; and
- the value of all distributions from the combined property made for the purposes of the individual property and the purpose and date of each distribution.

The board must also maintain records on the combined property, which parallel the records for the individual property:

- the value of each individual property that becomes part of the combined property and the date on which it becomes part of the combined property;
- the value of the combined property that becomes part of the combined property, the date on which it becomes part of the combined property and details of the individual property to which the contributed property relates;
- the amount of revenue received by the combined property, the amount allocated to each individual property and the date of each allocation;
- the amount of the expenses paid from the combined property, the amount allocated to each individual property and the date of each allocation; and
- the value of all distributions from the combined property made for the purpose of an individual property and the purpose and date of each distribution.

The regulation places a significant record keeping obligation on the organization, for which the board of directors is responsible. It is not clear whether or not the regulation has any retrospective effect. The regulation seems to be future-oriented. What happens to the situation where the funds are already combined? Does the organization need to un-combine those funds? Recreate the records needed? Obtain a court order to remedy the apparent breach of fiduciary duties? As of the date of writing, these matters had not been litigated. Accordingly, an Ontario organization that has combined its contributed property may want to seek legal advice on this issue. For charitable organizations in other jurisdictions, common law precludes commingling of assets. Absent legislation permitting such commingling, organizations and their directors may be held in breach of trust where this practice occurs.

CHAPTER 7

Members and their Relationship with the Organization

A   OVERVIEW

This chapter reviews the relationship between the members and the organization. The relationship is essentially contractual in nature, whether or not the organization is an unincorporated association or a corporate entity. The nature of the contract is based both in the common law and, with corporate entities, in statute.

The common law has generally focussed its attention on two areas: the property and civil rights of a member, and procedural matters. To some extent, the two areas are inter-related. The courts want to ensure that a decision by the organization or its officers and directors does not improperly adversely affect the property or civil rights of the members. The courts also want to ensure that where there is an adverse effect, appropriate procedures are in place and that they are followed when rights of membership are changed or membership is terminated or suspended.

Incorporating statutes include a number of provisions that govern membership. The statutes provide for the establishment of membership qualifications. They also set out or provide for a number of membership rights. The rights are there, in part, to ensure that the organization carries on its activities in accordance with its objects and with the desires of the members. Therefore, the members have a right to vote, to information and to attend meetings.

The statutory provisions with respect to co-operative corporations reflect the principles of co-operatives and their democratic nature. That statute provides more substantive and procedural rights for members, especially where occupancy rights in a not-for-profit housing co-operative are involved.

B   INTRODUCTION

Charitable and not-for-profit organizations can only carry out their objects through their officers, directors or trustees, and their members. In many cases, the underlying purpose for the organization, especially a not-for-profit organization, may be to provide goods and services to their members. The relationship between the members and the organizations is a pivotal one and often not well understood. The relationship between an organization and its members is contractual in nature. This contractual relationship exists where the organization is an unincorporated association or a corporate entity incorporated as a corporation without share capital or a co-operative corporation without share capital.

Notwithstanding the importance and prevalence of charitable and not-for-profit organizations in Canadian society, there are few cases that examine the relationship between organizations and members.[1] The cases are usually old ones and are primarily concerned with rights to property or the benefits of an insurance policy or similar member service. The Supreme Court has dealt with the relationship in a few cases. In *Senez v. Montreal Real Estate Bd.*,[2] for example, the Court concurred with the comment that "equates the by-laws of such corporations to provisions of a contractual nature". In that case, a member of a real estate board was expelled from the organization. The salesperson, as a result, lost access to services that were available to members. Membership in the real estate board was not, however, mandatory for a salesperson to carry out his or her trade. The regulation of real estate salespersons was undertaken by a public body authorized by legislation to do so. Membership in the board was voluntary, albeit very useful. The expelled member sued for breach of contract and in tort.

Mr. Justice Beetz favourably quoted a commentator:

> In general, only the members of the corporation are subject to the by-laws and their consequences; they exist and have their authority merely by virtue of the application of a sort of contractual agreement; they are a type of adhesion contract.

A breach of the by-laws, by either a member or the corporation itself, would be a breach of contractual obligations. The Court continued that:

> When an individual decides to join a corporation like the [Montreal Real Estate] Board, he accepts its constitution and the by-laws then in force, and he undertakes an obligation to observe them. In accepting the constitution, he also undertakes in advance to comply with the by-laws that shall subsequently be duly adopted by a majority of members entitled to vote, even if he disagrees with such changes. Additionally, he may generally resign, and by remaining he accepts the new by-laws. The corporation may claim from him arrears of the dues fixed by a by-law. Would such a claim not be of a

---

1   See *Senez v. Montreal Real Estate Bd.* (1980), 35 N.R. 545 at 557 (S.C.C.), where Mr. Justice Beetz comments on the "relatively rare precedents that are to be found on this or similar points".
2   *Ibid.*, at 555 to 557.

contractual nature? What other basis could it have in these circumstances? In my view, the obligation of the corporation to provide the agreed services and to observe its own by-laws, with respect to expulsion of a member as in other respects, is similarly of a contractual nature.

The "terms of the contract" will vary from organization to organization. The constituting documents and by-laws will be the major basis for the contractual terms.[3] The by-laws will set out who may be a member and what rights and privileges a member has in the organization. Organizations that have a statutory basis, such as corporations without share capital or co-operative corporations without share capital, will have significant provisions set out in the legislation or provided for in the legislation. These provisions deal with both substantive rights, for example, right to the audited financial statements, and procedural rights, such as how by-laws may be enacted or amended. In other cases, the courts have developed terms as part of the common law for charitable and non-profit organizations. The common law terms of the contract have tended to be more procedural than substantive in nature. For example, if significant property or civil rights are at issue, the courts will require the corporation to comply with an appropriate degree of "natural justice" before expelling or suspending a member.

C COMMON LAW PROVISIONS OF THE CONTRACTUAL RELATIONSHIP

Common law development has been restricted, for the most part, to two areas of concern: property and procedural rights. As with all common law, it exists in the absence of any specific statutory or other provisions to the contrary.

I PROPERTY RIGHTS

A member has the right to expect that the organization's property will be used in accordance with the provisions of the contract, as set out in the constituting documents. For example, a member may join an organization because of his or her agreement with the objects of the organization. The member has an interest in ensuring that the property is used to carry out those objects. If the organization undertakes fundamental changes to the objects or activities, the member has an interest in ensuring that any changes are undertaken in accordance with the rules established by the organization and its members or by statute.

---

[3] The Ontario Court of Appeal, in *Berry et al. v. Pulley et al.* (2000), 48 O.R. (3d) 169 (C.A.) commented that for unions the union constitution is not a typical or conventional contract. Rather, they have their own particular or special juridical character.

Property may be held by a corporate entity in its own name or by an unincorporated association in trust or on behalf of the members. In the case of an unincorporated association, unless the constituting documents provide otherwise, the common property will be vested in the members of an organization for the time being and held in accordance with the organization's rules. The "general property of the common assets is, ... in the members for the time being, subject, of course, to the provisions of the contract under which they are associated together".[4] Where the understanding is that no individual member would have an interest in the property, aside from usage as a member, a former member would have no rights with respect to the property. He or she could not, therefore, require that the property be partitioned or that chattels be divided up among the various members.[5] If the officers of the unincorporated association have a legal right to dispose of the property, the members cannot obtain, for example, an injunction to stop the disposition.[6] Of course, if the by-laws of the organization provided for membership approval of any sale of property, the situation would be different. With respect to any disposition those by-laws would have to be complied with.

The court will intervene to ensure that an organization's property is properly administered. Unincorporated associations may use "trustees" to hold the property of the association which cannot be held in the name of the association. Where the trustees refuse to administer the property for the benefit of the members, as beneficiaries of the trust, the court has the ability to remove the trustees and appoint persons who will.[7] Similarly, if the trustees divert the property from the purposes set out in the association's constitution, the court may also intervene by injunction.[8] A member, in contesting the actions of a trustee holding the association's

---

[4] *Underwriters' Survey Bureau Ltd. v. Massie & Renwick Ltd.*, [1940] S.C.R. 218, [1940] 1 D.L.R. 625; *Re Sons of Temperance of Ont.* (1926), 8 C.B.R. 49 (Ont. S.C.). For a more recent case, see *Wawryniak v. Jagiellicz* (1988), 65 O.R. (2d) 384, 51 D.L.R. (4th) 639, 31 E.T.R. 45 (C.A.). The cases will, however, turn on the facts of each case and on the provisions in the constituting documents. For example, in *Jubilee Local No. 6 v. Carmen's Council Section "A"*, [1920] 3 W.W.R. 781, 56 D.L.R. 318 (Man. T.D.), the remaining assets on dissolution were repayable to the original contributors who were still members in good standing.

[5] *Hofer v. Waldner*, [1921] 1 W.W.R. 177 (Alta. T.D.); *Polish Veterans Second Corps. v. Army, Navy & Airforce Veterans in Can.* (1978), 20 O.R. (2d) 321 (C.A.).

[6] *Gold v. Maldaver* (1912), 4 O.W.N. 106, 6 D.L.R. 333 (H.C.).

[7] *Brewster v. Hendershot* (1900), 27 O.A.R. 232 (C.A.).

[8] *Kozlowski v. Workers' Benevolent Society of Can.*, [1933] 2 W.W.R. 593, [1933] 4 D.L.R. 652 (C.A.); *Kaik v. Boraski*, [1926] 3 D.L.R. 916 (Sask. K.B.); *Brylinski v. Inkol* (1924), 55 O.L.R. 369 (H.C.); *Vick v. Toivonen* (1913), 4 O.W.N. 1542, 12 D.L.R. 299 (T.D.); *Kowalchuk v. Ukrainian Labour Farmer Temple Assn.*, [1935] 1 W.W.R. 529, [1935] 2 D.L.R. 691 (C.A.).

property, must prove to the court that he or she is a member.[9] He or she must have some legal interest to sue in his or her own name.[10]

There are circumstances, however, where a group of members of an unincorporated association may have a right to the property being held in trust. If, for example, a majority of members vote, in accordance with the organization's constitution, to change the fundamental principles of the organization, those members who adhere to the original principles may be entitled to the property.[11] The court is to review the nature of the original association as the guide for making its decision.[12] The objectors, however, must show that property rights are affected in order for the courts to intervene.[13] The changes must also be sufficiently fundamental that the organization becomes, for all intents and purposes, a different organization.[14]

The courts will not usually intervene if the changes have been made in accordance with the law and with the constitution of the organization, be it an unincorporated association or a corporation.[15] A change may negatively affect a member's personal interest but, provided that it was adopted in good faith and in accordance with the rules governing the organization, the court will not interfere with the internal affairs of the organization.[16]

The situation is different for charitable organizations. Because all of the property of the organization — whether a trust, unincorporated association or corporate entity — must be used exclusively for charitable purposes, the property is impressed with a charitable trust both at common law and, in Ontario, by the *Charities Accounting Act*.[17] The property may not be used for any purposes other than those set out in the trust

---

[9] *Kozlowski v. Workers' Benevolent Society of Can.*, [1933] 2 W.W.R. 593, [1933] 4 D.L.R. 652 (Man. C.A.).
[10] *Huegli v. Pauli* (1912), 26 O.L.R. 94, 4 D.L.R. 319 (H.C.).
[11] *Hennig v. Trautman*, [1926] 1 W.W.R. 912, [1926] 2 D.L.R. 280 (Alta. T.D.). But, see *Trow v. Toronto Humane Society*, [2001] O.J. 3640, September 10, 2001, Ontario Superior Court of Justice and *Toronto Humane Society v. Milne*, [2001] O.J. 3890, October 2, 2001, Ontario Superior Court of Justice.
[12] *First German Evangelical Lutheran Zion's Congregation v. Reiker*, [1921] 1 W.W.R. 794 (Sask. T.D.); *Stein v. Hauser* (1913), 5 W.W.R. 971, 15 D.L.R. 223 (Sask. T.D.). Where two organizations result from dissent among the members, the court will vest the assets in the members who adhere to the original purposes of the organization, *Wirta v. Vick* (1914), 6 O.W.N. 599 (Div. Ct.).
[13] *Whelan v. Knights of Columbus* (1913), 5 O.W.N. 432, 14 D.L.R. 666 (H.C.).
[14] See *Itter v. Howe* (1896), 23 O.A.R. 256 (C.A.), which speaks of destroying the identity of the original organization.
[15] *Heine v. Schaffer* (1905), 2 W.L.R. 310 (Man. K.B.); *Brendzij v. Hajdij*, [1927] 1 W.W.R. 301 (Man. C.A.); *Ont. Grand Commandery, Knights of St. John v. Goldkie* (1921), 20 O.W.N. 86 (C.A.).
[16] *Baker v. Independent Order of Foresters* (1897), 28 O.R. 238 (H.C.), affd. (1911), 24 O.A.R. 585 (C.A.); *Whelan v. Knights of Columbus* (1913), 5 O.W.N. 432, 14 D.L.R. 666 (H.C.); *Anderson v. Gislason*, [1920] 3 W.W.R. 301, 53 D.L.R. 491 (Man. C.A.).
[17] R.S.O. 1990, c. C.10.

document or the incorporating documents. The charitable purposes for which the trust is established may only be amended in accordance with the law, such as an application for *cy-pres*. The courts have an inherent jurisdiction to oversee charitable trusts and the Attorney General or, in Ontario, the Public Guardian and Trustee, acts as *parens patriae* over the charitable trust.

II PROCEDURAL RIGHTS

The procedural rights of the members of an organization should be set out in the constituting documents or the by-laws. In general, if there is a dispute, the courts will consider the organization to be a domestic forum and will permit that forum to resolve any disputes before any judicial remedy may be sought in the courts.[18] The dispute may relate to the rights and privileges of a member, and how they may be exercised, or to the suspension or termination of a membership or any rights of membership.

The contractual nature of the relationship between members and the organization also places obligations on the members. The organization has a right to expect that the members will comply with the terms of the contract. The organization may, therefore, discipline its members or suspend or terminate membership in accordance with its own rules and natural justice. The courts may intervene in a dispute where the member's property or civil rights are at issue and natural justice has not been followed.[19] The rationale appears to be that a member joins an organization voluntarily and the relationship is contractual in nature. Membership in a voluntary organization is not the same in nature as membership in a public body that a person must belong to in order to carry on a particular profession, trade or business. Provided that the domestic forum has not acted in bad faith, has acted in accordance with natural justice (unless the rules expressly provide otherwise), and has acted in accordance with the organization's own rules, the courts will defer to the domestic forum, especially if the rules make the domestic forum's decision final.

Natural justice is a common law development that is intended to protect the procedural rights of persons. Although it is more usually considered in the context of administrative law, the basic premises of natural justice have been applied by the courts to domestic forums and the relationship between members and organizations. Natural justice includes several elements. First, the person whose rights are to be affected should receive notice of the date and time of any hearing that will decide those rights. Second, the notice should set out the grounds or reasons for the

---

[18] *Ash v. Methodist Church* (1900), 27 O.A.R. 602 (C.A.), affd. (1901), 31 S.C.R. 497; *Gummerson v. Toronto Police Benefit Fund* (1905), 11 O.L.R. 194 (C.A.); *Kemerer v. Standard Stock & Mining Exchange* (1927), 32 O.W.N. 295 (C.A.).

[19] *Lakeside Colony of Hutterian Brethren v. Hofer*, [1992] 3 S.C.R. 165.

hearing and the proposed change, termination or suspension. Third, the person whose rights are to be affected should have the opportunity to make submissions. Fourth, the decision maker or tribunal should not be biased.

There is no overall rule about what the specific contents of natural justice are. For example, should the person be able to make oral submissions or just written submissions? Should the hearing be in public? Who should hold the hearing? Must the decision maker hold a hearing or can it resolve the matter in private? The courts will take into account the nature of the organization, the nature of the right and its impact on the member, and the rules or practices of the organization in determining what was required by natural justice in any given situation. Thus, it will not intervene and overturn a decision to expel a member solely on the grounds of bias or reasonable apprehension of bias where by tradition, dogma and contract, the life, religion and belief of a religious group were strictly integrated and structured. To do so would make the organization impotent to deal with its membership.[20]

D STATUTORY PROVISIONS OF THE CONTRACTUAL RELATIONSHIP

I ELIGIBILITY FOR MEMBERSHIP

(1) Introduction

An applicant for letters patent automatically becomes a member of the corporation upon incorporation.[21] Unless the letters patent, supplementary letters patent or the by-laws state otherwise, there is no limit to the number of members the corporation may have.[22] Persons may be admitted by a resolution of the board of directors or as provided for in the letters patent, supplementary letters patent or the by-laws.[23]

(2) Types and Qualifications for Admission

Members are an essential part of most non-profit and charitable organizations. Unlike "for profit" entities, such as business corporations, members tend to be active in the affairs of the organization. Shareholders in a business corporation, by comparison, tend not to be as active in the affairs of the corporation. Members are volunteers who support the objects of the organization and share a common interest with other members. The objects are not-for-profit in nature and intended to benefit the pub-

---

[20] *Lakeside Colony of Hutterian Brethren v. Hofer* (1994), 93 Man. R. (2d) 161 (Q.B.).
[21] R.S.O. 1990, c. C.32, s. 121.
[22] *Ibid.*, s. 123.
[23] *Ibid.*, s. 124.

lic. Shareholders are investors who are seeking a return on investment, not public benefits. Because of these differences, applicants for membership may need to meet certain eligibility criteria in order to become members.

Membership qualifications are common for charitable and not-for-profit organizations. There may also be more than one category or class of members, each having different voting rights.[24] Membership is deemed to be nontransferable, to lapse and to cease on the member's death, resignation or otherwise in accordance with the by-laws for suspensions or termination for failure to pay fees.[25] The by-laws should provide for a degree of natural justice where a membership or membership rights may be suspended or terminated.

The statutes provide some guidance on membership criteria. Subsection 286(1) of the Ontario *Corporations Act* requires that all directors be or become members of the corporation. Subsection 284(1) provides that the applicants for incorporation become members of the corporation and its first directors. Corporations may also be members of a corporation without share capital, unless the letters patent, supplementary letters patent or by-laws provide otherwise.[26]

The statutes provide for broad powers for by-laws with respect to membership. The Ontario statute provides greater guidance in this area than the federal statute, which is generally silent. However, at the federal level the model by-law provides for similar matters. Industry Canada's policies on membership tend to have the same effect as the Ontario statute because the Minister's approval of all by-laws is required under the *Canada Corporations Act*.

Section 129 of the Ontario Act and s. 155 of the federal Act permit by-laws to be enacted governing the admission of persons as members. Classes of membership may be designated and terms and conditions may be established for each class. Section 130 permits the directors to pass by-laws which divide the membership into groups either territorially or on the basis of a common interest. The election of directors may also be held on the basis of these groups or numbers in each group. A by-law under s. 130 must be confirmed by at least two thirds of the votes cast at a meeting called for that purpose.

There is no limit to the number of members that may be admitted, unless the letters patent, supplementary letters patent or by-laws provide otherwise. Practically, if admission is by resolution of the board of directors under subs. 124(1) of the Ontario Act, control over the numbers will rest with the board. However, there must be at least three members in an Ontario corporation.[27] The letters patent, supplementary letters patent

---

[24] *Ibid.*, ss. 120 and 125.
[25] *Ibid.*, subs. 128(1).
[26] Para. 155(2)(a), *Canada Corporations Act*, R.S.C. 1970, c. C.32, and para. 129(1)(a) of the Ontario *Corporations Act*, R.S.O. 1990, c. C.38.
[27] R.S.O. 1990, c. C.38, s. 311.

and by-laws may also provide for *ex officio* members.[28] Membership is not transferable unless the letters patent, supplementary letters patent or by-laws provide otherwise.[29]

If the membership admission procedures are set out in the letters patent or supplementary letters patent, the procedures will be mandatory and cannot be amended by by-law. If the procedures are set out in the by-laws, the directors could amend the by-laws, subject to the membership confirming the by-law amendment at a general meeting. If the letters patent or supplementary letters patent provide that membership decisions are to be made by the board, this authority may be delegated by by-law to an executive committee pursuant to s. 70 of the Act where there are at least six members of the board.

As a practical matter, most organizations have rules for admission which focus on the organization's objects, purposes and activities. The criteria may be limited to the applicant agreeing to subscribe to the organization's objects, or the criteria may be more detailed. The criteria could be more extensive and be intended to or have the effect of restricting membership. It is not uncommon for membership in an organization to be restricted to persons with a common interest, background or professional status or qualification. Some organizations require new members to be sponsored by existing members.

Any restrictions to membership should not, however, be contrary to human rights legislation.[30] If the organization falls within the regulatory regime of a ministry or department of government, there may be restrictions that apply to membership or limitations on the types of restrictions that may apply. In some cases, membership may carry, implicitly or explicitly, economic rights. This situation is particularly prominent in professional and trade associations. An unjustifiable restriction may be challenged if it infringes on an economic or similar right.[31] The loss of a professional qualification may be valid grounds for expulsion.[32]

---

[28] *Ibid.*, subs. 124(2).
[29] *Ibid.*, s. 128.
[30] See, for a judicial discussion of this issue, *Blainey v. Ont. Hockey Assn.* (1986), 54 O.R. (2d) 513 (C.A.), revg. (1985), 52 O.R. (2d) 225; *Can. Trust Co. v. Ont. Human Rights Comm.* (1990), 74 O.R. (2d) 481 (C.A.).
[31] See *Arrow 1st Cdn. Realty Inc. v. Winnipeg Real Estate Bd.* (1991), 72 Man. R. (2d) 64 (Q.B.); *Ritholz v. Optometric Society (Man.)* (1957), 18 D.L.R. (2d) 514 (Man. Q.B.). Membership in a real estate board and real estate associations and access to certain services provided by the boards and associations has been reviewed by the Competition Bureau. In 1989, a Consent Order was entered into governing this relationship with the Canadian Real Estate Association.
[32] *Parker v. Lethbridge Real Estate Bd. Co-op Ltd.* (1983), 49 A.R. 279 (Q.B.), affd. (1986), 70 A.R. 61 (C.A.).

II SPECIFIC RIGHTS OF MEMBERSHIP

Members have a number of rights by virtue of their membership in the organization. In the case of corporations, these rights will be set out in the statutes, the letters patent, any supplementary letters patent and the by-laws. The rights of members of trusts and unincorporated organizations will usually be set out in the terms of the trust and in the memorandum of association and any by-laws, rules or practices. No matter the legal character of the organization, members have or should have the right to vote, to obtain information and to attend meetings.

(1) Right to Vote

The right to vote is the underlying method for members to maintain control over the direction of the organization. The degree of control will vary from organization to organization and will depend to a large extent on the by-laws and the needs of the organization. Section 125 of the Ontario Act provides each member with one vote, unless the letters patent, supplementary letters patent or by-laws provide for more than one vote or for no vote for classes of membership. Paragraph 155(2)(b) of the federal Act requires that the by-laws include provisions regulating rights of voting. The model by-law includes provisions in this area.

The right to vote comes into play in four important areas. Under s. 129(2) of the Ontario Act, a by-law passed by the board of directors is effective until the next annual meeting unless it is confirmed, amended or revised by the members. A majority of votes cast at the meeting is necessary to confirm the by-law. Subsection 130(2) provides that no by-law under subs. 130(1) is effective until it has been confirmed by two-thirds of the votes cast at a meeting called for that purpose.

The members also usually vote for the election of the directors. Section 287 requires that the directors be elected by ballot or in such other manner as the by-laws prescribe. The election shall occur annually, unless otherwise provided for in the letters patent or supplementary letters patent. As noted above, directors may be elected on a class of membership basis pursuant to a by-law enacted under s. 130. If provided for in the letters patent, supplementary letters patent or by-laws, the members may also directly elect the officers of the corporation.[33]

A member may also vote by proxy. Section 84 provides that a member is entitled to vote by proxy. The proxy holder need not be a member of the corporation. The by-laws may, however, establish the requirements for proxies.[34] The corporation may, for example, require that proxies be filed with the secretary prior to the holding of the meeting. The federal statute does not specifically address proxies; however, the policies and model by-law of Industry Canada do.

---

[33] R.S.O. 1990, c. C.38, subs. 289(3).
[34] *Ibid.*, para. 129(1)(i).

(2) Right to Information

A right to vote is meaningless if the member does not have a right to relevant information about the affairs of the organization. The annual meeting is usually the primary source of information, both financial and on the activities of the organization. The financial statements must be submitted by the directors and the auditor must report to the members on the financial statements and the financial position of the corporation.[35] Members also have a right of access to the books and records of the organization under ss. 299, 300, 304 and 305 of the Ontario statute. The rights of access are more restrictive under subs. 111.1(1) of the *Canada Corporations Act*.

How much, what information and accessibility to information may sometimes become an issue. In *Trow v. Toronto Humane Society*,[36] Justice Rivard reviewed a by-law that had been passed at a previous annual general meeting which reclassified members as either "active" or "sustaining". Only active members would be entitled to vote at meetings of members. The board of directors subsequently confirmed only 12 individuals as "active" and all others were "sustaining". The right to vote, therefore, was effectively removed from more than 1,000 members and limited to 12 members— the directors. The by-law and its validity was challenged by some of the sustaining members.

The Court was concerned with how the proposed by-law had been initially presented to the members. The materials sent by the president to members indicated that it was a standard by-law adapted to the specific needs of the THS. It noted that "a reading of the draft By-Law 2 sent with the notice would not have led members to the conclusion their right to vote was being taken away."[37] The Court continued, with important comments on what the right to information and the right to vote means:

> A member of a corporation is entitled to receive not only notice of the meeting, but it is each member's right to receive with such a notice, sufficient information to permit him to come to a reasoned decision as to whether or not he should support the proposal under consideration.
>
> Sufficient information did not accompany the notice in this case which would have led a member to know he was being asked to support a by-law which would ultimately take away his right to vote.
>
> It is therefore declared that By-Law 2 is invalid due to lack of material disclosure to members of the Society.

---

[35] *Ibid.*, s. 96 and s. 132, *Canada Corporations Act*, R.S.C. 1970, c. C.32.
[36] [2001] O.J. No. 3640, Ontario Superior Court of Justice, September 10, 2001.
[37] *Ibid.*, at para. 14.

> There will also be an Order setting aside the Resolution of the Board of Directors ... which removed the vote from all members, save for the members of the Board of Directors. The right to vote for members of the Society is restored ... .[38]

The Court, however, declined to appoint an interim trustee, although it acknowledged that it had the authority to do so as part of its inherent jurisdiction.

The litigation did not end there. In *Toronto Humane Society v. Milne*, the Court dealt with a situation in which notice of a general meeting had been provided "within the strict confines of the times set out for notices of meetings."[39] The notice was sent by the vice president of the board, as was her power, but not by the board which is the usual procedure. Some members questioned the adequacy of the information and proxy circulated with the notice, and whether that information and proxy should have been sent to all members. The Court noted that the Toronto Humane Society had been embroiled in conflict for some time — indeed, dating back to the 1980s.[40]

The Court noted that a fight for control of the board was emerging, one that would evolve into a proxy fight. The adequacy of the information provided and who received the information was in issue. The applicants before the Court:

> ...point to the differential treatment of members, in terms of the material sent to them, as a ground for finding the meeting improperly constituted. They point to the partisan nature of the letter some members received as giving a flawed and inadequate history of matters, thus depriving a member of the ability to make an informed decision about the matters to be voted on at the AGM. They also suggest that the general proxy included does not permit a member to vote against any resolution, and thus is flawed. Although they concede that the timing of the notice is technically adequate, they raise concerns about the general lack of fairness in the timing, in that it deprives other members from putting forward alternate nominees to the board. I share these concerns.[41]

The Court commented further on the litigation that "What has emerged from the litigation, however, is a clear statement from this Court that it has the inherent jurisdiction to direct and control the administration of charities, of which the Society is one". The Court then

---

[38] *Ibid.*, at paras. 15 to 18.
[39] [2001] O.J. 3890, Ontario Superior Court of Justice, October 2, 2001, at para. 2.
[40] The 1986 matter also led to litigation, *Re Public Trustee and Toronto Humane Society*, (1987), 60 O.R. (2d) 236, which remains an important case on the role of the court and Public Guardian and Trustee, and on the interaction between the law of charities and corporate law with respect to charitable corporations.
[41] *Ibid., Toronto Humane Society v. Milne*, at para. 7.

quoted from the earlier decision of Rivard, J. that "such power ought to be exercised where charitable trusts are not being properly administered, where funds are being mismanaged or where the trustees of the funds are breaching their fiduciary obligations."[42] The Court commented further, following upon the decision made by Rivard, J., that "I find it no less important that each member receive sufficient information, and indeed, time, to make an informed decision about the proposed resolution. That is particularly so when the resolution concerns the removal of directors". Furthermore, "the deficiencies in the materials, and their being forwarded to only some of the members coupled with the effective lack of time for a response combine to make the notice of meeting defective".[43]

The Court, in two decisions within the space of a few weeks, clearly found that technical compliance may not be enough. There must be both procedural and apparent fairness to comply with the obligations to members and to respect their rights. Interestingly, the Court relied upon its inherent jurisdiction over charities — regardless of their legal status as corporate or non-corporate entities — to provide it with authority to make the decisions that it did.

(3) Right to Attend Meetings

Members usually exercise their rights to vote and to obtain information at meetings, either the annual meeting or general meetings called for a particular purpose. Many organizations have regular monthly meetings at which the affairs of the organization are reviewed and discussed. The use of proxies permits members to exercise rights at annual and special meetings, although they may be unable to attend the meeting in person.

The first annual meeting must be held no later than 18 months after incorporation[44] and subsequently not more than 15 months after the last preceding annual meeting. Directors may call a general meeting at any time provided that notice of the general nature of the business is given to the members.[45] A minimum of 10 per cent of the members entitled to vote at the meeting may request that the directors call a meeting. They must specify the general nature of the meeting which shall be set out in the notice calling the meeting.[46]

Section 93 governs the handling of meetings in the absence of other provisions in the by-laws. A notice of meeting must be given not less than 10 days in advance of the meeting to each member, usually by mail. A notice of meeting for a charitable corporation may be given by publication of the notice at least once a week for two consecutive weeks prior to

---

[42] *Ibid.*, at para. 8.
[43] *Ibid.*, at para. 9.
[44] R.S.O. 1990, c. C.38, s. 293.
[45] *Ibid.*, s. 294.
[46] *Ibid.*, s. 295.

the meeting in a newspaper or newspapers circulated in the municipality or municipalities in which the majority of the members reside.[47]

Meetings must be held at the head office, unless the by-laws provide otherwise. Typically, a by-law will provide that meetings may be held at any place in Ontario. Only the letters patent or supplementary letters patent may authorize a meeting to be held outside of Ontario.

(4) Terminating and Suspending Membership

The Ontario and federal *Corporations Act* do not set out the rules for terminating or suspending membership. The by-laws may do so, but are not required to. Unless the by-laws provide otherwise, a member would be able to terminate his or her own membership by providing notice to the secretary. It is prudent for the by-laws to establish a process for suspension and termination of members.

In any event, the basic rules of natural justice will probably be applicable to any hearings to suspend or terminate a membership. A member has a right to procedural fairness, including notice of any hearing and the grounds for which the suspension or termination is to occur, an opportunity to make representations and an unbiased tribunal.[48] Where the member of a golf club cut down prized trees, the organization had a justified concern with the behaviour and the failure of the member to rectify the situation. The Court refused to intervene where the board extended to the member the appropriate degree of procedural fairness in terminating the membership.[49]

Any provisions that will restrict rights and privileges of members, especially property rights, will be strictly construed by the courts.[50] However, in the absence of an infringement of natural justice or the rules of the organization, or a biased tribunal, the courts will consider the organization a domestic tribunal and will not usually intervene. Where there have been infringements, all internal remedies must usually be exhausted before the courts will intervene.[51]

---

[47] *Ibid.*, subs. 133(2).
[48] *Lakeside Colony of Hutterian Brethren v. Hofer*, [1992] S.C.R. 165, revg. (1991) 77 D.L.R. (4th) 202 (Man. C.A.); *Sosnowski v. Polish Fraternal Aid Society of St. John Cantius* (1988), 55 Man. R. (2d) 222 (Q.B.); *Wollmann v. Hofer* (1989), 63 D.L.R. (4th) 473 (Man. Q.B.).
[49] *Barrie v. Royal Colwood Golf Club*, August 9, 2001, Doc. 01/2857, Edwards J. B.C.S.C. unreported decision of the British Columbia Supreme Court. In that case, the member also attempted to transfer responsibility for the problem to another person, which the Court saw as conduct unbecoming a member of the club and was a legitimate consideration for the board in making its decision to terminate the membership.
[50] *Maillé v. Union des ouvriers boulangers* (1897), 12 Que. S.C. 524; *Cannon v. Toronto Corn Exchange* (1880), 5 O.A.R. 268 (C.A.).
[51] *Kemerer v. Standard Stock & Mining Exchange* (1927), 32 O.W.N. 295 (C.A.); *Essery v. Court Pride of the Dominion* (1882), 2 O.R. 596 (C.A.).

(5) Co-operative Corporations without Share Capital

The relationship between a co-operative corporation and its members is similar to that of corporations without share capital and their members. It is also contractual in nature, but there are some statutory provisions that are included to implement the principles of co-operatives.

(a)   Membership Qualifications

As with corporations without share capital, membership qualification may be set out in the incorporating documents or in the by-laws. Subject to the articles or by-laws, s. 63[52] provides that anyone 16 years of age or older may apply to the co-operative's board of directors for membership. Corporations, both business and corporations without share capital, may also be members. The by-laws may require a member to pay a fee or to make a member loan to the co-operative. This member loan is a major method of raising monies for a co-operative.

(b)   Membership Rights

Members have similar statutory rights as do members of corporations without share capital. A member, under s. 76, for example, has a right to one vote. However, no proxies are permitted but, a corporation may authorize — under corporate seal — one of its officers or directors to vote on its behalf. The members may also require, under s. 70, that a by-law or resolution be placed before the membership for a vote. If the co-operative's membership is divided into groups, these groups may elect delegates who in turn vote on their behalf for the directors although the delegation is not mandatory. In addition, co-operatives may be established using two or more "stakeholder groups". These multistakeholder group co-operatives may be used where each stakeholder group has a different interest but it makes sense to merge into one organization to work together.[53]

A dissenting member may also have certain rights under s. 69 of the Act to obtain a refund of his or her loan to the co-operative corporation. This right may be exercised where a resolution was passed by the directors and confirmed by the members with respect to the sale, lease or exchange of property, an agreement of amalgamation, the conversion of the co-operative corporation to business corporation or a co-operative with share capital, or the transfer to the laws of another jurisdiction.

---

[52] R.S.O. 1990, c. C.35.
[53] *Ibid.*, para. 24(1)(b).

A member has a right to be notified of and to attend the meetings of the co-operative.[54] The co-operative must hold an annual meeting pursuant to s. 77 within 15 months of the last meeting. At the annual meeting, the members have the right to hear and examine the auditor's report on their co-operative's financial position and the results of its operations.[55] The co-operative must provide the members with the financial statements at least 10 days before the meeting.

The members may attend any other meetings called by the directors under s. 78. They may, in accordance with ss. 70, 71 and 79, require that a meeting be called by the directors to deal with a resolution or by-law requisitioned by the members.

(c)   Terminating Membership

(i)   Voluntary Leaving by the Member

Co-operatives are voluntary associations and, as such, members may leave a co-operative. Under s. 67, a member must provide six months' notice to the secretary. If the member was required to provide a member's loan, the member has a right to repayment along with any interest owing within six months. The member may, however, choose to continue the loan if the co-operative agrees under subs. 67(4). The directors have the authority to delay repayment of the loan where it is in the best interests of the co-operative. If the repayment is delayed, it must be repaid within five years and by at least 20 per cent each year.[56]

(ii)   Administrative Termination by the Co-operative Corporation

Membership in a co-operative corporation without share capital may be terminated under subs. 49(3) of the Act, subject to s. 67, by the co-operative administratively in two circumstances. Because members are intended to be active, a membership may be terminated if the member has not used the co-operative for two years. A corporate membership may be terminated if the member is about to be dissolved. Any members' loans must be repaid to the members with any interest owing.

(iii)   Expulsion of a Member by the Co-operative Corporation

The co-operative corporation may also move under s. 66 of the Act to expel members. That section sets out detailed requirements before a

---

[54] *Ibid.*, s. 75. The meeting should be held at the co-operative's head office unless the by-laws provide for the meeting to be held elsewhere in Ontario. The articles of incorporation may authorize a meeting to be held outside Ontario.

[55] *Ibid.*, ss. 127 and 128.

[56] *Ibid.*, subs. 64(6). Under s. 67, the directors may also be prohibited from making any repayments if the co-operative is insolvent, would become insolvent or is otherwise detrimental to the financial stability of the co-operative.

member may be expelled. Given the nature of the relationship, which may involve supplies, housing or employment, the detailed procedures make sense. They would also appear to meet the requirements of natural justice that the courts have imposed on corporations and unincorporated associations where written rules were not available or followed.

A member may be expelled by resolution of the majority of the board at a meeting called for that purpose. The meeting may not be held within 30 days of the annual meeting. The member must receive written notice at least 10 days prior to the meeting setting forth the grounds for the proposed expulsion. The member has a right to appear and to make submissions at the meeting personally or by agent or counsel. If the directors pass the resolution, the secretary must notify the member in writing by registered mail of the notice of expulsion.

If the member is expelled, the co-operative must repay the member's loan with any interest owing within one year. Under s. 67, a member may not be expelled if the co-operative is insolvent or the repayment would be detrimental to the financial stability of the co-operative.

A member has the right to appeal the expulsion at the next general or annual meeting of the members. The members may confirm or overrule the board's decision by majority vote. The member must appeal in writing within 21 days of receiving his or her expulsion notice.

The expulsion of a member in a housing co-operative requires additional procedures. Because membership will usually involve occupancy rights, ss. 171.8 and 171.23 were enacted to protect the occupancy rights of a member. If the member does not have occupancy rights, the member may be terminated or expelled in the way discussed above. If the member has occupancy rights, these rights may be terminated only if his or her membership in the co-operative is terminated at the same time. The occupancy and membership rights may be terminated only if the member no longer lives in the member unit or for grounds stated in the by-laws. The procedures are detailed and set out in s. 171.8. A judge, in reviewing an application for the termination of membership and occupancy rights, may consider whether or not the by-law is reasonable. If there is, however, no evidence that the by-law is unreasonable, the judge ought not to dismiss an application for terminating membership and occupancy rights.[57]

---

[57] See *Ryegate (Tecumseh) Co-operative Homes Inc. v. Stallard*, April 4, 2000, Doc. 898-1997, Campbell, Soubliere, Cunningham JJ. Ont. Div. Ct. and *Tamil Co-operative Homes Inc. v. Arulappah*, May 10, 2000, Doc. C32908, Labrosse, Doherty, Austin JJ.A. Ont. C.A.

CHAPTER 8

Taxation and Charitable and Not-for-Profit Organizations

A   OVERVIEW

Taxation, (income tax, consumption tax, property tax) and other assessments by governments are major considerations to both profit and not-for-profit organizations. The type of legal structure chosen for an organization may be affected by the tax implications. Charitable and not-for-profit organizations are no different in this regard.

The members will have identified objects which they would like the organization to achieve; how to do so in the most efficient and effective manner will necessitate a consideration of how to minimize the amount and type of taxes the organization will have to pay. On the other hand, organizing the affairs of an organization so that it is exempt from the payment of taxes has its own costs. For example, the organization cannot be structured to make profits and distribute those profits to its members.

The courts and governments have long recognized that charitable and not-for-profit organizations provide substantial benefits to the community. If the government replaced the services, facilities and activities provided by charitable and not-for-profit organizations, significantly greater governmental expenditures would result. Without charitable and not-for-profit organizations, the public would suffer a loss to its economic and social life.

In recognition of the importance and value of charitable and not-for-profit organizations, they receive benefits under the various taxation statutes. These benefits may be exemptions from taxation in total (such as income taxation) or for certain activities related to the charitable and not-for-profit organizations (such as retail sales tax). In the case of income taxation, charitable organizations that are registered charities have additional privileges that other organizations do not have, primarily the ability to issue receipts to donors for income tax purposes. They are also eligible to receive a rebate on the portion of the goods and services taxes that they pay.

This chapter reviews the major taxing statutes and their application to charitable and not-for-profit organizations. It reviews the federal *Income*

Tax Act[1] and the exemptions that are provided to charitable and not-for-profit organizations. The chapter also discusses registration as a charitable organization, the advantages and disadvantages, the application process and what must be done to maintain registration, including compliance with the disbursement quotas and annual filings. Registration of public and private charitable foundations is also discussed. The Ontario *Corporations Tax Act*[2] provides exemptions to many charitable and not-for-profit corporations. Provincial corporate taxation is an area that is overlooked by some not-for-profit corporations.

Consumption taxes are a second type of taxation that affect charitable and not-for-profit organizations. There are two major forms of consumption taxes: the goods and services tax or the harmonized sales tax under the *Excise Tax Act*[3] and retail sales taxes under the *Retail Sales Tax Act*[4] and similar provincial statutes. Charitable and not-for-profit organizations may be required not only to pay the taxes on their purchases but also to collect the tax on sales and remit the collected amount to the government.

A third type of taxation is property taxation, principally under the *Assessment Act*,[5] which was substantially amended in the late 1990s in Ontario — several times to fix various serious adverse impacts, including on charitable organizations. There are some exemptions from property taxation available for charitable or not-for-profit organizations which organizations should consider using.

There are many myths about taxation in the sector. Some believe that registered charities are exempt from all taxes, which is far from the situation in law or fact. On the other hand, there are exemptions and rebates for which charitable or not-for-profit organizations may be eligible, but do not use or obtain. The directors have an obligation to take reasonable steps to structure their activities to take advantage of the tax exemptions and rebates and to minimize the payment of taxes and similar imposts. In doing so, of course, they must keep their focus on the purpose of the organization and not artificially create situations, the intention of which is solely to obtain tax benefits. In addition, directors ought to keep in mind that there is a difference between tax minimization in accordance with the law and tax evasion or improper tax avoidance.

---

[1] R.S.C. 1985, c. I (5th Supp.).
[2] R.S.O. 1990, c. C.40.
[3] R.S.C. 1985, c. E-15 [as am. S.C. 1990, c. 45].
[4] R.S.O. 1990, c. R.31.
[5] R.S.O. 1990, c. A.31, as am.

B FEDERAL INCOME TAX ACT

I EXEMPTIONS

The *Income Tax Act* has two major influences on charitable and not-for-profit organizations. First, it exempts those organizations from the payment of taxes on their income if they are registered as a charitable organization or if they fall within the definition of not-for-profit for purposes of the Act. This exemption may also provide exemptions under other statutes, such as the Ontario *Corporations Tax Act*. The rationale for the exemption is that the organizations are not intended to make profits (which is what is normally taxed as income of business corporations) and they provide benefits to the public.

Second, the Act permits registered charitable organizations to issue receipts for income tax purposes to individuals and to businesses that donate money or goods to the charitable organization. This provision encourages individuals and businesses to donate to charitable organizations so that the organizations have the resources necessary to carry out their objects. Other non-charitable organizations, such as certain amateur athletic associations, have a similar registration scheme.

(1) Not-for-profit Organizations

The *Income Tax Act* provides for separate exemption regimes for not-for-profit organizations and charitable organizations. Not-for-profit organizations are exempt from the payment of income tax on their income under para. 149(1)(l) of the Act. The subsection defines a "non-profit" organization as:

> (l) a club, society or association that, in the opinion of the Minister, was not a charity within the meaning assigned by subsection 149.1(1) and that was organized and operated exclusively for social welfare, civic improvement, pleasure or recreation or for any other purpose except profit, no part of the income of which was payable to, or was otherwise available for the personal benefit of, any proprietor, member or shareholder thereof unless the proprietor, member or shareholder was a club, society or association the primary purpose and function of which was the promotion of amateur athletics in Canada.

The definition is a negative one in that a not-for-profit organization is one that is not a charity. Thus, if the Minister forms the opinion that the organization is, in fact, a charitable organization under para. 149(1)(l), the organization will be required to comply with the various reporting requirements and restrictions on use of funds provided for under the Act. For example, although a charitable organization may not use its funds for political purposes, a not-for-profit organization can, provided the activities are within the scope of its objects. If the organization is, in the opinion of the Minister, a charitable organization and it has not complied with the requirements for charitable organizations, it may not be eligible for exemption from payment of income tax. Some not-for-profit organizations will, therefore, include in their objects a non-charitable object in order to avoid the possibility of being classified by the Minister as a "charitable organization".

The Canada Customs and Revenue Agency has published an Interpretation Bulletin[6] which sets out its interpretation of para. 149(1)(l) and related provisions. In order to qualify under that exemption, the organization must comply with the following conditions:

- it is not a charity;
- it is organized exclusively for social welfare, civic improvement, pleasure, recreation or any other purpose except profit;
- it is in fact operated exclusively for the same purpose for which it was organized or for any of the other purposes mentioned above; and
- it does not distribute or otherwise make available for the personal benefit of a member any of its income unless the member is an association which has as its primary purpose and function, the promotion of amateur athletics.

Interestingly, if the organization is a "charity" but is not registered as a charity (or its registration has been revoked), it will not be considered to be a "non-profit organization" and will not be exempt from taxation.

The CCRA will make a determination on the basis of the facts of each situation. It will review the instruments creating the organization (letters patent, constitution, by-laws, memoranda of agreement and so forth) to determine what its purposes are. But it will also look to what the organization actually does and how it carries out its purposes and its activities.

The Interpretation Bulletin comments that "social welfare" means the provision of assistance for disadvantaged groups or for the common good and general welfare of the community. "Civic improvement" includes enhancements in value or quality of a community or civic life. The types of activities would appear to be fairly broad and include encouraging the establishment of new industries in a community. The CCRA does comment that care must be taken with these purposes to ensure that the purposes are not charitable such that the organization is a charity (unless, of course, the organization is registered as a charity). A typical method of doing so is to include one or more objects or purposes that are clearly not charitable — such as political lobbying — but which remain not-for-profit.

---

[6] "Non-Profit Organizations", IT-496R, August 2, 2001.

"Pleasure or recreation" is also broadly interpreted to include those things that provide "a state of gratification or a means of refreshment or diversion". The definition includes social clubs, sports clubs and other clubs that are organized and operated to provide facilities for the enjoyment of members and their families.

The final category is for "any other purpose except profit". This category may be used for a wide variety of activities or objects, including those that have an ultimate purpose of improving the business conditions and profitability of other organizations. This category includes an association that is organized to advance the educational standards within a particular industry or profession. An organization would probably not qualify, however, if its main purpose and activities was to sell the goods or services of its members and receive a fee or commission in relation to the sales promoted. The Canada Customs and Revenue Agency considers that type of organization to be an extension of the members' sales organization and therefore a commercial operation. A residential condominium corporation will also normally be considered to be a not-for-profit organization where it is incorporated pursuant to the relevant provincial legislation and is not operated as a business.

The Canada Customs and Revenue Agency uses several indicators in assessing whether or not an organization is operated exclusively for not-for-profit purposes or is carrying on a trade or business. The fact that the organization may be incorporated as a corporation without share capital and has only not-for-profit objects is not decisive. The Canada Customs and Revenue Agency looks to the activities of the organization and how it is operated, not just its objects. These indicators include the following:

- the organization's activities are a trade or business in the ordinary meaning such that it is operated in a normal commercial manner;
- the organization's goods or services are not restricted to members and guests but are more broadly available;
- the organization is operated on a profit basis rather than a cost recovery basis. This indicator does not prohibit an organization from making an income in excess of its expenditures. However, the material part of the excess must not be accumulated each year and the balance of accumulated excess must not be greater than the organization's reasonable needs. If the excess is greater than the organization's reasonable needs, the Canada Customs and Revenue Agency will consider the organization to be operated on a profit basis and it would not be eligible for the exemption; or
- the organization is operated in competition with taxable entities carrying on the same trade or business.

The accumulated excess issue is problematic for some not-for-profit organizations. An organization may want to accumulate an excess in order to protect itself from reduced revenues in the future, either anticipated or unanticipated. The accumulated excess may also be a cushion against unforeseen expenses. However, the organization — and its officers and directors — need to recall the underlying purpose of the exemption. It is to provide an increased ability for not-for-profit organizations to carry out activities that will fulfil their objects and that are for the public good. The assets of an organization should, therefore, be devoted to its activities. On the other hand, the organization and its officers and directors must be cognizant of the need to be financially responsible in managing the affairs of the organization. Financial responsibility includes providing a reasonable level of financial flexibility for the future.

The Canada Customs and Revenue Agency would appear to recognize this need. It assesses each case on the merits. The Interpretation Bulletin notes some of the considerations that the Canada Customs and Revenue Agency will take into account in making its determination. For example, the Canada Customs and Revenue Agency will be concerned if the accumulated excess is used for purposes that are unrelated to the organization's objects: long-term investments to produce income; enlarging or expanding its facilities for normal commercial operations; or making loans to members, shareholders or non-exempt persons. It will also look at how the accumulated excess was created. The amount, pattern and source of the revenue that resulted in the accumulated excess is considered. Whether or not the excess income occurs on a regular, annual basis or an occasional basis is also relevant.

The test set out in the Interpretation Bulletin has not received much judicial review. The Tax Court, however, did review the test in *L.I.U.N.A., Local 57 Members' Training Trust Fund v. R.*[7] The Tax Court concluded that the organization must be doing more than earning "passive income". The earning of the income must be an operating motivation and a focus of its activity. Although the case was not appealed by the Canada Customs and Revenue Agency, it may be distinguishable. Arguably, one of the purposes of the accumulated excess in that case was to provide the long-term financial stability and income necessary for the training trust fund to carry out its objects.

If the organization is accumulating an excess, it would be prudent for the officers and directors to be in a position to demonstrate how any accumulated excess occurred and why it is justifiable. For example, the organization should be able to demonstrate that: the excess was accumulated from non-commercial activities; that the level of excess is reasonable, given the nature of the organization and its activities; and that the organization has a plan on how to use the excess. The organization should avoid distributing the excess in any way to its members by way of loan, dividend or otherwise.

The ability of an organization to distribute its income to its members, either directly or indirectly, would normally disqualify the organization as a not-for-profit organization. If the organization's constituting docu-

---

[7] [1992] 2 C.T.C. 2410, 92 D.T.C. 2365 (T.C.C.).

ments permit it to do so, the Canada Customs and Revenue Agency will consider it to be organized on a profit basis and not exclusively for not-for-profit purposes. Similarly, if the winding-up provisions of the organization permit the organization to distribute income to a member, it will not be eligible for the exemption for not-for-profit organizations.[8]

Members may receive certain types of payments or benefits without causing the organization to be disqualified as a not-for-profit organization under the Act. A member may be paid, for example, a salary or wage, fees or honoraria for services provided to the organization. Any amounts must be reasonable and consistent with the amounts paid for similar services in an arm's-length relationship. The organization may also pay expenses related to attendance at conferences, meetings and conventions as delegates for the organization to further its aims and objectives. Special provisions exist for payments to athletes who are members of an organization that promotes amateur athletics in Canada.

A not-for-profit organization is not required to file an annual return under the Act, unless it has certain types of income. Subsection 149(5) overrides the general exemption for not-for-profit organizations under para. 149(1)(l). If the not-for-profit organization's main purpose is to provide dining, recreation or sporting facilities for its members, income from property in excess of $2,000 will be taxed both at the federal level and the provincial level. The organization would file an annual T3 Trust Tax Return. Subsection 149(5) deems the organization to be a trustee of an *inter vivos* trust for the property that gives rise to the income. The types of income that are included in making the calculation, however, are limited to property income, such as rental income from renting space for parties or events, interest on any investments of membership dues, and so forth.[9]

A not-for-profit organization may also be required to file an annual return with the Canada Customs and Revenue Agency under subs. 149(12). That subsection requires a not-for-profit organization to file an annual T1044 Return if one of three events occur: if it receives more than $10,000 in interest, rentals or royalties; if it has more than $200,000 in assets at the end of the preceding fiscal period; or if it was required to file the return in any preceding fiscal period. This provision is applicable for fiscal periods ending after 1992.[10] The subsection also applies after the fact; the organization is required to file if, at the end of the fiscal period, it falls within the subsection's criteria.

Subsection 149(1) provides exemptions to a number of other persons and activities. For example, a municipal authority or public body that is

---

[8] See "Winding-Up of a Non-Profit Organization", IT-409, February 27, 1978, for information on how to windup a not-for-profit organization without losing the exemption status.
[9] See, for a fuller discussion of this issue, "Non-Profit Organizations — Taxation of Income from Property", IT-83R3, October 31, 1990.
[10] S.C. 1994, c. 7, subs. 88(4).

performing a function of government in Canada is exempt from paying income tax under para. 149(1)(d). Under para. 149(1)(i), corporations that were constituted exclusively for the purpose of providing low-cost housing accommodation for the aged are exempt. A not-for-profit corporation for scientific research and experimental development, subject to certain restrictions, is exempt under para. 129(1)(j). These exemptions may be applicable to some not-for-profit organizations in addition to the general exemption in para. 149(1)(l).

(2) Charitable Organizations

Section 149.1 of the Act recognizes two types of charities that are exempt from income taxation:

- a charitable organization, all the resources of which are devoted to charitable activities carried on by the organization itself. No part of its income may be payable to or otherwise be available for the personal benefit of a proprietor, member, shareholder, trustee or settlor. In addition, more than 50 per cent of the directors, trustees, officers or similar officials must be at arm's length. A charitable organization may be established as a corporation, an unincorporated association or a trust;
- charitable foundation, which is constituted and operated exclusively for charitable purposes. No part of its income may be payable to or otherwise be available for the personal benefit of any proprietor, member, shareholder, trustee or settlor. Charitable foundations may provide funds to charitable organizations or other "qualified donees" so that those organizations may carry out their charitable activities. A charitable foundation must be either a corporation or a trust.

There are, in turn, two types of charitable foundations. A "public foundation" is a foundation where more than 50 per cent of its directors, trustees, officers or similar officials are at arm's length and not more than 50 per cent of its capital was contributed by one person or the members of a group of persons who are not at arm's length. In the case of a charitable foundation that was registered before February 15, 1984, the capital contribution rate is 75 per cent. A "private foundation" is not a public foundation. In general, a private foundation is one that is established for philanthropic purposes by a wealthy individual or family. A private foundation may also be established in part for tax planning purposes.

II REGISTRATION AS A CHARITABLE ORGANIZATION OR CHARITABLE FOUNDATION

(1)   Advantages and Disadvantages

There is no requirement that a charitable or not-for-profit organization apply for registration as a "registered charity". Many organizations that carry out charitable activities or activities that are charitable in nature are not registered. There are a number of advantages to registration, however, which should be considered by the organization:

- the organization may issue receipts for income tax purposes to donors, which is an incentive to the donors to give money or goods or to increase the value of the donation;
- registration is not certification by the Canada Customs and Revenue Agency that the organization is using the money or goods donated wisely, but it does add credibility to the organization. In addition, the Canada Customs and Revenue Agency does conduct periodic audits on registered charities to ensure compliance with the *Income Tax Act*;[11]
- the organization is automatically exempt from taxation under Part I of the Act;
- it avoids the Minister determining under para. 149(1)(l) that it is a charity. If the organization applies for registration and is refused registration, this fact will be *prima facie* evidence of the Minister's opinion on its charitability. Some organizations will include an object that is clearly not a charitable object in order to obtain the refusal;
- the organization will benefit from special provisions that apply to registered charities with respect to the Goods and Services Tax or Harmonized Sales Tax;[12]
- the organization may be exempt from other taxation, including corporate income tax under the Ontario *Corporations Tax* Act[13] and certain retail sales taxes under the Ontario *Retail Sales Tax Act*[14] or from charging certain retail sales taxes under that Act; and

---

[11] R.S.C. 1985, c. I (5th Supp.).
[12] For further information, see the Canada Customs and Revenue Agency — Customs and Excise publications, "GST/HST Information for Charities", RC4082, July 8, 1998 and "GST/HST Information for Non-profit Organizations", RC4081, April 14, 1999.
[13] R.S.O. 1990, c. C.40, s. 57.
[14] R.S.O. 1990, c. R.31 and O. Regs. 1012/90 and 1013/90.

- the organization may more readily qualify for other benefits. Charitable foundations, for example, usually provide their funds to registered charitable organizations. Charitable organizations (including charitable foundations) may qualify for a lottery or bingo licence.

There are some disadvantages to registration which should be taken into account before a decision is made to apply for registration. These include:

- the organization must devote all of its resources to its charitable activities. A number of activities are prohibited or restricted. Political lobbying, for example, is limited to activities that are ancillary and incidental to the charitable purposes of the organization;[15]
- the organization must make annual filings with the Canada Customs and Revenue Agency. Certain of the information will be accessible to the public and the Canada Customs and Revenue Agency is considering making more information available;
- the organization must have a formal constitution, be incorporated or be a trust, which may increase legal expenses. In the case of a foundation, it must be a trust or corporation;
- none of the property of the organization may be distributed to the members. On dissolution or winding up of the organization, the property must be distributed to another charitable organization after payment of any debts or liabilities; and
- the Public Guardian and Trustee in Ontario uses registration as a charitable organization as one of the tests to determine whether or not the organization falls within the supervisory jurisdiction of the Public Guardian and Trustee under the *Charities Accounting Act*.[16]

The application process is usually straightforward, provided that the necessary ground work has been done and the supporting documentation is included with the application. The application is made by an "Application for Registration" (Form T2050), which is readily available from the Charities Directorate, Canada Customs and Revenue Agency or the District Taxation Office.

---

[15] Subsection 149.1(6.1) of the *Income Tax Act*, R.S.C. 1985, c. 1 (5th Supp.). See, for a discussion, Information Circular 87-1, "Registered Charities — Ancillary and Incidental Political Activities", February 25, 1987.

[16] R.S.O. 1990, c. C.10.

The registration application process for charities under the Act is, at first blush, a complicated one. Much of the operational aspects of the application process and compliance itself are set out in Interpretation Bulletins and Information Circulars issued by the Canada Customs and Revenue Agency and its predecessor, Revenue Canada. Although these Bulletins and Circulars do not have the force of law, as statutes or regulations do, they are important statements of how the Canada Customs and Revenue Agency interprets and applies the law. Generally, complying with the Interpretation Bulletins and Information Circulars means that the organization is in compliance with the law, subject to the facts of any particular case.

Equally important, complying with the "regulator's" understanding of the law is useful in the relationship with that regulator. There may be circumstances in which an organization may want to challenge the regulator's interpretation or application of the law. A challenge can be done through a number of mechanisms, including through litigation. There is certainly nothing improper in carrying through with an appropriate challenge that is in the best interests of the organization. The Interpretation Bulletins are only one interpretation of the law, albeit one that is usually persuasive at the very least. It may be that the Canada Customs and Revenue Agency's interpretation or application of the law is incorrect in general or in the context of a specific set of facts.

If there is value in doing so, the organization could consider an appropriate challenge. The challenge may be done at the administrative level or in seeking comments on a specific fact situation. If these approaches do not resolve the matter, litigation may be an appropriate route for the charity. Care must be taken, however, in not doing so in a manner that would jeopardize registration. For example, it is usually not advisable to act as if the law did not exist and wait for the Minister to issue a notice to revoke a registration. This approach is very risky and exposes the directors and officers to potential personal liability.

(2) Application Process

The Canada Customs and Revenue Agency is responsible for the registration process for charitable organizations. That Agency, an agency of the Government of Canada, monitors registered charities for compliance with the law and provides information about charities to the public. It also provides information to charities and others about registration and compliance.

The application process is not a complicated one but it can take time. Ambiguity or vagueness can delay the application, as will incompleteness. The Agency needs to be satisfied that the applicant:

- is a charity, as that word is defined in law,
- has objects or purposes and activities that are charitable, and
- will carry out its activities in accordance with the law.

A registered charity enjoys substantial privileges in Canadian society, not the least of which is the ability to issue receipts for income tax purposes to individuals and corporations for donations. The registration has other benefits with respect to other forms of taxation, including Goods and Services Tax, property assessments (for some charitable organizations) and retail sales tax. Registration as a charitable organization is a condition for most grants from registered charitable foundations and for many government grant programs. At the very least, registration makes it easier to demonstrate that the organization is a charity than if it were not registered. Registration is a form of imprimatur that is used by others. The fact that the Canada Customs and Revenue Agency has determined that an organization is "charitable" for purposes of income tax legislation is very persuasive to others that the organization is "charitable" for their purposes.

The Canada Customs and Revenue Agency is, for many, the issuer of a "seal of approval", albeit not in a legal sense. It is not legally liable for the activities of registered charities nor for any assumptions or presumptions that others may have with respect to registration. Nevertheless, the Agency does take its role seriously and in recent years additional resources have been devoted to the charity division. It has become more active in monitoring and compliance and some charities have been vocal in their objections. On the other hand, these actions will benefit all charities in the long run.

The application process is designed to assist the Agency in making the determination whether or not an applicant is eligible for registration as a charity — either as an organization or as a foundation (public or private). The process assumes that the applicant knows what it is doing. There are opportunities for clarification and redrafting, but applications should be complete and readily understandable. First and foremost, the objects and activities must be clearly charitable.

The Canada Customs and Revenue Agency has issued a number of Interpretation Bulletins, Information Circulars and Brochures to assist organizations to apply for registration or for registered charities to comply with the law. The application process has become more sophisticated and detailed in recent years, in part no doubt to reflect the increased level of public interest in registered charities and the need for accountability to the public. Registering a Charity for Income Tax Purposes[17] is one of the primary documents to use in completing the Application to Register a Charity under the Income Tax Act.[18]

The Canada Customs and Revenue Agency sets out in Registering a Charity its standards for review. An organization must be established and operated for charitable purposes and devote its resources to charitable activities. In addition, the charity must be resident in Canada. It cannot use its income to benefit its members.

---

[17] T4063.
[18] T2050.

A charity must also meet the public benefit test to demonstrate that:

- its activities and purposes provide a tangible benefit to the public;
- those people who are eligible for benefits are either the public as a whole or are a significant part of the public as a whole. They cannot be a restricted group or share a private connection, such as a social club or professional association; and
- the activities must be legal and cannot be contrary to public policy.

These standards are based on the common law definition of charitable, as it has developed in Canada.

What is or is not "charitable" is discussed in greater detail in Chapter 1 of this text. In brief, a charitable object or activity must fall within one of the four categories that the courts have identified:

- relief of poverty,
- advancement of education,
- advancement of religion,
- purposes beneficial to the community which the courts have decided are charitable.

A number of activities are not charitable and may disqualify an organization from registration. For example, the *Income Tax Act* prohibits the income of a registered charity from being payable or otherwise available to benefit personally a proprietor, member, shareholder, trustee or settlor of the organization. The organization will not be eligible for registration if, for example, it distributes income to its members. Similarly, under the common law, an organization is not charitable if one of its purposes are political in nature.

The objects of an organization are typically set out in its governing documents. These documents establish the organization as a legal entity — an association, corporation or trust. The legal nature of an association is a complex one as it is not a "person" in law. Similarly, a trust is not a person in law but each of the trustees are persons in law and the trust can only act through its trustees. In any event, an unincorporated association is recognized under the *Income Tax Act* and has a limited "personality" for other purposes.

The governing documents must have the following elements to be considered by the Canada Customs and Revenue Agency for registration as a charity:

- Trust Document:

    - name of the trust;

- names of the original trustees;
- purpose for which the trust is established;
- rules governing the administration of the trust funds by the trustees;
- provision requiring that the money received from the trust will be expended only on the purposes set out in the trust document;
- process for the replacement of trustees;
- effective date of the trust; and
- signatures of at least three trustees.

- Constitution (unincorporated association):

  - organization's name;
  - organization's objects or purposes;
  - clause stating that it will carry out its purposes without gain for its members and any profits or other accretions shall be used solely to promote its objects;
  - organization's structure, i.e., officers;
  - process for the replacement of directors and officers;
  - effective date of the document; and
  - signatures of at least three directors.

A corporation's letters patent will already include these elements and, in some cases, additional information. These are the minimum requirements and many organizations or trusts will have additional elements and provisions to meet their needs.

Many organizations will be established with the view of applying for registration. The process can be time-consuming and expensive, especially if revisions are required. The Canada Customs and Revenue Agency will review draft governing documents provided all other information and documents required on the application form are included. The Agency's comments on the draft governing documents may be used to clarify or revise the governing documents before the members take the next step of incorporation — formally establishing the trust or unincorporated association. Changing the terms of a trust document can be particularly difficult and expensive, and, may require a court order.

The Agency is not bound by its comments on draft documents. The legislative scheme does not provide for any appeals until the application itself has been reviewed and a determination made on it. Nevertheless, the draft document approach is a useful one and will often save time and expense. It permits changes to be made based upon the written comments from the Agency. The process that has been established is one more akin to a courtesy than one with any formal legal rights attached to it. The Agency will also only review the materials in draft form once; the next time must be through a formal application both for a new organization or an existing one that wants to amend its governing documents to make itself eligible for registration.

The application was revised in 1999. It is comprised of a series of questions (24) which may be answered on the form itself or with attachments. Most of the information is available to the public if the application is approved and the organization becomes registered. The public availability of information is an important part of public accountability both of the Agency itself and of the registered charities. This increased level of publicly available information reflects the increased public interest in charities and similar organizations.

The application should be completed by either a person in a position of responsibility with the organization, such as its president, or by its legal representative appointed to do so. At least two individuals who are authorized to sign on behalf of the organization must sign the application, such as the president and secretary or treasurer. These individuals will normally be directors and officers of the organization. The application must be complete, and include any required attachments, before it will be reviewed. The Agency strongly urges applicants to make sure that they have worked out all of the details and have a clear idea of what the organization will do and how it will operate before an application is submitted. A delay will occur if the application is vague, ambiguous or unclear.

In addition, although not noted by the Agency, the application will provide the Agency with its first impression of the organization. An incomplete application, one that is missing mandatory documents or that is unclear will not leave a good impression. Decision-making with respect to applications for registration is based upon the materials that are filed. There is seldom a pre-existing working relationship between the applicants and staff. Even if there is one, staff at the Agency must assess the application on its merits, not on any relationship that may exist. If, however, there are significant problems with the application, those problems may give rise to concerns about the credibility and ability of the organization and its officers and directors to manage a charity in accordance with the law.

The application is comprised of 24 questions in six parts. Each part is discussed below:

(a)   Part 1 — Identification of Applicant

This part asks about the current legal and trade or operational name of the applicant. The legal name will be the name set out in its governing documents. Some organizations will also use a shorter version for operations or operate under a different but related name.

If the organization operated under a different name in the past, that name must be disclosed. If the organization already has a Business Number, it is to be included. An organization may have a Business Number because it is registered for GST/HST purposes (a separate registration scheme) or have employees. The use of a Business Number does not mean that the organization is carrying on business, rather it is a single number used to identify the organization for various purposes.

The application also requests a complete address for mailing purposes. Organization will often have applied for registration or corresponded with the Charity Division. If so, information about the previous contact. If the organization had been registered and the registration was revoked, it must provide the Business Number or registration number of the organization at the time, the date of revocation and the reason for revocation. The most common reason for revocation is a failure to file the annual information return within six months of the organization's fiscal year. Other reasons include carrying on non-charitable activities, changing the governing documents to include non-charitable objects, and issuing improper receipts for income tax purposes. An organization may voluntarily request that its registration be revoked if, for example, it is merging with another organization or decides to wind up its affairs.

(b)   Part 2 — List of Applicant's Directors or Trustees

The individuals who are elected or appointed to manage the affairs of the organization are usually called directors, trustees, officers, governors or have similar names. The name of the position will be set out in the governing documents, such as the by-laws. The applicant must submit a list of the individuals (first and last names) and their position. Additional names or initials must be used to identify each individual if any of the individuals have similar names, e.g., John Edward Doe and John Frank Doe. The name of the religious leader is to be included for organizations that are religious congregations, even if that individual is not a director or trustee.

(c)   Part 3 — Organizational Structure

(i)   **Internal Division**

The applicant may be an internal division of a registered charity. If so, the division will operate under the governing document of the parent organization. The parent organization will typically exercise one or more powers, such as approval of the internal division's budget, holding title to property used or managed by the internal division, signing all contracts, loans or agreements affecting the internal division. It will also have the authority to create internal divisions. The application from an internal division must include a certificate from the parent organization signed by a director or trustee confirming the division's status as a branch, section, parish or congregation or other division of the parent. The certificate must also provide the officially recognized names of both the parent and the internal division in full and the effective date when the relationship was created. The internal division must submit an acknowledgment, signed by at least two officials of the division confirming that the members of the internal division operate under the governing document of the parent organization.

(ii) Independent Organization

If the organization is not an internal division of a parent organization, it must have its own governing documents. The organization may be incorporated, in which case it must provide a copy of its incorporating documents, usually letters patent. Copies of all amendments or supplementary letters patent must be also be included. A certificate of good standing or similar document from the incorporating authority must be submitted if the organization has had five or more fiscal year ends between the day it was incorporated and the date of submission. An applicant for re-registration must include a certificate in all cases.

(iii)   Unincorporated Associations

There are a few different types of unincorporated entities that may be registered. They may be established by a constitution, trust deed (in the case of a trust), a will or otherwise. A copy of the organization's constitution, trust deed or other constituting document must be submitted as part of the application. At least three current directors or trustees must sign the copy certifying that it is a true copy of the current constituting document under which the organization operates. The certification must also include the effective date of the document and of the signatures.

If the organization also has by-laws in addition to the incorporating documents, constitution or trust deed, a copy signed by at least two current directors or trustees must be submitted. The effective date of the by-laws and the date that each signed by the by-laws must be indicated.

A number of organizations own land or will own land or buildings or intend to do so to carry out their objects. The applicant must indicate if it owns or intends to own real property. If the organization is not incorporated it would not normally be able to hold title to real property and must do so through a legal person. The application must include the name of the legal person who will be holding title in trust for the organization. The trust deed should include provisions for the replacement of the trustees and for the registration of the trust deed against title under the real property laws of the province in which the real property is held.

(iv)   Designation

The Minister must designate a charity as a charitable organization, private foundation or public foundation. The designation is based upon the information provided in the application. To some extent, the designation will depend upon both the purposes of the charity and on the relationship among the directors or trustees. A charitable organization, generally speaking, carries out charitable activities; a charitable foundation provides funds to charitable organizations from the income earned on the foundations assets.

A public foundation gives more than 80 per cent of its income annually to other qualified donees. Qualified donees include other registered charities and some other entities, such as municipalities. It must be established either as a corporation or a trust. An unincorporated association is not eligible to be a public foundation. Less than 50 per cent of its directors or trustees are related persons and at least 50 per cent of its funds are from donors who are not related persons. A public foundation may also carry out its own charitable activities.

A private foundation is similar to a public foundation. It may either carry on its own charitable activities or give funds to qualified donees. An unincorporated association is not eligible to be a private foundation. A private foundation is one in which (a) 50 per cent or more of its directors or trustees are related persons or otherwise do not deal at arm's length with each other, or (b) more than 50 per cent of its funds are received from one person or group of persons who do not deal with each other at arm's length. A private foundation may not carry on any business activity at all, whereas a public foundation and a charitable organization may carry on related business activities.

"Related person" and "arm's length" are concepts in tax law and other areas of law, such as securities law.[19] An arm's length relationship is one in which each party acts independently of the other. "Non-arm's length" relationships are ones, therefore, in which people act or are considered to act in concert with each other. Typically, non-arm's length relationships include individuals who are related to each-other by blood, marriage, adoption, common law relationships or close business ties.

A "related person" has a similar definition. The brochure notes that individuals can be related to each other by marriage, blood, adoption, common-law relationship or by a close business or corporate association. A close business or corporate association could arise where two or more individuals are business partners or one is an employer and the other an employee. Individuals or groups of individuals may also be related to a corporation in which they have a controlling interest. The people related to those individuals or groups of individuals may, in turn, be related to the corporation. If so, they are not considered to be acting at arm's length to each other.

Question 12 of the application form is intended to provide the Minister with the information necessary to make a decision about designation — assuming, of course, that the organization is otherwise eligible for registration. It asks whether or not the organization was formed for the purpose of giving more than 50 per cent of its income to qualified do-

---

[19] See also "Meaning of Arm's Length and Interpretation" Interpretation Bulletin, IT-419R, August 24, 1995, "Corporations: Association and Control" Interpretation Bulletin, IT-64R, August 14, 2001, for a fuller discussion of these concepts and application by the Canada Customs and Revenue Agency.

nees, such as other registered charities. Although there are other entities that fall within the definition of qualified donees, such as municipalities, in most cases the grants will be to registered charities. The Question also asks about the relationship among the directors and trustees and if 80 per cent or more are in a non-arm's length relationship. If they are, the relationship must be disclosed. Similarly, if the organization received or will receive more than 50 per cent of its funds or other assets from one source or from a group of persons who are not arm's length from each other, this fact must be disclosed. The identity of the source and the relationship of the donors, if a group of non-arm's length donors, must also be disclosed.

Issues around arm's length and related persons are important. If an organization wants to be registered as a charitable organization and not as a private foundation, for example, it must take the appropriate steps to ensure that a sufficient number of the directors or trustees are independent of each other. If there is a business relationship among the directors or trustees, this fact may have an impact upon the Minister's designation decision. For example, if one of the directors is an employer of another director, that relationship could (but not necessarily would) be sufficient to conclude that those two directors are in a non-arm's length relationship. The facts of each case are relevant to this determination. Essentially, the underlying issue is whether or not they are seen to be acting or will be acting in concert with reach other.

The potential impact is significant. For example, if the organization is registered as a private foundation instead of as a public foundation or charitable organization, it cannot carry on any business activity, whether ancillary and incidental to its objects or not. The operation of ancillary and incidental business activities are often important sources of revenue for charities and a legitimate method of fundraising.

(d)   *Part 4 — Information about the Activities of the Applicant*

(i)   **Description of Activities**

In Canada, the government and the courts have placed substantial emphasis upon not just the objects or purposes of the organization but also the organization's activities in determining whether or not the organization is "charitable" for purposes of the *Income Tax Act*. This approach has had a ripple effect in other areas of the law. The approach makes sense as the actual or proposed activities of the organization are a test of how it will carry out its charitable objects or purposes. But, at times, especially at the start, organizations may not readily know in detail what their activities will be. Organizations develop and respond to community needs. In addition, the reality is that activities are often determined by both the organization's ability to raise funds and the source of those funds. A $100,000 donation to operate a soup kitchen may mean that the organization carries out its object to relieve poverty by operating a soup kitchen.

Question 13 of the application requires the applicant to describe the activities that it will undertake to achieve each of the objects set out in its governing documents. Sometimes, especially for newer organizations, this exercise may be difficult. The objects may have been broadly drafted in order to provide room for the organization to grow or so as not to restrict it and its activities, yet allow it to remain charitable. Nevertheless, organizations should, at the very least, consider the types of activities that it might undertake as it develops its objects. It may be that the implementation of some of the objects will be staged over a period of years; if so, the organization should have made this decision before it applies for registration. If the organization intends to use other qualified donees, such as other registered charities, it must provide details about the resources it intends to make available to those qualified donees to assist in carrying out their charitable activities.

The Agency expects a substantial amount of detail about the activities and takes the position that it needs the detail to make its assessment. It needs to have a clear understanding of what an organization intends to do to demonstrate that it is charitable. For example, if the organization is to establish a community centre, the Agency wants to know, at a minimum, the following information:

- membership requirements;
- the kind of facilities and services to be provided, such as indoor and outdoor sports facilities, meeting rooms, daycare services, catering services and banquet hall facilities. If the organization intends to provide catering services, banquet hall facilities or similar services and facilities, the organization needs to take care to ensure that these services and facilities are ancillary and incidental to its objects. If, on the facts, the community centre is more business than charitable, it would not be eligible for registration and, if registered, could be subject to revocation proceedings. Furthermore, in Ontario, the organization must be able to demonstrate that its use of real property is to carry out its charitable objects. The *Charities Accounting Act* restricts charitable organizations from owning real property for investment purposes and requires that the real property be disposed of in an orderly manner. The *Charitable Gifts Act* also limits charities to a 10 per cent interest in the shares of a business. However, if the business activities are ancillary and incidental to the charitable objects, as opposed to an investment in a separate entity, the organization would appear to be in compliance with that statute;
- the centre's schedule of events. The request for this type of information would appear to be overly cautious on the part of the Agency and does not reflect the evolving nature of community centres. Community centres develop over time and often the ab-

sence of a community centre is the reason why certain events and activities do not occur. Arguably, scheduling the centre's events is putting the cart before the horse, because it is very much a "build it and they will come" scenario. Nevertheless, the applicant should at the very least know the types of events that will occur and who the potential users are. A prudent organization would have carried out a feasibility study and that study should provide some of the requested information;

- the percentage of time reserved for sports compared to other kinds of activities, whether sports facilities will be available to all, whether coaching or instruction will be compulsory, whether certain sports will be specifically reserved for special groups of people, such as "gifted" or semi-professional players. Because sports and the promotion of sports has not been recognized as a charitable object for purposes of the *Income Tax Act*, care must be taken in developing this aspect of the community centre's activities.[20] The courts have recognized certain types of sports activities as being charitable if intended to advance education of youth or to promote health and well-being for the disabled or seniors as part of modern day relief of poverty. The comment made above about scheduling events applies to this information request; and

- the activities that will be organized by the community centre itself rather than by community groups. Again, details may be difficult to provide given the nature of community centres, but the organization must have some sense and information in order to proceed at a practical level. If it cannot answer this type of question, it should reassess its own business plan.

A similar analysis could be undertaken for the other examples used by the Agency or for other types of charitable activities. The key is to provide accurate information but to do so in manner that is consistent with the law on what is or is not charitable. In addition, it is essential that the organization have collectively thought through how it wants to implement its objects. Sometimes, the reverse approach is the better route to take — deciding on the activities the organization wants to undertake and drafting the objects around those activities, assuming that both the activities and objects are charitable.

---

[20] The Divisional Court in Ontario has recognized the promotion of amateur sports, to a limited extent, as a charitable object in *Re Laidlaw Foundation* (1984), 48 O.R. (2d) 549, 18 E.T.R. 77, 13 D.L.R. (4th) 491, 6 O.A.C. 181 (Div. Ct.). However, there is no similar case for purposes of the *Income Tax Act*.

(ii) Political Activities

Question 14 asks about the political activities of the organization. Most charitable organizations would not normally have political activities. By their nature, political activities are not charitable. However, at common law, an organization may carry out political activities that are ancillary and incidental to its charitable objects. The classic example used is where a children's aid society lobbies for improvements to the legislation to protect the interests of children. This political lobbying is consistent with its objects. Any political activity must be non-partisan, so support for a political party or candidate for election is not permitted.

The Canada Customs and Revenue Agency permits up to 10 per cent of a charity's resources to be used for non-partisan political activities to influence law, policy and public opinion on matters related to its charitable objects or purposes.[21] The common law is less specific but would seem to be consistent with the Agency's approach.

The application form requires the applicant to provide details on the type of political activities it expects to undertake. It must also explain how these activities will achieve the organization's objects or purposes. The applicant must provide estimates on the percentage of its resources that will be used for its political activities — human resources, financial resources and physical resources.

If the organization intends to carry out lobbying it may be required to register as a lobbyist under either the federal *Lobbyist Registration Act*[22] or similar provincial legislation, such as the Ontario *Lobbyist Registration Act, 1998*.[23] An organization that intends to include information about its lobbying efforts in the application (which it must do if it does intend to carry out political lobbying) should review the federal and Ontario legislation, depending upon at which level of government the organization expects to carry out lobbying activities. Some municipalities, such as the City of Toronto, have also expressed an interest in a lobbyist registration by-law.

The public policy behind the lobbyist registration schemes is to ensure that there is public accountability and transparency with respect to decisions that affect public policy and public law. Lobbyist registration brings, to some extent at least, the "backroom" influencing of public policy into public view. The statute does not differentiate in principle between lobbying efforts by or on behalf of businesses and those of charitable and not-for-profit organizations. However, charitable and not-for-profit organizations have not historically considered themselves to be

---

[21] See also Information Circular IC87-1 Registered Charities — Ancillary/Incidental Political Activities and the draft RC4107, "Registered Charities: Education, Advocacy, and Political Activities".
[22] R.S.C. 1985, c. 44 (4th Supp.).
[23] S.O. 1998, c. 27, Schedule. The Ontario legislation is a schedule to a statute entitled the *Lobbyist Commissioner and Lobbyists Statute Law Amendment Act*, 1998.

the same as "business lobbyists". Nevertheless, lobbying efforts for purposes of business or for charitable and not-for-profit organizations are both included under the federal and Ontario statutes. There are differences between the two statutory schemes and, to some extent, between the requirements for businesses as opposed to charitable and not-for-profit organizations. The principle behind the schemes remains and those completing the application for registration need to ensure consistency and compliance with both the *Income Tax Act* requirements and the federal and Ontario lobbyist registration statutes.

(iii) Fundraising

Fundraising is an essential activity for charitable organizations but it is not in and of itself a charitable activity. The purpose of fundraising, both occasional and regular, is to raise the funds necessary to undertake the charitable activities of the organization to fulfill its charitable objects. Without funds, it is very difficult — if not impossible — to provide the benefits to the public that the public justifiably expects.

The public also expects that the charitable organization will devote its resources primarily to carrying out its charitable objects or purposes, not to raise funds. A charity needs funds but normally, its pith and substance should not be to raise funds. There may be exceptions for organizations that have specific projects that require substantial funds to carry out its object or purpose for defined periods of time or for foundations that raise funds for public hospitals. However, even in these cases, it is essential to be able to demonstrate that the organization is there to carry out charitable activities, that it is doing so and will continue to do so.

Questions 15 and 16 ask for information about the organization's occasional and regular fundraising activities. Occasional fundraising is described as occurring on an irregular or intermittent basis, such as annual or semi-annual bingo, auctions, a Christmas craft sale, an annual walk-a-thon or an annual mail campaign. If the organization intends to sell goods or services, at these events, it should describe those goods and services. It should also describe the different types of fundraising it intends to employ, how often and the anticipated proportion of volunteers. The use of volunteers has an impact on both eligibility for registration and on the exemption for GST/HST purposes. If a professional fundraiser is to be used, the applicant must describe the relationship, including method of payment.

Similar information is to be provided for regular fundraising events, whether they are regular bingo events, the operation of a bookstore or daycare centre or similar activities. If the organization intends to develop and maintain a regular program to solicit donations, it must disclose that fact and what it intends to do. If it intends to sell goods or services, details on the goods or services must be provided. Again, it must also indicate the percentage of people involved who will be volunteers.

From a practical point of view, it is difficult for many organizations to provide the type of information in the detail requested. However, the application requires the organization to focus on this issue, which may be beneficial in the longer term for the organization. For example, too often, organizations get started without having considered how their activities will be funded. Or, whether or not an organization will have the resources and expertise available for certain types of fundraising activities. Whether or not its members and donors are comfortable and supportive of, say, charitable gaming or direct solicitation. It is better to have thought these issues out earlier rather than later.

(e)   Part 5 — Financial Information

The application requires detailed information about the next fiscal period of the organization. If the organization is already operating, the financial information would typically be included in its budget for the upcoming year. If not, the information would be similar to a *pro forma* statement. Part 6 of the application also requires an applicant to provide its financial statements for its previous fiscal period, although these financial statements will normally be kept confidential and do not form part of the file that is available to the public. The Annual Charity Return for registered charitable organizations provides the charity with the option of consenting to the release of its annual financial statements.

The Agency requires very detailed financial information about the upcoming fiscal period. It recognizes that not all categories of information will be applicable to all organizations and that amounts will be approximations. Nevertheless, the applicant must take care and should spend a considerable amount of time developing this financial information and answering Questions 17 and 18 of the application.

The organization should also be able to connect the financial transactions (receipts and disbursements) with the information provided earlier in the application. For example, the applicant should be able to connect revenues to the fundraising activities or disbursements to the description of charitable activities. Similarly, the answers about source of funds in Question 12 dealing with the designation of the organization should be consistent with the answers given on source of revenues in Question 17.

Question 17 asks for information about both receipts and disbursements. The types of receipts include:

- occasional fundraising events;
- regular fundraising events;
- gifts from individuals not already included from, for example, an annual mail campaign;
- gifts from registered charities not already included from, for example, a fundraising campaign with public or private foundations — the name of the charity is to be included if known;

- gifts from other organizations and businesses not already included;
- government grants or contracts. A contract would normally be for the provision of goods or services, such as housing and support for young offenders; and
- revenues from other sources. These revenues would include membership dues, interest, dividends and so forth.

Receipts may be cash or in-kind in nature. Receipts also include loans or proceeds from the sale of capital assets. The amount of the receipt should be the "gross" amount and not the "net" of any costs associated with obtaining the receipt. Disbursements are all cash outlays for any purpose, including for fundraising purposes. Disbursements include the following expenditures:

- occasional fundraising event costs, such as promotional material, cost of goods, postage and so forth;
- regular fundraising event costs, including the cost of goods, bingo hall rentals and so forth;
- gifts to beneficiaries, which may be scholarships or grants, money spent on food to be provided to the poor or for the purchase of clothing to aid victims of a natural disaster;
- gifts to qualified donees, which may be cash or goods, such as equipment. If known, the names of the qualified donees should be provided;
- remuneration and benefits, including salaries, wages, commissions, bonuses, fees and honoraria and the fair market value of any benefits, such as private use of car or office space;
- accounting and legal fees;
- occupancy costs, such as rent, mortgage payments, maintenance, heat, hydro, insurance and so forth;
- supplies and equipment not already included, such as office supplies, telephones and other items used by specific types of organizations, such as shelving for a library;
- printing and publications not already included for information brochures, annual report and other publications that are distributed without charge;
- transportation costs, such as the purchase and maintenance of motor vehicles for use in carrying out charitable activities or in administration;
- social events not already included, such as a party for volunteers. Each anticipated event should be accounted for separately; and

- other disbursements not already included, such as bank charges, with an explanation.

The application also asks for disbursements outside Canada to be separately identified. If any funds or resources are to be disbursed outside of Canada, the organization must identify where and how much is to be spent in each location. The organization should ensure that it complies with the Agency's requirements for disbursements outside Canada.[24]

Organizations may also have a number of assets or expect to have assets at the end of its fiscal period. The application form asks for the anticipated approximate value those assets will have at the end of the next fiscal period. Similarly, it is also to provide comparable information about anticipated liabilities. The assets would include cash, investments and fixed assets, which are to be specified. Liabilities include mortgages, loans and notes payable (which may be for the fixed assets) and other amounts payable.

The organization may, in certain circumstances, have or anticipate having financial transactions with its directors or trustees. These transactions may include loans or a landlord/tenant relationship. The common law generally prohibits many kinds of financial transactions on the basis that a director or trustee has a fiduciary obligation to the organization, one that is particularly acute in dealing with charitable property. A financial relationship between the registered charity and the director or trustee may be contrary to the common law and cause the organization to be ineligible for registration.

There are circumstances in which such relationships may be permitted. For example, if the organization has obtained a court order authorizing the relationship, such as a loan to one of its directors, the relationship may not be a problem. Nevertheless, great care must be exercised in any situation in which a director or trustee is in a financial relationship with the organization. This relationship may be either direct or indirect. The Agency will want information for both a direct relationship and one that is through an intermediary. For example, if an individual is a director of the organization and also on the board of a business company that rents space from the organization, the Agency will want details about the terms of the lease, such as size of space, fair market value rent and the monthly rent.

(f)   Part 6 — Confidential Information

This part sets out certain confidential personal information about the directors or trustees of the applicant. Based on the list of directors or trustees, the applicant must provide the home address, telephone num-

---

[24] See RC4106, "Registered Charities: Operating Outside Canada".

ber and occupation of each director or trustee. Another question asks for the business address or physical location of the organization, which may be the same as the mailing address set out in Part 1. The telephone and facsimile numbers are also requested. Similar information about the location of the books and records, and about the authorized representative of the organization is required. If the authorized representative is a director or trustee already identified, only the name needs to be provided. The Agency will only provide information to the person or persons who are identified as the organization's authorized representative. It is important, therefore, to keep the Agency aware of who is or who is not the authorized representative, especially where elections result in changes.

The applicant is also requested to provide copies of minutes, newspaper clippings, fund-raising materials, pamphlets, brochures, videos or other materials that illustrate its work and purposes. The intention is to provide an overall picture of the organization that is as comprehensive as possible. If the organization has been operating for over a year, a separate copy of its financial statements are to be included. These financial statements will supplement the financial information set out earlier in the application. If they were not prepared by an independent auditor, they should be signed by the treasurer. At a minimum, financial statements will include a statement of receipts and disbursements, and a statement of assets and liabilities for a fiscal period. The statements should also show the sources of income and how it was spent.

The Part 6 information is confidential and will not be made public except where required by law or, in exceptional circumstances, where it is permitted by law. These circumstances include legal proceedings under federal or provincial statutes that provide for the imposition or collection of a tax or duty, pursuant to a court order or under authority of certain federal statutes.

The application must also be certified as correct and completed by two persons authorized to sign on behalf of the organization. These individuals must, of course, be in a position to sign such a certification and would hold positions, such as president or treasurer, within the organization.

(g)   Summary

The registration of an organization as a charity is an involved process. It is largely a legal one that requires considerable thought by the organization's officers, directors and members. The Canada Customs and Revenue Agency has, over the last few years, developed a more detailed review process partly in response to demands for greater public accountability from charities. Whereas previously, the application was relatively easy to complete, it now takes time and effort. The application and its process require the officers, directors and members of the organization to think through what its objects and activities are going to be. They must make decisions — if not for all time, at least initially — on a wide variety of topics, including fundraising, methods of carrying out activities and what those activities will be.

C ONTARIO CORPORATIONS TAX ACT

I INTRODUCTION

The Ontario *Corporations Tax Act*[25] applies to all corporations operating in Ontario. The Act is largely integrated with the federal *Income Tax Act* but not to the same degree as exists for personal income taxation. Corporations are obliged to file and pay tax on their income, unless they are exempted from doing so under the Act.

II EXEMPTION

The Act provides a number of exemptions from the payment of corporate income tax and the filing of corporate income tax returns (unless the corporation is otherwise required to file by the Minister of Finance). The exemptions are similar to those provided under the federal *Income Tax Act* and, indeed, largely incorporate the federal exemptions by reference to the relevant provisions in the federal statute. Paragraph 57(1)(a) of the provincial Act adopts much of s. 149 of the *Income Tax Act* for exemption purposes. Paragraph 57(1)(b) exempts certain not-for-profit organizations that the Minister has determined are not charities within s. 149 of the *Income Tax Act* but which otherwise meet the requirements of the *Corporations Tax Act*.

Section 149 of the *Income Tax Act* exempts from taxation a wide variety of corporate entities, including municipal authorities; labour organizations; mutual insurance corporations; limited dividend housing corporations; pension corporations; and farmers' and fishermen's insurers. These types of organizations are not-for-profit in nature but are beyond the scope of this text. The major exemptions under s. 149 that are incorporated by reference into the *Corporations Tax Act* are the following:

- registered charities, including charitable organizations, charitable foundations and their divisions that are properly registered with the Canada Customs and Revenue Agency pursuant to para. 149(1)(f);
- not-for-profit organizations, such as a club, society or association, that is not in the opinion of the Minister a charity within subs. 149.1(1) of the *Income Tax Act*. The organization must be organized and operated exclusively for social welfare, civic improvement, pleasure, recreation or for any other purpose except profit.

---

[25] R.S.O. 1990, c. C.40.

The organization must not, in the taxation year, distribute any part of its income to any proprietor, member or shareholder or appropriate any of its funds or property in any manner to or for the benefit of any proprietor, member or shareholder. The only exception to this requirement on distribution is for an organization whose primary purpose and function is the promotion of amateur athletics in Canada. This exception mirrors the *Income Tax Act*'s exemption for amateur athletics.

Subsections 57(2) and (3) set out rules on computing income for the taxation year in which the distribution is made. The corporation will be required to pay income taxes on the amount that it distributed or is deemed to have distributed. Subsection 57(2) applies, for example, in a reorganization or winding-up of the organization where it no longer qualifies for the exemption;

- co-operative housing corporations without share capital are exempt if they are not subject to federal income tax in the year or any previous year.[26] This rule, however, does not apply to other co-operative corporations without share capital, which may be required to pay corporate income tax. They may or may not be tax exempt depending upon the purposes of their incorporation and operations and whether or not they have distributed income or appropriated property for the benefit of the members.

Some "profits" earned by the housing co-operative are excluded from determining whether or not the corporation is subject to federal income tax. For example, interest earned on an operating or reserve fund is excluded — provided that fund is not maintained at an unreasonably high level; profits from rentals to non-members —if, substantially, all gross revenues are derived from dealings with members; profits from dealing with members; and rental income derived from non-members which has been allocated to members. Ontario uses the federal rules in determining whether or not a previously exempt corporation should be subject to Ontario corporate taxes. However, under the Ontario rules, interest earned on operating or reserve funds is included in the computation even if the funds are not unreasonably high.

Clearly, the rules are complicated and care must be taken in how the co-operative corporation structures its operations. Importantly, once the exemption is lost, the corporation is subject to the *Corporations Tax Act* for all subsequent tax years;

---

[26] Information Bulletin, April 1980, Ministry of Revenue.

- housing corporations that are exempt under paras. 149(1)(i) and (n) of the *Income Tax Act* are exempted under the *Corporations Tax Act*. These corporations are primarily institutional housing corporations and low-cost housing for the aged.

Subsection 12(10) of the Act also authorizes the removal of the exemption that is provided under the *Income Tax Act* that would otherwise apply under the *Corporations Tax Act*. By regulation, the exemption has been removed for specific corporations.

The list of exemptions is not exhaustive of the exemptions and exceptions that are provided for under the *Corporations Tax Act*. Integration with the *Income Tax Act* is not complete and the relationship between the two is, at times, strained. However, the policy would appear to be to have as much consistency as possible. For registered charities, that consistency is present. For other types of charitable organizations or not-for-profit organizations, the level of consistency will vary.

In any event, it is important that organizations also consider the tax implications under the *Corporations Tax Act* as well as the *Income Tax Act* in developing and implementing their activities. The organization's exemption from paying corporate income tax and from filing annual returns may be at risk. Once that exemption is lost in a given tax year, it is lost for all subsequent tax years.

D   CONSUMPTION TAXES

I   GOODS AND SERVICES TAX/HARMONIZED SALES TAX

(1)   Introduction

The Goods and Services Tax (GST) was imposed as an amendment to the *Excise Tax Act*[27] in 1990 and came into effect on January 1, 1991. The GST replaced the federal (or manufacturers') sales tax which had previously been assessed under that Act. The major changes brought about by the GST are that it applies to most goods and services sold in Canada and requires most sellers of those goods and services to register under the Act and to collect and remit the taxes to the federal government.

---

[27] R.S.C. 1985, c. E-15. The GST/HST provisions are set out in Part IX of the Act. The Canada Customs and Revenue Agency has prepared two useful publications for charitable and not-for-profit organizations — "GST/HST Information for Charities", RC4082, July 8, 1998 and "GST/HST Information for Non-Profit Organizations", RC4081 Rev. The Canada Council and the Canadian Conference of the Arts have also prepared a good review of the GST on arts organizations that is applicable and useful to other charitable and not-for-profit organizations, "Introduction to the GST for Arts Organizations".

The GST has been harmonized in a number of provinces into a single consumption tax of 15 per cent. The Harmonized Sales Tax (HST) is imposed in Nova Scotia, Newfoundland, New Brunswick and Quebec. In Quebec, the HST is administered by the provincial government.

As with all taxation programmes, changes occur to reflect the experience and public policy. The GST/HST rules for certain registered charities were changed as of January 1, 1997. Public institutions that were registered as charities, such as a school authority, public college, university, hospital authority or a local authority determined to be a municipality are dealt with separately by the Canada Customs and Revenue Agency — presumably due to the size of their operations and the high level of public funding provided directly to these institutions. This chapter is focussed on registered charities that are not "public institutions".

Charity for purposes of GST/HST includes organizations that are registered as Canadian amateur athletic associations for income tax purposes. As noted earlier, these associations are not charitable at common law but there is a comparable registration scheme. Charities, "not-for-profit" organizations, municipalities, school authorities, hospital authorities, public college or university. The definitions are critical but sometimes become confusing. Nevertheless, classification as a "public service body" provides benefits to both registered charities and not-for-profit organizations.

The GST/HST is charged throughout the production and distribution process in Canada. The GST/HST is set at 7 per cent on the sale of most goods and on the provision of most services as the product moves through the system. It is a multi-stage tax: the tax is assessed and collected at each stage of production and remitted by the supplier that sold the goods or services. That supplier then claims an input tax credit on the amount that it paid to the suppliers from whom it purchased goods or services and forwards the difference to the government. If the amount paid as an input tax credit exceeds the amount assessed and collected in a particular reporting period, a refund is paid to the supplier. The final purchaser, usually a consumer, will pay 7 per cent, or 15 per cent in participating provinces, on the purchase price for the goods or service but cannot, of course, claim any input tax credit or refund because he or she is not a supplier.

(2) Exemptions

There is a distinction between two types of supplies, be they goods or services — taxable goods and services and exempt. Most supplies of goods and services are taxable supplies. However, the GST/HST provides for two categories of taxable supplies. Some taxable supplies are taxed at 7 per cent (15 per cent for HST) and others are taxed at 0 per cent. "Zero rated" supplies include goods and services exported from Canada, basic groceries (other than restaurant meals, takeout foods, alcohol, snack foods and sweetened baked goods), certain financial services, prescription drugs and medical devices, and several other types of goods.

Other supplies are exempt from taxation. These supplies include health care, child care, legal aid services, educational instruction, most domestic financial services and specified residential housing. In addition, certain supplies provided by charities, not-for-profit organizations and governments are also tax exempt.

The distinction between a taxable supply, including one that is "zero-rated", and an exempt supply is important. A supplier may not claim an input tax credit on the sale of supplies that are "exempt" from taxation. However, the supplier may claim an input tax credit on the sale of any supplies that are "zero-rated".

Not all suppliers are required to register under the Act. If the supplier has sales of less than $30,000 per year, the supplier may elect not to register. However, the supplier will not be able to claim any input tax credit on the goods or services that it sells. This exemption applies to charitable and not-for-profit organizations that supply taxable goods and services. However, if the charitable or not-for-profit organization is a "public service body", the small supplier limit is $50,000. As registered charities and not-for-profit organizations are included in this definition, there is an additional benefit for these smaller organizations that provide taxable goods or services.

A registered charity may also be exempt as a small supplier if it has gross revenue of $250,000 or less. Gross revenue includes business income, donations, grants, gifts, property income and investment income less any amount considered to be a capital loss for income tax purposes. For a registered charity, this amount will be included in the *Registered Charity Information Return* which is filed each year by a registered charity. The gross revenue figure calculation may be based on more than one fiscal year. For example, if the organization is more than two years in operation, it can calculate the gross revenue for the previous two fiscal years. If the amount is $250,000 or less in either of those fiscal years, it does not need to register.

If the organization is registered for GST/HST purposes and falls within either the $50,000 taxable supplies or $250,000 gross revenue exemption, it may apply for the cancellation of the registration. An organization may also voluntarily register for GST/HST purposes. The organization will be required to collect the GST/HST but it may also claim the input tax credits. For some organizations, the paperwork of being registered may be outweighed by either the cash-flow for the input tax credits or the net difference between the GST/HST rebate and the cost of being registered.

One of the costs of registration for GST/HST purposes may be, however, customer satisfaction or convenience. In addition, as many of the goods and services provided by registered charities and not-for-profit organizations are exempt from GST/HST, input tax credits cannot be claimed for those goods and services. Some goods and services are exempt regardless of who provides them (long-term residential accommodation, child-care services for children 14 years of age or younger, personal-care services for children, underprivileged individuals or individuals with disabilities). If the supplier is a charity, then most services, sales of used and donated goods, short-term residential accommodation (less than one month) and meals-on-wheels programmes are exempt. As of January 1, 1997, parking space rentals, short-term facility rentals (such as halls for weddings), catering services for private functions (such as weddings) and the total admission to fundraising events where receipts for income tax purposes may be issued for any part of the ticket price are also exempt for charities.

Fundraising is an important exemption. Most goods and services sold or provided for a fundraising activity that are not otherwise covered by exemptions after January 1, 1997 are exempt. The major exception is if the goods or services are sold or provided (or the clients are entitled to receive) regularly or continually through the year or significant part of the year. The Guide identifies a few examples of each — greeting cards at Christmas would be exempt, but goods sold at a tuck shop would not be exempt under this broader exemption. If the organization were registered for GST/HST purposes, it would be required to collect the 7 per cent or 15 per cent tax.

If the cost charged to the purchaser is the same as what it cost the organization registered for GST/HST purposes, no additional GST/HST needs to be collected. This case occurs where the organization is simply flowing through its direct cost (including any GST/HST paid) to the ultimate purchaser without adding any additional amounts for profit or other costs. The organization may choose whether or not to have the sales either taxable or exempt. The cost to the purchaser, though, must be an all inclusive amount, including the GST/HST and cannot separate out the purchase price and tax in order to qualify for this exemption.

No GST/HST is payable on revenues from the sale of lottery, break-open or raffle tickets.[28] Bingo games and casino or social gaming events also benefit from an exemption on the sale of bingo cards or the bets. An admission charge (if any) will also be exempt if volunteers run the event, take the bets and the bingo or casino night is not held in a commercial hall or temporary structure used primarily for gambling activities. Note, however, that admission fees are not generally permitted for bingo events.

Recreational programs primarily for children 14 years of age or under are also exempt form GST/HST. Similarly, if the charity supplies goods or services for no amount, it will be exempt with few exceptions. GST/HST also does not apply to grants or subsidies or to personal or corporate donations. On the other hand, these revenues do not affect a

---

[28] This exemption does not apply to any lottery tickets sold for a provincial or interprovincial lottery corporation. The GST/HST is included in the purchase price.

charity's entitlement to GST/HST rebates or for input tax credits. Sponsorships may also be exempt from GST/HST, unless the payment is made primarily (50 per cent or more) for advertising on television or radio or in a publication issued by the charity.

There are several exemptions that are available to not-for-profit organizations. If the organization is registered for GST/HST purposes, it does not need to collect GST/HST on admission to a place of amusement if the maximum amount charged is $1.00 or less. Tickets sales to performances or athletic events are exempt if at least 90 per cent of the performers, athletes or competitors are not paid directly or indirectly for participating. Reasonable amounts as gifts, prizes or compensation for travel and incidental expenses will not be considered payment. Cash prizes at professional golf tournaments would normally make the ticket prices taxable.

Several other situations are also exempt from collecting GST/HST. If the goods or services are supplied for free, they are exempt. Fundraising activities are exempt for most sales if the organization is not in that business, is not selling alcoholic beverages or tobacco, has salespersons that are volunteers, and the cost is $5.00 or less for each item and the goods are not sold at an event where similar goods are sold by persons in that business. A typical example is the sale of chocolate bars to raise money. Admission to gambling events are exempt if 90 per cent or more of the functions are carried out by volunteers and the bingo or casino night event is not held in a commercial hall or temporary structure that is used primarily for gambling activities. Similarly, lottery, break-open and raffle ticket sales are also exempt (unless for a provincial or interprovincial lottery corporation). The direct cost exemption discussed above for charities also applies to not-for-profit organizations.

Memberships in a club are taxable if the main purpose of the club is to provide dining, recreational or sporting facilities to its members. Other memberships are exempt provided the membership benefits are limited to indirect benefits available to all members, the right to receive certain dispute resolution services, the right to vote or participate in meetings, the right to receive or acquire goods and services at an additional fee at fair market value, the right to receive discounts for goods or services if the total value is less than 30 per cent of the membership fee, and the right to receive periodic newsletters, reports or other publications if the value is less than 30 per cent of the membership fee or the publication only provides information on activities and financial status of the organization.

The provision of food, beverages or short-term accommodation to relieve poverty, suffering or distress is also exempt from the collection of GST/HST by organizations that are registered for GST/HST purposes. Meals-on-wheels programmes, recreational programmes for children primarily 14 years or younger, or programmes primarily for individuals who are underprivileged or disabled are similarly exempt. Donations, grants and sponsorships are often exempt. However, there may be complex situations with respect to the tax treatment of transfer payments from governments if the supply, property or service is for public use.

(3) Registration

(a)   Collecting and Paying the GST/HST

In making this decision, the organization should balance the real benefits to it. For example, if it primarily supplies goods or services that are exempt from the GST/HST, there may be little benefit for the expenses incurred in registering and complying with the GST/HST. One of the considerations should also be the anticipated effect that it will have on the persons to whom the goods and services are supplied. Can those individuals, for example, afford the additional 7 per cent or 15 per cent? Would the payment affect fundraising initiatives? Is the additional paperwork going to be too burdensome on the organization?

If the organization decides to register and collect the GST/HST, the legislation requires that the GST/HST registration number be included on invoices or sales slips and that the GST/HST be set out separately on the invoices or sales slips if the customer requests. In most cases, customers of charitable or not-for-profit organizations are unlikely to require the sales slip for their own GST/HST purposes because they will not be suppliers.

The invoice or sales slip must include different levels of information depending upon the size of the sale. If the sale is under $30, it must include: the name of the organization or its trade name; the date on which the GST/HST was paid or became payable; and the total amount paid or payable. For sales between $30 and $150, the organization's GST/HST number, the items that are subject to GST/HST and the total amount of GST/HST charged must be shown. The GST/HST may be included in the price but the customer must be advised of this inclusion on the invoices, sales slip or display sign. For sales over $150, the purchaser's name or trading name, the terms of sale (cash or credit) and a brief description of the goods or services must be included.

(b)   Filings

Registrants are required to file a GST/HST return for each reporting period, whether or not the registrant made any sales of taxable goods and services, collected any GST/HST, paid any GST/HST or claimed a refund or a rebate. Reporting periods are monthly, quarterly and annually, however, since January 1997, most charitable organizations are assigned an annual reporting period. The charity may change the reporting period by applying to the CCRA.

Most charities will use the net tax calculation method to calculate GST/HST payable. Charities, under this method, will remit 60 per cent of the GST/HST collected and claim input tax credits on a limited number of items. The charity will be able to claim the 50 per cent rebate available to public service bodies on the GST/HST paid where an input tax credit was not claimed.

The Special Quick Method of calculating tax payable that is used by other public service bodies is no longer available to charities. A charity may, however, use a simplified rebate calculation. The charity may also elect to opt out of the net tax calculation method if it makes supplies outside of Canada, has zero-rated sales in the ordinary course of business or if 90 per cent or more of its sales are taxable.

The default is the net tax calculation method. If another method is being considered, the charity ought to seek expert advice on what the most appropriate method is for them. Different methods will have their own legal and practical advantages and disadvantages. A board of directors and management ought to know and understand the options and their implications, both immediate and over a longer period of time.

The net tax calculation will be used by most charities that are registered for GST/HST purposes. It involves three steps. The first step is the addition of the GST/HST charged (whether collected or not) on taxable sales. This step can be complicated, depending upon the types of goods and services supplied and issues such as real property or capital property tax adjustments. In any event, for many charities, the calculation for step one is relatively simple — add up the amount of the GST/HST charged on sales and remit 60 per cent of that figure. Step two involves a calculation of the input tax credit that the organization was entitled to claim from a previous reporting period when the net tax calculation method was not used. The third step is subtracting the amounts from the first two steps. The organization would be able to claim the 50 per cent rebate on the remaining GST/HST paid.

A charity that does not use the net tax calculation method must apply to do so. It would use the general rules applicable to all GST/HST registrants or the Simplified Input Tax Credit Method that is available to all registrants. Essentially, the charity would determine the input tax credits that it paid and subtract that amount from the GST/HST collected. It would normally pay the difference.

Most charities are eligible to apply for a percentage of the GST/HST they pay on purchases and expenses for which they cannot claim an input tax credit. As noted earlier, public institutions operate under a different regime and are not eligible for these rebates. Charities that are not registered for GST/HST purposes may apply for a rebate on the GST/HST paid or owed on eligible purchases and expenses. Charities that are registered may apply for the rebate on eligible purchases and expenses that are not eligible for an input tax credit. In the case of most registered charities, who use the net tax calculation, they qualify for a rebate of 50 per cent that are not included as an input tax credit the net tax calculation.

If the charity does not use the net tax calculation, it can claim for general operating and overhead expenses for which input tax credits cannot be claimed, allowances and reimbursements to employees and volunteers engaged in exempt activities, supplies bought to produce exempt goods to sell and merchandise for sale at fundraising events, and capital property that is intended primarily for use in exempt activities.

There are also many purchases and expenses that are not eligible as the activity is not exempt. For example, memberships in a dining, recreational or sporting club are not eligible for a GST/HST rebate. Similarly, alcoholic beverages supplied with a meal, tobacco products, goods and services purchased to provide long-term accommodation (unless at least 10 per cent for specified groups) and others are not exempt.

Charities that are not registered for GST/HST purposes will normally apply for the rebate each year, but may apply twice in any fiscal year. They may apply for up to 4 years. However, it is incumbent upon directors to ensure that the application for a rebate is made in a timely manner and not to wait for the full 4 years. Charities that are registered for GST/HST purposes will apply when they file the GST/HST return, which is normally on an annual basis.

The CCRA has also developed a simplified method to calculate the rebate for public service bodies, such as charities. The charity does not need to keep track of GST/HST paid or owed to suppliers for each invoice, although it is necessary to separate out GST from HST taxable purchases. If taxable purchases at the rate of 7 per cent for GST or 15 per cent for HST were no more than $2 million in the previous fiscal year, and the reasonable expectation is that the amount will not be more than $2 million in the current fiscal year, the charity may use the simplified method. The charity must also not have taxable sales in excess of $500,000 in the immediately preceding fiscal year and cumulative sales in the current fiscal year cannot exceed $500,000.

If the charity is eligible, it calculates the GST/HST rebate by adding the GST/HST included on all purchases and expenses at 7 per cent GST or 15 per cent HST. It may also add a number of other amounts, such as reasonable tips, import duties, reimbursements to employees and volunteers and non-refundable provincial taxes and fees. Zero-rated supplies (such as salaries) and other supplies that are not subject to the GST/HST are not to be included. The total taxable purchases is multiplied in step two by 7/107 for GST purchases or 15/115 for HST purchases if the charity is resident in a participating province. If the charity is not resident in a participating province, the charity multiplies the HST purchases by 7/115. These amounts are added and further multiplied by 50 per cent. Any provincial tax that is collected separately, such as in Ontario, is not to be included in the purchase price.

There are, of course, a number of complicating factors and considerations to the calculations. These will depend upon the activities of the charity and the types of purchases and sales that it makes. For example, a rebate is available for property or services removed from a participating province. The sale or lease of real property has its own rules with respect to input tax credits or rebates. If there is a change in commercial use by more than 10 per cent cumulatively, other steps must be taken.

Not-for-profit organizations may also be eligible for a public service body rebate, whether or not they are registered for GST/HST purposes. In order to qualify, the not-for-profit organization must receive — in that fiscal year or the previous two fiscal years — at least 40 per cent of its total revenue from government funding. If the organization qualifies, then a similar regime is in place for it to claim the rebate as for a charity. Given the nature of the types of goods and services that a not-for-profit organization may legally provide, the calculation of the rebate may be substantially more complicated. It may be necessary, for example, to allocate expenses and revenues with respect to commercial activities more precisely.

A qualifying not-for-profit organization may also elect to use the Special Quick Method for calculating the GST/HST payable if it is registered. Otherwise, the organization may use the methods that are generally available to businesses. With the Special Quick Method, the organization does not need to track the end use of the purchases — those that were for commercial activities and those that were for exempt activities. This method will, obviously, reduce the amount of paperwork that is necessary to complete the GST/HST filing by registrants.

As with charities, a not-for-profit organization that is registered for GST/HST purposes will have significant book-keeping requirements, regardless of the method of calculation that may be used. Because only qualifying not-for-profit organizations may apply for the 50 per cent public service body rebate, there may be a stronger incentive for not-for-profit organizations to register for GST/HST purposes. In any event, GST/HST is complicated and often requires expertise to take advantage of exemptions and to avoid making errors that may be costly in the short term or on an audit.

II ONTARIO RETAIL SALES TAXES

(1) Introduction

All of the provinces except Alberta levy a general provincial sales tax on the purchase of "tangible personal property" or on the user of a taxable service or participate in the HST (Nova Scotia, Newfoundland, New Brunswick and, in Quebec, the GST and provincial sales tax are administered in a similar manner by Quebec). Any person who, in Ontario, offers goods for sale, provides taxable services or who charges admission to a place of amusement must obtain a vendor's permit from the Ontario Ministry of Finance (Revenue) under the *Retail Sales Tax Act*.[29] The ven-

---

[29] R.S.O. 1990, c. R.31. There are other forms of retail sales tax, including the *Tobacco Tax Act*, R.S.O. 1990, c. T.10, the *Gasoline Tax Act*, R.S.O. 1990, c. G.5, and the *Fuel Tax Act*, R.S.O. 1990, c. F.35, which may apply to a charitable or not-for-profit organization if they are involved in the sale, as an ancillary or incidental activity, in tobacco products

dors are required to collect, as agents of the province, and remit the appropriate sales tax on the sale of the goods or taxable services.[30]

The Ontario provincial sales tax does not apply to personal property or services in the following circumstances:

- the purchase of tangible personal property that is intended for resale;
- the sale of tangible personal property or taxable services to consumers who reside outside of Ontario; and
- the sale of tangible personal property or taxable services that are exempt by the Act or under the regulations. These specific exemptions include the necessities of life (food, certain clothing, prescription medication) and a variety of other exemptions based on the person making the purchase or the personal property or service being purchased.

(2) Exemption

(a) Charitable Organizations

Charitable and not-for-profit organizations may be both purchasers and vendors, depending on the transaction. As purchasers, the organizations are liable to pay the sales tax; as vendors, they are required to levy, collect and remit the tax on behalf of the government. The Act and Regulations provide a number of exemptions that are applicable to organizations that are based on their status as a charitable or not-for-profit organization. These exemptions include the following:

- admission to a place of amusement — Subsection 2(5) imposes a tax on the admission price for any entertainment, event, dance, performance or exhibition staged or held. Registered charities are exempt from collecting this tax under subs. 9(2) if the performance is staged or held under the auspices or sponsorship of the registered charity. There are other situations in which there is an exemption that may also apply to charitable and not-for-profit organizations, such as if the performers are not remunerated. Subsection 9(2) provides a list of other organizations that may also be exempt under this provision, including an educational institution, a labour organization and an agricultural society;
- fundraising events — Subsections 22(1) and (2) of O. Reg. 1013/90 under the Act exempt the collection of taxes on any sales

---

or fuel. However, in most cases, the *Retail Sales Tax Act* will be the more usual provincial consumption tax that affects charitable or not-for-profit organizations.

[30] *Retail Sales Tax Act*, s. 10.

at certain fundraising events operated by a religious, charitable, benevolent or not-for-profit organization. Not-for-profit organization is defined in s. 1 of the Regulation. The events must not be operated on a regularly scheduled basis and the organization must have paid to the Minister of Finance an amount equal to the amount of tax that would have been payable had the organization purchased the tangible personal property for its own consumption and use. Retail sales taxes must be paid and collected on the sale of any prepared food products that are sold at the fundraising event;
- sale of prepared food products — Subsection 22(3) of the Regulation exempts the payment of the sales tax on prepared food products if the person purchases the products as part of a program and they are provided for a nominal charge to persons who are disabled, disadvantaged or underprivileged or who because of age or an infirmity require support;
- used clothing and footwear — Paragraph 20 of subs. 7(1) of the Act exempts used clothing and footwear from sales tax if it is sold by a religious, charitable, benevolent or not-for-profit organization. The clothing and footwear must be sold in one transaction and the total consideration cannot exceed $50;
- equipment for religious institutions — Paragraph 53 of subs. 7(1) of the Act exempts specified equipment used by the institution for worship or school. The type of equipment that is exempt is set out in s. 1 of O. Reg. 1012/90; and
- publications — religious, charitable and benevolent organizations' publications are exempt from sales tax under subs. 7(1) of the Act.

The Act and Regulations also provide other exemptions that are not dependent upon the legal status of the organization but on the activity or transaction itself. These exemptions may be applicable to a charitable or not-for-profit organization. The organization should examine the exemptions to determine if any are applicable or if the organization could structure its operations to fall within the exemption.

The Regulation provides the Minister with the authority, under section 14, to rebate to the governing body of a religious, charitable or benevolent organization, amounts in respect of tangible personal property incorporated into a building or structure. The section provides a method to calculate the amount. It also excludes certain public institutions from the rebate program and requires certain leasehold terms if the land is not owned by the organization.

(b)   Not-for-profit Organizations

Not-for-profit organization is defined in s. 1 of O. Reg. 1013/90 as a club, society, association or any group organized and operated exclusively for social welfare, civic improvement, pleasure or recreation or for any other purpose except profit. No part of its income may be paid to or otherwise be available for the personal benefit of any organizer, trustee, officer or member. Reasonable compensation may be paid, however, to those persons, employees, performers or others for work and services actually performed by them. Registered charities are not considered to be not-for-profit organizations. Not-for-profit organizations may benefit from the exemptions for fundraising events and the sale of used clothing, footwear and publications.

E   PROPERTY TAXES

I   ASSESSMENT ACT

The *Assessment Act*[31] provides the statutory basis for municipalities to assess and collect property taxes. The Act requires that land and buildings be assessed at market value or similar basis. A property tax is applied to that assessment using a rate. The rate will differ in Ontario depending upon the class or sub-class of property, i.e., commercial, industrial, residential/farm and so forth. Different provinces use different language, but the basic concept is similar.

The Act was substantially revised in the late 1990s in Ontario. Amendments were necessary to correct problems for charities and to provide them with relief from taxes that were owing.[32] For example, a key revision was the elimination of the "business occupancy tax" which applied to businesses but not charities. The general property tax was enhanced to incorporate the business occupancy tax, which then became payable by charities. The amount would either be payable directly or indirectly through lease payments. An amendment was necessary to put in place a mandatory rebate program to qualifying charitable organizations. The process is complicated and it is far from clear whether all eligible charities understand and benefit from this process.

Under s. 3 of the Act, all real property in Ontario is liable to assessment and taxation. A number of categories of real property are, however, exempt from taxation. The list of exempt real property is lengthy and does not necessarily follow a consistent approach. The use of the real property and the character of the owner or user of that property appear to be factors in what real property is included in the exemption.

---

[31] R.S.O. 1990, c. A.31, as am., see *infra*, note 32.
[32] *Fair Municipal Finance Act*, 1997, S.O. 1997, c. 5, *Fair Municipal Finance Act, 1997* (No. 2), S.O. 1997, c. 29.

There is no blanket exemption for charitable or not-for-profit organizations. The amendments in the late 1990s also attempted to clarify the wording of some of the exemptions.

The most relevant exemptions for charitable and not-for-profit organizations are the following:

- land that is owned by a church or religious organization or leased to it by another church or religious organization and that is a place of worship and the land used in connection with it, churchyard, cemetery or burying ground, or 50 per cent of the assessment of the principal residence and land used in connection with it of the member of the clergy who officiates at the place of worship so long as the residence is located at the site of the place of worship;[33]
- land owned, used and occupied solely by not-for-profit philanthropic, religious or educational seminaries of learning, or, land leased and occupied by any of them, if the land would be exempt from taxation if it was occupied by the owner. This paragraph applies only to buildings and up to 50 acres of land;[34]
- property owned, occupied and used solely and only by The Boy Scouts Association, The Canadian Girl Guides Association, any provincial or local association, or other local group in Ontario that is a member of either Association or is otherwise chartered or officially recognized by it;[35]
- land owned, used and occupied by a not-for-profit philanthropic corporation for the sole purpose of a house of refuge, the refor-

---

[33] Para. 3 was revised to clarify what lands were exempt. Under the previous wording, it seems that the exemption for cemeteries would extend to cemeteries that are operated for a profit, according to *Memory Gardens Ltd. v. Waterloo (Township)*, [1955] O.W.N. 424 (H.C.). The new wording applies to 2001 and subsequent tax years.

[34] Under the previous wording of this paragraph, a ballet school operated by the National Ballet School benefited from this exemption, *National Ballet School v. Assessment Commissioner No. 9 et al.* (1979), 25 O.R. (2d) 50 (S.C.), but a union training centre did not, *Regional Assessment Commissioner et al. v. Zangari et al.* (1985), 8 O.A.C. 294 (Div. Ct.). Similarly, under the previous wording for a comparable paragraph, camps that were used primarily for religious purposes will also be exempt. However, if the primary purpose is recreation and not religious instruction, the lands will not be exempt. See, for examples, *Re Mizrachi Organization of Can. v. Ennismore (Township)*, [1973] 1 O.R. 465 (H.C.); *International Bible Students Association of Canada et al. v. Halton Hills (Town) et al.* (1986), 57 O.R. (2d) 42 (Div. Ct.); *Augustinian Father (Ontario) Inc. v. Regional Assessment Commissioner Region No. 14 et al.* (1985), 52 O.R. (2d) 536 (H.C.).

[35] *Assessment Act, supra*, note 31, para. 10.

mation of offenders, the care of children or a similar purpose but excluding land used for the purpose of a day care centre;[36] and
- land owned, used and occupied by The Canadian Red Cross, The St. John Ambulance Association or any charitable, not-for-profit philanthropic corporation organized for the relief of the poor if the corporation is supported in part by public funds.[37]

The similar corporation must also be supported, in part at least, by public funds and the lands owned by the institution and occupied for its purposes. The exemptions under the provision include three distinct categories: for the relief of the poor; the two listed charitable organizations; and "any similar incorporated institution".[38] This exemption has been the subject of extensive litigation as organizations attempt to fall within the requirements of the Act. The courts have attempted to rationalize the cases, but not always with success.[39] In *Re Kitchener-Waterloo and North Waterloo Humane Society and City of Kitchener*[40] the Court concluded that "philanthropy" is confined to love of one's fellow man and exertions for his/her well being. It does not extend to animals. A not-for-profit nursing home operated for the relief of the poor is a "similar incorporated institution"[41] but a planned parenthood organization is not. Its services are of a public benefit but they are not directed to the relief of the poor.[42] Poor does not necessarily mean destitute. In deciding whether or not an institution is organized for the relief of the poor, the onus is on the institution to establish some economic deprivation or need and that its purpose is to relieve it.[43] The relief of the poor must be the primary purpose for the organization. If the obvious and controlling purpose is not to relieve the poor, but to provide homes for the aged, the organization is not exempt.[44] The amount and form of public support that it receives is also a relevant consideration. The public support must

---

[36] *Ibid.*, para. 11.
[37] *Ibid.*, para. 12.
[38] *Cencourse Project Inc. v. Regional Assessment Commissioner for Region 27 and Corporation of the City of Windsor* (1991), 5 O.R. (3d) 349 at 356 (Gen. Div.).
[39] *Ibid.*, at 356 where Zalev J. comments, "I am not sure that can be done successfully. It seems to me that what is required is a balancing of all the various factors, all of which are of varying degrees of importance".
[40] [1973] 1 O.R. 490 (C.A.).
[41] *Stouffville Assessment Commr. v. Mennonite Home Assn. of York County*, [1973] S.C.R. 189.
[42] *Re Planned Parenthood of Toronto v. Toronto (City)* (1979), 27 O.R. (2d) 666 (C.A.).
[43] *Auburn Retirement Village of Peterborough Inc. v. Peterborough (City)* (1983), 22 M.P.L.R. 173 (Ont. Co. Ct.); *London (City) v. Byron Optimist Sports Complex Ltd.* (1983), 23 M.P.L.R. 10; *Cencourse Project Inc. v. Regional Assessment Commissioner for Region 27 and Corporation of the City of Windsor* (1991), 5 O.R. (3d) 349, at 357 (Gen. Div.).
[44] *Pentecostal Benevolent Assn. of Ont. v. Scarborough (Borough)* (1979), 26 O.R. (2d) 552 (H.C.); *Cencourse Project Inc. v. Regional Assessment Commissioner for Regions 27 and Corporation of the City of Windsor*, *supra*, note 43, at 357.

be direct and not indirect support. In *Les Soeurs de La Visitation D'Ottawa v. Ottawa*,[45] the Court found that public support meant that funds were provided directly from the treasuries of the federal, provincial or municipal governments.[46]

There are other exemptions from taxation set out in s. 3 of the *Assessment Act*. They apply to particular types of organizations: children's aid societies; public institutions, such as libraries; and types of real property, such as battle sites and exhibition buildings. Under s. 4 of the Act, a municipality may also exempt, by by-law, the land of a religious institution that is used for recreational purposes. The exemption only applies, however, to the municipal assessment and not to that of the school board or local improvement rates.

Performing arts organizations obtained a significant benefit in the 1997 amendments. An exemption was created for lands used as a live theatre containing less than 1,000 seats. The theatre must be used predominantly to present live performances of drama, comedy, music or dance. The exemption does not apply to land used as a dinner theatre, night club, tavern, cocktail lounge, bar, striptease club or similar establishment. In order for a building that was not previously a live theatre to qualify, there must be modifications to the building.[47]

(1) Other Taxes

The *Provincial Land Tax Act*[48] also applies to real property in Ontario. That Act provides for the assessment and payment of a tax in unorganized territories where a municipality is not incorporated. Section 3 of the Act provides for exemptions similar to those under the *Assessment Act*. An organization will also be subject to taxes under the *Land Transfer Tax Act*[49] on the purchase of real property in Ontario.

---

[45] (1951), 2 D.L.R. 343, at 353; see also *Stouffville Assessment Commr. v. Mennonite Home Assn. of York County, supra*, note 41.

[46] See also *Light-Haven Home Inc. v. Regional Assessment Commissioner, Region No. 31 v. Bruce Mines (Town)*, unreported decision, March 23, 1995, Doc. RE4807/94, Mandel J. Ontario Court (Gen. Div.).

[47] *Tax Credits to Create Jobs Act, 1997*, S.O. 1997, c. 43, which added para. 26 to s. 4 of the *Assessment Act* exemptions.

[48] R.S.O. 1990, c. P.32.

[49] R.S.O. 1990, c. L.6.

CHAPTER 9

Supervision of Charitable Organizations

A OVERVIEW

Charitable organizations receive substantial benefits under the law. As a result, a number of government agencies and the courts are interested in holding them accountable for their activities and their expenditure of charitable funds. The importance of accountability has been enhanced in recent years through the Ontario Law Reform Commission's *Report on the Law of Charities*[1] and the "Broadbent Report".[2] These reports also encouraged the Government of Canada to review its own legislation and to work with the voluntary sector towards improvements to the accountability structure for charitable and not-for-profit organizations.[3] The accountability structures are under review and changes can be expected over the next several years. However, existing methods of accountability are likely to remain in place, albeit adapting as change occurs to the overall structure.

This chapter reviews the role of the Public Guardian and Trustee (formerly called the Public Trustee) and the courts under common law, the *Charities Accounting Act*[4] and the *Charitable Gifts Act*.[5] The chapter also discusses the doctrine of *cy-pres* and its use in amending the terms of a trust when it can no longer be carried out. The final part lists various statutory powers that the courts have available to use in carrying out a supervisory role. These statutory powers are a continuation of the courts' inherent jurisdiction over charitable trusts and charitable organizations that hold those trusts.

---

[1] Ontario Law Reform Commission, (Toronto: Queen's Printer, 1996).
[2] "Panel on Accountability and Governance in the Voluntary Sector", *Building on Strength: Improving Governance and Accountability in Canada's Voluntary Sector*, Final Report (Ottawa: February, 1999).
[3] Voluntary Sector Task Force, Privy Council Office, *Engaging the Voluntary Sector*, February 18, 1999 and Voluntary Task Force, Privy Council Office, *Partnering for the Benefit of Canadians: Government of Canada – Voluntary Sector Initiative*, June 9, 2000.
[4] R.S.O. 1990, c. C.10.
[5] R.S.O. 1990, c. C.8.

B ROLE OF PUBLIC GUARDIAN AND TRUSTEE

I INTRODUCTION

The Crown, as represented by the Attorney General, is at common law a protector of the charitable organization. The role of the Crown began to evolve with the decline of the Church's control over charities and charitable trusts in the sixteenth century. At the same time as the ecclesiastical courts lost their jurisdiction over increasingly secularized charitable trusts, the Chancellor's Court obtained its jurisdiction through the operation of trust law. The Crown's role of *parens patriae* or the protector of the property of a charitable trust grew along with the role of the Chancery Courts. The rationale for the Crown's supervisory role is that the property is not given to a particular person but for the benefit of the general public.[6]

The Crown's role was historically exercised by the Attorney General. In Ontario, since 1915, the Public Guardian and Trustee has taken on the supervisory responsibility with the enactment of the *Charities Accounting Act*. It is exercised in the public interest to ensure that the charitable purposes for which the charitable organization was established are carried out. In addition, the Public Guardian and Trustee has a role under the *Charitable Gifts Act*. That Act limits a charitable organization's ownership of a business and sets out a process to administer any ownership that exceeds the limit.

The Court has commented on the role of the Public Guardian and Trustee in *Re McNab*:[7]

> By way of brief explanation, the role of the Public Trustee in proceedings like these has both an historical and statutory emanation. The duty of law officers of the Crown to intervene to protect the interests of charities has a long history in our law. Presently, in Ontario, specific statutory provision permits the Public Trustee to intervene and to be heard in any proceedings i) where no one appears to represent a charitable institution; ii) where a beneficiary is not named in a will and, iii) where a discretion is given to the executor or trustee as to the choice of beneficiaries.

Although this case was concerned with the disposition of a life insurance policy, it is reflective of the Court's approach generally to the importance and role of the Public Guardian and Trustee in charitable matters. In the *McNab* case, the Court concluded that "the Public Trustee

---

[6] E. Moore, "Submissions to the Ontario Law Reform Commission Project on the Law of Charities", (1990), 9(4) The Philanthropist 12, at 18.
[7] [1995] O.J. No. 2581, Ontario Court of Justice (Gen. Div.), August 4, 1995, *per* Stach, J., at para. 15.

was constrained to pursue the matter and should have costs ... out of the insurance proceeds on a solicitor and client scale".[8]

II CHARITIES ACCOUNTING ACT

The courts have recognized the Public Guardian and Trustee's role at common law. However, that role also has a statutory base under the *Charities Accounting Act*. In *Re Baker*,[9] the Public Guardian and Trustee's role was challenged by an applicant for a variation of a trust. The Court examined the role of the Public Guardian and Trustee and concluded that, under the Act, the Public Guardian and Trustee was required "to guard the public interest in bequests for such purposes by monitoring the disposition of the property bequeathed."[10] The statute itself set out a scheme by which notice had to be served on the Public Guardian and Trustee. The Court continued that:

> ... the statute casts the Public Trustee in the role of invigilator of the executor or trustee, so that, in the case of a trust for a religious, educational, charitable or public purpose, the public interest will be safeguarded and, of course, that public interest demands that the religious, educational, charitable, or public purpose contemplated by the testator be adhered to. ... Historically, in Chancery matters involving charities the Attorney-General acted on behalf of the Crown as *parens patriae* in representing all the objects of the charity ... In my opinion, the scheme of the Charities Accounting Act imposes upon the Public Trustee the duties that, otherwise, in the absence of that Act, would have fallen upon the Attorney General.

The judge continued that if he were wrong in his interpretation of the Act, the Public Guardian and Trustee would have a role in the proceedings as *amicus curiae* or friend of the court.

The Public Guardian and Trustee interprets the Act as applying to all charitable organizations, including corporations and unincorporated associations, and not just those created by trust deed or a bequest.[11] Although charitable corporations or unincorporated associations are not necessarily "trustees", they are considered to be trustees who are holding funds that are the subject of a charitable or purpose trust. Subsection 1(2) of the Act, for example, provides that:

---

[8] *Ibid.*, para. 30.
[9] (1984), 47 O.R. (2d) 415, 17 E.T.R. 168.
[10] *Ibid.*, at 174.
[11] Ontario Ministry of Consumer and Business Services and the Office of the Public Guardian and Trustee, *Not-For-Profit Incorporator's Handbook* (Toronto: Queen's Printer, 2000), at 43 and 46-7. See also P. Reynolds, "Administration of the Charities Accounting Act" in *Legal and Tax Issues Affecting the Charitable Sector* (Toronto: The Canadian Centre for Philanthropy, 1988).

Any corporation incorporated for a religious, educational, charitable or public purpose shall be deemed to be a trustee within the meaning of this Act, its instrument of incorporation shall be deemed to be an instrument in writing within the meaning of this Act, and any real or personal property acquired by it shall be deemed to be property within the meaning of this Act.

The Public Guardian and Trustee has also taken the position that charitable corporations are trustees for the purpose of the common law on the grounds that a charitable organization is not able to function without the decisions taken by the officers and directors. The corporation has a fiduciary role with respect to the property that is impressed with the charitable trust and, therefore, the officers and directors have a similar fiduciary role. The Public Guardian and Trustee recognizes that "there are some areas where trust law and corporation law and also income tax law overlap resulting in some gray areas"; however, its approach is usually from a trust law perspective.[12] The practical impact on charitable organizations is that the Public Guardian and Trustee places the onus on the organization and its officers and directors to prove that the organization is not a charity if the legislation appears to deem it to be a trustee of the charitable property.

A charitable organization must, pursuant to s. 2 of the Act, inform the Public Guardian and Trustee of its existence within one month of its creation by a trust document, a will, letters patent, or other written instrument. In the case of an Ontario letters patent corporation, the Public Guardian and Trustee would normally have been advised as part of the procedures used to incorporate charitable corporations. The charitable organization must furnish any information that the Public Guardian and Trustee requests. The Public Guardian and Trustee usually requests the following information:

- copies of the complete letters patent, trust document, will or other written document that created the charitable organization, and any subsequent documents, such as supplementary letters patent, that alter the legal structure of the charitable organization;
- the street and mailing address of the organization and the names and street addresses of the officers and directors or trustees;
- all legal and popular or common names or acronyms by which the charity is known or identified;
- the registration and business identification numbers assigned by Canada Customs and Revenue Agency for charitable donation tax credit purposes. If no numbers have been assigned or it is subse-

---

[12] Reynolds, *supra*, note 11 "Administration of the Charities Accounting Act", at 2.

quently revoked, this information and an explanation is also to be provided.[13]

The Public Guardian and Trustee may also request information and materials about the administration or management of the charitable organization. The directors are required to provide this information, including any financial information, such as financial statements.

There would appear to be at least one category of charitable organizations that may not fall within the Act in any substantive measure. A public hospital that intends to use its funds, with the approval of the Ministry of Health, to build a medical arts building for specialists' offices and other health-related services falls under the supervisory jurisdiction of the Ministry of Health. In *Re Centenary Hospital Assn.*,[14] the Court concluded that the Public Guardian and Trustee did not have supervisory powers over the hospital and that the interest in a building that was to be rented out was not an interest in a business under the *Charitable Gifts Act*.[15] The Public Guardian and Trustee's supervisory role was limited to any specific gift or bequest that was made to the hospital and not over all of the property held by the hospital for charitable purposes.[16]

The Court concluded that the Public Guardian and Trustee was a statutory body and, as such, had only those powers that were provided to it. Given the legislative history of the supervision of public hospitals, a general supervisory role for public hospitals was not granted to the Public Guardian and Trustee. That role was vested in the Ministry of Health. In any event, the Court also found that the building was only an ancillary activity to the hospital's charitable undertaking. Notwithstanding the overall results, the Court did also note that at least one section of the *Act* would apply to a public hospital in this circumstance.[17]

Section 6 permits the Court to order an investigation based upon a complaint by a member of the public. The Public Guardian and Trustee may be ordered by the Court to investigate the affairs of a charitable organization where there was a *prima facie* case that the funds were not being used as required. The complaint must be based on reasonable and probable grounds deposed to under oath and it must set out facts to show that the public interest requires an investigation. In *Stahl*,[18] the Court expressed some concerns about the potential for abuse:

---

[13] *Not-for-Profit Incorporator's Handbook*, *supra*, note 11, at 47.
[14] (1989), 69 O.R. (2d) 1 (H.C.).
[15] R.S.O. 1990, c. C.8.
[16] See also *Re Incorporated Synod of the Diocese of Toronto and H.E.C. Hotels Ltd. et al.* (1987), 61 O.R. (2d) 737 (C.A.), in which specific legislation which permitted the charitable organization to own land not being used or occupied for its charitable purposes took precedence over the *Charities Accounting Act*.
[17] *Re Centenary Hospital*, *supra*, note 14, at 16.
[18] *Stahl v. Ontario Society for the Prevention of Cruelty to Animals* (1989), 70 O.R. (2d) 355; *Re Schoen* (1987), 19 C.P.C. (2d) 110 (Ont. Dist. Ct.).

The Charities Accounting Act provides a means by which citizens may bring to the attention of the appropriate authorities any perceived impropriety in the solicitation or procurement of funds by a charity or in the manner in which such funds have been dealt with or disposed of.

It takes little imagination to see how this Act might be made a means of harassment of organizations that, by definition, are engaged in benevolent endeavours.

To prevent abuse of the Act, no investigation of the matter complained of is initiated unless the particulars of the complaint are reduced to writing, submitted to a judge of this Court and that judge is of the opinion that the public interest can be served by an investigation of the matter complained of.

Certain questions arise:

1. How is the complaint brought to this Court?
2. Who, if anyone, should be given notice that the matter has been placed before this Court?
3. What form should the evidence take before the Court?
4. What standard of proof does the Court apply in making its decision?

The Court is also cognizant of the costs that are involved for a charitable organization in any investigation or passing of accounts. In *Boldrini v. Hamilton Naturalists Club*,[19] the Court commented:

Generally, inquiries under the Act should be based on reasonable and probable grounds and not conjecture, surmise, groundless accusations or conclusions.

The Court must remain mindful that an investigation under the Act is disruptive and costly.

The Act is clear that the granting of an Order is governed by the public interest being served and not that of the complainant.

The Court in *Re Stahl* adopted the process set out in *Re Schoen*. The Court noted that the complaint must be in writing and "be specific so that the Judge will be able to determine exactly what is the basis of the complaint and as to whether the public interest is served by an investiga-

---

[19] [1995] O.J. No. 3321, Ontario Court of Justice (Gen. Div.), October 18, 1995, at paras. 3 to 5.

tion thereof."[20] It is not to be based on conjecture, surmise, groundless accusations or groundless conclusions.[21] The complaints must have a reasonable and probable grounds basis, given the costs and disruption that will occur. An investigation is an extraordinary remedy. In summary, the Court commented that:

> Keeping those principles in mind, it is my view that in an application under s. 6, the complainant should set forth fully and succinctly every wrongdoing of which he complains as to the manner of soliciting and procuring funds and as to the manner in which such funds are dealt with or disposed of. The facts (being reasonable and probable grounds), upon which such complaints are based, should be deposed to by the complainant under oath as well as any facts upon which the complainant avers that the public interest will be served by an investigation of the matters complained of.[22]

The Court has dealt with its role and its relationship with that of the Public Guardian and Trustee. For example, in *Asian Outreach Canada v. Hutchinson*:[23]

> The court has an inherent jurisdiction to intervene if charitable funds are misapplied. This jurisdiction is supplemented by the provisions of the Charities Accounting Act which, also, confer powers and impose responsibilities on the Public Guardian and Trustee. Section 6 of the Act specifically authorizes the court to direct the Public Guardian and Trustee to investigate written complaints delivered by any persons to a judge of this court with respect to the manner in which a person or organization has solicited or procured funds by way of contribution or gift from the public for any purpose, or as to the manner in which any such funds have been dealt with or disposed of. Section 6, like most of the provisions of the Act, creates machinery and provides procedures and does not significantly extend the jurisdiction of the Court over the matters to which it refers except to the extent that it authorizes the court to direct the Public Guardian and Trustee to conduct investigations. The nature and extent of any such investigation is for the Public Guardian and Trustee to decide. If the statute did not exist, the Court would, I believe, have power to request the Attorney General to investigate. Section 6 is expressed not to apply to the solicitation of funds by any "religious or fraternal organization" but there is, at least, a question whether the corporate bodies here are religious organizations of the kind contemplated. Moreover, other sections of the Act may well be applicable during, or at the termination of, this litigation if it appears that funds donated for charitable purposes have been improperly dissipated by, or in, the proceedings.

---

[20] *Re Schoen, supra,* note 18.
[21] *Ibid.*
[22] *Ibid.*
[23] (1999), 28 E.T.R. (2d) 275 (Ont. S.C.J.).

Cullity, J continued with respect to the legal nature of "charitable corporations" and trust property in an attempt to clarify some of the issues:

> Although, as charitable corporations, AOC, AOI and AOIC are deemed to be trustees for the purposes of the Charities Accounting Act, they do not necessarily hold all their property, including funds solicited from the public, in trust in the technical sense: Re Centenary Hospital Association ... Re Christian Brothers of Ireland in Canada ... . Statements to the contrary have been made from time to time but such statements are inaccurate and misleading to the extent that they suggest that those entities are merely corporate trustees incapable of beneficial ownership of property. The confusion that has sometimes arisen is a consequence of the fact that the equitable jurisdiction of the Court includes both the enforcement of trusts and the supervision of charities whether the latter are established under wills or trust instruments inter vivos, or as corporations. As many of the general principles applied by the courts in supervising charitable trusts have also been applied to charitable corporations there was a tendency, particularly in the 19th Century cases in England, to find the basis of the jurisdiction over charities in the law of trusts. This does not appear to be correct historically and it is clear that it does not represent the present state of the law in this jurisdiction. Charitable corporations own property beneficially and person who make gifts to them for their general purposes are presumed, prima facie, to intend to make outright gifts and not gifts in trust for such purposes. Moreover, the fact that, in supervising charitable corporations, principles that are also applicable to charitable trusts are very often applied, does not mean that all the implications of corporate personality and the requirements of corporate law are to be ignored. The difficulty is to determine how the principles interact and to identify the situations in which the inherent jurisdiction may, in effect, override the rules applicable to corporations in general. The difficulty is particularly acute when the interpretation of statutes that refer to trusts and trustees, on the one hand, or to corporations, on the other is in issue: see, for example, Re Public Trustee and Toronto Humane Society ... .
>
> As legal persons with the capacity to have legal rights and duties, the corporate charities in this case are not to be considered merely as conduits for the flow of charitable funds. Like other corporations, they have interests which they are entitled to protect by seeking the intervention of the Court. However, in the exercise of the Court's discretion, the interests of the public generally and the interests of those who provide financial support to AOC, AOIC and AOI must, I believe be taken into consideration as well as the principles that apply when interlocutory orders, and other equitable remedies, are sought by persons who are not charities.[24]

---

[24] *Ibid.*, at paras. 27 and 28. See also *Oblates of Mary Immaculate-St. Peter's Province v. Ontario (Public Trustee)* [1994] O.J. No. 2757, Ontario Court of Justice (Gen. Div.), November 28, 1994 in which Chadwick, J. noted that s. 2 of the *Charities Accounting Act* and a court

The courts have attempted to address the confusion with respect to the law of charities. However, that confusion continues both with respect to the nature of "charitable corporations" and the role and responsibilities for supervision of charitable organizations in general. The case law would appear to have limited the role of the Public Guardian and Trustee with respect to certain charities that are supervised or regulated by other government agencies. Do the legal principles set out in *Re Centenary Hospital* apply only to public hospitals or do they extend to comparable public institutions, such as universities, school boards and colleges that are also charitable?

Yet, notwithstanding the apparent constraints on the Public Guardian and Trustee under s. 6 of the *Charities Accounting Act*, there remain considerable powers of supervision. The Court has also been careful to retain its own inherent jurisdiction in any cases. The *Charities Accounting Act* provides, it seems, a mechanism for the public to cause the wheels of supervision to move. It is a nicety but not necessary; the Court, in its view, already has the jurisdiction.

The Public Guardian and Trustee has another source of authority for its supervisory role. If there are any concerns about the administration or management of the charitable organization or its property, the Public Guardian and Trustee may, under ss. 3 and 4, require that the charitable organization pass its accounts in the Ontario Court of Justice. This passing of accounts is intended to ensure that the purposes for which the charitable organization was created — to carry out the charitable purposes set out in its objects clauses — are fulfilled.[25]

In some cases, a charitable organization may request that the court pass its accounts. This application would be made to obtain the court's approval for the conduct of the charitable organization and its officers, directors or trustees. For example, it has been used where there was a question about the charitableness of an activity,[26] to determine if payment of honoraria when a charitable organization was dissolved was appropriate,[27] and to order the return of funds improperly loaned to a business.[28] But the court exercises discretion whether or not to order any passing of accounts. If, the court's view, such passing of accounts would not serve a useful purpose or provide "further illumination", it will decline to make the order.

The Public Guardian and Trustee may also request that the charitable organization correct any problems identified in the passing of accounts,

---

hearing into the protection and preservation of assets or the operation and management of the corporation and its assets is a narrow one and does not extend to the protection of interest of the intervenors.

[25] See, for an example, *Re Cdn. Foundation for Youth Action* (1977), 1 A.C.W.S. 282.
[26] *Re Laidlaw Foundation* (1984), 44 O.R. (2d) 549 (Div. Ct.).
[27] *Re Faith Haven Bible Training Centre* (1988), 29 E.T.R. 198. See also, *Re David Feldman Charitable Foundation* (1987), 58 O.R. (2d) 626, where the Court refused to pass the accounts.
[28] *Re Burns*, [1988] O.J. No. 2001, November 28, 1988, Ontario Surrogate Court.

audited financial statements or in any other additional information requested by the Public Guardian and Trustee. If the problem is not corrected, the Public Guardian and Trustee may advise the Minister of Consumer and Business Services with respect to a charitable corporation (who may move to dissolve the corporation) or the Canada Customs and Revenue Agency. An application may also be made to the court for the election of a new board of directors under court supervision where the existing board is not able to carry out its obligations or refuses to comply with the requirements of the law.

III CHARITABLE GIFTS ACT

The *Charitable Gifts Act* is primarily concerned with the operation of business activities by charitable organizations. This topic is, of course, an important one. The rationale for the operation of a business activity — to make money — is often obvious to boards of directors. The rationale as to why such business activities should be restricted or even prohibited is not as easily recognized.

The predecessor legislation became law in Ontario in April 1949. The Hon. Leslie M. Frost, then Treasurer, introduced Bill 169, "An Act respecting certain charitable and other gifts" on March 25, 1949. The Bill had three rationales according to Mr. Frost, which were inter-related:

- Succession Duties — Ontario had made changes to the *Succession Duty Act* to encourage people to donate portions of their estate to charities. The amendments provided relief from duties on such gifts.
- Safeguards — it is necessary to put into place safeguards to ensure that the charitable intent is carried out.
- Provincial Interests — the province became interested in the trust because of the exemption from duties. The provincial taxpayer, therefore, had a right to be assured that the charitable purposes are carried out. Mr. Frost noted the requirement to file financial statements under the *Charities Accounting Act*. The financial statements permitted the public access to information about the operations of the charities.[29]

Mr. Frost identified "the principal problem arises where a business either in its entirety or a controlling interest therein is given to a charitable foundation or trust."[30] He then noted the trustees may appoint themselves as directors, managers or officers of the businesses and have effective control over the business and over their successors. For Mr. Frost,

---

[29] *Ibid.*, at 1335-63.
[30] *Ibid.*, at 1336.

this situation was real and had a negative effect on the policy objectives of succession duties. One of the policy objectives was to break up economic concentration of wealth and force distribution and sale of assets, which was necessary and desirable in an economy like Ontario's.

Mr. Frost continued with four problems that are created by this situation:

- the trustees and their successors are in effect given the right to appoint themselves and their successors as directors, managers and officers of such businesses for all time. It quite naturally follows that relatives connected with either the testator, founder or the trustees would be logical successors,
- owing to the fact that, generally, no specific charities are named, it follows that the trustees may operate these trusts according to their own ideas and they may or may not be interested in operating such businesses for any profit other than their own salaries and fees. In other words, the charitable object may become secondary to the interest of the directors, managers and officers who would be by themselves and their successors the trustees in perpetuity,
- in the result, the huge exemptions which are given under The Succession Duty Act from taxation are not effectively devoted to any charities. The charitable intent becomes secondary,
- from an economic point of view, such a result would, without regulation, no doubt become a menace to competitive business and provide extremely unfair competition to businesses which are endeavoring to pay taxes and provide dividends for shareholders.

The best scrutiny, according to Mr. Frost, to ensure the proper operation of any company or business is that provided by shareholders who are interested in it. The *Charitable Gifts Act* was intended to ensure that this approach was the result.

It is far from clear what is or is not covered by the *CGA*. This confusion arises from two factors:

- the obscure language (a point noted by the Ontario Law Reform Commission)[31] used in the statute, and
- the paucity of judicial interpretations and applications of the statutes or of other analyses of the statutes.

---

[31] *Report on the Law of Charities*, (Toronto: Queen's Printer, 1996), at 600.

The phrase "given to or vested in a person in any capacity for any religious, charitable, educational or public purpose" is particularly confusing. A strict interpretation of the wording leads to very unusual circumstances. For example, shares in business corporations that issue securities are commonly held by financial institutions and stock brokers for the benefit of their clients. These institutions could be holding shares on behalf of several "charities", which cumulatively amount to more than 10 per cent interest in a business. It would appear on the face of the *Charitable Gifts Act* that it would be required to dispose of the excess.

While this situation and result is unlikely to occur (or to be recognized), it does illustrate the uncertainty of the scope of the statute. There are no clear demarcations in the statute and the language is difficult to interpret. What is an "interest"? A share is probably an "interest" in the business. But para. 2(4)(c) would seem to expand an interest to other forms of securities and to investments that are not securities and that do not provide any material control over the business entity.

What is meant by a "business"? While many would consider a business to be an ongoing legal entity, such as a corporation or a partnership, the statute does not define "business" in that way. A reasonable interpretation could prohibit two performing arts organizations from being partners to produce a series of shows that have as one of the purposes "gain or profit". Arguably the condition precedent "given to or vested in" would eliminate this situation from coverage; but for the statute to have what appears to be the intended scope, "vested in" would need to be liberally interpreted.

The Act also takes an interesting approach with respect to the types of organizations that are to be covered —"religious, charitable, educational or public purpose". At common law, "charitable" includes the relief of poverty, the advancement of education, the advancement of religion and other purposes beneficial to the community. This common law definition was certainly known in 1949. Arguably, the addition of the words "religious ... educational or public purpose" was intended to expand coverage beyond "charitable" to include other purposes that are not charitable at common law. For example, not all educational institutions are "charitable" or are intended for the "advancement of education", as that head of charity was defined in 1949 or 1959.

Does the legislation cover those institutions? Or does it cover organizations that have a "public purpose", such as service clubs, that are not charitable? While common sense would suggest that it was not the intention of the government of the day to include those types of entities, it is not clear whether or not the legislation does.

The statute covers "corporations", which could be "charitable corporations" or "not-for-profit corporations" or business corporations. However, modern incorporation legislation in Ontario and Canada has eliminated the requirement for objects or purposes in the articles of incorporation. Any of these corporations could have one or more purposes. In the case of charitable corporations, all of their purposes must be charitable. However, not-for-profit corporations are not so restricted. The Act does not expressly require that all of the purposes must be "charitable"; rather, subs. 2(1) refers to "any religious, charitable, educational or public purpose".

There is another significant issue. What types of transactions are covered by the Act? The statutes refer to both "given to" and "vested in". However, it is possible to contemplate other methods by which a charity may acquire an interest in a business. For example, it may purchase the interest. While it is probable that a purchase is included in the concept of "vesting", that result is not certain. Supporting the argument, though, is the difficulty to demonstrate ownership of an interest unless that ownership has "vested" in some manner.

On the other hand, the *Ballard Estate v. Ballard Estate*[32] does provide some argument to support the position that a purchase of an interest is not covered. If the phrase "given to or vested in" is read conjunctively, arguably the two conditions must be met before s. 2 of the Act is triggered. Until the "gift" is "vested", the Act does not apply in this interpretation.[33]

However, if there is no gift but rather a purchase which is then "vested" in the charity, is s. 2 triggered? At the very least, there is an argument to make that the *Charitable Gifts Act* does not cover this situation — or if it does, it does so in a very convoluted manner. The Court of Appeal does comment in the *Ballard Estate* case about the purposes of the *CGA* and those comments are not directly supportive of this interpretation. But the Court was not deciding a case involving a purchase but rather a gift.

The scope of the legislation is not clear from at least four perspectives:

- what amounts to an "interest"?
- what is a business?
- what types of transactions are covered? and
- what types of legal entities are covered and at what point in the regulatory regime?

The Public Trustee in 1983 provided comments on the purpose and administration of the Act, noting that, because there is a requirement for charities owning more than 50 per cent of a business to report to the Public Trustee, that it is assumed by many that the Public Trustee supervises the Act. He continued:

---

[32] (1991), 3 O.R. (3d) 65 (C.A.).
[33] Although "or" is often read disjunctively, Mr. Justice Osler appears to consider it to be conjunctive in *Re Centenary Hospital* in which he summarizes an argument that "the term 'vested in' ... is roughly equivalent to what is sometimes expressed, unfortunately in my opinion as 'gifted to'" and later comments that this argument has some weight. While Osler, J. does not expressly read "gifted to or vested in" conjunctively, it seems that it would be necessary to arrive at this conclusion.

That may be so, but I do not feel that the legislation is clear on this point. In practice we receive only about one enquiry each year about this statute.[34]

It is interesting to review some of the fact situations that "troubled" the Public Trustee in 1983. For example, he was troubled

> by such situations as arise when hospitals operate gift stores or parking lots for profit; medical foundations raise part of their funds by providing medical services for a fee; physical fitness organizations operate summer camps; and political or religious groups operate learning centres where guests pay a fee and are entitled to use a gymnasium, sauna baths or sailboats while they are attending seminars.[35]

He then listed several examples that had come to the attention of the Public Trustee and for which, presumably, action was taken:

- a charitable organization in the fitness field considers incorporating a squash club in the adjoining premises with the intention that the club will be operated for profit,
- a charitable organization promotes as ancillary to its charitable purpose, an enterprise that becomes profitable and then seeks to separate that enterprise from the charitable purpose but with the charitable organization having 100 per cent of the issued capital stock,
- a charitable organization finding that one of its ancillary businesses turns out to be profitable, wishes to sell that business and take back a promissory note for the full amount or a large part of the purchase price.

He continued that "It is my opinion that the act requires clarification and requires more direct and meaningful enforcement provisions".[36] The Public Trustee then noted one suggestion that has been made to avoid the *Charitable Gifts Act*. Two foundations could be set up so that every six years one foundation would convey all its assets to the other. He also noted the suggestion that was promoted by Mr. Frost in his first reading speech as an appropriate way of dealing with shares, i.e., that 11 charitable foundations each own less than 10 per cent of the business.

The Public Trustee did subsequently challenge hospitals and their operations of certain types of ancillary businesses, as noted above. In *Re Centenary Hospital*,[37] the Public Trustee was unsuccessful in prohibiting

---

[34] A.J. McComiskey, Public Trustee, "The Role of the Public Trustee", (1983), 6 Philantrop. 9, at 13.
[35] *Ibid.*, at 14.
[36] *Ibid.*, at 15.
[37] (1989), 69 O.R. (2d) 447 (H.C.J.).

hospitals from carrying on certain businesses. The Court concluded, in part, that the Public Trustee as a statutory authority did not have all of the common law powers of the Attorney General with respect to charities. The Public Trustee's authority was limited to the powers granted by the statute. Furthermore, the Court concluded that hospitals were regulated by another statutory regime, the *Public Hospitals Act*.

The then Public Trustee's approach seems to be inconsistent with the reality of today. It is common for charitable organizations to carry on business activities. There are likely few hospitals in Canada that do not operate gift shops, parking lots, coffee shops or similar business entities either directly or indirectly to raise funds for its charitable purposes. From a governance perspective, it would appear to be prudent to isolate the business risks associated with the operations of a business into a for-profit or not-for-profit corporate structure.

Similarly, many universities, hospitals, community colleges and similar educational institutions, especially those involved in research and development, have "interests" in "businesses" in order to commercialize the intellectual property derived from the research and development. Indeed, federal and Ontario public policy and funding agreements encourage universities to retain interests in the businesses.

This approach, though, is consistent with how the Public Trustee applied the *Charitable Gifts Act*. Staff wrote that an applicant for letters patent under the Ontario *Corporations Act* for a charitable corporation "should also be aware of other provincial legislation governing charities such as: the *Charitable Gifts Act* (which restricts the owning and operating of businesses".[38] He continued that subs. 2(2) of the *Charities Accounting Act*:

> ...is reinforced by the Charitable Gifts Act and obligates a charity to account for its owning or controlling or operating other corporations. This would only occur if a business was donated to the charity and would not allow a charity to buy a controlling interest in a business. Even then, any more than a 10% interest in a business must be disposed of.[39]

The Attorney General directed the Ontario Law Reform Commission in 1989 to provide recommendations on the law of charities. The Public Trustee commented to the OLRC that:

> There are four interrelated aspects of charities' business activities that are of particular concern to us: risk; trustees' liability; conflict of interest; and objectives, values and ethics. There are other aspects, such as unfair competition and self-perpetuating oligarchic control of businesses, that no

---

[38] P. Reynolds, "Administration of the Charities Accounting Act", in A. Arlett, *Legal and Tax Issues Affecting the Charitable Sector* (Toronto: Canadian Centre for Philanthropy, 1984), at 4 of Tab 7.

[39] *Ibid.*, at 5 and 6.

doubt are of concern to others but that we think are more properly addressed by those others.[40]

Interestingly, those other concerns appeared to have been of substantial concern to Treasurer Frost and formed part of the rationale for the 1949 legislation.

The Public Trustee's concerns focussed on conflicts of interests and the role of trustees. It continued:

> There is also the conflict of interest. We have had occasion during the last two years to review a large number of charities' business activities and business-activity proposals. In almost every instance in which the business activity was unconnected to the charity's purposes, except by application of profit to those purposes, we have found serious, material, real conflicts of interest of which the charitable trustees apparently either have been unconscious or have not appreciated the significance. ... It should be noted that substantially all of the provisions of the Charitable Gifts Act, R.S.O. 1980, c. 63, are concerned with the relationships between a charity having a business interest, its trustees and the business, i.e., conflict of interest.[41]

The Public Trustee recommended to the OLRC that provisions of the *Charitable Gifts Act* related to the relations between the charities, their trustees and charities' businesses should be retained.

There has been surprisingly little case law with respect to the *CGA*. There may be a number of reasons for this fact, including the lack of knowledge about it. In addition, the Public Guardian and Trustee has generally taken a complaints-based approach to enforcement rather than an active approach.

Most of the cases have not interpreted or applied the legislation. These cases, instead, were concerned with the appropriate fees to be paid for the administration of an estate. There was a sense that the *Charitable Gifts Act, 1949* made the administration of some estates more cumbersome and legally convoluted, requiring greater legal and estate administration fees.[42]

The High Court of Justice did examine the *Charitable Gifts Act* in *Re Centenary Hospital*. In that case, as noted above, the Public Trustee was not successful in ensuring that its supervisory role applied fully to public hospitals. The Court found, in particular, that the hospital's interest in a building that was to be rented out was not an interest in a business under the *Charitable Gifts Act*. The Public Trustee's supervisory role was limited

---

[40] (1991), 10 Estates L.J. 277, at 284.
[41] *Ibid.*, at 285.
[42] See *Re Mason Estate*, [1951] O.J. No. 40 (H.C.J.) and *Re Atkinson*, [1952] O.R. 685 (C.A.). The *Re Mason Estate* case does note that until the shares are vested in the trustee, the Act does not apply. A similar approach was taken by the Court with respect to the Ballard estate in *Ballard Estate v. Ballard Estate*, (1991), 3 O.R. (3d) 65 (C.A.).

to any specific gift or bequest that was made to the hospital and not over all of the property held by the hospital for charitable purposes.

The only other substantial judicial interpretation of the *Charitable Gifts Act* is by the Ontario Court of Appeal in *Ballard Estate v. Ballard Estate* in which Mr. Justice Finlayson provided the oral judgment of the Court.[43] He stated:

> The purpose of the Charitable Gifts Act is to prevent charitable corporations or trusts, other than religious institutions, from owning, holding or controlling, directly or indirectly, more than a ten per cent interest in a business that is carried on for profit or gain. The legislation is aimed at ensuring that charities are not used as a means of sheltering a business enterprise, that is to say, of creating a situation where the tax privileges conferred upon charities are employed as a means of building up a business, or otherwise sustaining it: see Waters, Law of Trusts in Canada, supra at pp. 635 and 636.
>
> There is much to be said for the position of the Public Trustee that the trust indenture was skilfully drafted to avoid the effects of the Charitable Gifts Act for a maximum period of 21 years. The shares of HEBL and MLGL do not have to vest in the Harold E. Ballard Foundation until the division day and that date is defined as potentially occurring 21 years after the death of the testator. This complies with the rule against perpetuities as set out in s. 16 of the Perpetuities Act, R.S.O. 1980, c. 374.
>
> It follows from this, submits counsel, that if the option is triggered and exercised by Knob Hill sometime prior to January 1, 1996, it will result in a purchase of the shares under Clause VII of the will and this will advance the division day and bring s. 5 of the Charitable Gifts Act into play. That, he says, is the true effect of the granting of the option.
>
> However, I am only concerned with whether the granting of the option is a present disposition made pursuant to s. 2 of the Charitable Gifts Act. In my opinion it is not, and therefore, s. 5 does not apply so as to require the approval of a judge.

The comments of the Court are, with respect to the application of s. 2, *obiter*. However, Finlayson's comments would be considered in any judicial interpretation of the coverage of s. 2 given the nature of the litigation and the senior level of the Court of Appeal.

The Ontario Law Reform Commission provided the most thorough review of the statutes and commentary on them. It commented:

---

[43] (1991), 3 O.R. (3d) 65 (C.A.).

The *Charitable Gifts Act* restricts severely the extent to which charities may own businesses ... "Interest in a business" is defined in a somewhat obscure, but inclusive way.[44]

The Commission also notes:

Although the justification for the Act was very narrowly focussed on protecting the revenue and saving charities from possible abuse, the scope of its prohibition is incredibly wide. It may even preclude a charity from running a related business. We return to a fuller discussion of the statute below; then we simply note this obvious discrepancy between its intended and its actual target.[45]

The Commission continued:

The *Charitable Gifts Act* is unclear as to which types of ownership interests are regulated. It appears to cover ownership interests in corporations than run businesses, ownership interests in trusts than run businesses, and charities running businesses directly. If that, indeed, is the intention with respect to the scope of application of the statute — and it was our assumption above that it is — then the statute may be seeking to address two quite distinct issues, neither of which is made explicit and neither of which, in our view, is addressed adequately. One objective might be to ensure that the fiduciaries of entities controlled by a charity fulfill their fiduciary obligations to the entity so that the charity's investment in the entity maintains its value. A second objective might be to ensure that charities themselves do not breach the exclusively charitable standard by running businesses directly.

In the Commission's view, the first objective is poorly addressed in the statute. The general prohibition against owning a greater than ten percent interest in a business is both too broad and too narrow a rule. It is too broad because it precludes all charities from owning a greater than ten percent interest in an entity when the proper target of the regulation should be merely the enforcement of the fiduciary duties owed to these entities. It is too narrow because it does not pick up all situations in which a breach of these fiduciary duties is a real possibility. We suggest a better set of rules below.

With respect to the second possible objective — to control for breaches of the exclusively charitable standard — the ten percent is simply wrong. It suggests that it is not permissible for a charity to carry on what we have called "related" and "subordinate" commercial activity. This is clearly misguided.

---

[44] *Report on the Law of Charities, supra,* note 31, at 600.
[45] *Ibid.*, at 601.

There are two further difficulties with the Act. First, it appears that the statute may apply only to "gifts" of interests of businesses to charities and, therefore, not to acquisitions. If the objectives of the legislation are as just set out, there is no reason why the provisions of the Act should apply only to gifts of more than ten percent interests of businesses to charities.

Second, there is an implicit contradiction, alluded to above, between the *Charitable Gifts Act*, which prohibits a greater than ten percent interest in a business, and the provisions of the *Charities Accounting Act*, which requires corporations controlled by charities to furnish financial and other information to the Public Trustee. As stated above, it seems that the provision of the *Charities Accounting Act* implicitly contemplate a possibility which is prohibited by the *Charitable Gifts Act*. This is a minor criticism, however, because it is possible to read the provisions of the *Charities Accounting Act* so that they apply only to corporations in which the controlling interest was purchased as opposed to being received by gift (on the assumption that the *Charitable Gifts Act* applies only to interests greater than ten percent, which are obtained by gift) and, where the interest is acquired by gift, only to the interim period between the date of the gift and the date of the required disposition. Although that reading of the provision achieves some measure of consistency between the two statutes, the distinctions required to achieve consistency have little merit. Rather, it seems more likely that the cause of the inconsistency is the fact that the *Charitable Gifts Act* was hastily drafted and hastily enacted.[46]

Not surprisingly, the Commission recommends the repeal of the *Charitable Gifts Act* and its replacement by more appropriate legislation to govern investments in businesses by charities. Unfortunately, the Government of Ontario has failed to take any steps towards this strong recommendation.

It is a short statute that is primarily concerned with ensuring that charitable organizations are not carrying on business. It also serves to discourage charitable organizations from placing funds at risk in capital markets. The directors and trustees do not have a duty to maximize the return on the investment of the charitable organization's property; rather, they have a duty to protect the interests of the charitable organization, both in the short and the long term. Capital markets provide a higher level of risk than is sometimes appropriate for some charitable organizations.

The Act prohibits charitable organizations from owning more than 10 per cent of the shares of a business. If the charitable organization receives a gift or bequest of an interest in a business that is greater than 10 per cent, the directors or trustees are empowered and directed by s. 2 to dispose of the surplus within seven years of the receipt of the gift or bequest. A judge of the Ontario Superior Court of Justice may, under s. 3,

---

[46] *Ibid.*, at 602-603.

extend the seven-year period if it would be prudent to do so or if the extension would benefit the charitable organization. This could occur, for example, where the disposition of the shares could result in a lower overall benefit to the charitable organization by reducing the per share price received. Furthermore, pursuant to s. 4, as long as the interest is greater than 50 per cent, the directors or trustees and the Public Guardian and Trustee must determine by June 30 of each year the amount of the profits earned by the business which will be distributed to the charitable organization.

C DOCTRINE OF CY-PRES

The doctrine of *cy-pres* arises out of the court's inherent supervisory jurisdiction over charitable trusts. Under the doctrine, the court may alter the terms of the trust where the trustees cannot apply the property for the charitable purpose to one that is as near as it may be to the intended purpose of the settlor of the property.

The court's jurisdiction is based on the principle that the court has a role in assisting the settlor and the trustees to preserve the trust. Although the courts will not write the terms of the trust, they will support the intent of the trust.[47] The doctrine of *cy-pres* is one method by which the courts may support the overall intent of the settlor of the trust when the terms of the trust cannot be complied with by the trustees. As noted above, "trustees" in this situation would include a corporation or unincorporated association that is holding property and is impressed with a charitable trust or purpose.

The courts will not, however, apply the doctrine out of expediency alone or without taking into account the position of the Public Guardian and Trustee. Although it may be expedient, for example, to alter the terms of the trust to avoid estate duties, that is not sufficient grounds to do so. The court is to exercise its jurisdiction sparingly and only in those cases where the Attorney General or Public Guardian and Trustee, acting in its role as *parens patriae* has approved.[48]

The cases have reviewed the doctrine and when it will or will not be applied in some detail. The general rule appears to be that the doctrine could be applied to a particular charitable purpose if it is or becomes impossible, impractical or illegal to carry out the particular purpose. In some cases, the court was concerned with whether this impossibility, impracticality or illegality existed at the time of the establishment of the charitable purpose or occurred afterwards. For example, if a will provided for a bequest to a particular charity but that charitable organization did not exist, the bequest had to indicate a general charitable intent. If, however, the property had vested and the charitable purpose became

---

[47] *Re Baker* (1984), 17 E.T.R. 168, at 178-180 (Ont. H.C.).
[48] *Ibid.*, at 180.

impossible or impractical or illegal subsequently, there was usually no need to determine what the testator's intent was.[49]

The first line of cases seem to arise most often where a bequest is being contested. In *Lapointe v. Ont. (Public Trustee)*,[50] the Court noted that Canadian case law "on occasions, searched unnecessarily in cases of supervening failure, for a general or paramount charitable intent". Whether this search is necessary will depend upon the perspective that the court has of the property. If the court views the charitable purpose as being the relevant consideration, and not the legal entity that holds the property, there does not appear to be a need to find a supervening failure. The property vests in the charitable purpose. The court's role in this perspective is to support the charitable purpose by applying the doctrine so that the charitable purpose is administered by an appropriate legal entity.

A trust may have been practical or legal when it was created. A change in public policy or in the economic and social conditions of society may, however, make it impossible or illegal for the trustees to carry out the terms of the trust. Lord Simonds, in *Nat. Anti-Vivisection Society v. Inland Revenue Commrs.*,[51] commented that:

> A purpose regarded in one age as charitable may in another be regarded differently. ... But this is not to say that a charitable trust, when it has once been established can ever fail. If by a change in social habits and needs, or, it may be, by a change in the law the purpose of an established charity becomes superfluous or even illegal, or if with increasing knowledge it appears that a purpose once thought beneficial is truly detrimental to the community, it is the duty of the trustees ... to apply to the court ... and ask that a *cy-près* scheme be established.

The Ontario Court of Appeal in *Canada Trust v. Ont. (Human Rights Comm.)*[52] adopted this argument in applying the doctrine to a scholarship programme that was contrary to public policy. In this case, a charitable trust was established to provide scholarships to individual students. The recipients were restricted to persons who were white, Protestant and British subjects. The Court found that these restrictions were contrary to public policy, as set out in human rights legislation and the Constitution. The majority decision found that changing social attitudes had made the charitable trust impracticable to carry out in the original manner planned by the settlor. The Court concluded, however, that the trust

---

[49] See *Re Fitzpatrick; Fidelity Trust Co. et al. v. St. Joseph's Vocational School of Winnipeg et al.* (1984), 16 E.T.R. 221 (Man. Q.B.) and *Weninger Estate v. Cdn. Diabetes Assn.* (1993), 2 E.T.R. (2d) 24 (Ont. Gen. Div.) for a discussion of these cases.

[50] (1993), 1 E.T.R. (2d) 203 (Ont. Gen. Div.). See also *Re Daley Estate* (1987), 27 E.T.R. 291 (Sask. Q.B.).

[51] [1948] A.C. 31 at 74 (H.L.).

[52] (1990), 38 E.T.R. 1 (Ont. C.A.).

should not fail and that the *cy-pres* doctrine could be applied. It did so by deleting the restrictions based on prohibited grounds and thereby permitted the general charitable intent to advance education or leadership through education to be implemented.

Mr. Justice Tarnopolsky agreed in the result with the majority opinion; however, he took a different approach with respect to the application of the doctrine. In his judgment, he looked to whether or not there was a general charitable intent on the part of the settlor, not to determine what would be the most appropriate scheme, but to determine whether or not there was a charitable trust. It would appear, however, that the law in Ontario is that once the charitable purpose is established, the intent of the settlor is relevant only in developing the appropriate scheme.

Whichever approach is taken, the doctrine of *cy-pres* is available only where the property can no longer be applied to the charitable purpose for which it is vested. In Ontario, the Public Guardian and Trustee is the appropriate respondent in an application to the Ontario court for the establishment of a *cy-pres* scheme. As a practical matter, it is unlikely that the court would grant the application or devise a scheme without the Public Guardian and Trustee's consent or agreement. Prior to providing such consent or agreement, the Public Guardian and Trustee may require the applicants to comply with any outstanding obligations under the *Charities Accounting Act* or the *Charitable Gifts Act*, or to pass the accounts.

D JUDICIAL SUPERVISION

The courts have a substantial role in the supervision of charitable organizations. This role is an outgrowth both of the common law and by statute. As discussed in Chapter 1, the courts have been largely responsible for defining "charity" and in restricting its application to those objects and activities that the courts consider to be "charitable". They did so in carrying out their inherent jurisdiction over charitable trusts and charitable organizations that hold those trusts.

This inherent jurisdiction is not dependent upon statutes such as the *Charities Accounting Act* or the *Charitable Gifts Act*. Although those statutes may provide for procedural matters or for powers and responsibilities to others, such as the Public Guardian and Trustee, the overall jurisdiction is one that the courts have developed and now guard. Those statutes may also address specific substantive issues, such as the ability of a charitable organization to hold shares of a business, these types of issues were within the domain of the courts in any event. The statutes may express a different policy or a more developed policy on the issue, but they do not attempt to take away any of the court's inherent jurisdiction.

Courts have periodically discussed the inherent jurisdiction and its relationship to other regulators. The *Asian Outreach Canada v. Hutchinson*[53] case reviewed above is one such example. Another, also involving the Public Guardian and Trustee, is *Ontario (Public Guardian and Trustee) v. AIDS Society for Children (Ontairo)*.[54] Mr. Justice Haley comments that:

> The Court has an inherent jurisdiction to direct and control the administration of charities. The acquisition of that power is described by Professor Waters in Law of Trusts in Canada ...
>
>> It was in the Court of Chancery that the law of charities grew, primarily in the sixteenth to eighteenth centuries; there the privileges in relation to perpetuity, certainty and scheme-making were fashioned. This jurisdiction has remained to the present day, handled in contemporary times by the superior courts of each common law jurisdiction who are the successors to the old Court of Chancery.
>
> There is no specific administrative control over charities imposed by legislation to the extent that charities are registered or supervised by any government agency, other than the indirect control exercised under the Income Tax Act through permitting the issuing of receipts for income tax purposes. However, as Professor Waters notes ...:
>
>> But the Crown also had a role to play as parens patriae. Under its prerogative power, it was a protector of the interests of charities and therefore concerned with the maladministration of charitable trusts. Primarily the Crown was thus concerned to see that funds were properly handled, and that expenditures were only made upon trust objects. It would also sue to recover charitable funds which had been fraudulently made available to third parties. This responsibility of the Crown devolved upon the senior law officer, the Attorney General as one of his many tasks, and for three centuries at least the Attorney General has discharged it, first in England and then later in all other common law jurisdictions where his counterpart, or a nominee like the Public Trustee, has assumed the role.[55]

Haley J. then reviews the formalization of this prerogative power in the *Charities Accounting Act* in Ontario in 1915, a position that is consistent with *Re Centenary Hospital* and other cases. However, it is clear that the prerogative power remains in existence in other Attorneys General. He continues:

---

[53] (1999), 28 E.T.R. (2d) 275 (Ont. S.C.J.).
[54] [2001] O.J. No. 2170, Ontario Superior Court of Justice, May 25, 2001 *per* Haley J.
[55] *Ibid.*, at paras. 18 and 19.

Under the statute the Public Guardian and Trustee is given notice of charitable bequests or donations of property, of passing of accounts affecting charitable property, of applications for probate and of actions to set aside a will. *The Crown, however, has no supervisory capacity per se.* The jurisdiction resides in the court to order the PGT to carry out investigations and to make reports to the court upon which the court may order a passing of accounts or make such other order as it may decide. The court's inherent jurisdiction is confirmed in section 11(2) of the Courts of Justice Act, R.S.O. 1990, chap. C.43. [Emphasis added].[56]

The Court was clearly laying out its jurisdiction - one that exists in part because of the absence of any other supervisory or regulatory authority. He continues with a review of the "corporate versus trustee" issue for charitable corporations, concluding that:

> Since the charitable corporation is not a "trustee" in the true sense it must be considered at the very least a "fiduciary". The beneficiaries of the AIDS Society in the sense of trust law would be the children for whom the hospice is to be built. However, there is also a relationship between the Society and the public from which it seeks and obtains funds for its charitable purpose. ....
>
> It is in this sense that the court in its inherent jurisdiction and within the framework of the Charities Accounting Act has required a charitable corporation to act in accordance with its charitable purposes and to intervene if charitable funds are misapplied. ... There is an implicit acknowledgement that the fiduciary owes a duty to the public in general which supports the privileges extended to charitable corporations and to the public in particular which turns over its money to the charitable corporation for the charitable purposes it wishes to support.
>
> In this case the court has exercised its inherent jurisdiction and the specific provisions under the Charities Accounting Act to require the Society to pass its accounts and for that purposes has called in the Public Guardian and Trustee to represent the public interest.[57]

At first blush, this case seems to be one of a number of cases that have involved the exercise of the inherent jurisdiction of the court as massaged by the *Charities Accounting Act*. Arguably, the case goes beyond this approach. It seems to be articulating a robust role for the courts, at least in Ontario, in which the machinery of government (Public Guardian and Trustee) is available to it to protect the charitable funds and to ensure the protection of the public interest — both that of donors and the beneficiaries. Given the costs of litigation, its limitations and the confu-

---

[56] *Ibid.*, at para. 20.
[57] *Ibid.*, at paras. 25 and 26.

sion entailed in the concept of a "charitable corporation", it is arguable that this approach is not the most efficient and appropriate one for the supervision of charitable organizations (including charitable corporations). However, the failure of provincial governments throughout Canada to develop a more appropriate policy response to the issues leaves the matter within the inherent jurisdiction of the superior courts — as supplemented or reinforced by statutory powers. In the absence of any such response, the Court is clear:

> This Court does have the inherent jurisdiction to direct and control the administration of charities. Such power ought to be exercised where charitable trusts are not being properly administered, where funds are being mismanaged or where the trustees of the funds are breaching their fiduciary obligations.[58]

A judge of the Ontario Superior Court of Justice has a number of statutory powers that may be used in the supervision of a charitable organization. These powers include the following:

- to make any order or determination necessary to carry out the *Charitable Gifts Act*;[59]
- to extend the period that a charitable organization may hold more than 10% of an unrelated business;[60]
- to determine the annual profit of a business if the charitable organization and the Public Guardian and Trustee cannot agree;[61]
- to establish the terms of a sale of a charitable organization's interest in a business when made to a non-arm's length purchaser;[62]
- to direct a trustee to comply with the *Charities Accounting Act*; to remove a trustee and appoint another person to act in his or her stead; to direct a trustee to pay any funds in his or her hands into court; to give direction about the future use of a charitable organization's property; or to impose a penalty of a fine or imprisonment;[63]
- to order the Public Guardian and Trustee to investigate any charitable organization's solicitations, on application of any person;[64]

---

[58] *Trow v. Toronto Humane Society*, [2001] O.J. 3640, September 10, 2001, Ontario Superior Court of Justice, at para. 21.
[59] R.S.O. 1990, c. C.8, s. 8
[60] *Ibid.*, subs. 3(3).
[61] *Ibid.*, subs. 4(5).
[62] *Ibid.*, s. 5.
[63] *Ibid.*, s. 5.
[64] *Ibid.*, s. 6.

- to order and to give directions to a charitable organization on the sale of land that is no longer required by the charitable organization and the use of the proceeds;[65]
- to order the appointment of a new trustee or trustees;[66]
- to vest any property in a charitable organization;[67]
- to provide an opinion, advice or direction to a trustee on any question respecting the management or administration of the trust property or assets;[68]
- to pass, examine and audit the accounts of a charitable organization;[69]
- to exercise the court's inherent jurisdiction with respect to charitable organizations and the law of charity.

The courts may also exercise powers under the incorporating statutes to resolve disputes or to make orders to comply with the incorporating legislation. Other laws of general application may also be enforced through the courts by civil suit or through a prosecution.

---

[65] *Trustee Act*, R.S.O. 1990, c. T.23, s. 15.
[66] *Ibid.*, s. 4.
[67] *Ibid.*, s. 14.
[68] *Ibid.*, s. 60.
[69] *Charities Accounting Act* R.S.O. 1990, c. C.8, s. 23 and s. 3.

CHAPTER 10

Fundraising

A   INTRODUCTION

Fundraising is a critical activity for most charities and not-for-profit organizations. Without funds, these organizations could not carry out their activities. Without fundraising, Canadian society, and others throughout the world would not obtain the benefits from a vibrant charitable and not-for-profit sector — a sector that operates in most areas of our lives.

Fundraising, though, does not occur in a vacuum. The charitable and not-for-profit sector is part of Canadian society and operates within its legal, political and social structure. Canadians have certain expectations of charities and not-for-profit organizations. These expectations may not be clearly articulated, but they are readily apparent to most — especially when something goes wrong. When a charitable or not-for-profit organization falls short of the expectations, it becomes readily apparent.

It is necessary for the charitable or not-for-profit organization to carry out its activities and to fulfill its objects. It is not, however, the reason why most organizations were created. Officers and directors need to ensure that an appropriate balance is achieved in the organization's priorities. While it needs to raise the funds necessary to deliver its goods and services, a charitable or not-for-profit organization cannot devote or use its resources such that the organization's purpose becomes solely or primarily to raise funds.

There is no clear, unequivocal point at which this event may occur. In some cases, when the organization is undergoing severe financial constraints, the officers and directors may, by necessity, focus on fundraising. Arguably the officers and directors would be negligent if they did not do so in certain circumstances. There are also some organizations whose essential purpose is to raise funds for other organizations. Hospital foundations, for example, fall into this category of organizations. But even with these types of organizations, there is a fundamental rationale for their existence — to raise funds not for the sake of raising funds but to provide funding for hospitals to carry out their charitable activities.

Accountability is another key factor in the development and maintenance of a strong, positive reputation in the community. There are three elements of accountability. The first is relatively well-known and involves traditional financial accountability. Organizations must be able to "account" for the funds through the establishment of proper accounting books and records, financial statements (audited or unaudited depending on the circumstances) and operating in accordance with generally accepted accounting principles. Organizations and their officers and directors are also legally accountable to the organization's membership for their management of the affairs of the organization.

There is a third and increasingly important form of accountability. Charitable and not-for-profit organizations must be accountable to the public and their communities for how funds are raised, the use of those funds and their priorities. This form of accountability reflects society's more sophisticated and developing understanding of the role of charitable and not-for-profit organizations in Canadian society. It also recognizes that society has high expectations of these organizations, expectations that must not only be met but be shown to have been met.

Society may hold charitable and not-for-profit organizations accountable for fundraising activities and use of funds in a number of forums. In some cases, there are formal, institutional structures that have been put into place by legislation or by the common law. The Ontario Public Guardian and Trustee, for example, has a statutory role under the *Charities Accounting Act*[1] and the *Charitable Gifts Act*.[2] The superior courts in the provinces have a common law role to play in the supervision of charities, which is sometimes supplemented by legislation. Similarly, the Canada Customs and Revenue Agency plays an essential role with respect to taxation and the exemption from taxation of certain types of fundraising under the *Income Tax Act*[3] and the *Excise Tax Act*.[4]

Charitable and not-for-profit organizations are also held accountable in the court of public opinion. The community will assess organizations against their expectations. It is critical, therefore, for organizations to account to the public for their use of the funds, ensuring to the extent possible that the funds were raised through appropriate methods and that they are expended on appropriate activities.

There are a wide variety of fundraising activities available to organizations. An organization needs to identify those that are acceptable to it, its supporters and, in context of its activities and reputation, the community in which it operates. Fundraising by door-to-door solicitations is a traditional form of fundraising in Canada. This type of fundraising is, however, under pressure given public concerns with safety. Using children, therefore, to go door-to-door in the evening may be considered a questionable method to raise funds. More recent forms of fundraising, such as charitable gaming, may be appropriate for some charities, but for others it raises serious moral and ethical issues.

---

[1] R.S.O. 1990, c. C.10, as amended.
[2] R.S.O. 1990, c. C.8.
[3] R.S.C. 1985, c. I (5th Supp.).
[4] R.S.C. 1985, c. E-15, as am. S.C. 1990, c. 45.

Society has also begun to identify new concerns and issues. For example, many donors have become concerned about the use of their personal information. They want to protect their privacy. Activities, such as sharing or renting lists of names, that were common and acceptable at one time are now being re-examined and are no longer as accepted. Intellectual property has also become an issue — both in the use of the intellectual property of others by charitable or not-for-profit organizations and the protection of the organization's intellectual property. Society places greater emphasis on the value of intellectual property now than it did only a few years ago.

Efficiency is another topic that has become prominent in recent years. The community expects charitable and not-for-profit organizations to be efficient in their fundraising and in their use of funds. While few, if any, expect the organizations to be ruthlessly efficient and business-like, organizations that have inexplicably high "administrative costs" are not viewed with favour. Donors are also more inclined to make larger donations if they are satisfied that the donation will meet the needs of more than just one charity or not-for-profit organization. It is more efficient to build one theatre that meets the needs of most of the community's performing arts groups than to build a theatre for each group.

A charitable or not-for-profit organization exists to carry out its objects. It can do so, though, only through humans. An organization, whether incorporated or unincorporated, may have an existence in law but it is an artificial entity — it exists because its members established it and the law recognizes that it exists. In the case of a corporation, the law recognizes a broader existence than it does for unincorporated organizations. Nevertheless, in both cases, the organization has a purpose and that purpose is achieved through the actions of its officers, directors, members, employees, volunteers and agents.

The officers and directors provide the organization with its overall direction. In law, they are accountable for the actions (and failures to act) of the organization. The level of accountability and the extent to which any individual officer or director will be liable will depend upon the facts and the law of each case. These types of assessments by the courts and by regulators are not done in isolation. It is essential for each officer and director to be diligent in carrying out their own respective functions to ensure that they can demonstrate that they did their jobs, that they are accountable and that they did what they ought to have done in the circumstances.

This level of due diligence is particularly important when an organization is raising funds for its activities. Asking the public for money moves a charitable or not-for-profit organization into another level of accountability. If an organization can fund its activities solely through membership fees or other similar assessments from within, the courts and regulators do not usually interfere. There are, of course, exceptions where fraud or other criminal activities may occur, or where the transactions or activities have tax implications. But the overview by the courts or by a regulator, such as the Public Guardian and Trustee in Ontario, or by another government body, such as the Canada Customs and Revenue Agency, will be minimal.

Once an organization goes outside to seek monies from others, the donors also expect accountability. They expect that any solicitation will comply with the law and that the funds will be used for the purposes for which the donation was made. They expect that the organization will have in place the appropriate accounting and financial records and systems to protect their contributions. They expect that the information provided to them is accurate. They also expect that their dealings with the organization will be open and honest and that any privacy concerns are respected. They will look to the officers and directors of the organization to ensure that these expectations are met.

B ROLE OF DIRECTORS

The directors must meet the expectations of the members of the organization, the courts and regulators, and donors in any fundraising activities. In order to do so, these individuals must have a solid understanding of the organization and the "rules" of fundraising. These rules are both legal in nature but also practical.

The courts look to the directors for accountability even in situations in which the fundraising has been contracted out. This point was clearly illustrated in *Ontario (Public Guardian and Trustee) v. AIDS Society for Children (Ontario)*:[5]

> The position of the directors of the Society is equally clear. The directors stand in a fiduciary relationship to the Society and are therefore required to act in such a way as to support and further the objects of the Society as a charitable institution. The directors through the corporate structure control the acts of the Society. Do they also stand in a fiduciary relationship to the public and can therefore be said to have a fiduciary duty of care to the public in the same manner as the Society?

Justice Haley quotes from the oft-quoted reasons of Danckwerts J. In *Re The French Protestant Hospital*,[6] noting that "the corporation is completely controlled under the provisions of the charter by the governor, deputy governor and directors, and that those are the persons who in fact control the corporation and decide what shall be done. It is plain that those persons are as much in a fiduciary position as trustees in regard to any acts which are done respecting the corporation and its property ... Therefore it seems to me plain that they are, to all intents and

---

[5] [2001] O.J. 2170, May 25, 2001, Ontario Superior Court of Justice, at paras. 29 to 32.
[6] [1951] 1 Ch. 567, at 570.

purposes, bound by the rules which affect trustees". Haley J. continues with respect to the AIDS Society situation:

> On this basis the directors of the Society stand in the same relationship to the public as does the Society. It is a fiduciary relationship. There is no suggestion on the facts in this case that the agreements made by the directors for the Society with the fund-raising agencies were not at arm's length. The effect of entering into those agreements is still to be determined either in this judgment or on the passing of accounts. However, it must be kept in mind that a fiduciary relationship may have been breached whether or not a loss occurs. In Hamilton v. Wrights (1842), 9 Cl&F. 111. Lord Brougham said at p. 123:
>
>> There cannot be a greater mistake than to suppose ... that a trustee is only prevented from doing things which bring an actual loss upon the estate under his administration. It is quite enough that the thing which he does has a tendency to injure the trust; a tendency to interfere with his duty.
>
> Therefore the answer to Question 1: is the Society and/or its directors responsible as fiduciaries to the public for all the funds collected from the public including the gross amount of funds received by The Brown Baker and the Canadian Programs and Promotions Inc.? is Yes.

This case is an important one in the areas of fundraising. It articulates a very strong view — one that probably ought not to be surprising — that the funds solicited from the public for charitable purposes are "trust funds". As a result, the organization and the directors have fiduciary responsibilities for those funds. Where this case may have expanded the relationship — including that of the directors — is consideration that the fiduciary responsibilities appear to extend (i) to the public in general, and not just to the beneficiaries of the charitable trust, and (ii) to all of the funds solicited, including any funds retained by a third party fundraiser. Directors need to understand the rules of fundraising, both to do their job and to protect themselves.

The first practical rule of fundraising is to "know your organization". The officers and directors of a charitable or not-for-profit organization cannot make prudent and reasoned decisions about fundraising unless they understand the purposes of the organization, its financial position, its human resources (both employees and volunteers), its charitable activities, its strategic plan, its needs, its opportunities and its strengths and weaknesses. Fundraising is not an isolated activity; it should fit into the overall objectives of the organization and lead to improved effectiveness. The fundraising activities themselves need to be cost effective, which will often depend upon the resources that are available to the organization and its context. Fundraising should also increase public awareness of the organization and its objects and activities, and support or enhance its reputation.

Directors have a legal responsibility with respect to fundraising. Directors have a fiduciary duty to the organization. In addition, for charitable organizations, the directors have a duty that is akin to being a trustee. The general duties of directors have been summarized by the Public Guardian and Trustee in Ontario as follows:

> Directors and trustees must handle the charity's property with the care, skill, and diligence that a prudent person would use. They must treat the charity's property the way a careful person would treat their own property. They must always protect the charity's property from undue risk of loss and must ensure that no excessive administrative expenses are incurred.[7]

Although not explicitly stated, the reputation of an organization — charitable or not-for-profit — is also one of its "assets". Fundraising practices that damage the reputation of an organization will likely reduce public support for the organization and ultimately the resources available to it to carry out its objects. Fundraising practices that result in high costs, such as percentage-based commissions, may cause a charitable organization to have excessive administrative expenses. An organization that undertakes a poorly designed fundraising campaign will probably have poor results and may incur losses. Inadequate monitoring of the campaign by the board of directors may result in poor returns or even losses. In a worse case situation, improper fundraising activities may lead to investigations under the *Charities Accounting Act*[8] or other legislation.

The second practical rule, therefore, is that directors must be involved in the fundraising campaign. This involvement includes:

- the identification of specific needs for and uses of the funds that are raised,
- the fundraising goal,
- the options that will be considered,
- the development of the campaign, including objectives, budget, types of activities and resources needed. The campaign needs to be relevant to the specific organization. It should not simply adopt campaigns or activities used by others, which do not necessarily reflect the needs or resources of the organization or its legal authority and mandate,
- the establishment of fundraising policies, including the adoption of ethical standards,

---

[7] *Charities Bulletin No. 3 — Duties, Responsibilities, Powers of Directors and Trustees of Charities*, (Toronto: Office of the Public Guardian and Trustee of Ontario, July, 1999).
[8] R.S.O. 1990, c. C-10.

- the decision to use (or not to use) professional fundraisers (either employees or consultants) and the selection of the professional fundraiser,
- approval of the detailed campaign,
- assisting in the fundraising campaign, including making donations and providing services,
- ongoing monitoring of the campaign and approval of adjustments where necessary,
- ensuring that the appropriate books and records are maintained,
- ensuring that the campaign is carried out in accordance with the law and ethical standards and making corrections where necessary to do so,
- carrying out a "post-mortem" and identifying strengths, weaknesses, and opportunities for future campaigns. Each campaign or activity should be reviewed to ensure it met the objectives, was consistent with the established policies and enhanced the organization.

Part of any fundraising campaign development should be a legal review.[9] The review is an assessment of the legal risk associated with a fundraising activity or campaign. It should include both legal and accounting issues. The directors should receive the results of the legal review and consider it as part of the board's decision to approve the campaign or activity.

The review should include an analysis of the organization's documents. For example, some letters patent for Ontario corporations without share capital include provisions that effectively prohibit the corporation from participating in charitable gaming. If so, any decision to do so would be *ultra vires* and the directors could be held personally liable. Prior to that organization participating in charitable gaming, amendments to its letters patent would be necessary, which must be approved by the members at a meeting called for that purpose. If the fundraising includes the carrying on of a business activity, the directors must be satisfied that the business activity falls within the objects of the organization and, if a charitable organization, that it does not contravene any restrictions on charities carrying on business.

Any legal review should look both at the objects and powers of the corporation, but also at the by-laws and any relevant resolutions of the board or members. Of course, the review should also identify any legal restrictions, prohibitions or requirements for the fundraising activity. For example, an organization requires a licence to conduct and manage a

---

[9] See, for a discussion of the need for a legal review aimed at lawyers, T.S. Carter, *Looking a Gift Horse in the Mouth — Avoiding Liability in Charitable Fundraising*, Law Society of Upper Canada, Second Annual Estates and Trust Forum, November 24, 1999.

lottery; any sale of food products must comply with health protection legislation; or municipal by-laws may require that the organization obtain a permit to occupy public property for an event.

The legal review should also set out any risk management steps that ought to be taken by the directors with regard to the contemplated fundraising. For instance, these steps may include obtaining liability insurance for the organization, or — where permitted by legislation — for the organization's directors and officers. Specific measures to ensure adequate oversight of the fundraising effort may also be recommended.

Mistakes will be made; the board's role is to minimize the chance of mistakes by careful and prudent planning and monitoring and by identifying those mistakes, correcting them and avoiding them in future campaigns. Nobody expects perfection; but it is essential that the directors, as individuals and collectively as a board, be able to demonstrate that the fundraising was carried out with integrity, in an efficient and effective manner, responsibly and in accordance with the law and ethical standards. Ultimately, the directors must show that the fundraising has enhanced the financial position of the organization, enabled it to carry out its objects and supported or improved its reputation.

C   ETHICAL STANDARDS

I   BACKGROUND

The "legal" rules of fundraising are not necessarily the same as the "ethical" rules. As in other aspects of life, what a person can do legally is not always the same as what that person ought to do. Ethical behaviour is an increasingly important component of the rules for charitable and not-for-profit organizations. Ethical standards are developing in response to the demand for greater accountability and openness in fundraising. While there is no overall consensus on what is ethically permitted and what is not for all situations, there are some general statements about ethical behaviour for which there is a consensus.

The Ontario Law Reform Commission examined the charitable and not-for-profit sector and in 1996 issued its *Report on the Law of Charities*.[10] The Commission examined fundraising as part of its review and made a number of recommendations. For example, it recommended that a new law be enacted to police not-for-profit fundraising.[11] The *Report* also recommended that charitable gift annuities be regulated and that investments in active businesses which are unrelated to and are not ancillary or incidental to a not-for-profit purpose be prohibited. It did suggest that

---

[10]   (Toronto: Queen's Printer, 1996).
[11]   Fundraising is discussed in Chapter 18 ("Specific Areas of Regulatory Concern: Fundraising, Investments, Political Activity, and Privileges") and the recommendations with respect to fundraising are summarized at 636 of the *Report*.

these activities could be carried on by a separate, taxable corporate entity.[12]

The OLRC Report generated substantial discussion in the sector. The Report, together with other factors, resulted in several major charities establishing the Panel on Accountability and Governance in the Voluntary Sector in 1997. The Panel issued its final report, *Building on Strength: Improving Governance and Accountability in Canada's Voluntary Sector*[13] in 1999. It commented that fundraising is "under enormous public scrutiny". It noted that the "solicitation of funds is the only contact that many people have with voluntary organizations and their impression of the sector is shaped by this".[14]

The Panel concluded in its report that accountability, in general, required at minimum the following:

- establishing an appropriate mission and/or policy priorities and ensuring their relevance,
- sound management of funds received from donors and governments and of expenditures,
- effective organizational governance (including structures and processes for managing human resources), and
- the outcomes, quality and range of their programs and services.[15]

The Final Report is lengthy and covers a wide range of topics and issues. The work started by the Panel was continued by a Government of Canada/Voluntary Sector Joint Initiative.[16]

Given the importance of fundraising, the Panel specifically addresses this topic in some detail. It notes that fundraising is necessary for organizations to have the monies to carry out their objects. It also comments on some of the other less obvious goals of fundraising. It is an opportunity to engage people in their work and for individuals to facilitate the voluntary work of others. It provides, therefore, an opportunity for people to make a contribution to others, to issues or to programs that are important to that individual. The Panel comments that "philanthropy is

---

[12] *Ibid.*, at 636.
[13] The Panel was established by the Voluntary Sector Roundtable and was chaired by the Hon. Ed Broadbent. The Panel issued a Discussion Paper, *Helping Canadians Help Canadians: Improving Governance and Accountability in the Voluntary Sector* in May 1998. It held a number of public forums to discuss the issues and received submissions from many organizations. The Final Report was also influential in leading the Government of Canada to initiate its own process for addressing the needs of the voluntary sector.
[14] *Building on Strength*, at 33.
[15] *Ibid.*, at 15.
[16] See *Working Together: A Government of Canada/Voluntary Sector Joint Initiative*, Report of the Joint Tables, August 1999.

about more than collecting dollars; it is also about building communities of interest and support".[17]

These multiple objectives of fundraising are consistent with how properly developed and organized fundraising campaigns operate. They also raise the stakes for accountability and the need to be accountable to the community. A fundraising campaign can be and ought to be more than just raising money. Ethical fundraising, therefore, becomes that much more important to the success of any campaign and to the long-term success of the organization. A campaign that is perceived to be "unethical", albeit legal, will damage not only the specific campaign but also the organization itself and possibly other related or even unrelated campaigns and organizations.

The Panel identified three primary issues of accountability for fundraising. These are:

- promoting ethical fundraising by voluntary organizations,
- promoting ethical conduct by for-profit fundraisers, and
- educating the donor.[18]

It recognized two ways to encourage ethical fundraising — government regulation and self-regulation. These two ways are not mutually-exclusive, but rather are part of any mature industry in a modern society. Reliance solely on government regulation is not sufficient; directors and senior management must ensure that their organization's fundraising is not only in compliance with the law set out in government regulation. They must also participate in self-regulation. Self-regulation can occur through participation in umbrella organizations, such as the Canadian Centre for Philanthropy and complying with the "rules" established by those organizations.

Furthermore, each organization needs to self-regulate itself by establishing its own policies. These policies could build on the ethical standards that have been adopted but reflect the unique context or characteristics of the organization. For example, some organizations for religious, ethical or cultural reasons object to charitable gaming. The organization may decide not only to not participate in charitable gaming but also to refuse funds that were earned through charitable gaming. The board of directors and the organization's officers are responsible for ensuring compliance and addressing the concerns of their members and the community.

The Panel on Accountability and Governance strongly encouraged boards of directors to adopt a code for ethical fundraising and financial

---

[17] *Building on Strength.*, at 32-33. See also L. Eagen, *Overview of Fundraising Management*, 2nd ed. (Toronto: National Program in Fundraising Management Delivery Consortium, 1999) at 1-12 to 1-13.
[18] *Building on Strength*, at 33.

accountability. It commented favourably upon the code developed by the Canadian Centre for Philanthropy, which is reviewed below. There are other codes that have been developed by other organizations, some of which are also discussed below. The Panel noted that boards ought to formally adopt a code of ethical fundraising that addresses the following elements:

- respect donors' rights to disclosure of truthful information and their rights to privacy,
- investigate complaints promptly and fairly, and report results of the investigation to the complainant,
- responsibly manage funds entrusted by donors, and
- report their financial affairs accurately and completely.[19]

There are differences among the various codes of ethical fundraising. The Panel identified two significant differences that distinguish the Canadian Centre for Philanthropy's code from some of the others. The CCP code prohibits two practices that a number of charities employ:

- retaining a fundraising company and paying that company a percentage of the donations or sponsorships. This approach to fundraising is often used by smaller charitable or not-for-profit organizations. Too often, the bulk of the monies raised end up with the company and not with the organization. Organizations are tempted by this approach for many wrong reasons. For example, the organization is often guaranteed a specific amount for which it is not expected to do much. It does not need to find volunteers to do the mailings or telephoning, the company will do it; it does not need to handle the cash, the company will do it; it does not need to do the books of account, the company will do it. Of course, if the for-profit corporation carries out these functions, the organization will usually have no control over the activities of the company or over the funds. It will be held accountable legally and in the public's mind for the actions of the professional fundraiser, but would not be in a position to ensure compliance with the law or with ethical standards and the legitimate expectations of its members, the public, donors and the courts and regulators;
- selling of donor lists. The public is increasingly concerned about privacy. The selling of donor lists is perceived to be unethical by many donors. The selling of donor lists to businesses is particularly difficult for the public to accept. Donors may begrudgingly

---

[19] *Ibid.*, at 36.

accept mail soliciting donations from another charity, but advertising from a business using a mailing list sold to it is another matter. On the other hand, cooperation among organizations is often desirable and cross-usage of donor lists will sometimes assist. Modern technology does permit both privacy and cooperation, without the selling of donor lists. Furthermore, donor lists have been developed by the organization and are an asset of the organization. The selling of the donor lists may be seen as an imprudent action by the directors.

The Panel also discusses ethical conduct by commercial fundraisers. Professional fundraising is part of many campaigns and legitimately so. Professionals bring an expertise that is important and may assist in keeping costs of fundraising down and increase the level of donations. They will also help the organization to meet all of the objectives of fundraising, including making the connections among people and developing the organization's reputation and public awareness.

The decision to use a professional fundraiser and the choice of professional are important and ought to be made by the board of directors. In some cases, the decision and choice may be constrained by law. For example, in charitable gaming in Ontario, any professional would need to be registered as a gaming supplier under the *Gaming Control Act*.[20]

The Panel focussed on professional fundraisers who operate as a business. These for-profit businesses develop and manage a campaign. The Panel recommended that these types of commercial fundraisers be licensed and bonded if they collect more than $25,000 in revenues. This recommendation was based on the Alberta legislation, which is discussed in more detail below.[21] It also recommended that commercial fundraisers comply with a professional code of conduct.

The Canadian Centre for Philanthropy's *Code* covers fundraising in a comprehensive manner. It is divided into three main sections — Donors' Rights, Fundraising Practices and Financial Accountability — and sets out specific requirements for an organization to meet. The Canadian Centre for Philanthropy lists those charities that have adopted and have agreed to comply with the *Code*. In order to be included on the list, a charity's governing board must pass a resolution adopting the *Code* and committing itself to adherence to it.

The adoption of the Centre's or a similar code should not be seen as the end of the board's activities. The *Code* is an important contribution to ethical fundraising. Its effectiveness, though, is dependent upon boards ensuring compliance with it. The boards should also build on the *Code*

---

[20] S.O. 1992, c. 25, as amended.
[21] *Charitable Fund-Raising Act*, S.A. 1995, c. C-4.5, as amended. See also the Manitoba *Charities Endorsement Act*, C.S.M.

with fundraising and accountability policies that reflect their organizations' context, history and resources.[22]

D   DEVELOPING THE STRATEGY

I   INTRODUCTION

The development of a campaign strategy is a responsibility of the board of directors and an organization's management.[23] There are a number of resources available to assist the board and its management to do so and this chapter is not intended to replace these resources. Rather, the intention is to highlight in a general manner what ought to be in a campaign strategy and the steps that are usually taken to develop it. The details of the strategy will, of course, be dependent upon the nature and context of the organization and the community in which it operates.

II   TYPES OF FUNDRAISING ACTIVITIES

Fundraising is evolving and, to be successful, must always take into account the context in which campaigns and activities occur. Having said that, there are only a few major types of fundraising activities. Success or failure will depend upon selecting the correct type of activity that is appropriate to the organization, the purpose for the fundraising and the prospective donors or sponsors.

The following are the key fundraising activities:[24]

- Grants — the grants may be received from governments, corporations or foundations. Grants usually are made for specific purposes or projects, such as a building or to fund certain activities. As a result, grants will come with conditions, some of which may restrict the use of the funds. If so, accounting systems must be in place to ensure that any restricted funds are dealt with in accordance with the conditions. Restricted fund accounting is discussed in Chapter 5. Granting bodies will also sometimes require that the recipient sign an agreement, which may include repayment provisions or staged funding as a project proceeds.

---

[22] The Canadian Centre for Philanthropy has published *Interpretation Guide: The Ethical Fundraising & Financial Accountability Code* to assist organizations to understand and comply with the *Code*. It, along with other resource materials, are available at the CCP's website — www.ccp.ca.
[23] Eagen, *Overview of Fundraising Management*, at 4-4 to 4-6.
[24] L.V. King and K. Shipley, *Fundraising Approaches I*, 2nd ed. (Toronto: National Program in Fundraising Management Delivery Consortium, 1999), at 1-31 to 1-44.

- Personal Solicitation — personal solicitation is usually done one-on-one, with a board member or volunteer asking peers for a donation. This type of campaign is very labour intensive and the volunteers need to be well-trained and knowledgeable about the organization and the use of the funds. There is some risk with this type of activity because of the potential for misunderstanding or agreements between the donor and the volunteer which would not be acceptable to the organization or the board. This risk is reduced with training and ensuring that the volunteers keep to the script and refer any questions for which they do not know the answer to appropriate staff. For example, a volunteer should not be responding to questions about tax implications of a donation, other than providing basic information. In addition, volunteers must respect the donor's "rights" under the *Ethical Fundraising & Accountability Code*.
- Door-to-Door Canvassing — door-to-door canvassing has been a very popular form of fundraising in Canada, especially for larger organizations in healthcare and research, or for local schools and similar organizations. It is labour intensive and there are some risks arising from individuals walking door-to-door in neighbourhoods. It is important to ensure that the canvassers are not put into dangerous situations and that they are trained in how to deal with the public. Certainly, children and youth should be accompanied by an adult when canvassing. Given the nature of the one-on-one nature, organizations must also ensure that the materials are accurate and that the canvassers are properly trained, stick to the script and do not provide advice to the prospective donor. If the prospective donor requires further information, he or she should be referred to a responsible person within the organizations.
- Direct Mail — mailings to prospective donors, usually from a mailing list that has been developed by the organization or rented or exchanged for the specific purpose can be a good method to raise funds and develop public awareness. As discussed earlier, selling donor lists is not considered to be an ethical practice. Direct mail campaigns can be very sophisticated targeting recipients to be effective. These campaigns can be expensive and in some cases are used to build a donor list; the second mailing is when the organization will see a return on the investment.
- Telemarketing — telemarketing can be an effective method to raise funds, but problems with telemarketing have raised issues for both governments and for organizations. Done correctly, it is labour intensive and requires significant support. As with direct

mail, it is sometimes used to develop a donor list for future use. The *Competition Act* and the Alberta *Charitable Fund-Raising Act* apply to telemarketing and are both discussed below.
- Advertising — public or targeted advertising can be successful to increase awareness and to encourage donations. However, it can be expensive to develop appropriate advertising and there are regulatory requirements for broadcast media.
- Sale of Goods or Services — organizations can raise substantial funds from the sale of goods or services to members or to the public. In some cases, sales are a natural part of the charitable activities of an organization, i.e., rental of rooms in a charitable nursing home or sale of tickets by a charitable theatre group. The sales of goods and services though gives rise to the potential for liability, especially in those situations in which the goods or services may cause injury. There may also be legal requirements with respect to the sales. For example, the sale of liquor requires a licence or special occasion permit. Any sale of food must comply with the provincial health requirements. If the organization is a registered charity, it must also ensure that if the sales are considered to be a business activity that it is related to its charitable objects.
- Special Events — there are a wide variety of special events, including dinners, auctions, various "a-thons" and so forth. They provide entertainment to prospective donors or encourage volunteers and prospective donors to engage in activities. Special events may involve considerable risk, especially where liquor or physical activity are involved.
- Corporate Sponsorships — sponsorships are different from donations in that there is a benefit flowing to the sponsor from the sponsorship. Sponsorships are often part of a corporation's advertising or public relations budget. The sponsorship may be for an event or an activity or for such things as a newsletter. In some campaigns, organizations may combine sponsorships of special events and of the campaign brochure with personal solicitation. Alternatively, a corporation could sponsor the production of the fundraising brochure that is used for personal solicitation or for direct mail. Since a business derives a benefit from a sponsorship, a charitable tax receipt should not be issued for such contributions. The business may, however, be able to write off the contribution as an operating expense.
- Planned Giving — planned gifts involve a number of mechanisms that are used to "plan" the donation, such as insurance policies, wills and trust agreements, in which the organization is the bene-

ficiary. In many cases, the organization will benefit on the death of the individual or on some specific event triggering the gift being realized.
- Charitable Gaming — charitable gaming can be very lucrative for organizations but there are legal and financial risks. In addition, charitable gaming is not acceptable to all volunteers or prospective donors for moral or religious reasons.

The type of campaign will often depend upon the underlying reason for raising funds. Typically, funds will be raised for one or more of the following four reasons:[25]

- operating expenses and to support existing programs and activities,
- projects which have specific budgets and anticipated results,
- capital purchases. Typically, capital campaigns are the "bricks and mortar" campaigns to build new or renovated buildings. However capital assets also include such items as information technology,
- endowment funds, which are intended to provide stable ongoing funding for an organization for its operating expenses.

Different types of fundraising campaigns are more appropriate for the different uses of the funds. The board ought to consider the use of funds in assessing what type of campaign and fundraising activities to use.

III Professional Fundraisers

(1) Deciding to Use and Selecting a Professional

The decision to use professional fundraisers is one that ought to be made by the board of directors. It may act on the advice of the organization's senior management, if any, but it is a decision that the board should take. There are several good reasons to retain professional fundraisers either on staff or as independent contractors. There are also poor reasons to do so. The better reasons focus on the obtaining of skills, expertise and knowledge that are not otherwise available to the organization and on the transfer of those skills, expertise and knowledge to the organization over time.[26]

A good fundraiser will also inform the board about the risks involved, the chances of success and, importantly, the likelihood of failure. No fundraising campaign is without risk — financial, legal or to the organi-

---

[25] Eagen, *Overview of Fundraising Management*, at 3-2 to 3-3.
[26] K. Wyman, *Planning Successful Fund Raising Programs*, 2nd ed. (Toronto: The Canadian Centre for Philanthropy, 1991).

zation's reputation. The board needs to understand what those risks are and how to minimize them. If the expertise is not available within the organization to do so, a fundraising consultant can assist the board to understand and address these risks.

The board should consider using a professional fundraiser, either a consultant or an employee, where one or more of the following factors apply to the organization and its proposed campaign:

- the fundraising campaign or project is outside the organization's (board, volunteers and employees) experience or expertise,
- the campaign or project requires technical expertise or knowledge that is either not readily available or there is a need for additional assistance,
- an independent feasibility study is required to determine if the campaign or project will be successful and to provide advice on timing or changes to a proposed campaign or project,
- specific functions need to be done and a specialist is required or best able to carry out the functions. These functions may range from training to copyediting.[27]

There are essentially three types of fundraisers:

- professionals who provide advice on fundraising campaigns, activities, strategy and so forth. These professionals may also provide services with respect to the drafting of materials, placement of advertisements and other similar "backroom" activities,
- professionals who carry out fundraising activities, including those who solicit for funds and charitable gaming service suppliers,
- professionals who sell goods and services on a profit-sharing basis with an organization. In recent years, an increasing number of organizations have used events such as book sales which are operated by businesses and the businesses provide a share of the proceeds to the organizations.

Which type of fundraiser is selected will depend upon the needs of the organization and the legal context. In some cases, the use of professionals may be counterproductive. For example, professional canvassers may cause prospective donors to reconsider making a donation but they certainly have a right to know whether or not the individual canvassing is being paid to do so. However, in other circumstances, the professional may be regulated, as in charitable gaming, and it would be difficult if not

---

[27] Eagen, *Overview of Fundraising Management*, at 4-9.

impossible for regular fundraising activities to occur without them, such as for bingos.

There is a wide variety of fundraising consultants. The types of functions that a fundraiser will undertake may be narrow and technical or may involve very broad areas, including strategic planning. Some are operational in nature whereas others limit their activities to planning. Whatever the nature of a specific consultant's area of expertise and activity, the board must remain accountable and responsible for any campaign and for the actions of the fundraiser on behalf of the organization. A good consultant may help to assess the organization's strength and weaknesses, opportunities for fundraising or review a proposed fundraising campaign. They can also advise on whether or not the project will garner the type of support that is needed and, if not, what should be changed to improve the chances of success.

The major ethical codes established by both charities and by professional associations do not support commission-based remuneration. If the consultant proposes that it be paid on a commission basis, it may be time to eliminate that consultant from the list being considered. The major exception to this "rule" is in charitable gaming. The terms and conditions of licences assume that the gaming services supplier will be remunerated on the basis of the proceeds for bingo and break open tickets. In raffles, there appears to be more flexibility to use a fixed fee approach for the planning services related to larger raffles.

It is equally important to find the type of consultant that will be a good match for either the organization, the type of campaign that is being considered, or the types of fundraising activities that are being included in the campaign. The board should carry out at least some preliminary work to determine the type of consultant that is needed and canvass the sector for suggested consultants.

References from both successful and unsuccessful campaigns should be asked for and followed-up. Although it is rarer to receive references about unsuccessful campaigns, that information is also useful. Not every project is a success; it is important to understand why and to adapt in the future.

Organizations should be particularly concerned about fundraising businesses that share the proceeds with the organization. The organization needs to assure itself that the type of products being sold are consistent with the image that the organization wants to project. In addition, depending upon what the relationship is, the organization may be jeopardizing its charitable status if it is seen to be "in business" where that business is not related to the organization's charitable objects. In certain circumstances, the purchasers may believe that the organization is the vendor and may turn to that organization to remedy any problems with the goods or services. There is significant potential for liability for injuries or damages that the purchaser may suffer in those situations.

The board, in selecting a consultant should know how long the consultant has been in business and what its qualifications are. It is also important to know who will actually be working on the project and who will be responsible for the product. The board needs to be conscious of costs, including what the estimated fees will be and the basis for their calculation and an estimate for expenses that are to be reimbursed or paid directly by the organization. The board must know what the "budget" will be and how it was determined and who approves costs. Timelines are equally important; a project may be on budget but if it is too late to meet the timing for a campaign, it may be wasted effort and money. The board also needs to know about previous clients and projects, both for reference purposes and with respect to qualifications. One of those qualifications is why the consultant wants to work with that organization or on that type of campaign. The board must be able, at the end of the selection process, to justify its choice of one consultant over the others.

(2) Contracts with a Professional

Any relationship with a professional fundraiser should be documented by a contract in writing. If the fundraiser is an employee of the organization, the relationship should also be set out in the employment agreement and in the job description. The contract with the professional fundraiser who is not an employee should set out the following information:

- the roles and responsibilities of the consultant and of the organization,
- the services that are to be provided by the fundraiser and what assistance will be provided by the organization,
- the remuneration to be paid, the basis on which it is calculated and when it is to be paid,
- the delegations of authority and who will provide instructions to the consultant,
- that the fundraiser is not the organization's agent and that it must distinguish between it and the organization in all dealings with the public and with regulators,
- the ownership of intellectual property and, most importantly, of any donor lists that are developed and what uses may be made of those lists, trade-marks and copyright,
- what requires the board's approval. The board should retain substantial approval over the direction of the campaign and over public materials and any filings with regulators. The board needs to keep in mind at all times the reputation of the organization and the overall strategic plan for the organization in making any decisions,

- assurances that the work will be carried out to a high professional standard and in accordance with the relevant ethical codes and professional codes of conduct and all relevant laws,
- the fundraiser specifically agrees to comply with any codes of conduct and policies that the charity has adopted or developed and to carry out its duties in accordance with the laws of Canada and of any relevant province and municipality,
- the right of the organization to inspect the fundraiser's premises to verify the methods of solicitation and compliance with the codes of conduct and policies and to examine all relevant books and records, including financial records,
- budget for the work to be carried out by the consultant and what costs require board or other approval before those costs are incurred. It is important to keep in mind that expenses cannot be excessive,
- method to resolve any disputes,
- schedules for when work is to be started and completed, recognizing that flexibility is necessary in many campaigns or fundraising activities,
- conflict of interest provisions to ensure that any conflicts are identified early on and addressed,
- control over donations. There would be few situations — if any — in which any organization would agree to relinquish control over the funds that are received from any fundraising campaign. The organization must also retain full control over the issuance of any receipts for income tax purposes,
- termination of services. Sometimes, no matter how careful the planning has been, termination of the relationship will become desirable. If so, the organization needs to make sure that its interests are protected in any such termination prior to the completion of the contract. An organization would want to terminate the contract if, for example, the fundraiser uses any false or misleading solicitation practices.

The nature of the contract can become important. In certain circumstances, the contract may be void or voidable, notwithstanding the court's general reluctance to interfere with the freedom of the parties to contract.[28] Whether or not a contract is void or voidable will depend upon the facts, but it is certainly not an area into which most charitable organizations will want to step.

---

[28] *Ontario (Public Guardian and Trustee) v. AIDS Society for Children (Ontario)*, [2001] O.J. No. 2170, May 25, 2001.

IV STEPS IN A CAMPAIGN

Any fundraising campaign — whether it is for a specific project, annual or for planned giving — has a number of steps, some of which have already been discussed. The board of directors and management of the organization must be involved in all steps of the campaign.[29] In order to be involved, the directors need to understand what these steps typically include. The steps include the following:

- identifying why a campaign is needed, i.e., the purposes for which the funds will be used, to attract new members or volunteers, to build a donor base for future use, to increase public awareness of the organization or charitable purpose or issue;
- assessing fundraising strategies;
- determine whether or not the campaign is for operating, projects, capital, endowment purposes or a combination of these;
- preparing the draft case for support;
- identifying and rating prospective donors;
- feasibility review;
- campaign leadership;
- budget preparation;
- development of the action plan and who will do what, when and where;
- implementing the campaign, including the recruitment and training of volunteers, cultivating of the donors and prospective donors, securing the donation and following-up on prospective donors, donor appreciation, collecting donations and following-up on pledges, ongoing accounting, and reporting the results.

The final step of any fundraising campaign, successful or not, is the post-mortem review. The board must be able to determine what the effective methods are to raise funds. This assessments starts with the post-mortem review.

E   COMPLIANCE WITH THE LAW

I   BACKGROUND

In most provinces, there is no single statute that applies to organizations to regulate fundraising or to establish standards on how to raise funds.

---

[29] See for a more detailed description and discussion M.C. Stuart, *Strategic Management of Fundraising Campaigns*, 2nd ed. (Toronto: National Program in Fundraising Management Delivery Consortium, 1999), at 1-1 to 1-14.

The Alberta *Charitable Fund-Raising Act*[30] is the most comprehensive in Canada and Manitoba's *Charities Endorsement Act*[31] does apply to public fundraising activities for charitable purposes. Saskatchewan has also considered legislating in this area.[32] Generally, statutory provisions may apply or may not apply depending upon the facts of the situation, including the type of fundraising that is being carried out, the mechanism to do so (telephone versus personal solicitation), whether or not any "sale" is part of the fundraising activity, the timing of the transaction and whether or not the funds are being raised for charitable as opposed to not-for-profit purposes.

This section discusses a number of federal and provincial statutes that apply generally to fundraising activities. In other chapters, statutes that apply to specific types of transactions or forms of fundraising are discussed.

II COMPETITION ACT

The *Competition Act*[33] is federal legislation and applies throughout Canada. The purpose of the legislation is to maintain and encourage competition in Canada. As part of this purpose, the Act also makes certain practices illegal. The Act was enacted under the federal criminal law power and, as a result, offences are treated as being criminal in nature.

Due to the large number of complaints received both at the provincial and federal level, amendments[34] were enacted to make certain deceptive telemarketing practices and false and misleading representations illegal under the *Competition Act*. These amendments were proclaimed in force in early 1999.

The first amendment included "the raising of funds for charitable or other non-profit purposes" in the definition of "business" for purposes of the *Competition Act*. This definition brings under the Act organizations (both charitable and not-for-profit) and their officers, directors and agents, and any professional fundraisers acting on behalf of the organization. The definition of "telemarketing" in s. 52.1 includes interactive telephone communications for any business interest, which would include fundraising.

The Competition Bureau commented that the definition of "business" was changed to include fundraising for charitable and other not-for-profit purposes. It commented further that "this amendment clarifies that persons engaged in fundraising efforts will be covered by the de-

---

[30] S.A. 1995, c. C-4.5, as amended.
[31] R.S.M. 1987, c. C60.
[32] *Canadian Fund-Raiser*, November 21, 2000.
[33] R.S.C. 1985, c. C-34, as amended.
[34] S.C. 1999, c. 2, s. 12.

ceptive telemarketing and deceptive marketing practices provisions".[35] The provisions would apply not only to the organization but also those who act on its behalf.

The person who engages in telemarketing must disclose in a fair and reasonable manner at the start of the telephone communication the identity of the person on behalf of whom the communication is being made (i.e., the charitable or not-for-profit organization) and of the price of any product that is being promoted and any material restrictions, terms or conditions applicable to its delivery. Fundraising under the guise of carrying out market research or public opinion surveys (commonly known as "frugging"), when conducted by telephone, contravenes this provision and exposes an organization to criminal prosecution. If the corporation commits an offence, the officers and directors who were in a position to direct or influence the policies of the corporation are parties to and guilty of the offence. If the offence is committed by an employee or agent of the corporation, that is sufficient proof that it was committed by the corporation.

The amendments to the *Competition Act* also create an offence with respect to certain types of contests and lotteries or that purport to be a contest or lottery. The offence is in addition to any *Criminal Code* provisions with respect to the conduct or management of a lottery scheme. It is an offence to conduct or purport to conduct a contest, lottery or game of chance, skill or mixed chance and skill where:

- the delivery of a prize or other benefit is or is represented to be conditional on the prior payment of any amount by the participant, or
- adequate and fair disclosure is not made of the number and approximate value of the prizes, of the area or areas to which they relate and of any fact within the person's knowledge that effects materially the chance of winning.

Any promotional materials with respect to lotteries should, therefore, disclose the number and value of prizes and any available information that materially effects the chances of winning. Winners are to be chosen randomly or on the basis of skill.[36] Where the fundraising activity is a lottery scheme, these types of issues are also addressed in the terms and conditions issued with each licence to conduct and manage a lottery scheme.[37] Furthermore, promotional contests are also regulated under s. 74.06 of the *Competition Act*. It must also be complied with and is complementary to the specific provisions dealing with telemarketing of-

---

[35] *Improvements to the Competition Act — Deceptive Telemarketing*, Competition Bureau, March 18, 1999.
[36] Subsection 52.1(3).
[37] Charitable gaming and the terms and conditions to licences are discussed in Chapter 5.

fences. It also indirectly requires that the distribution of the prizes not be unduly delayed.[38] The Information Bulletin issued by the Competition Bureau with respect to promotional contests sets out what is considered to be adequate and fair disclosure.[39]

The Competition Bureau has commented that contests in which the prize is a percentage off the price of a product or is "free" if another product must be purchased will be considered to contain a condition of prior payment to receive the prize. The cost of a postage stamp necessary to mail an entry will not be considered a condition of prior payment, but long distance charges and 1-900 charges may be.[40]

It is also an offence for any person who engages in telemarketing to make a representation that is false or misleading in a material respect.[41] In a prosecution, the general impression conveyed by a representation shall be taken into account.[42] As a result, where the information contained in the materials is literally accurate but the overall impression misleads or is false, the organization can still be convicted.

There are two other offences dealing with the offering of products. A product cannot be offered at no cost or at below fair market value in consideration for the supply or use of another product unless fair, reasonable and timely disclosure is made of the fair market value. Similar disclosure must also be made of any restrictions, terms or conditions applicable to its supply to the purchaser.[43] Thus, an organization could not offer a product for free when its supply is tied to the purchase of another product without disclosing the fair market value of the first product. If there are any restrictions, terms or conditions, those must also be disclosed. It is also an offence to offer a product for sale at a price grossly in excess of its fair market value where delivery of the product is or is represented to be conditional on prior payment to the purchaser.[44]

These two offences are probably not relevant for most fundraising activities used by organizations. However, there may be circumstances in which an organization does sell, either as part of its carrying on business, or as part of a fundraising activity. The Competition Bureau's Information Bulletin sets out the Bureau's views with respect to pricing matters.[45] If the organization is otherwise carrying on business, it must, of course, comply with the *Competition Act* as would any other business operator. The issue may also arise if the organization has entered into an arrangement by which a business uses the organization's name to sell goods or services and shares the proceeds with the organization.

---

[38] Para. 74.06(1)(b).
[39] *Promotional Contest*, Information Bulletin, Competition Bureau, July 28, 1999.
[40] *Telemarketing*, Information Bulletin, Competition Bureau, September 22, 1999, at 5 to 6.
[41] Para. 52.1(3)(a).
[42] Subsection 52.1(4).
[43] Subsection 52.1(3)(c).
[44] Subsection 52.1(3)(d).
[45] *Supra*, note 40, at 5.

There are due diligence defences, but it is best to ensure that there is no need to refer to those defences much less to need to rely upon them. Organizations should, therefore, be very cautious in using telemarketing for fundraising purposes (either for donations or for the sale of goods or services) and ensure that the information provided is complete and accurate. Furthermore, it is essential that the organization have in place, monitor and ensure compliance with policies and practices with respect to accuracy of information and the timely disclosure of information about the identity of the organization. In addition, it is important that those engaged in the telemarketing have a script from which they work and do not deviate and, of course, that that script does not mislead or deceive. The organization must be able to demonstrate that it has done so and has corrected any problems in a timely manner and each officer and director that they have carried out their duties in that regard.

Section 52 establishes another offence. It is an offence for a person "for the purpose of promoting, directly or indirectly, the supply or use of a product or for the purpose of promoting, directly or indirectly, any business interest, by any means whatsoever, knowingly or recklessly make a representation to the public that is false or misleading in a material respect. A representation is deemed to have been made to the public if it is made, for example, in the course of door-to-door or telephone selling to a person as ultimate user. It would apply, therefore, to any representation made by a charity that sells chocolate bars or similar goods door-to-door, by telephone or using "donation" boxes in stores. In order to obtain a conviction, it is not necessary for the Crown to show that any person was in fact deceived or misled by the representation. As a result, it is important for the organization — and the officers and directors — to show that the information is not misleading or deceptive and the best way to do so is to ensure that it is accurate.

Although the *Competition Act* applies only to certain types of transactions, it would be appropriate for charitable and not-for-profit organizations to structure their solicitations and similar materials with that Act in mind. It would not be prudent or appropriate for an organization to comply with respect to the transactions that fall under the Act but decide to adopt or carry on policies and practices that do mislead or misrepresent for transactions that are outside the scope of the statute. This type of approach would be unethical. In addition, from a practical perspective, it would be very difficult to ensure that materials that do not comply are not accidentally used in fundraising activities that are under the Act. The fact that the organization has two sets of materials would also be evidence against the organization and its officers and directors in any prosecution with respect to intent to mislead or deceive. Similarly, the donor who was misled or deceived could use that evidence to substantiate any claim against the organization or its officers and directors.

All fundraising materials should accurately describe the charity and its activities and the purposes for which donations will be used. The individuals who will be dealing with the public (whether volunteers, employees or professional fundraisers) need to be trained and to use the written materials as the basis for their personal solicitations or door-to-door or telephone solicitations. They should disclose at the start for whom they are soliciting and the purpose of any telephone call or canvassing. The board should establish a very clear policy that the organization and all those who act on its behalf shall not make any false or misleading statements or representations and ensure that all volunteers, employees and professional fundraisers are aware of and comply with this policy. The board must also put in place measures to monitor compliance with the policy and to ensure that any failures to comply are brought to the board's attention in a timely manner and are corrected in a timely manner.

III PERSONAL INFORMATION PROTECTION AND ELECTRONIC DOCUMENTS ACT

The *Personal Information Protection and Electronic Documents Act*[46] sets out standards for the collection and use of personal information of donors and others. The Act is discussed in more detail in Chapter 6. For purposes of fundraising, the Act will apply to situations where an organization is involved in "commercial activity". Some fundraising activities will fall within the usual sense of "commercial activity", such as sales of used clothing and so forth. However, it is important to note that Parliament specifically included in the definition "the selling, bartering or leasing of donor, membership or other fundraising lists".

IV INTELLECTUAL PROPERTY

There are two major forms of intellectual property that will be of concern in fundraising activities — copyright and trade-marks. These issues are also discussed later in this chapter as they relate to the use of the internet. There are other forms of intellectual property, such as patents and industrial designs, but charitable and not-for-profit organizations are not likely to use or infringe intellectual property in these areas as part of a fundraising campaign or activity.

The *Copyright Act*[47] applies to original works. Copyright in Canada is automatically created in the author of a work, although the author or somebody acting on his or her behalf may register copyright.[48] Copyright is the legal right:

---

[46] S.C. 2000, c. 5.
[47] R.S.C. 1985, c. C-42, as amended.
[48] See *A Guide to Copyright* (Ottawa: Her Majesty the Queen in Right of Canada (Industry Canada) 2000) for a good review of copyright law. Industry Canada also publishes a number of very useful publications related generally to intellectual property and which are available from its website at "cipo.gc.ca".

- to copy a work,
- to produce or reproduce a work,
- to permit somebody else to copy or produce or reproduce a work.

There may be copyright in literary works (books, pamphlets, poems and other works consisting of text and computer programs), dramatic works, musical works, artistic works (paintings, photographs, sculpture, maps and so forth). The work must be "original" in order for copyright to exist. Copyright may also exist in a performance, a communication signal (such as a television broadcast) and sound recordings.

Copyright is important in fundraising from three perspectives:

- if an organization wants to use in whole or substantial part works created by another person, it must have permission from that other person to do so. Typically, permission is granted in writing by a licence for which a royalty is paid. In some cases, collectives have been established to manage the issuance of licences, to collect the royalties owing and to enforce the copyright holder's legal rights. For example, if the organization wanted to use a song or part of a song in its fundraising campaign, it would need to obtain the rights to do so from the Society of Composers, Authors and Music Publishers of Canada (SOCAN) or a similar rights organization in the relevant jurisdiction. Similarly, if the organization wanted to use a poem or other text, it would obtain the licence from the Canadian Copyright Licensing Agency (CANCOPY) or similar rights organization in the relevant jurisdiction. A failure to obtain a licence and to pay the appropriate royalty may result in legal proceedings against the organization when the copyright holder enforces his, her or its rights. The organization may also lose its investment in any materials that were created if the court orders the destruction of the materials;
- the author of the work holds the copyright in most cases. The major two exceptions to this general rule are:
  - if the work is created by an employee the copyright belongs to the organization, unless there is an agreement to the contrary. It is important to ensure that the employee is an employee and not, say, an independent contractor or a volunteer,
  - if the work is created by another person under commission to the organization, unless there is an agreement to the contrary. However, for the work to fall into this exception, the organization must have paid consideration for the copyright. To be safe, an agreement for services, such as adver-

tising copy, should indicate that copyright in the product will be held by the organization.

The author of the work may also transfer the copyright to the organization, a third way for the organization to obtain the copyright. Any assignment must be in writing. The author may do so for consideration or as a "gift". If the author is to receive a receipt for income tax purposes, there should be an independent appraisal as to the fair market value of the copyright,

- enforcement of copyright by the organization. Some businesses or others may attempt to use works for which the organization has a copyright. The *Copyright Act* provides the organization with remedies to cause these persons to cease from doing so. The organization may want to take such steps where, for example, somebody is purporting to be acting on behalf of the organization or who is reproducing the organization's materials for their own benefit.

Generally, copyright lasts for 50 years after the death of the author. The length of the copyright becomes a bit more complicated when dealing with photographs, sound recordings and so forth. Regardless of the medium or the type of work, it is important to clarify who has copyright and whether or not that copyright remains in force before the organization makes use of any work that has copyright.

The author of the work also have common law and by statute "moral rights" in the work, even if he or she no longer has copyright in the work. The moral right prohibits anybody from distorting, mutilating or otherwise modifying a work without the permission of the author if it would be prejudicial to the reputation of the author. Similarly, the moral right prohibits the work being used in association with a product, service, cause or institution in a way that may be prejudicial. The author may "waive" his or her moral rights, but cannot sell them. If the organization intends to use a work that was created for it and for which it holds the copyright, it may want to ensure that it also obtains the waiver of moral rights so that it has the flexibility that it feels may be necessary for fundraising purposes. The waiver may be general or specific in nature. The moral right continues until the copyright expires.

There are a number of works or parts of works in which copyright does not occur. For example, there is no copyright in facts, ideas or news. The copyright does not exist in the idea but in how that idea is presented. Copyright does not exist in materials that are in the public domain, i.e., where the copyright has expired. The usual example for public domain are the works of Shakespeare. There may be, though, copyright in a reproduction of the works of Shakespeare. Copyright also does not exist in names, slogans, short phrases or methods of teaching.

There may be, though, an ability to trade-mark certain of these under the *Trade-Marks Act*.[49]

The registration of a trade-mark is intended to protect the identity of a corporation or organization. The registration provides legal title to the intellectual property. A trade-mark is a word, symbol, design or combination that is used to distinguish the wares or services of one person from those of another. The underlying intention of a trade-mark is that it represents both the provider and the reputation of the provider.

There are three major types of trade-marks:

- ordinary marks — words or symbols that distinguish the wares or services of a specific firm or individual. Many organizations have logos or other marks that distinguish them from other organizations or even businesses,
- certification marks — these marks indicate that a ware or service meets a defined standard. The mark is owned by one person who licences its use by those who meet the defined standard. The Canadian Centre for Philanthropy's "Imagine" mark is an example of a certification mark in this sector,
- distinguishing guise — a product may come in a unique shape or package, which is readily identifiable.

A trade-mark to be registered, cannot be clearly descriptive of the product, deceptively misdescriptive or designate a place of origin. Similarly, words in another language that are descriptive of the product cannot be registered. The proposed trade-mark cannot be confusingly similar to a registered trade-mark or pending trade-mark and may not incorporate a prohibited mark.

A trade name is not automatically a trade-mark. In order to be registered as a trade-mark, a trade name must be used as such. It must be used to distinguish the wares or services provided by that organization from others.

As with copyright, the owner of a trade-mark may have a common law right to use it. However, that common law right may be reduced if somebody subsequently registers a trade-mark. Registration is *prima facie* evidence that the registered holder is the owner of the trade-mark. The registered holder does not have to prove ownership in a dispute; rather the person challenging the registration must prove ownership.

The registration of a trade-mark can be expensive and time consuming. Often, businesses will retain a trade-mark agent to handle the registration process. The registration is valid for 15 years and is renewable every 15 years. The registration also only protects the organization's

---

[49] R.S.C. 1985, c. T-13. See *A Guide to Trade-Marks* (Ottawa: Her Majesty the Queen in Right of Canada (Industry Canada) 2000).

rights in Canada. Nevertheless, if the organization has developed a distinctive trade-mark it may want to protect the intellectual property in that trade-mark.

An organization, as with copyright, must take care if it uses the trade-mark of somebody else. For example, if the organization wants to show the public that a business is supportive of the campaign by including that business's trade-mark, it must obtain the permission of the business to do so. The organization should consider registering those trade-marks that it believes will prove valuable to it.

V CHARITIES ACCOUNTING ACT AND CHARITABLE GIFTS ACT

In Ontario the *Charities Accounting Act*[50] and the *Charitable Gifts Act*[51] are the two major statutes that deal with charitable organizations. Both are administered by the province's Public Guardian and Trustee and both are older style statutes. They are not comprehensive legislation and were subject to significant review and recommendations by the Ontario Law Reform Commission in 1996.[52]

The applicable provisions primarily are directed at addressing problems in fundraising after they occur. For example, s. 6 of the *Charities Accounting Act* allows any person to complain to a judge of the Superior Court of Justice "as to the manner in which a person or organization has solicited or procured funds by way of contribution or gift from the public for any purpose, or as to the manner in which any such funds have been dealt with or disposed of". The Court can direct the Public Guardian and Trustee to carry out an investigation into the matter and has broad powers to do so. The Public Guardian and Trustee shall report in writing to the Attorney General and to the judge who ordered the investigation. The judge may then order a passing of accounts in question and s. 23 of the *Trustee Act*[53] applies. Section 6 does not apply to fraternal or religious organizations.

Section 10 of the *Charities Accounting Act* establishes a similar statutory authority for a complaint with respect to an allegation of breach of trust. Two or more people may allege a breach of trust involving a charitable purpose to a judge of the Superior Court of Justice. The judge may make an order as the Court considers just, including an order directing the Public Guardian and Trustee to carry out an investigation. The report is submitted to the court and to the Attorney General.

There is a specific power under s. 4 of the Act with respect to the use of property, fund or money. If the charitable organization is not using the property, fund or money as directed by the will or other instrument, the Public Guardian and Trustee may apply to a judge of the Superior

---

[50] R.S.O. 1990, c. C.10, as amended.
[51] R.S.O. 1990, c. C.8.
[52] *Report on the Law of Charities* (Toronto: Queen's Printer, 1996).
[53] R.S.O. 1990, c. T.23.

Court of Justice to direct compliance. The order could also remove the executor of the estate or the trustee and appoint some other person, provide directions on future investment, disposition and application of the property, fund or money, and impose a penalty (financial or imprisonment) for any default, misconduct or disobedience by the executor or trustee. Trustee is defined in the Act as including a corporation incorporated for "religious, educational, charitable or public purpose".[54]

A donor could also complain under s. 3 of the Act. The Public Guardian and Trustee may require an executor or trustee to submit the accounts of dealings with the property to be passed and examined and audited by a judge of the Superior Court of Justice. As with the other remedies under the Act, this one is time-consuming and potentially expensive. It also is more reactive and does not provide very clear directions in the statute.

The *Charitable Gifts Act* is primarily aimed at the disposition of an interest in business. If a charitable organization receives an interest in business, under s. 2 of that Act it must dispose of that interest if it is more than 10 per cent interest in the business. This requirement does not apply to an organization of any religious denomination. The remainder of the Act sets out the process for disposition over a period of time, supervision by the court and for enforcement. This Act would come into effect if, for example, a charity were to receive a donation of shares in a business that were more than 10 per cent of the issued shares. It must dispose of the shares that are in excess of the 10 per cent limit.

A comparable provision is included in s. 8 of the *Charities Accounting Act* for real property. That section requires that any person who holds land for a charitable purpose shall do so only for the purpose of actual use or occupation of the land for the charitable purpose. Thus, if a charitable organization were to receive real property as a donation, but it could not use or occupy that land for its charitable purposes, it is obliged to dispose of it. If it does not do so, the land can be vested in the Public Guardian and Trustee who will then dispose of it.[55] This issue becomes important when considering whether or not to accept a gift of land.

VI CHARITABLE FUND-RAISING ACT

Alberta's *Charitable Fund-Raising Act*[56] was enacted in 1995 and is the most comprehensive in Canada. It regulates both fundraising activities and those who fundraise, including organizations and professional fundraisers. The statute also provides significant investigation and enforce-

---

[54] *Charities Accounting Act*, subs. 1(2).
[55] The Court in *Re Centenary Hospital Assn.* (1989), 69 O.R. (2d) 1, 33 E.T.R. 270, 59 D.L.R. (4th) 449 (H.C.), additional reasons at (1989), 69 O.R. (2d) 447 narrowed the scope of this provision as it applied to hospitals, which are regulated under other legislation.
[56] S.A. 1995, c. C-4.5, as amended.

ment powers. It is, depending upon how it is administered and the resources allocated for it, a comprehensive regulatory statute which deals with fundraising as an activity that ought to be regulated in the public interest.

Section 2 sets out two purposes for the legislation:

- to ensure that the public has sufficient information to make informed decisions when making contributions to a charitable organization or for a charitable purpose, and
- to protect the public from fraudulent, misleading or confusing solicitations and to establish standards for charitable organizations and fund-raising businesses when making solicitations.

The Act applies to both organizations and professional fundraisers ("fund-raising business"). The definition of "charitable organization" is broad and would include organizations that are entirely charitable and those that have "a charitable purpose".[57] Similarly, the definition of "charitable purpose" is very broad, but does exclude a purpose that is part of a business.[58] The Act does not apply to solicitations made to a member or his or her family, for goods or services that are to be used for the charitable organization's administration or some other non-charitable purpose, or a solicitation in respect of charitable gaming.[59] A solicitation is covered if it is made by the charitable organization or its volunteers or employees or by a fund-raising business or that business's volunteers or employees on behalf of the charitable organization.[60]

Section 4 identifies four circumstances to which Part 1 of the Act apply. That Part is concerned with soliciting contributions. These circumstances are:

- solicitations made by a fund-raising business,
- solicitations made by a charitable organization that uses a fund-raising business to make solicitations on its behalf or to manage or be responsible for solicitations made by or on behalf of the charitable organization,
- solicitations made by a charitable organization in its financial year if the charitable organization intends to raise, as a result of those solicitations, gross contributions of $25,000 or more from persons in Alberta during that fiscal year,

---

[57] Subsection 1(1).
[58] *Ibid.*
[59] Section 3.
[60] Subsection 1(2).

- solicitations that are made after the gross contributions exceed $25,000 from persons in Alberta during that fiscal year, regardless of the intentions of the charitable organization.

It is not clear if the Act applies to persons outside of Alberta where a fund-raising business is used. On the face of the statute, it would appear that it does. It is not clear how the organization makes the transition from an intention to receive gross contributions under $25,000 to the situation in which it in fact receives contributions in excess of $25,000.

Part 1 of the Act sets out certain requirements for solicitations, regardless of who does the solicitation. Under s. 5, a solicitation by telephone may be carried out only between 8:00 a.m. and 9:00 p.m. Section 6 requires that information be provided to the prospective donor prior to the acceptance of any contribution where the solicitation is done in person or over the telephone. That section also applies to solicitations that are made through printed material, television or other media. The following information must be disclosed:

- the name of the charitable organization making the solicitation or on whose behalf the solicitation is being made,
- the charitable purpose for which the contribution will be used,
- the charitable organization's estimate of the costs of making the solicitations and the activities directly related to making the solicitations and the charitable organization's estimate of the contributions that it will receive as a result of the solicitations. These estimates must be presented one after the other without intervening information in between,
- the address of the charitable organization and, if incorporated, the charitable organization's place of incorporation,
- the name and telephone number of a contact person in the charitable organization to whom the person being solicited may direct any inquiries, and
- if the charitable organization uses a professional fundraiser to make solicitations on its behalf or to manage or be responsible for solicitations made by or on behalf of the charitable organization,
    - the operating name and full legal name of the professional fund-raiser, and
    - how the remuneration of the professional fundraiser is determined.[61]

This information must be provided orally or in writing.

---

[61] Section 4, Alta. Reg. 95/95, as amended to 175/96.

The charitable organization or fundraising business is required to maintain financial records of its operations in Alberta and of its solicitations made in Alberta for at least three years after solicitations are made.[62] The charitable organization must prepare its audited financial statements or financial information return in accordance with the regulations.[63] Section 9 sets out the information that must be provided to any person who requests it, including a copy of the most recent audited financial statement or financial information return, the portion of the gross contributions used directly for charitable purposes in the last financial year, an estimate for the current financial year, reasonable detail about where and how the contributions received as a result of the solicitation will be spent, and the disclosure information required under s. 6. The charitable organization may charge a reasonable fee for the copy of the financial statement or information return.

A person who makes a solicitation must give a receipt to the person making the contribution, if requested to do so.[64] This receipt appears to be separate from a receipt for income tax purposes under the *Income Tax Act* issued by registered charities. Section 11 statutorily establishes that the contributions received by a fundraising business or its employees are held in trust for the charitable organization. It is not clear what the trust status of contributions received by "volunteers" of the fund-raising business is, but it is unlikely that this situation would arise very often. That trustee must deposit the funds within three days of receipt (not including Saturdays and holidays) into an account in Alberta in the charitable organization's name. The account must also be under the charitable organization's control.

Part 2 of the Act establishes a registration scheme for both charitable organizations and fundraising businesses. Registration is not required for a charitable organization if its fundraising activities are outside the monetary threshold set out in s. 4. Organizations that are not incorporated but are affiliated with another charitable organization that controls the contributions are not required to be registered.[65]

The charitable organization is prohibited from using a fundraising business to make solicitations on its behalf or to manage or be responsible for solicitations unless the organization is registered.[66] Sections 14 to 15 set out the requirement to provide the Minister with information and the grounds for the Minister to refuse a registration, which focus on the organization or its principals, directors or managers having committed an offence within the last five years under the Act or any law, criminal or otherwise, that indicates unsuitability to deal with contributions. A failure

---

[62] Section 7.
[63] Section 8. The requirements are set out in ss. 6 and 7 of Alta. Reg. 95/95, as amended to 175/96.
[64] Section 10.
[65] Section 12.
[66] Section 13.

to pay a fine or an order under the *Fair Trading Act* are also grounds to refuse registration.

The Minister may also impose terms and conditions on any registration. Section 16 requires the Minister to notify the organization of the Minister's intention to refuse the registration or renewal or the imposition of terms and conditions. The organization may make submissions to the Minister. If the Minister decides to refuse, written reasons must be provided to the organization.

A similar scheme is in place for fundraising businesses. It cannot provide fundraising solicitation services unless it is licensed under the Act.[67] Sections 23 and 24 parallel the grounds and process for registration of a charitable organization. Section 27 also requires the fundraising business to stop its activities if the security that the business has provided to the Minister is not in force.

Section 27.1 is important and clarifies ownership and control over donor lists. That section makes it clear that the list of names and other information about persons who have given a contribution that is compiled by the fundraising business is the property of the charitable organization. Furthermore, it is under the exclusive control of the charitable organization. No fundraising business that compiles a donor list may use or deal with it except with the written permission of the charitable organization.

The Act also requires that there be a fundraising agreement between the fundraising business and the charitable organization. The charitable organization may not use a fundraising business and a fundraising business may not provide its services unless there is an agreement in place and in force that complies with s. 29 of the Act.[68] Section 29 requires that an agreement be in writing and include the following:

- all terms and conditions between the parties respecting the fundraising, including the duties and responsibilities of both parties,
- the estimated amount of contributions to be received and an estimate of expenses and costs,
- the remuneration to be paid to the fundraising business, which must be a specific amount of money, a specified percentage of gross contributions or a combination of the two,
- the methods of soliciting contributions to be used,
- if the solicitations will involve selling goods or services, a description of the goods or services and the specific price for which they will be sold,
- the location of the account of the charitable organization into which the monetary contributions are to be deposited,

---

[67] Section 21.
[68] Section 28.

- the charitable organization's address and the name and telephone number of a contact person for the charitable organization and similar information for the fundraising business,
- any matter provided for in the regulations.

Section 29.1 of the Act gives the Minister the power to establish standards of practice relating to fundraising carried out by charitable organizations and fundraising businesses. All principals, directors, managers and employees of the charitable organization whose main responsibility is to make solicitations or to manage or be responsible for solicitations must comply with the standards of practice. The principals, directors and managers of the charitable organization must take reasonable steps to ensure that employees who are covered by this provision comply with the standards. A fundraising business and its principals, directors, managers and employees must comply with the standards of practice. It appears that all principals, directors, managers and employees of the business must comply, regardless of their duties.

Part 3 of the Act applies to "donor fundraisers". This type of business states or implies that all or a portion of a purchase price for a good or service will be donated to a charitable organization or be used for a charitable purpose.[69] That Part requires the donor fundraiser to make the donations or use the funds for the purposes represented, prohibits it from making false representations about its relationship (if any) with a charitable organization and requires that it provide specified information to any person who requests it.

The enforcement provisions of the Act are set out in Part 4. The inspection and investigation powers are standard types of powers used in other regulatory schemes. Charitable organizations and fundraising businesses have obligations to provide books and records to inspectors and may be subject to orders that are akin to search warrants. The Minister may initiate an investigation on receipt of a complaint or when the Minister considers it necessary. The Minister also has powers under section 40 to issue orders that effectively freeze bank accounts. The Minister may also suspend or cancel a licence or registration, or impose terms and conditions on the licence or registration under s. 42.

Part 5 sets out a number of additional offences and other requirements. For example, s. 43 prohibits the making of a false statement of fact or misrepresentation of any fact or circumstance in a solicitation. Section 49 allows a person who made a contribution to apply to the court for an order compelling the charitable organization to return the contribution to the donor or to use the contribution for the charitable purpose for which it was donated. This statutory remedy is a potentially very powerful one for donors and highlights that charitable organizations have duties towards donors.

---

[69] Section 30.

Section 51 provides for penalties under the Act. The fine is a minimum of $1,000 and may be as high as $100,000 or three times the amount that the defendant acquired as a result of the offence, whichever is greater. There is also the potential for a term of imprisonment for up to two years. The principals, directors, managers, employees or agents of a corporation are guilty of the offence if they authorized the contravention or failed or assented to it or acquiesced or participated in it. In addition, under s. 52, a justice that convicts a defendant of an offence may on application of the aggrieved person order that the defendant pay compensation to that person. Clearly, the risks of liability entailed in not complying with the Act are great.

As noted above, the Act permits the Minister to establish standards of practice for fundraising. Standards were established on April 1, 1999 after consultation and are based on the *Code of Ethical Principles and Standards of Professional Practice* developed by the National Society of Fund-Raising Executives.[70] The Standards are as follows:

- Charitable organizations and fundraising businesses must comply with all relevant municipal, provincial and federal laws,
- Charitable organizations and fundraising businesses must advocate, within the organization, adherence to all applicable laws and Standards of Practice,
- The principals, directors, managers and employees of charitable organizations and fundraising businesses that must comply with these Standards must effectively disclose to their organization all conflicts of interest and all situations that might be perceived as a conflict of interest,
- Charitable organizations and fundraising businesses must give donors the opportunity to have their names removed from lists that are sold, rented, or exchanged with other organizations,
- Charitable organizations and fundraising businesses must not disclose any personal and confidential information about donors or prospective donors outside the work environment, and within the work environment only as appropriate,
- Charitable organizations must, to the best of their ability, ensure that contributions are used in accordance with donors' intentions and obtain the explicit consent of a donor or the donor's representative before altering conditions of a gift,
- Charitable organizations must use accurate and consistent accounting methods that conform to the appropriate guidelines

---

[70] Carter, *"Looking a Gift Horse in the Mouth" — Avoiding Liability in Charitable Fundraising*, at 68.

adopted by the Canadian Institute of Chartered Accountants (CICA),
- Charitable organizations and fundraising businesses must not take unfair advantage of a donor or prospective donor for their own advantage or benefit.[71]

VII CHARITIES ENDORSEMENT ACT

This Manitoba statute prohibits an organization from canvassing the public unless it has been authorized to do so.[72] The authorization is issued by the Minister if it is to be valid throughout the province of Manitoba or by the mayor or reeve of a municipality or other person or body appointed for that purpose by the council of the municipality.[73] The legislation is very broad and includes promotional agencies (professional fundraisers), door-to-door and telephone canvassing, advertising and so forth. There are exceptions for organizations that solicit only from their members.[74]

The Act also indirectly governs professional fundraisers, or promotional agencies. An authorization shall not be granted if the organization retains a promotional agency unless the terms of the contract are disclosed to the authority issuing the authorization. The contract must also set out the payment as a fixed sum or as a percentage of net profit, which is subject to the approval of the authority issuing the authorization. The authority also has a right to financial information from the promotional agency, including audited financial statements, with respect to the fundraising.[75]

F DEFINING "GIFT"

The question of what is or is not a "gift" is an important one in fundraising, especially for registered charities that intend to issue an official receipt for income tax purposes. The Canada Customs and Revenue Agency sets out three conditions for there to be gift for income tax purposes:

- the donor transfers ownership of property (cash, or gifts in kind such as goods or land) to a registered charity;
- the transfer is voluntary; and

---

[71] *The Charitable Fund-Raising Act — Information for Charities and Donors Tipsheet*, Alberta Government Services, September 1999, at 6 to 7.
[72] Section 2, R.S.M. 1987, c. C60.
[73] Section 1.
[74] Subsection 2(2).
[75] Subsection 2(6). Subsection 2(7) makes any contract that is not authorized invalid.

- no benefit is provided to the donor or a person selected by the donor unless the benefit is of nominal value.[76]

"Nominal value" is not defined but the Agency comments that it would consider a benefit to be nominal if its fair market value is less than 10 per cent of the gift up to a maximum of $50. If the fair market value cannot be determined for any benefit, then the Agency will not consider the benefit to be of a nominal value and the contribution will not be a "gift". For example, the fair market value of an opportunity to meet a celebrity cannot be determined, therefore, any donation that includes this benefit could not be receipted. Similarly, the Agency's position is that if the value of the benefit is dependent upon usage by the donor (such as an ongoing discount at a bookstore), fair market value cannot be determined, the benefit is not of "nominal value" and the charity would not be permitted to issue a receipt for income tax purposes.[77]

The issue of what is or is not "nominal value" is not always an easy one to determine. There has been periodic misconceptions, according to the Agency, about when the nominal value determination is needed and when it is not. A donor who supports a symphony may still be issued a receipt for income tax purposes, provided the donor does not directly receive something in return.[78] The donor may still continue to enjoy the symphony after making the donation.

The courts have periodically commented on what is or is not a "gift". The approach taken by the Canada Customs and Revenue Agency and set out above, not surprisingly, generally adopts the case law. For example, in *The Queen v. Zandstra*, the Court commented that "a gift is a voluntary transfer of property owned by a donor to a donee, in return for which no benefit flows to the donor".[79] This approach was also followed in *Woolner v. The Attorney General of Canada*.[80] In that case, the Federal Court of Appeal concluded that parents received a "material benefit" where they wanted their children to receive an education in a Christian school. The parents donated each year to the school, a registered charity, which issued receipts for income tax purposes. The children of the donors received bursaries to attend the school. The Court concluded that the donation was made to obtain a material advantage. The donation met the first part of the legal definition, i.e., it was voluntary, but it did

---

[76] *Tax Advantages of Donating to Charity*, RC4142, at p. 6. See also paragraph 15(f) of *Gifts and Official Donation Receipts*, Interpretation Bulletin IT-110R3.
[77] *Ibid.*
[78] *Registered Charities Newsletter*, Newsletter No. 9, June 6, 2000.
[79] [1974] C.T.C. 503, 74 D.T.C. 6416 (F.C.T.D.). See also *The Queen v. Burns*, [1988] 88 D.T.C. 6101 (F.C.T.D.); affd. [1990] 90 D.T.C. 6335 (F.C.A.).
[80] (1999), 99 D.T.C. 5722 (F.C.A.) which followed *The Queen v. McBurney*, [1985] 2 C.T.C. 214, 85 D.T.C. 5433, 62 N.R. 104, 20 E.T.R. 283 (F.C.A.).

not meet the remaining conditions. The contributions were made with the anticipation of a benefit or advantage of a material nature.[81]

Arguably, the receipt for income tax purposes issued to a donor is of material benefit or advantage. Clearly, many donors may make a donation with the anticipation of obtaining the receipt for use in reducing the taxes that are payable on income. However, the court has found that this advantage is not considered to be a benefit for purposes of the common law definition of "gift".[82] However, there must still be an underlying charitable intent or motive on the part of the donor. The tax benefit alone cannot be the basis for the gift if a receipt for income tax purposes is to be issued by a registered charity.[83]

A charity may find it difficult to assess what is the true motive of a donor. One clue, based on the case law, as to the motivation of a donor is if he or she is attempting to donate gifts-in-kind that are in excess of fair market value or refuses to permit an independent appraisal on the gift-in-kind.

As noted above, the Court has held that a gift is a voluntary transfer of property. The transfer is gratuitous and "not as the result of a contractual obligation without anticipation or expectation of material benefit".[84] It is not entirely clear to what extent, therefore, a charity can enforce a promise to make a donation. Is the promise to make a donation a "contract"? Under contract law, there must be "consideration" or an exchange of value between two parties for a contract to be enforceable. If so, does the existence of a "contract" necessarily mean that there is no "gift"? In most cases, a gift that is part of a contractual obligation probably is not a "gift" for charitable and taxation purposes. However, "the mere fact that a person has made a contractually binding promise to make a gift may not ... necessarily deprive it of its character as such when it is made".[85] A gift will ordinarily proceed, though, from "a detached and disinterested generosity".

---

[81] See also, in a different context, *Dupriez v. Canada*, [1998] 98 D.T.C. 1790 (T.C.C.). In that case, the court quoted from *McBurney* that:
> In a borderline case involving dispute as to whether a particular transaction constitutes a gift ... the presence or otherwise of the usual attributes of a gift will provide the reference point for answering the essential question. The fact that in the instant case all prospective adoptive parents made a contribution of a substantial and identical amount indicates an operation which is not in the nature of a gift but involves the performance of a contractual obligation assumed by the prospective parents in order to become adoptive parents.

[82] *Friedberg v. Canada*, [1992] 1 C.T.C. 1, 92 D.T.C. 6031, 135 N.R. 61 (F.C.A.).

[83] *Dutil v. Canada*, [1991] 95 D.T.C. 281 (T.C.C.).

[84] Sexton J.A. in *Woolner*, at 4 adopting the test in *McBurney*.

[85] *Tite v. M.N.R.*, [1986] 2 C.T.C. 2343, 86 D.T.C. 1788 at 1790 (T.C.C.) quoting from an Australia case.

In situations where the donation was part of a larger contractual relationship, the courts would not usually recognize it as a "gift".[86] This approach makes sense because the contractual relationship presupposes that the donor is receiving a benefit from the "gift" and thus is not transferring the property out of "detached and disinterested generosity" but in order to obtain a benefit.[87] The donation may, however, be a legitimate business expense if the donation was made for the purpose of producing income.[88]

Establishing the value of a gift-in-kind is essential. Often, the value of a gift-in-kind is not readily apparent and there may be significant and legitimate disagreements as to the true value of a gift. The Canada Customs and Revenue Agency recommends that gifts be appraised before a tax receipt is issued to a donor. The appraisal should be done by an independent appraiser with expertise and knowledge to appraise the fair market value of the gift-in-kind. The Agency does recognize certain exceptions to the use of an independent appraiser. If staff of the charitable organization is familiar with the type of property, he or she could do the appraisal if the following conditions are met:

- the value of the gift is $1,000 or less,
- an independent appraiser cannot be reasonably located, or
- the appraisal involves unreasonable expense, even though the value of the gift might be more than $1,000.[89]

The Agency also cautions charities about using appraisals provided by a donor if the appraisal seems high, the person who did the appraisal sold the property to the donor, the staff of the charitable organization are not familiar with the type of property, or the type of property is unusual or difficult to appraise.[90]

This advice is consistent with the case law with respect to determining the value of gifts-in-kind. A number of these cases arose out of "art donation schemes" or "scams" in which the appraisals were far in excess of the fair market value of the gift. In one instance, the charity itself sold the property to the donor and provided a receipt for tax purposes for a portion of the sale price. The charity's position was that the art was val-

---

[86] *Hudson Bay Mining and Smelting Co. Ltd. v. R.*, [1986] 1 C.T.C. 484, 86 D.T.C. 6244 (F.C.T.D.).
[87] But see *Jabs Construction Limited v. M.N.R.*, [1999] 99 D.T.C. 729 (T.C.C.) in which a very complex settlement to litigation resulted in a "gift" to a private charitable foundation that was recognized by the court as a gift. This case would appear to turn on its unique facts.
[88] See *Olympia Floor & Wall (Que.) Ltd. v. M.N.R.*, [1970] Ex. C.R. 274, C.T.C. 99, 70 D.T.C. 6085 (Ex. Ct.) And *Impenco Ltd. v. M.N.R.*, [1988] 1 C.T.C. 2339, 88 D.T.C. 1242 (T.C.C.).
[89] *Registered Charities Newsletter*, Newsletter No. 9, June 6, 2000.
[90] *Ibid.*

ued at, say, $250 but was sold for $500 and therefore it could issue a receipt for income purposes for the difference of $250.

In *Dutil v. Canada*,[91] the Tax Court of Canada addressed the issue of fair market value. The taxpayer donated a painting to a charitable organization and claimed a value of $5,500 but the taxpayer had only paid $1,100. Two expert appraisers for the Minister valued the painting at $1,275. At no point did the taxpayer take possession of the painting and the Court concluded that he, in effect, had purchased a tax deduction.

Mr. Justice Dussault commented that "in establishing the fair market value of an item, the courts have several times noted that an expert must not only demonstrate competence and impartiality or professional independence, but must provide an opinion based on objective criteria".[92] He continued that the definition of "fair market value" has also been well established. He accepted the following definition, which was adopted in *Friedberg*:

> The highest price, expressed in terms of money or money's worth, obtainable in an open and unrestricted market between informed and prudent parties, acting at arm's length, neither party being under compulsion to transact.[93]

The Court continued about the legislative objectives. It compared this case to others in which the transaction amounted to a contract between the donor and the donee (the charity). It commented that "the facts of the instant case are different, since the financial benefit the appellant wished to receive would have come not from the donee itself but from a third party, the government, in the form of a tax deduction claimed". It continued that:

> Our tax system provides for the deduction of a charitable gift within the limits determined by the Act, when such a gift is made to a recognized body. It may thus be regarded as a normal consequence [tax deduction] intended by the legislature in order to encourage such gifts. However, it may be seriously doubted whether such a gift even exists in the true sense when the taxpayer's sole motivation is clearly to enrich himself, not impoverish himself. If Friedberg ... is used as authority for the argument that this may nevertheless be the result of a gift, it is still true that it is the exception and not the rule. Comparable circumstances would also have to be shown. In that case, three independent appraisers, whose expert opinions were accepted by the Court, were called on and the taxpayer had in any case decided to go ahead with purchasing and donating collections ... In the in-

---

[91] (1991), 95 D.T.C. 281 (T.C.C.).
[92] *Ibid.*
[93] *Ibid. Friedberg* was appealed to the Federal Court of Appeal. The definition adopted by the Court was from R.W. Wise, "Fair Market Value Determinations — A Few More Requirements", (1983), 31 Can. Tax. J. 337.

stant case, in my opinion, the quest for an unwarranted tax benefit leaves little doubt that there was no intent to make a gift, as is indicated by the fact that by his own admission the appellant had to have a receipt in an amount greater than that spent if the transaction was to be a "tax benefit" to him.

This case, by its nature, focussed on the taxpayer and the implications for him where the receipt for tax purposes identified a value that was not "fair market value" and could not be supported. Indeed, the nature of the scheme was such that there was no real "gift" being made by the donor but rather an arrangement the sole purpose of which was to create a "tax benefit". On the facts of this case, the Court even considered the matter to have been a misrepresentation or false statement or circumstances that amounted to gross negligence on the part of the taxpayer. In those circumstances, the Minister could assess a penalty in addition to the amount of tax that was otherwise payable. The Court agreed.

What are the implications for the charity? First, these facts put into question the good faith of the charity itself in issuing a receipt for tax purposes that was far in excess of the true fair market value of the property. Second, proposed amendments to the *Income Tax Act* could result in penalties to the charitable organization for misrepresenting the value of the gift.[94]

There is also another possible implication for the charity. If this scheme was initiated or proposed by the charity to prospective donors, that donor would have suffered damages. The donor could have a legitimate claim against the charity for causing those damages. Whether or not the donor's complicity was sufficient to exculpate the charity is an issue, but it is not one that is worth the legal expense to find out. In addition, the situation would cause other prospective donors not to donate to the charity at all because they do not want to be associated with such schemes and charities that promote or participate in such schemes. Finally, the issuance of receipts for income tax purposes in those circumstances would put the registration of the charity at risk.

The making of a gift is not always a simple matter. There are also a number of technical matters for a gift to be made. For the transfer of property to occur, three steps must be completed:[95]

- intention to give the property,
- delivery of the property, and
- acceptance of the property.

---

[94] The federal Budget Speech, 2000, proposed adding s. 163.2 which would permit the assessment of a penalty for misrepresentation.
[95] A. Drache, *Canadian Taxation of Charities and Donations* (Toronto: Carswell, 1999), at 11-22 to 11-23.

If any of these three steps are not completed, there is no legal transfer of the property and the gift would fail. In addition, there may be legal impediments to one or more of these steps being validly and legally completed. For example, a gift made by an individual who was, at the time the gift was made, mentally incompetent, may be voidable because the individual did not have the capacity to form the intent to donate the property.

The property must also be delivered to the recipient of the donation. Without the delivery, there may be a pledge or promise to transfer the property but insufficient action has taken place to show that a donation was made. In some cases, there may be other legal requirements to demonstrate that delivery has occurred. For example, in the case of a donation of a motor vehicle, it may be necessary for the registration of the motor vehicle to have been transferred. Although the change in registration is not, strictly speaking, a "change in ownership", it is good evidence of the intention of the parties, especially the "donor" to transfer the property. In addition, without this change in registration, the organization may not be in a legal position to use the property. It would not be able, for example, to obtain a licence for a motor vehicle.

Acceptance is the third action that must occur for the transfer of property to be valid. A charitable or not-for-profit organization may not want to accept every donation that is made to it for several reasons:

- the donation may not be consistent with the objects and powers of the organization. For example, a donation of a piece of medical equipment would probably not be consistent with the objects of an art gallery,
- acceptance of the donation may be voidable or improper. As discussed above, an individual who is not mentally competent cannot form the intent to make the donation and if this situation is known to the organization, it ought to refuse the donation,
- the donation may be questionable. An unfortunate practice at one time was for charitable organizations to accept donations of gifts-in-kind with appraisals established by the donor. While there may be circumstances in which the appraisal is acceptable, in most cases, as discussed above, appraisals ought to be made by and received from independent appraisers,
- the donation may be illegal. For example, donations of certain types of products may be restricted by international agreements or by law. These types of agreements and laws are increasingly common for cultural properties and for products created from endangered species,
- the donation may be tainted. This could occur if the donor is donating property. An environmental assessment would be appropriate whenever real property is being donated. Under environ-

mental legislation, the owner of the property is liable for the cost of any clean-up regardless of how or when the contamination occurred. If the directors or officers do not exercise due diligence, they could also be personally liable or be subject to prosecution if, for example, the contamination continued and due diligence had not been exercised.[96]

In the case of personal property, such as equipment, the organization may want to ensure that the property meets any standards, or that usage is legal in Canada. An organization should not accept, for example, equipment that is dangerous or that does not meet minimum standards for such equipment either for its own use or for sale to others. There is potential liability on the organization if it does use such equipment. In the case of food products, in Ontario, the *Donation of Food Act*[97] provides some protection to the directors, employees, volunteers and agents of the charity and to the person who donated the food, but not directly to the charity. In any event, it is obviously preferable to avoid situations in which somebody might become ill from donated food.

The organization should also consider whether it has the capacity to manage any donation of property. In the case of real property, could the organization use the property in its activities? If not, it may be required to dispose of the property at common law or by statute.[98] Does the organization have the resources to insure the property and to maintain it? If not, the organization may want to refuse the donation or accept on condition that it could sell the property. If the donation is shares, can those shares be readily marketed?[99]

- if the donation is not within the criteria established by the organization. Museums and art galleries will often have established policies on what types of donations they will accept for inclusion in the collections. If a donation of art is outside the criteria, it may decide to accept it on the basis that it would be sold to raise funds for the operation of the gallery or for the endowment fund. In

---

[96] See *R. v. Bata Industries Ltd.* (1993), 9 O.R. (3d) 329 (Prov. Div.); vard. (1993), 14 O.R. 354 (C.J.) and reversed in part on appeal (1995), 127 D.L.R. (4th) 439 (Ont. C.A.) in which directors were successfully prosecuted for pollution caused by an operating factory.

[97] S.O. 1994, c. 19. Alberta has enacted, but not proclaimed, similar legislation with the *Charitable Donation of Food Act*, S.A. 1999, c. C-4.3.

[98] For example, in Ontario, a charity must dispose of any real property that is not used for charitable purposes. See section 8, *Charities Accounting Act*, R.S.O. 1990, c. C.10. The *Charitable Gifts Act*, R.S.O. 1990, c. C.8 restricts ownership of the shares of a business.

[99] S. Lalani, "Looking a Gift Horse in the Mouth", (1999), 14 The Philanthropist 42 at 47.

some cases, organizations have established gift acceptance criteria for complex donations which further restrict the types of donations it will accept or set out procedures to make the assessment,[100]

- if the donation has restrictions that would be too onerous for the organization to comply with or that are illegal, the organization should decline the donation. Donors have a right to put in place restrictions on the use of funds or gifts-in-kind. But in some cases, these restrictions may so ham-string the organization that it either alters the nature and character of the organization or makes it impossible for it to fulfil the restrictions. In the worse case situation, the restrictions may be contrary to human rights legislation or would preclude a receipt for income tax purposes being issued.[101]

A board may want to consider limiting the authority of staff or volunteers to accept donations. Some organizations have put by-laws or resolutions in place that require the board of directors to formally accept a donation before the organization "accepts" it. These types of resolutions are particularly apt for museums, galleries and similar institutions that need to meet high standards in their collections. Ultimately, it will be the board of directors to whom the public, the courts and regulators will look to prevent problems and to rectify them when they do occur.

G CHARITABLE GAMING

I INTRODUCTION

The *Criminal Code*[102] permits charitable organizations to conduct and manage lottery schemes, provided they obtain a licence to do so. A licensee is permitted to use gaming suppliers and gaming assistants to provide goods and services for the operation of the lottery scheme. All of these activities are regulated by the terms and conditions to the licence and by the regulatory structure that is in place for gaming suppliers and gaming assistants.

---

[100] See Lalani, "Looking a Gift Horse in the Mouth" at 45 – 48 for a discussion of the Vancouver Foundation's *Gift Acceptance Criteria for Complex Gifts*.

[101] See *Canada Trust Co. v. Ontario Human Rights Commission, (sub nom. Leonard Foundation, Re)*, (1990), 74 O.R. (2d) 481, 12 C.H.R.R. D/184, 69 D.L.R. (4th) 321, 38 E.T.R. 1, 37 O.A.C. 191 (C.A.).

[102] R.S.C. 1985, c. C-34, as am. For a fuller discussion of charitable gaming, see D.J. Bourgeois, *The Law of Charitable and Casino Gaming* (Toronto: Butterworths Canada Limited, 1999).

This brief synopsis identifies the basic elements for legal gaming by charitable organizations. It considers the risks that are part and parcel of this form of fundraising and the ethical issues that arise from gambling. Charitable gaming is potentially a very lucrative form of fundraising — both in the amounts of money that can be raised and return on investment of resources, including volunteer time. Few golf tournaments or bake sales have the same level of return per volunteer hour as does charitable gaming.

On the other hand, charitable gaming can result in losses both financial and reputational. Some donors will reconsider their commitment to the charitable organization if it becomes active in charitable gaming. Charitable organizations should consider charitable gaming as a form of fundraising, but only after a thorough review of the types of lottery schemes that are available, the regulatory structure under which it will conduct and manage the lottery scheme, the investment that will be required (both financial and time) and the risks that are implicit in charitable gaming.

The most immediate risk is financial. Charitable gaming is gambling both from the perspective of the players and the charitable organization. It is possible and not uncommon for a charitable organization to lose at gambling. Although the odds, over time, are usually in favour of the charitable organization, there are factors that are beyond the control of the charitable organization. For example, sometimes the players are luckier than the house. Lottery schemes are designed to be in favour of the licensee, but the reality of odds is that they are just that — odds of winning and losing. Sometimes luck is on the side of the player in the short term. In a few cases, that luck may be the result of players cheating.

Weather will be a factor for some lottery schemes. A snowstorm prior to a bingo event could reduce the numbers of players able to attend. Or a special show on television may be more attractive that evening to many players than the bingo event. The licensee is, however, usually obliged to carry on with the bingo event regardless of the numbers in attendance. If the bingo sales are not sufficient to cover the prize board, the licensee has nonetheless a legal obligation to pay the prizes. It must do so by contract law and in accordance with the terms and conditions to the licence, with only a few exceptions.

Large raffles, with prizes totalling millions of dollars, are popular throughout Canada, but a number resulted in substantial losses for the charitable organization. The losses were due to a number of factors, including market saturation, inadequate market research, poor administration and excessive administrative costs. The losses reportedly put at risk the short and medium term ability of some charitable organizations to provide their programs. Although these situations were more spectacular because of the amounts of money involved, the inherent risk exists for any lottery scheme.

The financial risk and the nature of that risk will differ depending upon the type of lottery scheme that is licensed. Break open ticket lottery schemes are, if properly administered, less risky than large value raffles. The charitable organization may be licensed for, say, 20 boxes of break open tickets but the lottery scheme is structured so that it will receive a specified amount for each box. The prize board and costs are predetermined for break open tickets. There is a risk that not all of the boxes will be sold, due to market conditions, but it is not necessary to order all boxes at once. Alternatively, the licence period can sometimes be extended for a reasonable period to allow for the sale of the remaining boxes.

The flip side of the lower risk for break open tickets and the ability to manage the risk is, of course, the limited, predetermined financial return. With a bingo event, although a snowstorm may reduce the numbers and cause a loss for the charitable organization, it may also increase the numbers who attend or remain from the prior event. Larger numbers for a fixed prize board bingo event will mean increased profits. The prize board remains the same but bingo sales will increase, netting more monies for the charitable organization.

There are other risks that must be identified, understood and managed. These risks are sometimes less specific or easy to identify. Not everybody in society agrees with charitable gaming as a legitimate fundraising method. Although societal attitudes have changed over the last twenty years, in particular the last decade, for some people charitable gaming is an inappropriate method of raising funds for moral or ethical reasons. Sometimes the individuals will agree not to participate but will be neutral on whether or not the organization should obtain a licence. However, for some it will be sufficiently important that they will no longer be involved with the organization — as a member, volunteer or donor.

Individuals will hold and express their views on charitable gaming. Their views are legitimate and are deserving of consideration by the organization in making its decision on charitable gaming. Those views may be held by most members of the organization or by a sufficient number that the organization decides not to conduct and manage lottery schemes or certain types of lottery schemes. It is for each organization to make those decisions in a manner that is most appropriate for it.

There are also legal risks arising from charitable gaming. Gambling is contrary to the law in Canada, unless the activity falls within one of the exemptions in the *Criminal Code*. The charitable gaming exemption pursuant to paragraph 207(1)(b) of the *Criminal Code* comes with significant legal requirements. Failure to comply with those legal requirements may result in (and have resulted in) charges under the *Criminal Code* against the organization or its officers and directors. Even if the charges are not successful, the publicity alone may severely damage the reputation of the organization or its leadership such that others will not want to donate to it or volunteer for it.

There may be legal impediments to the charitable organization conducting and managing lottery schemes. It is not unusual, for example, for charitable organizations incorporated decades ago to have restrictions in their letters patent with respect to gambling, especially on the organization's premises. The letters patent must be examined to determine if there are any such restrictions. There may be other restrictions that will affect the decision, such as a donation that was conditional upon the charitable organization not conducting and managing lottery schemes. While this type of limitation would be out of the ordinary, it does occasionally arise.

The organization may also not be legally eligible for a lottery licence. Not all not-for-profit organizations will be seen as charitable and, as a result, will not qualify under the *Criminal Code* for a licence.

Organizations interested in charitable gaming must do their homework. Charitable gaming, while potentially lucrative, is not a fundraising panacea for all organizations. There are risks involved — financial, legal and public. Members or key donors may object to charitable gaming. The organization may not have the resources, financial or volunteers, or the expertise to conduct and manage a lottery scheme. It is important that the organization understand the context of charitable gaming and its ability to conduct and manage a lottery scheme before it applies for a lottery licence.

Equally important, an organization should consider the type of lottery scheme that is most appropriate to it. A charitable organization that has little or no experience with lottery schemes probably should not conduct and manage a large-scale raffle. If it does not have sufficient members, 19 years of age or older, it may not be able to conduct and manage a bingo. Experience, as with other forms of fundraising, is critical to an efficient and effective conduct and management of a lottery scheme that is in compliance with the law. It will help reduce the risks involved and increase the returns on investment of volunteer time and other resources. A charitable organization should usually start out with lower risk lottery schemes to get an understanding of the issues and expectations.

II *CRIMINAL CODE* AND CHARITABLE GAMING

Gambling and opportunities for gambling have expanded dramatically in Canada and throughout the world. There appears to be a greater acceptance of gambling as a source of funds for charitable organizations and for governments. But it remains illegal, unless conducted, managed and operated in accordance with the exemptions in the *Criminal Code*. The legal equation seems to be that people want to gamble but gambling is intrinsically harmful; as result, gambling needs to be restricted.

The courts appear to take a similar approach. In *R. v. Andriopoulos*, the Ontario Court of Appeal rejected a defence argument that gambling was no longer criminal in nature due to changing societal attitudes and the growth of gaming opportunities. The Court of Appeal did not agree and commented:

The essential fallacy of this proposition is in equating a lottery, licensed, conducted and managed by a province, to all forms of gaming and gambling ... . The business of organized gaming is the subject matter of the prohibitions, presumably because it invites cheating and attracts other forms of criminal activity. There is no evidence that public perceptions of commercial gaming have changed or that it is any less criminal in nature than it ever has been.[103]

The law with respect to gaming is fundamentally criminal law and, thus, within the constitutional jurisdiction of the Parliament of Canada. Provincial legislatures cannot alter the criminal law, although they have jurisdiction pursuant to s. 207 of the *Criminal Code* to license charitable and similar forms of gaming. The courts have long recognized this distinction. For example, in *Keystone Bingo Centre Inc. v. Manitoba Lotteries Foundation*, the Manitoba Court of Appeal stated:

> Keystone's operations contravened the provisions for a statute of parliament. Not even the legislature of Manitoba could give Keystone the colour of right to act in the manner in which it did. Even more so, the Government of Manitoba could not, by acquiescence or otherwise, create a proprietary interest in an illegal business.[104]

The Alberta Supreme Court took a similar approach in *LaRose v. Fleuty*.[105] The fact that a licence has been issued to an organization that was not charitable to conduct and manage a raffle was not sufficient to bring the raffle within the exemption of the *Criminal Code*. The Supreme Court of Canada has also reviewed the role of the provincial governments in the regulation of gaming. It upheld s. 207 on constitutional law grounds in *R. v. Furtney*.[106]

The provincial role in charitable gaming arises from subs. 207(1), which provides that:

> Notwithstanding any of the provisions of this Part relating to gaming and betting, it is lawful:
>
> (b) for a charitable or religious organization, pursuant to a licence issued by the Lieutenant Governor in Council of a province or by such other person or authority in the province as may be specified by the Lieutenant Governor in Council thereof, to conduct and manage a lottery scheme in

---

[103] Unreported decision, October 17, 1994, (Doc. No. CA 1671 C-16740, Ont. C.A.) *per* Catzman, Carthy, Osborne JJ.A).
[104] (1990), 76 D.L.R. (4th) 423, 60 Man. R. (2d) 191 (C.A.); leave to appeal to S.C.C. refused (1991), 78 Man. R. (2d) 160n, at 430 (S.C.C.).
[105] [1971] 5 W.W.R. 515, 5 C.C.C. (2d) 528 (Alta. S.C.).
[106] (1991), 66 C.C.C. (3d) 498, 8 C.R. (4th) 121 (S.C.C.).

that province if the proceeds from the lottery scheme are used for a charitable or religious object or purpose.

The private sector's involvement in charitable gaming is a limited one. Paragraph 207(1)(g) permits:

> any person, for the purpose of a lottery scheme that is lawful in a province under any of paragraphs (a) to (f), to do anything in the province, in accordance with the applicable law or licence, that is required for the conduct, management or operation of the lottery schemed or for the person to participate in the scheme.

Paragraph 207(1)(h) provides that it is also lawful for persons to make or print, send, transmit, mail and so forth those materials used in the lawful gaming activity.

All of these lawful activities, however, are conditioned — they must be carried out in accordance with the licence. Subsection 207(2) provides that:

> Subject to this Act, a licence issued by or under the authority of the Lieutenant Governor in Council of a province ... may contain such terms and conditions relating to the conduct, management and operation of or participation in the lottery scheme to which the licence relates as the Lieutenant Governor in Council of that province, the person or authority in the province designated by the Lieutenant Governor in Council thereof or any law enacted by the legislature of the province may prescribe.

A failure to comply with the terms and conditions of a licence is itself a criminal offence. Charges may be laid under subs. 207(3) of the *Criminal Code*. And they have been. For example, in *R. v. Hunt*, the Court commented:

> While, in a general way, the Gaming Control Commission was attempting under its mandate to supervise lottery funds and their disposition, nevertheless, the Commission had the power to pass the Terms and Conditions regulations they did, from time to time, including the terms either prohibiting or limiting the right of charitable organizations to pay sales commissions, whether wholly or partially out of non-lottery funds.
>
> I find no ambiguity in the regulations in question ...
>
> Section 207 of the Code gives the provinces sweeping and flexible powers for the creation, supervision and control of lotteries and, in s. 207(2), one finds a very broad power vested in the provinces to impose terms and conditions on the grant of licences. It ill behooves a court, I believe, to nit-pick at these powers which were so obviously created in the public interest.

The terms and conditions set out in this regulations were clearly intra vires the province and the court should allow a substantial measure of room to manoeuvre within these subordinate enactments. To me, the successive terms and conditions were legitimate experiments under the broad scheme propounded by the federal Parliament and should be enforced in their clear terms to allow the province to achieve legitimate public policy objects.[107]

The concept of "conduct and manage" is a critical one, but the terms are not defined in the *Criminal Code*. Several cases did attempt to interpret the phrase in context of specific fact situations. The terms and conditions of the licence, which are discussed below, are intended in part to ensure that the licensed charitable or religious organization conducts and manages the lottery scheme and does so in a prescribed manner.

In *R. v. Rankine*[108] the Court examined the phrase "conduct or manage", which was used at that time. Mr. Rankine was distributing interim receipts for a sweepstakes that was to take place in Australia. The sweepstakes was legal in Australia but not in Canada. The British Columbia Court of Appeal found that he had nothing to do with the issuance of the tickets and that he did not, therefore, conduct or manage the lottery scheme. It concluded, as a question of fact, that the appropriate person in Australia was conducting or managing the lottery scheme. Mr. Rankine's activities were minor services incidental to his primary functions as a salesperson.

The B.C. Court of Appeal decision was not followed in most other cases. However, the distinction made between activities that are in their nature "conduct or manage" and that are not was important. Essentially, the power of control over the lottery scheme became the focus of attention. In *R. v. Miller*,[109] the Court accepted the distinction but distinguished the *Rankine* case. It was not necessary for the individual to take part in the actual drawing of a winning ticket in order to conduct or manage the lottery scheme, although the drawing was an incident of conduct or management. The Court expanded on this approach in *R. v. Kinsmen Club of Windsor*[110] in which it identified several activities that would be considered incidents of "conduct or management" in context of a bingo game. The Court examined the following elements of the bingo game to determine whether or not the club was conducting and managing the lottery scheme.

---

[107] *R. v. Hunt*, unreported decision, January 20, 1998, Doc. GD98-426 *per* Killeen J. (Ont. Gen. Div.), at 9 to 11.
[108] [1938] 4 D.L.R. 201, 70 C.C.C. 354 (B.C.C.A.).
[109] [1951] O.W.N. 230, 99 C.C.C. 79, 11 C.R. 324 (C.A.).
[110] [1964] 1 C.C.C. 144 (Ont. Mag. Ct.).

This approach was also used in *R. v. Gladue*.[111] One of the individuals was a cashier and the other was the bingo caller. The Court convicted both, after reviewing the *Miller* and *Kinsmen* cases. It commented:

> The methods and equipment may be somewhat more sophisticated today than in 1963 but the common elements are essentially unchanged.
>
> The roles of "Cashier" and the "Caller" undertaken by each accused were essential to the conduct of the bingo event. The bingo event was clearly a scheme with the essential elements of a lottery scheme being present: consideration, prize and chance ... The term "conduct" certainly includes the physical operation of the event and each of the accused did, in fact, conduct the scheme described.[112]

The conduct and management of lottery schemes by a charitable organization is a critical condition to the exemption under the *Criminal Code*. The case law provides some guidance to licensees on what a charitable organization needs to do. The terms and conditions, though, provide substantially more detailed direction, direction which must be complied with by the licensee and any others who are providing services for the lottery scheme. The terms and conditions are reviewed below.

III Types of Lottery Schemes

Before a charitable organization decides whether or not to participate in charitable gaming, it needs to understand the types of lottery schemes that are available. They need to understand the basics of the lottery scheme before they can decide whether or not it is appropriate for their organization. For example, if the organization does not have sufficient numbers of *bona fide* members over 19 years of age, a weekly bingo event is probably not an appropriate lottery scheme. A break open ticket lottery scheme or an occasional raffle ticket lottery scheme may be more appropriate.

There are several types of lottery schemes that are licensed in Canada. Although each jurisdiction will have variations, the charitable gaming industry is a North American one and there are common elements to most games. There will be local differences that reflect cultural, political and market conditions. There are four major lottery schemes in charitable gaming — bingo, break open tickets (or "pull-tabs"), raffles and social gaming. Social gaming events are also known as casino nights and monte carlos.

Not all types of lottery schemes are available to charitable organizations. Subsection 207(4) prohibits anybody (including a charitable or-

---

[111] (1986), 30 C.C.C. (3d) 308 (Alta. Prov. Ct.).
[112] *Ibid.*, at 311. See also *R. v. MacKenzie* (1982), 135 D.L.R. (3d) 174 for a discussion of what amounted to "conduct" for purposes of a pyramid scheme.

ganization) other than a government of a province (or its Crown corporation) from conducting and managing a lottery scheme operated on a video device, computer or slot machine. That subsection effectively gives the provincial governments a monopoly over the most lucrative forms of gaming — slot machines, video lottery terminals and similar gaming devices.

Although several provinces, including British Columbia, Alberta, Manitoba and Ontario provide charitable organizations with access either directly or indirectly to the proceeds of these gaming devices, no province permits charitable organizations to conduct and manage lottery schemes using the devices. The access is provided in a few ways. For example, in Ontario and Alberta, some of the proceeds are used to fund charitable activities. Ontario and Alberta also conduct and manage an electronic form of bingo and the charitable organizations in the bingo halls receive funds from the proceeds of the electronic bingo. In Ontario, Super Star and Linked bingo are operated using charity volunteers and the relevant charities share in the net proceeds. It is likely that this type of arrangement will become increasingly important to charitable gaming because without it, charities will not have the benefit of the most lucrative areas of gaming. Indeed, in British Columbia, the approach announced in early 2002 seems to remove the charity from any direct role in the conduct, management or operation of bingo.

Bingo is the largest charitable gaming activity in most Canadian jurisdictions. It is often a social occasion and develops a loyal customer base. Players often play once or more a week. A bingo event will include several bingo games over a period of time, most often about two hours. Bingo is a lottery scheme where players are awarded a cash or merchandise prize for being the first player to complete a specified arrangement of numbers on pre-printed bingo cards. The numbers are selected on a random basis and called as they are selected by a bingo caller. Typically, the bingo game will have 75 balls with 75 different numbers, although 90 or 80 balls may be used in some halls. The balls are placed in a machine which mechanically selects a ball on a random basis. The randomness is achieved by a mechanical bingo blower that blows a ball into a shute. The ball is then "called" by the bingo caller and displayed. The verbal call is the official calling of the number. The ball is then dropped onto a board, which triggers the number to be displayed on a display board. The ball may also be displayed as it is called using a television camera and monitors. Both of these methods of display provide players with a sense of fairness and verification that the number called is, in fact, the number that was selected. The caller will select and call a ball approximately every six seconds. This time permits a typical bingo player to play up to 24 cards (six strips of three cards per strip). Some players can, of course, play more and others fewer cards.

Break open tickets are instant win lottery tickets and are commonly known as pull tabs, nevada tickets or "BOTs". BOTs are laminated cardboard tickets with "windows". The windows are perforated to permit the player to break open the window. Underneath the window are symbols, the correct combination of which will result in a cash prize. The cost of the ticket, the number of prizes, the number of tickets in a box or "deal" and the number of the prizes are all predetermined and approved as part of the approval and licensing process.

Raffles are a traditional form of gaming and so prevalent that sometimes the persons who are conducting and managing them do not consider them to be gaming or gambling. However, raffles are a game of chance and a lottery scheme — they involve consideration, chance and a prize. There are several types of raffles, the most common being the stub draw. The raffles tickets are paper tickets with two parts. The first half of the ticket will usually include the player's name, address and telephone number for future identification. It also includes a unique serial number for each ticket. This half is retained by the licensee and placed in a drum or other device. At a predetermined date and time, one or more such portions are selected and the number drawn is a winner. The second half is retained by the player at the time of purchase. It has a matching number. It will also include information about the licensee and the raffle itself, such as draw date, prizes and so forth. A "50/50" raffle is a form of raffle that is a common variation on the stub draw. It is often for smaller prizes. In this raffle, the player whose stub is drawn wins 50 per cent of the proceeds and the licensee retains the other 50 per cent.

Social gaming involves table games, such as blackjack, that are conducted and managed by licensees. In British Columbia and Alberta, video lotteries may also be conducted and managed by the provincial governments at the same sites. Social gaming in Ontario does not include either video lottery terminals or slot machines. Those lottery schemes are available at race-tracks and four charity casinos operated by the Ontario Gaming and Lottery Corporation without the participation of charitable organizations.

IV TERMS AND CONDITIONS TO LICENCES

(1) Authority for Terms and Conditions

The terms and conditions to licences are generally of two types — those that apply to all licences and licensees and those that are specific to a particular type of lottery scheme. In addition, a licensing authority may impose terms and conditions specific to a licensee to address issues and problems that have occurred previously or that may occur. The authority to impose terms and conditions is in subs. 207(2) of the *Criminal Code*.

The provinces provide for terms and conditions either pursuant to an order in council or through legislation. Although there are differences among the various terms and conditions to reflect policy and program decisions in each jurisdiction, the overall intentions for the terms and conditions are similar and cover comparable issues.[113] The discussion below is based on the terms and conditions in Ontario.

(2) General Terms and Conditions

(a) Introduction

The terms and conditions for lottery licences are issued for each type of lottery scheme.[114] There are, however, a number of terms and conditions that are common for most of the licences. These terms and conditions are generally related to the overall control over the lottery scheme, the financial management of the lottery scheme and compliance requirements.

The general terms and conditions require that the licensee be responsible and accountable for the overall conduct and management of the lottery scheme.[115] The licensee, therefore, shall control and decide all operational, administrative and staffing requirements for the lottery scheme.[116] Although the licensee may seek and obtain the advice of a gaming supplier with respect to these matters, it is the licensee that must make the decisions.

(b) Conduct of the Event

The licensee must also conduct and manage the lottery scheme in accordance with the law, such as the *Criminal Code* and the *Gaming Control Act, 1992*,[117] but also in accordance with all other federal, provincial and municipal laws.[118] As a result, if a charitable organization wanted to conduct and manage a rubber duck raffle, it must comply with all environmental laws. All advertising and sales must comply with the *Competition Act*. If a bingo event is being conducted and managed in the charitable organization's premises, those premises must be zoned under the municipal

---

[113] For a fuller discussion of the terms and conditions, see D.J. Bourgeois, *The Law of Charitable and Casino Gaming* (Toronto: Butterworths Canada Ltd., 1999).

[114] Terms and Conditions have generally been set out in documents called "Terms and Conditions" which are appended to each licence. Terms and Conditions have been prepared in Ontario for Social Gaming Event Licences (98/06), Raffle Licences (01/96), Regular and Special Bingo Event Licences (03/97), Super Jackpot Bingo Event Licences (97/03), Media Bingo Event Licence (03/95) and Break Open Ticket Licence (12/97). Unless otherwise noted, the discussion with respect to the general terms and conditions that are applicable to all licences is based on the Regular and Special Bingo Event Licences (03/97). It is important to note that terms and conditions are subject to more frequent changes than other legal instruments, such as regulations or statutes. These changes will reflect new policy decisions and address problems that have arisen with respect to lottery schemes or licences.

[115] Regular and Special Bingo Event Licence Terms and Conditions (03/97), section 1.1.

[116] *Ibid.*, section 1.2.

[117] S.O. 1992, c. 24, as am.

[118] *Supra*, note 110, section 1.5.

zoning by-laws for that purpose and all building code and fire code requirements must be met.

The licensee must also conduct and manage the lottery scheme in accordance with the information set out in the application and approved by the licence.[119] For example, an application for a regular or special bingo licence indicates whether it is for one bingo or a series of bingo events and, if so, for what time period. It will also set out the dates and times of the bingo event, including start and finish times and the total value of the prizes. The application will list the charitable or religious objects or purposes to which the proceeds are to be used in detail. The applicant must also provide its incorporation number (if incorporated), how long it has been in existence, the number of members, and, if it is registered as a charity, its registration number with the Canada Customs and Revenue Agency. The application must include the premises at which the bingo games will be conducted, including the name of the bingo hall operator, location and capacity, what equipment and services are to be included in the "hall rent" and what the proposed administrative expenses will be. The game schedule is to be attached for approval of the licensing authority. The members in charge must also be identified. The licensee cannot deviate from the information provided without obtaining an amendment to the licence.[120]

(c)   Bona fide Members

The licensee shall carry out its responsibilities through *bona fide* members of the organization or registered gaming suppliers.[121] Certain functions may only be carried out by *bona fide* members. Who is or is not a *bona fide* member has been an issue at various times. A number of situations have arisen where members of convenience have been used who are purported to be *bona fide* members of the organization. These individuals were, in fact, employees of the gaming supplier who became members for any organization for which they provided services, regardless of whether or not they even knew the name or purposes of the organization.

A *bona fide* member, for purposes of lottery licensing, is an individual who is eligible to be a member of the organization in accordance with the criteria for membership.[122] The criteria for membership are usually set out in the organization's letters patent, supplementary letters patent, by-laws, deed of trust, memorandum of association, constitution or similar document. The individual must also have been admitted as a member by the board of directors or whoever has authority to admit individuals as members. The individual's name and address should be on the organi-

---

[119] *Ibid.*, section 1.4.
[120] Application to Conduct and Manage a Bingo Lottery, (98/06).
[121] Terms and Conditions, section 3.2.
[122] AGCO Information Bulletin No. 018, February 12, 1999.

zation's register of members. In the case of corporations, the incorporating statutes require that a register be kept. Prudent organizations would do so in any event. The member must also remain a member in good standing, as provided for in the organization's documentation.

A *bona fide* member cannot, however, be only a member of convenience in order to circumvent the intentions of the lottery licensing process. An individual who is a *bona fide* member of any organization would not be a member out of convenience. He or she would usually have other functions within the organization or participate in the objects of the organization in ways other than just assisting in the lottery scheme. For example, a member of a service club, such as a Rotary Club or Knights of Columbus, would attend regular meetings and participate in other events. A member of a religious congregation would attend religious services. A member of a theatre group would participate in the productions as a member of the cast or crew or in similar functions.

The terms and conditions for each lottery scheme set out the specific requirements for that lottery scheme. However, in general terms, the *bona fide* members must supervise all activities related to the conduct and management of the lottery scheme, complete and file the required financial reports, ensure that the terms and conditions of the licence and any other conditions imposed by the licensing authority are complied with, keep and maintain records and carry out the required reconciliations with respect to the lottery event.[123]

The licensee, in order to carry out these functions, must have at least three *bona fide* members, over the age of 18 years, to be in charge of and responsible for the conduct of the bingo. These individuals must be continuously present during the event.[124] In the case of bingo, these individuals would normally sell the bingo paper to players, handle the cash, distribute bingo paper for games to runners to sell on the floor, and pay the prizes to the winners, usually using runners.

If the licensee also supplies the runners, a typical bingo event would require more than the minimum of three *bona fide* members. These additional individuals may be *bona fide* members, full-time employees of the licensee (whose functions are primarily not related to charitable gaming) or volunteers. The volunteers cannot receive remuneration or reimbursement for any out-of-pocket expenses.[125]

The licensee must also ensure that if it uses gaming goods or services supplied by a gaming supplier that that person is registered under the *Gaming Control Act*.[126] It shall not allow any person, including individuals

---

[123] *Supra*, note 115, section 3.1.
[124] *Ibid.*, section 3.1.
[125] AGCO Information Bulletin No. 022, November 30, 1999.
[126] *Supra*, note 115, section 3.5. Pursuant to section 3.6, the licensee shall not pay the wages of the employees of the bingo hall operator. The operator is responsible for all remuneration, including any statutory or other benefits, deductions and remittances with respect to all employees.

as gaming assistants, whose registration has been terminated, revoked, suspended or refused to participate in any way in the conduct or management of the event.[127]

The licensee decides how to staff a bingo event. It may use only *bona fide* members who volunteer their services to act as runners and the caller or it may use employees of the bingo hall operator as runners or the caller. If the bingo sponsors' association has entered into a memorandum of understanding with the hall operator that has been approved in writing by the licensing authority, the licensee may also use runners employed by the hall operator. The licensee would pay for those runners separate from the hall rent and only if there is a profit from the bingo event. The total payment, including GST, cannot exceed three per cent of the prize board and cannot be more than 40 per cent of the profits. The licensee may also use a combination of the three, where it considers it appropriate to do so.[128] The runners may only verify winners, award prizes obtained from the licensee and sell bingo paper for games during the bingo event.[129]

(d) Lottery Trust Account, Proceeds and Expenses

The control over the proceeds from the lottery scheme is a critical aspect of conduct and management. Those proceeds are "trust" funds to be used for the purposes set out in the lottery licence application and approved by the licensing authority. This requirement exists both at common law and by necessary implication of paragraph 207(1)(b) of the *Criminal Code*. In addition, s. 11 of Order in Council 2688/93 also requires that the proceeds be used for such purposes. Paragraph 11(1)(b) provides, as a term and condition of the licence, that:

> ... the gross proceeds from the lottery shall be used for the charitable or religious objects or purposes providing a direct benefit to the residents of Ontario as set out by the licensee in the application for a licence, less the cost of the prizes awarded and such reasonable and necessary expenses actually incurred in the management and conduct of the lottery, and such expenses shall be restricted to those set out in the terms and conditions of the licence.

The issue of what are "proceeds" at common law is not clear. Are "proceeds" the total amount bet by the players? or is it the amount that remains after the payment of prizes? or the net amount after the licensee fee has been paid? or after all expenses have been paid? The Order in Council seems to take the approach that gross proceeds is the amount bet by the players, out of which the prizes and expenses are paid. This

---

[127] *Ibid.*, section 3.6.
[128] *Ibid.*, section 3.2. See also AGCO Information Bulletin No. 022, November 30, 1999.
[129] *Ibid.*, section 3.4.

approach would, arguably, mean that all of the gross proceeds are subject to the "charitable trust". That charitable trust, in turn, would be conditioned by any lawful obligations that are owing that gave rise to the proceeds being available, i.e., the payment of prizes, licensing fees and expenses.

The court cases would appear to be generally, but not universally consistent, with this approach. In *R. v. Brampton*,[130] the Supreme Court of Canada seems to have considered "proceeds" to be stakes or bets but also the "commission" for the operator of the common gaming house. In the *Keystone Bingo Centre Inc. v. Manitoba Lottery Foundation*[131] case, the court referred to *R. v. Brampton* and concluded that "proceeds" were the profits generated from the gambling, but did not state exactly what was included. In *Keystone*, the court did seem to include even the profits from the canteen.

The more recent Nanaimo Community Bingo Association v. British Columbia (Attorney General)[132] looked to who had a share in the "proceeds". It seems to have included in what are "proceeds" those funds that were used to pay expenses of a bingo hall operator. This approach, of including in the definition of "proceeds" all funds flowing directly from the gaming activities, is also the one taken by the House of Lords in Payne v. Bradley.[133]

In any event, the definition of "gross proceeds" in section 1 of the Order in Council specifies that it means "all money and other things of value received by a person in the conduct of a lottery event". It is from these gross proceeds that the licensee pays the prizes and expenses. And it is these gross proceeds for which it must be able to account and to maintain appropriate books and records.

The licensee must have a lottery trust account that is used to make all deposits and all payments,[134] with a few exceptions peculiar to each lottery scheme. It holds these proceeds in trust for its charitable purposes as set out in its application for a lottery licence.[135] That lottery trust account may only be used for that purpose and other funds cannot be commingled with lottery trust funds.[136] There is one exception with respect to Superstar Bingo or similar games conducted and managed by the Ontario Gaming and Lottery Corporation.[137] The licensee may, in certain circumstances, use only one lottery trust account for all lottery schemes or use separate lottery trust accounts for all lottery schemes.[138] Any inter-

---

[130] [1932] 4 D.L.R. 209 (S.C.C.).
[131] (1990), 76 D.L.R. (4th) 423 (Man. C.A.).
[132] (1998), 52 B.C.L.R. (3d) 284, [1999] 2 W.W.R. 428 (B.C.S.C.).
[133] [1962] A.C. 343 (H.L.).
[134] *Supra*, note 115, sections 12.1 to 12.4.
[135] *Ibid.*, section 12.1.
[136] *Ibid.*, section 12.5.
[137] *Ibid.*, section 12.7.
[138] *Ibid.*, subsection 12.1(b).

est that is earned on the lottery trust account or accounts must be used for the licensee's approved charitable purposes.[139]

It may open one designated lottery trust account for each type of lottery scheme or for all lottery schemes that it conducts and manages. Each designated lottery trust account shall be maintained in the name of the licensee, in trust. The accounts shall have cheque writing privileges and monthly statements. All cheques are to be returned with the monthly statement.[140]

The licensee must pay all prizes and expenses incurred out of the gross proceeds from the lottery scheme.[141] There are some practical exceptions to this requirement. For example, if the licence fee is to be paid at the time of the issuance of a lottery scheme, the source of the funds for the first licence would need to be other than a lottery scheme. However, those funds for the payment of the licence fee would have to be reimbursed and accounted for from the lottery proceeds. Similarly, if the lottery scheme's proceeds are not sufficient to pay for the prizes, there is still a legal, contractual obligation to pay the prizes. The licensee may, with the approval of the licensing authority, use funds other than lottery proceeds to do so.

The situation is different with respect to gaming suppliers. Depending upon the circumstances, the supplier may not be in a legal position to collect on any outstanding debt arising from a lottery scheme that did not have sufficient proceeds to pay all prizes and expenses. For example, in the case of break open tickets, if the break open tickets do not sell, the basis on which payment is to be calculated and earned has not occurred. The commission is a maximum percentage to be paid based on sales. If a bingo event does not have a net profit after payment of the prizes, the bingo hall operator would not be able to collect any "rent". The rent to be paid is a maximum of 40 per cent of the "profits" from the bingo event.

In administering the lottery trust account, the licensee must have at least two signing officers who must be *bona fide* members of the licensee. These officers must sign the cheques. All withdrawals must be made only by cheque in order to provide a paper record for tracking and audit purposes.[142]

The licensee shall deposit all monies derived from the operation of lottery events into this account as soon as it is practical to do so. The deposits must be by deposit slip in order to create a paper trail. Although electronic transfers of funds are available at most financial institutions, to date, such transfers have not been approved for lottery proceeds. All withdrawals from the account shall be made by cheque, again to create a paper trail. The cheques may only be written to pay for expenses in-

---

[139] *Ibid.*, section 12.3.
[140] *Ibid.*, section 12.2.
[141] *Ibid.*, section 12.4.
[142] *Ibid.*, section 12.4.

curred in the conduct of the lottery, to disburse the net proceeds to members organizations (in the case of a licensee that is a bingo association) or to donate the proceeds in accordance with the lottery licence and approved use of proceeds. The donation of proceeds occurs frequently with service clubs whose charitable object is to support charitable organizations in their community.

Where only one lottery trust account is maintained for more than one lottery scheme, or where monies from Ontario Gaming and Lottery Corporation bingo-themed games, such as Superstar Bingo are deposited, the licensee shall maintain separate ledgers for each.[143] The ledgers shall outline the financial details for each type of lottery event conducted, by game and licence, including proceeds derived from each, expenses paid and a list of how the proceeds were disbursed.

There are limited number of circumstances in which the Registrar of Alcohol and Gaming may permit a licensee to move lottery proceeds from the designated lottery trust account to the licensee's operating account. If the licensee has only charitable objects and all its revenues are used solely to deliver its charitable activities, it may be permitted to transfer the proceeds to its operating account.

The licensee must apply for permission from the Registrar and satisfy the Registrar that it is eligible for this privilege. The Registrar will review the licensee's constituting documents, charitable programs, financial statements, annual reports and such other documents as are necessary to demonstrate that the organization is eligible. The licensee must also agree to additional terms and conditions, which are to be issued by the municipal licensing authority and/or by the Registrar.

The licensee must demonstrate that it has an accounting system and financial controls that will track the lottery proceeds and assure accountability for those funds. All expenses related to the lottery scheme itself must continue to be paid out of the lottery trust account. The transfer may occur only by cheque drawn on the lottery trust account. The cheque must include on it the licence number and the approved use of proceeds. Subledgers must be in place to track the approved transfer through the accounting system. In addition, all of its books and records must be readily available to the licensing authority.

(e)   Books and Records

The licensee must maintain the usual types of financial books and records that a business would maintain. Licensees must maintain those books and records for a minimum of 4 years.[144] However, other statutory requirements, such as taxing legislation, may require a licensee to maintain the books and records for longer periods. Books and records are defined in the terms and conditions as documents outlining financial

---

[143] *Ibid.*, section 12.6.
[144] *Ibid.*, section 11.3.

details of the lottery event. They include ledgers, subledgers, cheque books, cheque stubs, deposit books, deposit slips, bank statements, cancelled cheques, receipts, invoices and control sheets. Any other books and records used by the licensee are also included.[145]

The licensee shall obtain receipts for most of the expenses incurred.[146] There are some exceptions with respect to certain out of pocket expenses, such as honorarium for *bona fide* members. Typically, a licensee would keep and maintain invoices, receipts and other supporting documentation, ledgers and financial reports and statements. The financial reports would include the lottery licence report that is required to be filed. The licensee must, in any event, maintain detailed records of the disbursement of all proceeds derived from the conduct and management of the lottery scheme.[147]

The licensee shall provide unencumbered access to the licensee's books, records and other documents related to the conduct and management of the lottery schemes and the use of proceeds. It shall also deliver to the licensing authority within the time period specified by the licensing authority the licensee's books, records and other documents.[148] These books, records and other documents include, but are not limited to, those that are related to the conduct and management of the lottery schemes and to the use of proceeds. The licensing authority may also require the licensee to provide other materials for audit and investigation purposes. These materials could include, for example, any inventory that is being kept by the licensee under a licence. A similar requirement is also provided for in paragraph 11(1)(c) of Order in Council 2688/93.

(f)   Financial Reports and Financial Statements

The licensee shall provide the licensing authority with a financial report outlining the results of the lottery scheme, the expenses and use of proceeds. The financial report will include copies of all deposit slips (both sides, including the verification stamp by the financial institution). The financial report is to be filed within 15 days of the bingo or within 30 days of the expiry of any licence. Typically, the financial report will be filed before a new licence will be issued for ongoing lottery schemes such as bingos or break open tickets. The licensing authority may request further documentation about the lottery scheme, expenses and use of proceeds.[149]

Each year, the licensee shall file with all licensing authorities that issued it a licence the licensee's financial statements.[150] These financial

---

[145] *Ibid.*, definition of "books and records".
[146] *Ibid.*, section 11.1.
[147] *Ibid.*, section 11.2.
[148] *Ibid.*, section 11.4.
[149] *Ibid.*, sections 13.1 and 13.2.
[150] *Ibid.*, section 13.3.

statements are to be filed within 180 days of the licensee's year end. The financial statements are to include a summary of the financial information with respect to the receipt and use of lottery proceeds from all lottery schemes (and any Ontario Gaming and Lottery Corporation monies derived from bingo-themed lottery schemes, such as Superstar Bingo). The financial statements are also to show, either in the body or in notes, all the expenses, disbursements, net proceeds and use of net proceeds for each lottery scheme for which it was licensed. The licensee must also file a "compliance report" certifying that it has complied with the terms and conditions of the licence.

The type of compliance report and the level of audit or review of the financial statements will depend upon the amounts that are derived from the lottery schemes. If the licensee derived less than $50,000 from net lottery proceeds (including Ontario Gaming and Lottery Corporation bingo-themed lottery schemes), the financial statements must be prepared consistent with the recommendations of the *Canadian Institute of Chartered Accountants (CICA) Handbook*[151] and verified by the board of directors of the licensee. Where a licensing authority requires it, a compliance report must also be filed. It must be verified by the board of directors of the licensee.[152]

If the licensee had proceeds of $50,000 or more from lottery proceeds (including Ontario Gaming and Lottery Corporation bingo-themed lottery schemes) there are two options. A licensee that is otherwise required to obtain audited financial statements, such as a corporation without share capital incorporated under the Ontario *Corporations Act*,[153] the financial statements must be audited by a public accountant. The compliance report must be prepared by the public accountant in accordance with s. 5815 of the *CICA Handbook*.[154] If the licensee is not otherwise required by law to obtain audited financial statements, it must at minimum provide financial statements that have been reviewed by a public accountant in accordance with ss. 8100 (General Review Standards) and 8200 (Reviews of Financial Statements) of the *CICA Handbook*. The compliance report must be prepared by the public accountant in accordance with s. 8600 of the *CICA Handbook*.[155]

A licensing authority may also require other information, materials, financial statements, audited financial statements, review engagement reports, compliance reports or auditor's reports on compliance. The licensee is obliged to provide it to the licensing authority within the time period specified by the licensing authority.[156] The licensee may, however, use lottery proceeds to pay for the preparation of the annual financial

---

[151] *CICA Handbook* (Toronto: The Canadian Institute for Chartered Accountants, 1993).
[152] *Supra*, note 115, subsection 13.4(a).
[153] R.S.O. 1990, c. C.40, as am.
[154] *Supra*, note 115, subsection 13.4(b).
[155] *Ibid.*, subsection 13.4(c).
[156] *Ibid.*, section 13.5.

statements and compliance reports or otherwise as required under the terms and conditions. The expenses are not included in the expense maximums set out in the terms and conditions.[157]

Audits and review engagement reports may be expensive. In addition, the requirements have been enhanced in recent years to ensure accountability throughout the process. Similar enhancements have occurred in general in accounting of charitable organizations by the CICA itself. There are certain areas in any operation that are more critical than others, both for purposes of the financial statements and the compliance reports. This statement is not meant to suggest that full disclosure and full compliance is not required; rather there are some aspects that are considered by most people to be more important than others.

The public accountant has an important role to play and responsibility in ensuring accountability and proper use of funds. This role and responsibility arises out of their professional responsibilities in performing any audit or engagement review. As with other audits and engagement reviews, a significant level of professional judgment comes into play in carrying out the audit or engagement review. The *CICA Handbook* provides some direction and guidance to public accountants in this regard.

The scope of the audit or the engagement review is the responsibility of the public accountant, consistent with their professional obligations and the purposes of the audit or engagement review. As with any financial or compliance audit or engagement review, an auditor will not examine in detail all areas. There are certain areas of any lottery scheme and its conduct, management and operation that are more susceptible to direct examination. Compliance with other areas can sometimes only be deduced from other evidence; some areas are almost impossible to audit or review.

Nevertheless, an overall financial position and level of compliance can probably be obtained. While it may not be possible for the auditor to verify personally that a break open ticket dispenser was always at least one-half full, the auditor can review the procedures used to determine if the procedures are in place to ensure compliance. Alternatively, the auditor can, where warranted, make a visual check. This approach would not be possible, of course, if the auditor is not retained until after the year end.

Licensing authorities will normally be more interested in those terms and conditions that relate to proceeds and expenses than some others. This level of interest is appropriate given that the funds are "trust" monies that are derived from an exemption in the *Criminal Code* and expenses are strictly regulated. As a result, compliance with the books and records, reporting, banking and financial requirements are essential.

The person carrying out the audit, engagement review or review should assess compliance as against each of the terms and conditions. The compliance report should set out the findings for each term and

---

[157] *Ibid.*, section 13.6.

condition. Where a finding is not possible, the compliance report should note that fact and why. For example, the term and condition that requires that the dispenser be at least one-half full would be difficult to assess after the fact. The auditor could note that fact but that the licensee's procedures are adequate to ensure compliance in foreseeable circumstances.

If the board of directors is verifying compliance, they may, in fact, be in a better position to check on compliance on an ongoing basis. For example, while an auditor may not be able to check after the fact that the break open ticket dispenser was always at least one-half full, a director of a service club where the break open tickets are sold could do so on a regular basis. An auditor could also recommend to licensees, as part of their compliance report, that a director be assigned to do so and to report to the board on a regular basis. These reports could then be used by the auditor in the compliance report for that year.

The compliance report, whether prepared by a public accountant or by the board of directors, should identify clearly where any breaches or apparent breaches of the terms and conditions occurred. The licensing authority may use this information to develop special terms and conditions for the licences to ensure that the problems are addressed and resolved. The information may also be used to suspend, to cancel or to refuse a licence. These steps are usually left to situations where there has been an ongoing problem that has not been addressed and resolved by the licensee or where there is a serious problem, such as fraud, theft or use of unregistered gaming suppliers or gaming assistants.

The licensee should also use the information to correct any problems on their own because the board of directors and members in charge are potentially liable for any losses or damages that result from the problems. Turning a blind eye may be an initial reaction of some but it permits the problem to continue and to grow. Licensing authorities recognize that honest mistakes can happen. The reaction to the honest mistake and how it is corrected, or not corrected, is equally important in any assessment of eligibility and in what administrative or other action is appropriate.

Financial statements are another important tool to ensure accountability on the part of licensees. The financial statements, the notes to financial statements and supplemental information are important in determining eligibility for a licence — both initially and on an ongoing basis. The information should disclose in a clear and concise fashion the trust and other assets and liabilities relating to lottery events, the amount and source of lottery proceeds raised from both provincial and municipal licences, the use of the lottery proceeds, the objects of the organization and how those objects were being met by the use of proceeds. Specific types of licences will also have their own information requirements. For example, a bingo association would need to show the net proceed allocation to its members.

A licensee with less than $50,000 in lottery proceeds may have two signing officers of the lottery trust account sign the financial statements with respect to the lottery schemes. The board of directors must verify these financial statements. Where the amount is greater than $50,000, a public accountant must report on the financial statements, either by audit opinion or engagement review.

Financial statements should be prepared on an accrual basis and include at minimum a balance sheet, statement of proceeds and expenses and supplemental information and notes. The balance sheet should include lottery-related assets, such as lottery trust account, inventory (if any, such as break open tickets), prepaid lottery expenses and liabilities, such as amounts payable to gaming suppliers as at year end. The statement of proceeds and expenses should disclose the gross proceeds and the expenses for each type of lottery scheme during the period.

The supplemental information should include schedules or notes setting out the information on an event or licence basis. The licence number should be included in this information. The supplemental information should also include a list or schedule setting out in detail the use of the net proceeds. Given that the funds are trust monies and to be used only for the purposes set out in the licence application and approved by the licence, this schedule should relate the use of proceeds to the purposes.

Licensing authorities want to ensure, as do most licensees, that the funds raised from charitable gaming are used to fulfill the charitable objects of the licensee as approved in the licence. The financial statements are critical to providing the level of assurance that is needed — to the licensing authority, to the licensee and its members, and to the public through the licensing authority. The financial statements may disclose problems — ranging from inadequate record keeping to fraud and theft. As with compliance issues, it is important to identify and correct the problems.

(g)   Conflict of Interest

The Registrar has also established general conflict of interest guidelines, to ensure both the integrity of the lottery scheme and that players and the public perceive it to be so. Public confidence is essential for charitable gaming to be successful and to maintain the integrity of charitable organizations.

A member or principal officer of an organization should not be involved in approving the application for a licence. For example, a municipal councillor ought not to be involved in approving an application for a licence if he or she is a member of the organization, especially as an officer or director. He or she also should not sign the application.

Once the licence is issued, those persons who will be participating in the conduct and management of the lottery scheme should not have any interest in the outcome of it. They should not purchase a ticket or bingo card or place a bet.[158]

Individuals involved in the conduct and management of the lottery scheme should not have a direct or indirect personal interest in the proceeds. For example, the designated member in charge for a youth sports organization should not be a coach for the organization and receive payment for coaching services from the lottery proceeds. Similarly, the coach should not be a break open ticket seller for that licensee. A bingo hall manager or caller should not provide any services to licensees in the conduct and management of the lottery scheme, other than in his or her role as a gaming assistant. He or she should not, therefore, be a volunteer for the licensee at the bingo hall he or she manages or at which he or she calls.[159]

(3) Specific Terms and Conditions

Each type of lottery scheme will have specific terms and conditions that are related to the unique features or issues of that scheme. These terms and conditions will be concerned with the types of expenses and the maximum amounts that are permitted, operational aspects of the lottery scheme (such as staffing), approval for equipment, reporting requirements and the bingo sponsors' association. They are very detailed and should be reviewed before making a decision on which type of lottery scheme to conduct and manage.

This chapter will not review in detail the specific terms and conditions.[160] However, there are some provisions on the terms and conditions that are important in making a decision to conduct and manage that lottery scheme, in particular for bingo licences.

The bingo licensee has a number of responsibilities in the conduct and management of a bingo event. The licensee must ensure that:

- the bingo paper, supplies and equipment comply with the standards established by the Registrar,
- if personal bingo verifiers (an electronic device used solely as an aid to players) are available, they comply with the terms and conditions for use and are approved,
- only those games that are approved on the licence are played,
- the games are played in accordance with the rules of the game, including those rules that are applicable for the use of American currency,

---

[158] *Ibid.*, section 6.1.
[159] See the "Conflict of Interest Guidelines" in the *Lottery Licensing Policy Manual* for a further discussion of this topic at 17.21 to 17.22.
[160] See D.J. Bourgeois, *The Law of Charitable and Casino Gaming* (Toronto: Butterworths Canada Limited, 1999) for a fuller discussion of the specific terms and conditions.

- it verifies that the player has won the prize before it is paid out,
- any advertising complies with the terms and conditions and that the licensee is responsible for its design, placement and payment,
- the bingo hall operator complies with the terms and conditions of the licence, provides the goods and services that it is contracted to provide and payment is made in accordance with the terms and conditions,
- it files a complete and accurate bingo lottery report within 15 days of the bingo event. If the bingo hall is a pooling hall, there are special terms and conditions for licensees who participate in the pool.

Bingo sponsors' associations are mandatory in all bingo halls where more than one licensee conducts and manages a bingo. These associations help to balance the relationship between the bingo hall operator and the licensee. The associations act on behalf of the members and administer certain bingo events (super jackpot) and other lottery schemes, such as break open tickets, in the hall. It will also administer the agreement with the Ontario Gaming and Lottery Corporation with respect to certain lottery schemes in the bingo hall, such as Super Star and Link bingo.

V USE OF PROCEEDS

The *Policy Manual* provides guidance to lottery licensing authorities on both the legal and policy issues with respect to use of proceeds. In general, use of proceeds is based on the eligibility — if the organization is eligible, it may use the proceeds for its charitable purposes. There are some specific exceptions to this general position for particular types of lottery schemes. For example, the proceeds from a provincial break open ticket licence (P-BOTS) may only be used for direct delivery of services to residents of Ontario throughout Ontario. The proceeds may not be used for administrative expenses or for research purposes.

The use of proceeds will also depend upon the legal character of the organization. If the organization is exclusively charitable, it may use the proceeds to carry out any of its objects, subject to the approval of the licensing authority. If the organization is a not-for-profit organization but with a mixture of both charitable and non-charitable objects, it may use the proceeds only to carry out those objects that are charitable. A service club is typically an organization with both charitable and non-charitable objects. Its charitable objects are usually to donate monies to charitable organizations in their community.

An organization that is registered as a charitable organization or charitable foundation under the *Income Tax Act*[161] and files annually with the Public Guardian and Trustee under the *Charities Accounting Act*[162] will usually be considered to have exclusively charitable objects. However, the review of its use of proceeds does not necessarily end at that determination. The licensing authority must also be satisfied that it is only carrying out charitable activities and those charitable activities fall within the organization's objects. The test of charitableness is both a legal one and a factual one. This issue is discussed in Chapter 1.

The *Policy Manual* sets out a list of approved uses for each category of charity.[163] This list is based on the law of charities, policy considerations and experience with lottery programs. The approval of any use not included in the list, or for that matter of any use including those on the list, is at the discretion of the lottery licensing authority. In most cases, if the intended use identified in the application for the licence falls within the list of approved uses, it would normally be approved use of proceeds for that licensee. Municipal licensing authorities do, however, have the jurisdiction under the Order in Council to issue licences for the benefit of the residents of the municipality. As a result, a municipal council could decide to issue licences to organizations that will use the proceeds — within their charitable objects — for particular programs that the municipal council considers best meet the needs of the community.

The *Policy Manual* also establishes three categories of charitable organizations for lottery licensing and use of proceeds purposes.[164] Category 1 organizations are ones with only charitable objects. These organizations will be registered charities under the *Income Tax Act*. They may use lottery proceeds for most of their expenses, subject to other directions in the *Policy Manual* or the terms and conditions of the licence. In addition, the licensing authority may also restrict use of proceeds on Category 1 organizations.

Service clubs and similar organizations that raise funds for other organizations are Category 2 organizations. Typically, the service club will conduct and manage the lottery scheme with the intention of donating the proceeds to charitable organizations in their community. Those organizations, in turn, carry out their charitable objects. In certain circumstances, the licensing authority may approve the use of proceeds by the

---

[161] Section 149.1(1), R.S.C. 1985, c. I (5th Supp.). It is important to note that the *Income Tax Act* also provides for the registration of other types of not-for-profit organizations for income tax purposes. These organizations are not necessarily "charitable" notwithstanding that they are sometimes considered to be charitable. For example, the reason for the legislation of a distinct category of amateur athletic associations appears to have been because these associations were not considered to be charitable at common law at the time.

[162] R.S.O. 1990, c. C.10.

[163] "Eligibility and Use of Proceeds" *Lottery Licensing Policy Manual* (Toronto: Entertainment Standards Branch, 1993), c. 4.

[164] *Ibid.*, at 4-22 to 4-30.

service club if, for example, the club is providing charitable activities, such as a community centre space.

Category 3 organizations are ones that have a mixture of charitable and non-charitable objects. They raise funds for their own charitable activities. In some cases, all of their objects may be charitable but the organization has decided not to apply for registration as a charity under the *Income Tax Act* or the registration has not been approved at that time. The use of proceeds must be directly related to the organization's own objects and not those of other organizations.

H SPECIAL EVENTS

I GENERAL COMMENTS

Special events can be a lucrative method of raising funds in the short-term and to build relationships for the longer term. They can also be used to enhance public awareness of the organization and its purposes. On the other hand, there are potentially significant legal risks involved in special events, especially where physical activity, food or liquor are involved. As with all fundraising activities, there is also the risk of losses due to poor planning or implementation or events beyond the control of the organization. It does sometimes rain on a parade.[165]

The types of risk that may arise will depend upon the fundraising event. There are some events, however that have intrinsic risks and these events should not be used unless the organization has planned properly and has put protection from legal liability in place. The sale or service of alcoholic beverages, for example, is inherently risky. Similarly, sporting events in which guests participate create risks of physical injury. The sale or service of food also has potential to cause illness. Obviously, the risk of illness will vary depending upon the type of food served (hamburger versus vegetables), the weather conditions (hot weather versus milder temperatures), the hygienic conditions under which the food was prepared or served, and the potential allergies of the consumers.

Certain events may also involve specific legal requirements or authorizations. For example, the sale or service of liquor, with few exceptions, must take place in a licensed premises by a person licensed to sell and serve liquor. Provinces have enacted legislation that control the sale and service of liquor to the public. Some provinces permit organizations to obtain a liquor licence or special occasion permit (or similar authoriza-

---

[165] See H.K. Bjarnason and L.J. Cannell, *Organizing Events — Avoiding Risk and Promoting Safety* (Vancouver: Western Legal Publications (1982) Limited, 1999) for a step-by-step approach to organizing a variety of special events. For a discussion of the pros and cons of several types of special events, see K. Wyman, *Guide to Special Event Fundraising* (Ottawa: Voluntary Action Directorate, Multiculturalism and Citizenship Canada, 1990). Both of these texts have bibliographies with respect to special event fundraising.

tion) to sell or serve liquor.[166] The individuals who sell and serve the liquor may need to have taken training, such as a server intervention program or "Smart Serve" program.

The location of the event may also require a permit or other authorization. The use of municipal property, such as a street, will usually require permission of the municipal government. Municipalities may also require that an organization obtain a business licence or similar legal authorization to carry out certain activities, regardless of whether the activity occurs on public or private property.

In some cases, certain types of activity may be prohibited regardless of the municipal approval. For example, in Ontario, the *Safe Streets Act, 1999*[167] has probably made illegal a number of traditional fundraising events used in rural Ontario and smaller communities. That statute amended the Ontario *Highway Traffic Act*[168] to create new offences with respect to solicitation on public highways.

The statute also creates offences under the statute itself. For example, one form of fundraising involves firefighters "stopping" cars at an intersection and requesting the drivers to make a cash donation. This type of fundraising activity would appear to be an offence under the *Safe Streets Act*. Section 3 makes it an offence to "while on a roadway, solicit a person who is in or on a stopped, standing or parked vehicle". "Solicit" is broadly defined in section 1 to mean:

> ...to request, in person, the immediate provision of money or another thing of value, regardless of whether consideration is offered or provided in return, using the spoken, written or printed word, a gesture or other means.

Every person who contravenes s. 3 is guilty of an offence. Section 5 provides for a fine on conviction of not more than $500 for a first offence and not more than $1,000 and/or imprisonment of not more than six months for each subsequent conviction.

The amendments to s. 177 of the *Highway Traffic Act* create similar offences for a person who stops or attempts to stop a motor vehicle for the purpose of offering, selling or providing any commodity or service to the driver or other persons in the motor vehicle. It is not clear how this provision would affect the use of carwashes, for example, to raise funds.

---

[166] The following provinces permit some form of special licence or permit: British Columbia — *Liquor Control and Licensing Act*, R.S.B.C. 1996, c. 267; Alberta — *Gaming and Liquor Act*, S.A. 1996, c. G-0.5; Saskatchewan — *Alcohol and Gaming Regulation Act*, S.S. 1988-89, c. A-18.01, which is to be replaced by the *Alcohol and Gaming Regulation Act*, S.S. 1997, c. A-18.011 on proclamation; Manitoba — *Liquor Control Act*, R.S.M. 1988, c. L.160; Ontario — *Liquor Licence Act*, R.S.O. 1990, c. L.19; New Brunswick — *Liquor Control Act*, S.N.B., c. L.10; Nova Scotia — *Liquor Control Act*, R.S.N.S. 1989, c. 260; Prince Edward Island — *Liquor Control Act*, S.P.E.I., c. L.14.

[167] S.O. 1999, c. 8.

[168] R.S.O. 1990, c. H-8.

II Risk Identification and Risk Management

(1)   Step 1 — Risk Identification

The board of directors and the organizers of an event must identify the legal and other risks that may arise from the special event. Identification of the risks is the first step in:

- preventing or reducing the risks from occurring,
- laying off or transferring the risk to others either through insurance or waivers,
- preparing for risks during the event through planning, training and bringing appropriate personnel, including health care professionals.

Minimizing risk is important to avoid legal liability but also to ensure that participants enjoy themselves and that the public image of the organization is maintained or enhanced. A case of food poisoning not only leaves the organization open to liability, but it will also affect the willingness of others to participate in the future. It is simply good business to minimize the risks for the organization; and even more important, it avoids injury to others.

Identifying risks is sometimes difficult. One approach is to start with a detailed plan of what will occur, step by step, in the special event. The detailed plan should set out what the potential risks are from all perspectives — that of the volunteer, the participant, any observers, staff, professionals and the organization itself.

(2)   Step 2 — Risk Transference

A second substantial way to minimize the risks of liability to the organization is to lay-off or transfer the risk to others. This can usually be done through the purchase of insurance or from waivers.

(a)   *Insurance*

Insurance should cover both the damages that may be suffered by somebody but also the legal costs that may be associated with the defence and settlement of any claims. There are a number of insurance companies in Canada, each with their own insurance policies. Insurance is usually either general liability insurance, property insurance or for specific activities or risks.

An organization may purchase a general insurance policy for its activities each year. If so, the organization should check to make sure that the policy is sufficient for the special event. If it is not, the insurance should either be enhanced or separate coverage purchased for the special event. Depending upon the types of special events and their frequency, it may be less expensive to purchase coverage on an annual basis.

Insurance policies will also often include endorsements. An endorsement extends the coverage to specific types of activities, such as the sale and service of liquor. An endorsement to a general liability policy for the sale and service of liquor may be cheaper than purchasing a specific policy for two or three events. The insurance policy may also include cross-liability, which protects in situations where one participant may have a claim against another participant. Other types of insurance or endorsements that may be appropriate include the following:

- employer's liability if the organization is not contributing to a provincial workers' compensation insurance program,
- property insurance for property that is temporarily at a premises other than the usual location, i.e., where the organization's equipment is being used at the special event, or where others are bringing their equipment to the special event,
- automobile insurance for owned, leased or hired motor vehicles, non-owned vehicles and for volunteers and employees,
- cargo insurance, if the organization will be transporting materials or equipment,
- business interruption insurance, if the organization carries on business activities,
- cancellation insurance, where an event may be cancelled due to inclement weather,
- malpractice insurance for any medical personnel, whether volunteers or otherwise,
- prize indemnity insurance to cover any prizes for games of skill, and
- errors and omissions insurance for the officers and directors. Charities may be restricted in purchasing errors and omissions insurance without a court order as it may be seen to be a form of remuneration to the directors.

The organization should consult with an insurer or insurance broker to determine what insurance coverage is appropriate in general for the organization and for a special event. The list above is intended to identify some types of insurance coverage that are available; however, the organization will need to decide on coverage based upon the facts and context in which it operates. It may be, for example, that in order to use public property, the municipality will require the organization to carry $2 million in coverage and to name the municipality as an insured. Or there may be specialized insurance that is very expensive but for which there are alternatives.

The insurer or insurance broker should also advise the organization what risks are not covered by the comprehensive general liability policy and alternatives to address those risks. If the organization is conducting an event outdoors and there is a risk of environmental contamination, it may want to ensure that the insurance does not exclude this risk. Similarly, it is not unusual for policies to exclude injuries caused by criminal offences or human rights violations, such as sexual assault or harassment. If liquor is consumed, a specific endorsement is usually required. The organization should discuss its plan with its insurer or insurance broker so as to put into place the appropriate insurance coverage to minimize the risk of liability to the organization.

(b)   Waivers

Waivers are another method to transfer the risk — in this case not to a third person but back to the participant. Waivers, though, are far from fool-proof, especially if liquor is to be sold or served to participants. There are several types of "waivers":

- waiver — in which the signatory waives any rights to sue in case of injuries,
- release — in which the signatory releases the organization from any liability,
- indemnity — in which the signatory indemnifies the organization or agrees to reimburse the organization for any losses that it may incur as a result of his or her participation. This indemnity could be used, for example, if the signatory injures another player who in turns sues the organization, and
- acknowledgement of risk — in which the signatory acknowledges that the activity has inherent risks.

Each of these types of "waivers" has its own uses and limitations. For example, if the risks are not clearly pointed out to an individual, a court may very well not enforce an acknowledgement of risks or a release. Certainly, a document signed by somebody who is not of the age of majority will be very difficult to enforce. At the very least, the parent or guardian should sign the document on behalf of the child, but even in that case the court may be reluctant to enforce the waiver if the parent did not fully understand what he or she was signing. A document signed by somebody who was incapacitated by alcohol would be of doubtful value. Any consent to participate must be "informed consent" in that the person knows and understands the full nature of what he or she is consenting to, including the level and chance of risk. A person incapacitated by alcohol or drugs may not be able to give an informed consent.

An organization should seek legal advice in the preparation and use of any of these "waivers". The lawyer should prepare the document (which may incorporate the waiver, release, indemnity, and acknowledgement) and provide advice on how to use it and, equally important, when not to use it. The lawyer can advise on the options to waivers, such as using a sign posted in a prominent location or a statement printed on a ticket or brochure.

If the special event involves significant physical activity, such as a marathon, it may be appropriate to require participants to obtain a medical examination and to provide a medical certificate. An individual with medical problems probably should not participate in certain types of physical activities. If a medical doctor determines that the individual is not at risk, at least the organization can look to that doctor should something go wrong.

The medical information about the participant is also relevant in preparing for the event. The information is, of course, confidential and must be treated as such. However, organizers have a legitimate interest in ensuring that the medical support staff at, for example, a sporting event have access to relevant medical information about somebody participating in the event. For example, if the person is allergic to certain types of pain killers, that information would be important to know prior to treating somebody for an injury. An individual may also have a medical condition that endangers others. A decision may need to be made on the participation of that individual in the event and, if so, under what conditions or circumstances.

Information about medical conditions is very confidential and strong safeguards must be in place to ensure that it remains confidential. An organization that fails to protect the confidentiality of the information exposes itself to legal proceedings. Qualified medical practitioners are accustomed to collecting and using confidential medical information. One approach for organizations without their own medical staff is to retain medical practitioners or organizations such as St. John's Ambulance to provide the medical services at the special event.

(3) Step 3 — Preparing for the Risks

The best way to avoid liability is to prevent it or the factors that may give rise to an injury. This approach is beneficial to the organization and to the people who participate in any special event. Prevention involves:

- inspecting the property and equipment to be used in an event and ensuring that they are safe and appropriate for use by those at the event. The property should also have the appropriate washrooms, cleaning stations and so forth to meet the requirements to protect health,
- cancelling an event if the weather poses a danger or moving the event to another location. The weather conditions may also require special precautions, such as making sure that there is an

adequate supply of water to avoid dehydration or warm clothing to protect from the cold,
- addressing in advance situations that may be dangerous to some participants but not to others. For example, individuals in wheelchairs will have special needs in case of a fire,
- if any hazardous materials are being used, such as fireworks, appropriate security measures need to be in place. Use of hazardous materials should comply with the standards that are in place and only experienced and properly trained and accredited individuals should have access to or use them. For example, any person who uses fireworks should have the appropriate training and licence for pyrotechnics,
- is important for most events, especially where large crowds gather, if valuables are around or if the equipment can be tampered with causing a safety hazard. It is the organization's obligation to ensure that those attending an event are safe and secure. A security plan and the hiring of appropriately trained security staff or use of trained volunteers may be required,
- emergency planning is essential. Wherever people gather, there is the possibility of an emergency. Plans should include the use of trained volunteers or professionals for medical emergencies, fire and so forth.

The organization should put into place an incident reporting system for special events. This system is intended to ensure that the records are made and kept of any incidents that could give rise to a claim. The documentation is important for two reasons. First, it provides a record of what happened to whom, when, where and why. This record will be essential in determining what, if any, liability may exist for the organization or the participant. Second, it provides information to the organization about problems or potential problems that can be avoided for the next special event.

The incident reports should be made by the person in the organization who is most familiar with the incident. The information to be gathered should include what happened, when did it happen, who was involved, and where did it happen. The reports should distinguish between an incident that caused an injury from one in which no injury occurred and between serious and less serious injuries. The incident report should also include information about what the response was to the incident. For example, if the incident caused an injury, who called a medical practitioner at what time was he or she called and when that practitioner arrived.

The incident reports are potential evidence just as are similar documents. If the incident involved a criminal offence, the police may obtain a search warrant to seize it. If one participant injured another and is sued, the plaintiff or defendant may seek production of the document by the organization. If the organization is involved in a lawsuit it is likely that its insurer will want to review the incident report. The incident report should, therefore, be accurate but be limited to reporting on the facts and avoid making "judgments". The reports would not normally include "conclusions" about, for example, who is "at fault".

It is important that organizations not only plan for these situations but that they document that they have done so. The courts recognize that sometimes a participant or spectator will be injured in a special event. The cause of the injury, if it was beyond the reasonable control of the organization, may not result in legal liability. However, if the organization cannot demonstrate that it took reasonable steps to identify and prevent the risks, it could be held negligent and liable in whole or in part for the damages.

III PLANNED GIVING

(1) Introduction

Planned giving is, generally, an attempt by both the donor and the organization to maximize the benefits to the donor while attaining the charitable object of both the donor and the organization. The benefits to the charitable or not-for-profit organization are the receipt of a donation that it can use to carry out is objects; the benefits to the donor are usually tax-related or similar financial benefits. Often the planning for the gift may occur during the donor's lifetime, but the receipt of it by the organization will occur after the individual dies or at some other specified period.

Planned giving involves a number of legal and accounting issues. As a result, lawyers and accountants are often used to assist in designing a planned gift on an individual basis and to document that gift in a will, life insurance policy, annuity or trust agreement. The documents should reflect the individual circumstances of the donor and the recipient organization — although there will be commonalities among the plans and documents in order to comply with the law, industry practices and guidelines from the Canada Customs and Revenue Agency.

(2) Kinds of Planned Giving

(a) Bequests

Bequests in a will are a common method for individuals to plan their giving. The organization in that circumstance will need to prepare for the receipt of the bequest. The organization must ensure that its interests are protected under any will and by the person administering the estate.

A charitable or not-for-profit organization will not always know if it is named in a will. Sometimes, the name used in the will is not the legal name of the organization, which may complicate its ability to collect on the bequest. Where an organization is aware that an individual intends to leave it a bequest, the organization should attempt to ensure that the legal name is used so as to avoid potential legal issues with the bequest. Obviously, discretion should be used. If the organization's staff are involved in the planning of the gift, it will be easier to do so. If the organization is aware of potential bequests, it may want to maintain a confidential record so that appropriate follows-up may occur, including after the death of the donor.

The practice is to notify those named in the will of any bequests. An organization should, therefore, be notified by the solicitor or the estate administrator of any bequest. If the organization had maintained a record of potential bequests, it could follow-up with the estate's solicitor or administrator at an appropriate time on the bequest if it has not been notified. The organization might not be notified for a number of reasons, including a failure of the administrator to act in a reasonable period of time, confusion as to what organization is to be the beneficiary of the bequest or a dispute with respect to one or more of the bequests. Although not common, less honourable reasons may also be behind the failure to notify the organization of the bequest.

It is incumbent on the organization to take reasonable steps to ensure that the bequest is realized. For example, the organization should monitor the administration of the estate and periodically make enquiries of the estate solicitor or administrator. If the solicitor or administrator is not acting within a reasonable period, the organization should seek legal advice on how to ensure that the bequest is protected. Similarly, if there is a challenge or dispute to the bequest to the organization or a more general dispute which indirectly involves the bequest to the organization, legal advice should be obtained on how to protect the organization's interests.

The organization should also keep in mind its due diligence obligations with respect to property. If, for example, the bequest leaves the charity with real property, it must be satisfied that the property is not contaminated or otherwise inappropriate. If the property is otherwise satisfactory but cannot be used for charitable purposes, it may be required to sell the property. Similarly, in Ontario, a charitable organization may be required to sell over time any interests in a business that is left to it by bequest.

The directors of the organization are not relieved of their responsibilities around property merely because it is received by bequest. The directors must carry out their due diligence to protect the interests of the organization and its charitable purposes. It may be that the organization must decline the bequest in some circumstances for legal, ethical or other reasons. However, the directors should seek legal advice before making any decision to decline a bequest and may need to obtain the permission of the court, or the Public Guardian and Trustee in Ontario, before doing so.[169]

(b)   Life Insurance

A donor is eligible for a receipt for income tax purposes if he or she donates a life insurance policy to a registered charity. The policy must be assigned absolutely and the charity must be the beneficiary of the policy.[170] If the individual continues to pay the premiums, the amount paid is also eligible for a receipt for income tax purposes.[171]

The donation must be absolute and no right, privilege, benefit or advantage can accrue to the donor, other than the intended tax credit for the gift. Any consents that may be required as a result of a third party interest, such as a spouse or former spouse, must be obtained before the donation is absolute. All provincial legislation must be complied with in obtaining such consents.[172]

The cash surrender value of a whole life insurance policy at the time the gift is made is usually the amount of the donation. The cash surrender value includes the accumulated dividends and interest less any outstanding loans that have been made to the insured. If there is no net cash surrender value in the policy, a receipt for income tax purposes could not be issued for that part of the donation. Any future payments of the premiums would be eligible for an income tax receipt. If the donor repays any outstanding loan on the policy after it has been assigned absolutely to the charity, he or she may be entitled to a tax credit for that amount. However, any ongoing increases in the cash surrender value in the policy due to accumulated dividends and interest are not eligible for a receipt for income tax purposes.[173]

An organization may obtain an interest in a life insurance policy in several ways. The beneficiary of an insurance policy may be changed to the organization. The organization should agree to this change only if it is satisfied that the current beneficiary is not irrevocable or that the beneficiary has some other legal claim to the insurance proceeds. If the policy does not name a beneficiary other than the estate, that may be sufficient provided the transaction was not intended to avoid any lawful obligations to others, such as family members or creditors. The consent of these other people may be necessary and if so must be obtained before the donation will be recognized for income tax purposes. If the organi-

---

[169] See Ministry of Consumer and Commercial Relations and the Office of the Public Guardian and Trustee, *Not-for-Profit Incorporator's Handbook* (Toronto: Queen's Printer for Ontario, 1998) at 6.13, with respect to foregoing a bequest in whole or in part at the request of the next-of-kin.

[170] "Gifts by Individuals of Life Insurance Policies as Charitable Donations", IT-244R3 (Canada Customs and Revenue Agency, Sept. 6, 1991) at 1.

[171] *Ibid.*

[172] *Ibid.*, at 2.

[173] *Ibid.*, at 2.

zation purchases insurance in the name of a donor, the donor's consent will likely be required because it does not have any other interest in the life of the donor.

The organization may also want to consider having the ownership of the policy changed or transferred. If the organization becomes the owner of the policy, it can better protect its interests by, for example, ensuring that the beneficiary is not changed or by making payments on the policy if that becomes necessary in the future. In some cases, donors have not been able to keep up payments and the policy lapsed. The organization may have been in a position to make the payments from other revenues.

In some circumstances, it may be to the donor's advantage not to name the charitable organization as the beneficiary. A similar result can be achieved if the estate is the beneficiary of the insurance policy and the donor's will includes a bequest to the charitable organization for a comparable amount. For the donor, this approach may be useful tax planning because it permits certain "carry-back" provisions to occur. In addition, the death of the donor may trigger a number of deemed realizations, which then become taxable in the year of death. A sizeable donation of the insurance proceeds may help to reduce the tax impact of the deemed realizations.

However, one disadvantage of this approach is that the insurance proceeds do become part of the estate, which may be subject to probate and fees. The receipt of the funds will also likely be delayed until after the estate is wound-up. If the organization is the named beneficiary, it will receive the proceeds (absent unusual circumstances) in a short time period.

Which approach is more appropriate is a matter for analysis and advice on an individual basis. The donor may want to review his or her decision in the future (unless it was irrevocable) if there are financial and tax situations changes. In addition, the donor may want to consider the implications of s. 148 of the *Income Tax Act*. The donor's proceeds of the disposition of the life insurance policy will be the value of the policy at the time of the assignment, which is consistent with the basis of the calculation for purposes of the income tax receipt. If the proceeds exceed the adjusted cost basis of the policy, the donor is required to include that amount as income.[174]

Depending upon the sophistication of the organization's planned giving program, it may be the passive beneficiary of insurance policies or it may become involved in promoting insurance as a method of raising large amounts of money over a longer period. The organization could become involved in a group term plan in which donors purchase insurance policies with a view to making the charity a beneficiary. These types of schemes are complex and the charity must satisfy itself that the insurer is an appropriate insurance company with which it would want to be associated.

---

[174] *Ibid.*, at 2 and 3.

Whatever approach is taken, the charitable organization will be issuing a receipt for income tax purposes, and the amount must be included in its disbursement quota for the next fiscal year. As a result, the charitable organization should be able to ensure that its expenditures on charitable activities will be sufficient to meet its disbursement quota or that it has sufficient flexibility by bringing forward or carrying-back on the quota. The planning of the gift should, therefore, consider whether or not to make the donation subject to a ten-year trust or direction.

If the donation is subject to the ten-year trust or direction, the gift must be held for at least ten years and the donation will be exempt from the disbursement quota for that period. However, it is important to keep track of all such trusts or directions both for purposes of the organization's financial statements but also for inclusion in the disbursement quota calculation in the future.

The premiums paid in subsequent years could also be eligible for the ten-year trust or direction. The Canada Customs and Revenue notes that one way to maximize the exclusion is for the donor to require the charity to keep the policy, or property substituted from the policy, for at least 10 years after the last premium has been paid by the donor.[175] The property substituted from the policy would be the cash received as a result of the death of the insured (donor) or the surrender of the policy.

(c)   Capital Property

Several issues around the donation of capital property were discussed in earlier chapters. There are, however, a number of gifts of property that are made as part of a "planned gift", such as the donation of securities, art work or real property. The donation of capital property is also reviewed by the Canada Customs and Revenue Agency in Interpretation Bulletin IT288R2.[176] Interpretation Bulletin IT297R2, "Gifts in Kind to Charity and Others", discusses the Canada Customs and Revenue's position with respect to fair market value.[177]

(i)   Real Property

Real property sometimes is subject to debt, such as a mortgage. The mortgage may represent a significant portion of the fair market value of the property or be relatively minor. If the property includes a building, there may be substantial income derived from the property. If a donor seeks to give the property to a charity subject to the mortgage, the transfer is probably not a gift for which a receipt for income tax purposes may be given if the charity assumes the mortgage. The donor has re-

---

[175] *Ibid.*, at 3.
[176] As amended by "Explanation for Changes for Interpretation Bulletin IT288R2" January 16, 1995.
[177] March 21, 1990.

ceived a benefit as a result of the charity assuming the mortgage and the transfer would not be eligible to be treated as a gift.

It may be that the charity and the donor can arrange the transaction such that it is one for which a receipt may be issued, but both should seek legal and accounting advice before doing so.[178] The charity must also satisfy itself, even if some arrangement could be worked out that is eligible, that it can adequately pay the mortgage without jeopardizing its other charitable assets and, in Ontario, that it is in compliance with the *Charities Accounting Act*.

The Government of Canada has in recent years encouraged the donation of ecologically sensitive land. The measures are limited to only certain types of charities, but they are potentially useful for charitable organizations involved in conservation and environmental protection.

After 1996, a landowner could obtain a tax credit for up to 100 per cent of net income for a donation of land, including an easement, covenant or servitude (in Quebec), of lands certified by the Minister of Environment as being ecologically sensitive and deserving of conservation and protection. The amount of the donation was the fair market value of any restriction that is placed on the land as a result of the easement, covenant or servitude or the reduction of the land's fair market value by the restriction.[179]

The 2000 Federal Budget created stronger incentives for owners of such property to donate by decreasing the amount of capital gains that is realized on the making of the gift to one-third from one-half. The land must be certified by the Minister of the Environment (or designate) to be ecologically sensitive land and the conservation and protection of that land is important to the preservation of Canada's environmental heritage. The gift must be made to either Her Majesty the Queen in Right of Canada or in right of a province, or to a registered charity, other than a charitable foundation. If the donation is made to a registered charity, the charity must satisfy the Minister of the Environment that one of its main purposes is to conserve and protect Canada's environmental heritage.

(ii) Securities

The donation of securities is very complex. As noted previously, there are restrictions on the ownership of businesses by charitable organizations. Although a not-for-profit organization does not have the same statutory restriction, it should be careful that it is not considered to be, in effect, operating a "business" through a not-for-profit shell or be seen as a "holding company". In addition, once its net assets exceed $200,000,

---

[178] S.G. Mehinagic, "Gifts of Real Property Subject to Debt", *Gift Planning in Canada — A Supplemental Publication of Planned Giving Today*, Volume 5, Number 6 (April 2000), at 1.

[179] RC4142, "Tax Advantages of Donating to Charity", (Canada Customs and Revenue Agency, Oct. 4, 1999) at 10 and 11.

not-for-profit organizations are required to file an annual Information Return under the *Income Tax Act*.

The planned giving of securities has become increasingly common, especially during strong economic times. In addition, as the "new economy" grows, the value of new businesses also grow. The donation of securities has developed into an important method for owners of businesses to donate substantial sums of money through the donation of securities in their businesses. The 2000 Federal Budget increases the incentives for charitable giving of appreciated marketable securities that are traded on exchanges in Canada, the New York Stock Exchange, NASDAQ and many other foreign exchanges, or that are mutual funds or prescribed debt obligations. The improvements, intended to expire in December 31, 2001, are indicative of how the Government of Canada may continue periodically to provide incentives for the donation of securities to charities. Other measures had been put in place in 1996 and 1997 to be in effect until January 1, 2002. The Canada Customs and Revenue Agency noted that these incentives may become permanent "if it is seen to encourage charitable giving".[180] The October 2001 Budget indicated that these incentives would be continued.

There may be restrictions on how long an organization may or should hold onto the securities and its intentions should be part of the planning of the gift. Both the donor and the organization will usually benefit from legal and accounting advice in determining the best way and the most advantageous timing of the gift of securities or similar property.

(iii) Cultural Property

The donation of cultural property to designated Canadian institutions is the subject of Interpretation Bulletin IT407R4.[181] Certified cultural property is property of outstanding significance and importance to Canada for which a certificate has been issued by the Canadian Cultural Property Export Review Board. That Board is established under the *Cultural Property Export and Import Act*.[182] The gift of certified cultural property to a designated cultural institution in Canada exempts the donor from the capital gains on the donation and allows for a tax credit of up to 100 per cent of annual income with a five year carry-forward.[183] These types of donations will not be received by most charities in Canada, but are potentially very beneficial to cultural institutions. The provisions also encourage Canadians to donate certified cultural property to

---

[180] RC4142, "Tax Advantages of Donating to Charity", (Canada Customs and Revenue Agency, Oct. 4, 1999) at 8.
[181] "Dispositions of Cultural Property to Designated Canadian Institutions", November 7, 1996.
[182] R.S.C. 1985, c. C-51, as amended.
[183] IT407R4 at 1.

Canadian cultural institutions instead of selling it to purchasers outside Canada.

(d) Remainder Trusts

A charitable remainder trust (CRT) is one in which a person has use of the donated property and the organization will receive it upon death or other event triggering the transaction. Typically, the donor will create a trust to hold the property, such as a home, which will allow the donor to use or occupy the property. On his or her death, title to the property will be transferred to the charitable organization. This type of planned giving is more common in the United States than in Canada due, in part, to the difference in tax treatment.[184]

A charitable remainder trust may be created during the life of the donor or in the donor's will. In either case, before a receipt may be issued for income tax purposes, several requirements set out in the Canada Customs and Revenue Agency's Interpretation Bulletin[185] must be met. First, it must be a "gift" to the charitable organization. A gift is a voluntary transfer of real or personal property without consideration. The Interpretation Bulletin sets out several requirements:[186]

- the transfer must be voluntary and with no expectation of right, privilege, material benefit or advantage to the donor or a person designated by the donor. Given the nature of a "remainder trust", which does provide for either the donor or a person designated by the donor to use the property or receive the income from the property for a period of time, it would appear that this type of "benefit" is not caught by this requirement,
- the property must vest with the charitable organization at the time of the transfer. For a gift to vest, certain trust law requirements must be satisfied, which are also set out in the Interpretation Bulletin. For example, the charitable organization must exist and be ascertained and the size of the beneficiary's interests must also be ascertained. In order for the trust law requirements ("the three certainties") to be met, the beneficiary of the trust must also be known. In addition, the conditions attached to the gift must be satisfied before it vests,

---

[184] C. Chouinard, "Comparison of the Tax Treatment of Charitable Remainder Trusts in Canada and the United States", (1998) 14 *Philanthropist*, No. 3 at 3. See also E. Pearce, "Charitable Remainder Trusts", *Canadian Fund Raiser*, April 26, 2000 (Volume 10, Number 8), at 4.

[185] "Gift to a Charity of a Residual Interest in Real Property or an Equitable Interest in a Trust", IT-226R, (Canada Customs and Revenue Agency, November 29, 1991).

[186] *Ibid.*, at 2.

- the transfer must be irrevocable. In other words, once the transfer has occurred, the donor cannot "retrieve" it, and
- the charitable organization must eventually receive full ownership and possession of the property transferred, without any claim to use or the income from the property. This fact must be evident in the transaction and the documentation, including the trust deed.

The beneficiary of the trust (either the donor or a person designated by the donor) cannot encroach on the capital of the trust.[187] The capital would normally be the real or personal property, such as a building or securities. Encroachment occurs if the property is sold and the proceeds are given over to the beneficiary. Encroachment would defeat the purpose of the charitable remainder trust from a public policy and tax perspective. The rationale behind the ability to issue a receipt for income tax purposes is that the property donated will, once the "remainder" has expired, be exclusively available for charitable purposes. This rationale would be defeated if the capital was encroached.

The Agency takes the position that if the trust property is personal property, such as paintings, sculptures and other moveable property, certain precautions must be taken.[188] The *Interpretation Bulletin* does not specify what these precautions are, but with any property that is easily moved from one location to another, it is prudent for the charitable organization to ensure that its interests in the property are protected until the physical transfer and distribution of the property occurs. The charitable organization should prepare an inventory of the gift, ensure that the gift is insured and that the charitable organization is named as the insured, put in place appropriate monitoring of the gift and so forth.

The valuation of the gift is another critical step in the issuance of the receipt for income tax purposes. The CCRA recognizes that the method of valuation of the residual interest in real property or the equitable interest in a trust will vary according to the type of gift, the residual or trust interests in the property and the documentation. Typically, valuation will be based upon the fair market value of the property, the current rate of interest, the life expectancy of the beneficiary or the time specified for use by the beneficiary, and other relevant factors. It is generally easier to evaluate real property, especially over a longer period of time, than it is to place a value on personal property.[189]

A receipt for income tax purposes may be issued based upon the present value of the property if the gift is irrevocable. In addition, any use to be made by the donor must be deducted from the present value. This use is determined using a discount rate.

---

[187] *Ibid.*, at 2 and 3.
[188] *Ibid.*, at 3.
[189] *Ibid.*, at 3.

The Interpretation Bulletin does not specify a discount rate. A discount rate is used to calculate the "present value" of the gift, i.e., the value of the gift after deducting from it the use to be made of the gift until the remainder interest expires. The remainder interest will usually expire on the death of the beneficiary or on a specific date set out in the documents. Several approaches have been taken by charitable organizations, including the CCRA's prescribed rate, the long-term bond rate, prime rate, prime rate plus one per cent, or a mix of the prime rates of several financial institutions.[190] Whatever approach is taken, it is essential that the organization obtain professional advice and that it be able to substantiate the approach used and why it was appropriate. The calculation of the "life time" is another area for which professional advice is useful. At the very least, the organization should use industry-accepted mortality tables.

The gift of the property will usually give rise to a capital gain or loss. A reasonable portion of the adjusted cost base of the total property immediately before the disposition must be attributed to the residual interest and other interests at the time the gift vested. If the gift is made during the lifetime of the donor (*inter vivos* gift), the donor will be deemed to have received the proceeds of the disposition. If the gift is made in a will (testamentary gift), the usual rules for tax calculations in the year of death will apply.

The CCRA provides the following formula in determining the adjusted cost base of the residual interest:[191]

> Fair Market Value of Residual Interest (divided by) Fair Market Value of All Interests in the Property (multiplied by) Adjusted Cost Base of Total Property (equals) Adjusted Cost Base of Residual Interest

The taxation of income and capital gains during the period in which the property is subject to the remainder trust is an issue. The income and capital gains may be taxed in the hands of the trust or in the hands of the beneficiary. It may be possible to arrange matters such that the capital gains are payable to the charitable organization. If so, the gains would not be taxed because the charitable organization is exempt from income taxation. However, this area is very complicated and has some pitfalls that require expert advice.

There are a number of other issues that a charitable organization should consider before promoting charitable remainder trusts as part of its fundraising activities or accepting a gift that has a charitable remainder trust. For example, is the type of gift one that the charitable organization may accept? As discussed in previous chapters, there may be limitations on what a charitable organization may accept at common law, by statute or under its own incorporating or trust documents.

---

[190] E. Pearce, "Charitable Remainder Trusts", at 5.
[191] IT-226R, *supra*, note 185, at 4.

Second, is the property one with which the charitable organization wants to be associated? Is the property notorious or otherwise not acceptable to the organization? This situation could arise, for example, for a health charity in accepting shares of corporations that manufacture products that are known to be carcinogenic.

Third, does the property pass the usual "due diligence" tests? A charitable organization should probably avoid real property that is contaminated whether it is donated outright or subject to a remainder trust.

Fourth, the charity will need to consider the impact on its own registration status. For example, will it adversely affect its ability to meet its disbursement quota? If so, the charity (charitable organization or charitable foundation) may want to use measures to allow it to minimize the impact, such as obtaining the Minister's permission to accumulate for a specific purpose or using the "ten-year rule".

(e)   Annuities

Annuities are a life insurance product. An individual provides to an insurance company an amount of money and the insurance company agrees to make payments to the individual for life or a specified period of time. The insurance company invests the amount of money (capital) and based on an agreed upon interest rate, a specific amount is determined. The annuity over time pays out the capital and earned interest. In some annuities, the payments are pre-determined in amounts and time. In other cases, the insurance company agrees to make the payments for life. If the annuitant dies before the capital is paid out, the insurance company retains the remainder; if not, the insurance company must use other funds to make the payments.

One approach is for the donor to pay the capital to the insurance company, which in turn agrees to make annuity payments to the charity. This approach has the least risk for charities to benefit from annuities. However, other options include the donor transferring assets irrevocably to the charitable organization. The organization in turn agrees to make payments to the donor. The "gift" is the difference between what the annuitant would have received from an insurance company and what he or she is willing to accept from the charitable organization. This approach is risky for the charitable organization, especially if it agrees to do so for "life" as opposed to a specified period.

The charitable organization may minimize its risk by purchasing a separate annuity for the projected amount of the payments. If, for example, the donor is expecting to receive payments based on the earned interest and a percentage of the capital, the charitable organization could use a portion of the capital to purchase an annuity from a life insurance company. In this approach, the charitable organization will also receive the estimated donation now rather than in the future.

The value of the gift will depend upon the difference between the amount that the donor is expected to receive from the charity as an annuitant and the amount transferred. In making this determination, the Canada Customs and Revenue Agency requires that the charitable organization use the mortality tables in its *Interpretation Bulletin* for life annuitants. The mortality tables set out the age of the donor at the time of the donation and the number of expected annuity payments over the anticipated lifespan of the donor. Thus, if the annuitant donated $60,000 and is expected to receive nine $5,000 payments, $45,000 will be returned to the donor and thus the "gift" has a value of $15,000. By contrast, if the annuitant expects to receive 14 payments, he or she would receive back $70,000 and there would have been no gift.[192]

There are some potential legal issues around annuities. Charitable organizations may be able to offer annuities, but charitable foundations are not permitted to do so by the Canada Customs and Revenue Agency. Furthermore, the organization needs to examine its own incorporating legislation, letters patent, by-laws or other constating documents to ensure that it has the capacity to enter into the transaction. It will also need to ensure that it is not offending any laws with respect to securities or insurance, both of which are regulated industries. The Canada Customs and Revenue Agency specifically comments in *Interpretation Bulletin IT111R2* that it "does not sanction the issuance of annuities by a charity which is not authorized to undertake such an activity pursuant to its own constating documents".[193]

In Ontario, the Public Guardian and Trustee seems to take the position that Ontario insurance legislation prohibits a charity from issuing annuities unless it is also licensed by the Superintendent of Insurance under the *Insurance Act*. An insurance operation, though, is a business activity and not something that a charity would normally be permitted to carry on. The Public Guardian and Trustee notes that some charitable organizations may have the power to issue annuity contracts if it is included in private legislation incorporating them. Most charitable organizations would not have this power and it is not one that is ancillary or incidental to their objects.[194]

There are also practical matters that a charitable organization must consider if it were to become involved in the issuance of annuities. It may be liable for the payments to the annuitant if the trustee of the annuity is not financially able to make the payments. Should that occur, the direc-

---

[192] IT-111R2, "Annuities Purchased from Charitable Organizations", (The Canada Customs and Revenue Agency, Sept. 22, 1995) at 3. Note that the Individual Annuity Mortality Table used in this Interpretation Bulletin was from 1983 and that the Canada Customs and Revenue Agency issued a corrected version on February 10, 1997 as a Special Release.

[193] *Supra*, IT-111R2, note 192, at 1.

[194] Ministry of Consumer and Commercial Relations and the Office of the Public Guardian and Trustee, *Not-for-Profit Incorporator's Handbook* (Toronto: Queen's Printer for Ontario, 1998), at 23.

tors who approved of the scheme may have acted imprudently and could be held personally liable.

The payment of any fees must also be considered as part of the scheme and a failure by the directors to address this issue may give rise to liability. The financial institution would normally be entitled to fees and charges for handling the annuity and processing the payments. These fees and charges should be reasonable and provide demonstrable value to the charitable organization, especially given that the fees and charges will normally encroach on the capital.

For several reasons, the issuance of annuities by charitable or not-for-profit organizations is very risky, even assuming that they have the legal authority to do so. The gifting of annuities by a donor where the annuity is issued by an insurance company is, on the other hand, an approach that is beneficial to both the donor and the organization.

(f)   Interest-free Loan

A charitable organization may borrow from either a financial institution or from a donor. In the case of a financial institution, it will usually want to earn interest on that loan. A donor, however, may be willing to loan the funds without interest. At the end of the period, the donor will be paid back the loan. The charitable organization, in the interim, invests the loaned amount in appropriate investments and the interest or other income becomes revenue to the charitable organization. The donor may, later, decide to donate the amount loaned, at which time it becomes a donation for which a receipt for income tax purposes may be issued.

The charitable organization must also satisfy itself that it can "borrow" the funds. It may have restrictions in its letters patent, for example, that permit it to borrow only for operational purposes or as a mortgage. If so, it may be restricted in borrowing money from a donor even in this circumstance. If the organization is a private foundation, it may also be restricted from dealing with any person who is not at arm's length.

One approach to avoid some of these legal restrictions is to establish a trust. The donor loans the money interest free to the trust, which in turn invests the funds. Any revenue would be taxable in the hands of the beneficiary, but a charitable organization does not pay income tax. Thus, the revenue may be distributed to the beneficiary charitable organization(s).

I   INTERNET AND CHARITABLE AND NOT-FOR-PROFIT WEBSITES

The Internet provides charitable and not-for-profit organizations with another tool for fundraising and climbing the pyramid of giving. It is not "fundamentally" different from others tools that have been used over the years, but it has its own unique features and issues. The Internet can help organizations to build healthy relationships, which are essential to the pyramid of giving. To be successful, organizations will need to effectively use this tool.[195]

A website, if it is accessible to the target audiences, can assist organizations in several ways:

- as an effective marketing tool reaching large audiences at a relatively low cost,
- as a tool to cultivate donors or groups of donors by keeping them up-to-date on a regular basis on the organization's plans, activities, financial situation, planned giving initiatives and so forth,
- allows the development of chat rooms or other methods to exchange information and comment on matters of importance to the organization, its members and donors,
- provides a new method to solicit for donations and to raise funds, including sponsorships,
- provides a new mechanism to build the "mailing list" and to identify those donors who may be interested in planned giving.

Whatever its advantages, the decision to create an Internet site and to allocate the resources to it should be a thoughtful one and treated like any other similar investment. The organization must know what it wants and why and plan to maximize the returns on its investment in the website.[196] The same rules with respect to carrying on a business, political lobbying and so forth are also applicable to the Internet. The Internet does not transform the organization or take it outside the laws of Canada — it is another tool for the organization.

The Internet, though, does take the organization's reach outside of Canada in ways that were not readily possible before. Individuals in other countries will have access to the organization's website — which may be a good thing but also has some pitfalls. For example, if the content in the website is contrary to the laws of the other country, can the charitable organization be charged? While this question may be hypothetical, it is likely that the issue will arise as the Internet develops over the next several years. If the charity is "selling" into that other jurisdiction it may need to comply with the laws of that jurisdiction. Similarly, if the organization is soliciting funds through its website, it will need to make sure that it is complying with the laws of that jurisdiction. In Canada, for example, charities that solicit on their websites may be soliciting for purposes of Alberta and Manitoba law in those provinces.

---

[195] D. Jamieson, "Building Relationships in the Networked Age: Some Implications of the Internet for Nonprofit Organizations" (2000), 15 *The Philanthropist* No. 2, at 23.

[196] R. Oulton, "Treat Your Internet Program Like any New Business Venture: Plan, Measure and Evaluate Results for Long-Term Success", *Canadian Fund Raiser*, Volume 10, Number 10 (April 26, 2000), at 1.

The legal issue around jurisdiction is a complex one and far from settled. The case law to date, largely from the United States, seems to turn on whether or not the website transaction is "pushed" to residents in other jurisdictions or "pulled" by those residents. Thus, if there is any question, it is probably better for the website to require the person accessing the website to "pull" the information or transaction. Although far from fool-proof, the organization is less likely to be seen as transacting business or activities in that other jurisdiction. It may also want to consider the blocking of access to the website from certain jurisdictions, although this technology is not mature.

There are a number of intellectual property issues around websites, not the least of which are the use of domain names. Domain names may be and often are a form of intellectual property. For example, an organization could not normally use a trade-name of another person as its domain name. Charitable and not-for-profit organizations may want to ensure that others do not use their trade-names or trade-marks as domain names by registering the appropriate domain names and any relevant trade-marks in Canada and other jurisdictions.

Hyperlinking is an important method to connect various websites to each other. But, there may be copyright issues in doing so. Before including a hyperlink on a website, it is best to obtain the written permission of the owner of the website. Similarly, if a meta-tag is going to be used, that may be the trade-mark of the other person for which permission is required. The framing of and placement of hyperlinks or webpages may also be an issue if it places the other website or person in a poor light.

Organizations should ensure that they own the intellectual property in their website and its content. To do so, the contract with the website developer and the Internet service provider should clearly stipulate that the organization will own the intellectual property. The contract should also address control over the website, especially if the relationship is to come to an end for whatever reason. The organization needs to maintain and exercise control over how the website is operated and how it is developed. The website in this regard is no different from any other "publication" that the organization may produce and for which it will be legally responsible.

Issues of privacy and security should also be addressed. The use of cookies, for example, should be carefully reviewed — when to use them and when not to. The collection of data either through cookies or by requesting information from the person directly needs to be protected. Confidential information should be treated as such and measures put in place to ensure that it is protected. Security is related both to the protection of privacy and to the organization's need to make sure that its website is relatively secure and that measures are taken should problems occur.

The organization may want to consider a legal audit of its website. A legal audit would examine the Internet strategy, the development of the site and its contents, activities on the site, links to other sites, collection of information and legal disclaimers or other notices.[197]

The Internet is a valuable tool for charitable and not-for-profit organizations. It is one that has its own unique features, many of which are still being developed. It is, though, essentially another tool and the laws of the land do continue to apply.

---

[197] D.M. Adderly, "Website Legal Audits", *Internet and E-Commerce Law in Canada*, Volume 1, Number 1 (March 2000), at 1.

Appendix A

APPENDIX A CONCORDANCE OF LEGISLATION BY MAJOR ISSUES AND JURISDICTION
A — INCORPORATION STATUTES

Issue	Alberta	British Columbia	Manitoba	New Brunswick
	Societes Act, R.S.A. 1980, c. S.18	Society Act, R.S.B.C. 1979, c. 390	Corporations Act, R.S.M. 1987, c. C.225	Companies Act, R.S.N.B. 1973, c. C.13
Application	3-8	2-3	5-7, 10-12, 267, 270	4, 6-11, 16-18
Powers	10, 13-15	4, 16	15	14, 36-38
Members	4, 16-17, 21, 31	1, 5, 9, 39, 56-70	1, 43, 127-130, 133, 137, 274	16, 18, 49-53, 123, 101-103
By-Laws	5, 6, 11, 26	3, 6, 7, 23 and Schedule B	6, 275-277	7, 17, 130
Directors	23	3, 24-31, 66	6, 97, 100-102, 104, 106, 108-110, 113-115, 117-119	39, 87-100
Officers	23	7	116	94, 96
Books and Records	9, 24, 26, 31	11, 36-37, 39, 70, 89	20-22, 249-250	18, 104-111, 128
Auditor	21, 22	41-55	149, 155-157, 159-163	124

Issue	Newfoundland Corporations Act, R.S.N. 1990, c. C-36	Nova Scotia Societies Act, R.S.N.S. 1989, c. 435	Ontario Corporations Act, R.S.O. 1990, c. C.38	Ontario Co-operative Corpo- rations Act, R.S.O. 1990, c. C.35
Application	404-405, 418-420, 421, 423	3-9	4, 7, 9, 13-16, 22, 119, 133	4-12
Powers	27	10, 28	23, 59, 113	15, 50
Members	215-257, 419, 424-428	4, 14-15, 19, 27	84, 93, 96, 120-125, 128, 133, 293-295, 298, 311, 321	60-79
By-Laws	424, 429	6, 13 and Schedule B	59, 127, 129, 130, 132, 133, 286	21-24
Directors	161, 167-210, 302, 419, 420, 422, 428, 429	5, 16, 30	67, 69-71, 80-82, 127, 133, 283-288, 292	17, 85-110
Officers	202-203	2	69, 133, 289-291	17, 105-107
Books and Records	36-45, 258-261, 384	17-23	282, 299-305, 323	113-122, 128-137
Auditor	258, 264-278	19	94-97, 133, 159-163	123-128, 138-139

Issue	Prince Edward Island	Quebec	Saskatchewan	Canada
	Companies Act, R.S.P.E.I. 1988, c. C.14	Companies Act, R.S.Q. 1991, c. C.38	Non-profit Corporations Act, S.S. 1995, c. N-4.2	Canada Corporations Act, R.S.C. 1970, c. C.32
Application	6, 9-12, 89, 90	9-10, 218-219	5-13	9, 25, 28-29, 155
Powers	14, 15, 20	30, 31, 36	15-18	15, 16, 65
Members	57, 79	97-100, 216, 226	113-136, 137-141	33, 43, 102, 132
By-Laws	28, 78, 90	8, 77, 91	90, 91	155
Directors	22, 28, 64, 79	83-90, 92, 95, 219	88-112	93, 98-99, 155
Officers	53, 54, 90, 91	89	88-112	3
Books and Records	38, 50, 52-54, 79, 91	98, 104-109, 223	20-23, 264-275	109, 111.1-117, 138
Auditor		98	142-160	130-132

B — OTHER ISSUES

Issue	Alberta	British Columbia	Manitoba	New Brunswick	Newfoundland
Trustees	Trustee Act, R.S.A. 1980, c. T.10	Trustee Act, R.S.B.C. 1996, c. 463	Trustee Act, R.S.M. 1987, c. T160	Trustee Act, R.S.N.B. 1973, c. T.15	Trustee Act, R.S.N. 1990, c. T-10
Corporate and Income Taxation	Alberta Income Tax Act, R.S.A. 1980, c. A-31	Corporation Capital Tax Act, R.S.B.C. 1996, c. 73	Corporation Capital Tax Act, R.S.M. 1988, c. C226	Income Tax Act, R.S.N.B. 1973, c. 1-2	Income Tax Act, S.N. 2000, c.1-1.1
(See Note Below)	Alberta Corporate Tax Act, R.S.A. 1980, c. A-17	Income Tax Act, R.S.B.C. 1996, c. 215	Income Tax Act R.S.M. 1988, c. I10		
Property Taxation	Municipal Government Act, S.A. 1994, c-M26.1 School Act, R.S.A. 1980, c. S-3, Re-en. R.S.A. 1988, c. S-3.1, s. 254(1)	Assessment Act, R.S.B.C. 1996, c. 20 Assessment Authority Act, R.S.B.C. 1996, c. 21	City of Winnipeg Act, S.M. 1989-90, c. 10 Municipal Act, S.M. 1996, c. 58	Assessment Act, R.S.N.B. 1973, c. A-14 Real Property Tax Act, R.S.N.B. 1973, c. R-2	Assessment Act, R.S.N. 1990, c. A-18 Municipalities Act, S.N. 1999, c. M-24

B – OTHER ISSUES CONT'D

Issue	Alberta	British Columbia	Manitoba	New Brunswick	Newfoundland
		Municipal Act, R.S.B.C. 1996, c. 323 Taxation (Rural Area) Act, R.S.B.C. 1996, c. 448 Vancouver Charter, S.B.C. 1953, c. 55	Municipal Assessment Act, S.M. 1989-90, c.M226		St. John's Assessment Act, R.S.N. 1990, c. S-1
Sales Taxation		Social Services Tax Act, R.S.B.C. 1996, c. 431	Retail Sales Tax Act, R.S.M. 1987, c. R130	Harmonized Sales Tax Act, S.N.B. 1997, c. H-1.01	Retail Sales Tax Act, R.S.N. 1990, c. R-15

B – OTHER ISSUES CONT'D

Issue	Nova Scotia	Prince Edward Island	Quebec	Saskatchewan
Trustees	Trustee Act, R.S.N.S. 1989, c. 479	Trustee Act, R.S.P.E.I. 1988, c. T-8	Code of Civil Procedure, R.S.Q. 1991, c. C-25	Trustee Act, R.S.S. 1978, c. T-23
Corporate and Income Taxation (See note below)	Income Tax Act, R.S.N.S. 1989, c. 217	Income Tax Act, R.S.P.E.I. 1988, c. I-1	Taxation Act, R.S.Q. 1991, c. I-3	Income Tax Act, R.S.S. 1978, c. I-2
Property Taxation	Assessment Act, R.S.N.S. 1989, c. 23	Real Property Assessment Act, R.S.P.E.I. 1988, c. R-4	Cities and Towns Act, R.S.Q. 1991, c. C-19	Northern Municipalities Act, S.S. 1983, c. N-5.1
	Education Act, S.N.S. 1995-96, c. 1	Real Property Tax Act, R.S.P.E.I. 1988, c. R-5	Education Act, R.S.Q. 1991, c. I-13.3	Rural Municipalities Act, S.S. 1989, R-26.1
	Halifax Regional Municipality Act, S.N.S. 1995, c. 3		Municipal Code, R.S.Q. 1991, c. C-27.1	Urban Municipality Act, S.S. 1983-84, c. U-11

B – OTHER ISSUES CONT'D

Issue	Nova Scotia	Prince Edward Island	Quebec	Saskatchewan
	Municipality Act, R.S.N.S. 1989, c. 295		Municipal Taxation Act, R.S.Q. 1991, c. F-2.1	
Sales Taxation	Sales Tax Act, S.N.S. 1996, c. 31 Theatres and Amusements Act, R.S.N.S. 1989, c. 466	Revenue Administration Act, S.P.E.I. 1990, c. 54 Revenue Tax Act, R.S.P.E.I. 1988, c. R-14	Quebec Sales Tax Act, R.S.Q. 1991, c. T-0.1	Education and Health Tax Act, R.S.S. 1978, c. E-3

N.B. Provincial corporate and Income taxation statutes generally provide exemptions to corporations and other legal entities that are exempt from income taxation under s. 149(1) of the *Income Tax Act (Canada)*. Harmonized Sales Tax in Nova Scotia, New Brunswick and Prince Edward Island is administered by the Canada Customs and Revenue Agency and in Quebec by the Quebec government.

APPENDIX B

List of Addresses

The use of the internet has made the government more accessible. The federal and provincial governments are all committed to making services available to the public through the world wide web. Some governments are more advanced than others, but most have basic information accessible and many have forms, statutes, policies and other documentation on or through their websites. In addition, linkages to other websites is common, connecting many of the websites together in a readily accessible manner. Websites, however, do change to reflect reorganization or improvements to the sites.

1. Alberta

    Corporate Registry Office
    Department of Governments Services
    John E. Brownlee Building
    10365 — 97 Street
    Edmonton, AB T5J 3W7

    Telephone: (780) 427-2311
    Facsimile: (780) 422-1091
    Website: www3.gov.ab.ca/gs/services/cnfb/

2. British Columbia

    Corporate Registry
    Ministry of Finance
    2nd Floor, 940 Blanshard Street
    Victoria, BC V8W 9V3

    Telephone: (250) 356-7711
    Facsimile: (250) 356-6977
    Website: www.fin.gov.bc.ca/registries/default.htm

3. Manitoba

   Companies Office
   Consumer and Corporate Affairs
   1010 — 405 Broadway
   Winnipeg, MB R3C 3L6

   Telephone: (204) 945-2500
   Facsimile: (204) 945-1459
   Website: www.gov.mb.ca/cca/comp_off/

4. New Brunswick

   Corporate Affairs Branch
   Service New Brunswick
   City Centre, 432 Queen Street
   P.O. Box 1998
   Fredericton, NB E3B 5G4

   Telephone: (506) 453-2703
   Facsimile: (506) 453-2613
   Website: www.gnb.ca/snb/e/index.htm

5. Newfoundland

   Registry of Companies
   Department of Government Services and Land
   Ground Floor, East Block
   Confederation Building
   St. John's, NF A1B 4J6

   Telephone: (709) 729-3317
   Facsimile: (709) 729-0232
   Website: www.gov.nf.ca/gsl

6. Nova Scotia

   Registry of Joint Stock Companies
   Service Nova Scotia and Municipal Relations
   9th Floor, Maritime Centre
   1505 Barrington Street
   Halifax, NS B2Y 3K5

   Telephone: (902) 424-7770
   Facsimile: (902) 424-4633
   Website: www.gov.ns.ca/snsmr/rjsc/

7. Ontario

   Companies Branch
   Ministry of Consumer and Business Services
   2nd Floor, 393 University Avenue
   Toronto, ON M7A 2H6

   Telephone: (416) 314-8880
   Facsimile: (416) 314-4852
   Website: www.cbs.gov.on.ca/mcbs/english/company_infor.htm

   Licensing and Enforcement Division
   Financial Services Commission of Ontario
   5160 Yonge Street
   North York, ON M2N 6L9

   Telephone: (416) 226-7776
   Facsimile: (416) 590-7070
   Website: www.fisco.gov.on.ca

   Public Guardian and Trustee
   Charitable Property Division
   Suite 800, 595 Bay Street
   Toronto, ON M5G 2M6

   Telephone: (416) 326-1963
   Facsimile: (416) 326-1969
   Website: www.attorneygeneral.jus.gov.on.ca/html/pgt/pgthome.htm

8. Prince Edward Island

   Consumer, Corporations and Insurance Division
   Attorney General
   Shaw Building
   95 — 105 Rochford Street
   Charlottetown, PE C1A 7N8

   Telephone: (902) 368-4550
   Facsimile: (902) 368-5283
   Website: www.gov.pe.ca/oag

9. Quebec

   Direction des entreprises
   L'Inspecteur général des institutions financières
   800, place D'Youville
   Québec, QC G1R 4Y5

   Telephone: (418) 643-3625
   Facsimile: (418) 528-5713
   Website: www.igif.gouv.qc.ca/entreprises/personnes_morales/const_
      pers_morales.htm

10. Saskatchewan

    Corporations Branch
    Department of Justice
    2nd Floor, 1871 Smith Street
    Regina, SK S4P 3V7

    Telephone: (306) 787-2962
    Facsimile: (306) 787-8999
    Website: www.saskjustice.gov.sk.ca/branches/Corporations/nonprofit/
       nonprofit.htm

11. Canada

    Director
    Corporations Directorate
    Industry Canada
    9th Floor, Jean Edmonds Towers South
    365 Laurier Avenue West
    Ottawa, ON K1A 0C8

    Telephone: (613) 941-9042
    Facsimile: (613) 941-5781
    Website: www.strategis.ic.gc.ca

    Charities Directorate
    Canada Customs and Revenue Agency
    Ottawa, ON K1A 0L5

    Telephone: 1-800-267-2384
    Facsimile: (613) 952-6020
    Website: www.ccra-adrc.gc.ca/tax/charities/

APPENDIX C

Checklists

A   INITIAL INFORMATION

1. LEGAL STATUS

   What is the organization's current legal status?

   Are there any current constituting documents?

   Is the proposed legal status permanent or temporary? If temporary, what is the anticipated permanent legal status?

   Proposed Legal Status
   - i) Trust
   - ii) Unincorporated Association
   - iii) Corporate
     - a) Ontario Corporation without Share Capital
     - b) Ontario Co-operative Corporation without Share Capital
     - c) Canada Corporation without Share Capital

2. OBJECTS — LIST OF PROPOSED OBJECTS BY CATEGORIES
   - i) Not-for-profit
     - -
     - -
   - ii) Charitable
     - a) Relief of Poverty
       - -
       - -
     - b) Advancement of Religion
       - -
       - -
     - c) Advancement of Education
       - -
       - -

d)   Other Purposes Beneficial to the Community
-
-

Are any of the objects clauses that are pre-approved by the Public Guardian and Trustee for Ontario and Canada Customs and Revenue Agency appropriate?

iii) Unsure of Category
-
-

iv) Required Objects Given Nature of Organization, e.g. Special Corporation
-
-

3. NATURE OF THE ORGANIZATION

i)   Not-for-profit
   a)   General
   b)   Sporting and Athletic
   c)   Social Club
   d)   Service Club

ii) Charitable in Nature — Not Seeking Registration with Canada Customs and Revenue Agency as a Charity

iii) Charitable — Seeking Registration with Canada Customs and Revenue Agency as a Charity
   a)   Charitable Organization
   b)   Charitable Public Foundation
   c)   Charitable Private Foundation
      – List of Charitable Organizations to Support

4. PROPOSED NAME AND OPTIONS

i)   Considerations
   a)   English, French, Bilingual
   b)   Restrictions or Prohibitions
   c)   Consents for Use of Name
   d)   Government Approvals for Terms
   e)   NUANS — Ontario Biased (Ontario Incorporation)
      – Canada Biased (Federal Incorporation)
   f)   Business Name

ii) Check for Similar Names
   a) ONBIS Name Search at Companies Branch, Ministry of Consumer and Business Services
   b) Telephone Directories
   c) Trade and Business Directories

iii) Options
   -
   -
   -

5. HEAD OFFICE

   Address:
   Telephone Number:
   Facsimile Number:
   Website:
   Email Address:

6. CLUB HOUSE OR OTHER FACILITY

   Address:
   Telephone Number:
   Facsimile Number:
   Website:
   Email Address:

7. PERSONS ESTABLISHING ORGANIZATION

   Name:
   Address:
   Telephone Number:
   Facsimile Number:
   Email Address:
   Occupation:

   Consents Obtained?   Yes   No

8. FINANCIAL INSTITUTION

   Name:
   Address:
   Telephone Number:
   Facsimile Number:
   Contact Person:
   Email Address:
   Account Numbers:

i) Operating
ii) Trust
iii) Special Purposes

Signing Authorities

9. Proposed Auditors

10. Proposed Financial Year-End

11. Special Considerations

(i) Will the organization operate under the supervision or regulation of any ministry, department or agency of government?
(ii) If so, which ones?
(iii) If so, has prior approval been obtained? Has consultation occurred?
(iv) Have the objects been reviewed and approved?
(v) Will a club house or other facilities be maintained?
(vi) If so, do they conform to the municipal by-laws, building code, fire code, health protection and promotion regulations and other applicable legislation or regulations? Will the activities in the club house or other facilities conform to the law?
(vii) Will firearms be used? Have the police been consulted? Do all members have appropriate fire-arm registrations and certificates? Is there a policy and process in place to monitor compliance?
(viii) What will be the types of activities for the organization?
(ix) Are any of those activities inherently dangerous?
(x) Who will participate in the activities of the organization? Members? Non-members?
(xi) Will the organization be affiliated with another organization? A service club? Has the approval of the parent service club been obtained?
(xii) Is there an existing organization? Has it consented to the incorporation and undertaken to discontinue the use of the name within six months of incorporation?
(xiii) Will the organization apply for registration with Canada Customs and Revenue Agency as a "charitable organization"?

(xiv) If so, has CCRA been consulted?
(xv) Has the Public Guardian and Trustee for Ontario been consulted?

12. DIRECTORS/TRUSTEES:

Qualifications:
Numbers:
Election/Appointment Procedures:
Terms:
    i) Length
    ii) Restrictions
    iii) Rotating Directors

Ex Officio Director/Trustees:

Meetings:
    i) Quorum
    ii) Regular Meetings
    iii) Notice

Executive or Other Committees:
    i) Duties
    ii) Membership
    iii) Quorum
    iv) Regular Meetings
    v) Notice

Remuneration:
    i) Fees
    ii) Expenses

Indemnification:
    i) By-law Provisions
    ii) Liability Insurance
    iii) Comply with requirements under the *Charities Accounting Act*?

Powers:
Restrictions on Powers:
Duties:
Termination:

13. OFFICERS

Qualifications:
Titles:

Election and Appointment:
Remuneration:
- i) Fees
- ii) Expenses

Powers:
Duties:
Relationship to Directors/Trustees:
Indemnification:
- i) By-law
- ii) Liability Insurance
- iii) Compliance with requirements under the *Charities Accounting Act*?

Termination:

14. MEMBERS

Qualifications:
Classes or Divisions:
Fees and Dues:
- i) Initial
- ii) Annual

Termination of Membership:
- i) Grounds
- ii) Procedures

Rules and Regulations Governing Membership

15. MEETINGS

Notice Provisions:
- i) Annual General Meeting
- ii) General Meeting

Quorum:
Voting Rights:
Voting Procedures:
- i) Show of Hands/Ballot
- ii) Proxies

16. BY-LAWS

Are any matters usually in the By-laws to be included in the Letters Patent? e.g., borrowing powers, distribution of assets, directors (rotation, term, remuneration), membership qualifications?

17. POST INCORPORATION OR ORGANIZATION

- i) Initial Notice
- ii) First Meeting of Directors
- iii) Minute book
- iv) By-laws
- v) Appointment of Officers

B   CORPORATIONS

I   ONTARIO CORPORATIONS

1) Corporations Act
   - i) Completed Application for Letters Patent
   - ii) Fee
   - iii) Ontario-biased NUANS
   - iv) Approvals
   - v) Consents and Undertakings
   - vi) Special Considerations Addressed
   - vii) Supporting Documentation

2) Co-operative Corporations Act
   - i) Completed Application for Articles of Incorporation
   - ii) Fee
     - Name Reservation
     - Application for Articles of Incorporation
   - iii) Ontario-biased NUANS
   - iv) Affidavit of Verification
   - v) Form 3 Consent to Act as First Directors
   - vi) Consents and Undertakings
   - vii) Special Considerations Addressed

II   CANADA CORPORATIONS ACT

- i) Completed Application
- ii) Fee
  - Name Search if no NUANS
  - Application for Letters Patent
- iii) Canada-biased NUANS
- iv) Affidavit or Statutory Declaration of an Applicant
- v) Covering Letter from Applicants
- vi) Consents and Undertakings
- vii) By-laws
  - Corporation Directorate's Model By-law

- Previously Approved Customized By-law with Identifier
- New Customized By-Law with Directorate's Checklist Indicating sections of By-law that Address the Requirements

viii) Special Considerations Addressed
ix) Completed "Not-for-profit Checklist"

C   TRUST

1. Appointment and Discharge of Trustees
   i) Trust Instrument
   ii) Remaining Trustees
   iii) Membership
   iv) Beneficiaries
   v) Discharge or Termination

2. Numbers of Trustees

3. Qualifications

4. Powers in Addition to Those in *Trustee Act*
   i) Investment Powers
   ii) Administrative Powers
   iii) Depositive Powers

5. Notice to Public Trustee

D   CHARITABLE REGISTRATION

1. Resolution Authorizing Application
   i) Board of Directors or Trustees
   ii) Membership

2. Completed Application Form

3. Certified Copies of Documents which:
   i) Establish the Organization (letters patent, constitution, charter, trust document, by-laws);
   ii) State the Objects; and
   iii) Govern Its Operations

4. Statement of Activities and Programmes to be Carried Out by the Organization

5. Copies of Statements of:
   i) Receipts and Disbursements for Previous Fiscal Year or Period;
   ii) Assets and Liabilities

If organization not operating, proposed budget for first year or estimate of expenditures

6. List of Directors, Officers, Trustees (names, street addresses and occupations)

7. Notice to Public Trustee

E MAINTAINING THE ORGANIZATION

1. Books and Records
   i) Books of Account and Accounting Records
   ii) Constituting Documents
   iii) Members Registry
   iv) Registry of Securities for Co-operative Corporations
   v) Directors Registry
   vi) Incorporating Documents, By-laws and Resolutions

2. Financial Statements
   i) Budget
   ii) Audited Financial Statements
   iii) Co-operative Exemptions

3. Annual General Meeting of Members
   i) Notice of Meeting
   ii) Presentation of Minutes, Financial Statements and Auditor's Report
   iii) Election of Directors
   iv) Election or Appointment of Officers
   v) Appointment of Auditor

4. Board of Directors [or Trustees] Meetings

5. Minutes of Meetings
   i) Annual General Meeting of Members
   ii) Special General Meeting of Members
   iii) Board of Directors [or Trustees]
   iv) Committee Meetings

6. Registry of Members [for co-operative corporations without share capital, also registry of loans by members]

7. Filings

    i) Annual Return or Summary under the Corporations Information Act or the Canada Corporations Act
    ii) Notice of Change
    iii) Taxation Returns
        – Canada Customs and Revenue Agency
        – Registered Charity Return
        – Non-profit Return
        – Trust Return
        – Ministry of Finance Corporate Tax Return
        – Municipal Assessments
    (iv) Co-operative's Offering Statements

8. Due Diligence Review
    i) Risk Assessment
    ii) Internal Controls
    iii) Document Issues Being Addressed and How

APPENDIX D

Precedents

A   INTRODUCTION

Precedents are intended to be used as guides by lawyers and others in the preparation of legal and other documents. Each organization will have its own characteristics, background, requirements and desires, which should be reflected in the various documents. Precedents, therefore, should be adapted to the needs of the particular organization involved and not the other way around.

    A drafter should not feel restricted to using one set of precedents in preparing the documents for a particular organization. There may be relevant provisions that meet the needs of a proposed unincorporated association in the precedents in this manual for a corporation without share capital. Care must be taken to ensure that any documents comply with the statutory and common law requirements, the needs of the organization now and in the foreseeable future, and the objects of the organization.

    There are a number of legal requirements or prohibitions that may restrict organizations in the modification of precedents. For example, s. 155 of the *Canada Corporations Act* requires that all by-laws for corporations incorporated under that Act cover certain specified matters. The precedent for a by-law for a corporation incorporated under that Act provided in this manual includes the matters required by s. 155. The drafter should ensure that the by-law for any organization meets all the legal requirements that apply to the organization.

    Practical constraints should also be considered in the drafting of documents. The drafter should keep in mind the type of organization, its activities, the size of its membership, the members' experiences, the resources available to the organization and so forth while drafting the documents for a particular organization. As a general rule, the more simple the document is, the better it is. Similarly, the more plain language and the less legal terminology that is used, the better.

    It may be appropriate, however, to include some additional matters in by-laws that are covered in the legislation or the letters patent if that would assist the membership on a day-to-day basis. In the case of a trust document, a list of powers that the courts generally recognize or that are contained in the *Trustee Act* might assist the trustees in carrying out their duties.

The constituting documents are intended to establish the organization and to set out how it is to be operated. However, they are also intended to be used by the officers, directors, members and others. Again, the simple documents are easier for most organizations to use.

B   OBJECTS CLAUSES

I   NON-PROFIT

(1)   Athletics and Sports

The establishment and operation of an athletic and sports club for the following purposes:

- to promote an interest in athletics and sports among the members;
- to encourage organized athletics and sports;
- to promote better knowledge about safe practices in athletics and sports;
- to promote interest in health and physical fitness;
- to foster interest and participation in and to provide programmes to improve horse-breeding stock;
- to arrange for and to provide instruction, displays and exhibits on athletics and sports;
- to promote research into athletics and sports medicine;
- to teach and train members in athletics and sports;
- to provide opportunities and training for leadership, self-development and sportsmanship;
- to provide facilities for athletics and sports;
- to acquire, provide and maintain facilities for athletics and sports;
- to provide dining, meeting, changing and equipment facilities for members and their guests participating in athletics and sports;
- to grant prizes and awards of achievement;
- to arrange for athletic and sports competitions, games and tournaments; and
- for such other complementary purposes that are not inconsistent with these objects.

(2)   Arts

The establishment and operation of an arts club for the following purposes:

- to encourage an interest in and appreciation of artistic endeavours, including literature, dance, music, theatre, painting, sculpture, videos, movies, photography and live art;
- to promote the study of the arts;
- to study the arts and their practice;
- to promote and to provide lectures, concerts, classes and seminars in the arts;
- to arrange competitions and exhibitions;
- to grant prizes and awards of achievement;
- to arrange for juried competitions, exhibitions, showings and productions;
- to teach and train members in the arts;
- to study the arts and their practices;
- to encourage participation in the arts by students;
- to stimulate the enjoyment and understanding of the arts and to enrich the cultural life of the community;
- to promote and facilitate support of and participation in artistic and cultural activities in the community;
- to advance the knowledge of and about the arts;
- to protect the interests of artists;
- to co-operate with government departments and their agencies and other institutions to promote appropriate levels of funding for the arts and culture;
- to act as an umbrella organization for artists and arts groups in the community;
- to provide information to and to arrange for information sharing among members;
- to provide and operate facilities for education and instruction in the arts;
- to provide and operate facilities for a theatre, music hall and/or a gallery;
- to acquire, operate, provide and maintain facilities for the arts, including a theatre, music hall and/or an art gallery;
- to establish, equip, maintain and operate a facility for the arts, including by offering a theatre, music hall and/or an art gallery;
- to stage, provide for and conduct concerts, performing arts, visual arts, lectures and similar activities related to the arts;
- to represent the views of the members and to advocate the position of the organization before governments and other decision makers;
- to protect the artistic interests of its members by pursuing adequate facilities and funding for the arts;

- to act as a focal point for the artistic community and to promote its interests;
- to encourage excellence in the artistic community;
- to promote educational opportunities in the arts, including by providing scholarships, seminars, lectures, forums, courses and instruction;
- to establish, equip, maintain and operate a community centre for the arts providing workshops, programmes, drama, art, music, handicrafts, hobbies and recreation;
- to provide and operate facilities for studios, exhibitions and performances; and
- for such other complementary purposes that are not inconsistent with these objects.

(3) Business and Professional Organizations

The establishment and operation of an organization for the following purposes:

- to promote the interests and activities of the members;
- to provide a forum for the discussion of issues of importance or interest to the members;
- to attract business to the community;
- to attract customers to the business district and to establish an environment that will encourage customers and tourists to return to the business district;
- to promote and encourage fair dealings;
- to encourage and promote ethical behaviour among the members;
- to protect the character and status of the members of the profession;
- to provide mediation and arbitration services to resolve disputes among members and between members and their customers;
- to act as a mechanism to resolve disputes among members or between a member and a customer;
- to improve the standards of practice and qualifications of the members;
- to provide training programmes and skills upgrading programmes for members;
- to organize and promote educational opportunities for members;
- to organize cultural, social and recreational activities for members and their guests;
- to provide financial assistance to members and their families;

- to share information and opinions for the mutual benefit of the members;
- to prepare reports, studies, submissions and other documentation with respect to matters of importance to the members;
- to represent the members and to advocate the position of the organization before administrative tribunals, municipal government, provincial ministries, federal departments and their agencies;
- for such other complementary purposes that are not inconsistent with these objects.

(4) Community Organizations

The establishment and operation of a community organization for the following purposes:

- to develop and promote community spirit and understanding;
- to develop and operate recreational and athletic facilities for the members;
- to provide and maintain community facilities;
- to promote the interests of the community;
- to provide equipment for community centres and facilities for use by members and their guests;
- to acquire, provide, operate and maintain a community facility;
- to provide facilities for the enjoyment and pleasure of the members and their guests;
- to provide facilities for the enjoyment and pleasure of members of the community;
- to establish and operate a neighbourhood sports field;
- to promote organized athletics, arts, recreation and education for adults;
- to promote and provide for social services in the community;
- to organize cultural and recreational events for the members and their guests;
- to organize cultural, community and recreational activities;
- to encourage multicultural activities;
- to promote mutual understanding of the culture, difficulties, needs and opportunities of different groups in the community;
- to sponsor community festivals;
- to preserve and promote the traditions of the residents of the community;
- to conserve the natural habitat of wildlife, vegetation and the natural environment of the community;

- to gather and exchange information with respect to horticulture and botany;
- to promote the development of recreational activities compatible with the natural environment;
- to provide opportunities to participate in natural resource planning;
- to promote sustainable economic development;
- to promote public interest in the history and architecture of the community;
- to conduct historical and anthropological research and study;
- to maintain a library and museum;
- to promote co-operation among parents and teachers;
- to provide assistance to teachers and school boards in the delivery of extracurricular programmes;
- to encourage public support for the schools and education;
- to provide information to the public about the need for changes to the law;
- to promote changes to the law and law reform;
- to co-ordinate lobbying efforts with other organizations with similar objects;
- to hold conferences, symposia, meetings and exhibitions for the discussion of legal and political reform; and
- for such other complementary purposes that are not inconsistent with these objects.

(5) Fraternity and Sorority Organizations

The establishment and operation of a fraternity or sorority for the following purposes:

- to promote the interests of the members of the fraternity or sorority;
- to establish, maintain and operate a facility to provide accommodation, recreation and entertainment for members of the fraternity or sorority and their guests; and
- for such other complementary purposes that are not inconsistent with these objects.

(6) Service Clubs

The establishment and operation of a service club for the following purposes:

- to pursue the civic, commercial and social interests of the community;
- to provide a forum for the discussion of issues before the community;
- to promote international relations and welfare;
- to promote friendship and mutual understanding;
- to encourage social responsibility among the members;
- to promote ethical behaviour in business and the professions;
- to encourage social activities for the members;
- to encourage and carry out social and charitable work;
- to promote participation in civic activities;
- to promote good government and citizen participation in governing; and
- for such other complementary purposes that are not inconsistent with these objects.

(7) Social Clubs

The establishment and operation of a social club for the following purposes:

- to establish, maintain and operate a club house to provide social activities for members and their guests;
- to provide dining, meeting and similar facilities for members and their guests;
- to provide a reading room and library for members and their guests;
- to promote social discourse among the members;
- to organize social and cultural activities of interest to the members; and
- for such other complementary purposes that are not inconsistent with these objects.

II CHARITABLE

(1) Relief of Poverty

- to relieve poverty by providing food and basic supplies to persons without any visible means of support;
- to relieve poverty by providing financial assistance to persons in need;
- to provide financial assistance and support services to persons of low income in need of long-term shelter;

- to provide shelter for the homeless;
- to operate a food bank for the relief of poverty in the community;
- to deliver programmes for the relief of malnutrition;
- to relieve poverty by providing health services to persons in need;
- to provide recreational activities for children and youth of low-income families;
- to provide scholarships and bursaries to students from low-income families;
- to provide counselling and support services to persons of low income and their families;
- to relieve poverty by providing and assisting in community developed health care, transportation services, communications, water and sewage treatment and energy supplies in impoverished communities;
- to provide educational and instructional programmes to the community to promote health care and disease prevention;
- to establish and maintain an employment training centre for the unemployed and low-skilled workers;
- to provide basic skills training in agriculture and horticulture for community economic development purposes;
- to establish, maintain and operate a not-for-profit community employment and training centre for the long-term unemployed; and
- to liaise with other similar charitable and not-for-profit organizations and government departments and agencies in developing retraining and educational programmes for the unemployed.

(2) **Advancement of Education**

- to promote the advancement of education in the community;
- to provide literacy training programmes and classes;
- to promote the study of history by providing educational programmes, courses, seminars, conferences, symposia, materials and audiovisual materials for use by members of the public;
- to establish a research facility and laboratory for research into disease control and the study of disease prevention;
- to establish, maintain and operate a centre to promote innovation and technology and, without limiting the generality of the foregoing, to study, develop and perfect technology in the field of health care;
- to participate in all phases of education pertaining to health care, including the education of physicians, dentists, nursing staff and paramedical staff;

- to promote the advancement of education by providing scholarships to students continuing study and research in post-graduate programmes;
- to provide educational programmes to promote the understanding and awareness of the public of Canadian history; and
- to provide educational programmes in order to promote knowledge about teaching methods through research, education and publications.

(3) **Advancement of Religion**

- to preach and promote the teachings of the faith;
- to establish, support and maintain the missions and the missionaries of the religion in order to propagate the faith;
- to promote the advancement of the religion through education programmes, religious observance, tenets and doctrines associated with the faith;
- to establish and maintain a house of worship with services conducted in accordance with the tenets and doctrines of the faith;
- to organize and conduct seminars, lectures and courses for the advancement of the faith and the teachings of the faith;
- to preach, teach, promote, disseminate, advance, demonstrate and implement the tenets and doctrines of the faith within the community and throughout the province;
- to help and strengthen the members' adherence to the tenets and doctrines of the faith; and
- to establish and maintain a religious school of instruction for children, youths and adults.

(4) **Other Purposes Beneficial to the Community**

- to receive and maintain a fund or funds and to apply all or part of the principal and income, from time to time, to charitable organizations registered under the *Income Tax Act* (Canada);
- to establish and operate a community centre in the municipality of _____ , by providing workshops, programmes, athletics, drama, art, music, handicrafts, hobbies and recreation for the benefit of the general public;
- to establish, equip, maintain and operate a community orchestra in the municipality of _____ ; to educate and increase the public's understanding of and appreciation for the arts by providing performances in public places for the general public;

- to preserve the community's historical heritage by providing educational programmes to increase awareness;
- to purchase, maintain and preserve historical and heritage buildings and to keep the buildings open for viewing by the public;
- to preserve, protect and restore the natural environment in the municipality of _____ ;
- to encourage and promote an understanding of the natural environment by providing seminars, courses, public meetings and information;
- to promote an understanding of the dependence of humans on the environment through educational programmes, demonstrations and exhibits;
- to protect the natural environment and promote the preservation of the natural environment by providing information about the reduction, re-use, recycling and recovery of solid waste by the general public;
- to operate a community health centre in the municipality of _____ , by providing medical, health and supportive services for the general public;
- to provide supportive services for persons with disabilities by providing personal care, housekeeping, meals-on-wheels, shopping assistance and companionship;
- to provide life management counselling and supportive services to persons with disabilities;
- to undertake public education, information dissemination, family support services and to co-ordinate medical care and social services for persons suffering from debilitating disease;
- to promote nutrition and health in the municipality of _____;
- to organize, co-ordinate and direct medial support service programmes for persons with debilitating disease;
- to promote and support public research in the field of disease control and prevention;
- to co-ordinate health care and social services for persons with debilitating diseases and illnesses;
- to provide specialized social services to persons with debilitating diseases and illnesses;
- to conduct research into the causes of debilitating diseases and illnesses;
- to establish, maintain and operate a research facility for the study of debilitating diseases and illnesses;

- to provide programmes and co-ordinate support services for persons involved in substance abuse;
- to assist families of persons who abuse substances through counselling services and the dissemination of information about substance abuse;
- to provide treatment and recovery facilities to persons who abuse substances;
- to educate and create public awareness about the prevention of crime, protection of persons and property by conducting seminars and neighbourhood crime prevention programmes;
- to encourage and promote co-operation among the public and law enforcement agencies to solve crimes and to prevent crimes through information dissemination, seminars and public meetings;
- to provide immigrants and refugees with counselling services and language training;
- to provide an opportunity for adult offenders to reintegrate into society by offering a community-based residential programme, life and basic skills training, employment preparatory courses, personal care and substance abuse treatment; and
- to promote a better understanding within the community of adult offenders and to encourage community support and participation through education and information dissemination.

(5) **Objects Clauses Pre-Approved by the Public Guardian and Trustee for Ontario and the Canada Customs and Revenue Agency**

The Public Guardian and Trustee for Ontario has developed a number of "pre-approved" objects clauses that may be used by those establishing a charitable organization. These objects clauses have also been pre-approved by the Canada Customs and Revenue Agency for purposes of registration as a charity under the *Income Tax Act*. The objects clauses must be used without modification, other than where a specific faith or geographic area is to be included. All other requirements for incorporation or registration must, of course, still be met, including the mandatory special provisions for charitable corporations. Interestingly, the objects clauses are not necessarily grouped under one of the four heads of charity but generally along more functional lines.

(a) *Religious Organizations*
- To advance and teach the religious tenets, doctrines, observances and culture associated with the (specify faith or religion) faith.

OR

- To preach and advance the teachings of the (specify faith or religion) faith and the religious tenets, doctrines, observances and culture associated with that faith.
- To establish, maintain and support a house of worship with services conducted in accordance with the tenets and doctrines of the (specify faith or religion) faith.
- To support and maintain missions and missionaries in order to propagate the (specify faith or religion) faith.
- To establish and maintain a religious school of instruction for children, youths and adults.

(b)   Religious Schools

- To establish and maintain a religious school of instruction for children, youths and adults.
- To establish and maintain a religious day school.

(c)   Foundations

- To receive and maintain a fund or funds and to apply all or part of the principal and income therefrom, from time to time, to charitable organizations that are also registered charities under the *Income Tax Act* (Canada).

(d)   Services for Senior Citizens

*(i)   **Senior Citizens Centres***

- To relieve loneliness and isolation of the aged or to improve their mobility and fitness by establishing, operating and maintaining a senior citizens centre to provide recreation, education, cultural activities and other programs for senior citizens.

*(ii)   **Respite Services***

- To provide respite to persons caring for aged persons by providing temporary care to aged persons and by providing such services as housekeeping, meal preparation, nursing and shopping assistance.

*(iii)   **Home Care***

- To provide support services for aged persons including personal care, housekeeping, meals, nursing and shopping assistance.

(e) International Development

*(i) **Relief of Poverty***

- To relieve poverty in developing nations by providing food and other basic supplies to persons in need.

*(ii) **Health***

- To develop or promote public health in developing nations by educating and instructing the public on prevention of, and curative measures for, health problems and by researching and documenting changes in the health of the community.

*(iii) **Drinking Water***

- To improve the quality of drinking water in developing nations by constructing wells and water treatment, irrigation and sewage treatment systems.

*(iv) **Agriculture***

- To improve skills in forestry, agriculture and horticulture and to assist in the preservation of the environment in developing nations.

*(v) **Disaster Relief***

- To provide necessities of life to victims of disasters.

(f) Assistance for the Sexually/Physically Abused Child

*(i) **Education***

- To educate the public and professionals about prevention of, and responses to, child sexual abuse by offering courses, seminars, conferences and meetings and by collecting and disseminating information on that topic.

*(ii) **Counselling***

- To assist those affected by child sexual abuse through counselling and treatment programs.

(iii) Spousal Abuse

- To educate the public and professionals about prevention of, and responses to, spousal abuse by offering courses, seminars, conferences, meetings and by collecting and disseminating information on that topic

(iv) Counselling

- To assist those affected by spousal abuse through counselling and treatment programs

(v) Shelters

- To provide affordable and secure housing for women and the children of women who have been emotionally, physically or sexually abused or traumatized.

(g) Relief of Poverty

- To relieve poverty by providing food and other basic supplies to persons of low income, by establishing, operating and maintaining shelters for the homeless, and by providing counselling and other similar programs to relieve poverty.

(h) Programs for Physically or Mentally Disabled

(i) Residences

- To provide residential housing and a stable living environment to persons with disabilities.

(ii) Training Education and Counselling

- To provide life management counselling and other support services to assist persons with disabilities to become more independent in the community.
- To provide training for, and to assist in, the placement of persons with disabilities in employment.
- To provide support and encouragement to persons with disabilities by offering programs in individual development and integration into the community.
- To provide relief to persons with disabilities by developing and implementing recreation, education and social integration programs for the disabled.

(iii)   Community Education

- To educate the public on debilitating conditions and the needs of persons with disabilities by providing seminars and by collecting and disseminating information on that topic

(i)   Promotion of Health

(i)   Respite Services

- To provide respite to persons caring for aged, ill or disabled persons by providing temporary care to aged, ill or disabled persons and by providing such services as housekeeping, meal preparation, nursing and shopping assistance.

(ii)   Home Care

- To provide support services for aged, ill or disabled persons including personal care, housekeeping, meals, nursing and shopping assistance.

(iii)   Health Care Centre

- To operate a community health care centre by providing medical, health and support services for the general public.

(iv)   Health Care Co-ordination

- To coordinate health care and social services for people with debilitating diseases, illnesses and conditions.
- To provide social services to persons with debilitating diseases, illnesses and conditions.

(v)   Research

- To conduct research into the causes, controls and cure of debilitating diseases, illnesses and conditions.

(vi)   Mutual Support

- To provide support for those affected by debilitating diseases, illnesses and conditions by offering education and counselling and by establishing mutual support groups.

(j)   *Substance Abuse*

- To educate the public about the causes and effects of, and treatments for, substance abuse by offering courses, seminars, conferences and meetings and by collecting and disseminating information on that topic
- To conduct research for the benefit of the public into the causes of, and treatments for, substance abuse.
- To coordinate health care and social support services for persons affected by substance abuse.
- To assist persons in coping with the effects of substance abuse by offering education and counselling and by establishing mutual support groups.
- To provide a treatment and recovery facility for substance abuse clients and to provide medical and social support services at the facility.

(k)   *Preservation of the Environment*

- To organize or participate in environmental projects designed to:
    - preserve and protect flora and fauna;
    - preserve, protect and restore rivers; or
    - improve the urban environment.
- To educate and increase the public's understanding of the environment and its importance by offering courses, seminars, conferences and meetings and by collecting and disseminating information on that topic.
- To develop and provide programs promoting the protection and preservation of the environment through re-use, reduction, recycling and recovery of waste and to educate institutions, industries, businesses and individuals about efficient waste management systems.
- To conduct research relating to the environment and to disseminate the results of such research.

(l)   *The Arts*

- To educate and increase the public's understanding and appreciation of the arts by providing performances of an artistic nature in public places, senior citizens homes, churches, community centres and educational institutions and by providing seminars on topics relating to such performances.
- To provide instructional seminars on topics related to the performing and visual arts.

- To produce performing arts festivals for the purposes of educating and advancing the public's understanding and appreciation of performing arts and to educate artists through participation in such festivals and related workshops.

(m) *Community Centres, Immigrant Services, Literacy and Employment Training*

(i) **Community Centres**

- To establish and operate a community centre to be used for workshops, programs, athletics, drama, art, music, handicrafts, hobbies and recreation for the benefit of the general public.

(ii) **Immigrant Services**

- To provide education, counselling and other support services for immigrants and refugees in need, including language instruction, employment training, job search programs, translation services and information programs on Canadian culture and life.

(iii) **Employment Preparation, Training and Counselling**

- To establish, maintain and operate an employment training centre for needy unemployed and low skilled workers.
- To provide assistance to needy persons in drafting resumes, searching for employment and preparing for job interviews.
- To provide counselling to needy persons experiencing long term unemployment.
- To develop employment training and education programs for needy persons.

(iv) **Literacy**

- To provide literacy programs and classes to members of the public.
- To develop and provide education and training programs to persons who will conduct literacy training.

(n) *Low Cost Housing*

- To provide and operate not-for-profit residential accommodation and incidental facilities exclusively for:
    – Persons of low income;
    – Senior citizens primarily of low or modest income; or

– Disabled persons primarily of low or modest income.

III Co-operative Corporations

(1) Housing

- primarily to provide housing to the members of the co-operative; and
- to provide and operate housing with or without any public space, recreational facilities and commercial space or buildings appropriate thereto, mainly for persons of low or modest income.

C TRUST

I Basic Trust Document

THIS DECLARATION OF TRUST is made the   day of   200 :

John A. Smith
Jane B. Doe
Jean C. Blanc

(who are the "Trustees", which expression shall include the Trustee or Trustees for the time being of this Deed).

WHEREAS:

1) The ABC Reading Club is a not-for-profit organization which operates a club for its members and their guests;
2) The ABC Reading Club provides a facility for members and their guests to read newspapers, journals and texts for individual enjoyment and fulfilment;
3) The ABC Reading Club provides ancillary services for its members;
4) The members of the ABC Reading Club desire to establish a trust to hold and manage certain property for the benefit of the members.

NOW IT IS AGREED AND DECLARED as follows:

1. A trust is established in the name of the ABC Reading Club Trust ("ABC Trust") for the benefit of the members, from time to time, of ABC Reading Club.
2. The objects of the ABC Trust are:

(a) to operate the facilities known as the ABC Reading Room as a facility for members of the ABC Reading Club and their guests;

(b) to maintain and improve the ABC Reading Room for the enjoyment of the members of the ABC Reading Club and their guests;

(c) to purchase, obtain, maintain and dispose of newspapers, journals and texts for the members of the ABC Reading Club and their guests to read in the ABC Reading Room and for members to borrow on the terms and conditions set out by the Trustees;

(d) to raise revenue from the membership in order to operate, maintain and improve the ABC Reading Room.

3. The Trustees shall hold the capital and income of any cash, cheques, securities, investments, personal property, real property or other interests received or otherwise acquired for the ABC Trust upon trust used for the exclusive purpose of the objects of the ABC Trust.

4. The Trustees may invest in their names any monies or the proceeds of any property or interests received or otherwise acquired that are not required for the immediate purposes of the ABC Trust. The investments may be securities or other investments in which such trust monies or proceeds may by law be invested. The Trustees may, from time to time, deal further with the investments and may, from time to time, reinvest any amounts that are payable.

5. Any property received or otherwise acquired shall be vested in the Trustees.

6. The Trustees shall be a minimum of three and a maximum of seven.

7. The power of appointing new Trustees shall be vested in the surviving or continuing Trustees for the time being, excluding any retiring Trustees.

8. The following regulations shall govern the procedures of the Trustees:

(a) the Trustees shall hold meetings at least once every six months. The meetings may be at a place that the Trustees shall, from time to time, determine;

(b) any Trustee may, at any time, convene a special meeting of the Trustees provided at least seven days' written notice has been given to the other Trustees of the matters to be discussed and the time, date and location of the meeting;

(c) a majority of the Trustees shall form a quorum for any meeting of the Trustees;

(d) meetings may be held by conference call or by similar telecommunications or electronic means;

(e) the Trustees shall appoint by resolution one of the Trustees to be Chair. The Chair shall have a deciding vote in the case of a tie on any matter before the Trustees;

(f) any resolution of the Trustees may, from time to time, be rescinded or varied by the Trustees;

(g) the Trustees shall maintain a minute book. The proceedings of the Trustees shall be entered in the minute book. The Chair shall sign the minutes at the conclusion of each meeting or at a future meeting when the minutes have been duly confirmed by the Trustees; and

(h) the Trustees shall maintain books of account to record all money received and paid out by or on behalf of the Trustees.

9. The Trustees may, from time to time, open and maintain an account or accounts at a financial institution or institutions. The Trustees may at any time pay any monies forming part of the ABC Trust to the credit of the account or accounts or place the monies on deposit with any financial institution or institutions. All cheques and orders for payment shall be signed by the Chair and at least one other Trustee

10. The Trustees may be reimbursed for any reasonable expenses incurred personally in carrying out their duties as Trustees in fulfilling the objects of the ABC Trust.

11. The Trustees may establish terms and conditions of membership in the ABC Reading Club, for the use of the ABC Reading Room and its ancillary services, and for the borrowing by members of any newspapers, journals and texts.

12. The Trustees may engage any legal, accounting, library or other assistance that they consider appropriate to administer and preserve the ABC Trust and to operate, maintain and improve the ABC Reading Room. The Trustees may pay any fees, expenses or other charges with respect to the administration and preservation of the ABC Trust and the operation, maintenance and improvement of the ABC Reading Room and its ancillary services.

13. The Trustees may apply for incorporation as a not-for-profit corporation under the Ontario *Corporations Act*. The expenses related to the application may be paid from the ABC Trust. Upon incorporation, the ABC Trust shall be dissolved and the property shall be transferred to the corporation.

14. Upon dissolution of the ABC Trust, other than by incorporation, and after payment of all debts and liabilities, the remaining property of the ABC Trust shall be distributed to a not-for-profit organization with objects similar to the objects of the ABC Trust or to a public library.

IN WITNESS whereof this Declaration of Trust is signed and sealed this day of   , 200 .

Signed, sealed and delivered in the Presence of:	) _____) (Signature)) John A. Smith
_____ (Signature) Witness	) _____) (Signature)) Jane B. Doe) _____ (Signature) Jean C. Blanc

II CHARITABLE TRUST DOCUMENT

THIS DECLARATION OF TRUST is made the   day of   , 200 by:

John A. Smith
Jane B. Doe
Jean C. Blanc

(who are the "Trustees", which expression shall include the Trustee or Trustees for the time being of this Deed).

WHEREAS:

1) There is a need for educational opportunities for disadvantaged persons in the community;
2) It is desirable:
   (a) to provide scholarships and other forms of financial assistance to individuals who are financially disadvantaged and require financial assistance to obtain an education, and
   (b) to provide basic skills training and educational opportunities to disadvantaged persons in the community; and
3) It is desirable to establish a charitable trust fund to meet this need to the extent possible.

NOW IT IS AGREED AND DECLARED as follows:

1. A trust is established in the name of the ABC Educational Charitable Trust Fund ("ABC Trust Fund") for the benefit of persons who are financially disadvantaged and who are eligible and qualify for financial assistance and for educational programmes that benefit persons who are disadvantaged.
2. The objects of the ABC Trust Fund are, by such means as are charitable, to promote educational opportunities for disadvantaged persons in the community and, in particular:
   (a) to support, expand, promote and develop educational opportunities financially and otherwise for persons who are financially disadvantaged in the community;
   (b) to provide financial support to training and educational programmes for basic skills training and employment training;
   (c) to establish, operate and provide scholarships, bursaries, prizes and other financial assistance to persons who are financially disadvantaged; and
   (d) to solicit and receive donations, bequests, legacies and grants to establish and maintain a fund or funds and to disburse all or part of the capital of the fund or funds and their income to carry out the objects of the ABC Trust Fund.
3. The Trustees shall hold the capital and income of any cash, cheques, securities, investments, personal property, real property or other interests received or otherwise acquired for the ABC Trust Fund upon trust used for the exclusive purpose of the charitable objects of the ABC Trust Fund.
4. The Trustees may invest in their names any monies or the proceeds of any property or interests received or otherwise acquired that are not required for the immediate purposes of the ABC Trust Fund. The investments may be securities or other investments in which such trust monies or proceeds may by law be invested. The Trustees may, from time to time, deal further with the investments and may, from time to time, reinvest any amounts that are payable.
5. Any property received or otherwise acquired shall be vested in the Trustees.
6. The Trustees shall be a minimum of three and a maximum of seven.
7. The power of appointing new Trustees shall be vested in the surviving or continuing Trustees for the time being, excluding any retiring Trustees.
8. The following regulations shall govern the procedures of the trustees:

(a) the Trustees shall hold meetings at least once every six months. The meetings may be at a place that the Trustees shall, from time to time, determine;
(b) any Trustee may, at any time, convene a special meeting of the Trustees provided at least seven days' written notice has been given to the other Trustees of the matters to be discussed and the time, date and location of the meeting;
(c) a majority of the Trustees shall form a quorum for any meeting of the Trustees;
(d) meetings may be held by conference call or by similar telecommunications or electronic means;
(e) the Trustees shall appoint by resolution one of the Trustees to be Chair. The Chair shall have a deciding vote in the case of a tie on any matter before the Trustees;
(f) any resolution of the Trustees may, from time to time, be rescinded or varied by the Trustees;
(g) the Trustees shall maintain a minute book. The proceedings of the Trustees shall be entered in the minute book. The Chair shall sign the minutes at the conclusion of each meeting or at a future meeting when the minutes have been duly confirmed by the Trustees; and
(h) the Trustees shall maintain books of account to record all money received and paid out by or on behalf of the Trustees.
9. The Trustees may, from time to time, open and maintain an account or accounts at a financial institution or institutions. The Trustees may at any time pay any monies forming part of the ABC Trust Fund to the credit of the account or accounts or place the monies on deposit with any financial institution or institutions. All cheques and orders for payment shall be signed by the Chair and at least one other Trustee.
10. The Trustees may be reimbursed for any reasonable expenses incurred personally in carrying out their duties as Trustees in fulfilling the objects of the ABC Trust. No part of the capital or income of the ABC Trust is payable to or is otherwise available for the personal benefit of any Trustee.
11. The Trustees may establish by resolution the criteria for eligibility for financial assistance out of the ABC Charitable Trust Fund.
12. The Trustees may engage any legal, accounting or other assistance that they consider appropriate and are hereby authorized to pay all usual professional fees and other charges associated with the work done, with respect to the administration and preservation of the ABC Trust Fund.

13. The Trustees may apply for incorporation as a charitable corporation under the Ontario *Corporations Act*. The expenses related to the application may be paid from the ABC Trust Fund. Upon incorporation, the ABC Trust Fund shall be dissolved and the property shall be transferred to the corporation, provided that the letters patent for the corporation include a provision that upon dissolution any property remaining after payment of all debts and liabilities shall be distributed to a charitable organization in Ontario registered as a charity under the *Income Tax Act* (Canada).
14. Upon dissolution of the ABC Trust Fund, other than by incorporation, and after payment of all debts and liabilities, the remaining property of the ABC Trust Fund shall be distributed to a charitable organization in Ontario registered as a charity under the *Income Tax Act* (Canada).

IN WITNESS whereof this Declaration of Trust is signed and sealed this day of   , 200 .

Signed, sealed and delivered in the Presence of:	)	_____ (Signature) John A. Smith
_____ (Signature) Witness	)))))	_____ (Signature) Jane B. Doe _____ (Signature) Jean C. Blanc

III OPTIONAL PROVISIONS

(1) Administrative Provisions

The Trustees may appoint a solicitor or other person to be their agent and to receive and give a discharge for any money or valuable consideration or property receivable by the Trustees under the Trust.

The Trustees may insure against loss or damage any insurable property held by the Trustees and any premiums, taxes, fees or other charges arising from the insurance contract out of the income of the Trust.

The Trustees may enter into and renew any leases for real or personal property on terms that the Trustees consider reasonable and may pay any rents, taxes, fees or other charges arising from the lease out of the income of the Trust.

(2) Remuneration of Trustees

The Trustees may receive a reasonable fee or similar remuneration for acting as Trustees. The Trustees may, from time to time, set the amount of the fee or similar remuneration.

(3) Indemnification of Trustees

The Trustees, their heirs, executors and administrators and estate and effects shall be indemnified and saved harmless, individually and severally, from time to time and at all times from and against
  (a) all costs, charges and expenses which a Trustee sustains or incurs in or about any action, suit or proceeding brought, commenced or prosecuted against him or her for or in respect of any act, deed, matter or thing whatsoever, made, done or permitted by him or her, in or about the execution of the duties of his or her office or in respect of such liability; and
  (b) all other costs, charges and expenses that he or she sustains or incurs in or about or in relation to the affairs thereof, except such costs, charges or expenses as are occasioned by his or her own willful neglect or default.

The Trustees may obtain indemnification insurance for errors and omissions and may pay for this insurance out of the Trust.

(4) Investments

The Trustees may invest in any security or other investment in which trust monies or proceeds may by law be invested and in mutual funds or similar securities available from a financial institution.

(5) Amending the Trust

The Trustees may, from time to time, amend this Declaration of Trust as the Trustees consider necessary to fulfill the objects of the Trust.

D   UNINCORPORATED ASSOCIATION

I   Basic Memorandum of Association

1. The organization shall be called the ABC Reading Club.
2. The objects of the ABC Reading Club are:
   (a) to provide a reading room for the use of its members and their guests to read for enjoyment newspapers, journals and texts;

(b) to provide ancillary goods and services for use of its members, including seminars, lectures, photocopying and hospitality;
(c) to raise revenue to operate, maintain and improve the reading room from membership dues, fees for services and fines for breaches of the rules of the reading room and of the ABC Reading Club.
3. There shall be two classes of members:
  (a) Regular Class, who:
    i) are employees of ABC Industries Inc.;
    ii) apply for membership in the ABC Reading Club; and
    iii) are admitted by the directors.
  (b) Associate Class, who:
    i) are individuals other than employees, including the spouses and children of members;
    ii) apply for membership; and
    iii) are admitted by the directors.
4. There shall be five directors of the ABC Reading Club elected from among the members at an annual general meeting. The directors shall be responsible for the management of the affairs of the ABC Reading Club.
5. The directors may, from time to time, enact, amend or repeal, as they consider appropriate, by-laws to manage the affairs of the ABC Reading Club at a meeting of the board of directors called for that purpose. A by-law is effective only until the next annual general meeting of the members unless it is confirmed by a majority vote of members present at the annual general meeting or at a general meeting of members called for that purpose.
6. The directors shall elect from among themselves a president, vice-president and secretary-treasurer as officers of the ABC Reading Club.
7. The members may amend this Memorandum of Association at the annual general meeting or at a general meeting called for that purpose on one week's notice in writing. The purpose of the general meeting shall be given in any notice. A two-thirds majority of the votes cast at the annual general meeting or the general meeting, as the case may be, is required to amend the Memorandum of Association.
8. The members may dissolve the ABC Reading Club at a general meeting called for that purpose on one week's notice in writing. The purpose of the meeting shall be given in the notice in writing. Dissolution of the ABC Reading Club requires a two-thirds majority of the votes cast at the general meeting. Upon dissolution, any

assets remaining after payment of any liabilities shall be donated to another not-for-profit organization with similar objects in Ontario or to the public library.
9. The ABC Reading Club shall be carried on without purpose of gain for its members and any profits or other accretions to the organization shall be used solely to promote its objects.

Passed by the members of the ABC Reading Club this   day of   , 200 .

_____   _____   _____
(Signature)   (Signature)   (Signature)
John A. Smith   Jane B. Doe   Jean C. Blanc

II LONGER FORM OF MEMORANDUM OF ASSOCIATION

Name and Head Office

1. The organization shall be called the ABC Charitable Reading Room. Its head office shall be in the Town of Doone, Ontario.

Objects

2. The objects of ABC Charitable Reading Room are:
   (a) to promote the advancement of education by providing a reading room for disadvantaged persons;
   (b) to establish, maintain and operate a reading room for the benefit of the community and, in furtherance of that object, to provide ancillary and incidental services;
   (c) to promote literacy by providing classes to persons who have difficulty with reading and writing.

Members

3. Any person who supports the objects of the ABC Charitable Reading Room may be admitted as a member by the board of directors.

Directors

4. There shall be five directors of the ABC Charitable Reading Room elected from among the members at an annual general meeting. The directors shall be responsible for the management of the affairs of the ABC Charitable Reading Room. Any documents that require a signature may be signed by the President and the Secretary-Treasurer on behalf of the ABC Charitable Reading Room.

5. The directors may, from time to time, enact, amend or repeal, as they consider appropriate, by-laws to manage the affairs of the ABC Charitable Reading Room that are not inconsistent with the Memorandum of Association at a meeting of the board of directors called for that purpose.
6. Meetings of the board of directors shall be held on the second Wednesday of each month, unless a meeting is cancelled by the President with at least one week's notice. A quorum for a meeting of the board of directors shall be three directors. A meeting of the board may be adjourned with or without a quorum.
7. Decisions shall be made by a majority vote.
8. The directors shall elect from among themselves the following officers:
    (a) President, who shall chair all meetings of the directors and of the members; represent the ABC Charitable Reading Room in the community; have general supervision over the affairs of the ABC Charitable Reading Room; and perform such other duties as may be, from time to time, assigned to the President;
    (b) Vice-President, who shall act as President in the President's absence or if the President is unable to perform the duties; and perform such other duties as may be, from time to time, assigned to the Vice-President; and
    (c) Secretary-Treasurer, who shall maintain the financial records and books and registries of members, directors and officers; give notice to members and directors of meetings; prepare the financial statements and present them at the annual meeting of members; and perform such other duties as may be, from time to time, assigned to the Secretary-Treasurer.
9. The directors shall make arrangements for the financial affairs of the ABC Charitable Reading Room with a financial institution. Any cheques or other similar instruments require the signature of the Secretary-Treasurer and one of either the President or the Vice-President.
10. Meetings of the ABC Charitable Reading Room shall take place on the third Wednesday of every month, unless a meeting is cancelled by the President with at least one week's notice. Members may provide advice and guidance to the directors on the affairs of the Reading Room at a regular meeting. Quorum for a regular meeting shall be five members present in person. A regular meeting may be adjourned with or without a quorum being in attendance.

11. An annual meeting of the members shall be held during September of each year. Election of the directors, presentation of the financial statements and the Secretary-Treasurer's report and any other relevant business shall be conducted at the annual meeting.
12. All resolutions and motions shall be voted upon by a show of hands. A majority of the votes shall determine the resolution or motion.
13. An officer or director may be removed from office at a general meeting of the members called for that purpose on one week's written notice where two thirds of the members in attendance vote to remove the officer or director.
14. Any notice required to be given may be given personally, by facsimile transmission, by electronic mail or by mail. Notice given by mail shall be deemed to be given three days after it was mailed.
15. The members may amend this Memorandum of Association at the annual general meeting or at a general meeting called for that purpose on one week's notice. The purpose of the meeting shall be given in the notice.
16. The ABC Charitable Reading Room shall be carried on without purpose of gain for its members and any profits or other accretions to the organization shall be used solely to promote its objects.
17. No officer or director shall have an interest, direct or indirect, in any contract with the ABC Charitable Reading Room. If an officer or director becomes aware of an interest in contract or a proposed contract, he or she shall declare the interest to the board at the next meeting of the board. The officer or director shall not participate in the discussion of or vote concerning the contract or proposed contract.
18. The members may dissolve the ABC Charitable Reading Room at a general meeting called for that purpose on one week's notice in writing. The purpose of the meeting shall be given in the notice in writing. Dissolution of the ABC Charitable Reading Room requires a majority vote of all members present in person or by proxy. Upon dissolution, any assets remaining after payment of any liabilities shall be donated to another charitable organization with similar objects in Ontario.

Passed by the members of the ABC Charitable Reading Room this   day of ,   200 .

| (Signature) | (Signature) | (Signature) |
| John A. Smith | Jane B. Doe | Jean C. Blanc |

III BY-LAWS

Head Office

1. The head office of the ABC Reading Club shall be in the main office building of ABC Industries Inc., in the Town of Doone, Ontario or at such other place as the board of directors may, from time to time, determine.

Directors

2. The board of directors shall manage the affairs of the ABC Reading Club.
3. An individual is eligible to be elected a director if he or she:
   (a) is a member of the ABC Reading Club;
   (b) is at least 18 years of age;
   (c) is mentally competent;
   (d) does not hold a paid position with the ABC Reading Club;
   (e) is not bankrupt or insolvent.
4. The directors shall be elected by the members at the annual general meeting. The term of office shall expire at the next annual general meeting. An incumbent director is eligible for re-election.
5. A director shall cease to be a director upon his or her:
   (a) death;
   (b) resignation in writing; or
   (c) removal by a vote of the members.
6. A director may be removed from office by a majority of the votes cast by the members present at a meeting called for that purpose. The notice of meeting shall include the grounds for the proposed removal of the director.
7. The remaining directors, provided there is a quorum, may fill a vacancy on the board by appointment of one of the members to the board. If there is no quorum of directors, the remaining directors shall call a general meeting of the members for the purpose of electing directors.
8. The board of directors shall designate a day, time and location for regular monthly meetings of the board for the transaction of business. No formal notice of the regular meetings shall be required.

9. Any director may call a special board meeting on three days' written notice. The notice shall set out the purpose of the meeting.
10. A majority of directors shall constitute a quorum for a meeting of the board and for the transacting of any business, provided that there is a minimum of two directors present.
11. Decisions of the board shall be made by resolution or by motion. A resolution or motion shall pass if supported by a majority of the votes cast at the meeting. The chair of the meeting shall have a deciding vote in case of a tie vote.
12. Every director who has a direct or indirect interest in any contract or proposed contract with the ABC Reading Club shall:
    (a) declare his or her interest at the first meeting of the board after which he or she became aware of the interest;
    (b) request that the minutes of the meeting record the declaration; and
    (c) not vote on any resolution or motion concerning the contract or proposed contract and shall not participate in any further discussion concerning the contract or proposed contract.
    The other directors may require the director to leave the room during the discussion and vote.
13. The directors shall not be paid any remuneration for carrying out their duties as directors or as officers, other than being reimbursed for reasonable and necessary expenses incurred by them.

Officers

14. The officers shall be appointed by the directors at the first board meeting following the annual general meeting of the members. The term of office expires at the first board meeting following the annual general meeting of the board.
15. The officers shall have the following duties:
    (a) President — shall chair all meetings of the ABC Reading Club and of the directors; represent the Club in the community and with ABC Industries Inc.; have general supervision over the affairs of the Club; and perform such other duties as the Board may, from time to time, assign to the President;
    (b) Vice-President — shall act as President in the President's absence or if the President is unable to perform the duties; and perform such other duties as the Board may, from time to time, assign to the Vice-President;
    (c) Secretary-Treasurer — shall maintain the records, books of account, registries of members, directors and officers; give

notice to members and directors of meetings; prepare the Club's financial statements and present them at the annual meeting; and perform such other duties as the Board may, from time to time, assign to the Secretary-Treasurer.
16. An officer shall cease to be an officer upon his or her:
   (a) death;
   (b) resignation in writing; or
   (c) removal by the board of directors.
17. An officer may be removed from office by a majority of the votes cast at a meeting of the board called for that purpose. The notice of the meeting shall set out the grounds for the proposed removal.
18. The directors may fill any vacancy from among the directors remaining on the board, provided there is a quorum.

Members Meetings

19. The Annual General Meeting of the ABC Reading Club shall be held at 7:00 p.m. on the third Monday of September at the head office or at such other date, time and place as the board of directors sets out in the notice of meeting.
20. The notice of meeting shall be in writing and shall be sent to the members at least 14 days before the date of the meeting. The notice shall set out the agenda for the meeting.
21. The Annual General Meeting shall include the following agenda items:
   (a) presentation of the financial statements and the secretary-treasurer's report;
   (b) report of the board of directors;
   (c) election of the directors; and
   (d) such other business as may be properly brought before the meeting.
22. The directors may, by resolution, call a general meeting of the members by written notice sent at least three days before the date of the meeting. The notice shall set out the purpose of the meeting.
23. Decisions at the Annual General Meeting and at any general meeting shall be made by resolution or motion. A majority of the votes cast, unless otherwise provided for in the Memorandum of Association or the By-Laws, shall be required to pass a resolution or motion. The chair of the meeting has a second vote in case of a tie.

24. Quorum for a meeting of members is ten members present in person.
25. A member may not attend or vote at a meeting by proxy.

Termination of Membership

26. A member shall cease to be a member upon his or her:
    (a) death;
    (b) resignation in writing; or
    (c) termination by the members.
27. A member's membership may be terminated at a general meeting called for that purpose. The notice of meeting shall set out the grounds for the proposed termination of the member's membership. The member shall have the opportunity to make a presentation to the members at that meeting.

Signing of Documents

28. The board may, by resolution, appoint any person, from time to time, to sign documents on behalf of the ABC Reading Club. Absent a specific resolution, the President, Vice-President or the Secretary-Treasurer may sign documents on behalf of the ABC Reading Club.

Financial Affairs

29. The President and Treasurer are authorized to complete the banking of the ABC Reading Club. The banking may be conducted at a financial institution or institutions approved by resolution of the board.
30. The persons authorized to complete the banking are authorized to:
    (a) set up and operate the accounts;
    (b) execute any agreements with the financial institution to facilitate the banking arrangements;
    (c) deposit to the account of the ABC Reading Club all money, cheques and negotiable instruments payable to the Club;
    (d) issue receipts for property received by the Club;
    (e) make and sign cheques on behalf of the Club but only when two authorized persons sign the cheques together; and
    (f) other activities authorized by resolution of the board.

31. The financial year of the ABC Reading Club shall end on the 31st day of August unless it is otherwise changed by resolution of the board.

Reading Room

32. The board may establish rules for the use of the reading room and the ancillary goods and services. The board may determine if any member has breached the rules at a hearing called for that purpose. The notice of hearing shall be served on the relevant member or members who shall have a right to attend and make a presentation. The board may, by resolution, assess a fine for the breach of the rules. The fine shall not be greater than $10 for each breach.
33. The board may determine, from time to time, the reading materials and the ancillary goods and services that are to be provided in the Reading Room and may assess and collect fees for those goods and services.
34. The board may establish, from time to time, the dues for membership. The dues may be different for Regular and Associate Members.

Passed by the Board of Directors on the   day of   200 .

_____
Secretary
(Signature)

Confirmed by the Members on the   day of   200 .

_____
Secretary
(Signature)

E CORPORATIONS

I ONTARIO

(1) Applications for Letters Patent

The applicants for incorporation of a letters patent corporation must use the prescribed form. The precedents below set out the information that would be included on the prescribed form.

(a)   Not-for-profit Corporation

1. The name of the corporation is: ABC Reading Club
2. The address of the head office of the corporation is: 123 Main Street, Doone, Ontario, N2M 1A1
3. The applicants who are to be the first directors of the corporation are:

Name	Address
John Adam Smith	45 Red Road, Doone, Ontario, N2M 2A2
Jane Barbara Doe	56 Blue Drive, Doone, Ontario, N2M 2A3
Jean Charles Blanc	67 Black Road, Doone, Ontario, N2M 3A4

4. The objects for which the corporation is incorporated are:
    (a) to provide a reading room for the use of its members and their guests to read for enjoyment newspapers, journals and texts;
    (b) to provide ancillary goods and services for use of its members, including seminars, lectures, photocopying and hospitality; and
    (c) such other complementary purposes not inconsistent with these objects.
5. The special provisions are:

The corporation shall be carried on without the purpose of gain for its members, and any profits or other accretions to the corporation shall be used in promoting its objects.

6. The names and residence addresses of the applicants:

Name	Address
John Adam Smith	45 Red Road, Doone, Ontario, N2M 2A2
Jane Barbara Doe	56 Blue Drive, Doone, Ontario, N2M 2A3
Jean Charles Blanc	67 Black Road, Doone, Ontario, N2M 3A4

The application is executed in duplicate.

(b)   Charitable Corporation

1. The name of the corporation is: ABC Charitable Reading Room
2. The address of the head office of the corporation is: 123 Main Street, Doone, Ontario, N2M 1A1
3. The applicants who are to be the first directors of the corporation are:

Name   Address

John Adam Smith   45 Red Road, Doone, Ontario, N2M 2A2
Jane Barbara Doe   56 Blue Drive, Doone, Ontario, N2M 2A3
Jean Charles Blanc   67 Black Road, Doone, Ontario, N2M 3A4

4. The objects for which the corporation is incorporated are:
   (a) to promote the advancement of education by providing a reading room for disadvantaged persons;
   (b) to establish, maintain and operate a reading room for the benefit of the residents of the Town of Doone; and
   (c) to promote literacy by providing classes to persons who have difficulty with reading and writing.

5. The special provisions are:
   (a) the Corporation shall be carried on without the purpose of gain for its members and any profits or other accretions to the Corporation shall be used in promoting its objects;
   (b) the Corporation shall be subject to the *Charities Accounting Act* and the *Charitable Gifts Act*;
   (c) the directors shall serve as such without remuneration, and no director shall directly or indirectly receive any profit from their position as such, provided that directors may be paid reasonable expenses incurred by them in the performance of their duties;
   (d) the borrowing power of the Corporation pursuant to any by-law passed and confirmed in accordance with s. 59 of the *Corporations Act* shall be limited to borrowing money for current operating expenses, provided that the borrowing power of the Corporation shall not be so limited if it borrows on the security of real or personal property;
   (e) if it is made to appear to the satisfaction of the Minister, upon report of the Public Trustee, that the Corporation has failed to comply with any of the provisions of the *Charities Accounting Act* or the *Charitable Gifts Act*, the Minister may authorize an inquiry for the purpose of determining whether or not there is sufficient cause for the Lieutenant Governor-in-Council to make an order under subs. 317(1) of the *Corporations Act* to cancel the letters patent of the Corporation and declare it to be dissolved;
   (f) upon dissolution of the corporation and after the payment of all debts and liabilities, its remaining property shall be distributed or disposed of to charities registered under the *Income Tax Act* (Canada) in Canada;

(g) to invest the funds of the Corporation pursuant to the *Trustee Act*;

OR

(g) to invest the funds of the Corporation in such manner as determined by the directors, in making such investments the directors shall not be subject to the *Trustee Act*, but provided that such investments are reasonable, prudent and sagacious under the circumstances and do not constitute, either directly or indirectly a conflict of interest; and

(h) for the above objects, and as incidental and ancillary thereto, to exercise any of the powers as prescribed by the *Corporations Act*, or by any other statutes or laws from time to time applicable, except where such power is limited by these letters patent or the statute or common law relating to charities.

6. The names and residence addresses of the applicants are:

Name	Address
John Adam Smith	45 Red Road, Doone, Ontario, N2M 2A2
Jane Barbara Doe	56 Blue Drive, Doone, Ontario, N2M 2A3
Jean Charles Blanc	67 Black Road, Doone, Ontario, N2M 3A4

The application is executed in duplicate.

(c) *Social Club*

1. The name of the corporation is: Doone Social Club.
2. The address of the head office of the corporation is: 123 Main Street, Doone, Ontario, N2M 1A1.
3. The applicants who are to be the first directors of the corporation are:

Name	Address
John Adam Smith	45 Red Road, Doone, Ontario, N2M 2A2
Jane Barbara Doe	56 Blue Drive, Doone, Ontario, N2M 2A3
Jean Charles Blanc	67 Black Road, Doone, Ontario, N2M 3A4

4. The objects for which the corporation is incorporated are:
    (a) to establish, maintain and operate a club house to provide social activities for members and their guests;
    (b) to organize social and cultural activities of interest to the members; and

(c) for such other complementary purposes that are not inconsistent with these objects.
5. The special provisions are:
   (a) for the purpose of the objects of the corporation, to accept gifts, donations and bequests;
   (b) upon dissolution of the corporation and after payment of all debts and liabilities, its remaining property shall be distributed or disposed of to a similar organization in the Town of Doone or, if no such organization is considered appropriate by the then directors, to the Corporation of the Town of Doone or its successor.
6. The names and residence addresses of the applicants are:

Name	Address
John Adam Smith	45 Red Road, Doone, Ontario, N2M 2A2
Jane Barbara Doe	56 Blue Drive, Doone, Ontario, N2M 2A3
Jean Charles Blanc	67 Black Road, Doone, Ontario, N2M 3A4

This application is executed in duplicate.

(d)   Optional Provisions

(i)   Power Clauses

The following power clauses are examples of the types of power clauses that may be used to clarify the powers of the corporation. They may also be used in combination with powers to restrict the corporation or to provide that the corporation will not have the powers of a natural person where the members want the corporation to have only specified powers:

For the above objects and incidental and ancillary to those objects, to exercise any of the powers prescribed by the *Corporations Act* or by any other statute or law, from time to time applicable, except where such power is contrary to the statutes or law, and in particular, without limiting the generality of the foregoing:

Power to Accumulate:

(a) to accumulate from time to time part of the fund or funds of the corporation and income therefrom, subject to any statutes or laws from time to time applicable;

Power to Invest:

(b) to invest funds of the corporation in such manner as the directors may determine;

Power to Invest (Charitable Corporation):

(c) to invest funds of the corporation in such manner as the directors may determine in those investments authorized by the law for trustees;

Power to Solicit for Donations and Grants:

(d) to solicit and receive donations, bequests, legacies and grants, and to enter into agreements, contracts and undertakings incidental to the solicitation and receiving;

Power to Receive Personal Property:

(e) to acquire by purchase, contract, donation, legacy, gift, grant, bequest or otherwise, any personal property and to enter into and carry out any agreements, contracts or undertakings incidental to the acquisition, and to sell, dispose of and convey the same, or any part of the property, as the directors may consider advisable;

Power to Hold and Dispose of Real Property:

(f) to acquire by purchase, lease, devise, gift, or otherwise, real property, and to hold such real property or interest necessary for the actual use and occupation of the corporation or for carrying on the corporation's charitable activities, and when no longer necessary, to sell, dispose of and convey the real property or any part of it;

Power to Hire:

(g) to employ and pay such assistants, clerks, agents, representatives and employees, and to procure, equip and maintain such offices and other facilities and to incur such reasonable expenses, as may be necessary;

Power to Hire (Charitable Corporation):

(h) to employ and pay such assistants, clerks, agents, representatives and employees, and to procure, equip and maintain such offices and other facilities and to incur such reasonable expenses as may be necessary, provided that the corporation shall not pay any remuneration to a director in any capacity whatsoever;

Power to Co-operate with Other Charitable Organizations:

(i) to co-operate, liaise, and contract with other charitable organizations, institutions and agencies which carry on similar objects to that of the corporation;

Power to Co-operate with Governments:

(j) to enter into any arrangements, agreements or contracts that are consistent with the corporation's objects with any ministries of the Government of Ontario, departments of the Government of Canada, municipal governments, local authorities or federal or provincial agencies, boards and commissions or similar authorities, that the directors consider desirable to obtain, further or carry out the objects of the corporation;

Power to Pay Costs of Incorporation:

(k) to pay all costs and expenses of or incidental to the incorporation;

Power to Sue and Compromise Claims:

(l) to demand and compel payment of all sums of money and claims to any real or personal property in which the corporation may have an interest and to compromise or settle any such claims and to sue and be sued;

Power to Negotiate and Issue Instruments:

(m) to draw, make, set, endorse, execute, issue, negotiate or otherwise deal with negotiable or transferable instruments;

Incidental Powers:

(n) to do all such acts and things which are necessary or incidental for the attainment of the objects of the corporation.

(ii) **Restrictions on Powers**

(a) the corporation shall not have the capacity of a natural person;

(b) it shall not be lawful for the corporation directly or indirectly to transact or undertake any business within the meaning of the *Loan and Trust Corporations Act*; and

(c) the corporation may not borrow on the real property held by the corporation except upon the resolution of the members at a meeting called for that purpose and supported by at least 75 per cent of the members voting at that meeting.

(iii) **Directors**

Rotating Directors

The directors may be elected and retire in rotation, and the said first directors shall hold office until the first annual meeting of the members or until their successors are elected or appointed. At the first annual meeting of members, one third of the directors shall be elected for a one-year term, one third for a two-year term, and one-third for a 3-year term.

Thereafter, at each annual meeting of members, one third of the number of directors shall be elected for a term of three years unless elected or appointed to fill a vacancy in the board of directors of the corporation, in which case the director so elected or appointed shall be elected or appointed for the unexpired term of the director who has ceased to be a director and thus created the vacancy.

For purposes of this clause, a "year" shall commence on the date of election or appointment as director and shall terminate on the date of the next annual meeting of members at which directors are to be elected.

(iv) **Restrictions on Directors, Officers, Members**

(a) the corporation shall not directly or indirectly purchase from or lend money to any directors, officers or members, or any persons who are in a non-arm's-length relationship with the director, officer or member;

(b) directors and officers shall disclose in writing to the corporation and request to have entered into the minutes of the meeting of the board of directors the nature and extent of their interest in any contract between the director or officer or any person who is in a non-arm's-length relationship with the director or officer, and the corporation;

(c) no director or officer may serve more than two consecutive terms;

(d) no person shall be elected or appointed as director or officer until his or her election or appointment has the prior approval of;

(e) membership in the corporation shall be limited to 25 persons;

(f) the mayor of the Town of Doone shall be an *ex officio* member of the corporation and upon ceasing to hold office as mayor that individual shall cease to be a member of the corporation;

(g) membership in the corporation is restricted to individuals residing within the municipal boundaries of the Town of Doone;

(v) **Dissolution**

(a) upon dissolution of the corporation and after the payment of all debts and liabilities, the remaining property of the corporation shall be distributed among the members;

(b) upon dissolution of the corporation and after the payment of all debts and liabilities, the remaining property of the corporation shall be distributed to a corporation without share capital in Ontario with similar objects;

(c) upon dissolution of the corporation and after the payment of all debts and liabilities, the remaining property of the corporation shall be distributed to the public library board of the Town of Doone or its successors;

(d) upon dissolution of the corporation and after the payment of all debts and liabilities, the remaining property of the corporation shall be distributed to a charity registered under the *Income Tax Act*.

(vi) **Borrowing Powers**

Charitable Corporation

The board may:

(i) borrow money on the credit of the corporation;

(ii) issue, sell or pledge securities of the corporation;
(iii) charge, mortgage, hypothecate or pledge all or any of the real or personal property of the corporation, including book debts, rights, powers, franchises and undertakings to secure any securities or any money borrowed, or other debt, or any other obligation or liability of the corporation;
(iv) delegate the powers under this clause to an officer or officers of the corporation as the board considers appropriate;

provided that, except where the corporation borrows on the security of its real or personal property, its borrowing power shall be limited to borrowing money for current operating expenses.

Not-for-profit Corporation

The board may:

(i) borrow money on the credit of the corporation;
(ii) issue, sell or pledge securities of the corporation;
(iii) charge, mortgage, hypothecate or pledge all or any of the real or personal property of the corporation, including book debts, rights, powers, franchises and undertakings, to secure any securities or any money borrowed, or other debt, or any other obligation or liability of the corporation;
(iv) delegate the powers under this clause to an officer or officers of the corporation as the board considers appropriate.

(e) Supporting Documents

(i) **Consent and Undertaking**

BE IT RESOLVED that

1. John Adam Doe and others are authorized to apply for incorporation as a corporation without share capital under the name of ABC Reading Club Corporation.
2. The ABC Reading Club, an unincorporated organization, undertakes to discontinue the use of its unincorporated name within six months of incorporation of the new corporation.

I hereby certify this to be a true copy of the resolution of the members of the ABC Reading Club duly passed at a meeting of the organization on the   day of   , 200 .

Dated this   day of   , 200 .

(ii)   Consent of Individual

I, Edna Doone, residing at 14 Main Street, Doone, Ontario, N2M 1A2, hereby consents to the following name for use by a corporation to be incorporated — Edna Doone Reading Club.

Dated this   day of   , 200 .

_____
(Signature)

(f)   Changes to Incorporating Documents

(i)   Special Resolution Changing the Number of Directors

BE IT RESOLVED that

The number of directors of the ABC Reading Club Corporation, Ontario Corporation Number   , be increased from three to seven.

_____
(Signature)
President

I hereby certify this to be a true copy of the resolution of the members of the ABC Reading Club Corporation, Ontario Corporation Number, which was duly passed by two thirds of the members voting at a meeting of the corporation on the   day of   , 200 .

Dated this   day of   , 200 .

_____
(Signature)
Secretary-Treasurer

(ii)   Supplementary Letters Patent

1. The name of the corporation is:

   ABC Reading Club

2. The name of the corporation is changed to:

Doone Reading Club

3. Date of incorporation/amalgamation:

30 August 2001

4. The resolution authorizing this application was confirmed by the shareholders/members of the corporation on:

23 July 200

under s. 34 or 131 of the *Corporations Act*.

5. The corporation applies for the issue of supplementary letters patent to provide as follows:

Delete the following object:

(a) to provide a reading room for the use of its members and their guests to read for enjoyment, newspapers, journals and texts;

And replace with the following object:

(a) to provide a reading room for the use of its members;

Add the following special provision:

The members of the corporation must reside within the municipal boundaries of the Town of Doone.

This application is executed in duplicate.

ABC Reading Club

By/Per _____
    (Signature)
    Office

By/Per _____
    (Signature)
    Office

(2) Co-operative Corporations

(a) Incorporation Documents for a Co-operative Corporation without Share Capital

(i) Articles of Incorporation

1. The name of the co-operative is:

   ABC Co-operative Inc.

2. The head office is in:

   Town of Doone in the Regional Municipality of Waterloo

3. The address of the head office is:

   123 Main Street, Doone, Ontario, N2M 1A1

4. The number (or minimum and maximum number) of directors is: a minimum of three (3) and a maximum of ten (10).

5. The number (or minimum and maximum number) of directors each stakeholder group in a multi-stakeholder co-operative may elect is:

   Not Applicable

6. The first directors are:

Full Names incl. all given names)	Residential Address (give street, RR. number and municipality or post office)	Canadian Resident (yes/no)
John Adam Smith	45 Red Road, Doone, Ontario, N2M 2A2	Yes
Jane Barbara Doe	56 Blue Drive, Doone, Ontario, N2M 2A3	Yes
Jean Charles Blanc	67 Black Road, Doone, Ontario, N2M 3A4	Yes

Appendix D

7. Restrictions, if any, on the business the co-operative may carry on or on the powers the co-operative may exercise:

    The co-operative may not sell goods or services to non-members.

8. The amount of the minimum member loan, if any:

    Five hundred dollars ($500).

9. The restrictions of transfer of members' loans are:

    No member loan may be transferred without the consent of the directors, in the form of a resolution passed by the board.

10. The amount of the membership fee is:

    $25 annual membership fee.

11. The classes of membership, if any, are:

    Consumer members.
    Employee members.

12. The terms and conditions attached to each class of membership are:

    Consumer member — members of this class must purchase a minimum of $250 annually from the co-operative corporation; Employee member — members of this class must work annually in the co-operative store a minimum of 50 hours.

13. The stakeholder groups, if any, are:

    Not Applicable.

14. The terms and conditions for membership in each stakeholder group are:

    Not applicable.

15. Special provisions, if any, are:

Upon dissolution and after payment of all debts and liabilities, the co-operative corporation's remaining assets shall be distributed among the members in proportion to the patronage returns accrued to members during the five years prior to dissolution.

16. The names and residential addresses of the incorporators are:

Full Names incl. all given names)	Residential Address (give street, RR. number and municipality or post office)
John Adam Smith	45 Red Road, Doone, Ontario, N2M 2A2
Jane Barbara Doe	56 Blue Drive, Doone, Ontario, N2M 2A3
Jean Charles Blanc	67 Black Road, Doone, Ontario, N2M 3A4

These articles are signed in duplicate.

(ii) Affidavit of Verification

Affidavit of Verification

PROVINCE OF ONTARIO IN THE MATTER OF the *Co-operative*
REGIONAL MUNICIPALITY *Corporations Act* and the articles of
OF WATERLOO Incorporation of ABC Co-operative Inc.

I, John Adam Smith, of the Town of Doone in the Regional Municipality of Waterloo in the Province of Ontario make oath and say that:

1. I am one of the incorporators of ABC Co-operative Inc. and have personal knowledge of the matters herein deposed to.

2. Each of the incorporators who is a natural person signing the accompanying Articles of Incorporation in duplicate and each of the first directors named therein is 18 or more years of age.

3. The signatures of the incorporators affixed to the articles are their true signatures.

4. Each incorporator signing the accompanying Articles of Incorporation in duplicate is to be a member of the co-operative.

Sworn before me at Town of
Doone, in the Regional
Municipality of Waterloo

_____
(Signature)
John Adam Smith

this   day of   , 200 .

_____
(Signature)
Commissioner

(iii) **Consent to Act as a First Director**

Consent to Act as a First Director

I, John Adam Smith, residing at 45 Red Road, Doone, Ontario, N2M 2A2 hereby consent to act as a first director of ABC Co-operative Inc.

Dated this   day of   , 200 .

_____   _____
(Signature)   (Signature)
Witness   John Adam Smith

Affidavit of Witness

PROVINCE OF ONTARIO   IN THE MATTER OF the *Co-operative*
REGIONAL MUNICIPALITY   *Corporations Act* and the articles of
OF WATERLOO   Incorporation of ABC Co-operative Inc.

I, Jane Denise Jones, of the Town of Doone of the Regional Municipality of Waterloo in the Province of Ontario make oath and say that:

1. I was personally present and did see John Adam Smith sign the annexed consent to act as a first director of the ABC Co-operative Inc.

2. I am a subscribing witness to the said consent.

Sworn before me at the Town
of Doone in the Regional
Municipality of Waterloo

Signature
Jane Denise Jones

this   day of   200 .

_____
(Signature)
Commissioner

(b)   Optional Special Provisions

(i)   Not-for-profit Co-operative Corporations

   (a) The co-operative's activities shall be carried on without the purpose of gain for its members, and any profit or other accretions to the co-operative shall be used in promoting its objects;
   (b) The directors shall serve without remuneration and shall not receive, directly or indirectly, any profit from their positions as directors, but the directors may be paid reasonable expenses incurred in the performance of their duties;
   (c) Upon dissolution and after payment of all debts and liabilities, the co-operative's remaining property shall be distributed or disposed of to charitable organizations carrying on their activities solely within Ontario.

(ii)   Not-for-profit Housing Co-operative Corporations

   (a) The co-operative's activities shall be carried on without the purpose of gain for its members, and any profit or other accretions to the co-operative shall be used in promoting its objects;
   (b) The directors, and those directors who also serve as officers, shall serve without remuneration and no director shall directly or indirectly receive any profit or remuneration from his or her position as director or in any other capacity, provided that a director, including those who are also officers, may be paid reasonable expenses incurred in the performance of their duties; [or]
   (c) The directors, and those directors who also serve as officers, shall serve without remuneration and no director shall directly or indirectly receive any profit or remuneration from his or her position as director or in any other capacity, provided that a director, including those who are also officers, may be paid reasonable ex-

penses incurred in the performance of their duties. This provision does not apply to the remuneration which is paid to directors who occupy residential accommodation owned by the co-operative when employed by the co-operative on a part-time basis to perform routine maintenance, administration or operational tasks with respect to the accommodation and such part-time employment may be further defined or restricted in the by-laws with respect to time worked or quantum paid;

(d) The co-operative is a not-for-profit housing co-operative for the purpose of the *Co-operative Corporations Act*;

(e) No membership fee shall be charged to a geared-to-income occupant if such charge will act as a financial barrier to membership in the co-operative by the geared-to-income occupant;

(f) No member loan shall be required from geared-to-income occupants;

(g) Upon dissolution of the co-operative and after payment of its debts and liabilities, the remaining property of the co-operative shall be transferred to or distributed among one or more not-for-profit housing co-operatives or charitable organizations which carry on work solely in Ontario.

(iii) ***Multi-stakeholder co-operative corporations***

5. The number (or minimum and maximum number) of directors each stakeholder group may elect is:

    Stakeholder Group A: a minimum of two (2) and a maximum of three (3)
    Stakeholder Group B: a minimum of two (2) and a maximum of four (4)
    Stakeholder Group C: one (1)

13. The stakeholders groups, if any, are:

    The co-operative has three stakeholder groups:

    Consumer Stakeholders
    Employee Stakeholders
    Manufacturer Stakeholders

14. The terms and conditions for membership in each stakeholder group are:

Consumer Stakeholder:

Members of this stakeholder group must purchase from the co-operative corporation a minimum of $5,000 of product for personal or family consumption each fiscal year.

Employee Stakeholders:

Members of this stakeholder group must be employed by the co-operative corporation or by a member of the manufacturer stakeholders group.

Manufacturer Stakeholders:

Members of this stakeholder group must supply a minimum of $50,000 of goods or services to the co-operative corporation for sale to members of the consumer, employee or manufacturer stakeholders groups.

II FEDERAL

(1) Application for Letters Patent

(a)   General Not-for-profit

(i)   Application for Incorporation of a Corporation without Share Capital under Part II of the Canada Corporations Act

To: The Minister of Industry Canada

I

The undersigned hereby apply to the Minister of Industry Canada for the grant of a charter by letters patent under the provisions of Part II of the *Canada Corporations Act* constituting the undersigned, and such others as may become members of the corporation thereby created, a body corporate and politic under the name of:

ABC Reading Club Corporation

The undersigned have satisfied themselves and are assured that the proposed name under which incorporation is sought is not the same or similar to the name under which any other company, society, association or firm in existence is carrying on business in Canada or is incorporated under the laws of Canada or any province thereof or so nearly resembles the same as to be calculated to deceive, and that it is not a name which is otherwise on public policy grounds objectionable.

II

The applicants are individuals of the full age of 18 years with power under the law to contract. The names, addresses and occupations of each of the applicants are as follows:

(1) John A. Smith, 45 Low Street, Doone, Ontario, N2M 1A1, Office Manager.
(2) Jane B. Doe, 67 West Avenue, Milltown, New Brunswick, E1F 2G3, Engineer.
(3) Jean C. Blanc, 78 East Road, Wheateville, Saskatchewan, S2T 3U4, Technician.

The said John A. Smith, Jane B. Doe and Jean C. Blanc will be the first directors of the corporation.

III

The objects of the corporation are:

(1) to provide reading rooms throughout Canada for the use of members and their guests to read for enjoyment newspapers, journals and texts;
(2) to provide ancillary goods and services for use of its members, including seminars, lectures, photocopying and hospitality; and
(3) to raise revenues from membership dues, fees for services and fines for breaches of the rules of the reading rooms and of the ABC Reading Club Corporation to operate, maintain and improve the reading rooms.

IV

The operations of the corporation may be carried on throughout Canada and elsewhere.

V

The head office of the corporation is to be situated in the Town of Doone, Ontario.

VI

It is specially provided that in the event of dissolution or winding up of the corporation all its remaining assets after payment of its liabilities shall be distributed to an organization carrying on similar activities.

VII

The by-laws of the corporation shall be those filed with the application for letters patent until repealed, amended, altered or added to.

VIII

The corporation is to carry on its operations without pecuniary gain to its members and any profits or other accretions to the corporation are to be used in promoting its objects.

DATED at the Town of Doone in the Province of Ontario: this   day of   , 200 .

_____
(Signature)
John A. Smith

_____
(Signature)
Jane B. Doe

_____
(Signature)
Jean C. Blanc

(ii) **Optional Clauses**

Dissolution Clause

It is specially provided that in the event of dissolution or winding up of the corporation, all its remaining assets after the payment of its liabilities shall be distributed rateably amongst the members.

Borrowing By-Law

In accordance with s. 65 of the *Canada Corporations Act*, it is provided that, when authorized by by-law, duly passed by the directors and sanctioned by at least two thirds of the votes cast at a special general meeting of the members duly called to consider the by-law, the directors of the corporation may from time to time:

(a) borrow money upon the credit of the corporation;
(b) limit or increase the amount to be borrowed;
(c) issue debentures or other securities of the corporation;
(d) pledge or sell such debentures or other securities for such sums and at such prices as may be deemed expedient; and
(e) secure any such debentures or other securities or any other present or future borrowing or liability of the corporation by mortgage, hypothec, charge or pledge of all or any currently owned or subsequently acquired real and personal, movable and immovable property of the corporation, and the undertaking and rights of the corporation.

Any such by-law may provide for the delegation of such powers by the directors to such officers or directors of the corporation to such extent and in such manner as may be set out in the by-law.

Nothing herein limits or restricts the borrowing of money by the corporation on bills of exchange or promissory notes made, drawn, accepted or endorsed by or on behalf of the corporation.

(b)   Not-for-profit Corporation Charitable in Nature

(i)   Application for Incorporation of a Corporation without Share Capital under Part II of the Canada Corporations Act

To: The Minister of Industry Canada

I

The undersigned hereby apply to the Minister of Industry Canada for the grant of a charter by letters patent under the provisions of Part II of the *Canada Corporations Act* constituting the undersigned, and such others as may become members of the corporation thereby created, a body corporate and politic under the name of:

ABC Reading Club Corporation

The undersigned have satisfied themselves and are assured that the proposed name under which incorporation is sought is not the same or similar to the name under which any other company, society, association or firm in existence is carrying on business in Canada or is incorporated under the laws of Canada or any province thereof or so nearly resembles the same as to be calculated to deceive, and that it is not a name which is otherwise on public policy grounds objectionable.

II

The applicants are individuals of the full age of 18 years with power under the law to contract. The names, addresses and occupations of each of the applicants are as follows:

(1) John A. Smith, 45 Low Street, Doone, Ontario, N2M 1A1, Officer Manager
(2) Jane B. Doe, 67 West Avenue, Milltown, New Brunswick, E1F 2G3, Engineer
(3) Jean C. Blanc, 78 East Road, Wheateville, Saskatchewan, S2T 3U4, Technician.

The said John A. Smith, Jane B. Doe and Jean C. Blanc will be the first directors of the corporation.

III

The objects of the corporation are:

(1) to promote the advancement of education by establishing, maintaining and operating reading rooms for members of the public to use to read newspapers, journals and texts;
(2) to provide literacy training courses and educational programmes for disadvantaged persons;
(3) to provide opportunities for social discourse among the members and their guests; and
(4) to raise revenues from membership dues, fees for programmes and services, and fines for breaches of the rules of the reading rooms and of the ABC Reading Club Corporation to operate, maintain and improve the reading rooms.

IV

The operations of the corporation may be carried on throughout Canada and elsewhere.

V

The head office of the corporation is to be situated in the Town of Doone, Ontario.

VI

It is specially provided that in the event of dissolution or winding up of the corporation all its remaining assets after payment of its liabilities shall be distributed to one or more organizations in Canada carrying on similar activities.

VII

The by-laws of the corporation shall be those filed with the application for letters patent until repealed, amended, altered or added to.

VIII

The corporation is to carry on its operations without pecuniary gain to its members and any profits or other accretions to the corporation are to be used in promoting its objects.

DATED at the Town of Doone in the Province of Ontario this   day of   , 200 .

_____
(Signature)
John A. Smith

_____
(Signature)
Jane B. Doe

(Signature)
Jean C. Blanc

(ii)   Optional Clauses

Borrowing By-Law

In accordance with s. 65 of the *Canada Corporations Act*, it is provided that, when authorized by by-law, duly passed by the directors and sanctioned by at least two thirds of the votes cast at a special general meeting of the members duly called to consider the by-law, the directors of the corporation may from time to time:

(a) borrow money upon the credit of the corporation;
(b) limit or increase the amount to be borrowed;
(c) issue debentures or other securities of the corporation;
(d) pledge or sell such debentures or other securities for such sums and at such prices as may be deemed expedient; and
(e) secure any such debentures or other securities or any other present or future borrowing or liability of the corporation by mortgage, hypothec, charge or pledge of all or any currently owned or subsequently acquired real and personal, movable and immovable property of the corporation, and the undertaking and rights of the corporation.

Any such by-law may provide for the delegation of such powers by the directors to such officers or directors of the corporation to such extent and in such manner as may be set out in the by-law.

Nothing herein limits or restricts the borrowing of money by the corporation on bills of exchange or promissory notes made, drawn, accepted or endorsed by or on behalf of the corporation.

(c)   Charitable Not-for-profit Corporation

(i)   Application for Incorporation of a Corporation without Share Capital under Part II of the **Canada Corporations Act**

To: The Minister of Industry Canada

I

The undersigned hereby apply to the Minister of Industry Canada for the grant of a charter by letters patent under the provisions of Part II of the *Canada Corporations Act* constituting the undersigned, and such others as may become members of the corporation thereby created, a body corporate and politic under the name of:

ABC Reading Club Corporation

The undersigned have satisfied themselves and are assured that the proposed name under which incorporation is sought is not the same or similar to the name under which any other company, society, association or firm in existence is carrying on business in Canada or is incorporated under the laws of Canada or any province thereof or so nearly resembles the same as to be calculated to deceive, and that it is not a name which is otherwise on public policy grounds objectionable.

II

The applicants are individuals of the full age of 18 years with power under the law to contract. The names, addresses and occupations of each of the applicants are as follows:

(1) John A. Smith, 45 Low Street, Doone, Ontario, N2M 1A1, Office Manager
(2) Jane B. Doe, 67 West Avenue, Milltown, New Brunswick, E1F 2G3, Engineer
(3) Jean C. Blanc, 78 East Road, Wheateville, Saskatchewan, S2T 3U4, Technician.

The said John A. Smith, Jane B. Doe and Jean C. Blanc will be the first directors of the corporation.

III

The objects of the corporation are:

(1) to promote the advancement of education by establishing, maintaining and operating reading rooms for members of the public to use to read newspapers, journals and texts;
(2) to provide literacy training courses and educational programmes for disadvantaged persons; and
(3) to provide basic skills training and employment skills training for disadvantaged persons.

IV

The operations of the corporation may be carried on throughout Canada and elsewhere.

V

The head office of the corporation is to be situated in the Town of Doone, Ontario.

VI

It is specially provided that in the event of dissolution or winding up of the corporation, all its remaining assets after the payment of its liabilities shall be distributed to one or more qualified donees as defined under the provisions of the *Income Tax Act*.

VII

The by-laws of the corporation shall be those filed with the application for letters patent until repealed, amended, altered or added to.

VIII

The corporation is to carry on its operations without pecuniary gain to its members and any profits or other accretions to the corporation are to be used in promoting its objects.

DATED at the Town of Doone in the Province of Ontario this   day of   , 200 .

_____
(Signature)
John A. Smith

_____
(Signature)
Jane B. Doe

_____
(Signature)
Jean C. Blanc

(ii) Optional Clauses

Dissolution Clause

It is specially provided that in the event of dissolution or winding up of the corporation, all its remaining assets after the payment of its liabilities shall be distributed to one or more registered charitable organizations in Canada.

Borrowing By-Law

In accordance with s. 65 of the *Canada Corporations Act*, it is provided that, when authorized by by-law, duly passed by the directors and sanctioned by at least two thirds of the votes cast at a special general meeting of the members duly called for considering the by-law, the directors of the corporation may from time to time:

(a) borrow money upon the credit of the corporation;
(b) limit or increase the amount to be borrowed;
(c) issue debentures or other securities of the corporation;
(d) pledge or sell such debentures or other securities for such sums and at such prices as may be deemed expedient; and
(e) secure any such debentures or other securities or any other present or future borrowing or liability of the corporation by mortgage, hypothec, charge or pledge of all or any currently owned or subsequently acquired real and personal, movable and immovable property of the corporation, and the undertaking and rights of the corporation.

Any such by-law may provide for the delegation of such powers by the directors to such officers or directors of the corporation to such extent and in such manner as may be set out in the by-law.

Nothing herein limits or restricts the borrowing of money by the corporation on bills of exchange or promissory notes made, drawn, accepted or endorsed by or on behalf of the corporation.

(2) Affidavit

CANADA	IN THE MATTER OF the *Canada Corporations*
PROVINCE OF	*Act*
MUNICIPALITY OF	RE: Application for Incorporation under Part II in the name of ABC Reading Club Corporation

AFFIDAVIT

I, John A. Smith, in the Town of Doone in the Province of Ontario, make oath and say as follows:

1. I am one of the applicants herein.
2. I have knowledge of the matter, and the statements in the annexed application contained are, to the best of my knowledge and belief, true in substance and in fact.
3. I am informed and believe that each applicant signing the said application is of the full age of 18 years and has power under law to contract and that his or her name and description have been accurately set out in the preamble thereto.
4. The proposed corporate name of the company is not on any public grounds objectionable and that it is not that of any known company, incorporated or unincorporated, or of any partnership or individual, or any name under which any known business is being carried on, or so nearly resembling the same as to deceive.
5. I have satisfied myself and am assured that no public or private interest will be prejudicially affected by the incorporation of the company aforesaid.

SWORN before me at the
Town of Doone in the
Province of Ontario
this   day of   _____
200 .   (Signature)
                                   John A. Smith

A Commissioner, etc.

[This document may also be prepared as a Statutory Declaration under the *Canada Evidence Act*.]

(d)   *Covering Letter to Corporations Directorate*

(i)   Sample

Corporations Directorate
Industry Canada
9th Floor
Jean Edmonds Towers South
365 Laurier Avenue West
Ottawa, Ontario
K1A 0C8

Dear Sir or Madam:

Please find enclosed the following documents in application for the incorporation of ABC Reading Club Corporation under Part II of the *Canada Corporations Act*:

1. Application for incorporation (2 copies);
2. Affidavit of John A. Smith sworn before a commissioner for taking oaths;
3. By-laws (1 copy) that are the corporation's Directorate Model By-laws.
4. Canada biased NUANS name search report not more than 90 days old. [N.B. The applicants may also submit a cheque payable to the Receiver General in the amount of $15 as a filing fee for searching one proposed name. The filing fee for a bilingual name search is $30.]
5. Cheque for $200 payable to the "Receiver General for Canada".

The street address for the proposed corporation's head office is:

45 Low Street
Doone, Ontario
N2M 1A1

Please mail the letters patent to the above address when issued.

Yours truly,

A. Solicitor
23 High Street
Doone, Ontario
N2M 2A2

(e)   Optional Clauses

*(i)   **By-laws***

If the by-laws being submitted are the model by-laws prepared by the Corporations Directorate, one of the following clauses should be used depending upon the circumstances:

> previously reviewed standard by-laws bearing identifier no.;

customized by-laws that have not been previously reviewed without checklist being completed;

customized by-laws that have not been previously reviewed without checklist being completed.

(ii)   Urgency

The applicants may indicate if there are any urgencies with respect to the application. Any reasons for the urgencies and a time frame should be provided.

The application is urgent because the organization needs to be established as a corporation without share capital to apply for funding grants. The funding application is due within the next 60 days.

(2)   Application for Supplementary Letters Patent

(a)   Changing the Corporate Name

(i)   Application

To the Minister of Industry Canada

The application of ABC Reading Club Corporation:

1. Your applicant was incorporated under the *Canada Corporations Act* by Letters Patent dated the   day of   200 .
2. On the   day of   , 200 , a by-law was enacted, being By-law No.   of the by-laws of your applicant changing the corporate name of your applicant to ABC Reading and Training Club Corporation and authorizing an application for Supplementary Letters Patent to confirm the said change of name.
3. On the   day of   , 200 , said By-law No.   was sanctioned at a special general meeting of the members of the corporation duly called for the purpose of considering the same, by a vote of per cent of the members represented either in person or by proxy at such meeting.
4. The change of name as desired is not for any improper purpose and is not otherwise objectionable and is in the interest of the applicant.
5. The new name is not that of any known corporation or association incorporated or unincorporated or of any partnership or individual of any name under which any known business is being carried on, or so nearly resembling the same as to be calculated to deceive.

6. Your applicant is not in arrears in filing its annual summaries.

Your applicant therefore prays that Supplementary Letters Patent may be granted changing the corporate name of your applicant to ABC Reading and Training Club Corporation.

Dated at the Town of Doone, Ontario, this   day of   , 200 .

By/Per_____
     (Signature)
     President

By/Per_____
     (Signature)
     Secretary

(ii) **By-law**

A by-law changing the corporate name and authorizing application for the issuance of Supplementary Letters Patent to confirm the same.

BE IT ENACTED AND IT IS HEREBY ENACTED as By-law No.   of ABC Reading Club Corporation ("the corporation") that:

1. Subject to confirmation by Supplementary Letters Patent, the name of the corporation is hereby changed to ABC Reading and Training Club Corporation.
2. That the corporation be and is hereby authorized to make application to the Minister of Industry Canada for the issue of Supplementary Letters Patent confirming this by-law insofar as it relates to changing the name of the corporation to ABC Reading and Training Club Corporation.
3. That the directors and officers are hereby authorized and directed to do, sign, and execute all things, deeds and documents necessary or desirable for the due carrying out of the foregoing.

ENACTED this   day of   , 200 .

WITNESS the corporate seal of the said corporation.

_____
(Signature)
President

(Signature)
Secretary

Certified a true copy of By-law No.   of ABC Reading Club Corporation enacted by the directors the   day of   , 200   and sanctioned by a vote of not less than two thirds of the members present at a special general meeting of the corporation held on the   day of   , 200 .

(Signature)
Secretary

(iii) **Declaration of Officer**

DECLARATION of OFFICER

CANADA
PROVINCE OF ONTARIO
MUNICIPALITY OF DOONE

IN THE MATTER OF the application of ABC Reading Club Corporation for the issuance of Supplementary Letters Patent changing the corporate name

I, John A. Smith, of the Town of Doone, in the Province of Ontario do solemnly declare that:

1. I am the president of ABC Reading Club Corporation and as such have knowledge of the matters herein declared.
2. At a meeting of the directors of the said corporation held at the Town of Doone, on the   day of   , 200 , the by-law, two certified copies of which are hereto annexed, was duly enacted.
3. The said by-law was sanctioned at a special general meeting of the members of the said corporation held at the Town of Doone, on the   day of   , 200 , for the purpose of considering the same by   per cent of the votes cast in person or by proxy at such meeting.
4. Notice calling the said meeting of the members was mailed to all members of the said corporation on the   day of   , 200 , in accordance with the by-laws of the corporation respecting notice of meeting.
5. The statements in the annexed application are true in substance and in fact and the proposed change is *bona fide* and is considered to be in the best interest of the corporation.

AND I MAKE THIS SOLEMN DECLARATION conscientiously believing it to be true and knowing that it is of the same force and effect as if made under oath and by virtue of the *Canada Evidence Act*.

DECLARED before me at the
Town of Doone, in the Province
of Ontario this   day of   ,
200 .

                                             _____
                                             (Signature)
                                             President

Commissioner, etc.

(b)   *Application Amending or Varying Provisions of the Letters   Patent*

(i)   **Application**

To the Honourable Minister of Industry Canada

The Application of ABC Reading Club Corporation:

1. Your applicant was incorporated under the *Canada Corporations Act* by Letters Patent dated the   day of   , 200 .
2. On the   day of   , 200 , a by-law was enacted, being By-law No.   of the by-laws of your applicant, authorizing an application for Supplementary Letters Patent amending and varying the provisions of the Letters Patent incorporating your applicant by deleting Part VI of the Letters Patent which presently reads as follows:

It is specially provided that in the event of dissolution or winding up of the corporation, all its remaining assets after the payment of its liabilities shall be distributed to an organization in Canada carrying on similar activities.

and confirming the insertion of the following wording in its place:

It is specially provided that in the event of dissolution or winding up of the corporation, all its remaining assets after the payment of its liabilities shall be distributed to one or more qualified donees as defined under the provisions of the *Income Tax Act*.

3. On the   day of   , 200 , said By-law No.   was sanctioned at a special general meeting of the members of the corporation duly called for the purpose of considering the same, by a vote of

not less than   per cent of the members represented either in person or by proxy at such meeting.
4. Such Supplementary Letters Patent are not desired for any improper purpose and are deemed necessary and expedient in the interest of your applicant.
5. Your applicant is not in arrears in filing its annual summaries.

Your applicant therefore asks that Supplementary Letters Patent may be granted amending and varying the provisions of the Letters Patent incorporating your applicant in pursuance of the said By-law No.   .

DATED at the Town of Doone, Ontario, this   day of   , 200 .

By/Per_____
    (Signature)
    President

By/Per_____
    (Signature)
    Secretary

(ii)   By-Law

A by-law to amend and vary the provisions of the Letters Patent and authorizing application for the issuance of Supplementary Letters Patent to confirm the same.
BE IT ENACTED AND IT IS HEREBY ENACTED as By-law No.   of ABC Reading Club Corporation ("the Corporation") that:

1. Subject to confirmation by Supplementary Letters Patent, Part VI concerning dissolution is deleted and replaced by the following which reads:
It is specially provided that in the event of dissolution or winding up of the corporation, all its remaining assets after the payment of its liabilities shall be distributed to one or more qualified donees as defined under the provisions of the *Income Tax Act*.
2. That the corporation be and is hereby authorized to make application to the Minister of Industry Canada for the issue of Supplementary Letters Patent confirming this by-law insofar as it relates to amending and varying the provisions of the Letters Patent.
3. That the directors and officers are hereby authorized and directed to do, sign and execute all things, deeds and documents necessary or desirable for the due carrying out of the foregoing.

ENACTED this   day of   , 200 .

WITNESS the corporate seal of the said corporation.

By/Per_____
(Signature)
Secretary

By/Per_____
(Signature)
President

Certified a true copy of By-law No.   of ABC Reading Club Corporation enacted by the directors the   day of   , 200   and sanctioned by a vote of not less than two thirds of the members present at a special general meeting of the corporation held on the   day of   , 200 .

_____
(Signature)
Secretary

(iii) *Declaration of Officer*

DECLARATION OF OFFICER

CANADA	IN THE MATTER OF the application
PROVINCE OF ONTARIO	of ABC Reading Club Corporation
MUNICIPALITY OF DOONE	for the issuance of Supplementary Letters Patent amending and varying the provisions of the Letters Patent

I, John A. Smith, of the Town of Doone, in the Province of Ontario do solemnly declare that:

1. I am the president of ABC Reading Club Corporation and as such have knowledge of the matters herein declared.
2. At a meeting of the directors of the said corporation held at the Town of Doone, on the   day of   , 200 , the by-law, two certified copies of which are hereto annexed, was duly enacted.
3. The said by-law was sanctioned at a special general meeting of the members of the said corporation held at the Town of Doone, on the   day of   , 200 , for the purpose of considering the same by   per cent of the votes cast in person or by proxy at such meeting.
4. Notice calling the said meeting of the members was mailed to all members of the said corporation on the   day of   , 200 , in

accordance with the by-laws of the corporation respecting notice of meeting.
5. The statements in the annexed application are true in substance and in fact and the proposed change is *bona fide* and is considered to be in the best interest of the corporation.

AND I MAKE THIS SOLEMN DECLARATION conscientiously believing it to be true and knowing that it is of the same force and effect as if made under oath and by virtue of the *Canada Evidence Act*.

DECLARED before me at the
Town of Doone, in the Province
of Ontario this   day of   , 200..

                                     (Signature)
                                     President

Commissioner, etc.

(c) *Sample Letter to Corporations Directorate for Supplementary Letters Patent*

Corporations Directorate
Industry Canada
9th Floor
Jean Edmonds Towers South
365 Laurier Avenue West
Ottawa, Ontario
K1A 0C8

Dear Sir or Madam:

Please find enclosed:

1. Application for Supplementary Letters Patent for ABC Reading Club Corporation;
2. A statutory declaration of an officer attesting to the due passage of the by-law declared before a commissioner;
3. Two certified copies of the by-law enacting the change not more than six months old;
4. A cheque made out to the Receiver General for Canada in the amount of $50. [N.B. No fee if the Supplementary Letters Patent add a French or English version to the name.]
   If the Supplementary Letters Patent change the name, the following paragraph should be included:

5. A NUANS name search report not more than 90 days old [or a cheque in the amount of $15 as a filing fee for searching the proposed name, or $30 for a bilingual name].

Yours truly,

A. Solicitor
123 High Street
Doone, Ontario
N2M 2A2

(d) *Sample Letter to Corporations Directorate Requesting Minister's Approval for By-law Amendments*

Corporations Directorate
Industry Canada
9th Floor
Jean Edmonds Towers South
365 Laurier Avenue West
Ottawa, Ontario
K1A 0C8

Dear Sir or Madam:

Please find enclosed:

1. A request for the Minister's approval of a by-law amendment with respect to the following matters:
   (a) include the changes that have been made and to which sections;
   (b) the date on which the amendments were sanctioned by the members in accordance with the existing by-laws.
2. A consolidation of the existing by-laws.

Yours truly,

A. Solicitor
123 High Street
Doone, Ontario
N2M 2A2

F BY-LAWS

I ONTARIO

(1) Basic Organizational By-law

A by-law relating generally to the transaction of the affairs of the   , a corporation without share capital incorporated under the Ontario *Corporations Act* (Ontario Corporation Number   ).

Head Office

1. The head office of the corporation shall be in the   of   in the Province of Ontario. The directors may, from time to time, determine the specific location of the head office.

Fiscal Year

2. The fiscal year of the corporation shall begin on   of each year and end on   of the following year.

Seal

3. There shall be a corporate seal for the corporation. An imprint of the corporate seal is impressed in the margin.

   [N.B. A corporate seal is no longer required, but may be useful to have.)

Members

4. The following persons shall be eligible for membership in the corporation:
   (a) individuals who support the objects and activities of the corporation and who apply to the directors for admission and who pay the membership fee;
   (b) corporations, unincorporated associations and trusts that have similar objects and activities and that apply to the directors for admission and that pay the membership fee;
   (c) members of the immediate family of individual members who apply to the directors for admission and who pay the membership fee.
5. Annual membership fees are set at $10 for individual members, $25 for corporations, unincorporated associations or trusts, and

$5 for a member of the immediate family of an individual member. The directors may, from time to time, set another amount.
6. Every individual member in good standing and who has paid the applicable annual membership fee for that year is entitled:
   (a) to attend any meeting of the corporation;
   (b) to vote at any meeting of the corporation; and
   (c) to hold any office of the corporation.

   Members that are corporations, unincorporated associations or trusts are entitled to vote by proxy at the meeting. A member of the immediate family of an individual member is entitled to attend any meeting of the corporation.
7. A member may vote at a meeting by proxy in writing delivered to the secretary no later than 48 hours prior to the meeting.
8. Each member is entitled to one vote. The chair of the meeting is entitled to a casting vote in the event of a tie on any matter before that meeting that has been voted upon by the members.
9. Membership shall cease:
   (a) upon death of a member;
   (b) if the member has not renewed his or her membership and paid the applicable annual membership fee prior to or at the annual general meeting;
   (c) if the member resigns by written notice given to the secretary;
   (d) if the member no longer qualifies for membership in accordance with the by-laws; or
   (e) if the membership has been terminated by a vote of at least two-thirds of the members at a meeting duly called for that purpose. Notice of the meeting shall be served upon the member and shall set out the grounds for the proposed termination of his or her membership.

Meetings

10. The annual general meeting of the corporation shall be held no later than 18 months after the incorporation and no later than 15 months after the last annual general meeting in subsequent years. The following business shall be conducted at the annual general meeting:
    (a) reading of the financial reports;
    (b) election of the directors;
    (c) appointment of auditors and fixing or authorizing the board to fix the remuneration of the auditor; and

(d) any other business that may properly be brought before the meeting.
11. The directors may, from time to time, call a general meeting of the corporation.
12. The directors shall call a general meeting of the corporation if at least 10 per cent of the members of the corporation request that a general meeting be called.
13. Notice of the annual general meeting or of a general meeting shall be given to the members by the secretary at least seven days before the date of the meeting.
14. Quorum for the annual general meeting or for a general meeting of the corporation shall be six members of the corporation present in person or by proxy, provided that at least two members, other than directors, are present in person at the meeting.
15. Any meeting of the corporation may be adjourned to any time and from time to time. No notice shall be required for any adjournment. An adjournment may be made with or without a quorum being present.

Notice

16. Any notice required to be given under the Act, the Letters Patent, the by-laws or otherwise by a member, director, officer or auditor shall be deemed to have been given if it is:
(a) delivered personally to the person to whom it is to be given;
(b) delivered to the person's address as recorded in the corporation's records;
(c) mailed to the person's address as recorded in the corporation's records by prepaid ordinary mail; or
(d) sent to the person's address as recorded in the corporation's records by any means of prepaid transmittal, delivery or recorded communication

A notice shall be deemed to have been given when it is delivered personally or to the person's address, or three days after it was mailed or transmitted.
17. The notice shall specify the business to be attended to at the annual general meeting, the general meeting or the meeting.

Board of Directors

18. The affairs of the corporation shall be managed by a board of directors.
19. The board of directors shall appoint from among themselves a president, vice-president, secretary and treasurer who shall serve

until the next annual general meeting or until he or she is removed from office by resolution of the board of directors. The positions of secretary and treasurer may be combined into one position where the directors consider it appropriate.

20. The directors may, on behalf of the corporation, exercise all the powers that the corporation may legally exercise under the Act, the Letters Patent or otherwise, unless the directors are restricted by law or by the members from exercising those powers. These powers include, but are not limited to, the power:
    (a) to enter into contracts or agreements;
    (b) to make banking and financial arrangements;
    (c) to execute documents;
    (d) to direct the manner in which any other person or persons may enter into contracts or agreements on behalf of the corporation;
    (e) to purchase, lease or otherwise acquire, sell, exchange or otherwise dispose of real or personal property, securities or any rights or interests for such consideration and upon such terms and conditions as the directors may consider advisable;
    (f) to borrow on the credit of the corporation for the purposes of operating expenses, or on the security of the corporation's real or personal property; and
    (g) to purchase insurance to protect the property, rights and interests of the corporation and to indemnify the corporation, its members, directors and officers from any claims, damages, losses or costs arising from or related to the affairs of the corporation.

21. Each director shall be a member of the corporation at the time of his or her election or appointment, or within ten days of election or appointment and shall remain a member throughout his or her term of office. A director shall be at least 18 years of age. A director may not be an undischarged bankrupt nor a mentally incompetent person.

22. Each director shall be elected to hold office until the first annual general meeting after he or she was elected or until his or her successor shall have been duly elected. All directors shall retire at each annual general meeting, but each is eligible for re-election if he or she is otherwise qualified to be a director.

23. The directors may appoint a director to fill a vacancy, provided that a quorum of directors remains in office. If there is no quorum of directors, the remaining directors shall call a general meeting of the corporation to fill the vacancies.

24. The members of the corporation may elect a director or directors, as the case may be, by a show of hands or by ballot if requested by a member.
25. The members of the corporation may remove a director by a resolution passed by at least two thirds of the votes cast at a general meeting for which notice was given and may by a majority of votes cast elect at that general meeting any person who is qualified to be a director in his or her stead for the duration of the term.

Meetings of the Directors

26. A quorum for a meeting of the board of directors shall be four directors. The board may hold its meetings at any place in Ontario as it may, from time to time, determine.
27. Meetings of the board may be called by the president, the vice-president, the secretary or any two members of the board.
28. No formal notice of any meeting of the board shall be necessary if all the elected directors are present or if those absent have indicated their consent to the meeting being held in their absence.
29. The board may appoint a day or days in any month or months for regular meetings at an hour to be named. If regular meetings are scheduled, no additional notice is required. A meeting of directors may also take place without notice immediately after an annual general meeting or a general meeting to transact any business.
30. No error or omission with respect to notice for a meeting of the board shall invalidate the meeting or invalidate or make void any proceedings taken or had at the meeting.
31. The directors shall vote on any resolution arising at any meeting of the board. A majority of votes shall decide the resolution. In case of a tie vote, the chair of the meeting shall have a casting vote in addition to his or her original vote.
32. A declaration by the secretary that a resolution has been carried and an entry to that effect in the minutes shall be admissible in evidence as *prima facie* proof of the fact without proof of the number of proportion of the votes recorded in favour or against any resolution.

Officers

33. The officers of the corporation shall have the following duties:
    (a) President — chair all meetings of the corporation and of the board, when present in person and able; have general supervision of the affairs of the corporation; sign all by-laws

and execute any documents with the secretary; perform any other duties which the board may, from time to time, assign;

(b) Vice-President — exercise any or all of the duties of the President in the absence of the President or if the President is unable for any reason to perform those duties; and perform any other duties which the board may, from time to time, assign;

(c) Secretary — keep and maintain the records and books of the corporation, including the registry of officers and directors, the registry of members, the minutes of the annual general meeting, general meetings and meetings of the board, the by-laws and resolutions; have custody of the corporate seal; certify copies of any record, registry, by-law, resolution or minute; give any notices required for the annual general meeting, general meetings and meetings of the board of directors; and perform any other duties which the board may, from time to time, assign; and

(d) Treasurer — keep and maintain the financial records and books of the corporation; countersign all cheques or other payments with the President or the Vice-President, as the case may be; assist the auditor in the preparation of the financial statements of the corporation; and perform any other duties which the board may, from time to time, assign.

Indemnification

34. The corporation shall indemnify and save harmless the directors, their heirs, executors and administrators, and estates and effects, respectively from time to time and at all times from and against:

   (a) all costs, charges and expenses whatsoever that he or she sustains or incurs in or about any action, suit or proceeding that is brought, commenced or prosecuted against him or her, for or in respect of any act, deed, matter or thing whatsoever made, done or permitted by him or her in the execution of the duties of his or her office; and

   (b) all other costs, charges and expenses that he or she sustains or incurs in or about or arising from or in relation to the affairs except costs, charges or expenses thereof as are occasioned by his or her own willful neglect or default.

Amendments

By-laws of the corporation may be enacted, repealed, amended, added to or re-enacted by the directors in accordance with the provisions of the *Corporations Act*.

PASSED by the board of directors and sealed with the corporate seal this day of   , 200 .

_____   _____
(Signature)   (Signature)
President   Secretary

(2)   Optional Clauses

(a)   Rotating Directors

The directors shall be elected and retire in rotation as follows:

   (a) at the next annual meeting of the members of the corporation following the confirmation of this by-law, half of the directors shall be elected to hold office for a term of two years from their election or until the annual meeting after such date, whichever comes first;
   (b) at the next annual meeting of the members of the corporation following the confirmation of this by-law, half of the directors shall be elected to hold office for a term of one year from their election or until the annual meeting after such date, whichever comes first; and
   (c) directors shall subsequently be elected for a term of two years from their election or until the annual meeting after such date, whichever comes first.

(b)   Ex Officio Directors

The mayor of the town shall be an *ex officio* member of the board of directors without voting rights.

The board may, from time to time, appoint *ex officio* directors with or without voting rights.

(c)   Remuneration of Directors

The directors of the corporation shall serve without remuneration and no director shall directly or indirectly receive any profits from his or her position as such, provided that a director may be paid reasonable expenses incurred by him or her in the performance of his or her duties.

(d) Contracts

(i) Charitable Corporation

A director shall be disqualified if he or she has an interest, direct or indirect, in any contract or proposed contract with the corporation.

(ii) Not-for-profit Corporation

Every director shall declare his or her interest, direct or indirect, in any contract or arrangement or proposed contract or arrangement with the corporation, in the manner and at the time required by the Act and refrain from voting in respect to the contract or arrangement or proposed contract or arrangement if and when prohibited by the Act.

Every director who has any direct or indirect interest in a contract or proposed contract with the corporation shall:

(a) declare his or her interest at the first meeting of the directors after which he or she became interested or aware of any such interest;
(b) request that his or her declaration be recorded in the minutes of the meeting; and
(c) not vote on any resolution or participate in any discussion with respect to the resolution concerning the contract or proposed contract.

(e) Borrowing Powers

(i) Charitable Corporation

The board may:

(i) borrow money on the credit of the corporation;
(ii) issue, sell or pledge securities of the corporation;
(iii) charge, mortgage, hypothecate or pledge all or any of the real or personal property of the corporation, including book debts, rights, powers, franchises and undertakings to secure any securities or any money borrowed, or other debt, or any other obligation or liability of the corporation,
(iv) delegate the powers under this clause to an officer or officers of the corporation as the board considers appropriate,

provided that, except where the corporation borrows on the security of its real or personal property, its borrowing power shall be limited to borrowing money for current operating expenses.

(ii)   Not-for-profit Corporation

The board may:

(i) borrow money on the credit of the corporation;
(ii) issue, sell or pledge securities of the corporation;
(iii) charge, mortgage, hypothecate or pledge all or any of the real or personal property of the corporation, including book debts, rights, powers, franchises and undertakings, to secure any securities or any money borrowed, or other debt, or any other obligation or liability of the corporation;
(iv) delegate the powers under this clause to an officer or officers of the corporation as the board considers appropriate.

(f)   Banking Arrangements

The board shall designate the officers and any other persons who are authorized to transact the banking affairs of the corporation. The resolution shall provide to the designated officer or other person the power:

(i) to operate the corporation's accounts with the financial institution;
(ii) to make, sign, draw, accept, endorse, negotiate, lodge, deposit or transfer any cheque, promissory notes, drafts, acceptances, bills of exchange and orders for the payment of money;
(iii) to issue receipts for and orders with respect to the property of the corporation;
(iv) to execute any agreements with respect to the banking affairs of the corporation;
(v) to authorize any officer of the financial institution to do any act or thing on the corporation's behalf to facilitate the banking affairs.

The securities of the corporation shall be deposited for safekeeping with one or more financial institution or securities dealer, as the board may, from time to time, determine.

(g)   Agents and Employees

The board may appoint any agents and retain any employees that it considers necessary. The persons appointed or retained shall have the authority and shall perform the duties prescribed by the board.

The remuneration for any agents or employees shall be fixed by the board by resolution. The resolution shall be effective on the date set out in the resolution until the next general meeting of the members, at which time it shall be confirmed by resolution of the members. If the members fail to confirm the resolution, payments to the agents or employees shall cease to be made.

(h)   Committees

*(i)   **Executive Committee***

The board may establish and elect from among the directors an executive committee of the board. The executive committee shall have and may exercise the powers of the board in the management and conduct of the affairs of the corporation in accordance with any direction or restrictions provided in the board's resolution.

The executive committee shall consist of at least four members and shall have a quorum of at least three members. The executive committee may establish its own rules of procedure, unless those rules have been set out in the board's resolution.

*(ii)   **Other Committees***

The board may, from time to time, appoint any other committee or committees that it considers necessary or appropriate. The board shall, when appointing any committee, set out the purposes of the committee, its procedures and its powers, provided that the committee shall not exercise any of the powers or carry out any duties that are legally required to be exercised or carried out by the board of directors.

(i)   Not-for-profit Housing By-law Clauses

The following clauses may be used for not-for-profit housing corporations:

*(i)   **Contracts***

A director shall not have an interest, direct or indirect, in any contract or proposed contract with the corporation other than occupancy leases and agreements and, where applicable, part-time employment by a director who is a resident in the residential accommodation owned by the corporation.

*(ii)   **Cheques***

All cheques and other negotiable documents for the payment of money shall be signed by two signing officers, one of whom shall be the President, the Vice-President, the Treasurer or the Secretary.

(iii) **Resident Members**

Individuals who are residents in accommodation owned by the corporation are eligible for admission as full voting members.

II Federal By-Laws

Model Organizational By-Law Corporate Seal

1. The seal, an impression whereof is sampled in the margin hereof, shall be the seal of the corporation.

Head Office

2. Until changed in accordance with the Act, the head office of the corporation shall be in the Municipality of   in the Province of   .

Conditions of Membership

3. Membership in the corporation shall be limited to persons interested in furthering the objects of the corporation and shall consist of anyone whose application for admission as a member has received the approval of the board of directors of the corporation.
4. There shall be no membership fees or dues unless otherwise directed by the board of directors.
5. Any member may withdraw from the corporation by delivering to the corporation a written resignation and lodging a copy of the same with the secretary of the corporation.
6. Any member may be required to resign by a vote of three-quarters (3/4) of the members at an annual meeting.

Members' Meetings

7. The annual or any general meeting of the members shall be held within 30 days after the end of the corporation's fiscal year, in the city where the head office of the corporation is situated.
8. At every annual meeting, in addition to any other business that may be transacted, the report of the directors, the financial statement and the report of the auditors shall be presented and the auditors appointed for the ensuing year. The members may consider and transact any business either special or general at any meeting of the members. The board of directors or the president or vice-president shall have power to call, at any time, a general meeting of the members of the corporation. The board of directors shall call a special general meeting of members on written

requisition of members carrying not less than five per cent of the voting rights. Members present in person at a meeting will constitute a quorum.

9. Fourteen (14) days; written notice shall be given to each voting member of any annual or special general meeting of members. Notice of any meeting where special business will be transacted shall contain sufficient information to permit the member to form a reasoned judgment on the decision to be taken. Notice of each meeting of members must remind the member if he or she has the right to vote by proxy.

Each voting member present at a meeting shall have the right to exercise one vote. A member may, by means of a written proxy, appoint a proxyholder to attend and act at a special meeting of members, in the manner and to the extent authorized by the proxy. A proxyholder must be a member of the corporation.

10. A majority of the votes cast by the members present and carrying voting rights shall determine the questions in meetings except where the vote or consent of a greater number of members is required by the Act or these By-laws.

11. No error or omission in giving notice of any annual or general meeting or any adjourned meeting, whether annual or general, of the members of the corporation shall invalidate such meeting or make void any proceeding taken thereat and any member may at any time waive notice of any such meeting and may ratify, approve and confirm any or all proceedings taken or had thereat. For purpose of sending notice to any member, director or officer for any meeting or otherwise, the address of the member, director or officer shall be his or her last address recorded on the books of the corporation.

Board of Directors

12. The property and business of the corporation shall be managed by a board of directors, comprised of a minimum of three directors. The number of directors shall be determined from time to time by a majority of the directors at a meeting of the board of directors and sanctioned by an affirmative vote of at least two thirds of the members at a meeting duly called for the purpose of determining the number of directors to be elected to the board of directors. Directors must be individuals, 18 years of age, with power under law to contract. Directors need not be members.

13. The applicants for incorporation shall become the first directors of the corporation whose term of office on the board of directors shall continue until their successors are elected.

    At the first meeting of the members, the board of directors then elected shall replace the provisional directors named in the letters patent of the corporation.
14. Directors shall be elected for a term of   year(s) by the members at an annual meeting of members.
15. The office of director shall be automatically vacated:
    (a) if at a special general meeting of members, a resolution is made by   of the members present at the meeting that he or she be removed from office;
    (b) if a director has resigned his or her office by delivering a written resignation to the secretary of the corporation;
    (c) if he or she is found by a court to be of unsound mind;
    (d) if he or she becomes bankrupt or suspends payment or compounds with his or her creditor;
    (e) on death;
    provided that if any vacancy shall occur for any reason in this paragraph contained, the board of directors by majority vote may, by appointment, fill the vacancy with a member of the corporation.
16. The directors shall serve as such without remuneration and no director shall directly or indirectly receive any profit from his or her position as such; provided that a director may be paid reasonable expenses incurred by him or her in the performance of his or her duties. Nothing herein contained shall be construed to preclude any director from serving the corporation as an officer or in any other capacity and receiving compensation therefor.
17. A retiring director shall remain in office until the dissolution or adjournment of the meeting at which his or her retirement is accepted and his or her successor is elected.

Powers of Directors

18. The directors of the corporation may administer the affairs of the corporation in all things and make or cause to be made for the corporation, in its name, any kind of contract which the corporation may lawfully enter into and, save as hereinafter provided, generally, may exercise all such other powers and do all such other acts and things as the corporation is by its charter or otherwise authorized to exercise and do.

19. The directors shall have power to authorize expenditures on behalf of the corporation from time to time and may delegate by resolution to an officer or officers of the corporation the right to employ and pay salaries to employees. The directors shall have the power to enter into a trust arrangement with a trust company for the purpose of creating a trust fund in which the capital and interest may be made available for the benefit of promoting the interests of the corporation in accordance with such terms as the board of directors may prescribe.

    The board of directors is hereby authorized, from time to time
    (a) to borrow money upon the credit of the corporation, from any bank, corporation, firm or person, upon such terms, covenants and conditions at such times, in such sums, to such an extent and in such manner as the board of directors in its discretion may deem expedient;
    (b) to limit or increase the amount to be borrowed;
    (c) to issue or cause to be issued bonds, debentures or other securities of the corporation and to pledge or sell the same for such sums, upon such terms, covenants and conditions and at such prices as may be deemed expedient by the board of directors;
    (d) to secure any bond, debenture or other securities, or any other present or future borrowing or liability of the company, by mortgage, hypothec, charge or pledge of all or any currently owned or subsequently acquired real and personal, movable and immovable, property of the corporation, and the undertaking and rights of the corporation.
20. The board of directors shall take such steps as they may deem requisite to enable the corporation to acquire, accept, solicit or receive legacies, gifts, grants, settlements, bequests, endowments and donations of any king whatsoever for the purpose of furthering the objects of the corporation.
21. The board of directors may appoint such agents and engage such employees as it shall deem necessary from time to time and such person shall have such authority and shall perform such duties as shall be prescribed by the board of directors at the time of such appointment.
22. Remuneration for all officers, agents and employees and committee members shall be fixed by the board of directors by resolution. Such resolution shall have force and effect only until the next meeting of members when such resolution shall be confirmed by resolution of the members, or in the absence of such confirmation by the members, then the remuneration of such officers, agents or

employees and committee members shall cease to be payable from the date of such meeting of members.

Directors' Meetings

23. Meetings of the board of directors may be held at any time and place to be determined by the directors provided that 48-hours' written notice of such meeting shall be given, other than by mail, to each director. Notice by mail shall be sent at least 14 days prior to the meeting. There shall be at least one meeting per year of the board of directors. No error or omission in giving notice of any meeting of the board of directors or any adjourned meeting of the board of directors of the corporation shall invalidate such meeting or make void any proceedings taken thereat and any director may at any time waive notice of any such meeting and may ratify, approve and confirm any or all proceedings taken or had thereat. Each director is authorized to exercise one vote.

24. A majority of directors in office, from time to time, but no less than two directors, shall constitute a quorum for meetings of the board of directors. Any meeting of the board of directors at which a quorum is present shall be competent to exercise all or any of the authorities, powers and discretions by or under the by-laws of the corporation.

Indemnities to Directors and Others

25. Every director or officer of the corporation or other person who has undertaken or is about to undertake any liability on behalf of the corporation or any company controlled by it and their heirs, executors and administrators, and estate and effects, respectively, shall from time to time and at all times, be indemnified and saved harmless out of the funds of the corporation, from and against:
    (a) all costs, charges and expenses which such director, officer or other person sustains or incurs in or about any action, suit or proceedings which is brought, commenced or prosecuted against him or her, or in respect of any act, deed, matter of thing whatsoever, made, done or permitted by him or her, in or about the execution of the duties of his or her office or in respect of any such liability;
    (b) all other costs, charges and expenses which he or she sustains or incurs in or about or in relation to the affairs thereof, except such costs, charges or expenses as are occasioned by his or her own wilful neglect or default.

Officers

26. The officers of the corporation shall be a president, vice-president, secretary and treasurer and any such other officers as the board of directors may by by-law determine. Any two offices may be held by the same person. Officers need not be directors nor members.
27. The president shall be elected at an annual meeting of members. Officers other than president of the corporation shall be appointed by resolution of the board of directors at the first meeting of the board of directors following the annual meeting of members in which the directors are elected.
28. The officers of the corporation shall hold office for   year(s) from the date of appointment or election or until their successors are elected or appointed in their stead. Officers shall be subject to removal by resolution of the board of directors at any time.

Duties of Officers

29. The president shall be the chief executive officer of the corporation. He or she shall preside at all meetings of the corporation and of the board of directors. He or she shall have general and active management of the affairs of the corporation. He or she shall see that all orders and resolutions of the board of directors are carried into effect.
30. The vice-president shall, in the absence or disability of the president, perform the duties and exercise the powers of the president and shall perform such other duties as shall from time to time be imposed upon him or her by the board of directors.
31. The treasurer shall have the custody of the funds and securities of the corporation and shall keep full and accurate accounts of all assets, liabilities, receipts and disbursements of the corporation in the books belonging to the corporation and shall deposit all monies, securities and other valuable effects in the name and to the credit of the corporation in such chartered bank or trust company, or, in the case of securities, in such registered dealer of securities as may be designated by the board of directors from time to time. He or she shall disburse the funds of the corporation as may be directed by proper authority taking proper vouchers for such disbursements, and shall render to the president and directors at the regular meeting of the board of directors, or whenever they may require it, an accounting of all the transactions and a statement of the financial position of the corporation. He or she

shall also perform such other duties as may from time to time be directed by the board of directors.
32. The secretary may be empowered by the board of directors, upon resolution of the board of directors, to carry out his or her affairs of the corporation generally under the supervision of the officers thereof and shall attend all meetings and act as clerk thereof and record all votes and minutes of all minutes of all proceedings in the books to be kept for that purpose. He or she shall give or cause to be given notice of all meetings of the members and of the board of directors, and shall perform such other duties as may be prescribed by the board of directors or president, under whose supervision he or she shall be. He or she shall be custodian of the seal of the corporation, which he or she shall deliver only when authorized by a resolution of the board of directors to do so and to such person or persons as may be named in the resolution.
33. The duties of all other officers of the corporation shall be such as the terms of their engagement call for or the board of directors requires of them.

Committees

34. The board of directors may appoint committees whose members will hold their offices at the will of the board of directors. The directors shall determine the duties of such committees and may fix by resolution, any remuneration to be paid.

Executive Committee (Optional)

35. There shall be an executive committee composed of ____ directors who shall be appointed by the board of directors. The executive committee shall exercise such powers as are authorized by the board of directors. Any executive committee member may be removed by a majority vote of the board of directors. Executive members shall receive no remuneration for serving as such, but are entitled to reasonable expenses incurred in the exercise of their duty.
36. Meetings of the executive committee shall be held at any time and place to be determined by the members of such committee provided that 48-hours' written notice of such meeting shall be given, other than by mail, to each member of the committee. Notice by mail shall be sent at least 14 days prior to the meeting. (No less than two) members of such committee shall constitute a quorum. No error or omission in giving notice of any meeting of the executive committee or any adjourned meeting of the executive

committee of the corporation shall invalidate such meeting or make void any proceedings taken thereat and any member of such committee may at any time waive notice of any such meeting and may ratify, approve and confirm any or all proceedings taken or had thereat.

Execution of Documents

37. Contracts, documents or any instruments in writing requiring the signature of the corporation shall be signed by any two officers and all contracts, documents and instruments in writing so signed shall be binding upon the corporation without any further authorization or formality. The directors shall have power, from time to time, by resolution to appoint an officer or officers on behalf of the corporation to sign specific contracts, documents and instruments in writing. The directors may give the corporation's power of attorney to any registered dealer in securities for the purposes of the transferring of and dealing with any stocks, bonds and other securities of the corporation. The seal of the corporation when required may be affixed to contracts, documents and instruments in writing signed as aforesaid or by any officer or officers appointed by resolution of the board of directors.

Minutes of Board of Directors [and Executive Committee]

38. The minutes of the board of directors [and the executive committee] shall not be available to the general membership of the corporation but shall be available to the board of directors, each of whom shall receive a copy of such minutes.

Financial Year

39. Unless otherwise ordered by the board of directors, the fiscal year-end of the corporation shall be   (Date).

Amendment of By-laws

40. The by-laws of the corporation not embodied in the letters patent may be repealed or amended by by-law, or a new by-law relating to the requirements of subsection 155(2) of the *Canada Corporations Act*, may be enacted by a majority of the directors at a meeting of the board of directors and sanctioned by an affirmative vote of at least two thirds of the members duly called for the purpose of considering the said by-law, provided that the repeal or

amendment of such by-laws shall not be enforced or acted upon until the approval of the Minister of Industry has been obtained.

Auditors

41. The members shall, at each annual meeting, appoint an auditor to audit the accounts and annual financial statements of the corporation for report to the members at the next annual meeting. The auditor shall hold office until the next annual meeting, provided that the directors may fill any casual vacancy in the office of auditor. The remuneration of the auditor shall be fixed by the board of directors.

Books and Records

42. The directors shall see that all necessary books and records of the corporation required by the by-laws of the corporation or by any applicable statutes or law are regularly and properly kept.

Rules and Regulations

43. The board of directors may prescribe such rules and regulations not inconsistent with these by-laws relating to the management and operation of the corporation as they deem expedient, provided that such rules and regulations shall have force and effect only until the next annual meeting of the members of the corporation when they shall be confirmed, and failing such confirmation at such annual meeting of members, shall at and from that time cease to have any force and effect.

Interpretation

44. In these by-laws and in all other by-laws of the corporation hereafter passed unless the context otherwise requires, words importing the singular number of the masculine gender shall include the plural number of the feminine gender, as the case may be, and vice versa, and references to persons shall include firms and corporations.

PASSED by the board of directors and sealed with the corporate seal this day of , 200 .

_____   _____
(Signature)   (Signature)
President   Secretary

G MEETINGS

I Members

(1) Notice of Annual General Meeting

TAKE NOTICE that the annual general meeting of members of the ABC Reading Club will be held at 123 Main Street, Doone, Ontario on July 15, 200 , at 7 p.m., for the purpose of:

(a) receiving, considering and approving the financial statements for the previous financial year, together with the auditor's report;
(b) electing directors;
(c) appointing auditors and authorizing the board of directors to fix their remuneration;
(d) considering and dealing with the following proposed motions [optional, if there are any proposed motions];
(e) confirmation and sanction of the actions of the directors and any other matters that require the confirmation or sanction of the members;
(f) transacting such other business as may properly come before the meeting.

Members who will not be attending the meeting are requested to date, sign and return the accompanying proxy in the enclosed self-addressed envelope.

Only members in good standing are entitled to attend, participate in and vote at the meeting.

Accompanying this notice is a letter explaining the proposed motion [optional, if any proposed motions].

DATED this   day of   , 200 .

On behalf of the board of directors

_____
(Signature)
Secretary

(2) Notice of Special Meeting

TAKE NOTICE that a special meeting of the members of the ABC Reading Club will be held at 123 Main Street, Doone, Ontario on September 15, 200 ,   at 7 p.m. for the purpose of considering and confirming with or without variation or amendment as may be made at the meeting:

(a) a special resolution passed by the board on August 30, 200 , a copy of which is attached to this notice;

(b) By-law No.   amending the classes of membership in the corporation, a copy of which is attached to this notice.

Members who will not be attending the meeting are requested to date, sign and return the accompanying proxy in the enclosed envelope.

DATED this   day of   , 200 .

On behalf of the board of directors

_____
(Signature)
Secretary

(3)   Proxy

I,   , a member of the ABC Reading Club, hereby appoint   or failing him or her   as proxyholder for me, to attend, act and vote for and on my behalf at the annual general [or special general] meeting to be held on   200 , including any adjournments, and I hereby revoke all proxies previously given by me.

I authorize and direct the proxyholder:

1 (a) —   to vote for the election of the following individuals as directors [and officers]:
           or
   (b) —   not to vote for the following individuals as directors [and officers]:
           or
   (c) —   to abstain from voting for directors [and officers]
           or
   (d) —   to vote for directors [and officers] as the proxyholder in his or her absolute discretion considers advisable
           or
   (e) —   [(specify other authorization and instructions)].

2 (a) —   to vote for the confirmation of By-law No.   amending By-law No. 1 [or special resolution], with or without amendments,

or
(b) — to vote against the confirmation of By-law No. amending By-law No. 1 [or special resolution], with or without amendments,
or
(c) — to abstain from voting on the confirmation of By-law No. amending By-law No. 1 [or special resolution], with or without amendment
or
(d) — to vote as the proxyholder in his or her absolute discretion considers advisable.

3 (a) — to vote for the appointment of   as the auditors
or
(b) — to abstain from voting on the appointment of auditors.

4 (a) — to take action on such other business as may properly come before the meeting as the proxyholder considers advisable
or
(b) — to take the following action on such other business as may properly come before the meeting:

DATED this day of , 200 .

_____
(Signature)
Name of Member

(4)   Revocation of Proxy

I, , hereby revoke the appointment of   as my proxyholder with respect to the annual meeting of the ABC Reading Club to be held on 200 .

DATED this day of , 200 .

_____
(Signature)
Name of Member

(5)   Agenda for General Meeting

  1.   Opening of Meeting

  2.   Chair — appointment (if necessary)

3. Secretary

   (a) Proof of Notice of Meeting;
   (b) Report on Attendance, Including Any Proxies;
   (c) Determine If Quorum Present.

4. Approval of Agenda

5. Minutes from Previous General Meeting

   (a) Approval of Minutes;
   (b) Business Arising from Minutes.

6. Reports

   (a) Annual Report of Board of Directors;
   (b) Treasurer's Report;
       (i) Report;
       (ii) Financial Statements for Previous Financial Year;
       (iii) Budget for Current Financial Year;
   (c) Committee Reports.

7. Motions for Which Notice Has Been Given

   (a) Confirmation of Amendments to By-Laws;
   (b) Special Resolutions;
   (c) Confirmation of Actions of Directors;
   (d) Other Motions. [N.B. include confirmation of the remuneration of officers, agents, employees and committee members.]

8. Motions for Which Notice Is Not Required

9. Elections

   (a) Appointment of Scrutineers;
   (b) Nominations;
   (c) Speeches or Presentations from Candidates;
   (d) Election of Directors [and officers].

10. Appointment of Auditors

11. Other Business

12. Conclusion of Meeting

II BOARDS

(1)   Notice of Meeting

TAKE NOTICE that a meeting of the board of directors of the ABC Reading Club will be held on   , 200   at   a.m. [p.m.] at the head office [or at the following address].

DATED this   day of   , 200 .

By Order of the President

_____
(Signature)
Secretary

(2)   Waiver of Notice of Meeting

We, the undersigned directors of the ABC Reading Club, hereby waive notice of and consent to the holding of a meeting of the board of directors at the head office [or address] on   , 200 , at   a.m. [p.m.] and agree to ratify all resolutions passed and the business transacted at this meeting.

DATED the   day of   , 200 .

(3)   Agenda for Board Meeting

1. Open Meeting

2. Secretary

   (a)   Proof of Notice of Meeting;
   (b)   Determines if Quorum Present.

3. Minutes of Previous Meeting
   (a)   Approval of Minutes;
   (b)   Business Arising from Minutes.

4. Reports

   (a)   President;
   (b)   Treasurer;
   (c)   Committees.

5. New Business

6. Conclusion

III BALLOTS

(1) Election

(a)   Member's Ballot

I cast my vote for the following persons as directors:

1.
2.
3.
4.
5.
6.

I cast my vote for the following person as president [vice-president, secretary, treasurer, other officer]:

President
Vice-president
Secretary
Treasurer
Other officer

(b)   Proxyholder's Ballot

I hold proxy votes on behalf of   members who have appointed me as proxyholder for this purpose. A list of members for whom I hold proxies is attached and has been verified by the scrutineers for this meeting.

I cast   votes for the following persons as directors:
1.
2.
3.
4.
5.
6.

I cast   votes for the following person as president [vice-president, secretary, treasurer, other officer]:

President
Vice-president
Secretary
Treasurer
Other Officer

_____
Proxyholder

   proxy votes verified by:

_____
(Signature)
Scrutineer

_____
(Signature)
Scrutineer

(2)   **Motions**

(a)   *Member's Ballot*

I cast my vote   — for the motion
                    — against the motion

(b)   *Proxyholder's Ballot*

I hold proxy votes on behalf of   members who have appointed me as proxyholder for this purpose. A list of members for whom I hold proxies is attached and has been verified by the scrutineers for this meeting.

I cast   votes   — for the motion
I cast   votes   — against the motion

_____
(Signature)
Proxyholder

   proxy votes verified by:

_____
(Signature)
Scrutineer

_____
(Signature)
Scrutineer

(3) Scrutineers' Report

We, the undersigned scrutineers, report as follows:

1. The results of the election of directors [or officers] are:

    Candidates   Votes Cast

    Total Votes Cast

    In addition,   ballots were disallowed by us.

2. The results of the vote on the motion are:

    For the Motion
    In Person
    By Proxy
    Total For

    Against the Motion
    In Person
    By Proxy
    Total Against

    Total Votes Cast
    In addition,   ballots were disallowed by us.

DATED this   day of   , 200 .

_____
(Signature)
Scrutineer

_____
(Signature)
Scrutineer

H   PRECEDENTS FOR USE BY REGISTERED CHARITY

I   WRITTEN DECLARATION OF TRUST

Trust Declaration

Appendix D

To: ABC Educational Charitable Trust Fund
123 Main Street
Doone, Ontario
N2M 1A1

I,   , hereby direct the ABC Educational Charitable Trust Fund, a charitable organization registered under the *Income Tax Act* (Business Number   ) to hold my donation of $ in trust for a period of time of not less than ten years.

Official Receipt Number

Dated this   day of   , 200 .

_____
(Signature)
Donor
Street Address

II OFFICIAL RECEIPT

ABC Educational Charitable Trust Fund Receipt Number
123 Main Street
Doone, Ontario
N2M 1A1

Business Number

On the   day of   , 200 , ABC Educational Charitable Trust Fund received the sum of $ as a charitable donation from:

    John A. Smith
    45 Red Road
    Doone, Ontario
    N2M 2A2

This is an official receipt for income tax purposes issued at Doone, Ontario on the   day of   , 200 .

_____
(Authorized Signature)

Index

A

Accountability, 1, 2, 5, 113, 125-145, 169, 175, 208, 212-221, 233, 248, 265, 378. *See also* Directors
Association, 5, 37, 40-41, 50, 52, 85, 114-117, 176, 320, 323
Audit, 82, 95-98, 117, 119, 124, 134, 152-155, 248, 267, 441

B

Books and Records, 82, 84, 113-118, 121-124, 126-152, 190, 203, 299, 438-439
Broadbent Panel. *See* Panel on Accountability in the Voluntary Sector
Business Activities, 32-35, 140-144, 167-168, 207-209, 260, 265, 280-288, 360-370, 391, 398-412, 406-407
By-Laws, 47, 67, 71, 75, 81-112, 121, 176, 191, 215, 244, 290, 292, 297, 298, 383

C

Canada Corporations Act, 6-7, 37, 46-48, 52-53, 55, 70-75, 86, 89-90, 95, 97-98, 99-101, 103-104, 123-126, 183-187, 200, 223, 232-233, 254, 271, 296
Canada Customs and Revenue Agency, 1-3, 6, 8, 31-35, 64, 96, 113, 116, 130, 135, 147-176, 190, 196, 201, 203-204, 207, 221, 226, 246, 266, 268-269, 310, 311-313, 315-318, 320, 333, 341, 343, 354, 415, 417, 458, 461-463
Canadian Centre for Philanthropy, 386-390
Charitable
 definition, 6-27, 445
 objects and purposes, 3, 39
  advancement of education, 4, 9, 17, 19-21
  advancement of religion, 9, 18-19, 21-22
  other purposes of benefit to the community, 9, 19, 22-27
  relief of poverty, 4, 9, 17, 18-19
Charitable Gifts Act (Ontario). *See* Public Guardian and Trustee
Charitable Registration, 152-173, 314-334
 application, 317-334
 gifts, 157-164, 172, 331, 414-422
 information return, 162-173, 203, 337
 official donation receipts, 156-162, 331
Charitable Fund-Raising Act (Alberta). *See* Fundraising
Charities Accounting Act (Ontario). *See* Public Guardian and Trustee
Competition Act (Canada). *See* Fundraising
Conflict of Interest, 230, 236-238, 254-257, 443-444
Co-operative Corporations Act (Ontario), 38, 44-46, 49, 52-53, 55, 76-79, 86, 88-89, 95-97, 99-100, 103-104, 121-123, 181-183, 222, 224, 232, 303-305
Corporations Act (Ontario), 6, 37, 42-45, 49, 52-53, 55-70, 76-77, 86-89, 95-103, 117-121, 126, 163, 177-181, 187, 214, 221, 232-233, 254, 271, 277, 296
Corporations without Share Capital, 5, 37, 42-45, 46-48. *See also Corporations Act* (Ontario), *Canada Corporations Act*, *Co-operative Corporations Act* (Ontario)
Courts, 3-4, 9-18, 27-29, 39, 208, 221, 224-234, 290-291, 299-301, 353-360, 380-382
 supervisory role, 3, 29, 353-360, 372-376
Cy-pres, 39, 159, 176-177, 191, 294, 351, 370-372

D

Directors, 5, 49, 65, 75, 77, 81-82, 84, 87-89, 95, 98, 101-103, 119-120, 122-123, 125, 129, 144, 211-288, 379, 380-384, 389
 accountable boards, 248-253
 code of conduct, 257-258
 committees, 102, 248-249
 conflict of interest, 254-257
 duties and obligations, 230-234, 245-248
 effective boards, 241-248
 ethical standards, 384-389
 ex officio, 87, 102-103, 108, 191-192
 financial management, 265-267
 fiscal management, 276-278
 governance approaches, 212-221, 223, 242-243
 insurance and indemnification, 270-276
 investments, 280-288
 policies, 250-280
 privacy of personal information, 258-265
 program review, 278-280
 quorum, 82, 102, 107-108
 regulatory compliance, 267-270

Directors — *cont'd*
  rules of procedure or rules of order, 104-112
  standards of care, 221-228, 245-248
  statutory duties, 238-241

F

Financial Statements, 82, 95-97, 113, 120, 122-123, 125, 128-145, 203, 266-267, 330- 332, 439-443
  deferral method, 135-140, 266
  endowment funds, 136, 140, 197
  generally accepted accounting principles, 95, 127, 130-145, 219
  pledges, 138-139
  restricted fund method, 135-140, 193, 266
Fundamental Changes, 176-186
  amalgamation, 177, 180-181, 183, 186
  amendments, 177-178, 181-184
  dissolution, 178-180, 182, 184-185
Fundraising, 163, 165-167, 169-171, 174, 329, 330, 345, 377-469
  annuities, 464-466
  bequests, 454-456
  capital property, 458-461
  Charitable Fund-Raising Act (Alberta), 407-414
  Charities Endorsement Act (Manitoba), 414
  Competition Act, 398-402
  compliance, 397-414
  directors, 380-384
  ethical fundraising, 384-390, 394, 413, 423
  gift, 414-422. *See also* Charitable Registration
  loan, 466
  life insurance, 456-458
  planned giving, 454-466
  professional fundraisers, 392-396, 407-414
  remainder trusts, 461-464
  special events, 447-454
  strategic plan, 389-397

G

Gaming, 168-170, 329, 389, 392-393, 422-454
  Criminal Code of Canada, 422, 424-429, 431-432, 435, 441
  terms and conditions to a licence, 431-445
  types of lottery schemes, 429-431
Goods and Services Tax/Harmonized Sales Tax, 168, 307, 315, 322, 329, 336-344

Governance, 212-213, 248-253
Government, 2-3, 6, 22-24

I

Income Tax Act (Canada), 6, 8, 29, 48, 114-115, 118-119, 126, 135, 146-152, 155-176, 202, 208, 210, 217, 219, 307, 309-334, 446-447, 457
Industry Canada, 2, 47, 70, 183-186, 296, 298
Intellectual Property, 190, 196, 402-406, 469
Internet, 466-469
Investments, 143, 165, 174, 232, 280-288

L

Liability and Risk Management, 49-53, 55, 102, 221-222, 233, 239, 270-276, 449- 454

M

Meetings, 82, 84, 89-90, 97-98, 100-101, 113, 117, 119-125, 243-245, 248, 301
  rules of procedure or rules of order, 104-112, 113
Members, 41, 82, 84, 86-88, 90, 95, 98-100, 103, 113, 119-125, 289- 305
  eligibility, 295, 303
  information, 299-301
  liability, 49-53, 55
  meeting, 301-302
  procedural rights, 294-295, 302
  property rights, 291-294, 303-305
  vote, 298

N

Not-for-Profit
  definition, 6-8, 310-312
  information return, 173-175
  standard of care, 223-226
  taxation, 309

O

Objects, 41, 66, 84, 113, 168
Officer, 5, 82, 84, 88, 95, 103-104, 120, 125, 221, 230-234, 379. *See also* Director
Ontario Law Reform Commission, 2, 351, 365-369, 384-385
Organizational Changes, 186-202
  association model, 187-188, 190-195
  chapter model, 187-188, 195-197
  foreign activities, 202-207
  parallel foundation, 197-198
  strategic alliances, 186, 198-202, 203

P

Panel on Accountability in the Voluntary Sector, 2, 212-221, 266, 278, 351, 385-389
Political Activities, 30-32, 166, 171, 207-209, 328-329
Personal Information Protection and Electronic Documents Act (Canada), 258-265, 412
Public Benefits, 2, 7-8, 14-16, 18, 28, 32, 125, 175, 307
Public Guardian and Trustee (Ontario), 4-5, 35, 46, 56, 64, 67-69, 71, 95, 116, 118, 120, 177, 179, 180, 190, 201, 221, 226-228, 231, 237-238, 246, 254, 272, 316, 351-372, 373, 378, 382, 406-407, 465
   Charitable Gifts Act, 8-9, 33-34, 67-68, 142, 146, 208-209, 268, 326, 351-352, 360-370, 372, 375, 378, 406-407
   Charities Accounting Act, 4, 9, 24, 33, 47, 67-69, 71, 83, 102, 116, 146, 177, 190, 193, 208, 228, 231, 234, 238, 268, 272, 278, 286-288, 293, 326, 351, 353-360, 372-373, 375, 378, 382, 406-407

S

Statute of Uses, 1601, 3, 9-12, 15, 19, 24

T

Taxation, 5, 30, 240, 307-350
   consumption, 344-347. *See also* Goods and Services Tax/Harmonized Sales Tax
   corporate, 334-336
   property, 347-350
Terrorism, 203, 205-207
Trustee Act (Ontario), 40, 68, 116, 142, 146, 176, 190, 228, 236, 281, 282, 285
Trustees, 39, 48, 90, 114-117, 125, 221, 234
   duties and obligations, 230, 234-238
   standard of care, 226-230, 235
   See also Directors
Trusts, 5, 37-40, 49, 176, 319-320
   charitable trusts, 23-25